AGRARIAN REFORM AND
PEASANT REVOLUTION IN SPAIN

AGRARIAN REFORM AND
PEASANT REVOLUTION IN SPAIN, *1970*

Origins of the Civil War

by Edward E. Malefakis

NEW HAVEN AND LONDON, YALE UNIVERSITY PRESS, 1970

Copyright © 1970 by Yale University.

All rights reserved. This book may not be
reproduced, in whole or in part, in any form
(except by reviewers for the public press),
without written permission from the publishers.

Library of Congress catalog card number: 72–104618
International standard book number: 0–300–01210–1

Designed by Marvin Howard Simmons,
set in Caledonia type,
and printed in the United States of America by
The Colonial Press Inc., Clinton, Massachusetts.

Distributed in Great Britain, Europe, and
Africa by Yale University Press, Ltd., London; in
Canada by McGill-Queen's University Press, Montreal;
in Mexico by Centro Interamericano de Libros
Académicos, Mexico City; in Australasia by Australia
and New Zealand Book Co., Pty., Ltd., Artarmon,
New South Wales; in India by UBS Publishers'
Distributors Pvt., Ltd., Delhi; in Japan by John
Weatherhill, Inc., Tokyo.

To my mother, Despina
and to
the memory of my father, Emanuel

Contents

Tables

Maps

Preface

Most of the research and writing for this book was done during an eighteen-month stay in Spain in 1961 and 1962, and during whatever time I could spare from my teaching duties at Wayne State and Columbia universities in the years 1963 to 1965. I did some additional research in the United States in the summer of 1966 and spent the winter of 1967–68 grappling, often vainly, for solutions to a few especially difficult problems that troubled me. I am fairly well satisfied with the book as it now stands, although I wish that I could have learned more about the dynamics of peasant protest and fear that in some instances I may have been insufficiently generous in interpreting the exceedingly complex position of the Anarchosyndicalists and Socialists.

Needless to say, in the course of so many years I acquired a great number of debts both to persons and to institutions. I am especially grateful to three of my former teachers and colleagues at Columbia University, two of them in history and one in sociology. Shepard B. Clough suggested the topic and, with his usual kindness and patience, guided my research and writing of the book while it was in its dissertation stage. Rudolph Binion subjected my original manuscript to an exceedingly rigorous and intelligent scrutiny which enabled me to improve it considerably. As to Juan Linz, I have spent so many fruitful hours discussing with him the problems of Spain that I scarcely know any longer where his thoughts end and mine begin.

I am also particularly indebted to three Spaniards. Pascual Carrión, who for decades has sought to awaken Spain to the plight of its landless peasantry, devoted many long evenings to guiding me out of my ignorance. Ramón Bela, director of the Fulbright Commission, helped me more than he knew by his constant encouragement and good spirits, as well as by introducing me to persons who facilitated my work considerably. Angel Martínez Borque, then chief of planning of the Instituto Nacional de Colonización, provided invaluable assistance by allowing

me access to the archives of the Institute of Agrarian Reform and by placing at my disposal many of the facilities of the Instituto de Colonización.

My debt to several other persons is scarcely less great. Juan José
Vergara, of the Agronomic Institute of the University of Madrid, helped
educate me on some of the technical problems that accompany agrarian
reform. José Tudela and the late Manuel Jiménez Fernández generously
allowed me to draw on some of their vast knowledge. Gonzalo Anes
Álvarez and Salustiano del Campo Urbano, both of the University of
Madrid, went out of their way to assist me whenever they could. My
former colleague at Columbia University, Richard Weiss, gave generously
of his time in a moment of need. Burnett Bolloten, sometimes of Stanford
University, Josep Fontana of the University of Barcelona, and Raymond
Carr and Juan Martínez Alier of St. Antony's College, Oxford, provided
helpful criticisms of my manuscript. James Rial and Laurence Shoup,
graduate students at Northwestern, helped me prepare the index.

In reference to institutions, the Fulbright program and the Horace
Smith Fund of Springfield, Massachusetts—one of the small foundations
which collectively have done so much to advance the cause of higher
education in the United States—financed my stay in Spain in 1961–62.
The European Institute of Columbia University, and its director Philip
E. Mosely, gave me the financial assistance that made possible additional
research in the summer of 1966. The final revisions of my manuscript in
the winter of 1967–68 were supported through part of a grant from the
Social Science Research Foundation. I am also indebted to a number of
libraries, particularly to that magnificent research center, the New York
Public Library, as well as to the Hemeroteca Municipal and the library
of the Instituto de Colonización in Madrid.

There are a number of other persons and institutions to whom I would
render thanks if space permitted. Without their assistance, this book
could not have been written. A special position of honor, of course, must
be reserved for my wife, Mary Anne, and for my children. Like the
families of all scholars, it is they who have made the heaviest sacrifices
for the completion of this work.

E. E. M.

Northwestern University
Evanston, Illinois
October 1969

Regional Divisions

Regional classification is inevitably imperfect, because Spanish provinces do not correspond very closely to true agricultural units. The two major problems have been the placement of Salamanca and Logroño. By some standards the first should form part of Old Castile, not Estremadura, whereas the second should be united with Navarre and Alava or Old Castile rather than placed in the Aragon-Ebro region. I finally decided as I did in the case of Logroño because the amount of irrigated land and the crops grown in the province make its agricultural economy more similar to that of Aragon than of the other two regions. With Salamanca, aside from the resemblance of its property and social structure to that of Southern Spain, I was influenced by the fact that the agrarian reform legislation of the 1930s treated this province as more akin to Estremadura than Old Castile.

The reasons I separated "Northern," "Central," and "Southern" Spain as I did are explained in the text. So, too, is the necessity for placing the two industrialized Basque provinces of Guipúzcoa and Viscaya within the Biscay Coast region rather than with Navarre and Alava. I have anglicized the spelling of all provincial and regional names. In some cases (Córdoba, Sevilla, Zaragoza, Extremadura, Andalucía) this has meant changing the spelling as well as dropping the Spanish accents. In most cases (Cáceres, Cádiz, Málaga, Aragón, León) the spelling is the same, and anglicization has been achieved by eliminating the accents. In the latter cases I followed the example of such recent writers on Spanish affairs as Gerald Brenan, John Elliott, and John Lynch. I made an exception for Guipúzcoa, because of the difficulty of the name. Spanish spelling and accents have been retained for all subprovincial political units, whether counties or townships.

"Southern" Spain is always capitalized, because it always refers to the same thirteen provinces that were both *latifundista* and the object of special attention for the agrarian reform. This practice is also followed

——— *Latifundio* zone boundary
– – – – – Regional boundary
——— Provincial boundary

REGIONS

I	Galicia	VIII	Levante
II	Biscay Coast	IX	Southeast
III	Navarre-Alava	X	Estremadura
IV	Aragon-Ebro	XI	La Mancha
V	Catalonia	XII	Western Andalusia
VI	Old Castile	XIII	Eastern Andalusia
VII	New Castile		

REGIONS AND PROVINCES OF SPAIN

for such derivatives as "the South," "Southern owners," "Southern workers," and so on. "Northern" and "Central" Spain are always capitalized in Chapter I, since they always refer specifically to certain provinces.
In the rest of the book, I usually employ these words and their derivatives
in a looser sense and so do not usually capitalize them. I recognize that
a seeming inconsistency in capitalization results, and I apologize to the
reader for it. I also recognize that, with the province of Salamanca
thrusting so far northward, my category of "Southern" Spain is not in
fact very southerly. If these and other terminological problems of a similar nature sometimes prove infuriating to the reader, he should remember that they were far more so for me.

The geographical location of the regions I used are indicated on the
map on page xviii. The provinces included in each region are as follows.
It should be noted that, for technical reasons explained in the text, I had
to place the provinces of Burgos and Leon in a special category of their
own when discussing land tenure; only subsequently are they reintegrated
into Old Castile. Also, following a long-standing Spanish custom, I sometimes refer to Viscaya by the name of its capital city, Bilbao, and to
Guipúzcoa by the name of its capital, San Sebastian.

Galicia	*Old Castile*	*Estremadura*
La Corunna	Avila	Badajoz
Lugo	Burgos	Caceres
Orense	Leon	Salamanca
Pontevedra	Palencia	*La Mancha*
Biscay Coast	Segovia	Albacete
Guipúzcoa	Soria	Ciudad Real
Oviedo	Valladolid	Toledo
Santander	Zamora	*Western Andalusia*
Viscaya	*New Castile*	Cadiz
Navarre-Alava	Cuenca	Cordova
Alava	Guadalajara	Huelva
Navarre	Madrid	Jaen
Aragon-Ebro	*Levante*	Seville
Huesca	Alicante	*Eastern Andalusia*
Logrono	Castellon	Granada
Saragossa	Valencia	Malaga
Teruel	*Southeast*	
Catalonia	Almeria	
Barcelona	Murcia	
Gerona		
Lerida		
Tarragona		

Abbreviations

AEPA   *Anuario Estadístico de las producciones agrícolas* (statistical yearbook of the Ministry of Agriculture).

BIRA   *Boletín del Instituto de Reforma Agraria* (monthly bulletin of the Institute of Agrarian Reform).

CEDA   Confederación Española de Derechas Autónomas (coalition of Catholic parties headed by Gil Robles from 1933 to 1936).

CNT   Confederación Nacional de Trabajo (Anarchosyndicalist trade union from 1910 to 1936).

D.G.   (de Agricultura de Montes, and so forth), refers to Dirección General (de Agricultura, de Montes, and so forth).

DGP   Dirección General de Propiedades.

DGRA   Dirección General de Reforma Agraria.

D.S.   *Diario de las Sesiones de las Cortes Españolas* (record of Spanish parliamentary debates)

FAI   Federación Anarquista Ibérica (Anarchist action group that won control over the CNT in 1931–32).

FNAE   Federación Nacional de Agricultores de España (Anarchosyndicalist peasant federation from 1913 to 1918).

FNTT   Federación Nacional de Trabajadores de la Tierra (Socialist peasant federation from 1930 to 1936).

IRA   Instituto de Reforma Agraria (Institute of Agrarian Reform).

IRS   Instituto de Reformas Sociales (Institute of Social Reforms, which functioned from 1903 to 1923).

OT   *El Obrero de la Tierra* (FNTT's weekly journal).

PSOE   Partido Socialista Obrero Español (Spanish Socialist party).

REAS   *Revista de Estudios Agro-Sociales* (quarterly published after 1952 by the Instituto de Estudios Agro-Sociales).

UGT   Unión General de Trabajadores (Socialist trade union).

AGRARIAN REFORM AND
PEASANT REVOLUTION IN SPAIN

Introduction

The French Revolution proved to be the last great social upheaval in which the peasantry of northwestern Europe played an important role. As the basis of economic life in France, Germany, England, and the Low Countries shifted from agriculture to industry, the locus of revolutionary activity shifted with it. Long before the end of the nineteenth century the only significant threat to the social order of northwestern Europe came from the industrial proletariat. The peasantry no longer constituted a major revolutionary force.

The new rural tranquillity of northwestern Europe resulted in part from the French Revolution and the liberal reforms of the first half of the nineteenth century, which liquidated the ancient feudal claims that had previously burdened the peasantry. The peasants were transformed into small proprietors as they acquired full property rights to the land they had cultivated for so long. With the alien jurisdictions and oppressive dues of the past gone, the needs and interests of most of the rural population became conservative ones that could be met with relative ease within the existing social framework. As a consequence the peasants of France and Germany became loyal supporters of the new bourgeois society and remained immune to the appeals for its overthrow that attracted their city brethren. The French peasant, for example, refused in 1848 and 1871 to revive the spontaneous revolutionary alliance of 1789 with the Parisian radicals. Elsewhere in Europe the peasantry remained politically so submissive that Marx long seemed justified in his tendency to regard the industrial proletariat as the only truly revolutionary class.

The social balance established by the liberal reforms might easily have been upset, of course, had not the industrialization of northwestern Europe proceeded at a rapid rate. Not only did industrialization provide rich markets for agricultural produce; it also helped absorb the enormous increase in population that occurred everywhere in the world during the nineteenth century. Since surplus manpower could find employment in the cities, no important new discontented class arose in the villages. The countryside became a way station for the poor and landless on their path to the factory, shop, or mine. Because of industrialization, serious rural upheavals were avoided even in England and Prussia, the two northwestern European nations in which large landowners, not peasant proprietors, remained the dominant agricultural class.

On the periphery of northwestern Europe and in the non-European world, the same dramatic transformation to an industrial society did not occur; nor did the peasants achieve the same complete possession of the land. In these areas the overwhelming majority of the population remained in the countryside and participated so actively in social upheavals that it is not unreasonable to characterize the twentieth century as a century of peasant revolution. The Russian peasant, for example, did not sit by passively in 1905 and 1917 but tried to satisfy his craving for land by following the revolutionary lead of the city workers. Throughout Asia and Latin America—in Mexico, China, Cuba, and Vietnam—the turmoil of the past fifty years would be unimaginable were it not for peasant dissatisfaction. So important has the role of the peasantry become that it is increasingly sanctified in revolutionary theory. Lenin modified Marx by admitting the peasantry to equal revolutionary partnership with the industrial proletariat. New theories of guerrilla warfare now modify Lenin by assigning primacy to a militarized peasantry in the struggles for "national liberation."

In this process of historical development, as in so many others, Spain has stood between the two worlds of modern times. Like the northwestern European nations, it, too, altered many of the features of its traditional rural society during the first half of the nineteenth century. The few feudal claims that encumbered property in a nation where feudalism had never been firmly rooted were abolished. The old political jurisdictions of nobility and Church were swept away. Almost all of the Church lands were sold. Extensive tracts of common lands were also placed on the market. Noble properties lost their entailed status and were gradually transferred to untitled owners.

In most of the northern half of Spain, where the rural social structure during the *ancien régime* resembled that of France and western Germany in that the land was already effectively in the hands of small cultivators, the nineteenth-century reforms had social consequences comparable to those achieved in northwestern Europe, and small peasant proprietors emerged as the dominant rural class. To be sure, their position was not so favorable as that of their counterparts in northwestern Europe. The soils they tilled and the markets for their produce were not nearly so rich. Their sons could not so easily find employment in industry but had to be provided for on the land at the cost of fragmenting already small properties. The sluggish economy and the listless Spanish state made it difficult for them to obtain credit.

The poverty of northern rural society had important consequences for Spain in that cultural stagnation prevailed in areas that might otherwise have made a more positive contribution to national life. It also inevitably led to political strains, particularly when a fall in prices or a bad harvest threatened the small farmers with ruin. But the impoverishment of the northern small holders did not seriously threaten the existing social order. Like their more prosperous counterparts in France, Germany, and the Low Countries, they constituted a conservative, not a revolutionary, class.

It was not the standard of living but the illusion of independence which the possession of property gives that separated the nonrevolutionary from the revolutionary peasant. This conclusion is suggested by the historical experience of most of Southern Spain. There the nineteenth-century liberal reforms were either irrelevant or actually prejudicial to the bulk of the rural population, since the existing social structure that the reforms modified was not one in which small cultivators were already in effective possession of the soil but one in which landless workers predominated. No land was transferred to this class, whose dependence on the large owners increased as the latter took over the disentailed properties. As the population grew, the lot of the workers probably worsened. The escape to manufacturing available to the English field hand was lacking. Nor could the increase in population be absorbed by more intensive agriculture because of the relative poverty of the Spanish earth, the lack of prosperous markets, and the failure of the large owners to exploit fully those market opportunities that did exist. The labor surplus led to low wages. The low level of agricultural activity and the sporadic requirements for manpower characteristic of all farming resulted in long periods of unemployment.

Although their standard of living often was not significantly lower than that of many of the peasant proprietors of the north, it was these landless workers, together with some of the tenant farmers who also suffered from insecurity and dependence on the landowners, who tied Spain to the world-wide current of peasant revolution. The needs and interests of this massive rural proletariat were not the modest ones of the peasantry in northern Spain and northwestern Europe. Their demands dealt not with credit but with land, not with tariffs or prices but with a vague "justice." Such demands could be satisfied only with difficulty, if at all, in the existing social structure, because they fundamentally threatened the politically powerful large owners as the demands of the small peasant proprietors did not.

The tragic confrontation of classes in Southern Spain began to unfold after 1870 as the landless workers abandoned Catholicism and turned increasingly to the revolutionary philosophy of anarchism. By the turn of the century village uprisings, insurrectionary strikes, corp burnings, and other violent acts of protest had become endemic. At the end of World War I three consecutive years of labor strife shook Andalusia and Estremadura. Socialist labor unions began to compete with the Anarchists for peasant support. The alienation of the landless workers from the prevailing bourgeois society seemed complete. Southern Spain appeared doomed to a state of permanent instability in which the slightest relaxation of surveillance by the authorities or the slightest enthusiasm among the workers would quickly lead to a new period of conflict.

In 1931 an event occurred that promised to alter the course of the long struggle. The monarchy, which lacked the moral and political resources to deal with the agrarian problem, was overthrown because of urban middle- and working-class opposition. The Republican government that succeeded to power proclaimed as its purpose the regeneration of Spain and set out to conciliate the revolutionary peasant. For the first time in Spanish history a serious attempt at agrarian reform was inaugurated. Its consequences were not, however, the desired harmonization of classes but an intensification of social tensions that contributed first to the collapse of the progressive Azaña government, then to the radicalization of the Socialists, and finally—in 1936—to the outbreak of open and universal class warfare.

The primary purpose of this study is to discover why the agrarian reform of the Second Spanish Republic failed so completely. Because of the overwhelming political importance of the agrarian problem, the study is at the same time an examination of the origins of the Spanish Civil War. So as to place the historical narrative in proper perspective, however, I thought it wise to preface it with what might be considered a sociological analysis of land tenure and the structure of rural society in Southern Spain. This appraisal, which constitutes the first quarter of the book, proved considerably more difficult than I had expected. Spain is unlike most other European nations in that a commonly accepted body of statistical findings and detailed monographic studies does not exist. Most of the data available are so untrustworthy or so subject to controversy as to be almost worthless. The paucity of dependable alternative information led me to make my own analysis more rigorous than it might otherwise have been in a book whose primary concern is political. Those of my readers who cannot tolerate statistics may regret this decision and may even wish to skip directly to the historical narrative in Part II. I sympathize with them but could not omit entirely an attempt to quantify data, else this study, too, would have been guilty of what is the principal failing of so many histories: the recounting of events without proper regard to their social and economic bases.

Although my chief concern is Spain, I hope that my work may also have wider application. It seems to me that the Spanish experience has special relevance to one important aspect of the agrarian problem that agitates so many of the underdeveloped nations today. On both the popular and the official level, the Western world seems to have developed a singularly uniform ideal as to how this problem should be solved. The West hopes that enlightened bourgeois governments will come to power, ally themselves with whatever responsible trade union elements may exist, and deliver land to the peasantry. The redistribution of land is to take place within a democratic framework—that is, by means of parliamentary decisions that adjust the viewpoints of freely competing political parties and are administered through the normal bureaucratic apparatus of the state, with strict regard for due process of law. Former landowners will be guaranteed certain minimal rights. Settlement of the expropriated land will be conducted in accordance with technical criteria so that the new systems of cultivation may prove economically viable. It is recognized that all this will take time yet assumed that the land can be given to the peasants quickly enough to prevent them from turning to more violent solutions.

Few of the great agrarian reforms of the past have followed this pattern. Land reform frequently has been associated with terror, as in the Communist nations; with one-party rule or its equivalent, as in Egypt, Mexico, and occupied Japan; or with precipitous action in a revolutionary situation, as in Mexico once again, in Rumania after World War I, and in Bolivia. Only rarely has major land reform been attempted through constitutional, economically rational procedures within a democratic framework. The Spanish case stands as one of the few historical exceptions. In Spain the initial events followed exactly the pattern prescribed by the Western model for agrarian reform in underdeveloped nations today. Yet the consequence was not the stabilization of society but its destruction. The fundamental question thus arises as to whether the Western model is adequate. Was the Spanish failure due to special circumstances, or do democratic land reforms face obstacles that are likely to prove insurmountable? Is the liberal solution to the land problem a viable solution only under unusually propitious circumstances? These are some of the questions that will implicitly concern us in the second part of this book. But first we must turn to an analysis of the system of land tenure and the structure of the rural society that gave birth to a revolutionary peasantry in Southern Spain.

Part I

LAND TENURE AND
RURAL SOCIAL STRUCTURE

1: Land Tenure in Twentieth-Century Spain

The Importance of Agriculture

During the first sixty years of the twentieth century, Spain remained what it had always been: a primarily agricultural nation. This was true both economically and demographically. Until the mid-1950s, when a new era of industrial development began, agriculture was by far the largest single source of national income. In 1924, for example, agriculture and stock-breeding were estimated to have earned 42.8 percent of the total national income, whereas all extractive and manufacturing industries combined earned but 34.7 percent.[1] A 1935 survey of national wealth showed that the capital value of agriculture and forestry still exceeded the combined capital value of industry and mining by at least one-third.[2] Even after the beginning of the industrial boom of the mid-1950s, agriculture remained a strong rival for economic preeminence. In 1959, according to the official statistics that finally began to be compiled, agriculture and stockbreeding generated 24 percent of the Gross National Product, whereas forestry contributed 2 percent. By contrast, manufacturing industries accounted for 23 percent of the GNP. Only when the latter were combined with mining (2%) and with private construction and public works (4.6%) did the wealth produced by industrial processes surpass, by a slight margin, that earned from the soil. In 1960 these proportions remained identical.[3] Thus at the beginning of the seventh decade of the

1. Estimate of the Banco Urquijo as cited in Ramón Tamames, *Estructura económica de España* (Madrid, 1960), p. 525. The only other important income estimates of the period, those of J. Vandellós, assign a still higher place to agriculture. For these, see J. Vicens Vives, *Historia social y económica de España y América* (4 vols. Barcelona, 1959), vol. 4, pt. 2, p. 106.

2. Antonio de Miguel, *El potencial económico de España,* as cited in Vicens Vives, vol. 4, pt. 2, p. 106.

3. Instituto Nacional de Estadística (henceforth, INE), *Anuario Estadístico: 1961* (Madrid, 1962), p. 582, and *Anuario Estadístico: 1962* (Madrid, 1963), p. 254.

twentieth century, agriculture in Spain still nearly equaled in economic importance all forms of private industrial activity combined.

The dependence of Spain on agriculture was still greater and more prolonged when measured by the proportion of its population actively engaged in farming, stockbreeding, or forestry.[4] In four of the seven censuses completed between 1900 and 1960, the active agricultural population not only surpassed the industrial population but formed an absolute majority of the total active population; in the other three it constituted more than 40 percent. Even as late as 1960, 41.3 percent of the active population tilled the land.[5] In most of Spain the proportion of persons employed in farming and stockbreeding was even greater than these national averages indicate, because industry and commerce were concentrated in a very few provinces. In 1900, for example, the agricultural population constituted more than half the total population in forty-six of the fifty Spanish provinces: in thirty-six of these it accounted for more than 70 percent; in twelve, for more than 80 percent. In 1950 the situation was not radically different. Agriculturalists formed the majority of the population in thirty-six provinces: in eight of these they still represented more than 70 percent of the total. Even in the fourteen provinces where they no longer predominated, agriculturalists remained important: they constituted less than one-third of the total population only in the four industrialized provinces of Madrid, Barcelona, Bilbao, and San Sebastian.[6]

Because of this long preeminence of agriculture, an understanding of Spanish land tenure is essential to a comprehension of the economic, social, and political life of Spain. Control of the land until very recently implied control of the chief source of national wealth and determined the social position of most of the population. Given their importance, it is especially unfortunate that the sources of information on land tenure are so inadequate. The most recent survey, the Agricultural Census of 1962, did not concern itself with land ownership as such but only with

4. Spanish population statistics do not usually distinguish persons employed in agriculture and stockbreeding from those engaged in forestry. However, judging from the 1930 census, the only one in which a distinction was made, forestry workers account for only about 1.5 percent of the agricultural population, or approximately 0.7 percent of the total active population.

5. INE, *Anuario Estadístico: 1962*, p. 49. In 1960, 4.8 million out of 11.6 million employed individuals worked on the land. It is a sad commentary on the recent history of Spain that fewer people (4.6 million) were employed in farming in 1900. In absolute terms the agricultural population of Spain has actually increased during the past sixty years. Its decline in relative terms is due exclusively to the increase in the total active population.

6. Instituto de Cultura Hispánica, *Estudios hispánicos de desarrollo económico: La agricultura y el crecimiento económico* (2 parts, Madrid, 1956), pt. 2, pp. 348–54.

land use. Moreover, although it supplied information on the amount of land farmed by agricultural entrepreneurs, it did not provide any single index by which the value of that land might be determined. The 1953 and 1956 Encuestas Agropecuarias of the Farm Syndicates must be disqualified on other grounds. Extremely narrow in scope, they were not conducted on a scientific basis, so that the scanty findings they do present are not reliable. The Inventory of Expropriable Property compiled in 1933 is more interesting, because it refers entirely to the pre-Civil War period, with which we are principally concerned in this study, and contains information not available elsewhere. However, the Inventory does not encompass all lands but only those subject to the agrarian reform of the Second Republic. Moreover, since the Inventory has never been reduced to statistical terms it cannot be employed in the type of preliminary survey that this chapter purports to be. Only one source remains from which land tenure data suitable to our present purpose of providing a general overview of the property structure in Spain during the first half of the twentieth century can be drawn: the Cadastral Survey conducted since 1906 for purposes of taxation by the Ministry of the Treasury.[7]

Since the rest of this chapter is based chiefly on the Cadastre, some of the peculiarities of this land survey must be mentioned. The Cadastre was conducted with agonizing slowness and its results were published at exceedingly irregular intervals and in widely differing forms. Fairly complete findings were published in 1927 and 1930 for 22 million hectares in Central and Southern Spain, the only regions in which surveying had been done up to that time. In 1959, much less detailed data were published for 43 million hectares. This time the findings encompassed practically the whole of the land surface of Spain that was not covered by towns, roads, and rivers; therefore they included such northerly regions as Galicia, Asturias, the Basque provinces, Aragon, and Catalonia, in which surveying had not begun until after the Civil War.

This combination of circumstances presents the researcher with a dilemma. If he relies exclusively on the 1927 and 1930 figures, he can draw fairly reliable and detailed conclusions, but only for certain areas. If he relies instead exclusively on the 1959 data, he will be able to discuss land tenure in Spain as a whole, but his analysis will be rudimentary because the published data is so sketchy. I have sought to escape from this dilemma by disregarding the temporal differences in the two sets of data, using the 1927–30 data for the regions in which it was available and the 1959 data for the regions surveyed after the Civil War. This

7. For a more extensive discussion of all four sources of information on Spanish land tenure, see app. A.

procedure would obviously be unjustified had Spanish land tenure under-gone a fundamental change between the two periods mentioned. Because of the failure of political reform and the slowness of economic change before 1960, however, this did not occur. If my estimates for 1959 are correct in the tables that follow, it would seem that medium holdings had slightly increased, while large and small holdings had slightly de-creased in importance since 1927–30. Otherwise, the phenomena de-scribed by the Cadastre proved to be enduring, not transitory, and the data for either period can be taken as approximately valid for the other.

Aside from this temporal inconsistency, two other difficulties arise from my choice of method. First, because of the differences mentioned above in the quality of the data available for 1927–30 and for 1959, my conclusions for Central and Southern Spain are considerably more exact than those for Northern Spain or Spain as a whole, where I was forced to resort to rather rough estimates. Second, some of the regional divisions I employ in this chapter are themselves somewhat artificial; both "North-ern" and "Central" Spain are defined by when Cadastral data became available for them and so correspond only loosely to true geographic regions. This artificiality is unimportant, however, since the subregions are valid and can easily be rearranged into more meaningful classifica-tions in later discussion. Moreover, the critical category of "Southern" Spain is functionally useful both geographically and historically and will be employed not only in this chapter but throughout the book.

One final procedural matter must be explained. I have followed the Cadastre in dividing my analysis of land tenure into a discussion of land-holdings as such and a discussion of landowners. Although the two are obviously related, the connection is not so close as in the United States or Britain, where the entire property of an individual tends to be united into a single farm. In Spain a holding is not necessarily a farm in this sense; it is merely a parcel of land which is not contiguous to any other parcels owned by the same person.[8] Of the two types of Cadastral classi-fication, owners are the more important for our purposes, since their total property—not the individual units, or holdings, which together constitute that property—ultimately determines their political and economic power. Nevertheless, individual holdings must also be studied for two important reasons. First, possibly because of political considerations, the published Cadastral findings are much more complete on holdings than on owners. Many critical questions concerning owners can be answered only by projecting conclusions reached in examining holdings. Second, holdings reflect the physical organization of the land and decide to some extent the uses to which it can be put. An owner whose total property of 30 hectares

8. For further information on holdings, see app. A.

is divided into 50 separate, noncontiguous units faces problems quite different from those of an owner with a single 30-hectare farm.

Since the analysis that follows is fairly complicated, it might be wise to state explicitly what I will be trying to do in the rest of this chapter. My main purpose is to show how widely land tenure varies in different regions of Spain and to emphasize in particular the uniqueness of the large property structure of Southern Spain. I seek to achieve these ends first through a discussion of holdings and then of owners. Within each of these sections I subject the statistical data available to close scrutiny so as to ensure that raw numbers which have not been qualified do not mislead us. Data both as to size and taxable income are presented throughout since it is only by means of the latter (which provides a rough indication of the value of the land) that the true economic and social import of the former can be evaluated.

Regional Distribution of Landholdings

Spanish land tenure has two especially striking characteristics. (1) Holdings that are extreme in size and value predominate everywhere in Spain; medium-size holdings, in the sense of farms that in themselves will support (but not enrich) a peasant family, are relatively rare. (2) Pronounced regional differences exist as to which of the extreme types of holdings predominates: in some regions small holdings, none of which in itself will permit a peasant family to earn an adequate livelihood, are paramount; in other regions large holdings that require the constant use of nonfamily labor and produce considerable wealth are the normal units of exploitation.

Medium holdings, which in Spain may be defined statistically as those between 10 and 100 hectares,[9] occupy approximately one-quarter of the land surface of the nation (Table 1). They are most important in Catalonia and the two Basque provinces of Navarre and Alava, but even there they are probably not the predominant form of agricultural organization. In the rest of Spain medium holdings tend to be insignificant. In four of the eight regions of Central and Southern Spain, medium holdings occupy less than one-fifth of the land; in another three they occupy less than one-fourth. The single exception, the Southeast, is a false one, because the land is so arid there that holdings of medium size produce little income unless irrigated. Indeed, because medium holdings everywhere include a higher proportion of unproductive land than do small holdings,

9. See app. A for the problems encountered in deciding upon adequate statistical definitions for such loose terms as "small," "medium," and "large" holdings or owners.

TABLE 1   DISTRIBUTION OF MEDIUM HOLDINGS IN 1930 AND 1959

	Percent of Total Number of Holdings	Percent of Total Area	Percent of Total Taxable Income
Spain (1959)	0.8	24.9	21.5
North (1959)	0.4	21.5	18.6
Center (1930)	0.9	22.3	16.3
South (1930)	2.8	19.8	20.6
Northern Spain			
Galicia	0.1	11.4	9.8
Leon and Burgos	0.2	18.2	15.3
Biscay Coast	0.4	19.4	16.8
Aragon-Ebro	1.2	25.6	22.2
Catalonia	3.2	32.4	28.3
Central Spain			
Old Castile	0.4	14.1	13.6
New Castile	0.6	19.1	14.2
Levante	1.2	24.1	14.9
Southeast	4.2	34.2	25.2
Southern Spain			
Western Andalusia	4.5	20.3	22.1
Estremadura	2.3	21.4	22.1
La Mancha	2.4	18.2	15.9
Eastern Andalusia	2.6	19.2	19.8

SOURCES: The percentages for Central and Southern Spain were compiled from Pascual Carrión, *Los latifundios en España* (Madrid, 1932), Tables 1, 2, 5. For Spain as a whole and Northern Spain, the number of holdings was taken from Gabriel García-Badell, "La distribución de la propiedad agrícola de España en las diferentes categorias de fincas," *Revista de Estudios Agro-Sociales*, no. 30 (Jan.–March 1960), Table 2.

NOTE: I estimated the area and taxable income by methods described in Appendix B. Absolute figures are given in Appendix C, Tables A and B. For Spain as a whole in 1959, 439,404 medium holdings encompassed 10.7 million hectares and were assessed at 1.6 billion pesetas.

Medium holdings are 10–100 hectares. A hectare equals 2.471 acres, or 11,960 square yards.

the income from them and thus their real importance are everywhere less than their extent would indicate. In Spain as a whole, medium holdings occupy about one-quarter of the land but produce little more than one-fifth of the total taxable farm income. In Central and Southern Spain they account for less than one-sixth of the taxable income in four of the eight regions and for less than one-fourth in three others. In the rest of the nation they produce more than one-fourth of the agricultural income only in Catalonia. From whatever point of view the question is examined, the conclusion remains the same: Spain is not a nation of prosperous family-size farm units.

Extremely small holdings are as common as medium holdings are rare. In fact, they are the characteristic form of agricultural organization in most of the nation. On the average they occupy 46 percent of the land and earn 60 percent of the taxable income (Table 2). Their importance

TABLE 2   DISTRIBUTION OF SMALL HOLDINGS IN 1930 AND 1959

	Percent of Total Number of Holdings	Percent of Total Area	Percent of Total Taxable Income
Spain (1959)	99.1	46.5	60.2
North (1959)	99.6	63.3	71.1
Center (1930)	99.0	53.3	73.3
South (1930)	96.6	27.9	41.1
Northern Spain			
Galicia	99.9	78.7	83.2
Leon and Burgos	99.7	63.8	72.4
Biscay Coast	99.6	69.2	74.9
Aragon-Ebro	98.7	54.7	64.8
Catalonia	96.7	54.4	62.9
Central Spain			
Old Castile	99.6	66.1	77.1
New Castile	99.3	58.9	71.1
Levante	98.7	51.4	78.4
Southeast	95.5	33.4	62.0
Southern Spain			
Western Andalusia	94.6	22.4	34.8
Estremadura	97.1	27.4	35.4
La Mancha	97.3	34.8	57.2
Eastern Andalusia	96.9	26.4	49.4

NOTE: Sources and estimates are the same as for Table 1. Absolute figures are given in Appendix C, Tables A and C. For Spain as a whole in 1959, 53,547,993 small holdings (48.7 million of them under 1 hectare in size) encompassed 20.0 million hectares and were assessed at 4.4 billion pesetas.

Small holdings are under 10 hectares.

is very great in Central Spain, where they occupied more than half the land and controlled almost three-quarters of the taxable income in 1930. They are still more predominant in Northern Spain, where it seems likely that small holdings occupy more than 60 percent of the land and earn more than 70 percent of the taxable income. Indeed, in some Northern regions the degree of property fragmentation is staggering. The northwestern corner of the peninsula, above Portugal and to the west of San Sebastian and Soria, contains literally tens of millions of holdings of less than 10 hectares in size. In Galicia alone, where property fragmentation reaches its peak, such tiny parcels will number 15 million when the Cadastre is completed. By 1959 small holdings already outnumbered the total population of Galicia by almost 6 to 1; its total active agricultural population, by 26 to 1; and its peasant proprietor class, by 40 to 1.

Even these figures, striking though they are, do not convey the full implications of the extraordinary fragmentation of property in most of Spain. Although all parcels of under 10 hectares are included in the small-holding category for purposes of convenience, most of them do not begin to approach this size. On the average, almost 80 percent of the small holdings are in fact under half a hectare (1.24 acres) in size; more than 90 percent are less than a full hectare. In Galicia plots of less than half a hectare account for almost 93 percent of all small holdings; those of less than a hectare, for almost 98 percent. The situation is only slightly better in Leon and Burgos and along the Biscay Coast.[10] Nowhere in Spain, not even in Catalonia or in the South, do holdings of more than one hectare form a majority of all small holdings. Indeed, nowhere except in Southern Spain do units of more than 5 hectares constitute so much as 5 percent of all small holdings.[11] Thus, an extreme dominates in a category that is in itself extreme. The units included in the small holding category are usually not merely small but infinitesimal in size.

Small holdings are paramount in the land tenure systems of approximately two-thirds of Spain. They are also very common in the Southern third of the nation, where they constitute well over 90 percent of a lesser number of holdings of all sizes. Although much more numerous than other holdings, however, they are not the predominant form of agricultural organization in Southern Spain. Only in La Mancha did units of less than 10 hectares occupy so much as one-third of the land or earn so much as half of the taxable income in 1930. Medium holdings, though more important than in most of Northern and Central Spain, also were not preponderant. Southern Spain is the stronghold of the large estate. The degree of its preponderance varies according to the definitions chosen. For good land in a nonmechanized agricultural economy, 100 hectares may be considered an equitable statistical definition of farms that require continuous use of nonfamily labor and produce considerable wealth. Because much of the land in Spain is poor, however, many observers have

10. To summarize the situation in Northern Spain as a whole, there were 27.1 million holdings of all types in 1959. Of these, 27.0 million were under ten hectares. Of the small holdings in turn, 23.2 million were less than half a hectare, and only 0.15 million were between five and ten hectares (Gabriel García-Badell, "La distribución de la propieded agrícola de España en las diferentes categorias de fincas," *Revista de Estudios Agro-Sociales* [henceforth, *REAS*], no. 30 [Jan.–March, 1960], table 2).

11. Ministerio de Hacienda, Dirección General de Propiedades (henceforth, DGP), *Memoria de 1928* (Madrid, 1931), p. 123, and Pascual Carrión, *Los latifundios en España* (Madrid, 1932), table 1.

argued that the next level of classification used by the Cadastre, that of 250 hectares, is a more adequate definition of the large estate, one appropriate in all but marginal pasture or forest land.[12]

TABLE 3   DISTRIBUTION OF LARGE HOLDINGS IN 1930 AND 1959

	Percent of Total Number of Holdings	Percent of Total Area	Percent of Total Taxable Income
A. Large holdings defined as all those over 100 hectares			
Spain (1959)	0.1	28.6	18.7
North (1959)	—a	15.2	10.3
Center (1930)	0.1	24.4	10.3
South (1930)	0.6	52.4	38.3
B. Large holdings defined as those over 250 hectares			
Spain (1959)	—	16.9	10.1
North (1959)	—	8.0	4.9
Center (1930)	—	15.6	6.2
South (1930)	0.3	41.2	27.8
C. Regional analysis of holdings of over 250 hectares			
Northern Spain			
Galicia	—	4.6	3.0
Leon and Burgos	—	10.1	6.4
Biscay Coast	—	4.9	3.3
Aragon-Ebro	—	11.3	6.7
Catalonia	—	5.5	3.1
Central Spain			
Old Castile	—	14.4	6.0
New Castile	—	13.6	9.7
Levante	—	14.6	3.3
Southeast	0.1	20.5	7.4
Southern Spain			
Western Andalusia	0.5	46.0	32.1
Estremadura	0.2	35.8	28.7
La Mancha	0.2	38.8	21.6
Eastern Andalusia	0.2	43.3	21.5

NOTE: Sources and estimates are the same as in Table 1. Absolute figures are given in Appendix C, Tables A and D. In Spain as a whole in 1959, 49,323 holdings of over 100 hectares encompassed 12.3 million hectares and were assessed at 1.4 billion pesetas.

a. Unless otherwise stated, a dash (—) in this and all subsequent tables indicates less than 0.05 percent.

12. Carrión, for example, uses 250 hectares as his standard of measurement, whereas García-Badell uses 100 hectares. Neither figure would be adequate to describe a "large" estate in the United States or England, where agriculture is mechanized and farmers constitute a tiny fraction of the total population. In impoverished Spain, where population pressure on the land is very great, the use of the term "large" is perfectly justified, because estates of this size represent wealth far greater than that available to the average individual.

Whichever system of measurement is used, the unique importance of the large estate in Southern land tenure can easily be demonstrated (Table 3). If large estates are defined as those of over 100 hectares, they occupied almost twice as much land as did holdings of less than 10 hectares in Southern Spain in 1930. Precisely the reverse was true in the rest of the nation. In Central Spain large holdings were collectively less than half, and in Northern Spain less than one-fourth, as extensive as small holdings. Measured by the income they produced, large estates were less important in the South than the figures for size suggest, because more good land is usually included in small holdings. Only in Estremadura and Western Andalusia did large estates produce more income than small; in La Mancha they earned but half as much. Nevertheless, even by this standard the contrast with the rest of the nation remains dramatic. Not only were small holdings collectively more valuable in every region of Central and Northern Spain, but their taxable income ranged from 4.8 to 13 times that of the large estates.

The large estate is somewhat less important in the South if 250 rather than 100 hectares is adopted as its proper statistical definition, but the regional differences that distinguish Southern land tenure from that of the rest of Spain become still more pronounced. Even when so restrictively defined, large estates occupied half again as much land as small holdings in Southern Spain. By contrast, in Central Spain the area of large holdings was less than one-third, and in Northern Spain only one-eighth, that of small holdings. Estates of more than 250 hectares were collectively less valuable than holdings of less than 10 hectares in all Southern as well as in all Central and Northern regions; but in the South the taxable income of small holdings ranged from only 1.1 to 2.6 times that of the large, whereas in the rest of Spain small holdings produced from 8 to 28 times as much income.

The regional differences that separate Southern Spain from the rest of the nation are summarized in Table 4, where the number, area, and taxable income of large estates in the South are considered as multiples of these same factors in Central Spain.[13] Two of the conclusions that stem from the material presented should be stressed. First, I compiled the table on the basis of several different statistical definitions of the large estate so as to illustrate further the principle, implied above, that the higher the standard of measurement adopted, the greater the regional inequalities that usually appear. Thus estates of over 100 hectares occupy proportionately twice as much land in the South as in the Center, but estates of over 500 hectares are almost three times as extensive. The

13. The information available on Northern Spain was not sufficiently detailed to justify its use in these calculations.

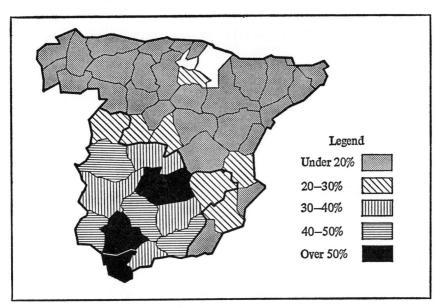

MAP 1. AREA OF LARGE (OVER 250 HECTARE) HOLDINGS

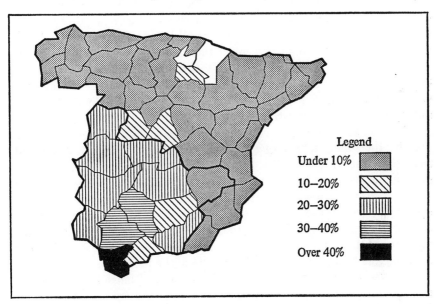

MAP 2. ASSESSED TAXABLE INCOME OF LARGE (OVER 250 HECTARE) HOLD-
INGS

Note: Sources and dates of reference of Maps 1 and 2 same as in Table 3.
Data unavailable for Alava and Navarre. The heavy interior line in these and all
subsequent maps indicates the boundary of Southern Spain.

TABLE 4   LARGE HOLDINGS IN SOUTHERN AS COMPARED TO CENTRAL SPAIN CIRCA 1930

Holdings (hectares)	Number of Holdings	Relation (Center = 100) Area Occupied	Taxable Income
Over 100	144	194	309
Over 250	200	239	372
Over 500	270	290	401
Over 1,000	359	420	393
Over 2,500	483	543	275

SOURCES: The categories under 1,000 hectares refer to 1930 and were compiled from Carrión, *Latifundios*, Tables 2, 3, 5. The categories over 1,000 hectares refer to 1927 and were compiled from DGP, *Memoria de 1928* (Madrid, 1931), pp. 121-34.

NOTE: The indexes are weighted to take into account the different amounts of land surveyed in Central and Southern Spain at each date. Over 100 hectare holdings occupied 43.7% of their total survey area and over 1,000 hectare 13.4%.

reason for this is that giant, as opposed to merely large, holdings increase in relative importance within the large-holding category as that category itself increases in importance. For example, in Central Spain giant holdings of over 500 hectares (1,236 acres) accounted for some 36 percent of the area and 34 percent of the income of all large holdings. In the South the proportions rose to 53 percent of the area and 44 percent of the income.[14] It is the giant holding, not any lesser type, that primarily accounts for the uniqueness of Southern land tenure. Once more, as was the case with small holdings in Northern Spain, an extreme predominates in a category that is in itself extreme.

The second interesting conclusion presented in Table 4 is that, except for the superestates larger than 1,000 hectares, the greatest regional disparity exists in the relative taxable income, not in the relative extension of the large estates. Large estates of under 1,000 hectares occupy from two to three times as much land in the South as they would in an equivalent area in the Center but earn from three to four times as much income, depending on whether 100, 250, 500 hectares is taken as the standard of measurement. This fact is significant because of its relevance to the agitated controversy as to the nature of the land in the large estates. Opponents of agrarian reform have traditionally dismissed the need for state action by arguing that the size of the large estates was meaningless because they consisted almost entirely of forest or poor pasture that could not be cultivated.[15] Advocates of reform, on the other hand, tend to for-

14. Compiled from Carrión, tables 2, 3, 5.
15. See, for example, a series of articles entitled "La leyenda negra andaluza" by José de las Cuevas in the influential newspaper *ABC*, 26 January–1 February

TABLE 5   DISTRIBUTION OF CULTIVATED LAND IN VARIOUS TYPES OF HOLDINGS IN 1927 AND 1962

1927		1962	
Size of Holding (hectares)	Income-Area Ratio	Size of Exploitation (hectares)	Percent Cultivated
Under 1	1.76	Under 1	81.4
1–5	1.26	1–5	72.6
5–10	1.32	5–10	72.4
10–50	0.99	10–50	76.2
50–100	0.92	50–100	66.2
100–250	0.84	100–200	49.7
250–500	0.76	200–500	32.3
500–1,000	0.73	500–1,000	20.9
1,000–5,000	0.50	Over 1,000	6.7
Over 5,000	0.27		

SOURCES: The 1927 figures are Cadastral data from DGP, *Memoria 1928*, pp. 125, 133. The 1962 data come from INE, *Primer Censo Agrario de España: Año 1962* (Madrid, 1966), p. 10.

get that the Cadastre surveys all types of land and regard every hectare as potentially arable so as to dramatize the need for legislative or revolutionary action.[16] Since both sides have used this ambiguity in the Cadastre findings for propagandist purposes, a systematic clarification of the relation between large holdings and uncultivated land is in order.

There can be no question that large estates generally include more than their share of nonarable land. This was conclusively proven by the Agricultural Census of 1962, which showed that only 26.6 percent of the area held by entrepreneurs who exploited less than 100 hectares was untilled, whereas 79.4 percent of the land in exploitations of over 100 hectares was not cultivated.[17] The same conclusion can also be reached through the Cadastral findings by comparing the ratio of taxable income earned by each type of holding to the area it occupied. Because agricultural land is usually much more valuable than pasture or forest, the higher the ratio of income to extension, the greater, proportionately, the amount of cultivated land included. The lower the ratio, the less the amount of such land present. Granted this assumption, it can be seen by referring to Table 5 that there is a steady decline in the proportion of ara-

---

1962. On a more sophisticated level, see Luis Marichalar, *La reforma agraria en España* (Madrid, 1931), passim, or, among foreign writers, William Foss and Cecil Gerahty, *The Spanish Arena* (London, John Gifford, 1938 [?]), pp. 22–32.

16. For example, Carrión, passim. On a less sophisticated level, see Cristóbal de Castro, *Al servico de los campesinos* (Madrid, 1931).

17. INE, *Primer Censo Agrario de España: Año 1962. Resumenes nacionales* (Madrid, 1966), p. 10.

ble land as the holding categories increase in size. Thus holdings of under 10 hectares consist primarily of arable land, but by the time one reaches estates of more than 5,000 hectares he is clearly dealing almost entirely with pasture or woodland. In some cases the differences in the ratios may be due partly to varying intensities of cultivation. On the whole, however, the way in which the taxable income is assessed and the uniformity of the decline in the income-area ratios both suggest that natural rather than human factors are responsible.[18]

Nor can there be any doubt that what was true for Spanish large holdings in general was also true for the Southern large estates. The 1962 Agricultural Census showed much more untilled land in large Southern exploitations than in small. The income-area ratio in the Cadastral findings is also unfavorable to the large holdings. Finally, a study of the specific location of large Southern estates suggests a positive, if irregular, correlation between such estates and nonagricultural land. For example, in Ciudad Real 33 of the 43 townships in which estates of over 250 hectares occupied more than half the land (and 13 of the 15 in which they monopolized more than three-quarters) were located in three mountainous counties. In Cordova the results are similar: 14 of the 20 municipalities in which 250-hectare units were dominant consisted primarily of pasture and woodland. In Seville the correlation was not as high, yet 15 out of the 29 townships in which 250-hectare holdings occupied half the land were also areas where more than half of the soil was not arable.[19]

The important question, however, is whether the relation between large estates and uncultivated land is greater in Southern Spain than in the rest of the nation. Although this question cannot be answered by township analyses, because information on this level is too difficult to obtain in most of Spain, all available means of measurement concur in proving that large estates are not more common in Andalusia and Estremadura because there is more forest and pasture land there.[20] In fact, it is clear that such estates include much less nonarable land in the South than elsewhere. Thus, according to the Agricultural Census of 1962, 64.8 percent

18. For further information on the assessed taxable income and its use as a rough indication of the nature of land, see app. A.

19. Based upon Carrión, pp. 107–09, 209–11, 223–26; Instituto de Reformas Sociales (henceforth, IRS), *Información sobre el problema agrario en la provincia de Córdoba* (Madrid, 1919), pp. 212–14; and an unpublished "Memoria" by the Provincial Delegation for Seville of the Institute of Agrarian Reform (folder 41/0–1, IRA archives).

20. In 1959, for example, the highest proportions of uncultivated land in Spain were recorded in Asturias (78.7%), Galicia (73.7%), the Basque provinces (63.8%), and Aragon (57.1%), precisely the regions in which property fragmentation was greatest.

of the area of large Southern exploitations were uncultivated, but in the rest of Spain 89.2 percent went untilled.[21] Or, to return to the Cadastral figures for 1930, estates of more than 100 hectares in Central Spain had an income-area ratio of 0.422, whereas the ratio for Southern large estates was 0.731, three-quarters again as much.[22]

The principal reason for the regional differences in the types of land included in the large estates seems to be that most of what the Cadastre records as large holdings in the rest of Spain are really municipal common lands composed primarily of pasture or forest, whereas most of the Southern large holdings are privately owned estates, many of which are arable. The question of corporate versus private ownership will be discussed in greater detail later in this chapter. The important point to be emphasized here is that large estates include proportionately the greatest amount of cropland precisely in those regions in which they are most dominant. Indeed, if this were not so the Southern large estates could scarcely have aroused such extreme political opposition. The general acceptance of the name *latifundio* to describe them suggests the hatred with which they are regarded. Nor is the use of this term entirely unjustified. Because large estates controlled some two and one-half to three times as much of the *cultivated* surface in the South as elsewhere (40.6 percent to 15.5 percent, according to the Agricultural Census of 1962), their importance in the social and economic life of Andalusia, Estremadura, and La Mancha was until recently comparable to that of the latifundia of the ancient Roman world.

Regional Distribution of Landowners

The distribution of holdings is in itself an adequate index of the system of land tenure only in those few nations in which a single owner normally farms a single plot of land. In Spain, where agricultural holdings are almost twice as numerous as the entire population, owners and holdings obviously are not conterminous.[23] The human aspect of Spanish land tenure must be discussed separately; our analysis of individual farming units must be followed by an examination of the way in which these units are combined into the property blocs that determine the social and economic power of their owners.

Unfortunately, Cadastral information is much less satisfactory on the

21. INE, *Censo Agrario*, p. 10, and provincial reports for the thirteen southern provinces.

22. Compiled from Carrión, tables 2, 3.

23. With the Cadastre not yet completed, 54 million holdings were reported in 1959. The population of Spain at the time was slightly over 30 million.

ownership of landed property than on individual holdings as such. The taxpayers listed by the Cadastre are for the most part not true agricultural proprietors in the sense of individuals who depend primarily on their lands for their livelihood. More than half of them are really gardeners—workers or shopkeepers whose chief income is derived elsewhere but who possess a small plot of land on which to grow a few vegetables for home consumption.[24]

A considerable proliferation of "owners" also occurs among those whose properties are larger and more valuable. In order to create manageable zones of investigation for its surveying teams, the Cadastre regards townships as isolated, self-contained units and records property only as it exists within each township. The individual whose lands are dispersed over several municipalities therefore is registered as an owner as often as there are municipalities in which he holds property. The resulting duplication of owners is probably greatest in Northern Spain, where townships tend to be small and holdings widely scattered.[25]

The fact that the Cadastre necessarily considers individual taxpayers, not family units, has similar consequences. Because it is common for a woman to retain title to the lands she brought as a dowry to her marriage, two owners often appear although a single family unit has exclusive use of the land. Again the duplication is probably greatest in Northern Spain, because there are so many more true peasant proprietors there.

This duplication of owners has an important consequence. Because the number of owners is exaggerated, the true size and value of the property of each is thereby understated. The effects of this distortion are probably greatest not in Northern Spain but among the large proprietors of the South. Although these individuals less often hold lands in several townships, when they do their properties in each are usually sizable.

24. Although no statistical definition can be completely accurate, it may safely be assumed that "owners" with total holdings of less than a hectare or an assessed taxable income in 1959 of less than 300 pesetas (i.e. whose real income from their lands was some 1,200 pesetas at a time when the average earnings for all employed individuals were approximately 39,000 pesetas) were really gardeners. In 1959, out of a total of 6.0 million Cadastral "owners," 3.1 million were gardeners under the area classification and 3.4 million under the income classification. Their properties accounted for only 2.7 percent of the area surveyed and 4.8 percent of the income assessed.

25. For figures on resident and nonresident owners, see INE, *Estadística de propietarios de fincas rústicas de España* (Madrid, 1951), p. 10. In Northern and Central Spain there were usually more than 50 nonresident owners for every 100 resident owners. In Southern Spain, only Salamanca and Toledo had more than 30 nonresidents for every 100 resident proprietors. Generally speaking, the smaller the municipalities in each province, the more often lands belonging to residents of neighboring municipalities were to be found in them.

Similarly, since the wealthy tend to marry the wealthy in Spain as elsewhere, when the spouse of a Southern large owner holds land in her name it is more often property of great consequence.[26]

The inadequacy of the Cadastral data is not limited to a gross overstatement of the number of owners and a consequent understatement of their true wealth. The system by which the ownership data are classified defeats any attempt to determine the exact relative importance of various types of proprietors. In dealing with holdings the Cadastre uses various dimensions of size as its basis for reporting both their income and their extension. For example, we learn that holdings of from 250 to 500 hectares occupy a certain area and earn a certain income. This method of reporting is not used for owners. Taxpayers are classified according to the size of their properties and according to the income these properties earn, but the two classifications are completely separate and lack a common basis of correlation. We know that a certain number of individuals own a certain amount of land but cannot determine what that land is worth. We also know that another group of individuals enjoy a certain income but do not know how much land is required to produce that income. The proprietor of 400 hectares of poor pasture may appear as a large owner in terms of area but as a medium owner in terms of income. Likewise, the owner of 40 irrigated hectares may seem a medium proprietor by area but a large proprietor by income.

Another equally important defect—one that affects Cadastral reporting of holdings as well as of owners—is the failure to distinguish between private and corporate ownership. As mentioned previously, many of the "large owners" are really municipalities whose lands are open to the use of all inhabitants, not private proprietors whose farms are dedicated to their individual profit. The importance of this distortion varies from region to region. Although municipal lands accounted for 17.4 percent of the national land surface in 1959, they occupied only 7.7 percent of the soil in Southern Spain and thus were of minor significance there. In Central and Northern Spain, on the other hand, they occupied 23.0 percent of the area and had considerable importance.[27] The effects of the distortion also vary according to which owner classification is being dis-

26. For example, a sampling of six latifundio provinces in the "Registro de la Propiedad" of the Instituto de Reforma Agraria shows that in 1933 only 4 of the 39 wives of noblemen who had property listed in their own name possessed less than 250 hectares; 7 owned between 250 and 500 hectares; 9, between 500 and 1,000; and 19, more than 1,000 hectares.

27. Compiled from Ministerio de Agricultura, D.G. de Montes, *Estadística forestal de España: Año 1959* (Madrid, 1961), p. 57. The low proportion of common lands in Southern Spain results from the effects of the nineteenth-century disentailments discussed in chap. 2.

cussed. Because common lands are usually very extensive, their presence can strongly affect the large-owner categories of the area classification. Perhaps half of the large owners by area in Northern and Central Spain and one-seventh of those in Southern Spain are not individuals but municipalities. In the income classification the effects are probably more dispersed and fall as much upon the medium- as upon the large-owner categories. This is because the common lands, though large, usually consist of pasture or forest, which has a low tax assessment. Thus perhaps 20 percent of the Northern and Central large-income holders and 5 percent of such holders in the South are municipalities.

These and other defects in the Cadastre are discussed at greater length in Appendix A. They limit but do not destroy the validity of the ownership data. In dealing with large owners two major considerations must be kept in mind. On the one hand the Cadastre overstates their relative importance because of its inclusion of gardeners. Not quite so small a proportion of the true owners as is usually reported holds so large a proportion of the land and income.[28] The disparity among individuals is also lessened somewhat because many of the large owners are really municipalities. On the other hand the Cadastre also understates the importance of the large owner. Because large owners often hold lands in several municipalities and effectively control properties registered in the names of their wives and children, they in fact possess much more land and a much greater total income than the Cadastre reports. The rather astounding extent to which this can be true is shown in Chapter 3 in a special study of family relationships among large owners in the province of Badajoz.

It is impossible to determine the extent to which this simultaneous overstatement and understatement cancel each other out in each region. One fact, however, is certain. Because the South has far fewer common lands and gardeners than elsewhere,[29] the factors that lead to an over-

28. Almost all of the secondary works on modern Spanish history, including such profound studies as Gerald Brenan's *The Spanish Labyrinth* (Cambridge, 1960), make the error of considering Cadastral "owners" as true owners. Although this error usually has little practical significance—even in comparison to other types of true owners, large owners hold a disproportionate amount of the land and income—it can lead to serious misinterpretation. For example, because he does not distinguish between gardeners and true owners, Brenan is led to say: "In that part of Spain which had been assessed by 1929, out of 1,026,412 landowners or tenants paying taxes, 847,548 earned daily less than one peseta" (p. 113). In fact, the latter group earned most of its livelihood from sources other than the land to which it held title. Its true income was not great, but it was certainly higher than one peseta.

29. The South is the only region in which Cadastral "owners" are less numerous than the total agricultural population. Thus in 1959 it had 1.4 million "owners" to a farm population of 1.8 million, whereas in the rest of Spain there were 4.6 million "owners" to an agricultural population of only 3.0 million.

statement of large-owner importance are least operative there. The Ca-dastre may exaggerate the property of large owners in Northern and Central Spain, but it unquestionably understates the possessions of large Southern owners. The regional differences within Spain are therefore even greater than Tables 6 and 7 show. The Southern large owners are economically even more powerful than the Cadastral findings indicate.

The fundamental conclusion that emerges from the Cadastral owner-ship data thus qualified is that the extremes that separate types of owners are much greater than those that separate types of holdings. Only the position of medium owners is roughly comparable to that of medium holdings. Small proprietors collectively control much less land and earn much less income than do small holdings. Large proprietors collectively control much more land and earn a much higher income than do large holdings. On the average, approximately 46.5 percent of the Spanish

TABLE 6   DISTRIBUTION OF OWNERS BY AREA IN 1959

	Gardeners and Small Owners		Medium Owners		Large Owners	
	A	B	A	B	A	B
Spain	91.7	19.7	7.5	27.9	0.8	52.4
North	93.9	32.7	5.7	29.0	0.4	38.3
Center	91.3	19.3	8.0	33.8	0.7	46.9
South	87.6	10.0	10.5	23.5	1.9	66.5
Northern Spain						
Galicia	96.4	51.3	3.5	31.9	0.1	16.8
Leon and Burgos	94.6	35.3	5.2	21.6	0.3	43.1
Biscay Coast	93.6	34.4	6.1	30.2	0.3	35.4
Aragon-Ebro	89.9	22.9	9.3	27.0	0.8	50.0
Catalonia	89.7	22.9	9.2	36.8	0.9	40.3
Central Spain						
Old Castile	89.9	19.8	9.4	39.0	0.7	41.2
New Castile	87.0	6.9	11.8	32.6	1.2	60.5
Levante	96.3	36.7	3.4	26.2	0.3	36.9
Southeast	88.6	20.5	10.2	31.8	1.2	47.6
Southern Spain						
Western Andalusia	85.8	5.7	11.7	22.4	2.5	71.8
Estremadura	88.4	10.4	9.6	21.4	1.9	68.1
La Mancha	87.2	11.7	11.2	25.8	1.7	62.4
Eastern Andalusia	90.4	17.3	8.4	26.1	1.2	56.5

SOURCE: The owner figures come from García-Badell, "Distribución de la propie-dad," Table 3.

NOTES: Area was estimated by methods explained in Appendix B. Absolute figures are given in Appendix C, Tables E and F. 1930 figures were not used for Central and Southern Spain, because on owner area they are no more detailed than those of 1959.

"A" columns indicate the percentage of all Cadastral owners formed by a given category; "B" columns, the estimated percentage of the total area held by that category.

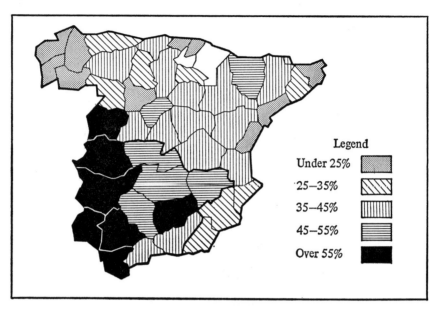

MAP 3. AREA HELD BY LARGE (OVER 250 HECTARE) OWNERS

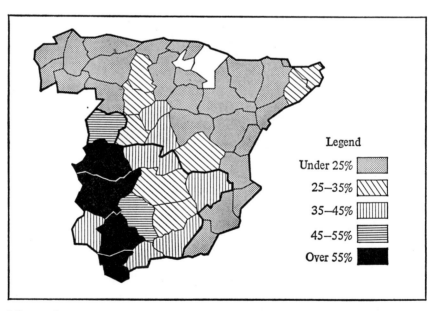

MAP 4. ASSESSED TAXABLE INCOME HELD BY WEALTHIEST OWNERS

Note: Source and data for Map 3 same as in Table 6, but only owners with over 250 hectares are included. Sources, categories, and periods of reference for Map 4 same as in Table 7. Data unavailable for Alava and Navarre.

TABLE 7 DISTRIBUTION OF OWNERS BY ASSESSED TAXABLE INCOME IN 1930 AND 1959

| | Gardeners and Small Owners | | Medium Owners | | Large Owners | |
	A	B	A	B	A	B
Spain (1959)	96.4	46.1	3.1	28.0	0.4	26.0
North (1959)	97.4	60.2	2.5	26.5	0.2	13.3
Center (1930)	96.8	47.9	2.7	28.0	0.4	24.2
South (1930)	93.0	25.4	5.4	24.0	1.5	50.7
Northern Spain						
Galicia	99.0	80.2	1.0	15.1	—	4.7
Leon and Burgos	98.7	72.4	1.2	17.7	0.1	9.9
Biscay Coast	96.5	58.5	3.4	31.1	0.2	10.4
Aragon-Ebro	95.7	53.0	4.0	28.2	0.4	18.8
Catalonia	92.9	40.1	6.5	39.4	0.6	20.4
Central Spain						
Old Castile	97.3	39.5	2.4	29.3	0.4	31.3
New Castile	95.4	39.9	3.9	27.1	0.7	33.0
Levante	97.0	56.7	2.7	27.5	0.3	15.8
Southeast	97.9	55.1	1.8	27.6	0.2	17.3
Southern Spain						
Western Andalusia	91.6	21.5	6.3	22.3	2.1	56.2
Estremadura	90.9	19.8	6.9	22.5	2.2	57.7
La Mancha	95.4	38.4	3.9	26.1	0.8	35.5
Eastern Andalusia	93.8	29.5	5.0	28.7	1.2	41.8

SOURCES: All statistics for Central and Southern Spain are compiled from Carrión, *Latifundios*, unnumbered table facing p. 86. Northern and national owner figures come from García-Badell, "Distribución de la propiedad," Table 5.

NOTES: Income was estimated by methods explained in Appendix B. Absolute figures are given in Appendix C, Tables G and H.

"A" columns indicate the percentage of all Cadastral owners formed by a given category; "B" columns, the percentage of the assessed taxable income held by that category.

soil in 1959 was organized into units of less than 10 hectares, but owners whose total properties did not surpass this figure controlled only 19.7 percent, or less than half as much (Tables 2 and 6). Only 28.6 percent of Spain was farmed in units larger than 100 hectares, but fully 52.4 percent, almost twice as much, was owned by individuals whose total holdings exceeded this size (Tables 3 and 6).[30] The gulf separating small

30. The disproportion between the area controlled by various types of large holdings and various types of large owners increases as the standard of measurement itself increases. At 100 hectares, owners control almost twice as much land as do holdings (52.4% to 28.4%); at 250 hectares, more than twice as much (42.4% to 16.9%); at 500 hectares, more than three times as much (32.6% to 9.7%); at 1,000 hectares, more than four times as much (22.0% to 5.0%); and at 5,000 hectares, more than five times as much (5.2% to 1.0%).

from large also widened in terms of income. If small holdings earned
60.2 percent of the taxable income, small owners earned but 46.1 percent
(Tables 2 and 7). Whereas large holdings accounted for 18.79 percent of
the assessed income, large owners earned 26.0 percent of that income
(Tables 3 and 7).[31]

What is true for Spain as a whole is also true for each of its regions.
In Central Spain holdings of more than 250 hectares occupied 15.6 percent
of the land, but owners in this category controlled 37.7 percent. Small
holdings in Central Spain earned 73.3 percent of the taxable income; small
owners, only 47.9 percent. The same pattern held in Southern Spain.
Small owners were collectively less important and large owners more so
even in the most highly fragmented regions of Northern Spain. In Galicia,
for example, three-quarters of the soil was organized into units of less
than 10 hectares, but barely half was owned by individuals whose total
holdings did not exceed this size. By contrast, though large holdings
scarcely existed in Galicia, large owners controlled 17 percent of the land
even there.

The conclusion is obvious. The *minifundista*, the small holder, is
much less predominant than the *minifundio*, the small holding, but the
latifundista is much more important than the *latifundio*. The unbalanced
nature of Spanish land tenure is accentuated when the human factor is
introduced. Small holders own fewer than half of the small holdings.
Large owners do not depend exclusively upon large holdings, with their
relatively higher proportion of poor lands, but also own many fertile
small and medium holdings. The possibilities for agrarian reform lie not
only in a breaking up of large estates but also in separating many minute
holdings from the property blocs into which they have gravitated.

Because this accentuation of the extremes occurs in a fairly uniform
manner throughout the nation, the regional variations that were noted in
examining individual holdings persist in approximately the same proportions when owners are discussed. Although small owners are less dominant
and large owners more dominant than small and large holdings, respectively, in Northern Spain, the region remains primarily one of small
peasant proprietors. In 1959 this class controlled almost as much land and
almost four times as much income as the large owners (Tables 6 and 7).
The same holds true to a lesser degree for Central Spain, where small
proprietors earned approximately twice as much income as did large owners in 1930. Both regions differed radically from Southern Spain, where a

31. Strictly speaking, this kind of analysis is incorrect, because the earnings of
large holdings by size are compared to those of large owners by income, not to those
of large owners by size. The capriciousness of the Cadastral classifications, however,
leaves no alternative.

few owners appropriated 66.5 percent of the land and 50.7 percent of the income. Not only did Southern large owners surpass the small-owner class in area and income; they surpassed all other classes of owners combined.

As mentioned earlier, the regional disparity is even greater than the Cadastral figures show because of their tendency to overstate large-owner property in Northern and Central Spain and to understate it in the South. This disparity constitutes the single central reality of Spanish land tenure, a reality that overrides the many local variations. Spain is divided into two broad areas: in the Southern third of the nation, especially in Western Andalusia and in Estremadura, large holdings and large owners predominate; in the remaining two-thirds of Spain large owners are not uncommon, but agriculture rests principally in the hands of small peasant proprietors who cultivate small holdings.

The boundary between the latifundio regions and the rest of the nation is an extremely important one in Spanish social history. Some of the fundamental facts of Spanish political life during the past century have been based upon this regional division. Where large owners were not predominant, agrarian unrest did not become universal or continuous but arose sporadically in response to special conditions and achieved general importance mainly during the breakdown of state authority during the first months of the Civil War. Where large owners monopolized the soil, agrarian unrest was endemic, constantly upsetting the political life not only of the South but also of the nation. Other social agrarian problems existed, to be sure, but they were converted into phenomena of national rather than local consequence only because they were nurtured by the profound dissatisfaction engendered by the central problem of the latifundios. Without the latifundios, it is inconceivable that either rural anarchism or revolutionary rural socialism could have developed the strength it achieved. Both figuratively and literally, the line that divided the Spain of agrarian revolution from the Spain of agrarian conservatism was essentially the same line that separated the latifundio regions from the rest of the nation.

Although the interrelation between the latifundios, social protest, and political action forms the main theme of this study, the regional disparity in land tenure is so pronounced that it is worth speculating briefly on its causes. An analysis of the historical and geographical setting of the latifundio system in Southern Spain will also begin to answer the question as to whether agrarian reform in the 1930s was a feasible solution to the social dissatisfaction this system had produced. The latifundios that consist of nonarable pasture or forest are not in question in this analysis, since large tracts of land of this kind obviously are necessary to earn their owners an adequate livelihood. Rather, the fundamental problem is whether natural conditions are so harsh in Southern Spain that, even when arable, land can successfully be cultivated only in large units by individuals who possess large quantities of capital. To what extent is the latifundio system on *agricultural* land—for, as mentioned earlier, it is the presence of the system on such lands which lends uniqueness to Southern land tenure—a product of geographical conditions and therefore essentially irreversible, and to what extent is it a product of history and thus at least partly alterable?

2: Geographical and Historical
Setting of the Latifundios

The Influence of Geography

Spain is divided into two principal parts by its systems of land tenure. There are also two distinct Spains from the point of view of climate—the rainy Spain and the arid Spain of popular parlance. All attempts to provide a geographical rationale for the latifundios ultimately invoke the latter division to explain the former. Large estates and large owners are said to be characteristic of the South, because "there is great risk of crop failure, more land is needed to feed a family and nothing grows without irrigation. Only a man with a large amount of land and capital can withstand such natural disadvantages over a long period of time." [1] Inevitably, it is argued, the small owner will collapse and the large owner will absorb his possessions. Thus the latifundios are not the product of historical circumstances but of harsh and irreversible climatic and geographical realities.

This argument cannot withstand close analysis. Spanish land tenure regions do not correspond very closely to climatic regions. The most exaggerated forms of the minifundios are indeed found in rainy Spain, where agricultural conditions are relatively favorable. It is also true that the latifundios are located entirely within arid Spain. However, the latifundio regions account for considerably less than half of arid Spain; in more than half, small holdings, not large estates, have somehow managed to survive as the predominant form of property. Rainy Spain, which constitutes less than one-fifth of the national land surface,[2] corresponds to only the

1. Ruth Way, *A Geography of Spain and Portugal* (London, 1962), p. 254.
2. The principal rainy regions (Galicia, the Basque Coast, Navarre, and Alava) cover 6.3 million hectares. Since the rainy area also extends along the Pyrenees and the southern slopes of the Cantabrian mountain chains, thus including small portions of provinces that I have listed as arid, the total surface of rainy Spain is approximately 10.0 million hectares, or about one-fifth of the total Spanish land surface of 50.0 million hectares.

Atlantic and Pyrenean provinces of what was called "Northern" Spain in our discussion of land tenure. The Catalonian and Aragonese provinces of "Northern" Spain and the whole of "Central" Spain fall within the arid four-fifths of the nation. The predominance of small property in the Levante and in Murcia may perhaps be attributed to the extensive irrigation systems that have long existed there. No such explanation will suffice for much of Catalonia, most of Aragon, and the whole of that immense region known as Old and New Castile which lies upon the great central plateau of Spain, the Meseta.

A number of methods must be used to document these assertions, since there is no single satisfactory criterion by which the natural agricultural potentialities of large regions can be judged. Climatic conditions offer perhaps the easiest gauge. Since agricultural potentialities are determined by the soil as well as by the climate, some analysis, however rudimentary, of soil conditions is also necessary. Finally, because there are so many imponderables, the ultimate criterion of natural fertility must be the comparative crop yields of various regions in lands on which man has not decisively altered natural conditions by the introduction of irrigation. All these tests are applied in the pages that follow.

Before beginning our discussion, a word of explanation must be offered. Although I shall drop the somewhat artificial categories of "Central" and "Northern" Spain—which had to be used in Chapter 1 because of the availability of Cadastral data—in favor of divisions that correspond more closely to true natural regions,[3] agricultural conditions vary so greatly that neither these new divisions nor any others that could be de-

3. The principal change was the transfer of the Aragon-Ebro and Catalan regions from "Northern" Spain to the Meseta-Ebro and Mediterranean Coast classifications, respectively. Another was the merger of Leon and Burgos with Old Castile in the Meseta-Ebro, to which region the two provinces belong both historically and geographically. The geographical tables differ from the land tenure tables in one other respect. The two Basque provinces of Navarre and Alava, which did not appear in the land tenure tables because their ancient *feuros* (constituted privileges) permit them independent tax administration, are now reported. The Basque provinces of Guipúzcoa and Vizcaya, which lost similar privileges because they resisted the Nationalists during the Civil War, continue to be included with the Biscay Coast provinces, which they resemble agriculturally. Needless to say, the problem of regional classification is a difficult one, because all information is collected on the basis of provinces, political divisions that do not always correspond with natural divisions. For example, Angel Zorrilla, *Introducción a la economía agrícola española en relación con la europea* (Madrid, 1960), adopts a more complicated classification, which differs somewhat from mine. It might also be mentioned that I will no longer capitalize "Northern" and "Central" Spain since these words no longer refer to specific regions, as they did in our discussion of land tenure. Since Southern Spain does refer to a specific region throughout the book, however, it continues to be capitalized. See the section on "Regional Divisions," pp. xvii–xix, for more details.

vised are perfectly satisfactory. For example, Catalonia enjoys considerably more rainfall than the Levante and Southeastern provinces with which I have linked it to form a "Mediterranean Coast" region. There is also some question as to whether Navarre and Alava are geographically sufficiently akin to the Biscay provinces and to Galicia to be classified with them in a "Cantabric Coast" region. Finally, in my "Meseta-Ebro" classification there are important climatic differences between what I call the "Aragon-Ebro" region and Old and New Castile.

To have paid strict heed to these many variations would have led to a proliferation of categories which could only have confused our discussion. Moreover, if the classifications I have chosen are not geographically impeccable, they are functionally useful. The Cantabric Coast classification encompasses the small-holding region that coincides with the rainy portions of northern Spain. The Mediterranean Coast classification corresponds to the region where small and medium holdings predominate despite vast areas of extraordinary aridity. The Meseta-Ebro classification includes all the other arid regions of Spain in which small and medium holdings are dominant. Southern Spain remains unchanged from the previous chapter; it encompasses the large-holding arid regions. The relation between these last two regions will be the focal point of our discussion, both because they account for most of the land and rural population of Spain and because they may be considered climatologically "normal" for that country. This focus of interest is reflected in my organization of material in the tables: I have presented subregional breakdowns for Southern Spain and the Meseta-Ebro alone; only over-all totals are given for the Cantabric and Mediterranean Coast regions.

Table 8 summarizes the climatic characteristics of the chief regions of peninsular Spain by indicating the average annual rainfall and the average temperature in each during a thirty-year period. Any discussion confined to these data is bound to be unrealistic, however. The rate of evaporation and transpiration by which moisture is removed from the soil must also be taken into account, because this determines the effectiveness of precipitation. Where specific measurements of evaporation do not exist, as is the case in most of Spain,[4] climatologists have devised alternate methods of estimating its influence. Since all of these are based on the fact that faster evaporation occurs at higher temperatures, they divide the average rainfall by the average temperatures to arrive at an "index of

4. For the few data available, see the excellent geographical handbook prepared by the Naval Intelligence Division of the English Admiralty, *Spain and Portugal, Volume I: The Peninsula* (4 vols. London, 1941), p. 90. In some areas evaporation is so rapid that Rafael del Cano, *Ante la reforma agraria* (Madrid, 1931), pessimistically speaks of an "upward rainfall."

aridity" which serves as an approximate guide to the effectiveness of precipitation. The index of aridity in Table 8 was calculated on the basis of the most widely accepted of these methods, that of de Martonne.[5]

TABLE 8   AVERAGE TEMPERATURE, AVERAGE ANNUAL RAINFALL, AND ESTIMATED ARIDITY IN 1901–30

Region and Number of Weather Stations	Average Annual Rainfall (millimeters)	Average Temperature (centigrade)	Estimated Index of Aridity
Spain (52)	620	14.2	25.6
Cantabric Coast (12)	1,075	13.1	46.5
Mediterranean Coast (11)	431	16.7	16.1
Meseta-Ebro (15)	461	11.7	21.2
Southern Spain (14)	536	16.0	20.6
Meseta-Ebro			
Old Castile (8)	503	10.8	24.2
New Castile (3)	442	12.6	19.6
Aragon-Ebro (4)	391	13.0	17.0
Southern Spain			
Western Andalusia (6)	672	17.6	24.3
Estremadura (3)	499	14.6	20.3
La Mancha (3)	343	14.1	14.2
Eastern Andalusia (2)	474	16.6	17.8

SOURCE: Rainfall and temperature data were taken from INE, *Anuario Estadístico: 1960* (Madrid, 1961), pp. 26, 30. E. de Martonne's Formula was used to derive aridity.

NOTE: The index of aridity is expressed inversely. Thus an index number of 25.6 indicates much *higher* aridity than one of 46.5.

Although the index of aridity is perhaps the most important single indicator of the limitations that climate per se imposes upon agriculture, it must not be used uncritically. A high index of aridity may result either when levels of rainfall are so low that even low temperatures will not counteract their effect or when temperatures are so high that even areas of normal rainfall will appear as arid. When high temperatures are primarily responsible for aridity, they bring with them certain compensatory advantages. Because periods of frost are rare, the growing season is

5. For the evolution of techniques of measuring the effectiveness of precipitation, see U.S. Department of Agriculture, *Climate and Man: Yearbook of Agriculture, 1941* (Washington, 1941), pp. 101–02, 546–48. It should be added that geographers like J. M. Houston, *The Western Mediterranean World* (London, 1964), pp. 29–30, have recently attacked de Martonne for ignoring the intensity of rainfall and its seasonal distribution. Since they offer no alternative general guide, however, de Martonne's formula must continue to be used as a rough gauge.

longer.[6] Because plants receive more heat, they grow more quickly within the longer season.[7] Because more plant species flourish in a warmer climate, a wider variety of crops can be raised.[8] None of these advantages exists when low rainfall rather than high temperatures is chiefly responsible for aridity. Growing seasons are short, plants grow more slowly, and there is less choice as to what can be planted. The presence of compensatory features must be kept in mind when comparing aridity figures for Southern Spain, where aridity results primarily from high temperatures, with figures for the Meseta-Ebro regions of central Spain, where aridity exists despite low temperatures and a slow rate of evaporation.

Table 8 is otherwise self-explanatory. The greatest extremes of aridity are recorded along the lower Mediterranean Coast, in the Levante, Murcia, and, above all, Almeria. The climate in these areas is so dry that only vines and certain tree crops can be grown competitively on unirrigated land. Southern Spain, except for La Mancha, enjoys considerably more rainfall than the rest of arid Spain, but its advantage in this respect is counteracted by its higher temperatures, which induce faster evaporation and transpiration, thus creating conditions of aridity roughly comparable to those in the Meseta-Ebro. Aragon and New Castile in the Meseta-Ebro resemble Estremadura and Eastern Andalusia in Southern Spain in occupying an intermediate position on the scale of aridity. In these regions grain crops can be raised competitively, but low yields and crop failures are frequent. The climate is most favorable to grain crops in the largest Meseta and Southern regions, Old Castile and Western Andalusia. In general, although the division of property in the Meseta-Ebro more closely resembles that of the rainy Cantabric Coast, its basic climatic characteristics have much greater affinity to those of Southern Spain.

The meager advantage of the Meseta-Ebro over Southern Spain when climate alone is examined disappears when soil conditions are taken into account. Rain that falls upon thin or sandy soil unable to absorb or retain it is obviously wasted even in those areas where the temperatures are not so high as to cause rapid evaporation. Rainfall under these circumstances may actually be harmful. If the soil is not sufficiently porous to absorb it, the water that runs off may carry away precious topsoil. If the soil is too

6. For example, in such typical Old Castilian centers as Burgos and Valladolid, the frost-free period normally extended from 25 April to 1 November and from 10 April to 31 October, respectively, from 1926 to 1935. By contrast, in Southern Spain Badajoz was free of frost from 5 February to 25 December and Seville from 15 January to 25 December. Zorilla, pp. 28, 78, 85, 93.

7. The thermal index (the number of growing days multiplied by the daily temperature) from 1926 to 1935 was 3,792 in Valladolid and 2,702 in Burgos. In Badajoz the index was 5,510 and in Seville 5,695. Ibid., p. 123.

8. See Table 12.

sandy to retain the water once absorbed and instead lets it percolate down into underground drainage channels, a leaching, or removal, of soluble minerals vital to fertility occurs.[9] The importance of the moisture-retentive qualities of the soil is evident. The problem that arises in dealing with them is that there are no scientific data by which their effects can be evaluated in large regions. One or two incidental factors, such as the degree of surface slope, which in turn has some influence on the rate of rainfall run-off, can be measured.[10] Specific areas of good soils can also be cited.[11] But no basis exists for a scientific analysis of the moisture-retentive qualities of the Spanish earth as a whole.

Where scientific standards are lacking, a pragmatic test must be applied. Approximately 14.5 million hectares, 77 percent of all unirrigated agricultural land in Spain, are devoted to the growing of herbaceous crops that must be sown annually. Of this total only some 500,000 hectares are planted with such nonrotation crops as tomatoes and potatoes. The other 14 million hectares are used to grow grains and the rotation crops associated with grains.[12] The moisture-retentive qualities of this immense area can be deduced from the frequency with which fallow land must be included in the rotation cycle. Fallowing has traditionally been regarded as the principal means by which dry soil can recover the moisture necessary to bear a crop.[13] If the soil cannot be seeded annually but requires frequent fallowing, then either the soil does not receive sufficient rainfall

9. Naval Intelligence Division of the English Admiralty, *Spain and Portugal, Volume III: Spain,* p. 181.

10. Because surface slope also affects erosion and the ease of plowing, the following data, compiled from INE, *Anuario Estadístico: 1960,* pp. 7–8, have some value even though the terms "mountainous," "hilly," and "plains" were not given statistical definitions. It will be noted that there is more level land in Southern Spain than elsewhere.

| | Land Surface | | | Total Land |
	Plains (percent)	Hilly (percent)	Mountainous (percent)	Area (thousands of hectares)
Spain as a Whole	46.7	31.9	21.4	50,474
Cantabric Coast	33.5	38.9	27.6	6,296
Mediterranean Coast	27.3	36.6	36.0	7,533
Meseta-Ebro	49.6	29.5	20.9	17,176
Southern Spain	55.9	30.4	13.7	18,241

11. Antonio Revenga Carbonell, *Comarcas geográficas de España* (Madrid, 1962), provides good summary descriptions of such regions.

12. Ministerio de Agricultura, *Anuario estadístico de la producción agrícola: Campaña 1959–60* (henceforth *AEPA: 1959–60*) (Madrid, 1961), pp. 370–71.

13. On the usefulness of fallow in moisture storage, see U.S. Department of Agriculture, *Soils and Men: Yearbook of Agriculture, 1938* (Washington, 1938), pp. 686–87, and *Land: Yearbook of Agriculture, 1958* (Washington, 1958), p. 57.

or it does not retain enough of the rain it has received to be continuously productive.

The frequency of fallowing has other, very real, consequences. The higher the proportion of bare fallow in the rotation cycle, the smaller the amount of land effectively at the disposal of the farmer. If an owner of 10 hectares can sow his fields only once every two years, he possesses not 10 but 5 hectares of useful land. If he can sow two years out of every three, his effective property increases to 6.7 hectares. Only if fallowing is not required at all does he enjoy full use of all 10 hectares. The frequency of fallowing is thus one of the chief determinants of the small farmer's natural capacity for economic survival. This is especially true because fallowing is so difficult and expensive a task. Though nothing is harvested, the fields must nevertheless be plowed to turn under the spontaneous growth that would otherwise cause soil moisture to be removed through transpiration. Thus the energies of the farmer and of his animals are expended without immediate compensation.

TABLE 9 RELATION OF SOWN LAND TO BARE FALLOW IN UNIRRIGATED ROTATION LANDS IN 1959

	Sown (percent)	Fallow (percent)	Ratio (fallow to sown)	Total Rotation Land (thousands of hectares)
Spain	63.3	36.7	0.580	14,544
Cantabric Coast	88.7	11.3	.128	973
Mediterranean Coast	54.7	45.3	.828	1,277
Meseta-Ebro	57.9	42.1	.727	5,637
Southern Spain	64.8	35.2	.543	6,444
Meseta-Ebro				
Old Castile	58.3	41.7	.715	3,229
New Castile	60.6	39.4	.650	1,224
Aragon-Ebro	53.8	46.2	.859	1,164
Southern Spain				
Western Andalusia	75.9	24.1	.318	1,655
Estremadura	59.7	40.3	.673	1,966
La Mancha	59.2	40.8	.689	2,176
Eastern Andalusia	70.8	29.2	.412	647

SOURCE: Ministerio de Agricultura *AEPA: 1959–60* (Madrid, 1961), pp. 370–71, 376–77. See n. 14 for further information.

NOTE: In this and all subsequent tables in which absolute figures are used, the national total is larger than the sum of the regions listed because it includes the Balearic and Canary Islands, which I have left out of consideration.

Table 9 clearly indicates that the conclusions suggested by Table 8 must be modified. If the Meseta-Ebro enjoys a slightly less arid climate, Southern Spain has soil better able to absorb and retain moisture and thus soil that is susceptible to more frequent productive use. For every 100 hectares planted in the Meseta-Ebro, 73 hectares of fallow are necessary, but only 54 hectares must be fallowed in Southern Spain. Of all rotation lands in the Meseta-Ebro, 58 percent are actually sown, whereas 65 percent of those in Southern Spain are planted. Except for the southeastern Mediterranean coast, where land must sometimes be fallowed for two successive years before it again becomes capable of bearing a crop, the lowest ratio of soil usefulness is registered in the Aragonese provinces of the Meseta-Ebro. Even in Old Castile, the Meseta region with the least arid climate, less than 60 percent of the land was sown, and for every 10 hectares sown, 7 required the expense of fallowing. By contrast, in Western Andalusia, the most important Southern region, 76 percent of the land was planted, and only 3 hectares of fallow were necessary for every 10 hectares sown. No other area of arid Spain approached the Western Andalusian ratio of soil usefulness. Only along the Cantabric Coast, where rainfall is extraordinarily plentiful, was this ratio surpassed.[14]

If neither climatic conditions nor the moisture-retentive qualities of the soil are significantly less favorable in Southern than in central Spain, only two possible geographical explanations for the latifundio system of the South remain: first, that other, essentially unmeasureable, factors such as the absence of organic materials in the Southern soil make agriculture unusually difficult in practice; second, that climatic conditions, though not especially unfavorable on the average, fluctuate greatly from year to year and cause an irregularity of production which the small farmer cannot long survive. Since these factors are too complex or ill-defined for direct analysis, their impact must be evaluated indirectly. One method of approach would be to select a single crop and examine its comparative yields in various parts of Spain. Wheat is the logical sampling choice because it is by far the most important Spanish crop. More than 4 million hectares, 32 percent of all unirrigated cropland that was sown, were planted with this grain in 1959. It is also the most valuable single crop, accounting in 1959 for 20 percent of the income earned by all Spanish

14. In compiling these ratios I included the Ministry of Agriculture's category of "annually sown lands not occupied" (by crops on the survey date of 1 May) under sown lands, on the assumption that they would be planted later in the year. Such lands constituted more than 5 percent of all rotation lands only along the Cantabric and Mediterranean Coasts. As another indication of the care with which Spanish statistics must be used, lands of this type were seriously misreported for Caceres (Estremadura) by the *AEPAs* for more than a decade. I have used post-rather than pre-Civil War figures, simply because the latter are more easily manageable. The proportions of fallow do not vary significantly from year to year but remain constant. For example, the *AEPA* of 1935, pp. 472–73, gives results almost identical to those presented here.

crops, whether grown on unirrigated or irrigated lands.[15] Finally, wheat is the most universal crop: 43 of the 50 Spanish provinces normally devote more than 10,000 hectares to its cultivation.[16]

TABLE 10   COMPARATIVE WHEAT YIELDS AND FLUCTUATIONS 1906–35 AND 1940–59

	Average Area Sown (thousands of hectares)	Fifty-Year Average Yield (metric tons)[a]	Fluctuation of Yields (percent)		
			0–20	20–40	over 40
Spain	3,826	0.83	52.8	31.2	16.0
Cantabric Coast	193	1.28	71.5	19.2	9.3
Mediterranean Coast	326	0.78	42.3	32.0	25.9
Meseta-Ebro	1,624	0.82	54.9	32.8	12.2
Southern Spain	1,683	0.79	51.4	30.0	18.6
Meseta-Ebro					
Old Castile	912	0.86	61.3	30.5	8.2
New Castile	378	0.74	53.7	35.5	10.8
Aragon-Ebro	336	0.83	38.8	36.0	25.2
Southern Spain					
Western Andalusia	505	0.97	47.9	28.1	24.0
Estremadura	444	0.79	57.8	28.0	14.2
La Mancha	551	0.64	48.8	31.0	20.2
Eastern Andalusia	183	0.75	53.1	37.4	9.4

SOURCES: Compiled from Manuel Torres Martínez, *El problema triguero y otras cuestiones fundamentales de la agricultura española* (Madrid, 1944), pp. 120–21, 275–85, and the *AEPAs* of 1941 to 1960.

NOTE: All figures are weighted (as is the case in all other tables) and refer to yields on unirrigated lands only.

a. A metric ton equals 2,205 pounds.

As is shown in Table 10, the average wheat yields during the fifty-year period from 1906 to 1935 and 1940 to 1959 tend to counteract somewhat the advantage enjoyed by Southern Spain when the frequency of fallowing was considered.[17] Although wheat yields approached the national average in two of the four Southern regions and far surpassed it in a third, the disastrously low yields of the provinces of Albacete and Ciudad Real in La Mancha pushed down the average for Southern Spain as a whole. Only Western Andalusia, which had by far the greatest average yield of any arid region in Spain, enjoyed a clear superiority over

15. *AEPA: 1959–60*, pp. 2, 370.

16. Ministerio de Agricultura, Servicio Nacional del Trigo, *La producción triguera nacional y rendimientos por hectárea del secano, por provincias, durante el quinquenio de intensificación de la producción, 1954–58* (Madrid, 1959), tables 3A, 3B.

17. The absence of statistics for 1936–39 was, of course, due to the Civil War.

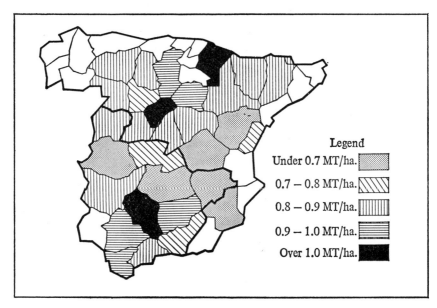

MAP 5. COMPARATIVE FIFTY-YEAR AVERAGE WHEAT YIELDS

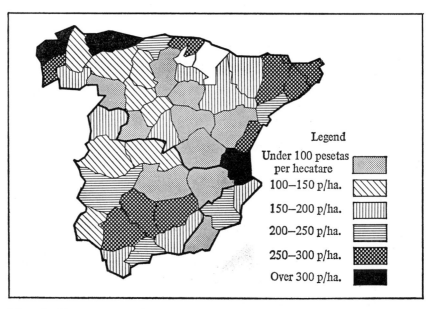

MAP 6. COMPARATIVE ASSESSED TAXABLE INCOME PER HECTARE IN 1959

Note: Sources and dates of reference for Map 5 same as in Table 10; provinces growing less than 40,000 ha. of wheat are omitted as unimportant. Source for Map 6 same as in Table 11; data unavailable for Alava and Navarre.

the Meseta-Ebro provinces. In this region, the heart of the latifundio district, the income potential of the small holder is much higher than that of his counterpart in Old or New Castile and Aragon even in grain lands, because he can use his property much more often and can count on higher yields when he cultivates. In Estremadura and Eastern Andalusia the situation is different. The advantage that small farmers in these regions enjoy because they do not have to fallow so often is counteracted by the somewhat lower yields they receive when they plant. The position of the small farmer of grain lands in most of La Mancha is clearly an inferior one. Except in the province of Toledo, he must fallow almost as often as the peasants of the Meseta-Ebro but must accept yields that are significantly lower.

The difficulties of economic survival in Southern Spain are more dramatically confirmed when fluctuations in wheat yields are considered. Although the South never had to endure the extreme variations that can occur in Aragon,[18] all of its regions except Eastern Andalusia experienced considerably more severe crop fluctuations on the average than did Old and New Castile. This was true even in the richest latifundio region, Western Andalusia, whose tremendous superiority in the frequency of land use and crop yields was, to some extent at least, counteracted by the great irregularity of production. In Estremadura, though fluctuations were less grave, the risks of survival were also significant for the small wheat grower. As for La Mancha, the instability of yields in Albacete and Ciudad Real confirms the position of these two provinces as perhaps the geographically least favored large region in unirrigated arid Spain.

Wheat is by far the most important single Spanish crop. Yet our conclusions would be misleading if we were to confine ourselves to it. The relative disadvantage, outside Andalusia, of the Southern small farmer when only grain crops are considered is often compensated by his less exclusive dependence upon such crops. As mentioned earlier, the hotter temperatures and longer growing season of the South permit a wider variety of crops than on the Meseta, where very cold temperatures prevail because of the high altitudes.[19] This is especially true in comparison to the richest and agriculturally most stable Meseta region, Old Castile. An owner of unirrigated land in Old Castile can plant only grains, legumes,

18. In Huesca, for example, the yield in 1949 was one-seventeenth that of 1946, one-sixteenth that of 1951, and one twenty-third that of 1954. The 1946 crop was four times as large as that of 1945; the 1954 crop was fourteen times as large as that of 1953.

19. The average altitude of provincial capitals in the Meseta-Ebro is 755 meters, as opposed to only 359 meters in Southern Spain (INE, *Anuario Estadístico: 1960*, p. 11).

and a few other annual crops such as potatoes. He cannot competitively grow such plants as cotton or corn, which have been transforming the economy of Southern Spain in recent years.[20] The cultivation of olives and of many types of fruit trees is also practically impossible in Old Castile. Vines can be raised, but not very profitably. The situation is somewhat better in New Castile and Aragon, where warmer climates permit the survival of the olive and improve the productive capacity of the vine. Even in these regions, however, the range of choice is far narrower than in Southern Spain. For example, fruits, vines, and olives in 1959 together accounted for only 10 percent of all unirrigated cropland in the Meseta-Ebro; by contrast, in Southern Spain they encompassed 24.1 percent, almost two and one-half times as much. To be sure, this natural advantage cannot be exploited to the fullest by the Southern small owner. Vines, olives, and fruit trees all require considerable capital reserves, because years must pass before such perennial plants are ready to bear yields. Nevertheless, as can be seen in more detail in Table 11,[21] the critical fact remains that the latifundio system has arisen in a multicrop region, whereas small holdings have survived, especially in Old Castile, in single-crop regions.[22]

This greater variety of crops, most of them more valuable than grain crops, together with other natural advantages, gives Southern Spain a very high position in the only uniform index of over-all land value which exists in Spain—the assessed incomes assigned by the Cadastre to the lands it surveys. Taken alone, these incomes are poor indicators of natural agricultural potentialities. Although they register enduring characteristics

20. In 1959, 131,944 hectares of unirrigated land were devoted to cotton in Southern Spain, but none was grown in the Meseta-Ebro. For corn the corresponding figures were 50,520 versus 2,740 hectares (AEPA: 1959–60, pp. 12, 266).

21. The percentages in Table 11, unlike those mentioned in the text, refer to all cropland, whether irrigated or unirrigated. The elevated percentage of annually planted lands is, of course, partly due to the enormous amounts of fallow lands which they include.

22. It might be wise to stress here that the latifundio system has not arisen because of these perennial crops. Although the initial capital investment necessary to grow vines, olives, or fruit trees is greater than that needed in grain lands, the impetus toward large-scale cultivation is more than counteracted, especially in the case of vines, by the intensive care necessary to keep the plants in effective production, care the small farmer is more likely to provide. Thus the 1962 Agricultural Census found that whereas 27.9 percent of the acreage for wheat and barley, the two principal grains, was attributable to farmers with more than 100 hectares, only 25.2 percent of the olives and 12.9 percent of the vines were so grown (INE, Censo Agrario, resumenes nacionales, pp. 13–15). Perennial crops are responsible for the latifundio system only in the indirect sense, which is explained in chap. 4, that by spreading manpower requirements over most of the year they made possible the day laboring class that could scarcely have survived if their services were needed only during the short sowing and harvest seasons of grain crops.

TABLE 11   DISTRIBUTION OF VARIOUS TYPES OF CROPLAND AND AVERAGE TAXABLE INCOME PER HECTARE IN 1959

	Total Cropland (thousands of hectares)	Unirrigated Cropland			Taxable Income per Hectare (pesetas)
		Annual Plants (percent)	Fruit Trees, Olives, Vines (percent)	Irrigated Cropland (percent)	
Spain	20,903	72.3	19.2	8.5	172
Cantabric Coast	1,247	83.1	8.9	8.0	241
Mediterranean Coast	3,023	47.7	32.4	19.9	243
Meseta-Ebro	6,843	83.0	9.3	7.7	118
Southern Spain	9,490	71.9	22.9	5.2	175
Meseta-Ebro					
Old Castile	3,626	89.5	5.6	4.9	108
New Castile	1,531	81.8	14.0	4.2	103
Aragon-Ebro	1,686	70.0	12.9	17.1	156
Southern Spain					
Western Andalusia	2,878	57.9	36.2	5.9	237
Estremadura	2,729	85.4	10.7	3.9	173
La Mancha	2,891	75.4	21.2	3.4	99
Eastern Andalusia	992	65.3	22.4	12.3	182

SOURCES: Compiled from *AEPA: 1959–60*, pp. 370–71, and García-Badell, "Distribución de la propiedad," Table 6.

of the land rather than the efficiency with which any given individual cultivates it in any given year, the assessed income figures are inflated enormously by long-range improvements that permanently transform the character of the land. The wealthiest agricultural region in Spain thus is not the Cantabric Coast with its abundant rainfall but the Mediterranean Coast, the region least favored by climate, where irrigation has achieved what nature had denied.[23] Nevertheless, in areas where irrigation does not play a major role, the taxable income figures provide an extremely useful gauge within which are reflected aridity, frequency of fallowing, insecurity of crop yields, and the other indicators of natural agricultural potentialities we have been considering. Since it is not possible to measure year after year every crop grown in Spain, these figures will serve to summarize our discussion of the relation between geographical conditions and systems of land tenure in the major regions of Spain.

As indicated in Table 11, land is on the average half again as valua-

23. As an indication of how profoundly irrigation can affect the Cadastral assessments, the average taxable income per hectare in Cordova in 1955 was 1,707 pesetas for irrigated and 313 pesetas for unirrigated cropland. For a discussion of the validity of using the assessed taxable income as an indicator of natural agricultural conditions, see app. A.

ble in Southern Spain as in the other great unirrigated region of arid
Spain, the Meseta-Ebro. Income from a hectare of land in the richest
Southern region, Western Andalusia, is more than twice that in the two
Castiles and approximates the incomes obtained along the rainy Cantabric
Coast or in the heavily irrigated Mediterranean provinces. The same is
true to a lesser degree for Estremadura. Even in La Mancha, where wheat
yields are so disastrously low and unstable, the value of the land approaches the level of the two Castiles once all crops are taken into consideration, as is done by the taxable income figures. To be sure, the differences in wealth between the Meseta and the South were not quite so
great before the introduction of such specialized crops as cotton in the
post–Civil War period. Nevertheless, even then all Southern regions except La Mancha enjoyed considerably higher assessed incomes than the
two Castiles.[24] In general, the income data confirm what most previous
measurements suggested. Agricultural conditions in Southern Spain are as
good as, and often better than, those in most other arid portions of the
nation.

What has been proven by comparisons with other regions may be
further substantiated by an examination of agricultural conditions within
Southern Spain itself. The region is a highly varied one, containing within
itself both the province with the second highest (Cordova), and the province with the second lowest (Ciudad Real), wheat yields in the nation. If
the latifundio economy originated and has endured primarily because of
geographical realities, it should be more developed in those Southern
areas where agricultural conditions are harshest. Yet, as can be seen in
Table 12, where the latifundio provinces are grouped according to their
relative fertility, the opposite is true. This is especially so if latifundio
strength is measured by the proportion of the total agricultural income
controlled by large estates and large owners, clearly the best single index
in unirrigated regions. In the seven geographically most favored provinces, owners and holdings controlled slightly more land and produced almost 40 percent more income than in the six least favored provinces.[25] To
return once more to the regional classifications we have been using,
Western Andalusia, the most fertile area in Southern Spain, has the most

24. In 1930 assessed income averaged 36.0 pesetas per hectare in the two
Andalusias and Estremadura, as against 31.6 pesetas in the two Castiles. The difference probably would have been greater had not the Southern assessments reflected
pre-World War I values (the Cadastre was largely completed in the South before
1917), whereas the Meseta assessments were established entirely during the 1920s
(Carrión, p. 74 and the unnumbered table facing p. 70).

25. The seven richest provinces are Cordova, Seville, Cadiz, Jaen, Badajoz,
Salamanca, and Granada. The six poorest are Malaga, Huelva, Toledo, Caceres,
Ciudad Real, and Albacete.

TABLE 12   NATURAL AGRICULTURAL POTENTIAL IN COMPARISON TO DEGREE OF LATI-
FUNDISMO IN SOUTHERN SPAIN

	Seven Most Fertile Provinces	Six Least Fertile Provinces
Natural Indicators		
Index of aridity	35.7	27.1
Proportion of fallow (percent)	31.9	41.1
Average wheat yield (metric tons)	0.90	0.66
Assessed income per hectare (pesetas)	226.5	117.2
Land Tenure Data (percent)		
Large-holding area[a]	42.2	39.9
Large-owner area[a]	55.4	52.7
Large-holding income[a]	30.5	22.5
Large-owner income[b]	56.1	40.8

NOTE: Sources and years of reference in each category are the same as those used in the corresponding tables.

a. Over 250 hectares.

b. Lands assessed at more than 5,000 pesetas in 1930.

strongly developed latifundio economy. Estremadura, which probably occupies second place in terms of favorable natural conditions (the higher taxable income of Eastern Andalusia is largely due to the extensive irrigation networks of Granada), is also second in degree of property concentration. La Mancha, the least favored region in terms of agricultural production per hectare (though not, because of its sparser population, in terms of per capita agricultural income), rivals Eastern Andalusia as the region in which the latifundios are least important. In short, the situation within Southern Spain is the same as in the nation as a whole. If a correlation exists between the latifundio economy and unfavorable natural conditions, it is as often as not an inverse one.

The importance of geography cannot be denied. Agricultural conditions are bad practically everywhere in Spain. Spain has the lowest rainfall and poorest soil in Western Europe. As can be seen in Table 13, its

TABLE 13   COMPARATIVE AGRICULTURAL CONDITIONS IN SPAIN AND OTHER MAJOR
EUROPEAN NATIONS IN 1930

	Percent of Fallow in Grain Lands	Wheat Yields per Hectare (metric tons)
Germany	7.6	2.37
England	6.8	1.99
France	12.3	1.73
Italy	18.0	1.41
Spain	49.4	0.97

SOURCE: International Institute of Agriculture, *The First World Agricultural Census* (*1930*) (3 vols. Rome, 1939), vols. 2, 3.

average wheat yields tend to be half those of France, England, or Germany and two-thirds those of Italy *when the land can be sown*. Since the need for fallowing means that the land can be sown only once every two years, the rest of Europe in effect enjoys wheat crops that are sometimes four to five times as great as those of Spain. These harsh geographical realities may reinforce the latifundio economy, once established, but because that economy is predominant in only one region of a universally impoverished nation, they most assuredly do not explain its origins or suggest its inevitability. Southern Spain differs too much within itself as to fertility and does not differ enough from most of the rest of the nation for such a causal thesis to be generally acceptable. The unity and the uniqueness of the South lie more in its history than in its geography. It is in the history, not the geography, of Southern Spain that the true roots of the latifundio system are more likely to be found.

The Influence of History

A detailed examination of the history of the South, a history that extends over more than two millennia, is clearly impossible in this study. Nor is so lengthy an analysis necessary to suggest the historical origins of the latifundio economy and to establish why it did not develop to the same extent in the Meseta portions of arid Spain. The hypothesis often associated with Claudio Sánchez-Albornoz but developed by a number of historians provides an acceptable substitute.[26] Essentially, it is argued that the bases for the modern systems of land tenure in Spain were laid during the reconquest of the peninsula from the Moors through an exceedingly complex interaction between royal power, the strength of the nobility and of the military orders, the size of the districts conquered in different periods, the methods by which they were won, the density and assimilability of the population in each region, and, finally, the ways in which each district was repopulated with new set-

26. In the discussion that follows I have relied heavily on *La reconquista española y la repoblación del país* (Saragossa, 1951), a symposium edited by José María Lacarra; Claudio Sánchez-Albornoz, *Le reforma agraria ante la historia* (Madrid, 1932), a brilliant, though polemic, synthesis prepared as a justification for the agrarian reform of the Second Republic; Julio González, *Repartimiento de Sevilla* (2 vols. Madrid, 1951), an exhaustive study of the reorganization of central Andalusia after its conquest; Ignacio de la Concha, *La "presura": La ocupación de tierras en los primeros siglos de la reconquista* (Madrid, 1946), a detailed study of this interesting custom. Excellent shorter accounts exist in Vicens Vives, vols. 1, 2, and in the articles by Luis G. de Valdeavellano on "Repoblación" and "Beheteria" and by José María Font on "Presura" in the *Diccionario de la historia de España* (2 vols. Madrid, 1952).

tlers. Because Southern Spain was conquered under quite distinct circumstances and repopulated under far different principles from the central Meseta, its systems of land tenure differ from those of the rest of arid Spain.

The theory—a kind of Turnerian "frontier thesis" positing a tendency toward lesser rather than greater social equality—is sufficiently fruitful to be worth a brief exposition. Most of the unirrigated portions of Spain were conquered in three quite separate stages by what eventually was to become the kingdom of Castile and Leon.[27] In the first of these stages, during the ninth and tenth centuries, the kingdom expanded from its original territory along the Biscay Coast into the region that stretches from the Cantabric Mountains to the Duero River and corresponds to the upper portions of what we called "Old Castile" when we discussed land tenure. This region, which had never been heavily settled, had been almost completely depopulated in the 740s and 750s by Alfonso I, who wished to create a no man's land to separate his realm from that of the then much more powerful Moslems. Since the Moors accepted this immense buffer zone and gradually retired to their southerly territories, which since Roman times had been more populated and wealthier than the north, adventurers from the Biscay Coast slowly began to feel safe in crossing the mountains to stake out claims in the man-made desert. What started as spontaneous private action became official policy after 850 under Ordoño I and Alfonso III. But because the resources of the crown were sufficient only for such major tasks as the rebuilding of cities, royal intervention never became dominant in the resettlement of the countryside.[28] Instead, the primacy of individual action was legally recognized and encouraged through a new custom known as the *presura*.

The presura resembles the legal devices adopted in other nations faced with the problem of peopling a deserted land. In essence it granted settlers free possession of the lands they occupied. This right could be exercised either by small settlers or by important men of the realm and by religious foundations. From the first group arose an im-

27. The kingdom of Castile and Leon grew out of Pelayo's band of Visigothic refugees but underwent innumerable fragmentations and reorganizations before it assumed its final form in 1230. I have not concerned myself with these many variations but refer to the kingdom as though it were always united and always known by the same name. Nor have I complicated the text by discussing the kingdom of Aragon, since it was responsible mostly for the conquest of the irrigated Mediterranean Coast. Small property flourishes there largely because the Moorish irrigation networks were not destroyed and the previously existing agricultural systems were permitted to continue.

28. Ignacio de la Concha in Lacarra, ed., *Reconquista y repoblación*, p. 210; Valdeavellano, "Repoblación," *Diccionario de la historia, 2,* 1019–20.

portant class of small free cultivators who knew no intermediaries between themselves and the crown. But even when the right of presura was exercised by members of the second group, only large domains, not servile conditions, appeared. Because the region was almost completely depopulated and still not entirely secure against Moslem forays, cultivators had to be offered attractive conditions if they were to be induced to migrate from the Biscay Coast or, as often occurred, from the Moorish territories to the South. A class of small permanent leaseholders in effective possession of the lands they tilled thus arose even within the large domains.[29]

To be sure, peasant freedom was seriously threatened toward the close of the tenth century as the Christian social order began to rigidify, the frontier to fill in, and enemy attacks (because of a temporary resurgence of Moslem ambitions) to increase. Yet the tradition of peasant independence was so strong that feudalism was not able to develop. Though the new conditions forced most of the small free cultivators to commend themselves to the protection of some lord, they did not thereby become his serfs. Instead, an unusual institution, the *behetría*, arose in which peasant communities had the right (which was usually more than theoretical) to replace the lord they had elected if his exactions became intolerable. In contrast to the rest of Europe, the lord in Old Castile tended to serve the community almost as much as the community the lord for most of the medieval era.[30] Though new dangers appeared in the fourteenth and fifteenth centuries, the tradition of freedom for the small cultivator who held de facto possession of his lands was on the whole preserved. The twentieth-century peasant proprietor of the upper Meseta owes his existence in large part to the fact that, through presuras and behetrías, his ancestors never completely lost their independence.

The second stage of the reconquest occurred between the 1020s and 1030s, when civil wars fractured the Caliphate of Cordova into an assemblage of petty principalities called *taifas*, and 1085, when the fall

29. De la Concha, La *"presura,"* pp. 62–63, 97–109, 114; Justo Pérez de Urbel in Lacarra, ed., *Reconquista y repoblación*, pp. 149–61; Sánchez-Albornoz, chap. 4. Regional differences in types of presura are best presented in Vicens Vives, *1*, 268, 299.

30. Luis G. de Valdeavellano, *Historia de España* (Madrid, 1952), p. 476; Vicens Vives, *1*, 314–15; Sánchez-Albornoz, chap. 4; Roger Bigelow Merriman, *The Rise of the Spanish Empire* (New York, 1918), *2*, 183. It should be stressed that behetrías were very common in Old Castile. According to Valdeavellano, "Behetría," *Diccionario de la historia*, *1*, 394, 600 of the 2,000 places recorded in the mid-fourteenth-century survey known as the *Libro de Meriendas de Castilla* enjoyed behetría status.

of Toledo frightened the Moslems into inviting from Africa the militant Almoravide sect, which stopped further Christian expansion for more than a century. During this period the Castilians advanced their frontier from the Duero to the Tagus River and almost doubled the size of their realm. Two important new territories were added to the old kingdom: the region that stretches from the Duero to the Central mountain chain and now constitutes the lower half of Old Castile, and the area between the mountains and the Tagus, which corresponds roughly to the western portions of New Castile, though it also includes the northern fringes of La Mancha and Estremadura.

The policies of repopulating these new territories were different from those followed north of the Duero and reflected the far more direct role the crown had played in the conquest. The spontaneous presuras, which had been universal in the north, were permitted only rarely. Instead, Alfonso VI and his successors retained greater royal control over colonization. The effects of this policy change were not harmful to the growth of small properties, however, because a strong noble class had not yet developed and the newly created municipal councils (consejos) to which the task of resettlement was delegated were relatively democratic.

In the Tagus valley the task of the consejos was relatively limited. The region had been fairly heavily populated both under the Visigoths and Moors and had passed to the Christians without appreciable devastation. Most of the old population, a large proportion of which consisted of Mozárabes (Christians who had retained their faith during the long centuries of Moslem rule), remained behind and were permitted to continue the cultivation of their lands, which were usually already organized into small holdings. On the relatively few abandoned lands, settlers from Castile were placed. After 1125 these settlers were joined by large new contingents of Mozárabes who fled from the Moorish south as a result of the general expulsion decreed by the Almoravides in that year.[31]

The colonization of the depopulated region between the Central mountain chain and the Duero was more difficult, but the resulting social structure was more or less the same. The municipal councils here were so strong that there was no need to allow noblemen to organize the settlements. New cultivators were attracted from all directions: from beyond the Duero in the north, from Navarre and Aragon in the east, and from the Almoravide domains in the distant south. Because the consejos had lands in excess, the terms of settlement were generous;

31. Vicens Vives, 1, 269–74; Julio González in Lacarra, ed., Reconquista y repoblación, pp. 164–74.

because colonists were not lacking, the fields did not remain abandoned. To quote a leading authority on the subject, although "much property belonged to single persons or families, the greater part was divided among many cultivators. Even in properties of the former type, the tendency was for those who actually tilled the land to be granted extensive privileges." [32] The tradition of small settlers in effective possession of their lands, which the presuras has established north of the Duero, was continued by means of the consejos to the south of that river.

The Castilian advance to the Tagus and the rise of the Almoravides, who were replaced after 1150 by an equally militant Berber sect, the Almohades, brought Moslem and Christian Spain into deadly confrontation. The buffer zone that had previously separated the two cultures was now gone. The sporadic raids of earlier centuries gave way after 1085 to a state of almost continuous warfare. Just as Almoravide and Almohade dominance had militarized Moorish society, so the new fears and ambitions engendered by the conquest of Toledo gave Christian society a stronger military bent than before. Following the example of the Crusaders in the recently subdued Holy Lands, the Castilians established three great military orders—Calatrava, Santiago, and Alcántara—between 1164 and 1183, when the Moorish-Christian struggle reached crisis proportions. These orders, together with such European orders as the Knights Templars, acted as the principal armies of the Christian kings during the great military breakthrough of the early thirteenth century. For the first time, a strong military caste had appeared whose collaboration had to be rewarded.

Prior to the thirteenth century the Christians had definitively conquered and repopulated only the extreme northern fringe of the areas that are today dominated by the latifundios. [33] The entire southern third of the peninsula fell to the Castilians suddenly and at one blow. The continuous campaigns of Alfonso VIII (1158–1214) culminated in the stupendous victory of Las Navas de Tolosa in 1212, which broke the

---

32. González in Lacarra, ed., *Reconquista y repoblación*, pp. 177, 181. Vivens Vives, 2, 66, 224, lays greater emphasis on the rise of large estates in this region, even within consejo areas, but agrees that their importance was partly nullified and that the basis for the rise of a small proprietor class was established because the cultivators held de facto control of the land through long-term leases.

33. Alfonso VII of Castile (1126–57) conquered vast stretches of land between the Tagus and the headwaters of the Guadalquiver but lost them to the Almohades after a few years. The spectacular raids of Alfonso I of Aragon (1104–34) covered still more territory but were even more transitory in their effects. The sub-Tagus region remained essentially Moorish until the thirteenth-century military breakthrough.

back of Almohade military might. To complete the disaster, rebellions followed which fragmented Moslem Spain once more into several petty principalities, none of them a match for Castile. By 1250 all these new *taifas* except for the Moorish Kingdom of Granada had been swept away. The situation of five centuries earlier was thus reversed. Christians now held the entire peninsula except for the elongated coastal kingdom of Granada, which was temporarily secure behind the barrier of the Sierra Nevada chain.

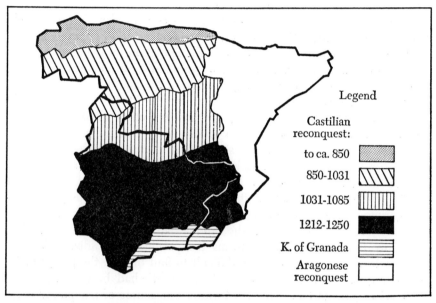

Legend

Castilian reconquest:

to ca. 850

850-1031

1031-1085

1212-1250

K. of Granada

Aragonese reconquest

MAP 7. STAGES OF THE CASTILIAN RECONQUEST

The area conquered between 1212 and 1250 was immense in size. Castile and Leon, which controlled some 200,000 square kilometers after the fall of Toledo in 1085, suddenly added 155,000 square kilometers.[34] An area almost as large as the entire former kingdom lay open for repopulation. The magnitude of the conquest deeply affected the social reorganization that followed. Even before the victory at Las Navas, the Castilian kings had placed themselves under heavy obligations to the military orders.[35] Faced with their inability to organize personally the

34. New Castilian conquests between 1225 and 1250 totaled 120,000 square kilometers (Vicens Vives, 2, 10). Another 30,000 square kilometers had been conquered in La Mancha by Alfonso VIII just before Las Navas, but they were precariously held and not repopulated until after 1212 (González in Lacarra, ed. *Reconquista y repoblación*, pp. 184–86).

35. In 1189, for example, Alfonso VIII recognized the right of the Order of

immense territories acquired, Fernando III and Alfonso X tended to exceed their obligations. The major cities remained under royal control through the establishment of strong municipal councils, but most of the countryside was turned over to the military orders and to individual nobles.[36] The proportion of land placed under nonroyal jurisdiction was greatest in La Mancha and Estremadura, where the orders had borne the brunt of the fighting. Enormous tracts also fell to the orders along the Andalusian frontier with the kingdom of Granada, especially after a 1263 revolt supported by Granada raised fears of a Moorish revival. In Andalusia as a whole, even though its urbanized central region remained mostly under control of the crown, considerably more than half the land fell under nonroyal jurisdiction.[37] Repopulation by strong men and military orders, rather than by presura or municipal councils, was the distinguishing feature of the reorganization of the South.

These extensive land grants in themselves might not have prevented the eventual growth of small property had not other factors also contributed. Although the South as a whole had been the most densely inhabited area of the peninsula since Roman times, the lands of the military orders were only sparsely peopled. Estremadura, an important grain-growing region under the Romans, had declined under the Moors. La Mancha had lost much of its population, because it was the chief battleground during the long period of warfare between 1085 and 1212. The 1263 revolt depopulated the Andalusian frontier with Granada, especially the area that today forms the province of Cadiz. Colonists to settle these regions were more difficult to find than in the past. Much of the surplus Christian population in the north had been used up in the resettlements of Old and New Castile. The source of manpower previously supplied by Mozárabe refugees from Moorish territories was now largely exhausted. Moreover, for those who did immigrate, there were alternative places of settlement in the cities of central Andalusia, from which the Moorish population had for the most part been expelled.

Calatrava to one-tenth of the land reconquered. The other orders received similar, though less specific, privileges (González, *Repartimiento de Sevilla*, 1, 24).

36. Valdeavellano tends to stress the gains of individual nobles. All other authorities, including González, who has made the most detailed study, stress the acquisitions of the military orders.

37. Vicens Vives, 2, 20. Vicens Vives goes on to say: "If the repopulation of Andalusia was predominately *latifundista* and *señorial*, that of lower Estremadura was exclusively of this nature. Many years passed without a single royal municipal council being created, and the king reserved very few lands for royal redistribution. The repopulation was exclusively in the hands of the military orders, which received almost the whole of the land, and of a few great magnates, both laic and ecclesiastical."

Thus, even had the military orders wished to place small settlers on their holdings, they would have experienced difficulties. As it was, the orders usually did not encourage immigration but were content to inaugurate a pastoral economy, less exigent of manpower than agriculture, on their lands.

Central Andalusia, where scarcity of population was not a major problem, evolved in the same direction for different reasons. The prosperity of the Guadalquivir valley under the Moors was predicated upon the markets for agricultural produce provided by highly developed urban centers. The Moorish cities had begun to decline even before the Castilian conquest because of the political instability and the decay of the silk industry. The conquest accelerated the decline, since the former population was driven from the cities and the new Christian settlers lacked the manufacturing skills necessary to continue production. Moreover, the diminishing demand for silks was accompanied by a growing market in northern Europe for an aspect of the Moorish inheritance which the Castilians were better able to exploit: the raising of Merino sheep. In contrast to Old and New Castile, the rural social structure of Christian Andalusia was shaped from the beginning by foreign demand for Spanish wool exports, a demand which continued for more than three centuries.[38]

The pattern which evolved in the frontier areas and Estremadura thus repeated itself in milder form in central Andalusia. Cultivated land for whose produce there was little demand gradually reverted to pastoral uses, and many of the small farms that dotted the Guadalquivir valley under the Moors disappeared. As for the latifundia, whether those that had survived since late Roman times[39] or the new ones that were now created, less economic pressure existed to force the leasing of plots to small cultivators who might thus have gained that effective control of

38. The question of the effect of sheepherding on the decline of intensive farming is a difficult one. Although woolgrowing never became as important in central Andalusia as in Old and New Castile, the fact that it coincided with the birth of a new social system may have caused it to have disproportionate influence in the shaping of the property structure. In Estremadura and La Mancha sheepherding was paramount from the start. Although it would be unwise to overstress the connection, it is worth noting that the Christian South and the Meseta (the association of sheepherders which dominated Spanish rural society until the eighteenth century) are historical twins. The former was definitively conquered in 1248 and 1264; the latter received the first of its monopolistic charters in 1278.

39. Some latifundia apparently had survived since Diocletian's time. Their number and size are not known. It is certain, however, that property in Andalusia was far less concentrated under the Moslems than it became under the Christians. On this question, see González, *Repartimiento de Sevilla*, 1, 12; and Vicens Vives, 1, 126, 168, and 2, 12–13.

the land which ultimately gave birth to much of the modern European peasant proprietor class.[40] Two other factors contributed to these developments. Although the urban Moorish populations of central Andalusia had been expelled, relatively more Moslems remained on the land than in any previous Castilian conquest.[41] The insecurity of these individuals in an increasingly alien regime left them little recourse other than servile acceptance of the changes imposed by their Christian masters.[42] Also, if the Christian South was never again in as great danger as in 1263, it remained the Spanish frontier with the Moslem world in Granada and Africa for another two centuries. Its precarious position was not conducive either to intensive farming or to the development of small property.

The joint effect of the servile rural population, the basic economic changes, and the fundamental political transformation that the appearance of a well-articulated military aristocracy implied was to incline Southern Spain in the direction of a latifundistic system of land tenure. Once established, this system tended to perpetuate itself. Church lands and those of the military orders belonged to corporate bodies and could not be sold. The noble domains were also protected against fragmentation by the custom of entail, which first became common at about the time of the conquest of the South. The temporary renaissance of Andalusian urban life after the discovery of America failed to reverse the tide. The system was already too well established, the nobility and Church were too powerful, and the economic boom was too irregular and short-lived. Nor did a redistribution of property occur after the early eighteenth century, when agricultural production once more began— this time definitively—to eliminate sheepherding as an important eco-

40. Thus, in contrast to the early latifundios of Galicia or Leon, the Southern estates were not only large domains in legal terms but were also farmed on a large scale. De jure ownership was not counteracted by a de facto division among settlers who could gradually convert their emphyteutic leases into full ownership rights. There is no adequate English expression by which this critical distinction can be expressed. In Spanish the concept of de jure ownership can be rendered by *dominio eminente* and the idea of de facto occupation by *dominio útil.*

41. In general the Moorish cities had to be conquered by force of arms, whereas the smaller towns and rural areas surrendered without resistance in return for treaties that guaranteed them certain rights. As a result the Moslem inhabitants were usually expelled from the cities but were allowed to remain and to keep their property in areas where treaties had been worked out. Although the 1263 rural revolts led to the revocation of many of the treaties, the cities of central Andalusia remained more depopulated of Moors than the surrounding countryside (González in Lacarra, ed., *Reconquista y repoblación,* pp. 195–96).

42. The importance of the presence of a servile population is especially emphasized by Sánchez-Albornoz, chap. 1, and by Brenan, p. 104.

nomic activity in Andalusia (though not in Estremadura). In short, no unique historical force arose powerful enough to counteract the unique historical tendencies established at the time of the reconquest. Long before the development of modern capitalistic conditions, with their premium on market opportunities and their ruthless penalization of the inefficient producer, the large owners of Southern Spain had secured an extraordinarily strong hold over rural society.

The effects of the reconquest and the early uniqueness of the Southern system of land tenure can be measured quantitatively only to a limited extent. One available gauge is the regional differences in various types of political jurisdiction. At the end of the eighteenth century, despite the centralizing efforts of the Spanish Bourbons and the deterioration of the military orders after Ferdinand and Isabella, royal jurisdiction still extended to far less than half the national land surface. Although nonroyal jurisdiction was strong everywhere, it reached its acme in the territories conquered by Castile in the thirteenth century. There, as can be seen in Table 14, the crown exercised direct control over only

TABLE 14   ESTIMATED CULTIVATED AREA UNDER VARIOUS TYPES OF JURISDICTION CIRCA 1797

	Royal Jurisdiction (percent)	Noble Jurisdiction (percent)	Church Jurisdiction (percent)	Total Cultivated Area (thousands of *aranzadas*)[a]
Thirteenth-Century				
Castilian Conquests	18.2	59.7	22.2	14,987
Rest of Spain	37.2	48.4	14.4	40,013
Ancient Province of:				
La Mancha	0.6	68.7	30.6	2,784
Estremadura	16.9	48.9	34.3	4,398
Toledo	23.7	55.7	20.6	2,768
Jaen	26.4	51.9	21.7	952
Cordova	23.5	72.6	3.8	1,247
Seville	26.8	68.2	4.9	2,838

SOURCE: Compiled from data in Rafael García Ormaechea, *Supervivencias feudales en España* (Madrid, 1932), p. 7.

a. An *aranzada* usually equaled 0.477 hectares.

an estimated 18.2 percent of the cultivated land area. In the rest of Spain, royal jurisdiction existed in villages encompassing 37.2 percent, or more than twice as much, of the cultivated area. Although the accuracy of these figures is far from certain, the regional differences they reveal are probably correct, since the same variations appear in other types of analyses drawn up at other times.[43]

Needless to say, the nobility and clergy owned as property only a small part of the vast territory over which they held jurisdictional rights. Yet it is safe to assume that property followed jurisdiction rather closely.[44] Since no general information existed on property holdings until after private jurisdictions were abolished in 1811, this assertion must be documented by retrospective evidence. The nine modern provinces that were conquered principally during the thirteenth century and now form the central core of the latifundio district occupy 26.8 percent of the land surface of Spain. Nevertheless, in the 1930s, 53.6 percent of the property of the *grandeza,* the most ancient and powerful noble class, was to be found in these nine provinces. This was twice as high a proportion as the grandeza should have owned if noble power had been uniform throughout Spain.[45] With Church lands, the evidence is much less conclusive. Yet here, too, some correlation seems to exist.[46]

The early monopolization of property by the nobility and the Church was also reflected in the rural class structure of Southern Spain. The earliest census that addressed itself to this question, the census of 1797, revealed a distribution of rural classes remarkably similar to that which exists today. As can be seen in Table 15, where the 1797 findings are reproduced, landowning peasants usually formed less than one-tenth of the total active agricultural population in the territories conquered by Castile during the thirteenth century. On the other hand the day laborers who worked the great estates of the nobility and clergy made

43. The figures in Table 14 were presented at the Cortes of Cadiz by the deputy Alvarez y López during the debate on the abolition of private jurisdictional rights. For other types of analyses pointing to the same results, see José Tudela, "Los señoríos jurisdiccionales de la España de Carlos III," *Revista de los Servicios Sociales-Agrarios* (December 1932), 1, 824–47, or Antonio Domínguez Ortiz, *La sociedad española en el siglo XVIII* (Madrid, 1955), p. 299.

44. On the impossibility of determining the exact relation between property and jurisdictional rights, see Vicens Vives, 2, 417–18. For the varying types of power held by jurisdictional lords see Rafael García Ormaechea, *Supervivencias feudales en España* (Madrid, 1932), pp. 8–12, or Richard Herr, *The Eighteenth Century Revolution in Spain* (Princeton, 1958), pp. 89–96.

45. Compiled from Instituto de Reforma Agraria, *Boletín* (March 1934), 2, 169. Of the 557,359 hectares of arable land held by the *grandeza* in Spain as a whole, 309,629 belonged to *grandes* in the nine provinces reconquered in the thirteenth century.

46. According to Pascual Madoz, as cited in Vicens Vives, vol. 4, pt. 2, p. 92, Church lands in the nine reconquista provinces during the *desamortización* were assessed at 30 percent of the value of all Spanish Church lands, slightly more than they should have been if uniform conditions prevailed throughout Spain.

up almost three-quarters of that population. In territories conquered at other times, the situation was usually reversed. Owners usually equaled or exceeded laborers in number, and an important tenant class, some of whose members later established full property rights over their lands, existed.[47] Clearly, the social imbalance of the contemporary South arose long before the age of mechanization, quick foreclosures, and intense economic competition.

TABLE 15   RURAL CLASS STRUCTURE AS REFLECTION OF PROPERTY STRUCTURE IN 1797

	Owners (percent)	Tenants (percent)	Laborers (percent)	Active Male Population (thousands of persons)
Spain	22.3	30.5	47.2	1,602
Original nuclei of the reconquest: Cantabric Coast	35.8	48.3	15.8	327
Castilian reconquest, first stage: to the Duero River	28.9	44.7	26.4	186
Castilian reconquest, second stage: to the Tagus River	18.7	33.1	48.2	190
Castilian reconquest, third stage: Southern Spain	8.0	17.7	74.3	375
Aragonese reconquests and Granada	22.9	22.9	54.1	542

SOURCE: Compiled from José Canga Arguelles, *Diccionario de Hacienda* (London, 1927), *4*, 55–56.

NOTE: I have adjusted the results reported for the ancient provinces of Murcia, Soria, and Toledo because they were reconquered in more than one stage.

The Southern peasant proprietor class, which had never had a chance to develop during the centuries that followed the reconquista, also failed to emerge from the *desamortización*, the drastic transformation of property relations which occurred throughout Spain during the first half of the nineteenth century. The purpose of the desamortización was to free land in a nation where property had been nontransferable for centuries because for the most part it belonged to corporate bodies or to the entailed nobility. This purpose was achieved by wiping out the huge agricultural holdings of the Church, reducing the extent of the still more immense municipal commons, and gradually diminishing the importance of the nobility by prohibiting entail.[48] Although these effects

47. The 1797 findings are not completely trustworthy, but again the general conclusions and regional differences they present are valid.

48. Unfortunately there is no good general study of the desamortización, and most of the monographic research that is now being conducted on the subject has

were universal, their impact varied from region to region. In northern and central Spain, where small proprietors were predominant, there were relatively few individuals wealthy enough to buy up the large blocs of territory that were auctioned. Furthermore, the peasant proprietors and the tenants who held emphyteutic leases had more often acquired the means by which they, too, might purchase some land. Finally, because small farmers often controlled the municipal councils, they could limit the sale of common lands to those portions that were genuinely surplus (as the desamortización laws provided) rather than permit a wholesale liquidation of the village patrimony. In the South, where large owners—the nobility, their retainers, and a new rural bourgeoisie—dominated economic and political life, the desamortización followed a different pattern. The day laborers who formed the bulk of the population could not bid for a share of the land sold. The *poderosos,* the wealthy persons who dominated village councils,[49] felt no self-interest in preserving as much of the commons as possible. Instead they tended to allow the alienation of all these lands, since they and their friends possessed the resources with which to buy them. As a result, although the desamortización brought about the transfer of enormous quantities of land everywhere, its ultimate effect was to reconfirm the existing rural social structure of each region.[50]

Although the desamortización remains the least studied of all pivotal events in Spanish history, sufficient quantitative evidence exists to suggest the fundamentally different course it followed in the South. The rapidity with which lands offered for sale were grabbed up by the poderosos is indicated by the fact that in 1845, nine years after the desamortización of the Church lands had begun, 65.6 percent of such lands had already been bought in the South whereas in the rest of Spain only 49.9 percent of the properties offered had been purchased. The proportion purchased was highest in the two regions—Western Andalusia and Estremadura—that had been conquered principally during the

---

not yet been published. Carmelo Viñas y May, *La reforma agraria en España en el siglo XIX* (Santiago, 1933), never good, is now completely antiquated. The same is true of J. M. Antequera, *La desamortización eclesiástica* (Madrid, 1885). For a brief description of the intellectual and political background to the desamortización, see app. E.

49. On the new southern "rural bourgeoisie" of the eighteenth century, see Domínguez Ortiz, pp. 281–82, and Herr, p. 107; on the *poderosos*, see Herr, pp. 109–10.

50. Although he tends toward a somewhat more favorable view of the desamortización than I do, Raymond Carr, *Spain: 1808–1936* (Oxford, 1966), pp. 273–75, is one of the few general historians who emphasizes that its effects varied according to the preexisting social structure in each region.

thirteenth century and formed the heart of the latifundio district. In the former, 74.0 percent of the Church lands offered had been purchased by 1845; in the latter, 71.7 percent.[51]

The spoliation of the common lands was even more decisive. The exact extent and composition of these lands prior to the mid-nineteenth century are not known. There is little doubt, however, that (because of the relative underpopulation of Spain) they were much more widespread than in other European nations and occupied a much greater area than any other kind of property. Nor is there any question that the *comunales,* the portions open to all village inhabitants, everywhere formed a far larger proportion of the common lands than the *propios,* the surplus lands rented to individuals which the desamortización laws ordered sold. Finally, it seems certain that common lands were as prevalent in the South as in any other part of Spain, or more so, though the report of the late-eighteenth-century intendant, Olavide, that two-thirds of the land in Seville belonged to its cities and towns was probably exaggerated.[52] Yet because the poderosos, who had long since monopolized the use of the best common lands, took advantage of the desamortización to convert them into their personal property, Southern common lands of all types were almost completely liquidated. If Southern Spain as a whole forms 36.1 percent of the land surface of the nation, the Southern common lands still in existence in 1959 formed but 16.9 percent of all common lands. If the nine provinces principally reconquered in the thirteenth century occupy 26.8 percent of the national territory, their common lands in 1959 made up only 10.6 percent of the total common land area.[53] The regional difference can be viewed in still another way. In Southern Spain common pasture and woodlands occupy but 18.4

51. Compiled from the findings of Pascual Madoz as cited in Vicens Vives, vol. 4, pt. 2, p. 92. It might also be noted that although Southern Church lands were valued at 30 percent of all Church properties, Southern financial reserves were so extensive that almost half (49.5%) of the money actually disbursed for purchases of ecclesiastical domains was paid by Southern buyers. One other interesting fact should also be mentioned. Although the Church lands were snapped up more quickly in Southern Spain, there is no support for the frequent assertion that they were obtained at unusually low prices because of collusion among the poderosos who handled the auctions. In the nation as a whole the price bid for lands was 231 percent of the price at which they had been offered. In Southern Spain the increase was 241 percent and in the rest of the nation 222 percent, a slight difference that indicates, if anything, that competition for purchases was more intense in the South than elsewhere.

52. Herr, p. 108.

53. Compiled from *Estadística forestal de España: Año 1959,* p. 57. The area of all Spanish common lands in 1959 was 8.0 million hectares. At least 280 Southern townships were left completely without common lands (ibid., p. 56).

percent as much area as privately owned pasture and woodland. In the rest of the nation public and private ownership are much more on a par: municipal pastures and forests occupy 62.9 percent as much area as privately owned lands of this sort.[54]

The desamortización, whose sweeping nature in the South was made possible by the structure inherited from the past, helped in turn to shape the cruel future that awaited the region. Villages made up their loss of revenue from the propios by taxing staple goods bought mostly by the poor. The loss of the comunales deprived the needy of firewood and pasture. The transfer of Church lands to private owners meant that those who worked them no longer benefited from the benevolent terms that the earlier, inefficient administration had allowed. The gradual sale of noble lands to the new bourgeoisie more often harmed than helped the landless, since their new masters, less secure and more ambitious than the old, often proved more rapacious. Other, more subtle, changes produced similar effects. The breakdown of the loose medieval definitions of property resulted in the loss of the right to glean after harvest and to graze animals on the stubble. The substitution of impersonal, universal legal principles for local customary codes often meant that the emphyteutic leases tenants had enjoyed were replaced by short-term leases that could be altered or revoked at will. In short, the transformation of property relations in Andalusia and Estremadura aided only the strong.

The story is a familiar one, common to many nations in which the old was giving agonized birth to the new. But in Southern Spain the inheritance of the past was such that the new society was born especially defective. Despite its faults the old society had at least achieved some level of stability in which resources matched the felt needs of the population and ideas did not contradict institutions. As a result of the desamortización, the great rise in population which coincided with it, and the intellectual revolution that accompanied both, the new society never struck the same balance. The history of Southern Spain after the mid-nineteenth century is the history of men trying to revise or destroy a property structure that men in earlier centuries—not geography—had created.

54. Ibid. An indication of how much more complete the Spanish desamortización was than similar property disinvestitures in other European nations is given by María-Pilar Laso and Erich Bauer, "La propiedad forestal en España," REAS (Oct.–Dec. 1964), p. 46. In Spain in 1925 the state and municipalities owned only 28.8 percent of all forest lands, as opposed to 54.5 percent in Germany, 50.0 percent in Italy, and 33.4 percent in France.

3: The Social Structure of Southern Spain: The Rural Oligarchy

The agrarian unrest in Southern Spain during the past century and the problems that confronted the agrarian reformers of the 1930s cannot fully be understood unless the social structure of the South is examined in greater detail. Since the property relations described in Chapter 1 determined the nature of the social system more than any other single factor, its main outlines should already be evident. Many essential characteristics of the system, however, cannot be comprehended except through direct analysis.

The difficulties encountered in trying to draw an accurate picture of Southern rural society are fully as great as those that hampered satisfactory investigation of land tenure. The problem is in itself a complex one, of course. As mentioned earlier, crops and natural agricultural conditions in Southern Spain vary greatly from province to province. Moreover, exact information is lacking on most aspects of rural life. There are few local studies of the type that enriches French and English rural sociology. Little is known about such critical matters as the rate of capital investment, the nature of market opportunities, the customary provisions of farm leases, or even the wages earned by day laborers. Indeed, for most of the modern era the very numerical composition of the principal social classes must be a matter of speculation. Like so much else in Spanish life, the national census in some ways declined in quality after the eighteenth century and ceased to include detailed rural occupational analyses. This lack is so fundamental that it may be taken as illustrative of the scarcity of other types of information as well. Between 1797, when the data presented in Table 15 were gathered, and the census of 1950, no information was collected on the number of tenants, sharecroppers, owner-operators, or farm laborers either in Spain as a whole or in any of its provinces. Each census recorded how many people were *agricultores,* but inexplicably failed to relate what kind of *agricultores* they were, even though the farm population formed a

majority of the total population for most of the period.[1] There is probably no other major Western nation in which such basic intelligence was
lacking for so long.

Given such obstacles, it is clear that the analysis of Southern rural
society which follows can be only a crude and uneven one. Some questions, such as the identity of the large owners and the incidence of
absenteeism among them, are dealt with at length, because I was fortunate enough to come upon a source from which detailed answers could
be extracted. Others, such as the ways in which the absentee estates
were administered, had to be treated superficially because I lacked information. Most of the discussion refers to the period circa 1930, but
occasionally data from other periods must be used. The material is presented in the form of separate analyses for each important social class.
The large landowners who dominated Southern society are examined
first. They and their allies form the subject of this chapter. Chapter 4
juxtaposes to this rural oligarchy the day laborers who became its
principal historical opponents. The discussion of the rural proletariat
concludes with an analysis of the intermittently revolutionary tenants
and sharecroppers, who in some regions actively influenced the course of
events.

The Identity of the Large Owners

The first fact that must be emphasized in trying to establish the
identity of the large owners of Southern Spain is that they were individuals, not corporations. The small amount of land left to Southern
municipalities after the desamortización of the nineteenth century has
already been mentioned and needs no further elaboration. The role of
Church lands, however, is still often misunderstood. The desamortización
was even more effective in wiping out the holdings of the Church than

1. The census of 1920, which attempted a very rudimentary differentiation,
constitutes a minor exception to this practice. The first major effort to classify at
least part of the rural population occurred in connection with the agrarian reform
of the Second Republic when a list of potential recipients of land was drawn up
by the Institute of Agrarian Reform. Unfortunately this census of the rural proletariat was lost during the Civil War. I was able to locate only a one-page
résumé, which presents incomplete results for forty-four provinces as of 1936. These
are reproduced in Table 24. Only recently has there been any reason to believe
that the intelligence gap is being closed. Aside from the Encuesta agropecuária de la
población campesina of the Farm Syndicates, which is discussed in the next chapter,
several other sources have appeared. Unfortunately the best of these date from
the 1960s, by which time the mechanization of agriculture and the exodus from
the countryside had become so great that the data obtained can no longer be
taken as indicative of the class composition of rural society in earlier periods.

in despoiling the municipalities of their commons. Because the Church never attempted to reconstitute its rural holdings, it remained virtually without landed property from 1870 onward. The few tracts held by ecclesiastical organizations in the early 1930s certainly did not amount to more than a fraction of one percent of the land area of Spain. In the province of Cordova, for example, Church lands of all types made up but 1,114 of the 404,993 hectares registered in the Inventory of Expropriable Property compiled by the Institute of Agrarian Reform in 1933.[2] In Seville fewer than 1,000 of the 589,781 hectares listed in the Inventory belonged to ecclesiastical groups. The situation was more or less the same in Cadiz, Caceres, and Badajoz. In Toledo Church holdings were somewhat more extensive but still totaled only 3,521 hectares. In all six provinces combined, Church property probably did not surpass 12,000 hectares. Usually Church holdings were so small and scattered that any attempt to arrive at a more exact total would be as disheartening as it is pointless. The only really sizable individual holdings in the six provinces were a 1,407-hectare plot in Alconchel (Badajoz), a 1,993-hectare estate held by a religious sanatorium in Velada (Toledo), and a 1,136-hectare farm owned by another sanatorium in Nambroca (Toledo). Despite frequent assertions to the contrary by writers on the Left during the Republic and Civil War, the day of the great Church estates was long since past.[3] And if the Church opposed the agrarian program of the Republic, it was for reasons other than its need to protect its own property.

The continued rural strength of the nobility, on the other hand, was not mythical, though it, too, was exaggerated in the public mind. Although the desamortización did not expropriate noble properties, it attacked them indirectly by prohibiting their entailment and subjecting

2. I have taken the data on Church properties from the Registro de la Propiedad, the central register in which the Institute of Agrarian Reform inscribed the owners and farms potentially subject to expropriation under the Agrarian Reform Law of 1932. This Inventory of Property is an invaluable source for any detailed study of Spanish land tenure. The principal items of information it contains include the name and noble titles of landowners, their place of birth, their age and civil status, the crops grown on each of their farms, the size of these farms, the means by which and the dates on which they were acquired, and, finally, the mortgages and other financial charges that encumbered each farm. I have used the Registro extensively in this chapter and in chap. 8. Special problems connected with its use are discussed in app. A. The Registro consists of 254 unpublished volumes. In this and all future references it should be understood that I used the volume or volumes pertaining to the province, county, or township mentioned.

3. This is not to say, of course, that the Church did not possess urban property, shares in industrial and financial corporations, state bonds, and other such forms of wealth.

them to the normal laws of inheritance. Since the inheritance laws followed the Napoleonic Code in ensuring to all heirs some share in the legacy, part of each noble estate tended to pass with each generation to members of the family who did not succeed to the family title. The rate of the resulting diminution in the property left to noble titleholders is impossible to estimate. It was certainly not as rapid as some observers would have us believe and in no sense guaranteed so speedy or inevitable a fragmentation of the large estates as to make agrarian reform superfluous.[4] All heirs had to share in the legacy, but they did not have to share equally. The law still permitted so much freedom in the drawing up of bequests that, theoretically, the favored heir in a family of four children might receive as much as three-quarters of the family estate.[5] Indeed, the dispersion of agricultural holdings might be avoided entirely if the obligatory shares of the lesser heirs were satisfied in some form of family wealth other than land. These safeguards helped retard the rapid division of ancestral estates which would have occurred had the triumph of egalitarian principles of inheritance been more complete. Yet a considerable erosion of noble holdings undeniably did take place over the course of time.

The prohibition of entail was also important because it removed the protection that noble families formerly enjoyed against the dissolution of their estates through the action of individual titleholders. Family lands could now be sold at will or seized in payment of debts. Again, the general effects of these new legal principles are not measurable, although several specific cases can be cited in which family estates were greatly diminished. The house of Medina Sidonia, one of the most powerful noble houses in the early modern period, was left with but 464 hectares of arable land in Cadiz by 1933.[6] The Torres Cabrera holdings, very extensive in the nineteenth century, were reduced to 572 hectares by the unsuccessful agricultural experiments of the scholar-

4. A good statement of this conservative viewpoint can be found in Foss and Gerahty, *The Spanish Arena*, pp. 31–32.

5. Spanish inheritance laws operated as follows. One-third of the inheritance had to be divided equally among all heirs. A second third could be either divided among all heirs or granted entirely to a favored heir. The final third could be distributed without restriction, either within or outside the family. Theoretically, then, the favored heir could receive all of the latter two-thirds of the inheritance and part of the first third as well.

6. These were the only holdings of the Duke of Medina Sidonia in the six provinces I studied in the Registro de la Propiedad. His total holdings throughout Spain must have been less than one thousand hectares, since his name does not appear in IRA, *La reforma agraria en España: Sus motivos, su eséncia, su acción* (Valencia, 1937), pp. 47–48, where all *grandes* whose national holdings surpassed that figure are listed.

agronomist who held the family title during the 1890s and 1900s.[7] In more recent years the immense holdings of the house of Medinaceli have been considerably diminished as the latest titleholder transferred his wealth to urban and industrial properties.

These losses were compensated to some extent, of course, by new acquisitions. But a sampling of land purchases in several counties and townships in Badajoz, Cadiz, Cordova, and Seville suggests that by the 1930s the new acquisitions of the nobility were no longer sufficient to counteract the forces leading to a dissolution of the noble domains. Although the rate of purchase varied widely from place to place, only 13.4 percent of the noble holdings in the sample area as a whole had been purchased by the existing titleholders. Almost seven-eighths of their property had passed down to them through various forms of inheritance. This was in direct contrast to the experience of their bourgeois counterparts, who had purchased 26.6 percent—or about twice as much—of the land they owned.[8]

Despite the erosive tendencies at work, the old noble domains had been so extensive that in 1933, some 120 years after the first disentailment laws were approved by the Cortes of Cadiz, the nobility remained a very important landowning class. Its collective holdings in primarily arable land—nonarable pasture and forest lands were usually not recorded in the Inventory of Expropriable Property[9]—amounted to more than half a million hectares in the six key latifundio provinces studied. As can be seen in Table 16, the nobility owned from one-sixth to one-eighth of all the land included in the Inventory in Badajoz, Cordova, and Seville. In Toledo, where I did not compute the total amount of land in the Inventory, the proportion was probably between one-eighth and one-tenth. In Cadiz and Caceres nobles may have controlled as much as one-fourth of all Inventory lands. Even if the properties of the small

7. Registro de la Propiedad, my analysis. I am indebted to Vicente Flórez de Quiñones, *notario* of Cordova, for this account of the decline in the Torres Cabrera fortunes.

8. The total area sampled in the four provinces was 711,015 hectares, of which 172,911 hectares had been purchased by their then owners. In general about twice as much property was sold in fertile as in mountainous areas. Most of the noble purchases took place in these fertile areas, which suggests that the nobility was in the process of modernizing itself.

9. The complex question of the nature of the land inscribed in the Inventory of Expropriable Property is discussed in app. A. In general only about one-third of the Inventory lands were nonarable, whereas about three-fifths of all Spanish lands are normally not cultivated. This proportion varied from province to province, however. In Badajoz and Caceres I have estimated that about 40 percent of the Inventory land was nonarable, in Toledo about 33 percent, in Cadiz about 30 percent, in Cordova and Seville about 25 percent.

and medium owners not registered in the Inventory are added to those of the Inventory owners, noblemen still retained an important share of the entire cultivated area in the six provinces. The proportions reported in Table 16 on this question are only rough estimates, because it is difficult to determine precisely how much nonarable land found its way into the Inventory for each province. Nevertheless it seems certain that the nobility held at least 8 percent of the total cultivated area in the six provinces. Were it possible to take into account the property of untitled family members rather than just that of titleholders and their spouses, the proportion of noble-connected property would increase still further.

TABLE 16   NOBLE HOLDINGS IN SIX KEY LATIFUNDIO PROVINCES IN 1933

	Noble Holdings	All Inventory Holdings	Cultivated Land	Noble Holdings as Percent of: All Inventory Holdings	Cultivated Land[a]
	(thousands of hectares)				
Badajoz	127	790	1,035	16.1	7.3
Caceres	166	—[b]	1,015	—	9.9
Cadiz	61	—	284	—	14.8
Cordova	61	405	644	15.0	7.0
Seville	72	590	833	12.3	6.6
Toledo	58	—	615	—	6.3
Totals and Averages	545	(1,785)	4,426	(14.6)	8.0

SOURCES: Compiled from the Registro de la Propiedad and *AEPA: 1959–60*, p. 369.
   a. Noble holdings in cultivated land were estimated in accordance with the provincial variations mentioned in n. 9. The proportion of noble property in Cordova would be higher if records for Bujalance, an important noble stronghold, were not missing. The Registro is also incomplete for Toledo.
   b. A dash indicates not computed.

The collective importance of the nobility is all the more impressive when it is remembered how few individuals composed that class. Most of the noblemen who held property were giant landowners. As explained in Chapter 1, the possession of 250 hectares of arable land is enough to establish a person as a large owner by Spanish standards. If he holds more than 500 arable hectares, he enters a special category that probably includes less than one-tenth of one percent of the active agricultural population. Yet, as will be noted in Table 17, more than three-quarters of the nobles listed in the Inventory for the six key latifundio provinces studied held more than 500 hectares in those provinces alone, without reference to their belongings in the rest of the nation. Fewer than one-fourth of the nobles listed had more moderate domains, and almost half of these were latecomers to the nobility whose titles were granted after the traditional ties between aristocratic rank and landed property had begun to break down. In the latter connection, the strong correlation between antiquity of noble title and the size of cumulative holdings should be stressed as further evidence of the tenacity with which large property, once established, maintains itself. The largest landowners were almost all nobles whose roots lay in the medieval or early modern period.[10] Only in the smaller-landowning categories did families ennobled after 1800 begin to play a role comparable to that of their more ancient peers.

TABLE 17 NOBLE PROPERTY IN SIX LATIFUNDIO PROVINCES BY SIZE AND DATE OF ORIGIN OF FAMILY TITLE

Date of Origin of Family Title	Size (hectares)				
	Over 5,000	1,000–5,000	500–1,000	Under 500	Totals
Prior to 1800					
Owners	19	52	31	22	124
Hectares	226,503	119,628	21,746	5,478	373,355
1800 to 1931					
Owners	2	19	12	19	52
Hectares	29,273	37,471	8,224	4,810	79,778
Analysis of pre-1800 Titles					
Prior to 1600					
Owners	9	7	7	5	28
Hectares	111,682	16,817	4,758	1,809	135,066
1600 to 1699					
Owners	7	26	15	8	56
Hectares	69,511	58,513	10,764	1,526	140,314
1700 to 1799					
Owners	3	19	9	9	40
Hectares	45,310	44,298	6,224	2,143	97,975

SOURCES: Registro de la Propiedad for Badajoz, Caceres, Cadiz, Cordova, Seville, and Toledo; Ministerio de Justícia, *Grandezas y títulos del reino: guía oficial* (Madrid, 1959–60); Felipe de Salvador, *Guía de la nobleza* (Barcelona, 1956).

Though the individual and collective power of the nobility was thus considerable, it would be false to exaggerate its position and to imply that this class still dominated rural life. The largest noble owner

10. A major exception to this rule was the Marquis of Comillas, who owned 23,720 of the 29,273 hectares that appear in Table 17 for the largest post-1800 noble owners.

in the six provinces studied was the Duke of Medinaceli, who held 30,906 hectares. The second largest, the Marquis of la Romana, had 24,297. The third largest, the Marquis of Comillas, owned 23,720. After this the totals fall off rapidly, as only eight other nobles owned from 10,000 to 16,000 hectares. For property holdings in Spain as a whole, information exists solely for the 99 *grandes* especially affected by the Agrarian Reform Law.[11] The largest grande owner—Medinaceli—held 79,147 hectares of primarily arable land throughout Spain. The Dukes of Peñaranda, Villahermosa, and Alba were his closest rivals with 51,016, 47,204, and 34,455 hectares, respectively. The Marquis of la Romana and of Comillas round off the list of the six grandes who held more than 20,000 hectares in Spain as a whole, with 29,097 and 23,720 hectares each.[12] All these figures are impressive, especially since they would probably be at least half again as large if the Inventory had included all purely pastoral and forestal holdings. Nevertheless they do not approach the levels of the noble domains that existed in Eastern Europe before World War I, when the holdings of several noble families had to be measured in the hundreds of thousands of hectares. Nor can they be compared to the gigantic haciendas of Mexico prior to 1910.[13]

A sense of perspective must also be maintained when noble holdings are considered collectively. If it is shocking that so small a group controlled approximately one-twelfth of the cultivated land in six enormous provinces, it was nevertheless only one-twelfth—not one-quarter

11. The lack of information on the rest of the nobility is not a particularly important handicap, however, because grandes tended to be the most important noble landowners. For example, 8 of the 11 nobles with more than 10,000 hectares in the 6 provinces studied in the Inventory were grandes; 7 of the 10 with holdings of between 5,000 and 10,000 hectares also held this exalted rank.

12. IRA, *Reform agraria en España*, pp. 47–48.

13. Indeed, the land tenure system of Mexico remained far more unbalanced than that of Spain even after decades of agrarian reform. Thus, in 1940, after the presidency of Cárdenas, Mexico had 9,697 privately owned holdings of more than 1,000 hectares each, which collectively occupied 61.9 percent of its total land surface. By contrast, in 1959, the 1,078 Spanish holdings of this type (many of which, moreover, were publicly, not privately owned) occupied only 5.0 percent of the total area. The disparity is no less pronounced when uncultivated land is left aside and only cropland is considered. In Mexico, holdings of over 800 hectares encompassed 28.4 percent of all crop land in 1950, whereas in Spain the corresponding figure could not have been much more than 2 percent. Even the very *worst* of the Spanish latifundio regions are not fully comparable to the Mexican *average*. Thus, holdings of over 100 hectares occupied 52.4 percent of all land in the thirteen latifundio provinces of Spain in 1930, and 72.3 percent of all land in Mexico as a whole in 1940. The figures for Mexico are taken from Elias H. Tuma, *Twenty-Six Centuries of Agrarian Reform: A Comparative Analysis* (Berkeley, 1965), pp. 121–22.

or one-half of the land—that they dominated. Moreover, since the nobility was not as strong either in the seven peripheral latifundio provinces,
whose Inventories I did not investigate, or in the small- and medium-
holding provinces of central and northern Spain, this class controlled a
considerably smaller proportion of the cultivated surface in the rest of
the nation. A reasonable estimate of noble property throughout Spain
would seem to be some 1.2 or 1.3 million hectares of primarily arable
land—that is to say, no more than 6 percent of the 21 million hectares
that are normally cultivated.[14] Many of the sponsors of agrarian reform
during the Second Spanish Republic did not fully appreciate this fact,
but seem to have operated under the illusion that the reform could be
completed primarily through an attack upon noble holdings.

The vast majority of the land held by large owners in Southern
Spain belonged to individuals without noble rank. A small portion of
this territory was owned by recent descendants of noble families who
had not succeeded to the family title. The rest pertained to individuals
whose ties to the nobility were so distant that they were no longer
meaningful or to persons without any noble connections whatever. The
origins of the purely bourgeois owners remain to be studied. Many of
them were descendants of families that had purchased land during the
desamortización, but a substantial number seem to have established their
fortunes at the turn of the twentieth century or during World War I.[15]

14. All these estimates are based on the assumptions that (a) noble holdings
as a whole were geographically distributed in the same way as the estates of the
grandeza, the only noble class for which national data exist, and (b) that the
relation between grande estates and those of the lesser nobility was uniform. Thus
72.1 percent of the total grande holdings in Southern Spain (256,336 out of
355,353 hectares) lay in the six key latifundio provinces studied in the Registro.
The grandeza's total Southern holdings in turn made up 61.5 percent of the 577,359
hectares it held throughout Spain (IRA, Boletín [March 1934], 2, 169). Since
grandeza holdings constituted 45 percent of total noble holdings in the six provinces
studied, the nobility as a whole would own 1,283,020 hectares in all Spain, if
both my assumptions are correct. It is possible that the lesser nobility in fact held
more land relative to the grandeza in northern and central than in Southern
Spain because of the different types of reconquest in each region (see chap. 2).
Even so, the nobility could not have owned much more than 1.6 or 1.7 million
hectares of Inventory property in all Spain, which, discounting the pasture and
forest lands included in the Inventory, would leave us with some 1.2 or 1.3 million
hectares of arable noble property.

15. Thus, a group of sheepherders who emigrated to Cordova from Soria in
the 1890s gradually acquired so much land as to become locally famous. Another
celebrated source of large owners in Cordova were the tenants of the Duke of
Fernán-Nuñez, whose favorable leases allowed them to accumulate the reserves
with which to purchase land in the campiña. My sampling of methods of property
acquisition in the Registro also suggests fairly high property mobility in the

Whatever their origins, the important fact is that although few of the bourgeois owners were ennobled, they gradually acquired a local importance comparable to that once reserved to the nobility. By intelligent purchases and carefully chosen marriage alliances, many bourgeois families acquired so much land that entire localities were converted into their personal fiefs. Countless cases of this sort can be cited, several of which involved fairly populous villages.

The province of Toledo may be taken as an example. In 1933, when the Institute of Agrarian Reform compiled its Inventory of Expropriable Property, a nonnoble owner controlled at least one-third of the 5,864-hectare township of Cabezamesala (pop. 1,261). In the larger township of Ocaña (pop. 6,387) four members of the Silva Soria family and three other owners together owned 59 percent of the municipality's 8,792 hectares. In Carpio de Tajo (pop. 4,390) three bourgeois proprietors controlled at least 38 percent of the 10,862-hectare municipal area. A brother of one of these proprietors owned the neighboring hamlet of Barciene in its entirety, as well as one-third of the township of Gerindote (pop. 2,079) and one-eighth of the municipality of Novés (pop. 2,023).

Toledo was not unique in the frequency of its bourgeois fiefs. In Caceres the monopolization of property was even more pronounced. Of the 11,368 hectares of Herreruela (pop. 1,031), 78 percent belonged to three bourgeois owners. In neighboring Membrío (pop. 2,294) 70 percent of the 20,870-hectare municipality was owned by five nonnobles, three of whom were brothers and two cousins. In nearby Solarino (pop. 2,637) a sister of one of the Membrío owners and two of the Herreruela proprietors collectively owned 72 percent of the 15,705-hectare township. A similar situation existed in Cañaveral (pop. 2,792), where two sets of cousins owned at least 80 percent of the town's 5,548 hectares. In the large municipality of Zorita (pop. 5,318) four members of the local Cano clan owned 28 percent of the 19,998-hectare municipal area.[16]

In the examples given there is an obvious tendency for many of the large owners to be related to each other. A fundamental question

twentieth century. As will be remembered, 26.6 percent of all bourgeois lands was purchased, not inherited. In fertile regions the rate of purchase often reached 50 percent.

16. All statistics were compiled from the Registro de la Propiedad. The percentages given are minimal estimates because the Registro inscribed primarily agricultural land, whereas I compiled the percentages on the basis of the total land surface of each municipality (statistics on cultivated land are not readily available on the township or county level). The population data all refer to 1930 and were taken from the census of that year. The method by which I deduce family relationships between individual owners is explained above in connection with Table 18 and in app. D.

arises as to whether this tendency also appears in larger areas. Were most large Spanish owners linked together in what might be called interlocking family directorates that dominated the rural economy on the provincial and interprovincial level, as well as in the township and county? This question cannot be answered for the whole of Southern Spain, much less for the entire nation: the tracing of individual holdings and family connections over such vast regions is too difficult a task. The prevailing pattern can be suggested, however, if interlocking ownership is examined in a single province. I selected Badajoz as my sample, because interlocking ownership there seemed somewhat less frequent than in Caceres and Toledo and somewhat more frequent than in the richer and more economically active provinces of Cadiz, Cordova, and Seville. Table 18, which summarizes the Badajoz situation, therefore presents a rough average on this question for the six key latifundio provinces studied.

The methodology used in drawing up the table is explained in Appendix D. Here we need mention only that although the extended

TABLE 18   FAMILY CONNECTIONS AMONG LARGE OWNERS IN BADAJOZ IN 1933

	Number of Sibling Groups	Number of Individuals	Number of Nobles	Hectares Owned
Twenty-five Extended Families	104	198	31	294,207
Isolated Sibling Groups	49	144	4	140.445
Unrelated Individual Owners	—	70	6	131,287
Totals	[153]	412	41	565,939
Analysis of Extended Families				
Stuart y Falcó, or Stuart	4	9	8	38,495
Salabert Arteaga, or Arteaga	4	13	3	28,383
Montero de Espinosa	13	19	1	27,325
Alvarez de Toledo	3	5	5	25,531
Sánchez Arjona	10	18	none	24,739
Fernández de Córdoba	6	7	5	21,973
Donoso Cortes, or Donoso	11	18	none	18,582
Cueva Godoy	3	17	none	18,508
Gragera	7	14	none	16,024
Sixteen smaller extended family groups	51	87	12	108,401

SOURCE: Registro de la Propiedad.

NOTE: The "Extended Family" totals are net and exclude duplications caused by intermarriage between groups. In calculating column 1 for the extended families, I have of necessity counted some individual owners as sibling groups (i.e., some sibling groups within the extended families consist of only one person). The "Unrelated Individual Owners" category includes only persons who owned over 1,000 hectares and had no obvious family connections with other large owners.

family groups include a wide variety of relationships, some of which may be quite distant, the sibling groups are unquestionably closely knit units of brothers and sisters. Also a few of the "isolated" (i.e., unrelated) sibling groups, as well as some of the largest individual proprietors (who are included in the table to round off its description of property concentration in Badajoz), were probably related to each other, but the evidence available was not sufficient for them to be listed as such.

The table is otherwise self-explanatory. It confirms that the pattern of interlocking ownership noted in the local examples also prevails in larger areas. Most of the large owners of Southern Spain are fairly closely tied to each other by blood and descend from relatively few family groups. The most affluent of these groups tend to have noble connections and are remnants of the former dominance of the nobility. The vast majority, however, are of more recent and purely bourgeois origin. Because of these interrelationships within and between families, as well as because so many large owners hold property in more than one township, the true concentration of economic power is far greater than was suggested by the Cadastral data discussed in Chapter 1. Under the artificial standards of measurement used by the Cadastre, some 1,800 or 1,900 individuals listed as large owners appear to dominate the land surface of Badajoz in 1930.[17] In reality, when the duplications inherent in the Cadastre are eliminated and the personal ties between large owners established, the rural economy of the province is seen to have been controlled, for all practical purposes, by some 400 individuals organized into roughly one-third as many sibling groups, most of which in turn were linked together into a handful of extended families. The 565,939 hectares that belonged to these few individuals and families constituted 26.6 percent of the total area of Badajoz and—even if 40 percent of the Inventory holdings are discounted as consisting of nonarable pasture or forest—at least 32.5 of its total cultivated surface.[18] The social and political implications of these figures are overwhelming. In 1930 Badajoz had a population of 702,418 persons, three-quarters of whom were directly dependent on agriculture for their livelihood. By owning one-third of the arable land in the province, the 412 individuals

17. In 1930, when only four-fifths of the province had been surveyed, the Cadastre listed 1,576 proprietors with over 250 hectares.

18. The total area of Badajoz is 2.1 million hectares; its total cultivated surface is about 1.1 million hectares. Had all of the nonarable property of the large family owners been included, they would probably be found to own 35 or 40 percent of the entire province. It might be added, to show how few people the agrarian reform of the Second Republic need have affected had it been more intelligently conceived, that the 412 individuals in Table 18 held 72 percent of all the land listed in the Inventory of Expropriable Property for the province.

and 153 sibling groups listed in Table 18 in effect governed the destiny of hundreds of thousands of people, even when their nonarable and extra-provincial holdings are not taken into account.

The popular conception as to the rural holdings of the Church was entirely mythical. Even the general view of the rural strength of the nobility was considerably exaggerated. But the nearly universal concern over the existence of a strongly latifundistic rural economy was not based upon illusion. Since the monopolization of the Spanish earth remained almost as complete as it had been in the centuries before the collapse of the *ancien régime,* it is not surprising that so many Spaniards were mistaken in their identification of the dominant rural class. The underlying reality of an intense concentration of property had remained so much the same that it obscured the fact that the chief beneficiaries of the existing social order were no longer the nobility or the Church but a new class of bourgeois owners.

The Inefficiency of the Large Estates

Property concentration is not necessarily bad in itself. A fundamental question that must be answered in assessing its social and economic consequences is what use the noble and bourgeois owners made of their property. The question is difficult to answer. The Inventory of Expropriable Property is of no help here, and there is a paucity of relevant information from other sources. One fact seems certain, however. Although some traces of the old stockbreeding mentality lingered on, most large owners of the Guadalquivir valley, the heart of the latifundio region, had begun cultivating most of their arable land by 1930 rather than allowing it to remain in pasture or using it for hunting preserves. As late as 1919 a government survey reported that 29,000 hectares of fertile land in Seville were still devoted to the raising of fighting bulls rather than to farming.[19] These were the last remnants of a dying system, however. The high prices for agricultural produce which prevailed from 1900 on and the Europe-wide scarcities generated by World War I caused many new lands to be put to the plow, a trend that was not reversed during the 1920s, when prices once more became uncertain.[20] By 1930 even the fighting bull ranches of Western Andalusia had

19. The survey results are summarized in Carrión, p. 360.
20. On this question see Juan Díaz del Moral, *Historia de las agitaciones campesinas andaluzas—Córdoba* (Madrid, 1929), pp. 3–21. This eminent authority, however, suffers from regional chauvinism, as well as from a love of paradox, which sometimes cause him to overstate the improvements made in the economy of Cordova from the 1890s to 1920, precisely the period in which the social situation was markedly deteriorating.

nearly disappeared,[21] and the Guadalquivir valley had taken on the character it maintains today of a region where almost all naturally fertile land is in fact cultivated. The same was true for most of Estremadura, La Mancha, and Eastern Andalusia, although in these regions poorer soils and a less favorable climate often make economically arable and nonarable lands difficult to distinguish. In general the stage of development today associated with South America, where naturally fertile land is left in pasture or is not used at all, had been superseded in Spain by 1930. As Constancio Bernaldo de Quirós, a leading advocate of moderate agrarian reform, put it, "The idea that the Andalusian countryside is uncultivated, with immense tracts of land given over to fighting bulls and to the hunting of deer and wild boar," had truly become "an antiquated and mistaken notion." [22] Had not Southern owners constantly increased the amount of tilled land from the early part of the nineteenth century onward, it is difficult to see how the considerable growth in population discussed in the next chapter could have taken place.[23]

However, even if the most extreme charge against the latifundios had long since ceased to be generally valid and most Southern large owners had begun to till their estates, there is little reason to believe that they cultivated them well. Every available standard of measurement suggests that the large domains were managed without initiative or imagination, that their owners failed to apply modern farming techniques, and that the rate of capital investment in the land was minimal. The large estates were no longer regarded chiefly as status symbols, but neither were their owners willing to expend the energy and take the risks necessary to exploit their full natural potentialities.

The use of fertilizers is one index of the degree of adaptation to modern farming techniques. According to the Statistical Yearbook of the Ministry of Agriculture in 1930, the South had the lowest rate of fertilizer consumption in Spain. In the irrigated provinces of the Levante, for example, an average of 221 kilograms of mineral fertilizers was used on each hectare of cultivated land. Unirrigated Catalonia and Aragon employed 168 kilograms per hectare. Along the Biscay Coast the ap-

21. Ministerio de Trabajo, Servicio de Parcelación y Colonización Interior, *La crisis agraria andaluza de 1930–31: Estudios y documentos* (Madrid, 1931), p. 31.

22. Ibid. Adolfo Vázquez Humasqué, first director of the Institute of Agrarian Reform, basically agreed. He estimated that at most 1.5 million uncultivated hectares—"and these not of first-class land"—could be put to the plow throughout Spain (*Información Española*, March 1931, pp. 52–53).

23. On the considerable increase in cultivated land and in productivity during the nineteenth century, see Vicens Vives, vol. 4, pt. 2, pp. 223–42.

propriate figure was 231 kilograms and in Segovia, 116 kilograms. By contrast, 48 kilograms of mineral fertilizers per cultivated hectare were used in Estremadura, 53 in Western Andalusia, 56 in La Mancha, and 63 in Eastern Andalusia. The latifundio regions used less than half as much fertilizer as the small-holding regions cited above, and except for Eastern Andalusia, none of them even remotely approached the average consumption rate of 70 kilograms per cultivated hectare which prevailed in Spain as a whole.[24]

A second index of modernity is the speed with which agricultural machinery is adopted. Although such machinery may not be cheaper to use in the short run where wage levels are very low, its employment has certain inherent advantages. For example, machines permit deeper plowing (a result much to be desired in the black soil regions of the Guadalquivir valley) and make possible the speedy conclusion of agricultural operations while natural conditions are most favorable. Because they can be used most effectively on large estates, not small farms, one would expect to find a great concentration of agricultural machines, especially of the heavier and more expensive type, in Southern Spain. This was not the case in fact. The South contains 45.5 percent of the cropland and 77.6 percent of the large agricultural domains in Spain.[25] Yet as can be seen in Table 19, only 32.3 percent of all tractors were lo-

TABLE 19   MECHANIZATION OF AGRICULTURE IN SOUTHERN SPAIN AS OF 1932

	Tractors	Harvesting Combines	Irrigation Pumps
Western Andalusia	905	47	1,168
Estremadura	79	8	412
La Mancha	256	3	462
Eastern Andalusia	78	none	1,140
Southern Totals	1,318	58	3,182
National Totals	4,084	335	29,443
Southern Spain as Percent of the Nation	32.3	17.3	10.8

SOURCE: *AEPA: 1932*, pp. 318–26.

cated there in 1932. The latifundio provinces account for 42.8 percent of the land sown in grains and 68.2 percent of the land in which grains

24. Cited by Carrión, p. 345. The large acreage devoted to olives in Western Andalusia might explain minor deviations from the national average in that region, but cannot justify so major a deviation as existed.

25. In 1959, 77.6 percent of the 6,913 holdings with a taxable income of more than 40,000 pesetas were located in Southern Spain. García-Badell, Table 4. For comparative cropland figures, see Table 11.

were sown in blocks of 40 hectares or more.[26] Yet these same provinces contained but 17.3 percent of the harvesting combines used to gather such crops in 1932. The size of the Southern large estates elsewhere would have counseled mechanization. Because of the sluggishness of their owners, however, they were still worked almost entirely with animal and human power at the time of the Second Republic.[27]

Irrigation is still another measure of the determination of man to improve upon nature, especially in the arid regions of Spain where irrigation may increase crops from three- to sixfold. Southern large owners have long been notorious for their disinterest in irrigation. Because they did not build private irrigation networks in the eighteenth and nineteenth centuries, Southern Spain (except for Granada, where the Moorish irrigation systems had survived) entered the contemporary era as the least irrigated of all Spanish regions in which irrigation is technically feasible. Because they refused to cooperate with the Hydraulic Confederations by which Primo de Rivera attempted to expand irrigation facilities in the 1920s through joint public and private action, these failed in Southern Spain. Finally, because Southern owners were unwilling to finance even such secondary irrigation works as the leveling of the earth or the construction of conduits, they often did not use already existing facilities. A particularly notorious instance of this kind occurred in the Gaudalete valley in Cadiz after the construction of the Guadalcacín Dam in 1910. Every government from that date until 1952 failed in its efforts to get the large local owners, most of whom were not nobles, to bring water from the principal canal to their farms.[28] The impasse ended only when the Franco government itself undertook the building of the necessary secondary works. For forty-two years a major state investment remained useless for want of the type of private cooperation which during the same period was transforming the economy of Aragon.

26. Servicio Nacional del Trigo, *La producción triguera nacional*, table 3A, and *La estructura de las explotaciones trigueras segun datos estadísticos de la cosecha de 1957*, table 1. If only owners who sowed more than 150 hectares—a level at which mechanization should become absolutely indispensable—are taken into account, the South contained 79.5 percent of the 150,800 hectares so used in Spain.

27. The immense region of Estremadura was especially slow in adapting to mechanization because of its reliance on the yuntero system (see chap. 4). In passing it might be added that while mechanization in the South would have caused short-term social problems since some workers would have lost their jobs, its long-range consequences would probably have been to stimulate the Southern economy and thus provide greater employment opportunities. This would certainly have been the case had mechanization been accompanied by irrigation.

28. Thus the Registro de la Propiedad in 1933 and an Instituto de Colonización pamphlet in 1952 both report about the same amount of unirrigated land in the Guadalcacín basin—some 9,700 out of a total of 11,700 hectares.

Some writers have justified the large Southern owners on the grounds that even the secondary works in modern irrigation schemes are so expensive that they may sometimes exceed the original cost of the land itself.[29] The same justification cannot be applied to the equally obvious lack of enthusiasm of the Southern owners for the small-scale, inexpensive irrigation that can be created by drawing water from wells or diverting it from local streams. In miniature projects of this type, irrigation pumps are usually necessary to move the water to the fields. Yet as can be seen by referring to Table 19, it was precisely in this category of mechanization that the South was most deficient. Only one-tenth of all the irrigation pumps in Spain were located in the South, and more than one-third of these were to be found in Eastern Andalusia, where a tradition of irrigation had been inherited from the Moors.

Other evidence is not lacking for the low standards of cultivation on the large Southern estates. As mentioned earlier, the long growing seasons, warm climate, and relatively abundant rainfall of Southern Spain permit an extraordinary variety of crops to be sown in that region. The hesitancy with which these crop possibilities were explored demonstrates the absence of managerial imagination and initiative. The South is the only region in Spain where cotton can be grown on unirrigated land; Southern cotton enjoys certain advantages even in irrigated soils. After the Civil War this potential monopoly began to be exploited, and the economy of Southern Spain, especially in the Guadalquivir valley, has been transformed as a result.[30] This same transformation might have occurred earlier had the large owners of Southern Spain displayed the initiative that had long enabled owners of all kinds in the Levante to exploit both domestic and world markets. Instead, Southern owners of irrigated land, where cotton might always have been competitively grown, preferred to sow traditional crops. Further, owners of unirrigated land, where cotton can be grown only at higher than world prices, never used their considerable political power to force the granting of subsidies that would make their cotton competitive on the domestic market. When the policy of government support which led to the considerable cotton acreage of the

29. This argument is eloquently expressed in Marichalar [Viscount of Eza], *Reforma agraria en España,* pp. 85–86, 90. Eza complains that the lack of credit rather than the lack of managerial initiative was chiefly responsible for the absence of irrigation in Southern Spain but does not explain why irrigation projects were successful in areas where credit facilities were even less developed than in the South.

30. In 1959, for example, cotton was sown on 207,515 hectares and accounted for 13.2 percent of the value of all agricultural production in Western Andalusia (*AEPA: 1959–60,* pp. 362–63, 266–67). By contrast, only 8,167 hectares of cotton were sown in Southern Spain in 1932.

1950s was finally inaugurated, it owed little to an awakening of Southern initiative. Rather, it resulted almost entirely from the cumulative effects on Spanish foreign reserves and economic thought of the Civil War, World War II, and the subsequent economic blockade of Spain.

The case of cotton has a lesser parallel in the production of rice. By 1959 Seville had become the only important rice-growing province outside the Levante; it devoted 14,500 hectares to that crop and accounted for 21.7 percent of the national production. In 1935, though agricultural conditions were the same, only 105 hectares of this extremely valuable plant were grown in the province. The story is the same in the other Southern provinces, where 1,465 hectares were sown with rice in 1959 but none had been planted prior to the Civil War.[31] Again the initiative in the post–Civil War transformation came not from local growers like those who had made rice a successful crop in the Levante long before the age of governmental economic intervention, but from the national exigencies created by the two great wars.

Corn is another crop whose cultivation in Southern Spain agronomists have long urged.[32] Here, too, the South holds a favored position, because it is the only area outside Galicia and the Biscay Coast where there is enough rain for corn to be grown on unirrigated land. Yet though a promising start was made after World War I, the quantities of land sown with this plant remained small—some 60,000 hectares in the 1930s and some 83,000 hectares in 1959.[33] Similarly, economists have long thought it possible for Southern Spain to follow the example of the Levante and convert itself into an important supplier of early market vegetables,[34] but local growers have ignored this possibility almost completely. Finally, the South has been deficient in planting such fruit trees as the almond and the carob for which it and the Mediterranean coastal region are alone suited by nature.[35]

Absenteeism and Systematic Leasing

The unwillingness fully to explore crop possibilities, the failure to cooperate in irrigation schemes, the exceedingly slow adaptation to mod-

31. Ibid., p. 18.
32. For example, Ministerio de Trabajo, *La crisis agraria andaluza*, pp. 27–30.
33. *AEPA: 1959–60*, p. 12. The figures refer to both irrigated and unirrigated land.
34. For example, Zorilla, pp. 272–74.
35. Enrique Alcaráz, "The Problems of Home Colonization," *Bulletin of Economic and Social Intelligence*, 26 (December 1912), pp. 182–83, and Carrión, pp. 319–20, place what seems to me to be excessive emphasis on the insufficient development of the Southern fruit economy.

ern farming techniques, all add up to a neglect so fundamental that it may be considered a type of moral absenteeism. Behind this moral absenteeism often lay a physical absenteeism. Southern owners did not invest much capital or energy in their farms, because in many instances they did not know, operate, or live on those farms. Absenteeism was especially common among the nobility. With few exceptions, noble owners traditionally have been absentee owners almost by definition. For example, among the 262 grandes who collectively owned 355,000 hectares of arable land in Southern Spain in 1933, only 14 had been born there and all of these came from large cities, not from the countryside. More grandes were born in the resort city of San Sebastian than in any of the Southern capitals. More were native to such French centers of international society as Paris, Biarritz, and Bayonne than to all the Southern capitals put together. But it was Madrid that was the overwhelming favorite of the grandeza. There were 177 grande families—thirteen times as many as were to be found in Seville, Cordova, Granada, Málaga, and Jerez de la Frontera combined—centered in that city in the 1930s.[36] Obviously it was not the location of their sources of wealth which determined grande residence but the location of the sites where that wealth might be spent most graciously.

The absenteeism of the lesser nobility was only slightly less pronounced than that of the grandes. The main difference was that the French stamping grounds for international society were less favored among them; the social, industrial, and political centers of Spain exerted the same attraction as they did for the great nobles. According to an analysis of noble residence circa 1955, 77.9 percent of the 1,265 members of the lesser nobility studied lived either in Madrid, Barcelona, San Sebastian, or Bilbao. Only 22.1 percent lived in primarily agricultural provinces, and these, for the most part, resided not on their farms but in the provincial capitals. In a sense, the latifundio provinces suffered less completely from the noble rural exodus than did other agricultural regions, because Andalusia includes a few large cities that enjoy a relatively active social life of their own. Nevertheless, only a small minority of the landowning no-

36. According to the Ministry of Justice decree of 15 October 1932, which listed the 262 grandes especially affected by the Agrarian Reform Law, the distribution of grande birthplaces was as follows:

Madrid	177	Valencia	6
Paris	12	Jerez	5
Barcelona	11	Palma de Mallorca	5
Biarritz and Bayonne	8	Others inside Spain	10
San Sebastian	7	Others outside Spain	14
Seville	7		

bility of Andalusia actually lived there. As for Estremadura and La Mancha, both regions had been almost entirely deserted by their native aristocracy.[37]

Absenteeism among bourgeois owners is much more difficult to assess. The problems that confront the researcher are discussed in Appendix D, where the methodology underlying Table 20 is explained. Here we

TABLE 20   EXTRAPROVINCIAL URBAN ABSENTEEISM IN CADIZ, CORDOVA, AND SEVILLE IN 1933

	Bourgeois		Combined Noble and Bourgeois	
	Total Property (hectares)	Percent Held by Absentees	Total Property (hectares)	Percent Held by Absentees
Total Sample Region	592,000	13.7	693,891	22.7
Fertile Guadalquivir counties	220,300	19.0	295,761	32.4
Poor Sierra Morena counties	291,900	9.3	309,610	14.1
Counties with mixed lands	79,800	15.5	88,520	20.3

SOURCE: Compiled from the Registro de la Propiedad.

NOTE: The counties included are listed in n. 38. For absenteeism among the large family owners of Badajoz, see the text. The bourgeois absentee property was almost evenly divided between persons born in major Southern capitals and those born in major northern capitals.

need note only that the table unquestionably understates the frequency of bourgeois absenteeism, because it entirely excludes owners born in the capitals of the provinces in which they held land and includes as extraprovincial absentees only persons born in those few cities in Spain which are so economically active or socially glamorous that their natives are extremely unlikely to migrate to the Southern countryside.

Aside from documenting the fact that absentee property forms a significant proportion of the total Inventory property even when absenteeism is so restrictively defined, Table 20 suggests one other important conclusion. The highest degree of absenteeism was not recorded in the poor

37. I am indebted to Professor Juan Linz, Department of Sociology, Yale University, for these data. Linz's figures for the places of residence of the lesser nobility are as follows: Madrid, 817; Andalusia, 175; Barcelona, 109; Valencia, 64; Basque provinces, 60; Estremadura, La Mancha and New Castile, 34; Old Castile, 6. Data on place of birth can be used almost interchangeably with data on place of residence when dealing with the nobility (though not with the bourgeoisie, as is explained in app. D). This is indicated by the fact that my findings on the grandeza correspond almost perfectly to those of Professor Linz, despite the different methods of measurement employed.

mountainous counties of the Sierra Morena chain, where, because agricultural possibilities are limited, there is less need for active management
on the part of the owner. Rather, urban absenteeism was most common
in the Guadalquivir valley, where the land is extremely rich.[38] Because
of this positive correlation between absenteeism and soil fertility, the
figures presented in Table 20 understate the importance of the long-
distance urban absentee in the economy of Southern Spain. Farms were
most neglected precisely in the regions where population density was
highest and where most agricultural produce could be grown, not in
peripheral areas where relatively few people and little wealth were involved.

One other pattern should also be noted. It would have been too difficult to trace variations in the degree of absenteeism among different
types of owners in the entire area encompassed by Table 20. If the rich
countryside around Cordova known as the *campiña* is taken as a guide,
however, it would seem that—in contrast to noble absenteeism, which is
relatively uniform—bourgeois absenteeism tends to increase with the size
of the holdings. Thus only about one-eighth (13.5%) of the campiña land
that belonged to bourgeois owners of less than 500 hectares was held by
long-distance absentees. Among owners of from 500 to 1,000 hectares,
the proportion rose to nearly one-fourth (24.0%), and among those whose
properties exceeded 1,000 hectares it climbed to almost one-third (32.9%)
of their total holdings. Further proof for this correlation between bourgeois absenteeism and large holdings can be found among the owners
who made up the interlocking family directorates in Badajoz (Table 18).
Because only the largest owners were included in these family groups,
the over-all rate of absenteeism was higher than would have been expected in such a relatively poor region. Even if local provincial capital
absenteeism is again excluded, 22.6 percent of the lands in Badajoz—as
compared to 13.7 percent in the sample area for Table 20—not owned by
nobles were held by urban absentees.

If the almost universal absenteeism that prevails among the nobility
is added to the partial absenteeism of the bourgeoisie, most of the tendencies discussed above are considerably exaggerated. Absenteeism itself
increases enormously, and its incidence in fertile areas rises. In Table 20,
for example, the percentage of land held by absentees jumped from 13.7

38. The fertile counties in Table 20 included Carmona, Marchena, Morón,
Écija, Osuna, and the nineteen townships that may be said to constitute the
campiña of Cordova. The mountainous counties were Cazalla de la Sierra, Fuenteovejuna, Hinojosa del Duque, Montoro, and Pozoblanco—as well as the giant townships of Hornachuelos, Obejo, and Villaviciosa. The mixed-quality townships were
Lora del Río, Lucena, Rute, Chiclana, Grazalema, and Medina Sidonia.

to 22.7 percent in the sample region as a whole, and increased from 19.0 to 32.4 percent in the fertile counties. The rise in absenteeism was probably equally spectacular among the largest owners. Thus among the large family owners of Badajoz, the rate of absenteeism leaps from 22.6 to 36.5 percent once nobles are taken into account.[39] Had it been possible to include absentees resident in the local provincial capitals, all these proportions would have been higher still.

The high rate of absenteeism has obvious relevance to the incidence of leasing. If an owner does not himself cultivate his lands, one of the ways in which he can derive income from them is by renting them to tenants. As can be seen in Table 21, at least 53.3 percent of the land

TABLE 21   PERMANENT LEASING IN SOUTHERN SPAIN IN 1933

	Area Leased	Total Area	Percent of their lands leased by:		
	(thousands of hectares)		Known Absentees	Other Owners	All Owners
Fertile counties	124	308	62.3	30.3	40.5
Mixed counties	28	84	49.6	29.6	33.2
Badajoz family owners	142	462	50.0	18.2	30.8
Mountainous counties	59	363	49.9	10.5	16.3
Totals and averages	354	1,216	53.3	19.5	29.1

SOURCE: Registro de la Propiedad.

NOTE: Only property leased continuously for a minimum of twelve consecutive years as of 1933 is included. The sample area is the same as in Table 20 except for the addition of the large family owners of Badajoz, as well as of several townships in the county of Sanlúcar la Mayor (Seville). These additions, together with variations in the number of unknowns, account for the differences in the total area figures of the two tables. In absolute terms, "Known Absentees" (from which category I continue to exclude owners born in the capital cities of the provinces in which they held land) leased 183,883 hectares, and "Other Owners" 169,617 hectares.

owned by absentees in the areas studied was leased.[40] Though nonabsentees and those whose absenteeism could not be proven from the evidence available did not lease to nearly the same extent, the practice was

39. The absolutes quantities for Badajoz are that 97,415 out of the total 433,000 hectares belonging to bourgeois owners whose birthplaces could be determined were owned by extraprovincial urban absentees. When noble property is added to bourgeois, 200,102 of 548,304 hectares were held by absentees.

40. This figure is minimal, because the Inventory of Expropriable Property registered leased lands as such only if they had been let continuously for twelve successive years prior to 1933. Lands leased for shorter periods and the yuntero-type lands that were intermittently leased for a year at a time were not included.

common among them also. Thus three-tenths of the total Inventory area was leased on a permanent, systematic basis. Because the rate of leasing, like the rate of absenteeism, rose as the quality of the land improved, its importance was in reality greater than these figures suggest. Only one-sixth of the Inventory land in the mountainous Sierra Morena was leased, but in the fertile Guadalquivir Valley the proportion rose to 40 percent.[41]

When all types of leased lands are taken into account—those that escaped registration in the Inventory as well as the permanently leased lands described above—the South had the highest rate of leasing of any of the arid regions of Spain where grain crops constitute the basis of the rural economy. This fact, which is documented in Table 22, is not gen-

TABLE 22   LEASING OF ALL KINDS ON CULTIVATED LAND IN SPAIN AS A WHOLE IN 1951

	Area Leased	Total Area	Percent Leased
	(thousands of cultivated hectares)		
Spain	7,664	21,076	36.4
Arid Central Spain	1,824	6,671	27.3
Arid Southern Spain	3,744	9,639	38.8
Rainy, Irrigated Regions	2,096	4,766	44.0
Arid Central Spain			
Old Castile	1,018	3,425	29.7
New Castile	406	1,637	24.8
Aragon-Ebro	400	1,609	24.9
Arid Southern Spain			
Western Andalusia	926	3,044	30.4
Estremadura	1,137	2,847	39.1
La Mancha	1,184	2,709	43.7
Eastern Andalusia	497	1,039	47.9

SOURCE: Compiled from Luis García de Oteyza, "Los regimenes de explotación del suelo nacional," *Revista de Estudios Agro-Sociales* (Oct.–Dec. 1952), Table 5. The figures include sharecroppers as well as tenants.

erally recognized and deserves some emphasis.[42] It was precisely because known absentees leased some two and one-half times as much of their

41. Juan Carandell, *Distribución y estructura de la propiedad rural en la provincia de Córdoba* (Madrid, 1934), pp. 24–27, also finds evidence that the rate of leasing was higher in the fertile than in the mountainous counties.

42. Aside from the 1951 survey used in Table 22, the great extent of Southern leasing is also indicated by the Cadastral data of 1928 (DGP, *Memoria 1928*, pp. 62, 92–99) and by the Agricultural Census of 1962 (INE, *Censo Agrario*, p. 39). The latter source suggests that if uncultivated as well as cultivated land is taken into account, the South surpasses even the rainy and irrigated coastal regions in the proportion of land leased.

lands as did resident owners that the incidence of Southern leasing far exceeded that of Old and New Castile and approached that of the Atlantic and Mediterranean coastal regions, where special factors—the extraordinary population pressure of Galicia, the vineyard economy of Catalonia, the high proportion of irrigated land in the Levante—were operative.

The prevalance of absenteeism also affected the ways in which leasing was actually carried out in Southern Spain. In the rest of the nation owners for the most part directly leased their lands in small plots to small tenants. In the South this degree of active management was more than the absentee owner was prepared to give. Rather, the large estates were usually leased intact to a single large tenant, the *arrendador* or *labrador,* who thereupon either cultivated the land himself through hired labor or subleased it in small plots to small tenant farmers.[43] The position of the arrendadores in the Southern social hierarchy was exceeded in importance only by that of the owners themselves. In a few regions, particularly in the campiña of Cordova, where the rate of leasing was extraordinarily high, they rather than the owners seem to have dominated daily life. Given the significance of the arrendadores, it is unfortunate that we know almost nothing about them. As far as I have been able to discover, there are no studies on such questions as their social origins, the amounts of property they possessed in their own right, the average length of their leases, or the degree to which they tended to displace the absentee owners over the course of time through the purchase of the estate. And although it seems safe to assume that the arrendadores usually cultivated the lands they leased directly rather than subleasing them to small tenants,[44] we have no way of determining the precise extent to which this was so.

Our ignorance is even more complete in relation to the hired administrators who handled the day-to-day operation of the absentee estates that were not leased. The number of farms operated by each administrator, the methods of remuneration, the amount of supervision exercised by owners, are all questions that we cannot adequately answer in our present state of knowledge.

Indeed, it is worth hazarding guesses only as to the over-all consequences of a system of agriculture in which arrendadores and hired administrators played so prominant a role. For some eminent observers these two groups mitigated the harmful effects that absenteeism might

43. As proof of larger scale leasing in the South, leased holdings there were 2.35 times as large as unleased in 1927 whereas in Central Spain they were only 1.39 times as large. Similarly, in 1951 small "protected" tenants held 22.1% of all leased lands in the South as against 59.3% in the rest of Spain.

44. On this question, see above, chap. 4.

otherwise have had on Southern agriculture. Absentees may have owned large estates, it is argued, but these estates were not necessarily neglected, because they were cultivated by resident arrendadores or administrators. This distinction between ownership and cultivation was probably what Díaz del Moral had in mind when he said in 1929 that "absenteeism is not and never has been an evil" in the campiña, precisely the region in which absentee-owned estates were most common.[45] Although the distinction is useful, particularly in destroying the popular myth that absentee estates were completely untilled, Díaz del Moral would seem to have gone too far. The resident arrendadores and administrators may indeed have been intelligent, technically knowledgeable, and interested in expanding agricultural production. Nevertheless the land was in the long run more neglected than if it had not been absentee-owned precisely because none of these qualities could enjoy free play. The arrendador might cultivate efficiently within the existing resources of the farm, but because he lacked security of tenure he could not undertake long-range improvements like the introduction of new crops. Similarly, the administrator did not command either the authority or the capital with which to essay a major improvement like irrigation.

Absenteeism also had negative social consequences that Díaz del Moral's statement overlooked. The administrator's task was to produce maximum profits for a distant master; the arrendador had some of his earnings drained away from him as rent. For both groups the temptation must have been strong to shift their burdens onto the shoulders of the day laborers and small tenants who actually tilled the land by paying the lowest possible wages and charging the highest possible rents. On balance, then, the introduction of new intermediaries between the owners and the workers almost inevitably increased the financial exactions of the rural oligarchy but did not necessarily enhance its efficiency in farming.

Nevertheless it would be a mistake to consider absenteeism as the sole—or even the basic—cause of the social ills of Southern Spain. If the absentees drained capital from the land, the resident owners were not distinguished for their eagerness to invest in it. And if a resident owner

45. Díaz del Moral, p. xiii. Some writers stress this statement in defense of the economic viability of the latifundio system. To my mind, such emphasis is mistaken. The phrase occurs in the introduction to *Agitaciones campesinas*, where the great Cordovese writer was engaged in ridiculing the "clichés" used by foreign observers to explain the social unrest, and was setting up the paradoxes that would serve as the background for his own masterful analysis. It should not be taken so seriously as some of his other, better-substantiated observations, particularly since during the Republic Díaz del Moral himself would lead a strong attack on systematic leasing, one of the inevitable consequences of absenteeism.

could more easily supersede the existing systems of agriculture through long-range improvements, he might also, paradoxically, farm less efficiently within those systems, since he was not accountable to a master who might discharge him, as was the hired administrator, nor did he need to make profit sufficient to support both himself and a distant lessor, as did the arrendador. For example, Pascual Carrión, perhaps Spain's most farseeing agronomist in the 1920s and 1930s, speaks of owners who preferred to farm their lands extensively rather than intensively because the extra margin of profit would not be sufficient to make it worth their while to undertake the heavier capital investments and labor recruitment that intensive farming would require.[46] The arrendador, on the other hand, might find intensive farming more attractive since the extra profit, however small, might provide the margin he needed to pay rent to the owner and still earn enough for himself.[47]

In the final analysis, then, absenteeism should not be seen as a social evil of an entirely new order. Its frequency in Southern Spain merely confirms what earlier evidence had suggested. Although a bourgeois class, not the nobility, now controlled most of the Spanish earth, this class displayed little of the enterprising spirit that distinguished its counterparts in northwestern Europe. Although the traditional pastoral economy had largely disappeared outside Estremadura and most arable land—with the notable exception of whatever land had to be irrigated in order to bear crops—was now cultivated, it was not farmed well. The large owner was not impervious to market opportunities, but neither did he fully exploit them or strive to create new ones. Modern agricultural techniques were no longer unknown, but neither were they eagerly adopted. Some of the profits were invested in the land, but most went to personal consumption, to urban investments, or to the purchase of still more land to elevate further the social status of the owner.

This list of criticisms might be extended, but the point is already clear. Because he preferred to accept low returns rather than to engage in active management, the large owner did little to raise the economic horizons of Southern Spain and lessen the impoverishment of its population. Admittedly the landowner was limited in what he could do, because the backwardness of the nation as a whole in turn hampered the full eco-

46. Carrión, pp. 341–43. I am grateful to Juan Martínez Alier for bringing this passage to my attention.

47. These "negative incentives" offered by absentee ownership may explain why the campiña of Cordova remained as productive as neighboring regions with a much lower rate of absenteeism. Systematic studies of investment and production on absentee and non-absentee estates are needed to shed light on this and other issues raised in our discussion.

nomic development of the South. Yet with a different spirit this obstacle might have been partly overcome, as it had been in the Levante. Had the large owners displayed imaginative concern and initiative, their monopolization of the Southern earth might truthfully have been justified on the grounds that they used the land more efficiently than anyone else could. As it was, their claims to greater efficiency rang hollow. The latifundio system did not bring the optimal production that both the capitalist and socialist worlds associate with large-scale operations. Rather than stimulating him to farm them well, the size of the latifundista's properties merely provided him sufficient reserves so that he could afford the luxury of farming them badly. In this sense economic as well as social and humanitarian considerations seemed to counsel agrarian reform. If the large estates were split up, not only would the existing wealth be more evenly distributed, but that wealth might eventually be expanded as the buffer of too much land, which sheltered the large owners from the consequences of their lax management, was removed.

There is another side to the coin, however. Though the nature of the rural oligarchy and its operation of the large estates may have made land reform economically justifiable in the long run, they did not thereby make it especially practicable, either in economic or political terms. Politically, the ownership of the Spanish earth was such that little land could be redistributed without arousing determined opposition. Spain lacked all of the advantages that have facilitated land reform in other nations. In contrast to the new continents of North and South America, neither the state nor the municipalities possessed arable land that might be delivered to the peasantry by executive fiat and without expropriation. In contrast to Greece in the 1920s or to revolutionary France, so little land belonged to the Church that the alternative route whereby the expropriation of individual property might have been avoided was also closed. In contrast to Rumania in 1918 and Algeria in 1963, no important quantities of land belonged to foreigners, so that none of the repercussions that would follow expropriation of personal property could safely be diverted outside the political framework of the nation. Nor did enough land in Spain belong to the nobility for significant agrarian reform to be possible on the basis of an antiaristocratic crusade alone. If land were to be distributed to the peasantry, there was only one group from which it could be taken: the bourgeois owners who in most essentials were fully integrated into the political structure of the nation and could not be expropriated except at the cost of attacking some of the basic principles of that structure.

Economically, two of the factors mentioned above have special relevance. First, because the large estates were cultivated mostly in large units and not divided among small tenants, the process of land reform could not consist, as it has in India and Japan, primarily of the transfer of titles of ownership to already functioning farm operators. New systems of production would have to be devised to replace the old, and the settlers who applied these systems would be drawn chiefly from the farm laborers, who were without tools, animals, and, above all, without experience in the independent management of the land. Second, since so little arable land still remained uncultivated, this experimentation would have to take place on land that was already productive, with the result that yields would inevitably fall until the new systems of cultivation were successfully established. This consideration assumes particular importance if it is remembered that despite the neglect of its large owners, the South nevertheless remained the richest unirrigated region of arid Spain (Chapter 2). The prevailing economic system was not an optimal one, but it was a functioning one. If it were disturbed there might be serious repercussions for the national economy. Thus, though a more universal distribution of property might eventually increase the prosperity of the South, it carried with it great immediate risks. There was no easy, sure road by which land reform might be achieved in Southern Spain. The same factors that counseled a redistribution of the land also militated against the success of any far-reaching program that might be inaugurated.

4: The Social Structure of Southern Spain: The Rural Proletariat

Occupational Distribution of the Rural Population

Before beginning our analysis of the rural proletariat it would be useful to examine briefly the relative size of the various social classes in the Spanish countryside. This is not easy to do with precision. As mentioned earlier, the necessary data are lacking, because none of the national censuses between 1797 and 1950 tried to classify the rural population by occupation. There is also the problem that in the lower reaches of the social hierarchy the classes tend to merge and are sometimes difficult to distinguish from each other. Thus a peasant proprietor will often supplement his income by renting a bit of land or entering into a sharecropping agreement. A tenant or sharecropper, in turn, may hire himself out as a day laborer whenever his own lands do not require his presence. Even the day laborer class defies rigid classification. At harvest everyone—the village barber, tailor, and shoemaker—works in the fields, whereas during slack periods those persons who normally depend on agricultural day labor take up odd jobs that have nothing to do with farming.

Despite these difficulties, enough data have become available since 1950 to permit a few rudimentary conclusions. In the brief survey that follows, I have relied chiefly on the 1956 Agricultural Census of the Farm Syndicates for two reasons. First, it was conducted before the massive mechanization of agricultural tasks and great rural exodus of the late 1950s and early 1960s and so analyzes social structures that still closely resembled those that existed prior to the Civil War. Second, the occupational definitions employed are more complete than those of other surveys and more successful in assigning individuals to the occupational category to which they primarily belonged.[1]

1. Results of the Junta Nacional de Hermandades's Encuesta Agropecuária: 1956 are reprinted in *Revista Sindical de Estadística* (First Trimester, 1959), pp. 4–5. Family operators are defined as those who do not use nonfamily labor for more

The relative position of any given individual in the rural social hierarchy can be roughly established by the degree to which he has access to the land and can hire others to work it for him. Table 23 is organized on

TABLE 23   OCCUPATIONAL DISTRIBUTION OF ACTIVE MALE AGRICULTURAL POPULATION IN 1956

	Total Active Male Population (thousands of persons)	Labor-employing Entrepreneurs		Family Operators		Hired Laborers	
		Own-ers	Ten-ants	Own-ers	Ten-ants	Perma-nent	Day
		(percent)		(percent)		(percent)	
Southern Spain	1,557	11.1	6.9	14.3	11.2	13.2	43.3
Rest of Spain	2,988	12.3	7.6	39.6	17.1	6.8	16.6
Analysis of Southern Spain							
Western Andalusia	603	11.6	5.3	12.0	7.0	12.2	51.7
Estremadura	369	9.7	6.4	15.9	16.0	14.9	37.2
La Mancha	314	11.9	7.6	15.8	10.8	19.9	34.1
Eastern Andalusia	271	11.9	9.5	15.5	14.4	5.3	43.3
Analysis of Rest of Spain							
Cantabric Coast	912	10.7	5.3	53.2	20.9	2.6	7.3
Mediterranean Coast	986	12.6	9.9	28.1	17.8	5.7	26.0
Meseta-Ebro	873	13.1	7.2	41.3	13.5	8.9	16.1

SOURCE: Junta Nacional de Hermandades, "Encuesta Agropecuaria de la población campesina: 1956," *Revista Sindical de Estadística* (First Trimester, 1959), pp. 4–5.

the basis of these two criteria. At the top of the social hierarchy stand the labor-employing agricultural entrepreneurs who own their own land. The large owners discussed in the preceding chapter as part of the rural oligarchy are included in this group. The vast majority of its members, however, must be thought of as middle or upper-middle class, for they did not hire workers by the tens or the hundreds but controlled only enough land to be able to employ at least one laborer on a permanent or semipermanent basis. The same might be said for the labor-employing tenants and sharecroppers. A small portion of this group consisted of the *arrendadores*, who properly should be considered as part of the rural

than 90 days a year. Permanent hired hands are workers employed by the same master for at least 180 days a year. I excluded female day laborers from Table 23 because their political and economic roles are so uncertain. I have not attempted local studies, because the Encuesta—although the best available in this period—is often so unreliable that it would be foolhardy to use it at any but the broadest levels, where local errors tend to cancel each other out. For more information on how the Survey and its predecessor in 1953 were conducted, see app. A.

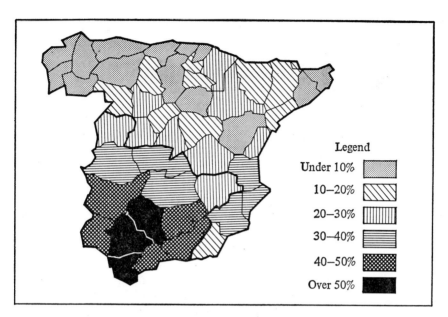

MAP 8. PROPORTION OF DAY LABORERS IN THE ACTIVE MALE RURAL POPU-
LATION IN 1956

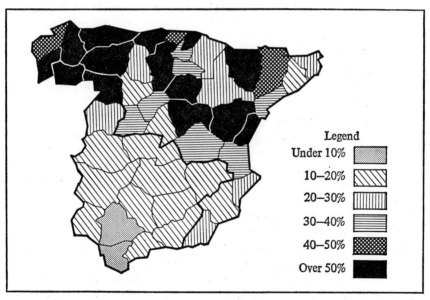

MAP 9. PROPORTION OF SMALL PEASANT PROPRIETORS IN THE ACTIVE MALE
RURAL POPULATION IN 1956

Note: Source for Maps 8 and 9 same as in Table 23. Permanent hired hands
are not included in Map 8; labor-employing owners are not included in Map 9.

oligarchy. The majority, however, was also middle class, commanding enough wealth and land to be able to hire only a few outsiders. The position of the middle-class tenants obviously differed from that of the middle-class owners, because they might conflict with the rural oligarchy over the terms under which they held their lands. Nevertheless their relative prosperity ensured that their opposition would be expressed through normal political channels rather than in association with revolutionary labor organizations. Middle-class tenants and sharecroppers may sometimes have supported Republican parties, but they did not play an important role in the upheavals that threatened Southern Spain.

Middle-class labor-employing farm operators formed approximately equal contingents in the rural populations of Southern Spain and of the rest of the nation. Once the oligarchs—more numerous in the South than elsewhere—are eliminated from the figures presented in Table 23, owners, tenants, and sharecroppers of this type make up from 15 percent to 16 percent of the population of the latifundio provinces and from 18 percent to 19 percent of the inhabitants of the small-holding regions. Thus the critical difference between these two great sectors of the nation arose not from the relative strength of their upper-middle classes but from the relative position of the lower-middle-class peasant proprietors who worked their farms exclusively with family labor. Peasant proprietors of this sort cannot be thought of as wealthy or even as comfortable in their circumstances, given the harsh agricultural conditions in most of Spain. Indeed, their poverty sometimes drove them into sporadic association with movements of revolutionary protest. Nevertheless, the small peasant proprietors on the whole were as important a force for social order in Spain as they have traditionally been in the rest of Europe. The weakness of this class in the South was the principal reason for the vulnerability of that region's rural social structure. Because so much of the soil was monopolized by the latifundios, small peasant proprietors accounted for only one-seventh of the agricultural population in Southern Spain. In the rest of the nation family farmers were almost three times as important. Forming 40 percent of the total agricultural population, they constituted by far the largest single social class. Once this class is added to the labor-employing upper-middle classes discussed earlier, the disproportionate revolutionary potentialities of Southern Spain become readily apparent. The inherently nonrevolutionary segments of rural society in northern and central Spain included 60 percent of the population, whereas the corresponding segments in Southern Spain encompassed only some 32 percent.

The difference between Southern Spain and the rest of the nation is probably accentuated once the class of small, family-farming tenants and sharecroppers is taken into consideration. This class, which had little in common with the larger, labor-employing tenants, was undoubtedly the most inconstant and disparate force in Spanish rural society. Its political attitudes seem to have depended entirely on the specific terms of the leases under which its members occupied the land in each region. If these terms were favorable, the small tenants added to the conservative balance. If, on the other hand, their use of the land was not secure or necessitated the payment of crushing rents, they tended to disturb that balance. Discussion of lease conditions and of tenant protest must await a later section of this chapter. Here it need only be stated that, with the possible exception of the *foreros* of Galicia and the *rabassaires* of Catalonia, the small tenants and sharecroppers of Southern Spain were much more rebellious than those of other regions, because the property structure permitted more frequent owner abuse. High rents, short leases, frequent subleasing, and, above all, the insecurities of the *yuntero* system in Estremadura combined to create widespread resentment. Thus whereas at least half of the small tenants in the rest of Spain may be considered part of the lower-middle classes in their fundamental acceptance of the existing social order, no more than one-third of those in Southern Spain should be so regarded. Only the relatively small numbers of this class in the South prevented it from becoming a more important revolutionary force in its own right.

The bottom of the social hierarchy consisted of those who themselves had no access to the land but worked it for others. These individuals by no means formed a single, united class. The most important point of differentiation among them was whether or not they were permanently employed. The permanent hired hands, though poorly paid and without property of their own, were usually able to tolerate their lack of true independence because of the security they discovered in their attachment to a particular master. For them the personal bonds of the precapitalist age had not been entirely broken. Thus, whether part of the teams that operated the large estates or isolated helpers of the middle owners, the hired hands differed in their loyalties from workers whose conditions of employment were less secure. During peaks of labor agitation, they might in self-defense be forced to join the local Anarchosyndicalist or Socialist unions.[2] Normally, however, they remained unaffiliated or joined the

2. During such times landowners sometimes even advised their permanent hired hands to join such unions so as to avoid troubles until the triumphant mood of the day laborers passed (Díaz del Moral, p. 369). The docility of the hired hands did not, of course, necessarily mean that they were personally devoted to their masters. As the excellent field study of the latifundio system in Cordova in the 1960s by Juan Martínez Alier (*La estabilidad del latifundismo* [Paris, 1968]) makes clear, strong resentments existed but did not usually translate themselves into actions.

rival Catholic societies that tried to still revolutionary worker protest. Because their circumstances made them the creatures of their masters, then, the herders, the plowsmen, and the field bosses should not be lumped together with the day laborers. For the most part they remained neutral in the social struggles that beset the Spanish countryside. On occasion they even acted more as a conservative than as a radical force.

The day laboring class also contained many individuals who sought to accommodate themselves to the field bosses and owners who might help them get jobs. Nevertheless the misery and insecurity of most day laborers in dry-farming regions was so great as to convert them into the only inherently revolutionary group in Spanish rural society. The central tragedy of Southern Spain was that because its latifundium heritage prevented the spread of small family-size farms, its largest social class consisted not of small proprietors but of landless day laborers. This class accounted for 43.3 percent of the Southern active rural population so late as 1956.[3] It was consequently more than two and one-half times as numerous as in the rest of Spain. If the relatively prosperous workers of the irrigated Levante are left aside, the disproportion becomes even greater. Day laborers were approximately four times as numerous in Southern Spain as in any other unirrigated region. They were as predominant in the South as peasant proprietors were elsewhere. Without their presence the revolutionary social protest of Southern Spain could not have achieved massive proportions. The occasional dissatisfaction of the poorer peasant proprietors would have passed without notice, and the agitation of the more insecure tenants and sharecroppers would have created disturbances of only local and temporary importance. The day laborers were the source from which sprang the social convulsions that swept Southern Spain. The specific reasons for their alienation, and the nature and limitations of their power, form the subject of the analysis that follows.

Landless Day Laborers

The very nature of agricultural production prevented the day laborer from achieving the prosperity that might have made him a contented member of Southern rural society. Unlike industry, agriculture does not provide constant employment; rather, it necessitates herculean efforts during certain seasons and calls for little labor during the rest of the year. For example, according to one official estimate, 51.4 percent of the labor required for the rotation crops of grains and legumes which occupy most

3. If female day labor is taken into account, the proportion of the agricultural population formed by day laborers would rise to 50.2 percent in Southern Spain as against only 21.8 percent in the rest of the nation.

of the cultivated surface of Spain is needed during the harvest months of June, July, and August. Another 12.0 percent is required during the main planting season, in October. Only 36.6 percent of the annual labor demand occurs during the other eight months of the year. When grain crops alone are grown the active periods are still shorter. In wheat production, for example, 58.7 percent of the yearly labor demand arises during the harvest period, from June to August, and another 20.6 percent during the plowing season, in October. Similarly, 77.3 percent of the yearly labor in the important olive industry is expended during the five months from January to May, when the harvest is collected and the trees are pruned. In vineyards 64.8 percent of the annual labor demand occurs during the three-month pruning season from February to April. When potatoes are grown 68.7 percent of the annual manpower is needed from June to August and from October to November. With sugar beets 55.4 percent of the labor is required in May, August, November, and December.[4] Only in irrigated lands, which in the warm climes of Spain are capable of bearing several crops a year, are labor demands fairly constant at all times.

The demand for labor can, of course, be regularized if a number of crops whose peak periods occur at different times of the year are grown. Indeed, if olives had not so frequently supplemented grains in Southern Spain, the physical survival of so large a day laboring class would have been impossible. In this sense the relative fertility of Southern Spain may have been as important as the *reconquista* in creating the latifundio system: less favored regions could not have supported the great numbers of unattached workers that the system requires. Nevertheless, because the climate favored some crops more than others and the large owners failed to explore all the possibilities that existed, Southern Spain experienced to a lesser degree the monocultivation that characterizes the rest of the nation. For example, more than 25 percent of the cultivated land in 1946 was devoted to a single crop, either wheat or olives, in eight of the thirteen latifundio provinces. In the other five provinces one of these two crops occupied from 19 to 25 percent of the cultivated surface. If the basis for measurement is crop groups whose primary labor requirements fall at the same times of the year rather than single crops, the degree of monocultivation becomes much higher. Even in 1959, after the introduction of cotton and other new plants, winter grains occupied at least 40 percent of the sown land in all latifundio provinces except Cordova, Jaen, and

4. Sindicato Vertical del Olivo, *El paro estacional campesino* (Madrid, 1946), pp. 46–53. E. Fuentes Quintana and J. Velarde Fuentes, *Política económica* (Madrid, 1959), p. 113, reports a similar distribution of the labor demand, as does *El paro obrero en Jaén* (supplement to nos. 27 and 28 of *Revista Sindical de Estadística*, (1952), 18–19.

Seville.[5] Crop diversification may be the ultimate solution to the social agrarian problem, as agronomists have stressed for so long, but in Southern Spain it has not yet reached the point at which it can provide constant employment.

The irregular seasonal distribution of the labor demand had two obvious consequences for the day laborer. First, he could not find work during a large part of the year. His day began at the labor shape-ups held in the village square, where the unemployed competed for the few jobs available. As often as not his day ended in the same village square or in the local tavern rather than in the fields where he had hoped to find work. The total number of workdays a field hand could expect during the year fluctuated widely from region to region. Most observers agree that the work period usually ranged from 180 to a maximum of 250 days—that is, from 60 to 80 percent of the 300 days that may be said to constitute a normal work year in underdeveloped nations. In regions of extreme monocultivation the period of employment often fell to as little as 130 to 150 days of each year. Southwestern Jaen, which is devoted almost exclusively to olive growing, has been especially infamous in this respect. Unemployment there was not only a recurrent feature of each worker's life but became his natural and habitual condition.

When the demand for labor is so small and its supply so large, low wages for those who succeed in finding employment are a second inevitable consequence. Comparative wage statistics for extended periods are difficult to secure in Spain, but an approximate average daily income for all employed individuals can be established by dividing annual income statistics by the 300 days that constitute the normal work year in most activities. In 1902, for example, the average income for all employed individuals was 4 pesetas a day,[6] but a field hand in Estremadura and Andalusia earned from 1.5 to 1.75 pesetas.[7] In 1913–14, when the Anarcho-syndicalist Federación Nacional de Agricultores announced as its goal a minimum wage of 2.5 pesetas for nonharvest labor, average daily earnings throughout Spain were almost 4.7 pesetas. A wave of strikes just after World War I raised nonharvest wages in Cordova to 3 pesetas,[8] but in-

5. Sindicato Vertical del Olivo, *El paro estacional campesino*, pp. 24–28; AEPA: 1959–60, pp. 344–45.

6. INE, *Primera mitad del siglo XX*, p. 139. This source was also used for the other average national earnings reported in the text. Since the INE figures include upper- and middle-class earnings as well as those of manual laborers, they probably overstate the income of industrial workers by approximately one-third.

7. Approximately four-fifths of the villages reported in IRS, *Resumen de la información acerca de los obreros agrícolas en Andalucía y Extremadura: 1902* (Madrid, 1906), paid wages of this amount.

8. Díaz del Moral, pp. 257–58, 337–38.

flation had meanwhile pushed the average daily income of all employed Spaniards to 10 pesetas. Nor was the pattern broken in the postwar period. In the winter of 1930–31 day laborers in Andalusia were being paid nonharvest wages of 3.5 pesetas, whereas average national earnings were 9 pesetas.[9]

Only during the harvest seasons, when the normal overabundance of labor was replaced by a sudden scarcity, did agricultural wages begin to approach the national average. The day laborer relied on his earnings during these seasons to accumulate the reserves that would carry him through the rest of the year. His own efforts were not enough to fulfill this purpose; all members of his family—his sons, his daughters, his wife —also had to search for work.[10] Yet at the same time as this collective family labor enabled him to live, the availability of cheaply paid child and female labor kept the wages of the male worker from rising to truly equitable levels even during harvest. The competition of migrant laborers had the same effect. Perhaps the chief supply of migrant labor was provided by near-by mountain villages, whose residents customarily descended to the fertile plains to share in the harvest before returning to reap their own poor and more slowly maturing crops. Migrant labor from northern Spain, especially from overpopulated Galicia, was also common during the Southern grain harvests, since these fell at times when the Gallegan farmer had little to do on his own small plots. During the Southern olive harvest the Gallegan influx was often supplemented by peasants from Old Castile who left their snow-covered fields in search of work. Finally, when Spanish migrant laborers proved insufficient, landowners turned to Portugal. The use of Portuguese labor, especially in Estremadura, was often the cause of bitter disputes between the rural proletariat and the rural oligarchy.[11] On every front, then, the Southern agricultural economy, which normally could hardly provide for its own workers, ended by providing for countless outsiders during harvest periods.

Because of this great influx of labor, harvest wages never rose to a point where they compensated for the wages lost during the long periods of unemployment or for the exceptionally low wages paid for nonharvest labor. The special harvest earnings of the day laborer and his family enabled him to survive, but only barely. Even under optimal conditions his

9. Ministerio de Trabajo, *La crisis agraria andaluza,* pp. 17, 29, 34.

10. Women formed an especially important part of the labor force during the olive harvest. According to the 1956 Agricultural Survey of the Farm Syndicates, more than half of the 418,462 women who worked on farms at least 90 days of the year were employed in the latifundio provinces.

11. For example, J. Polo Benito, *El problema social del campo en Extremadura* (Salamanca, 1919), pp. 14–15.

yearly income could not approach that of the rest of the population. In the 1918 strike wave in Bajadoz, for example, the demands of one union that sought 3.5 pesetas for normal work and 5.5 pesetas for harvest labor were regarded as extreme because they were so far above the prevailing wage levels.[12] Yet had these demands been granted, and had the workers been able to find the 160 days of nonharvest and the 90 days of harvest employment that must be regarded as maximal for Southern field hands, their annual income would have risen to only 1,055 pesetas at a time when average income in Spain had been driven by inflation to 2,923 pesetas.[13] To be sure, the discrepancy was usually not as great in noninflationary periods. Nor was there quite as great a difference between rural wages and those paid to factory employees, whose earnings cannot be separated from those of the middle and upper classes in the global income figures I have used as the basis for comparison. Nevertheless it may safely be assumed that the annual earnings of agricultural day laborers were seldom more than half and never more than two-thirds of those of even industrial workers.[14] This income gap was by no means entirely bridged by lower prices in the villages. Although rents were always cheaper, food —ironically—was always dearer in the pueblos of Spain than in its cities. The extent to which this was true is rather startling. According to the price index compiled at six-month intervals by the Ministry of Labor, food costs were higher in villages than in the major cities in 33 out of the 34 intervals between April 1914 and March 1931.[15]

Harvest wages permitted the day laborer to accumulate enough reserves to get him through normal years only. If a year was bad the laborer was left completely destitute and could survive only because of exceptional measures taken by the local and national authorities. One typical palliative for crisis years was proto-Keynesian in nature. Necessary public works such as bridge building and road repairs were customarily neglected until calamity struck, when they would be used to restore some approximation of an employment balance. If the crisis were severe, another palliative, the *alojamiento* system, was also applied. Under this system, perhaps the chief surviving trace of the paternalism that had mitigated economic hardships during the precapitalistic era, workers were assigned to owners who, whether or not they wanted their services, were expected to put them to work and pay them some small sum for the support of their families. Both measures were effective in short-term crises, but

12. Ibid., pp. 14–15, 46.

13. INE, *Primera mitad del siglo XX*, p. 139.

14. René Jupin, *La Question agraire en Andalousie* (Paris, 1932), pp. 67–68; Carrión, pp. 336–67.

15. Ministerio de Trabajo, *Boletín* (February–March 1931), pp. 234–35.

neither was adequate when crop failure and unemployment were serious or prolonged. Thus during the great drought of 1905–06, which left 100,-000 farm hands unemployed in Andalusia, the public works program, though subsidized by the national as well as by local governments, quickly exhausted its funds and was able to provide workers with a wage for only one day out of every three.[16] As for the alojamiento system, owner resistance against this archaic practice always stiffened as each crisis continued. Either the owners resorted to the device of dismissing their permanent hired hands and then taking them back as their contribution to the subsidy of the unemployed, or they claimed economic hardship and refused outright to accept unneeded labor contingents.[17]

The limitations of both these measures even as palliatives became more and more apparent as the number of day laborers grew. At the same time work crises became more frequent, since the increase in the labor supply depressed wages and led to more constant unemployment. It is difficult to document the extent of the growth in surplus agricultural manpower, because Spanish censuses have traditionally failed to distinguish the day laborer from the rest of the active rural population. Evidence that the increase was considerable lies in the fact that although the over-all population of Southern Spain rose at a much faster rate than that of Spain as a whole, the proportion of the Southern population dependent upon agriculture decreased more slowly than elsewhere. The rapid population growth of the South was due to the excessively high birth rates that seem characteristic of most underdeveloped societies.[18] Though the death rate was also high,[19] it by no means counteracted the effects of the birth rate. As a result the population gain of Southern Spain relative to that of the rest of the nation, a gain that began at least as early as 1797,[20] continued unabated during the twentieth century. In 1900, for example, the 5.3 million inhabitants of the South constituted 28.7 percent of the total national population. By 1930 its 7.1 million residents accounted for

16. *D.S.* 103, 7 March 1906, p. 3101.

17. Díaz del Moral, pp. 214–15; Ministerio de Trabajo, *La crisis agraria andaluza*, p. 167.

18. In 1933, for example, when the average national birth rate was 27.8 per thousand, birth rates in twelve of the thirteen latifundio provinces varied between 30.0 and 37.3 per thousand (*Anuario Estadístico: 1934*, pp. 46–47).

19. Ibid. Nine of the thirteen latifundio provinces exceeded the national death rate of 16.4 per thousand in 1933, in large part because of high infant mortality. Neither of these phenomena should be attributed to the latifundio system, however, since the Southern death rate was often equaled, and its infant mortality rate was usually surpassed, in the great small-holding center of Old Castile. As has been stated earlier, it was not so much material as psychological factors that separated the small peasant proprietor from the day laborer.

20. Vicens Vives, vol. 4, pt. 2, p. 19.

30.0 percent of the then 23.6 million Spaniards. Moreover, it was the latifundio provinces with the greatest proportions of day laborers which advanced most rapidly. Thus although the population of Salamanca, one of the least latifundista provinces, rose from a base of 100 in 1900 to only 106 in 1930, the population of Badajoz had meanwhile jumped to 135, that of Jaen to 142, that of Seville to 145, and that of Cordova to 147.[21]

The lethargic industrialization of Southern Spain could not keep pace with so rapid a population growth. Even during the 1920s, when the dictatorial regime of Primo de Rivera actively sponsored industrial development, the major Southern cities absorbed less than one-fifth of the 703,000 individuals by which the population of the South increased.[22] More than four-fifths of the increase was borne by essentially rural communities. Thus human pressure on the land constantly increased in absolute terms, though the proportion of the population engaged in agriculture constantly declined. This can best be illustrated by comparing the South to the nation as a whole. During the first fifty years of the twentieth century, the proportion of the population engaged in agriculture in Spain fell by 28.3 percent. Nevertheless, because the total population had meanwhile expanded by 50.5 percent, there were 500,000 more persons dependent on agriculture in 1950 than in 1900.[23] In the South the over-all population increase was 60.4 percent. Yet the proportion of the population dependent on agriculture declined by less than 10 percent in one of the thirteen latifundio provinces, by only 10 to 20 percent in seven others, and by less than 26 percent in four others. Only in Malaga did the decline exceed the national rate of population transfer from agriculture to industry and services.[24]

The increasing human pressure on agricultural resources might have been avoided despite slow industrialization had the Southern day laborer adopted the alternative of emigration, which long served as a safety valve for many European societies. Yet, whether because "the general prostration of the human being [caused] a pessimistic renunciation of the hope for betterment in any part of the world whatever" [25] or because the South-

21. D.G. del Instituto Geográfico, Catastral y de Estadística, Censo de la población de España: 1950 (Madrid, 1954), 1, XXII, LIII.

22. Ibid., pp. XLVII–LI. The population of Southern cities with more than 30,000 inhabitants increased by only 136,500 during the decade.

23. Jesús Prados, Los próximos veinte años (Madrid, 1958), p. 222. According to Prados, the male population employed in agriculture rose from 4,392,300 individuals in 1900 to 4,935,600 in 1950, but the proportion of the total working population that it represented fell from 66.3 percent to 45.6 percent.

24. Instituto de Cultura Hispánica, Estudios hispánicos, pt. 2, pp. 348–54.

25. Constancio Bernaldo de Quirós in IRS, La emigración obrera en España después de la Guerra (Madrid, 1920), p. 21

ern farm laborer preferred to combat the injustice of his situation rather than flee from it,[26] Andalusians and Estremadurans never emigrated in important numbers. This was an unusual and often ignored phenomenon. Though migration from Spain as a whole never matched Italian emigration, by the turn of the century it surpassed the exodus from such countries as Germany, Austria-Hungary, France, and England. However, Spanish agricultural emigrants originated almost exclusively in Galicia, the Levante, and the province of Almeria, not in the latifundio regions. From 1891 to 1895, for example, the emigration rate from Almeria was 20.6 per thousand; from Alicante, 13.8; from La Corunna, 12.2; and from Pontevedra, 11.5. During the same period the highest emigration rate of the latifundio provinces was registered by Cadiz with 7.1 emigrants per thousand inhabitants.[27] By 1912 the Almeria emigration rate had risen to 44.0, but the highest latifundio rate, now registered in Granada, was only 8.0.[28] During the four years of World War I the two greatest labor-exporting provinces in the Levante sent a total of 40,772 agricultural workers to

26. The thesis that the consciousness of an existing injustice that must be combatted is a greater deterrent to emigration than extreme poverty is brilliantly developed in J. S. MacDonald, "Agricultural Organization, Migration and Labour Militancy in Rural Italy," *The Economic History Review* (August 1963), pp. 61–75. In Italy, as in Spain, large landholding regions had a traditionally lower rate of foreign emigration than those in which the land was well divided. MacDonald suggests that this is because the enormous class distinctions in the former create an atmosphere of labor militancy which finds expression through revolutionary labor organizations aimed at the destruction of the existing social system. Where the land is fairly evenly distributed, no obvious enemy exists against whom protest might be focused, thus leaving emigration rather than militancy as the chief response. MacDonald refers only to foreign, not to internal, emigration, but his thesis seems applicable to both types of movement in Spain. Thus Almeria, where poverty is due to extreme aridity, had one of the highest emigration rates in Spain, whereas neighboring Malaga, where large estates are common, had one of the lowest. It is interesting to note that in the last few years, with the militancy of the Southern day laborer broken by the Franco regime, the latifundio provinces have finally become great labor exporters. For statistics on this, see Jesús García Fernández, "El movimiento migratorio de trabajadores en España," *Estudios Geográficos* (May 1964), pp. 139–74.

27. Marvaud, pp. 450–51.

28. Jupin, p. 93. For foreign emigration in this period, see also Vicens Vives, vol. 4, pt. 2, p. 34. It is surprising that though all these authors present statistical data in which the phenomenon is quite obvious, none seems aware that the emigration rate from the latifundio provinces was so low. A similar blindness characterized the national government in 1907, when the first modern agrarian reform bill was passed on the grounds that it would stem an emigration that was in fact almost nonexistent. The myth of a great exodus from the South in pre-Civil War Spain appears even in such recent writers as Eléna de la Souchère, *An Explanation of Spain* (New York, 1964), p. 106.

other nations. By contrast, the two greatest labor-exporting provinces in the latifundio belt had only 3,511 agricultural emigrants.[29]

Migration to other parts of Spain was no more common among the Andalusian and Estremaduran day laborers than was foreign emigration. The frequent assertion that the principal center of industrial anarchism, Barcelona, and the principal center of rural anarchism, Andalusia, were connected to each other by a constant flow of population from south to north is not borne out by census data.[30] In 1920 only 0.7 percent of the population of Barcelona was native to Western Andalusia and only 0.3 percent to Estremadura. In 1930 the figures were 1.1 percent and 0.9 percent respectively. Southern agricultural emigration to the other great Spanish metropolis, Madrid, was also insignificant. Natives of Western Andalusia accounted for 2.5 percent of Madrid's population in 1920 and 2.9 percent in 1930. For Estremadura the corresponding proportions were 1.5 percent and 2.3 percent. Nor was emigration to the lesser northern capitals of Bilbao, San Sebastian, and Valencia any greater. When the Southern day laborer sought industrial employment he went to near-by, not distant, mining and manufacturing centers. As a result the latifundio regions had by far the lowest net domestic emigration rate of any unirrigated area in arid Spain. From 1920 to 1930 the domestic emigration coefficient for Western Andalusia was 0.3 and that for Estremadura 2.7. During the same decade Aragon registered a coefficient of 5.9 and Old Castile one of 6.2.[31] In domestic as in foreign emigration, inhabitants of smallholding regions seemed much more prone to seek economic opportunity elsewhere than were residents of areas in which large estates predominated.

Since he did not choose to escape his desperate situation by emigration, the chief alternative that remained to the Southern day laborer was to fight for improvements in his existing conditions of work. Yet the in-

29. IRS, *Información sobre la emigración española a los países de Europa durante la Guerra* (Madrid, 1919), p. 52.

30. For an exposition of this thesis, whose corollary is that the Barcelona Anarchosyndicalist movement would have lost its militancy, because the workers were relatively well paid, had it not been for the constant influx of new and extremely embittered recruits from rural areas, see Franz Borkenau's introduction to José Martín Blázquez, *I Helped Build an Army* (London, 1939), and Brenan, p. 185. If such an influence existed, it was exerted by workers from Aragon and the Levante, both secondary Anarchist centers, not by those from Andalusia. The Aragonese contingent formed 6.7 percent of Barcelona's population in 1920 and 8.1 percent in 1930; natives of the Levante accounted for 12.7 percent and 13.2 percent. Many of the Levante natives, however, must have been merchants or white collar workers rather than factory laborers (D.G. del Instituto Geográfico, Catastral y de Estadística, *Censo de la población de España: 1930* [Madrid, 1932], p. LXXVIII).

31. *Censo de la población: 1930, ibid,* pp. LXV, LXXVIII.

struments at his disposal were limited. Political action remained inefficacious until the proclamation of the Second Republic in 1931. In part this was due to the general corruption of Spanish political life. Theoretically, Spain enjoyed one of the most democratic constitutions in Europe after universal male suffrage was established in 1889. In practice, the potential consequences of this suffrage were nullified by the tacit agreement between the two main Spanish parties to avoid genuine political conflict through controlled elections that allowed each party to rotate regularly in office. Though this agreement began to break down in the first decade of the twentieth century, for reasons discussed elsewhere, the electoral freedom that resulted was restricted to the major cities. In the countryside the local bosses who had managed elections in the past continued to control the vote. The pressures these *caciques* could apply were limitless in villages whose population was small, the majority of whose inhabitants were ignorant, and whose location was so distant from the principal centers of national life that the danger of unfavorable publicity was minimal. Opposition candidates were prevented from speaking, uncooperative voters were kept from the polls, the ballots cast were misrepresented, and, above all, men's jobs were made to depend upon their votes.[32] It was no accident that one local union in 1904 stated as the first principle of its founding manifesto: "We commit ourselves to serve [the owners] only in matters which are related to our work, without being obliged by the owners to vote for this or that idea whenever political struggles take place." [33]

Yet cacique power alone could not have voided the potentially massive rural vote if the peasantry had had a champion capable of convincing it that its traditional suspicion of parliamentary action was mistaken. The political apathy of the peasantry was never completely overcome because throughout the nineteenth century, when the modern political mold of Spain was being cast, the progressive elements in Spanish politics neglected peasant needs. Except during the short-lived First Republic of 1873, when Pi y Margall enunciated a program of land reform and wage legislation, the urban orientation and the philosophical presuppositions of all radical and Republican parties kept them from striving toward the formation of that powerful coalition which might have arisen between themselves and the peasantry.[34] By the turn of the century, when the

32. On the cacique system, see Carr, pp. 366–73, and Joaquín Costa, *Oligarquía y caciquismo como la forma actual de gobierno en España* (Huesca, 1927).

33. IRS, *Memoria acerca de la información agraria en ambas Castillas* (Madrid, 1904), p. 71.

34. C. A. M. Hennessy, *The Federal Republic in Spain: Pi y Margall and the Federal Republican Movement: 1868–74* (Oxford, 1962), passim, but especially pp. 15, 21–22, 200–01, 206.

progressive bourgeois parties began to take their first tentative steps toward attracting peasant support, a formidable obstacle to their success had appeared: the spread of anarchism in Andalusia. This movement, which denounced all bourgeois parties as equally evil and rejected the validity of all regular political action, voided the possibility of firm peasant support in the most densely populated agricultural region in arid Spain. For decades the electoral record of the progressive parties in Andalusia bore an inverse relationship to the strength of anarchism at any given moment. When anarchism waxed powerful most peasants stayed away from the polls and the Republican or radical vote fell below even what the caciques were normally willing to allow.[35] The Anarchist reaffirmation of peasant distrust of the electoral process also added to the difficulties the Socialist party experienced when, unlike the Anarchists, it decided to present candidates for municipal and national posts. As a result no peasant parties of the Eastern European variety appeared in Spain. Only among the *foreros* of Galicia and the *rabassaires* of Catalonia were a few minor steps taken in this direction. The creation of an active national coalition between the urban middle classes and the rural masses would have been difficult under the best of circumstances, of course. The ignorance of the day laborer, the cacique system, the variety of interests generated by the widely differing systems of land tenure in Spain, and the inherent conflict between some of those interests and the most cherished bourgeois principles in regard to the rights of property all militated against it. Nevertheless it was a tragedy for Spain that such a coalition was never essayed until it was too late, because the passions that found no political outlet eventually expressed themselves in more violent ways.

The frustration of the day laborer was rendered complete by his inability to bring basic improvements in his condition through the normal trade union tactic of the strike. Because of the peculiar nature of agricultural production, agrarian strikes are at the same time far less dangerous and potentially far more destructive than industrial strikes. For most of the year the worker has almost no bargaining power because there is so little demand for his labor. During the harvest seasons, however, the strike suddenly acquires a frightening potency. Industrial workers can at best

---

35. Díaz del Moral, pp. 132–33, 203, 238, traces this inverse relationship between Anarchist and Republican strength in Cordova from the 1880s to the 1920s. For example, in elections for municipal councilors in the capital city, Republican parties won nine seats in 1899, when the Anarchist movement was weak; only one in 1903, when the movement reached one of its early peaks; only two in 1905, when its strength, though waning, was still great. Not until 1909, when the rural Anarchist movement was again totally disorganized, did Republican groups once more win so many as nine seats.

threaten their employers with the loss of output during the period in which the factory or mine is closed. As soon as these reopen, production goes on as before. Protracted harvest strikes, on the other hand, can cause the employer to lose not only the output of a few weeks but that of an entire year, since the crop will rot if not collected. Moreover, if an agricultural strike extends to cowherds and shepherds, permanent capital as well as the whole year's produce may be destroyed, for the animals may stray or die.

This enormous power could be applied only rarely, however. The threat to livestock was in practice nullified, because the herders were usually permanent hired hands whose interests did not coincide with those of the day laborers and who seldom participated in strikes except under compulsion.[36] The threat posed by the harvest strike was also more theoretical than actual. The day laborers were so completely without financial reserves that they could not often stick to a strike decision at precisely the times in which they hoped to accumulate the earnings that would carry them through the long seasons of unemployment. The extraordinary power they held over the employers thus had its reverse side. Unlike an industrial strike, a harvest strike meant not hunger for a few days or weeks but possible starvation throughout the year. Moreover a protracted strike could always be broken by use of the abundant supply of blackleg labor provided by the migrant workers. These workers could not be organized and had to accept whatever terms of employment were offered because of their distance from their homes. Finally, even when circumstances somehow happily combined in such a way as to force employers to grant major concessions, these did not become permanent triumphs. As soon as the harvest was over the laborers were thrown out of work and all agreements came to an end. The gains registered did not apply either to the nonharvest periods that followed or to any future harvests. If the workers wished to retain the fruits of their triumph, they were forced to undertake the struggle anew. Thus agricultural locals struck several times each year during periods of labor excitement not solely out of perversity or extremism, but also because there were several individual short-term contracts to be decided.

Neither the Anarchosyndicalist nor the Socialist peasant unions were able to overcome these fundamental obstacles. Strike funds with which to finance long walkouts were unattainable, because the day laborer was so

36. One of the major objectives of Anarchosyndicalists during general strikes was to force herders to abandon their tasks. This often led to conflicts with the police, who sometimes even took over the guarding of livestock themselves when the strikers succeeded in driving the herders off. On these practices, see *D.S. 24, Legislatura de 1903*, pp. 363–66, and IRS, *Córdoba*, pp. 11–13.

impoverished that he could rarely afford dues.[37] Coordinated strikes by several villages, which might diminish the strikebreaking role of migrant laborers and disperse the police, were also unsuccessful. The population and the worksites in rural areas were too scattered to permit effective communication. Moreover, since the very survival of most mountain villages depended upon the earnings of harvest workers in the plains, they could not agree to stop the flow of migrant laborers.[38] Even the political concessions gained by the Socialists during the Second Republic proved insufficient, as will be seen. The drastic law by which they tried to block migrant labor caused such hardships that it had to be repealed. The permanent arbitration boards by which they sought to replace the sporadic, inconclusive, and isolated strikes with continuous collective bargaining were often defied by the owners. Favorable trade union legislation could not in itself bring the day laborer the power that basic economic and demographic realities denied him. Partly for this reason, the Socialists, who by the 1930s, had dropped the nationalization of industry as an immediate goal, increasingly insisted upon the expropriation and collectivization of landed property. When they discovered that their political influence was insufficient to bring about so drastic a change, they turned toward the revolutionary agitation that had always characterized the Anarchists. The transformation in the Socialists was symbolic of the transformation that occurred in most individual workers. The miserable lot of the day laborers under the latifundio system ensured that they would protest; their powerlessness to improve their condition through normal channels ensured that this protest would assume violent forms.

Impoverished Peasant Proprietors and Tenant Farmers

The day laborers were by no means the only impoverished group in Southern Spain. A great many small owners, tenants, and sharecroppers also suffered economic hardship. Since no statistics have ever been assembled on the precise earnings of individuals within these occupational groupings, it is not easy to distinguish those who lived in conditions of true misery from those who managed to maintain an adequate standard of living. The best quantitative guide we have on this question is prob-

37. The Anarchists, as a matter of principle, rarely charged dues. The Socialists expected small contributions, but these often were not paid. *El Obrero de la Tierra,* the Socialist peasant newspaper in the 1930s, listed in each issue several locals ousted for nonpayment of dues.

38. For example, the refusal of mountain villages to accept any limitations on the flow of migrant labor helped wreck the concerted strike effort in Cordova in 1919 (Díaz del Moral, pp. 393–400).

ably the Census of peasants who were so poor as to be eligible for settlement on expropriated land under the Agrarian Reform Law of 1932. This Census, which was in essence a register of the rural proletariat, was compiled by the Provincial Councils of the Institute of Agrarian Reform between 1933 and 1936 on the basis of reports submitted by the municipalities. As can be seen in Table 24, the Census was sadly incomplete at the

TABLE 24   CENSUS OF PEASANTS ELIGIBLE FOR SETTLEMENT UNDER THE AGRARIAN REFORM LAW IN 1936

Region	Number of Townships	% Reporting	Number of Eligible Peasants	% Workers	% Owners	% Tenants & Sharecroppers
Southern Spain	1,887	68.9	518,700	65.6	21.6	12.8
Rest of Spain	7,399	51.5	582,300	33.2	52.4	14.4
Analysis of Southern Spain						
Western Andalusia	393	86.3	219,600	75.6	15.7	8.7
Estremadura	767	82.7	162,300	56.0	25.1	19.0
La Mancha	385	56.9	87,900	57.7	31.4	10.9
Eastern Andalusia	342	31.9	48,900	66.9	18.6	14.3
Analysis of Rest of Spain						
Cantabric Coast	1,058	42.1	128,300	17.0	66.4	16.6
Mediterranean Coast	1,758	51.8	178,800	40.8	43.0	16.2
Meseta-Ebro	4,430	53.5	234,200	33.0	54.3	12.7

SOURCE: Mimeographed résumé found in the Archives of the Institute of Agrarian Reform. As in all previous tables, the regional totals do not add up to the national because I have omitted the Balearic and Canary Islands. See notes 39–41 for further details.

outbreak of the Civil War, particularly in central and northern Spain, where the Agrarian Reform Law did not immediately apply.[39] The definitions employed in compiling the Census were simple. "Workers" were all those who gained their livelihood in agriculture but owned no land whatever. Thus, this category included many permanent hired hands as well as day laborers. The "owners" and "tenants or sharecroppers" who qualified for inclusion in the Census were those with less than ten hectares

39. On the postponement of the application of the Agrarian Reform Law to northern and central Spain, see chap. 8. The Provincial Councils were supposed to verify the reports submitted by the municipalities, which may be one reason for the slowness with which the Census was compiled. In the mimeographed résumé that I discovered, no reports whatever had been received as of 1936 from five provinces (Alava, Barcelona, Guipúzcoa, Murcia, and Valladolid). The reports from seven other provinces (four of them in Old Castile) encompassed fewer than a third of the municipalities.

of unirrigated, or one hectare of irrigated, land at their disposal.[40] As can be seen in the table, approximately one-third of the rural proletariat in the South consisted of persons who owned, rented, or sharecropped land. In the rest of the nation, because of the relative scarcity of large estates and of the landless day laborers who worked them, the proportion rose to approximately two-thirds.[41]

To what extent were these owners, tenants, and sharecroppers subsistence farmers and to what extent did they take part in the market economy? I have not been able to devise any satisfactory method of answering these questions. The poorest among them obviously used their lands exclusively to grow food for their own consumption and relied upon occasional wage labor, either in agriculture or other activities, for their cash requirements. A majority, however, probably sold varying portions of their produce. For this reason, I have tried to discuss the influence of market conditions upon them in the analysis that follows. Moreover, since even the subsistence farmers owned some capital, in the form of animals and tools, and exercised a few managerial functions, at least to the extent of deciding how much seed to save and whether or when to perform agricultural tasks, I have adopted the term "impoverished entrepreneurs" whenever I have occasion to refer to the small owners, tenants, and sharecroppers as a group.

The numerical preponderance of small owners over tenants and sharecroppers within the impoverished entrepreneur sector of the rural proletariat is readily apparent. In Southern Spain, such owners were 75 percent more numerous than poor tenants, and in the rest of the nation some 260 percent more numerous. There can be no doubt as to the severe economic hardships that this enormous mass of people endured despite their possession of some land. State-sponsored credit facilities were almost nonexistent in the rural areas of Spain, and the large private banks were geographically inaccessible or too indifferent to the needs of the small peasant proprietor to provide an alternative source of funds. As a result, he was rendered dependent upon his wealthier neighbors who granted loans at usurious rates of interest.[42] Market conditions were also bad. Al-

40. As is explained in chap. 8, eligible owners were actually defined as those who paid less than fifty pesetas tax on their lands—about the amount that would have been due in the 1930s on ten hectares of average grain lands.

41. The proportion of owners and tenants in the Meseta-Ebro would probably have been closer to three-fourths had not Old Castile been so underrepresented (only 37.8 percent of the townships there reported as against 72.3 percent in New Castile and Aragon). The tenant and sharecropper figures would probably have been higher for the Mediterranean Coast had not both Barcelona and Murcia failed to submit reports.

42. Despite numerous minor improvements after 1906, all efforts (particularly

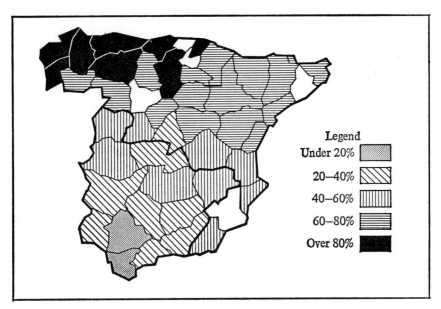

MAP 10. PROPORTION OF IMPOVERISHED ENTREPRENEURS IN RURAL PRO-
LETARIAT IN 1936

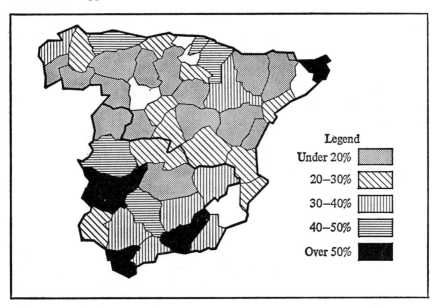

MAP 11. PROPORTION OF TENANTS AND SHARECROPPERS AMONG IMPOVER-
ISHED ENTREPRENEURS IN 1936

Note: Source and definitions for Maps 10 and 11 same as in Table 24. Impoverished entrepreneurs include tenants and sharecroppers as well as owners. No
data available for the five provinces left blank.

though the network of national highways was significantly expanded and improved by Primo de Rivera in the 1920s, the secondary and local roads on which the peasant relied to bring his produce to market frequently remained impassable. The cooperative movement, which in northern Europe had done so much to improve the bargaining position of the small producer, had remained weak in Spain except in Old Castile, where a number of small organizations were founded under Catholic auspices in the 1910s and 1920s.[43] Technical assistance was also practically unavail-

---

those of Santiago Alba in 1916 and 1918) for a major expansion of rural credit facilities failed. The Mortgage Bank, founded in 1873 primarily to service agriculture, dealt almost exclusively with urban property after 1900. A new central credit fund founded as a political gesture in 1917 was granted capital assets equivalent to only one-tenth of one percent of the combined value of agricultural and livestock production. Local loan institutions, or *positos*, existed in more than a third of Spain's 9,200 municipalities, but had such limited funds that their loans never exceeded one-fourth of one percent of the value of agricultural and livestock production (INE, *Primera mitad*, pp. 30, 51). The large private banks did not take up the slack. Most of the transactions required by the peasants were too small to be worth bothering with, many poor proprietors lacked clear titles to their lands because they could not pay the required legal registration fees, and most small tenants had no property that could serve as collateral. In consequence, the small entrepreneurs usually depended on local moneylenders who, in the province of Carceres at least, normally charged 5 percent interest per *month,* and often raised their rates in the months just before harvest, when the demand was greatest because the peasants had exhausted their earnings from the previous year (IRS, *Subarriendos y arrendamientos colectivos de fincas rústicas* [Madrid, 1921], pp. 9–10). Obviously, loans at such interest could not be used to finance long range improvements on the farm, but were taken only when required for immediate survival.

43. Like the positos, cooperatives were numerous but ineffective. In regard to their numbers, local rural associations of various types, most of which performed some cooperative functions (though perhaps only half were pure cooperatives), totaled 1,157 in 1909, over 2,000 in 1914, and 4,266 in 1933. Their ineffectiveness can be illustrated by two examples. First, aside from whatever small amounts they could collect from their members, the Catholic associations (which probably accounted for more than half the total number) relied for funds primarily on the Catholic-sponsored Bank of Leo XIII. Yet in the first seven years of its existence, from 1905 to 1912, the Bank loaned an average of less than 300,000 pesetas annually to its affiliates. Second, even so late as 1933 the combined capital assets of all local associations amounted to only 99 million pesetas, or 23,000 pesetas per association and 178 pesetas per member. Their economic debility also assured that none of the cooperatives, with the exception during the Primo de Rivera era of those grouped into the National Catholic Agrarian Confederation, would play a significant political role despite their large membership (442,206 in 1927 and 555,609 in 1933). During the 1900s and 1910s, two publications of the International Institute of Agriculture, the *Bulletin of the Bureau of Economic and Social Intelligence* and the *International Review of Agricultural Economics,* periodically carried excellent reports on the cooperatives (as well as on the official credit institutions discussed in note 42). See

able to the small peasant. The few regional agricultural schools that were established under state sponsorship in the 1900s and 1910s survived, but in a moribund condition. The network of village demonstration centers that had been planned to supplement the schools was never created.[44] In consequence, the small peasant proprietor was left defenseless before the periodic crises that followed a bad crop year or a drop in the prices of agricultural products. At best, his dependence upon the village money-lenders was increased. At worst, he might lose his lands to his creditors or to the State in default of taxes.[45]

Besides the hardships that the smallest of the peasant owners endured in their roles as proprietors, they were also exposed to other types of adversities. These originated in the additional roles they were obliged to assume because their tiny plots usually did not produce enough to enable them to survive. For part of each year, many small owners worked as day laborers for their wealthier neighbors, or moved to regions where the crop cycle was different from their own in search of work.[46] Alternately, a large number supplemented their income by renting additional land or entering into sharecropping agreements. In 1962, somewhere between one-quarter and one-third of the poorer owner-operators also acted as tenants or sharecroppers.[47] Prior to the Civil War, when leases were much easier to secure, the proportion was undoubtedly

---

also Ministerio de Agricultura, *Censo estadístico de sindicatos agrícolas y comunidades de labradores* (Madrid, 1934).

44. Another of the improvements authorized during the reform period of 1905–09, the agricultural extension schools and village demonstration centers either were never founded or vegetated miserably for lack of funds and of any real interest on the part of the state (Jean Costedoat-Lamarque, *La Question agraire en Andalousie* [Paris, 1922], pp. 103–19).

45. The increase in the taxes paid on the land, which resulted from the stricter registration procedures inaugurated by the Cadestre, was another of the problems that faced the small owner after 1900. Approximately one percent of all rural properties were seized annually in default of taxes—about half a million parcels, according to the International Institute of Agriculture, *International Review of Agricultural Economics*, 82 (May 1916), 101, out of a total of some fifty million parcels. This threat could have been ended without much cost to the State by the exemption of the smallest taxpayers, as was to be done after the Civil War by the Franco regime.

46. On the question of migrant labor, see the preceding section of this chapter.

47. INE, *Censo Agrario: Resumenes nacionales*, pp. 37–38, shows that 23.1 percent of all owners either rented or sharecropped additional lands. Since the poorer proprietors depended on supplementary agreements of this type much more often than the richer, the proportion among them must have been at least one-third in the nation as a whole, and more than one-fourth in Southern Spain, where (because so much land was monopolized by the large estates) the proportion for all owner-operators was 17.3 percent.

higher.[48] We have already examined the fate that the small owners were likely to experience in their roles as day laborers. It would be worthwhile to turn now to a brief discussion of the conditions they would encounter as tenants or sharecroppers, particularly as this discussion would also serve as an analysis of these two occupational groupings in themselves.

As independent entrepreneurs who were expected to provide their own seeds, tools, and animals, as well as to market their own produce, the tenants experienced all of the hardships that resulted from the inadequate credit, market, transportation, and educational facilities that were mentioned in our discussion of the small owners. Because the tenants did not own the lands they farmed, however, they also bore several other burdens. Since most of these are obvious, they do not require detailed description. In addition to earning enough to support their families, tenants had also to contribute to the livelihood of the owners from whom they leased. In most cases, the rents paid seem to have been equivalent to the value of at least one-quarter of the average crop produced on the farm.[49] The tenant did not gain security of tenure for his payments. The majority of contracts seem to have been verbal, not written, and thus could easily be broken by the owners. In those cases in which the length of the lease was specified in legally enforceable terms, the contracts were for short periods which rarely exceeded four years. Nor did the tenant have the freedom to cultivate the farm in the most efficient manner possible, since he had no right to reimbursement for any improvements he may have made when his contract terminated or he was expelled. In bad crop years, the tenant had to endure all the losses because reductions of rent for crop failure were practically unknown. The lease that was held by a tenant could not be assumed by his sons in the case of his death or disability without the consent of the owner. If the owner died or sold his farm, the new owners usually could

48. Since the end of the Civil War, all small tenants (i.e. those who produce the equivalent of less than four metric tons of wheat annually) have enjoyed fixity of tenure and other advantages which have caused owners to become much more reluctant to lease. This has been especially true in Southern Spain, because of the prohibition of the subleasing agreements under which many of the large estates had been worked. Thus, prior to 1936 there was probably a greater intermixture of functions in the South than is suggested by the 1962 figures used in note 47.

49. During the Republic, the conflict over lease legislation was waged in large part over the prohibition of rents that exceeded the assessed income—usually one-fourth or one-third of the real income—on which the land tax was based. In passing, it might be noted that as part of their rent, tenants were often obliged to pay the taxes (usually 12 or 13 percent of the assessed income) on the farms they worked. This meant that they, and not the large owners, bore the burden of the increased taxation mentioned in note 45.

renounce all existing leases and take over the land for their own use or turn it over to new tenants.[50]

The position of the sharecroppers—who probably constituted somewhere between one-quarter and one-third of the individuals listed in the "tenants and sharecroppers" column of Table 24[51]—is somewhat more difficult to describe. In many countries (the southern part of the United States, for example) the sharecropper has traditionally been more akin to a permanent hired hand than to an independent entrepreneur in the sense that the owner provided all the instruments of cultivation, closely supervised the work that was done, extended credit on which the sharecropper lived until harvest, and then marketed the crop, from the proceeds of which he paid the sharecropper a fixed portion. The sharecropper contributed only his labor. In Spain, although sharecropping of this kind was not uncommon, owners usually contributed far less, and the sharecropper far more, of his time and equipment to the process of production. In some cases, a sharecropping agreement meant only that the owner would contribute some of the newer farming aids, such as commercial fertilizer, to ensure that the harvest (and thus his portion of it) was as large as possible. In other cases, the owner might contribute seeds as well. In still others, he might also provide the animals or the

50. My description of lease conditions is in large part based on the demands made for corrective legislation in the various reform proposals of the 1920s and 1930s. Two excellent sources on this question are IRS, *Subarriendos y arrendamientos colectivos,* and the responses, some of which were published, of various organizations to a questionnaire on lease conditions circulated by the Primo de Rivera government in 1926.

51. The Peasant Census of 1933–36 (Table 24) did not distinguish sharecroppers from tenants. The Encuesta Agropecuária of 1956 (Table 23), which did, showed them to be 36.3 percent of the total number of non-owner-operators who relied on family labor. In the South, this figure rose to 47.1 percent, the highest proportion of sharecroppers in any but the Mediterranean Coast region. The conclusions that might be drawn from these figures are misleading for the pre-Civil War period, however, because the special protection give to small tenants after 1940 (see note 48) caused many owners to shift to sharecropping agreements. In six Southern provinces that I used as a sample, for example, the amount of cultivated land leased to tenants decreased by 31 percent, while the (much smaller) amount worked by sharecroppers increased by 367 percent between 1928 and 1951. If similar changes occurred in the relative position of the tenants and sharecroppers themselves, then the latter could not have been more than a third as numerous as the former in Southern Spain prior to 1936. My data proceed from DGP, *Memoria: 1928,* and Luis García de Oteyza, "Los regimenes de explotación del suelo nacional," *REAS* (October–December 1952), table 5. The 1962 Agricultural Census, though not strictly comparable to the 1928 data because it includes uncultivated land, also seems to support this conclusion.

plow.[52] There is no way of determining what the average contribution of the owner was at different times or in different regions of Spain. An indication of how low this contribution tended to be, however, can be found in the legislation of the 1930s, when a sharecropping agreement was deemed to exist so long as the owner supplied 20 percent of the costs of production.[53] So small a contribution did not spare the share-cropper entrepreneurial risks that confronted the small owner or tenant, nor justify in his eyes the large portion of the crop—usually half—that had to be paid to the owner at harvest.

Since many small tenants and sharecroppers, like many small owners, were often forced to seek wage labor to supplement their earnings, their interests also coincided to some extent with those of the day laborers. These various subdivisions of the rural proletariat were further inter-related in that day laborers might sometimes find themselves functioning as sharecroppers,[54] and many individuals who had once been primarily small entrepreneurs would be reduced by the loss of their properties or leases to complete dependence on wage labor.[55]

The grievances that the small entrepreneurs acquired while fulfilling their primary roles, together with the injustices to which their ties to the day laborers exposed them, were sufficient to cause them to associate themselves periodically with the revolutionary labor organizations that sprang up in the Spanish countryside after 1870. When this occurred, the force of the resultant peasant protest was often notably increased since the entrepreneurs were usually more disciplined than the day laborers, enjoyed somewhat greater social status, and were not quite so isolated from the holders of power in their communities. They also possessed a certain degree of economic independence which rendered them slightly less subject to the hardships that would accompany a long strike or dismissal from a job. In Cordova, for example, the labor dis-turbances which followed World War I were most acute in villages with large numbers of impoverished owners and tenants, rather than in those in which the entire population consisted of day laborers.[56] The

52. For specific examples of the extraordinary variety of sharecropping agree-ments that existed, see IRS, *Subarriendos y arrendamientos colectivos,* passim.

53. On this question, see chap. 8.

54. Workers were sometimes allowed to grow melons, onions, chick peas, and other such secondary crops under sharecropping agreements on land that had been fallowed in preparation for the primary crop. During his field study of the latifundio economy in Cordova during the early 1960s, Juan Martínez Alier concluded that ap-proximately 15 percent of the workers he encountered were part-time sharecroppers of this sort.

55. See, for example, the report of the Workers' Society of Sierra de Fuentes (Caceres) in IRS, *Subarriendos y arrendamientos colectivos,* pp. 60–61.

56. Díaz del Moral, pp. 301–02.

role played by the *yunteros* in Estremadura during the Second Republic also suggests the strength that small entrepreneurs could add to the revolutionary effort. Finally, the repeated efforts of both the Anarcho-syndicalist and Socialist labor organizations to attract members from among them indicate that their contribution to the struggle was respected.[57]

This considerable revolutionary potential of the impoverished entrepreneurs rarely actualized itself to the same degree as it did among the day laborers, however, nor did their grievances, though genuine, usually present so grave a threat to the existing social order. Why was this so? In the first place, although they possessed numerous ties to the day laborers, the small entrepreneurs never seem to have developed a firm sense of identification with their less fortunate brethren. Among the small owners, this may have resulted partly from their inability to personalize to the same extent as the other occupational groupings the struggle for survival in which the entire rural proletariat was engaged. The problems they encountered—in their roles as market producers, at least—were those of unstable prices, lack of credit, excessive taxation, and poor roads. All these appeared to stem from the eternal nature of things, not from the rapacity of any given individual. Assaulted by impersonal forces, but lacking a specific antagonist upon whom they could blame their misfortunes, the small owners were less often able to generate the moral indignation that sustained the more easily personalized resentments of the day laborers, small tenants, and sharecroppers.[58]

A less subtle psychological barrier also separated the impoverished entrepreneurs of all types from the day laborers, who were in so many ways their natural allies. The ownership or rental of a tiny plot of land gave to its occupants a certain status that they were loath to forgo. Rather than tie them to the field hands, into whose ranks adverse circumstances might so easily force them, the small owners' and tenants' precarious hold on land seems more often to have bred in them a contempt for those who were less successful. In the post–World War I disturbances in Cordova, for example, the entry of small entrepreneurs into the revolutionary organizations gave the protest much greater immediate

57. On the attitude of the anarchosyndicalists, see my discussion in the next chapter of the *minifundio communal* doctrine adopted at their 1919 Congress. The national Socialist organizations were particularly eager to attract small owners and tenants, as will be shown in Part II of this work. On the attitude of some local societies, see Díaz del Moral, pp. 302–03.

58. On the importance to the growth of revolutionary sentiments of the ability to focus resentments against specific individuals or an unjust society, see the thesis presented in note 26 of this chapter.

force than it otherwise would have had, but also subjected it to a very rapid decline as the superiority which they felt toward the day laborers began to manifest itself.[59] Since human insecurity and the capacity for disdain are apparently limitless, the same type of status considerations also undoubtedly inhibited a closer union between the owners and tenants, or between both of these and some of the less independent sharecroppers.

Economic as well as psychological factors also contributed to the inability of the various subgroupings of the rural proletariat to achieve a firm alliance. Several tactical errors on the part of the workers' organizations might be mentioned, particularly their tendency to define the general strikes that became common after 1900 so rigidly as to prohibit the small entrepreneurs from continuing to cultivate their own land, as well as from reporting for work at the other, incidental jobs they might hold.[60] Another important reason (and one more inherent in the structure of the rural economy) was that although the interests of the small entrepreneurs coincided with those of the field hands insofar as they often supplemented their incomes by wage labor, they also conflicted with them insofar as, in their roles as entrepreneurs, they occasionally themselves hired help to work their lands. This latter phenomenon was more frequent than would be expected for two reasons. Because of the uneven labor requirements characteristic of agriculture, the small entrepreneur might need outside help during harvest and other peak seasons of the year even though normally his holdings were insufficient to absorb his family's capacity for labor. Also, particularly in the mountainous regions, the small entrepreneur's search for supplementary jobs might lead him to migrate to other regions for protracted periods, leaving to others some of the work that was required on his own plot.[61]

We are fortunate to have statistical proof for this somewhat surprising admixture of roles. According to the 1962 Agricultural Census, 76 percent of all owners, tenants, and sharecroppers who held less than

59. Díaz del Moral, pp. 389–91.

60. In the Cordova disturbances of 1917–20, small owners and tenants were at first expected to abandon their farms completely during strikes. Only after acrimonious debate at a regional congress held in May 1919 were they given the right to guard—but not to work—their plots (Díaz del Moral, p. 304). In the nationwide harvest strike sponsored by the Socialists in 1934, small owner and tenant members were not allowed to work their lands until the strike had clearly been defeated (see chap. 12).

61. To the extent that the small entrepreneurs performed wage labor outside their municipalities as migrant workers, rather than inside, they were further cut off, both psychologically and in terms of common economic interests, from the day workers of their localities.

five hectares of land worked their plots entirely with family labor. But 11.8 percent of such entrepreneurs filled up to one-quarter of their labor requirements with hired help, another 5.4 percent used wage labor for anywhere between 25 and 75 percent of their work needs, and a final 6.8 percent employed outside help to do more than three-quarters of the farm tasks. Among entrepreneurs with from five to twenty hectares the proportions for each category rose to 16.1 percent, 9.0 percent, and 6.3 percent, respectively.[62]

These several factors combined to give the small entrepreneurs an ambiguous position in the revolutionary struggle and caused the workers' organizations, despite the recurrent efforts mentioned above to recruit them, to regard them with suspicion.[63] Those who were primarily (insofar as the extraordinary intermingling of roles that characterized the lower strata of the rural population can be disentangled)[64] small proprietors were unquestionably the least given to violent protest. Their heavy preponderance among the rural poor of central and northern Spain assured that those regions—particularly Old Castile and parts of the Cantabric Coast where the rise of an active Catholic social movement alleviated some of the economic pressures upon them and reinforced their ideological ties to the existing order—would not experience severe social convulsions. In Southern Spain, numerous small owners took part in the disturbances of 1917–20 and 1931–36, but they participated more as individuals than as a self-conscious group, and their contributions to the struggle were usually ephemeral.

62. INE, *Primer Censo Agrario de España. Año 1962. Resultados provisionales: Tercera parte: Anexo* (Madrid, 1964), pp. 61–62. The corresponding proportions for medium-sized properties (20 to 100 hectares) were 19.8 percent, 18.9 percent, and 14.4 percent, respectively, and for large properties (over 100 hectares) 7.0 percent, 17.0 percent, and 50.1 percent. The figures on the numbers of workers employed on each size of exploitation (p. 58) point to similar conclusions. It should be noted that about half of the farms under five hectares that employed hired labor, and perhaps two-thirds of those between five and twenty hectares in size, were not irrigated.

63. In Cordova, for example, many locals stretched their definitions of the word "worker" so as to be able to admit purely subsistence farmers, but persons with more than two or three hectares of property often continued to be excluded (Díaz del Moral, p. 304). In Estremadura during the same period (1917–20), most peasant unions refused to accept owner and tenant members (Polo Benito, p. 15). A survey of 36 Socialist locals in the mid-1920s found that 24 did not admit smallholders because they "worked too hard," lacked a sense of "union," and adopted the attitudes of the employers "too easily" (International Labor Organization, Studies and Reports. Series K, No. 8, *The Representation and Organization of Agricultural Workers in Spain* [Geneva, 1928], pp. 193–95).

64. This intermixture of roles can scarcely be exaggerated. In my attempt to create "ideal types," I have probably not done complete justice to it. For a good corrective (though perhaps it goes too far in the opposite direction), see Martínez Alier's *La estabilidad del latifundismo*.

The revolutionary propensities of the tenants, and of some of the more independent sharecroppers, were considerably more pronounced. Aside from their greater insecurity of tenure, the extra economic exactions that burdened them, and the stronger moral basis their grievances acquired because they could be focused against specific persons, two more transitory circumstances helped guarantee that their opposition to the established order would be greater than that of the small owners in the 1930s. The abandonment of traditional, precapitalistic lease arrangements, which had assured the occupants of the land semipermanent tenure at fixed rents, had mostly been completed during the nineteenth century. Nevertheless, the legal bases for the traditional conception had not been fully destroyed until the promulgation of the Civil Code in 1889, and the last vestiges of the older systems of tenancy were still being uprooted—often to the accompaniment of strong protest and much adverse publicity—in the 1920s.[65] The early part of the twentieth century, then, witnessed the final stages of a long process of historical transition in which the memory of privileges lost accentuated the resentment of tenants who were exposed to increasingly unfavorable conditions.

Of greater importance, however, was the economic impact of World War I on Spain. The prices of agricultural produce soared and were accompanied by sharp increases in the rents charged.[66] When the boom ended, however, rents did not fall back to their prewar levels. The tenants found themselves caught in a tight economic squeeze, particularly if they were unfortunate enough to have used their momentary gains during the boom to buy land at high prices.[67] In Southern Spain, because so much of the land was monopolized by the latifundia, the wartime rise in rents seems to have been especially severe, and their postwar decline particularly slow. Although the total amount of land rented increased, the demand for leases was so strong that every advantage lay with the large owners and the large tenants who rented whole estates and then subleased all or parts of them to smaller tenants and share-

65. In 1905, for example, Unamuno wrote against "those who evict whole villages" in the process of changing over to the newer type of leases (F. G. Brugera, *Histoire contemporaine d'Espagne: 1789–1950* [Paris, 1953], p. 335). A particularly interesting account of a conflict over the abandonment of the older type of lease arrangements in a large village (1,373 families) of Granada in 1920 can be found in José Morote y Greus, *El Soto de Roma* (Granada, 1921). The nobility, which had failed to uproot the traditional leases during the nineteenth century when the climate of opinion was more propitious, bore the brunt of most of these criticisms.

66. The inflationary effects of World War I on Spain are discussed in greater detail in chap. 5.

67. Adolfo Vázquez Humasqué, "El problema agrario español," *El Trimestre Económico*, 7 (1940), 470–75.

croppers. The increase in the incidence of subleasing was especially pronounced since some of the large farm managers sought to escape the labor troubles and wage raises that characterized the period from 1917 to 1920 by working the estates through sharecroppers rather than with large labor gangs.[68]

Yet if the tenants and sharecroppers had more reason than the small owners to combat the existing rural structure, they generally did not adopt so revolutionary a stance as the day laborers. For a brief period, in 1920 and 1921, subleasing in Southern Spain overshadowed all other rural social problems as a political issue, but this occurred less because of the strength of agitation among the tenants themselves than because the reform of lease conditions was more compatible than a widespread redistribution of land to the moderate politicians whose anxiety for action of some sort had been stirred by the peasant upheavals of 1917–20.[69] During the remaining years of the 1920s, improvement of the status of the tenants was a favorite theme both of the Catholic rural organizations and of Primo de Rivera.[70] Yet the ineffectiveness as revolutionaries of these impoverished entrepreneurs was once again confirmed after 1931, when, as will be seen, the agrarian problem was fought out primarily on the basis of the wages, working conditions, and need for land of the day laborers, not on the lease provisions which were the central concern of the tenants and sharecroppers. In most regions of Spain, these members of the rural proletariat were too isolated from each other and from the day laborers, as well as too closely tied to the rural society in which their rented lands and semi-independent status gave them some stake, however minor, to be able to assume a decisive role in the revolutionary struggle that developed.

68. Subleasing, which had earlier been prohibited under Spanish law, began to become customary in the latter half of the nineteenth century (Constancio Bernaldo de Quirós, *Los derechos sociales de los campesinos* [Madrid, 1928], pp. 64–65). It increased considerably after World War I when owners who had previously leased directly sought to place an intermediary between themselves and the newly restive peasants, and farm managers of all sorts tried to escape labor difficulties by turning to sharecroppers as much as possible. Given this insecurity on the part of the farm managers, the rents charged might have been beaten down had the small tenants and sharecroppers been able to unite among themselves instead of competing for the lands offered (Polo Benito, p. 63). As it was, rents quickly became excessive, and the relative newness of the system made them seem all the more unjust. IRS, *Subarriendos y arrendamientos colectivos* abounds with lists of grievances from villages throughout Southern Spain.

69. I refer particularly to the unsuccessful efforts of Ángel Ossorio y Gallardo, the liberal Catholic leader.

70. Primo de Rivera launched a major inquiry into lease conditions in 1926, made tenant farmers the chief beneficiaries of a limited land reform scheme in 1927, and sponsored an intelligent general lease law in 1929. See app. E for more details.

There were, however, three major exceptions in which tenants or sharecroppers managed to establish a clear identity and fought as a self-conscious group for specific ends. Two of these exceptions arose outside Southern Spain, and may be regarded as particularly acute manifestations of the conflict mentioned earlier between the traditional conception of lease relationships and the new capitalistic conceptions which emphasized the unrestricted rights of the owner over property.

This conflict existed in especially pure form among the parties involved in the extraordinarily complex *foro* relationships of Galicia. The foro dated back to the Middle Ages when most of the land in Galicia belonged to the Church. Originally revocable, the foro was converted in the course of time to a hereditary lease which obliged the occupant to pay a fixed ground rent, but otherwise left the land completely at his disposal since he could not be evicted from it. The rapid population rise of the late seventeenth and the eighteenth centuries greatly increased the value of the land, making it more profitable for the original occupants, the *foreros,* to sublease it than to farm it themselves. The rents paid by the subtenants, the *subforados,* rose so rapidly that the titular owner, the Church, tried to regain control of what was now a considerable source of income by reasserting the revocability of the foro. The foreros resisted and, after nearly a century of litigation, were successful in that a royal decree of 1763, without ending the residual ownership rights of the Church, permitted them to continue their possession of the land. With poetic justice, however, the decree passed on to the subforados the privileges the foreros had enjoyed as to noneviction and fixed rents.

The Church was removed from the controversy when the foreros bought up its residual rights during the nineteenth century desamortization. But now the foreros and subforados began to re-enact the conflict that had earlier been played out between the foreros and the Church; the latter started to regard the land as their own by reason of long occupancy, and the former sought to evict them so as to regain complete control. Lawsuits abounded, particularly after the Civil Code of 1889 firmly established the principle of the undivided control of property. By 1905 the actual occupants of the land had begun to withhold rents. In the atmosphere of unrest that followed World War I large-scale demonstrations occurred which encouraged the revolutionary labor organizations to hope that the foro might serve as their point of entry into Galicia, otherwise not easily susceptible to organization. This hope was not to be fulfilled. A series of decrees by the Primo de Rivera government in 1926 and 1927 settled the dispute in principle by granting to the actual occupants of the land the right to buy out the foro. The problem continued into the Republican era, but only in the sense of demands either for the abolition of the foro without compensation to the titleholders, or for the establishment of special credit facilities that would assist the poor peasants to buy it back. Whether the conflict would have become virulent even without the initiative of Primo de Rivera is debatable.[71]

The *rabassa morta* controversy of Catalonia was decidedly less anachronistic, thought it too stemmed from ancient usages. Since the Middle Ages, but particularly since the eighteenth century expansion of winegrowing in Catalonia, it had been customary for property owners to grant waste lands to peasants called *rabassaires,* who would plant vineyards on them and pay part of the produce as rent. The relationship long remained harmonious because the rents were not excessive and the leases remained valid for the forty or fifty years that the newly planted vines survived.[72] During the last two decades of the nineteenth century, however, the balance was upset as the phyloxera blight destroyed the old vines and obliged growers to plant expensive American shoots. The contracts which had seemed equitable when applied to the old European plants now began to appear unjust since the American vines lived an average of only twenty-five years, yet required the same long period of growth before they would bear fruit and more costly precautions against disease thereafter. At the same time the owners, following the general late nineteenth-century pattern of an assertion of property rights that had been stimulated by the promulgation of the Civil Code, and pressed by the rabassaires to contribute more than they had in the past, particularly toward the purchase of the new vines, began to try to transform the traditional rabassa morta contracts into more normal sharecropping agreements that would give them larger portions of the crop and be more susceptible to their control.

The conflict was initially joined in the early 1890s, but had subsided by the turn of the century. The new crisis that might have arisen

71. It seems doubtful that the foro controversy could have assumed overriding political importance even in the fervid atmosphere of the 1930s, because the peasants of Galicia were not so well organized as the *rabassaires* of Catalonia, enjoyed more independence from the titular owners, and did not have an autonomous government easily susceptible to their pressure. An excellent brief description of the foro dispute, which at the same time illustrates the hopes held by the revolutionary organizations for it, appears in the Communist party pamphlet, *El problema agrario y la lucha de los campesinos* (Barcelona, 1932), pp. 13–16.

72. The low rents and long leases compensated for the fact that the rabassaire would not receive any income from the vines during the first six or eight years, while they matured. *Rabassa morta* means "dead vine" in Catalan, an apt name for the controversy.

with the dying out of many of the original American plantations during World War I was avoided because the high price of wine permitted the owners and cultivators to agree on new contracts which allowed satisfactory returns to both parties. The postwar drop in prices led to a reopening of the controversy, however, which became all the more serious after 1931 when the new Republic adopted principles favorable to the rabassaires but failed to give a definitive solution to the problem. By 1933, the rabassaires, who in any case had recently come to enjoy considerable political power because of their ties to the dominant Esquerra party, began to turn to mass demonstrations and sporadic acts of violence to compel the autonomous Catalan government to adopt legislation which would oblige the owners to sell them the land under favorable terms. In 1934, during the constitutional conflict that developed with Madrid over this legislation, the reaction of the rabassaires was so fierce as to border on the revolutionary. Yet in the final analysis, the rabassaires proved not to be revolutionaries. They accepted without open resistance the unseating by Madrid of the Catalan government which had defended them, and achieved the ownership rights they sought only after that government was restored by legal means in 1936. Throughout the controversy the rabassaires never sought close collaboration with the Anarchosyndicalists who controlled the urban workers, but acted almost exclusively through their own more moderate organization. None of this should be surprising, for the rabassaires were relatively prosperous rural bourgeoisie who were in conflict with the existing society over a single issue. Consequently, there was no urge for the establishment of utopias among them, and no reason for the continuation of the struggle once their limited demands had been satisfied.[73]

The third major group of tenants or sharecroppers who established a clear identity and engaged in self-conscious protest was quite different from the other two. By dint of its extreme poverty and of its location in Southern Spain, it was also the only tenant group whose protest was to be closely coordinated with that of the day laborers during the 1930s. In Badajoz and Caceres, the two key provinces of Estremadura, stock-

73. The political repercussions of the rabassaire controversy are covered at length in all general histories. I deal with the controversy only in passing, both here and in chap. 12, because it was not directly connected with the truly great agrarian problem of Spain, that of the completely impoverished peasant, particularly in the South. The rabassaires were much richer, much better organized, had more limited objectives, and were immune to all efforts of the revolutionary organizations— whether Anarchosyndicalist, Socialist, Communist, or Trotskyist—to recruit them. The best analysis of the question probably appears in a very recent book that I was not able to consult: Albert Balcells, *El problema agrari a Catalunya: 1890–1936. La Questió Rabassaire* (Barcelona, 1968).

breeding had remained a much more important part of the rural economy than elsewhere in Southern Spain.[74] This was due partly to the fact that the two provinces, hard by the Portuguese border and not containing any important cities, were more completely cut off from markets for agricultural goods than other regions; partly to the unusually pronounced failure of the large owners to develop irrigation facilities or experiment with new crops; and partly to the relatively poor quality of the soil, not as propitious to plant growth as the rich soils of Western Andalusia. In many of the great estates of Badajoz and Caceres, particularly those in the less fertile areas, a unique pattern of land use had developed which blended stockbreeding activities with the raising of grain crops. The person in charge of the estate as a whole—either the owner himself or a single large tenant to whom it had been rented— acted primarily as a stockbreeder, but subleased to small tenants or sharecroppers portions of the land on which they grew a single crop, and then moved on to new sectors of the estate where they repeated the process while the land that they had earlier worked reverted to pasture.[75]

This rotation of lands was beneficial to the main operator of the estate both because he derived an extra income from the parcels he subleased and because the periodic plowing of the land improved its quality as pasture when it reverted to grazing. The system was less beneficial to the subtenants, or *yunteros,* (as they were called because they usually owned a team, or *yunta,* of mules which they used in plowing). First, because so large a proportion of arable land was given over to stockbreeding, the demand for leases on the land that was actually cultivated was even greater than in the rest of Southern Spain, and the owners or main tenants had still greater freedom to set whatever terms they wished. Second, because the owners enjoyed an alternative use of the land in that they could allow it to remain in pasture for longer than usual, they did not depend exclusively on the rents they received,

74. In Estremadura during the 1920s, stockbreeding accounted for 24.1 percent of the total value of all agricultural and livestock production, whereas in the rest of Southern Spain it accounted for only 14.9 percent. For Spain as a whole, the figure was 19.7 percent. See Carrión, the unnumbered tables facing pp. 320 and 340.

75. In the frequently employed four-field system, for example, portion A of the estate would be turned over to several sharecroppers for fallowing in the first year, while portions B, C, and D remained in pasture. In the second year, the sharecroppers would grow a grain crop on field A and fallow B, while animals grazed on C and D, as well as on the stubble of A. In the third year, A would revert to pasture while B was sown and C fallowed. In the fourth year, C would be sown and D fallowed. The cycle would start over again in the fifth year as D was harvested and A fallowed. Five- and six-field systems were not uncommon, and in the poorest land, a seven- or eight-field cycle might even be used.

as did owners who leased purely agricultural land. Consequently, they could break any widespread resistance on the part of the subtenants without much financial sacrifice by the simple expedient of refusing to allow new leases.

The system of land use also had psychological consequences. Aside from making the yuntero subject to more frequent revision of his lease terms, the "floating" leases to constantly changing parcels did not permit him the same degree of identification with a given piece of land that helped give a sense of status to tenants and sharecroppers in other regions. Of greater importance, the vast tracts of untilled land devoted to pasture were a constant aggravation to the yunteros who did not have enough land to work, and a constant reminder that additional land was readily available if only the injustices of the existing society could be eradicated.[76]

Thus, an explosive situation existed in that persons who were essentially independent, at least to the degree that they owned draft animals and raised major crops without much supervision or assistance, were subjected to high rents and great insecurity while lands on which they might have applied their labors lay in pasture. During the 1930s, a combination of circumstances in which the yunteros first received what seemed to be permanent rights to the land from the liberal Azaña government, and then saw these rights diminished and finally destroyed by the more conservative governments that followed, intensified the latent tension and converted the yunteros into a fiercely revolutionary group which on several occasions even surpassed the day workers of Andalusia as a force for social disorder.

In Badajoz and Caceres, in particular, there can be no doubt as to the primacy of the revolutionary role of the yunteros in the 1930s. Though considerably less numerous than the simple day laborers even in these two provinces, they constituted a proportion of the rural proletariat more than twice as large as that of tenants and sharecroppers in the rest of Southern Spain.[77] Their numbers, together with their greater discipline and self-

76. The yunteros and their problems are discussed repeatedly in chaps. 9–14, because of the great political importance they assumed during the Republic.

77. In the 1936 Census of Peasants, impoverished tenants and sharecroppers made up 21.8 percent of the rural proletariat of Badajoz and Caceres, as against 9.9 percent in the rest of Southern Spain (and 13.7 percent in the nation as a whole). In Southern Spain, only Granada, with its labor-intensive irrigated farming, had a comparable proportion. Western Andalusia, whose great estates were worked mostly with labor gangs, had by far the lowest proportion (see Table 24)—particularly the province of Seville where the figure was only 4.6 percent. These regional differences remained operative after the Civil War, although they may be diminishing as stock-breeding becomes less important in the economy of Badajoz and Caceres. The 1956 Encuesta Agropecuária (Table 23) showed tenants and sharecroppers to be almost

reliance, were sufficient to give them the leading position that tenants and sharecroppers in Andalusia and La Mancha were never to acquire.

Two final points should be mentioned before ending our discussion of the rural social structure and moving to an analysis of the way in which the struggle over the agrarian question actually unfolded. First, one of the major problems of modern Spanish historiography is to explain the rather pronounced geographical division of the Spanish proletariat (urban as well as rural) between the Anarchosyndicalists and the Socialists. As will be seen in the next chapter, where I undertake a fairly detailed description of the historical development of the two movements, I have not been able to discover any really satisfactory hypothesis.[78] In the context of our present discussion, however, it is worth noting that the Anarchosyndicalists tended to achieve their greatest success in regions where day laborers were overwhelmingly predominant, and the Socialists in regions in which there was a greater mixture of occupational groupings. Thus, in Cadiz, Cordova, Huelva, Malaga, and Seville—the latifundio provinces dominated by the Anarchosyndicalists—day laborers constituted 78.1 percent of the rural proletariat registered in the 1936 Peasant Census, whereas in Granada, Jaen, and the six provinces of Estremadura and La Mancha—where the Socialists were dominant—they accounted for only 58.1 percent.[79]

This occupational differentiation may help to explain the more constant intransigence of the Anarchosyndicalist groups, their more exclusive reliance on overt revolutionary action, and their greater tendency to experience abrupt rises and falls in membership. Among the Socialists, the somewhat greater proportion of small tenants and owners contributed to the greater moderation which characterized their move-

twice as numerous in these two provinces as in the rest of Southern Spain, while the Agricultural Census of 1962 indicated that they were only one-third again as numerous.

78. The older explanations (used by writers like Gerald Brenan and Constancio Bernaldo de Quirós) which rely on a dichotomy between the emotional, "Mediterranean" temperament of the Andalusian peasant and the more realistic outlook of the inhabitant of the Meseta, or see anarchism as a new expression of the old sentiment of regional separatism, are obviously inadequate. Aragon, which is neither especially "Mediterranean" in temperament nor given to particularly strong separatist feelings, went Anarchosyndicalist while other regions in which one or the other of these characteristics was more pronounced went Socialist. A more prosaic hypothesis is needed, one which would revolve around the influence of the large cities on the surrounding countryside, and on which movement happened to be recruiting in a given area at the time when it awakened socially.

79. These figures are approximate since there was a certain degree of intermixture between the two movements in each province, particularly in the mountainous regions of Cordova, Seville, and Malaga. In Granada, most of the peasants were never organized (see Table 35), but to the extent that they were, the Socialists rather than the Anarchosyndicalists predominated.

ment, but permitted it to act with greater discipline on such decisive occasions as the nationwide harvest strike of June 1934 and the massive seizure of lands in Badajoz on 25 March 1936. The differences between the two organizations should not be exaggerated, of course, since day laborers constituted the vast majority of the members in both, and their problems and policies had as many similarities as they did differences. Nevertheless, insofar as the tactics and objectives of the Anarchosyndicalist and Socialist rural organizations diverged, the divergence resulted as much from the occupational dissimilarities which characterized their followers as from their frequently conflicting ideologies.

The final point that should be mentioned is a restatement and extension of what was said earlier in this chapter concerning the increasing pressure of the population on the land in Southern Spain because of the failure of day laborers to emigrate to other regions. As was noted in Table 11 (Chapter 2), the South, by a considerable margin, is the richest of the arid regions of Spain in terms of the value of agricultural production per hectare. If the value of this production is compared to its population, however, a quite different conclusion emerges. The assessed taxable income, which as mentioned enables us to transcend yearly fluctuations of production by offering a rough average value of the land over long periods, was 175 pesetas per hectare in Southern Spain and only 118 pesetas in the Meseta-Ebro in 1959. Nevertheless, because of the high birth rates in the South and the failure to emigrate, the value of agricultural production per person actively engaged in agriculture there was only 2,022 pesetas as against 2,289 pesetas in the Meseta-Ebro region.[80]

This datum should not change our conclusion that the rural disorders of the South resulted more from the inequalities and injustices of its social system than from poverty as such. Sectors of the Cantabric Coast, particularly the extraordinarily overpopulated region of Galicia, had a far lower (1,665 pesetas) value of production per person but did not thereby become important centers of agitation. Yet the fact remains that the heavy pressure of the population on the land in Southern Spain made any easy solution to the existing social tension all the more unlikely. Not only were the patterns of land use and ownership not especially propitious, either economically or politically, for agrarian reform (see the concluding paragraphs of Chapter 3); even if such reform were to be effected it could not in itself satisfy the demands of the excessively large population for an adequate standard of living.

80. The assessed taxable income figures are taken from García-Badell, "La distribución de la propiedad," REAS, no. 2 (Jan.-March 1960), and the population figures from the Encuesta Agropecuária of 1956.

Part II

AGRARIAN REFORM AND
PEASANT REVOLUTION

5: The Agrarian Problem Prior to the Republic

Peasant Unrest up to 1875

At first glance it appears paradoxical that Spain, which throughout early modern times enjoyed the greatest domestic tranquillity in Europe, became in the nineteenth century the nation most prone to revolution. From the time of the *comuneros* revolt in 1521 to the expulsion of the French in 1814, the only important domestic upheavals were primarily regional in origin—those by which Catalonia and Aragon tried to secure autonomy and Portugal succeeded in reestablishing its independence. The religious wars and political convulsions that shook Europe during the three centuries from Luther to Napoleon stopped short at the Pyrenees.[1] Yet the paradox is more apparent than real. The domestic peace of the nation reflected stagnation rather than fruitful harmony. The inevitable day of reckoning arrived when the ossified Spanish social order proved unable to adjust to the changes generated by the French Revolution and by the industrial transformation of England.

It was the political structure of Spain which was first called into question. The unifying force formerly exerted by the monarchy broke down after 1815 as the European-wide battle between constitutionalism and absolutism was fought with unusual bitterness in Spain. Economic stability was simultaneously upset by the loss of the South American colonies and by the material damage inflicted during the Napoleonic Wars, which in Spain alone took the form of a continuous struggle capable of laying waste to a nation. In the new atmosphere of disorder, institutions upon which internal peace had once rested asserted them-

1. These three centuries of domestic tranquillity should be stressed, because many intellectuals attribute the continuous disorder since 1815 to supposedly inherent attributes of the Spanish "national character." Spaniards were not rebellious by nature because of an exaggerated individualism; they became rebellious by circumstance because of the collapse of the political and social balance of the ancient régime.

selves as divisive forces. This was the case with the army, formerly non-political, now deeply involved in each of the disputes that shook Spain. The Church also entered the political arena in defense of absolutism.

The result of these fundamental changes was a series of *pronunciamientos*, popular revolts, and civil wars which constantly threatened public order during the sixty-year period from 1814 to 1874. Of all these events, only the period of prolonged crisis that began in 1868 need concern us here. A widely supported pronunciamiento easily overthrew Queen Isabella and the Bourbon line, but the attempt to reorganize Spain as a truly constitutional monarchy under a new royal house proved more difficult. After several candidates had rejected it, Amadeo of Savoy finally accepted the unstable throne in 1870. The wisdom of his initial hesitations was confirmed in 1873 when the increasingly unmanageable situation forced him to abdicate. Upon his abdication the accumulated hatreds of a half century of dissension burst forth and brought chaos. The Republic that succeeded Amadeo by default was unable to control events. In the north the Carlists intensified their struggle for the restoration of absolutism and clericalism. In the south and along the Mediterranean Coast, the Federal Republican movement degenerated into a series of Cantonalist insurrections as several cities declared their independence from the Madrid government. Throughout the nation the urban working classes began to organize and agitate. Inevitably, the army intervened to restore order. After a year in which the defunct Republic was retained as the façade behind which a military directorate ruled, the Bourbons were restored to the throne.

The Restoration proved surprisingly successful. Bourgeois political passions were exhausted. The excesses of the Cantonalists discredited the Federal Republicans and other radical groups. The brief flurries of labor activity, especially the bloody clash in Alcoy, frightened the middle classes by raising the specter of "Red" atrocities and social revolution. The long absence of effective political authority convinced both liberals and conservatives of the dangers of intransigence and led to greater cooperation between them. The Restoration monarchy also learned from the experience and helped preserve the new-found balance by its willingness to work within constitutional forms. In short, the years 1868–74 marked a turning point in Spain similar to that marked by the revolutions of 1848–49 in northwestern Europe. A long lull ensued in the permanent civil war that seemed to have engulfed the nation. Not until 1917 was the political structure of Spain again seriously threatened. Not until 1931 was the monarchy again overthrown.

During the sixty years of turbulence from 1814 to 1874, the rural social structure of Spain had remained essentially unchallenged except insofar as it was the object of the modernizing efforts of the liberals, who initiated the various phases of the desamortización during their brief tenures in office. The rural masses, who had even less of a tradition of independent action than other Spanish social classes, remained passive amid the general upheaval. Spain had never known a Wat Tyler, a jacquerie, or a peasants' revolt of the type against which Luther fulminated.[2] The peasantry had not participated in a decisive capacity even in the comuneros revolt of the early sixteenth century. It had made its power felt only in the guerrilla struggles against Napoleon and in the Carlist War of 1833–40, and then it had acted not in opposition to, but in defense of, the traditional order.[3] Throughout most of the nineteenth century the Spanish peasant seemed more akin to his brothers of the Vendée than to those swept by the *grande peur*. Breaking the mystical bonds that tied him to Church and king was to prove much more difficult than had been the case with the urban middle and working classes.

Although the new concepts of liberty and equality may have had unsettling effects as they filtered down to the peasantry, the first signs of agrarian unrest coincide not with any of the liberal revolts but with the disentailment of the Church and municipal lands which the liberals initiated. As mentioned earlier, the desamortización clearly worsened the lot of the peasants in Southern Spain, contrary to the intentions of its sponsors.[4] Its affirmation of the individualistic nature of property deprived the poor of many rights they had enjoyed under the earlier collectivistic conception. Its transfer of lands from the Church and nobility to bourgeois owners was usually followed by a worsening of the terms under which the peasantry worked the land. Its sale of the common lands led to an increase in municipal taxes, which fell most heavily on the poor because they were almost invariably levied on basic items of

---

2. Díaz del Moral, for example, was unable to discover any important peasant revolt in Cordova prior to the nineteenth century, except for the celebrated insurrection of Fuenteovejuna. The only general peasant risings in Spanish history, those of the *payeses de remensa* in the fifteenth century, were limited to Catalonia.

3. The contrast in the peasant reaction to the two French invasions of Spain in 1808–14 and in 1823 dramatically illustrates this point. Against Napoleon's huge armies, many peasants fought for Church and king, but ten years later they allowed the Duke of Montpensier's small force to cross Spain without opposition in pursuit of the liberals who had tried to force the king to accept constitutional rule.

4. See the concluding paragraphs of chap. 2. Joaquín Costa, *La tierra y la cuestión social* (Madrid, 1912), pp. 14–15, sums up the effect of the enclosure of private property and the sale of Church and municipal lands in these words: "Those goods were the bread of the poor, their gold mine, their reserve funds, we might even say the Bank of Spain of the destitute working classes. The desamortización . . . has meant the assault of the governing classes upon this Bank."

consumption.[5] At the same time the small rural industries by which many peasants had supplemented their incomes gradually began to be demolished by the rise of large-scale urban competition.[6] Yet neither these new urban industries nor the intensified agricultural production that was the positive achievement of the desamortización sufficed to give employment to the peasants who had been displaced or to those who were being added to the labor force as Spain followed Europe in experiencing a sudden and prodigious population growth.[7]

The coincidence of so great a transformation of the rural economy with the rapid rise in population and the revolution in political ideas inevitably produced disturbances. As early as the 1830s banditry increased and could not easily be suppressed, because the peasants regarded the bandit as a popular hero who gave expression to the dissatisfaction they themselves felt. In 1840 peasants in several neighboring villages in Malaga moved to a new level of protest and seized former common lands. In 1857 a group of Fourierists attempted to arouse the rural masses near Seville by attacking outposts of the Guardia Civil and burning records of common land sales in the municipal archives. Although the Fourierists failed to precipitate a general rising, Rafael Pérez del Álamo, a social republican, almost succeeded a few years later. In 1861 this "Spanish Spartacus" attracted a mob of peasant followers which at times may have numbered as many as 10,000 as he made his way up the Genil river valley to take the city of Loja in Granada. Nor were the disturbances limited to Southern Spain. Important peasant risings also occurred in Castile and Aragon in 1855 and 1856.[8]

The remarkable feature of these risings is not that they occurred

5. Municipalities were not empowered to tax land, the principal form of wealth. The income from the land tax went mostly to the national, not the local, government.

6. For the effect of large-scale production and trade on a specific village, see Julian Pitt-Rivers, *The People of the Sierra* (London, 1954), pp. 3–5.

7. The population of Spain nearly doubled during the nineteenth century, rising from some 10 million in 1800 to 18.5 million in 1900. The greatest increases occurred after mid-century and undoubtedly contributed to the intensified agrarian unrest that began then. As mentioned in chap. 4, the rise was particularly great in Western Andalucia.

8. On peasant disturbance during this period and up to 1900, see Constancio Bernaldo de Quirós, *El espartaquismo andaluz* (Madrid, 1919), and *Bandolerismo y delicuencia subversiva en la baja Andalucía* (Madrid, 1913); E. J. Hobsbawm, *Primitive Rebels* (Manchester, 1959); V. G. Kiernan, *The Revolution of 1854 in Spanish History* (Oxford, 1966), pp. 177–78, 213–14; Brenan, pp. 139, 156–57; Carrion, pp. 20–21; Hennessy, *Federal Republic in Spain*, p. 57; José Termes Ardévol, *El movimiento obrero en España: La Primera Internacional* (1864–1881) (Barcelona, 1965).

but that they had no sequel. Peasant dissatisfaction had become a reality, but it had achieved neither the strength nor the self-consciousness necessary to threaten seriously the existing social structure. Not only had the mob that joined Pérez del Álamo gathered accidentally and without prior planning; it also dispersed without fighting as soon as troops were sent against it. This passivity continued even when the unseating of the Bourbons a few years later inaugurated a long period of political instability during which peasant claims might successfully have been pressed. Repeatedly rumors spread throughout Andalusia of an impending social revolution to recover the common lands and break up the large estates. But the opportunity passed with only brief risings in a few isolated villages, risings that collapsed as soon as they encountered the slightest opposition.[9] The peasantry neither aligned itself with any of the bourgeois revolutionary movements nor forced the leaders of these movements to seek peasant support.[10] The diffuseness of peasant resentment and its lack of organization made any important social changes impossible. And when the middle classes were reconciled to the Restoration monarchy after 1875, it seemed that the democratic and social revolutions would never coincide.

Rural Anarchism and Anarchosyndicalism

The rural masses began to become self-conscious only after the first great wave of middle-class revolution had passed. The instrument of their awakening was the philosophy of anarchism, whose seeds had been sown in Spain in 1868 during the visit of Bakunin's envoy, Giuseppi Fanelli. In describing the impact of anarchism in Southern Spain, most observers have resorted to religious analogies.[11]

There is a considerable amount of justification for this practice. The fervor anarchism aroused among the militants who formed its cadres gave it the power to survive repeated persecutions which had characterized early Christianity. The mass of its followers were not nearly so constant in their devotion but from time to time proved capable of such

9. For a record of the villages in which risings occurred, see Hennessy, pp. 57, 210; Hobsbawm, p. 77; and Díaz del Moral, pp. 70–77; and Termes, pp. 93–95.

10. Pi y Margall seems to have been the only important bourgeois leader sympathetic to the peasantry and aware of its potential significance. On his attempted land reform legislation, see Hennessy, pp. 15, 21–22, 200–01, 206.

11. Díaz del Moral particularly favors such analogies with the result that his interpretations are occasionally overly romantic. Nevertheless, his brilliant study of peasant agitation in Cordova undoubtedly remains the most important single work on the psychology of Spanish anarchism. All the standard English accounts (Brenan, Hobsbawm, Borkenau) are deeply indebted to him.

extraordinary enthusiasm that the millennial movements that had largely by-passed Spain during the Middle Ages visited it in Anarchist guise during the modern era. The functions of the priest were performed for the Anarchists by the *obrero consciente*. A Scripture sprang up in the movement's newspapers and pamphlets, from which the convert memorized and recited long passages. A system of morality with both general and specific precepts was devised to guide the believer. Above all, a concept of cosmic justice and a day of universal, miraculous salvation for all was preached. A moment would come in which the oppressed would spontaneously rise against their masters. It would usher in a new earthly paradise which would surpass the heavenly paradise proclaimed by Christianity, since all men, not merely those who had been saved, would enjoy it. After the Revolution all men would be filled with the same dazzling truth that illuminated the soul of the convert and, forgetting their former selfishness, would live together in perfect harmony—without property, without government, without any other form of coercion—in a new world from which man's inhumanity to man would be eradicated forever. So strong was the faith and so innocent its adherents that, reportedly, a believer once approached a landholder from whom all property was to be taken to ask him, "Señorito, when will the Great Day come?" in the expectation that the señorito awaited this day with the same eager anticipation.

The religious fervor of Andalusian anarchism had organizational consequences as well. Its emphasis on the total regeneration of society caused it to despise such limited goals as better wages and made it less susceptible to the reformist currents that affected other working-class movements. Its belief in miraculous causation and its insistence upon the full freedom and equality of each human personality led it to reject hierarchical organization, bureaucratic procedure, and realistic planning. Finally, its loathing of all forms of government caused Anarchists to refuse to present candidates for office, to vote in elections, or otherwise to participate in the normal political life of the nation.

None of these characteristics should be overemphasized, of course.[12] Rural anarchism remained a regional movement that did not penetrate any other area of Spain so decisively as it did Western Andalusia. Even in that unfortunate region, where the conditions of life constantly reinforced its extremist tendencies, anarchism from time to time seemed about to settle down to a more stable existence in which limited gains would become its real goals and more careful organization its chief mode

12. For example, Termes Ardévol's study of the First International in Spain offers many indications that the anarchists were not always so messianic in their actions as Díaz del Moral would suggest.

of operation. Yet this evolutionary process was never completed. Both because of the desperation of its followers and because of its own exalted vision, the violent and irrational heritage of anarchism was never entirely overcome. A distorted, unbalanced, and destructive society had given birth to a movement which, despite the nobility of most of its ideals and many of its leaders, was also often to prove unbalanced and destructive.

Neither these characteristics of rural anarchism nor the strength of its hold upon the rural masses was immediately apparent. The movement gained 28,000 adherents in Andalusia from 1869 to 1873, but so rapid a growth was not unusual in such troubled times. Moreover, most of the early members were artisans, not peasants.[13] A more substantial peasant following was acquired by secret proselytization during the period of repression that followed the Restoration. When working-class movements were again legalized in 1881, farm workers accounted for almost half the Andalusian membership and constituted the largest single occupational grouping in the new Anarchist Federation.[14] Yet this success was also short-lived. The extremism of some of the peasant groups, who advocated the adoption of Malatesta's tactics of the "insurrectionary deed," sowed dissension in the Federation. More important, it provided the local authorities in Andalusia with an excuse for launching the savage Mano Negra repressions of 1883, which drove rural anarchism back into the wilderness from which it had so recently emerged. For the next two decades the movement remained dormant. Its subterranean existence could not be forgotten, because peasant resentment still made itself felt in acts that ranged from recurrent crop burnings to the celebrated revolutionary assault by some four thousand peasants on Jerez de la Frontera, one of the largest cities in Spain, in 1892. Yet for the most part the rural disturbances were sporadic, small in scale, and limited to the provinces of Cadiz and Seville.[15]

13. Díaz del Moral, pp. 412–13, 425. The Andalusian peasantry does not seem to have been significantly more active in the upheavals of 1873 than it had been in the lesser disturbances of 1868, before Fanelli made his fateful journey to Spain.

14. By September 1882, 20,915 of the 57,934 members were agricultural workers, mostly from Andalusia. The rapid penetration of the countryside is also evident in the fact that locals existed in 130 different Andalusian villages or towns. Total Andalusian membership (38,349) still far exceeded that of Catalonia (13,201), or Valencia (2,355). (*Congreso de la Federación de Trabajadores de la Región Español celebrado en Sevilla en 1882* [Barcelona, 1882], pp. 64–72, 93).

15. Besides the authorities already mentioned, the following works are valuable for the late nineteenth-century history of anarchism: Diego Abad de Santillán, *Contribución a la historia del movimiento obrero español* (Mexico, 1962); Gabriel Jackson, "The Origins of Spanish Anarchism," *Southwestern Social Science Quarterly*

The movement not only survived these early failures but emerged after the turn of the century as a more effective force than before. Nothing had been done to ameliorate the lot of the peasants, which may have worsened as the population continued to grow and the landowners became less paternalistic in outlook. Moreover, anarchism revitalized itself by incorporating some features of the new theory of syndicalism, which had spread southward from France. In the industrial region of Barcelona, it was the syndicalist emphasis on the creation of large-scale revolutionary labor unions which proved most fruitful. By accepting the Syndicalist principle of mass organization, Catalan anarchism overcame the tactical sterility of its previous individualistic orientation and laid the basis for its capture in the next two decades of the urban proletariat of Barcelona.[16] In the countryside, where the dispersion of the population and the strength of village particularism made the establishment of large-scale unions more difficult, syndicalism nevertheless had an important impact because of its concept of the general strike as an instrument of revolutionary action. For a few years this concept fulfilled in Andalusia the functions of a Sorelian social myth. The Andalusian peasant became convinced that if the workers displayed their enormous power by simultaneously abandoning work, the established classes would be demoralized and the revolution would triumph.

Whether because of the long accumulation of peasant grievances or because of the magical qualities attributed to the general strike, the reemergence of rural anarchism in 1903 brought with it more continuous and widespread labor agitation than any previously recorded in Andalusia. The most serious outbreaks occurred in the traditional Anarchist strongholds of Seville and Cadiz, especially in the villages of Morón de la Frontera and Alcalá del Valle. The strike movement also spread for the first time to Cordova in the upper Guadalquivir valley, though there it was less violent, since anarchism was less firmly rooted, the workers had unusually naïve notions as to what a work stoppage in itself could accomplish, and the local authorities tried to appease the strikers with wage concessions. In 1904 strikes broke out anew in Andalusia.[17] But this time peasant resistance also appeared in other regions, even those in which the latifundio economy was not predominant. For the first time, bitter strug-

(September 1955), pp. 135–47; and, above all, Renée Lamberet, *Mouvements ouvriers et socialistes: L'Espagne (1750–1936)* (Paris, 1953).

16. Carr, *Spain: 1808–1939*, p. 445.

17. For the 1903–04 difficulties in Andalusia, see Marvaud, *Question sociale en Espagne*; Segismundo Moret, *El problema social-agrario en España* (Madrid, 1910); Abad de Santillán, pp. 502–03; Díaz del Moral, pp. 194–212; and the speech of Alejandro Lerroux in D.S. 101, 18 December 1903, p. 3180.

gles over the right to organize were fought in such provinces of Old Castile as Avila, Zamora, Palencia, Leon, and Valladolid.[18] For the first time,
Socialist labor organizations began to compete with the Anarchists for
peasant support.

Although the local authorities were unable to revive the public
hysteria that had permitted them to carry out the brutal repressions of
the Mano Negra, they exerted constant pressure against the strikers.
Workers' centers were closed. Labor leaders were arrested and deported.
Troops sometimes performed the agricultural task that the strikers had
abandoned. Above all, the Guardia Civil provided protection for strikebreakers.[19] Under this constant pressure, labor agitation began to
diminish toward the end of 1904. A mood of despair once more swept over
the workers as the strike proved unable to fulfill the great expectations
held for it. The final blow to worker enthusiasm was dealt by the extraordinary drought of 1905, which was especially severe in Andalusia
and reduced the workers once more to the elemental preoccupation of
ensuring physical survival. Yet the new spirit of independence which had
motivated the strike wave of the previous years did not totally disappear.
Before the turn of the century so great a threat of famine would have
caused the workers to throw themselves on the mercy of the wealthy[20]
or join in the processions in which holy images were conducted through
the fields to pray for rain. Now, "the immense majority invoked neither
charity nor the name of God" but crowded around the *ayuntamientos* demanding bread and entered farms in groups to force owners to grant them
work.[21] Although the new outburst of violence that threatened in the
spring of 1906 did not occur, bloodshed was only barely avoided during a

18. The difficulties in Central Spain are described in IRS, *Ambas Castillas*.
This report is especially valuable because it reproduces some of the correspondence
on the strikes between local authorities and the Ministry of the Interior.

19. For repressive measures employed, see especially IRS, *Ambas Castillas*,
pp. 17–18, 37–39, 54–55, 66–71, 75–78.

20. According to the Count of Torres Cabrera in Unión Agraria Española,
Cuarto Congreso Regional celebrado por la Federación Bética-Extremeña (Madrid,
1905), p. 9, Cordovese workers had responded to a similar drought in the 1880s by
distributing a handbill which said, "The working class, convinced that certain ora-
tors are carrying it to perdition and that it does not possess either the means to support itself or the intelligence to lead itself, appeals not to the authorities but to the
established and enlightened classes, for bread and for advice, offering them in return
an eternal gratitude." Though perhaps Torres Cabrera embroidered upon it, this
incident demonstrates the extraordinary change in peasant attitudes, since a similar
plea in 1905 would have been inconceivable.

21. Díaz del Moral, pp. 214–16. The word *ayuntamiento,* often used to refer
to the government of a municipality, is here employed in its alternate meaning of
"town hall."

demonstration in Morón (Seville) and, outside Andalusia, in Fraga (Saragossa), a clash between the Guardia Civil and the local unemployed left five peasants dead and four others wounded.[22]

The recovery of economic prosperity in 1907 neither restored amicable relations nor permitted the strike movement of 1903–04 to recover its lost momentum. A curious lull, which was to last for a decade, ensued in the class warfare of the Spanish countryside. On the one hand, it was to this period that landowners in Cordova later traced the loss of the remaining good faith between workers and employers. Workers refused to exert themselves and productivity declined drastically, with the result that piecework had to be extended to break the slowdown.[23] On the other hand, there was little overt labor activity and the local unions were unable to regain their former influence. In Cordova—which may be used as an example, since its labor history has been so thoroughly documented by Díaz del Moral—only one Anarchist society could claim any real popular support during the period from 1905 to 1910. Otherwise, organized anarchism either disappeared from the province or survived only in the form of small committees.[24] On the national level the infrequency of overt worker protest was revealed in the strike statistics compiled by the newly created Institute of Social Reforms. In the six years between 1905 and 1910 only nineteen agricultural strikes were officially recorded in the whole of Spain.[25] These figures should probably be dou-

22. *D.S.* 103, 7 March 1906, pp. 3100–02.

23. This complaint appears repeatedly in the responses of landowners in Cordova to a 1919 questionaire that asked them to state the origins of the agrarian disturbances then sweeping the province (IRS, *Córdoba*, pp. 73–144).

24. Díaz del Moral, pp. 222–24.

25. IRS, *Estadística de las huelgas*, volumes for the dates mentioned. As a result of the strike wave of 1903–04, the Institute of Social Reforms was commissioned to investigate the causes, duration, intensity, and outcome of all Spanish strikes, whether in agriculture or industry. The Institute's functions were taken over by the Ministry of Labor in 1923, so that a continuous strike record exists from 1905 to 1936. Unfortunately the value of this source of information is limited for three reasons. First, strikes were strictly defined so that spontaneous walkouts, demonstrations, riots, and other working-class upheavals were deliberately ignored. Second, probably because of insufficient funds and personnel, the Institute did not take official cognizance of many strikes that actually occurred. Third, the Institute analyzed fully only a portion of the strikes it reported as having taken place, with the result that its data on the number of strikers involved and work days lost are even less complete than its record of the number of strikes that occurred. These deficiencies were probably most pronounced in connection with agricultural strikes, since these took place in so many more scattered and obscure localities than did industrial strikes. For example, neither the Morón demonstration nor the Fraga strike found its way into the Institute's report for 1906. The best discussion of the Institute's methods of gathering information is probably the introductory section of the 1907 report.

bled or trebled to take into account the many strikes which the Institute left unrecorded, but the level of strike activity nevertheless remains inconsequential. Even the great bloodletting during the *semana trágica* in Barcelona in 1909 had no effect on the torpor of the rural masses.

The important new departures in labor organization after 1910 did not decisively alter the situation. The Anarchosyndicalist Confederación Nacional del Trabajo (CNT) organized in that year was eventually to prove the first lasting national federation in Anarchist history, but its immediate impact was not great. After recruiting some thirty thousand members, the CNT declined drastically when a series of strikes failed in Barcelona in 1912. The Federación Nacional de Agricultores de España (FNAE), founded in 1913 as the agricultural counterpart to the CNT, did not experience even so momentary a success. The instability of this organization, the first to attempt to unite all Spanish peasants as an independent group, was such that it changed its headquarters three times during its first three years of existence. Its membership was never large; after three years of proselytizing it had only 2,400 adherents in the whole of Spain. Nor was the ineffectiveness of the FNAE and CNT counteracted on the local level, though there, too, an important organizational drive was under way. In Cordova fifteen new locals were established between 1910 and 1914, but none was able to initiate significant popular protest.[26] On every front Spanish anarchosyndicalism appeared to have been rendered powerless. Strike activity increased sufficiently over the 1905–10 period to give cause for continued concern. Yet the ninety agricultural strikes reported by the Institute of Social Reforms between 1911 and 1914 were no real danger to social order, since they were neither as numerous nor as virulent as those of 1903–04.[27] The great wave of labor unrest that was sweeping Europe on the eve of World War I largely by-passed Spain.

The reasons behind worker inertia in this period are unclear. The lack of a new social myth capable of galvanizing worker feelings may serve as a partial explanation. The fervor aroused by the concept of the general strike in 1903–04 had diminished after the failures of those years. The Syndicalist strain had become too strong to permit an abandonment of trade union structure and a return to the earlier Anarchist tactics of secret societies that prepared insurrectionary deeds. Both the CNT and FNAE continued to regard strikes and sabotage as means toward the ultimate end of social revolution, but they now also stressed more prosaic objectives such as the abolition of piecework, the promulgation of a minimum

26. Díaz del Moral, pp. 258–59; Manuel Buenacasa, *El movimiento obrero español: 1886–1926* (Barcelona, 1928), p. 56.
27. IRS, *Etadística de las huelgas: Memoria de 1920*, p. 10.

wage law, and the establishment of an eight-hour day. The emphasis in both, but especially in the FNAE, was on better organization, more careful planning, and united action rather than on spontaneous upheaval.[28] In one sense this policy of caution and moderation was successful. The FNAE, for example, experienced none of the massive persecution that wrecked the first two Anarchist Federations, and it succeeded in proselytizing much of the previously unorganized Levante.[29] But the price of this success was that the FNAE became progressively weaker in the pivotal area of Andalusia, where extremism rather than moderation thrived.[30]

The effects of the lack of a social myth were buttressed by the uninterrupted economic prosperity Spain enjoyed after 1910. This prosperity increased greatly after the outbreak of World War I, since Spain remained neutral and assumed the fortunate role of supplier to the belligerents. From 1900 to 1936 Spain enjoyed a favorable balance of trade in only five years; four of these were war years.[31] Agriculture especially prospered because of a succession of exceptionally good crop years.[32] The competition for jobs in rural areas decreased as an industrial boom attracted many workers to the cities. Consequently, though strike activity continued to rise, it did not reach intolerable heights. The Institute of Social Reforms recorded twenty-three agricultural strikes in 1915, thirty-five in 1916, and forty-six in 1917; but until the last few months of 1917 these strikes were scattered and unimportant.[33]

28. On the timidity of the CNT and FNAE during this period see Buenacasa, p. 56; Díaz del Moral, pp. 257–58; Brenan, p. 178.

29. Brenan, p. 179, considers the FNAE's conversion of the Levante as its major achievement. Other indications of its extra-Andalusian interests are its initial choice of headquarters (Barcelona and Tarragona) and the fact that only two of its six congresses were held in Andalusia; the rest convened in Catalonia, Aragon, or the Levante.

30. Even some of the Andalusian locals that had helped found the FNAE dropped away from it. For example, it retained only 290 members in Cordova in the fall of 1917 (Díaz del Moral, p. 259).

31. In 1915, 1916, 1918, and 1919 Spain enjoyed a total trade surplus of 760 million pesetas. The only other favorable year, 1930, can hardly be counted as such, since the surplus amounted to only 9 million pesetas (INE, *Primera mitad del siglo XX*, p. 94).

32. The average wheat harvest rose from 3.3 million metric tons in 1904–14 to 3.9 million metric tons in 1915–18. The important olive industry also enjoyed the best harvests in history (ibid., pp. 32, 37).

33. IRS, *Estadística de las huelgas*, volumes for 1915, 1916, and 1917.

The Trienio Bolchevista and Its Aftermath

Three factors combined to end the long truce and inaugurate the extended period of trouble known as the *"trienio bolchevista."* The increased external demand for Spanish goods and the closing of foreign sources of supply stimulated economic activity but also exerted inflationary pressures. The cost of living more than doubled between 1914 and 1920, with three-quarters of the increase occurring after the spring of 1917.[34] Because wages did not keep up with the abrupt post-1917 price rise, the new-found prosperity of the working classes suddenly vanished. For example, a village in Cordova reported that although the normal daily wage of a field hand rose from 2.25 pesetas in 1913 to 3.25 in early 1919, the cost of living had meanwhile soared from 2.57 to 4.55 pesetas, thus leaving the worker with a greater deficit than before.[35]

The inflationary crisis coincided with and contributed to a grave political crisis. The Restoration system, which since 1875 had emasculated political dissension by means of controlled elections that permitted the two major parties to alternate regularly in power, gradually broke down after 1900. The old Conservative and Liberal parties began to splinter after the death of their leaders, Cánovas del Castillo and Sagasta. The Socialist, Republican, and Catalan regional parties, none of which would abide by the old rules of the game, all increased in power. The accession to the throne of Alfonso XIII in 1902 further unsettled political life, since the young man wanted to be an "active" king and sometimes meddled in governmental affairs. The result was that political disputes were no longer so easily compromised as before but began to be fought out. Nor could majority coalitions be easily formed, so changes in government became common.[36] The process was exacerbated as the memory of the ignominious defeat in the Spanish-American war and the dramatic

34. Ministerio de Trabajo, *Boletín* (March 1931), pp. 234–35, reported that village food costs rose from 100 in 1909–14 to 220 in September 1920. The period of greatest inflation was from April 1917 to November 1918, when the food cost index rose from 126 to 179. Similar price increases occurred in other items of consumption. INE, *Primera mitad del siglo XX*, pp. 145–50, reports a general increase from 100 to 223.4 in all wholesale prices from 1913 to 1920.

35. IRS, *Córdoba*, pp. 166–67.

36. In the 27 years between the Restoration and the accession of Alfonso XIII, 17 different cabinets held office, all but 6 of which were headed by Cánovas del Castillo or Sagasta. The 6 exceptions were mostly caretaker ministries that together governed for less than three and one-half years. By contrast, 18 different cabinets, commanded by 13 different individuals, held office in the 15 years between 1902 and 1917. An even greater breakdown of authority followed as 15 different cabinets, headed by 8 different men, sat between 1917 and Primo de Rivera's coup in 1923.

confirmation of the inconsequence of Spain during the First World War led to a public questioning of Spain's entire past and future.

Inflation, which injured the salaried middle class as much as the workers, combined with these long-range factors to create a situation in which the political structure of Spain was seriously threatened for the first time since 1875. The immediate crisis was short-lived, to be sure. In 1917 there were a number of bourgeois demonstrations against the high cost of living.[37] At the same time officers' juntas were formed which aroused the hope that the army might return to its pre-Restoration liberalism. A political framework for the opposition was established in July as Republican, Socialist, and Catalan deputies united in a "Renovation" movement, met as a rump parliament in Barcelona and called for a freely elected Cortes and a new constitution. The Socialists tried to push matters in late August by proclaiming a nation-wide general strike in support of the movement. At this decisive moment the army proved loyal to the Monarchy and crushed the strike with considerable bloodshed. Army opposition, the conciliatory tactics of the king, and internal disputes split the Renovation alliance. The immediate crisis passed when the relatively free elections of February 1918 did not produce the expected majorities for the remaining Renovation parties. Yet the questions that had been raised could not be entirely shelved. And though the revived current of middle-class rebellion was not itself to achieve success until fifteen years later, its initial expression in 1917–18 indirectly aided the growth of working-class protest. The extravagant promises and accusations that filled the air aroused Anarchosyndicalist expectations. Moreover, by undermining the confidence of the Madrid government the crisis ensured that its policies against the unfolding labor unrest would be neither strong nor consistent.

The impact of the Bolshevik Revolution, which occurred just as the Spanish political crisis was passing its height, completed the preconditions for the trienio bolchevista by providing the social myth that had been lacking for so long. It would be difficult to overestimate the influence of this distant event. The March Revolution aroused little notice among the Spanish working classes: at the Fifth Congress of the FNAE, held less than two months later, there was only one passing reference to it.[38] But the October Revolution generated so much hope and excitement that the Anarchist press was filled with such incantations as: "Prepare yourselves, workers of Spain; from one moment to the next the

37. On bourgeois demonstrations over the high price of bread, see Jorge Montojo Sureda, *La política española sobre trigos y harinas: Años 1900–45* (Madrid, 1945), pp. 17–28, 113.

38. Díaz del Moral, app. 6, especially p. 473.

clarion of justice may sound." [39] And at the Sixth FNAE Congress of December 1918, held more than a year after Lenin took power, the Russian example still permeated all discussion.[40]

Thus though Spain did not feel the shock of the World War, it anticipated and shared in the great social convulsions that swept postwar Europe. For three consecutive years, from 1918 to 1920, labor agitation without precedent shook the nation. The official strike statistics tell only a small part of the story, for the information-gathering machinery of the Institute of Social Reforms, never perfect, broke down almost completely under the flood of data.[41] Yet even these incomplete statistics are revealing. From 1914 to 1917 an annual average of 231 strikes of all kinds were reported, 32 of which were in agriculture. The total number of strikes reported rose to 463 in 1918, to 895 in 1919, and, finally, to 1,060 in 1920. The pattern was the same for agricultural strikes: these also doubled in each of the first two years of the trienio and increased still further in 1920. In 1918 agricultural strikes numbered 68, in 1919 the Institute reported 188, and in 1920 it listed 194.[42] Spanish agricultural strikes in 1920 exceeded in number (though probably not in intensity) even the rural walkouts in Italy, which were to contribute so heavily to Mussolini's rise to power two years later.[43] The Institute's statistics on the number of strikers involved and the number of work days lost, though especially incomplete, reveal a similar trend. The days lost in strikes of all sorts rose from 1.8 million in 1917 to 7.3 million in 1920; and the number of strikers, from 71,400 to 244,700. The number of agricultural days lost meanwhile increased from 43,735 to 369,256; and the number of strikers, from 8,587 to 27,514.[44]

39. *La Voz del Cantero,* 11 March 1918, as quoted in Díaz del Moral, p. 283.

40. Díaz del Moral, app. 7, especially pp. 493, 498, 512, 514, 515. Buenacasa says: "For many of us . . . the Russian Bolshevik was a demigod" (p. 71).

41. For example, the Institute reported only 30 strikes in Cordova during 1918–19, wheras Díaz del Moral listed 184. A similar breakdown of the data-gathering process occurred during the Second Republic, when the Socialists alone claimed to have participated in 929 rural strikes between April 1931 and July 1932, whereas the official statistics listed 145 agricultural walkouts by all groups.

42. IRS, *Estadística de las huelgas: Memoria de 1920,* p. 10.

43. IRS, *Huelgas y 'Lock-Outs' en los diversos paises* (Madrid, 1923), p. 65, states that 192 rural strikes occurred in Italy during 1920.

44. These figures far understate the real situation, because they are based upon strikers and workdays lost only in those strikes for which the Intitute could obtain complete information, not on all strikes it knew to have occurred. Thus from 1917 to 1920 the Institute took official cognizance of 2,664 strikes—although probably at least twice as many had actually taken place—but reported fully on only 1,259. The absence of data was probably most common in agricultural strikes, hence the low proportion of total strikers and days lost. Díaz del Moral, for example, gives one

The agrarian upheavals of the trienio bolchevista were too complex and have been too little studied to permit any detailed analysis here. Certain basic characteristics may be mentioned, however. First, although Andalusia remained the center of events, there was also serious peasant unrest in other regions. The organizational drive of the FNAE from 1913 to 1917 finally began to pay dividends as Anarchosyndicalist locals sprang up both in the Levante and Aragon. In 1919 there were at least thirty-three such locals in Valencia alone;[45] moreover, according to the IRS statistics, Valencia surpassed all but the three Andalusian provinces of Seville, Cordova, and Jaen in the number of strikers involved and work-days lost in agricultural walkouts. In Aragon, Saragossa was the center of the upheavals; in 1919 it ranked fifth in the number of workdays lost by rural strikes, and in 1920 it rose to second place after Seville.[46] In both these regions, then, anarchosyndicalism spread outside the cities for the first time and established itself as an important force in the countryside. In Andalusia, where rural anarchism was already deeply rooted, it consolidated its position so completely as to become a nearly universal and ineradicable force. In Cordova, for example, workers' organizations existed in 61 of the 75 townships and claimed a membership of 55,382 out of a total active rural population of 130,000.[47] As one writer put it, if local unions had been established in most Andalusian villages by 1903–04, by 1918–20 most landless Andalusian peasants had become members.[48]

Second, although labor protest became more intensive and universal, it was not much better coordinated than before. The initiative always remained with the locals despite the existence of national organizations. The FNAE experienced a considerable growth in membership but remained powerless to provide any real unity. In December 1918, as a move toward greater synchronization of rural and industrial protest, the

the impression that many more than 27,514 agricultural workers were striking in the province of Cordova alone.

45. CNT, *Memoria del Congreso celebrado en el Teatro de la Comedia de Madrid, los días 10 al 18 de diciembre de 1919* (Barcelona, 1932), pp. 23–28. Most of the Valencia locals were to be found in the unirrigated portions of that province, not in the rich, irrigated *huerta*.

46. IRS, *Estadística de las huelgas: Memoria de 1919*, pp. 256–57, and *Memoria de 1920*, pp. 336–37. These rankings should not be taken literally, of course, since IRS statistics were especially inadequate on strikers and days lost. The Guadalquivir valley clearly remained the center of peasant protest.

47. Díaz del Moral, pp. 570–72. The proportion of union members in the peasant population was probably somewhat lower than these figures indicate, because some of the affiliates were artisans. Also, although most of the unions were Anarchosyndicalist, a few were Socialist.

48. Carrión, p. 414.

FNAE voted to disband and merge with the CNT.[49] This simplification of the organizational structure had no practical effects. Peasant strikes in one part of Spain remained uncoordinated with those elsewhere, and the great gulf between the industrial and rural sectors of the CNT was still not bridged. As in the past, industrial and rural upheavals each followed their own rhythm.

The failure on the national level was matched on the regional level. Toward the beginning of the troubles, in May 1918, Andalusian workers formed a Regional Federation within the CNT. Though the Federation functioned for a time, it proved unable to synchronize the spontaneous local walkouts.[50] Unified strikes were successful only on an ad hoc basis within smaller areas. This was proven in Cordova where, because the greatest degree of local unity was achieved, the agrarian upheavals became the most serious in Spain. On three separate occasions between October 1918 and May 1919 village particularism was temporarily overcome as from 26 to 34 of the 75 townships in the province simultaneously went out on strike. Yet even at moments of greatest enthusiasm, worker strength was compromised by internal dissensions and the traditional Anarchist lack of a principle of authority. Because there was also no attempt to coordinate action with industrial or rural unions in other provinces, in the end the agitation in Cordova was easily crushed by a military expedition. Though it had shattered political stability in an entire province for a year (a total of 184 agricultural strikes occurred in 1918–19; for most of the period varying degrees of martial law had to be imposed), the Cordovese movement, on the whole, was a failure.[51]

In agrarian affairs, then, the CNT was usually unable to give the general strike any broader context than that which prevailed in 1903–04, before a firm organizational structure had been created. The Syndicalist influence helped modify other aspects of the Anarchist heritage, however. Surprisingly, the period of greatest rural upheaval in Spain's history was also a time of relatively little physical violence. Bloodshed could not be entirely avoided, of course, given the tensions that prevailed. In the Cordova strikes described above, armed clashes between the Guardia Civil and strikers occurred in eight villages. In the worst of these, the guardias left four peasants dead.[52] At times the strikers alone were re-

49. Buenacasa, p. 76; Brenan, p. 180.

50. Lamberet, p. 108; Díaz del Moral, pp. 173, 262, 315, 327; Buenacasa, pp. 57, 164.

51. Díaz del Moral devotes most of his magnificent work to the 1918–19 strike movement in Cordova. An excellent brief description of its early phases also appears in IRS, *Córdoba*, pp. 11–16.

52. Díaz del Moral, p. 366.

sponsible for the bloodshed, as in a Seville walkout of May 1920, when they murdered two strikebreakers. Damage to property also occurred; farms were occasionally burned and agricultural machinery sometimes destroyed.[53] Nevertheless the strikers generally stayed within the bounds of normal strike activity. Their demands were not always reasonable, but their methods were usually restrained. Mass invasions of farms by squatters who wished to cultivate them never became widespread, even during the early months of the trienio, when the authorities usually hesitated to employ force. There were few burnings of churches or of property registers. The open village insurrections of the past did not occur; there were no takeovers of ayuntamientos, no proclamations of village independence, no major clashes with the military forces.

The relative orderliness of the rural strikes reflected the predominant mood in the CNT as a whole. The moderate current that had appeared in the labor movement of the extreme Left after 1910 continued to develop during the trienio under the leadership of Salvador Seguí and Angel Pestaña. The CNT supported the Bolshevik Revolution and provisionally associated itself with the Third International; it rejected many of the concessions the state was willing to make, especially toward the institutionalization of the labor struggle through arbitration boards; it refused to supplement its strike programs by political action and continued to strive for the overthrow of bourgeois society. Nevertheless, the CNT was willing to rely on mass, open labor union agitation rather than on the insurrectionary tactics of small secret groups, either of the contemporary Bolshevik or of the earlier Anarchist variety. It inspired no violent demonstrations that might lead to bloodshed of the *semana trágica* type.[54] It engineered no open revolutions like those that were sweeping Germany at the time or those that were to become characteristic of the Second Spanish Republic. It refused to sanction even the type of factory occupations that Italian workers were to undertake in 1920.[55]

The effects of the CNT's moderation can also be seen in the agricultural program it adopted at its Second Congress, held in Madrid in December 1919. Besides emphasizing its interest in recruiting landowning peasants as well as landless tenants and workers, the CNT also moved away from its former goal of collectivistic exploitation of the land. Operating on the same statistical data used by Bernstein against Kautsky in the Revisionist battle that raged in prewar Socialist circles,[56]

53. *The Times* (London), 12 May and 5 June 1920.
54. Brenan, p. 177.
55. Barcelona militants urged a massive occupation of factories in response to the general lockout of November 1919 but were refused by the principal CNT leaders because of the danger of bloodshed. Buenacasa, pp. 84–87.
56. These were the 1895–1907 German statistical reports, which suggested that

the Congress sanctioned the doctrine of the *minifundio comunal*. Although this doctrine continued to reject the personal acquisition of the means of production and insisted that the land remain the property of the community as a whole, it permitted the land to be worked individually in small plots as well as collectively in large units. To the populist conception of a parceling of the great estates the CNT opposed its own *parcelación comunista*.[57] A fundamental change toward a broader and more flexible doctrinal position appeared to be in the making.

Thus though the "Bolshevik triennium" of 1918–20 revived in much more substantial form the specter that Pérez del Álamo had first raised half a century before, it also left room for hope that in coming of age anarchosyndicalism had learned restraint. Like all working-class movements, anarchosyndicalism seemed to be proving subject to the contradictory yearnings best expressed by one CNT rural local when it said: "All we workers, even though we abominate property, desire it because it liberates us from need." [58]

The hope that the Anarchists might eventually be absorbed into the existing social order was not to be fulfilled, because the moderate trend

---

small properties were more efficient than large and that contrary to expectation, small farms were not disappearing under the impact of capitalism.

57. CNT, *Memoria del Congreso de 1919*, pp. 324–29. Under the minifundio comunal system, all factors of production would be owned in common—the land, machines, credit facilities, and so on—but the land would be tilled individually. Earlier Anarchist theory had not entirely excluded the possibility of individual exploitation, but by formally resolving in its favor the 1919 Congress took possibly the most open stand for individualism in Anarchist history. This did not mean that the CNT accepted nonrevolutionary land settlements, however. It continued to reject partial land reform schemes on the grounds that the small plots given workers "awaken in the individual a profoundly egotistical instinct, killing his rebelliousness and destroying the solidarity and good will which should exist among the exploited in order to combat the capitalist regime" (ibid., p. 322).

58. Response of the Fernán-Nuñez local to an IRS questionnaire (IRS, *Córdoba*, p. 156). The agonizing dilemma that faced the Anarchosyndicalists in their simultaneous desire for land and their theoretical rejection of partial, nonrevolutionary settlements was illustrated at the Castro Congress of May 1919. Asked to support a Socialist demand for the immediate turnover of state, municipal, and badly cultivated lands to workers' syndicates, a majority at Castro decided "not to beg lands from the ruling classes, since we are irreconcilable enemies of authority and property. If we wish land, let us act like the Russian bolsheviks." Yet on the theme, "What means shall we use to avoid unemployment crises?", the same congress resolved that it should "demand lands for use of the syndicates" (Díaz del Moral, p. 335). At times the theoretical stance was so rigid that local societies actually refused lands offered to them (ibid., p. 375). The same phenomenon was to recur frequently during the Second Republic. In the end, the refusal of land was self-defeating and may help explain the relatively slow growth of the Anarchosyndicalist rural unions during the first years of the Republic.

in the CNT was reversed just as it was articulating itself. Events in Barcelona, which had become an unquestionably more important Anarchist center than Andalusia, were primarily responsible for this fatal relapse. The Catalan industrialists, having failed to crush the CNT by lockouts and the formation of rival trade unions, turned after November 1919 to the use of *pistoleros* who assaulted the workers, shot their leaders, and bombed their centers. Since the police and Army collaborated with the employers, the CNT's chief means of defense was to organize pistolero squads of its own. The tragedy of the struggle that ensued was symbolized by the murder in March 1923 of Salvador Seguí, who had been largely responsible for CNT restraint during the trienio, and the retaliatory assassination of the Cardinal Archbishop of Saragossa. Two years earlier retaliation had also taken the life of Eduardo Dato, the third Spanish prime minister assassinated by Anarchist sympathizers in a quarter of a century. More than a thousand persons in all were killed or wounded in Barcelona before the mutual terrorism was halted in September 1923.[59] Toward the end, both industrialists and CNT leaders lost control over events. Deaths from socially motivated acts of violence in Spain as a whole averaged about 63 from 1917 to 1922; in the first ten months of 1923, 154 killings were reported.[60] The contemporaneous disorders in the streets of Italy and Germany had required as a precondition the enormous dislocations of the Great War. Spain needed no such momentous external cause.

As in Italy and later in Germany, persons were not the only victims of the postwar violence. Though the street battles in Barcelona were not so directly politically oriented as those inspired by the Fascists in Italy and by various rightist groups in Germany, they, too, aided in the destruction of parliamentary rule. First challenged by the bourgeois Renovationists in 1917, then confronted with the labor unrest of the trienio bolchevista, and finally forced to recognize its impotence in checking lawlessness in perhaps the most important city of Spain, the constitutional regime was in a shaky position indeed. Its paralysis was completed by the fact that king and parliament, the two chief elements in the system, could no longer work together. The fragmentation of the old political parties and the growth of a Republican and Socialist opposition made the Cortes no longer amenable to the King, who resorted to playing the Army off against the parliament.

The issue that provided a focus for other conflicts and eventually

59. Stanley Payne, *The Spanish Revolution* (New York, 1970), pp. 57–61, estimates that Barcelona accounted for about 70 percent of the 533 persons killed and 1,243 wounded in Spain between 1917 and 1923 in such incidents.

60. Ibid.

brought the constitutional regime to its destruction was the disastrous military defeat suffered in June 1921 at Annual in Spanish Morocco. Both the king, who was said personally to have urged the course of action followed by the defeated commander, and the army, whose incompetence was brutally revealed by the slaughter of eight thousand men by native rebels, were deeply implicated. The question of the day became how fully the Annual disaster should be investigated. After considerable hesitation the Cortes risked authorizing a complete investigation by a commission of enquiry. A week before its report was to be published, on 13 September 1923, the military governor of Catalonia, Miguel Primo de Rivera, issued a pronunciamiento against "slimy political intrigues that take as a pretext the tragedy of Morocco" and "social disorders that are ruining agricultural and industrial production." Though the King had not participated in planning the coup, he hastened to accept it. The Cortes was dismissed, the Constitution of 1876 suspended, and the dictatorial rule of Primo de Rivera sanctioned. In a trip to Italy later in the year, Alfonso introduced Primo de Rivera to Victor Emmanuel as "my Mussolini." [61]

In fact, though he adopted some of the corporative principles of Italian Fascism in an effort to provide a philosophical rationale for his rule, Primo de Rivera was not a Mussolini. His government was authoritarian, not totalitarian. He did not understand the uses of demagoguery, was not concerned with building a fanatical party following, and had no messianic dreams of reconstructing under a new image either Spain or mankind as a whole. Primo de Rivera aimed only at modernization and renovation; his goals otherwise were the traditional ones of social discipline within a hierarchical order. Since his methods for achieving these ends were also relatively gentle, his rule was not altogether unfavorable for Spain. With the help of the French, the Moroccan revolt was crushed. A vast program of highway construction and irrigation works expanded the economic infrastructure of the nation, though the prodigality with which it was accomplished saddled the state with great debts. Social peace was restored not merely by suppressing all workers' organizations but by cooperating with one of them, the Socialists, in developing institutional means for collective bargaining in industrial disputes. And though the improved international situation aided him considerably, Primo de Rivera's economic policies brought a long period of uninterrupted prosperity to Spain.

The damage that Primo de Rivera's rule inflicted was more subtle. By giving the army a taste of power he reestablished its tradition of open

61. Brenan, pp. 74–76.

intervention in political affairs which had been dormant since 1875. By suppressing without cause the Mancomunidad agreement of 1914, which granted to Catalonia a degree of self-government, he exacerbated Catalan nationalism. By limiting his amelioration of abuses to the industrial sphere and neglecting fundamental rural social legislation, he killed the promising start made by the Cortes of 1921–23 toward agrarian reform. Finally, to return to our point of departure, by disbanding the CNT and driving it underground, he completed the process of radicalization which had begun during the street fighting in Barcelona. A new type of leader had been bred during this fighting who resembled the early Anarchist militants more than the trade union leaders of the trienio bolchevista. With the prohibition of CNT trade union activity during the seven years of the dictatorship, these new men, within whose souls the gunman complemented the saint, expanded their influence. During one of the last public meetings of the CNT, at a Regional Congress held in Cordova in July 1923, a step toward a more rigid doctrinal position had been taken by the rejection of minifundio comunal of 1919 and the affirmation of collective exploitation as the only means by which land should be cultivated after the Revolution.[62] In 1927 an event which would prove still more ominous occurred. At a meeting in Valencia the new leaders helped form a clandestine group, the Federación Anarquista Ibérica (FAI), which was to act as the vanguard of the proletariat by destroying reformist tendencies in the CNT and by organizing it as a revolutionary force once liberty of action was again permitted. In the long struggle within Anarchist ranks between mass trade union protest and insurrectionary tactics by small secret societies, the latter policy was in the ascendancy once more.

In the short run the 1923 coup turned out to have helped, not hurt, the liberal cause. The king was discredited even among many of his own followers by his violation of the constitution. Republican ranks were thereby strengthened, especially among the intellectuals and the youth. Primo de Rivera's attempt to stifle Catalan autonomy ensured that populous Catalonia would also withdraw its support from the monarchy. The cacique system by which elections had been managed since 1875 was disrupted as the dictator replaced local authorities with his own nominees. Without this combination of circumstances, the Second Republic could not have come into being in 1931. Yet though its birth

62. Ibid., p. 181. The change in the CNT's position may have been influenced by the failure of many small owners in the postwar period and by the increased ascendancy of industrial workers in the CNT as the rural locals fell away after 1920. A bitter struggle over this question had previously occurred at a CNT Levante regional congress in 1922 (Díaz del Moral, p. 205).

would otherwise have been delayed, its legacy might have been more favorable. The ideological divisions in the Republic might have been less severe and its rejection of the past less complete had not Primo de Rivera interrupted the process of political evolution which had begun in the last parliaments of the constitutional monarchy. The agrarian reforms that failed in the turbulent atmosphere of 1931–36 might have succeeded had less drastic reforms preceded them while the political structure and the economic prosperity of Spain were still intact. The CNT might have limited itself to massive strikes instead of turning to a policy of continuous insurrection against the new Republic. Finally, the Army might not have had either the excuse or the precedent for launching a new pronunciamiento in 1936, which this time would carry Spain into a destructive Civil War.

Rural Socialism

Until the trienio bolchevista the history of Spanish rural protest remained for all practical purposes the history of rural anarchism. The Socialists did not establish any important peasant following prior to that great period of labor agitation, and even then their influence was not in any sense comparable to that of the CNT. Not until the Second Republic did Spanish socialism escape the role of junior partner among the rural masses.

The limited agrarian strength of the Socialists was in part a reflection of their general weakness. Though introduced to Spain during the same period of political flux as anarchism, socialism did not immediately prosper. The first nucleus disappeared with scarcely a trace in 1874. A new start was made when a Socialist party was founded in 1879, but it attracted few followers. Nor did the publication of a newspaper after 1886 and the establishment of a national trade union, the Unión General de Trabajadores (UGT), in 1888 significantly alter the situation. The First Anarchist Federation had attracted 45,633 adherents within two years of its creation, and the Second Federation, 57,934 members within a single year. The UGT, on the other hand, still claimed only 6,276 followers in 1895, and most of these came from only two centers: Madrid and Bilbao. Though membership began to rise noticeably after 1898, the UGT did not unite so many as fifty thousand members until the wave of labor unrest in 1903–04.[63] It first acquired more than 100,000 associates in 1912, but by July 1918 membership had again sunk to 89,601. Only as the trienio bolchevista unfolded did the UGT achieve truly mass propor-

63. Marvaud, p. 454.

tions. By 1919 membership exceeded 200,000; in July 1921 it reached a predictatorship height of 240,113.[64] Yet though Spanish socialism had finally come of age, its strength still seemed puny in comparison to that of the CNT, which counted 699,369 members in December 1919.[65]

However, the slow progress of the UGT as a whole does not in itself adequately explain the organization's initial failure to penetrate the countryside more decisively. Spanish socialism was long handicapped by the indifference toward the peasantry which had characterized its spiritual founder. Marx's philosophy, based on the assumption of rapid industrialization, did not encompass the realities of the Mediterranean world. Except in some of his earliest writings, as *The Eighteenth Brumaire of Louis Napoleon,* he regarded the new industrial proletariat as the principal revolutionary class. The burden of his later work was that relatively little could be expected from agricultural workers, who were emasculated by their ignorance and sunk in the "idiocy of rural life." Thus whereas the Seville Congress of the Second Anarchist Federation in 1882 stressed its rural orientation by addressing its manifesto to the workers of the world from "these fertile banks bathed by the Guadalquivir, where nature throws forth her gifts with full hands . . . but where the terrible cancer of *latifundismo* is most developed; from this privileged Sevillian soil, a true paradise for the few, a positive inferno for the many," [66] the first important Socialist statement of principles, drawn up during the following year, failed to mention the agrarian problem.[67] Although agricultural workers represented at the Seville Congress made up more than one-third of the total Anarchist membership, peasant unions in the UGT normally contributed only 3 or 4 percent of that organization's total strength prior to 1900. During the upheavals of 1903–04 the situation altered slightly as the 6,309 associates of the UGT's 42 agricultural locals accounted for slightly more than 10 percent of its total membership.[68] In the early months of the trienio the proportion was still roughly the same: for example, only 9,040 of the UGT's 89,601 adherents were agricultural workers in July 1918.[69]

Yet if the Socialists built slowly, they built well. Marx, especially as

64. INE, *Anuario Estadístico: 1932–33,* p. 671.
65. CNT, *Memoria del Congreso de 1919,* pp. 11–34.
66. *Congreso de la Federación de Trabajadores de la Región Española,* p. 104.
67. Jaime Vera, *Informe presentado a la Comisión de Reformas Sociales por la Agrupación Socialista Madrileña en al año 1883* (Paris, 1962). The official party program drawn up in 1879 also did not specifically mention the land problem (Juan José Morato, *El Partido Socialista Obrero Español* [Madrid, 1918 (?)], pp. 107–17).
68. Marvaud, p. 65.
69. INE, *Anuario Estadístico: 1921–22,* pp. 308–09.

he came to be interpreted by most of his followers in Western Europe, had given socialism the discipline and the sense of historical causation which anarchism always lacked. Marx's belief in a final day of judgment and the establishment of an earthly paradise may have betokened mysticism and millennarianism, but his means toward those ends were more prosaic, rational, and realistic than those of the Anarchists. The Revolution would succeed only when its precondition, the active alienation of the majority of the people, had been brought about by historical evolution. The new society would not spring full-grown from individual acts of violence or from poorly organized mass demonstrations. Such acts could only dissipate labor strength and invite repression. The proletariat must continually haunt the bourgeoisie with the specter of revolution, but this specter must remain only a specter until the proper historical moment arrived. Only then should the carefully prepared and closely united proletariat rise in overwhelming numbers to strike the final blow against a society that for the most part would already have destroyed itself through its own internal contradictions. In short, the Revolution was placed at the end, not at the beginning, of a long chain of cause and effect. And in this chain, indirect causation rather than direct action would be principally responsible for bringing communism into being.[70]

This de facto postponement of the Revolution had two major consequences in Spain. First, although the rationalism of socialism delayed its spread among the unsophisticated Spanish working classes, it also spared the movement the persecutions and the extraordinary fluctuations in fortune experienced by the Anarchists. Socialist growth was slow, but it was steady. Second, since secret planning for immediate millennia did not preempt the Socialist mind, it was open to other influences. The specter of communism might just as well haunt the bourgeoisie from within the halls of parliament as from outside—hence Socialist willingness to use the traditional forms of political action which the Anarchists always rejected. Workers would remain permanently united in labor organizations only if some of their immediate needs were thereby secured —hence Socialist acceptance of nonrevolutionary strikes aimed only at the improvement of wages or working conditions. Nor did they consider all bourgeois groups equally bad, since some favored reform more than

---

70. There is, of course, a considerable difference between the tenor of Marx's theoretical writings and his commentaries on specific revolutions (e.g. the Spanish rising of 1854 or the Paris Commune) since his enthusiasm for action often carried him to interpretations that cannot easily be reconciled with his systematic theoretical work. In this section I am referring to Marx's theory, certainly the truly unique (though, especially since Lenin, not necessarily the most influential) aspect of his vast contribution to human thought.

others—wherefore the agonizing Socialist decision to cooperate with, instead of indiscriminately attacking, the Republicans.[71]

Because socialism was only dogmatic, not fanatical, dogma gave way to reformism in practice and the immediate humanitarian concerns of its philosophy won out over its messianic elements. The passage of time, which Marx expected would bring socialism over closer to the Revolution, served only to push the revolutionary goal into the background for many of his followers. This transmutation of values affected most Western European Socialist parties, of course, but its acceptance in Spain was surprising, given that country's backward social and economic conditions. The extremist currents that might have plagued Spanish socialism gravitated instead to anarchism and syndicalism. No Lenin arose within the party itself to dispute the moderating influence of Pablo Iglesias, its guiding spirit from its foundation until his death in 1925. Prior to 1933 the Socialist party of the economically most retarded Western European nation, Spain, stood together with that of the most advanced, Germany, in its emphasis on evolutionary means and its acceptance of most of the values of bourgeois liberalism.

These characteristics all became operative in rural socialism once the Marxist prejudice against the peasantry was overcome. The importance of the rural masses first seems to have been appreciated during the upheavals of 1903–04, when several agricultural locals were founded in northern and central Spain, the regions in which industrial socialism was already rooted. Organizers did not seriously begin to recruit in Southern Spain, where the Socialists had no important following among industrial workers, until about 1910.[72] They were totally unsuccessful in Seville and Cadiz, where the old Anarchist allegiance was too strong to be broken. They were unable to convert the *campiña* of Cordova, since this area was also closely tied to a city in which Anarchist influence was predominant. In the mountainous townships of Cordova, however, and in the Andalusian provinces of Jaen and Granada, they were more successful. But the Socialists prospered most in the non-Andalusian regions of the latifundio belt. Several locals were established in La Mancha, and in

71. The struggle over whether to cooperate with the Republicans took up most of the decade from 1900 to 1910. It was decided when the shock of the semana trágica in Barcelona caused Pablo Iglesias to shift his position in favor of cooperation. Though electoral alliances were again temporarily abandoned in 1920 because of a momentary upsurge in revolutionary feeling among the party rank and file, the spirit of collaboration had become well established (Morato, pp. 228–86).

72. Díaz del Moral pp. 162, 238. Other signs of the heightened Socialist interest in rural affairs include the party's adoption of its first detailed agrarian program at its 1912 congress (Morato, pp. 275–79).

Estremadura the Socialists became the dominant organized rural force.

Socialist penetration of all these areas was still so slight during the trienio bolchevista that this period served more to consolidate the UGT's precarious foothold than to give it an opportunity for a display of overwhelming power. Only in Cordova and Estremadura did Socialist labor agitation assume serious proportions, and even there UGT control was not complete. In Cordova several Socialist locals participated in the ad hoc congresses that coordinated strike action throughout the province, but the chief momentum unquestionably came from the Anarchosyndicalists.[73] In Badajoz and Caceres, the only provinces besides Cordova in which UGT peasant membership rose to more than ten thousand even at the height of the trienio, Socialist influence was stronger. Nevertheless, many of the disturbances there seem to have resulted more from the explosion of elemental peasant passions than from Socialist planning. Much later than Andalusia, Estremadura finally experienced the widespread labor protest that had been threatening since the latter part of the nineteenth century; peasant unrest, however, did not yet assume the massive proportions it was to achieve during the Second Republic, nor was it so well organized by the Socialists as it was to become.[73]

By the close of the trienio Socialist neglect of the rural masses had ended completely. Interest in peasant recruitment was so strong that the creation of a separate peasant federation within the UGT was seriously discussed for the first time. Although this federation did not materialize immediately, agricultural workers had already become the most numerous occupational grouping in the UGT, surpassing even the miners and construction workers who previously had constituted the bulk of the Union's followers. Prior to July 1918 peasants had never numbered more than one-tenth of the UGT membership; by 1919 they made up almost one-third of its total strength. Nor was this support ephemeral. As in the industrial field, once Socialist influence was established it proved much less prone to the extraordinary ebbs in fortune that characterized anarchism. The UGT peasant following fell away in some localities as the enthusiasm of the trienio passed, but in most areas it remained intact and even increased slightly in numbers. In May 1920, 61,327 of the UGT's 211,342 members belonged to 359 agricultural locals. In August 1922, a time of general labor exhaustion, rural locals numbered 510 and united 65,405 of the UGT's 208,170 associates.[75] The "cold and dry Socialist

73. Díaz del Moral, pp. 317–23. The Socialist unions in Cordova tried to launch a coordinated strike of their own in December 1918 but failed.

74. Despite its Catholic bias, Polo Benito, *Problema social,* is the best treatment I have encountered of the trienio in Badajoz and Caceres.

75. INE, *Anuario Estadístico: 1921–22,* pp. 308–09.

voices, a thousand leagues from the hearts of the workers," [76] required more time to take effect than did the messianic exhortations of the Anarchists, but because their message was more realistic, it permitted a more constant loyalty.

The rationalistic nature of socialism also enabled it, after the trienio had passed, to continue its struggle in the political arena from which the Anarchosyndicalists continued to debar themselves. Now fully committed to agrarian reform, the Socialists played an important role in the effort of the Cortes of 1921–23 to enact agrarian legislation. When this effort failed they continued to exert pressure on Primo de Rivera, with whom their opportunism permitted them to collaborate. Nor did the Socialists desist when Primo de Rivera allowed them concessions only in the industrial field while refusing to sanction major social improvements in agriculture. In 1927, the same year in which the FAI, which was to carry the CNT back to a policy of insurrectionism, was secretly organized, a Socialist party congress created an Agricultural Secretariat to study rural problems and prepare legislative proposals for the moment when parliamentary life would return to Spain. Having begun with little interest in the peasantry, the Socialists had ended as the political force most deeply committed to agrarian legislation.

During the 1927 Socialist Congress one local deputation eloquently summed up its plea for continued interest in agrarian affairs by saying:

> So long as one does not sow in the fields, the cities will bear no fruit. So long as we do not bring ideas to the villages, the city and the countryside will remain enemies. You, the Congress, know what this means. Politically, it means that an enormous force which could be a friend is not because we leave it to the mercy of any petty cacique. In revolutionary terms, it means the constant threat of failure. The peasantry is the dead weight which inclines the balance.[77]

In truth, the seeds had already been sown, and the long sleep of the Spanish peasantry was already over except in such regions as Old Castile, where the illusion of independence which small property brings would never allow it to end. Nor was the peasantry any longer a "dead weight" that would tip the balance against movements of protest which originated in the cities. Though agrarian protest had shown itself to be inconstant, difficult of organization, and incapable of sustained effort, the pre-

76. Díaz del Moral, p. 224. This author, writing in a period before the Socialists achieved full strength, tends to be contemptuous of them.

77. PSOE, *Convocatoria y orden del día para el XII Congreso Ordinario del Partido* (Madrid, 1927), p. 12.

dominant impression of the previous fifty years had been one of increasing self-consciousness and power. The extent of the transformation that had occurred since 1868 was to be demonstrated when a new middle-class revolution succeeded in overthrowing the Monarchy in 1931, only to find itself confronted with the no longer imaginary threat that it might be overtaken by a social revolution in which the peasantry would play a major role. As for the Socialists, who sympathized with the new democratic Republic, they discovered that their chief problem was no longer whether they could organize the rural masses but whether these masses, once organized, could be controlled.

6: The First Months of the Republic

The Proclamation of the Republic

The fall of the Primo de Rivera dictatorship in January 1930 left a political vacuum in Spain. The Restoration system of government had been destroyed by the 1923 coup, and the efforts of Alfonso XIII to revive it proved vain. After a year of popular unrest under interim governments, Alfonso agreed to call municipal elections as a prelude to national elections that would restore constitutional rule. The municipal balloting of 12 April 1931, registered Republican sentiment of such surprising strength, however, that the position of the crown became untenable. Without seriously attempting to recruit support for new extraconstitutional measures that would void the election results, Alfonso fled the country on April 14. A Republic was immediately proclaimed.

The peaceful nature of the political transformation must be emphasized. Although the urban middle classes and the urban proletariat played the decisive role in the sense that their votes gave the Republican candidates their sweeping majorities in the cities, the collapse of the monarchy was less the work of any single class than a result of the weakening of support for Alfonso in practically every segment of society. Thus, politicians of the old Restoration parties had tried to raise revolts against Primo de Rivera and then, when the king attempted to restore constitutional rule, they compromised his position by refusing to cooperate with him except on their own terms. Segments of the army had also contributed to the weakening of the monarchy, some by their opposition to Primo, others by their flirtation with pro-Republican revolts, and still others by their refusal to act against the electoral results of April. The police and the judiciary had also played a part, both in their lax suppression of demonstrations and in their acquittal of major opponents of the crown who had been brought to trial in the previous year. And if the Catholic press continued to support Alfonso to the end, it quickly welcomed the new regime. Although many of the actions mentioned resulted from grave miscalculations as to their ultimate effects, the acquiescence of the ruling classes to the overthrow of the monarchy also testified to the fact that they shared in the vague regenerationist urge that had dominated Spanish thought since 1900 and were willing to accept a Republic that they thought would be moderate.[1]

At first the expectations of the established orders did not seem mistaken. The Provisional Government that assumed power was composed of a number of political groups that had gathered at San Sebastian in August 1930 to plot the overthrow of the king. Although the San Sebastian coalition was united in its desire to democratize Spain by restoring parliamentary rule and removing what earlier generations had called the "traditional obstacle" of the crown, it had not worked out uniform social, economic, regional, or religious policies.

The right wing of the coalition consisted of the Progressives, whose leaders, Niceto Alcalá Zamora and Miguel Maura, had probably been the most politically prominent of the San Sebastian figures during the transitional period. These two men constituted the chief assurance that the new regime would not be politically adventurous. Had not the king himself violated the constitution, it is doubtful that the Progressive chiefs would have developed any quarrel with him. As it was, they abandoned their earlier monarchical allegiances and supported a moderate Republic in which honest elections and the independence of the Cortes would be ensured together with a limited degree of ecclesiastical, regional, and social reform.

The center of the coalition was formed by a party with a mixed heritage, the Radicals. In the early 1900s the Radicals had passed through a vituperative anticlerical phase during which they tried to attract working-class support. In later years the party—together with its leader, Alejandro Lerroux—had lost its sense of purpose. Among the propertied classes it had acquired the reputation of being tractable, whereas among Republican purists the prestige of this oldest and largest of Republican factions was shattered by charges of opportunism and corruption.[2]

1. For the truly astounding extent to which the established classes—and Alfonso himself—contributed to the downfall of the monarchy, see especially the memoirs of Berenguer, Maura, Mola, and Romanones. The attitudes of the army are best described in Stanley Payne, *Politics and the Military in Modern Spain* (Stanford 1967), pp. 224–65. Carr, pp. 591–602, is also helpful in establishing the atmosphere of the times. As an Anarchosyndicalist manifesto was later to point out, "If the monarchy had applied its laws with the rigidity and brutality which the Republican governments" were to display against the CNT, Maura and other conspirators would probably have been shot (quoted in *El Sol*, 26 July 1931).

2. For the extraordinary distrust and contempt with which the Radicals were

To the left of the Radicals lay four newly constituted urban middle-class groups: the Republican Action party of Manuel Azaña; the Radical Socialists of Marcelino Domingo and Álvaro de Albornoz; a Catalan regional party, the Esquerra; and a Galician regional party, the ORGA. The members of these groups were for the most part rebels from parties—the Radicals, the Reformists of Melquiades Álvarez, the Catalan Lliga—that had lost their original political fervor. The Republican Action and Radical Socialist factions were distinguished also by their ties to the Spanish intellectual and journalistic worlds. Aside from a willingness to grant greater regional autonomy—the indispensable prerequisite for an alliance of the Esquerra and ORGA to the nonregional groups—the four parties shared in common anticlericalism and a more intense, though not more precisely defined, desire to regenerate Spain than was characteristic of the other bourgeois groups.

The only working-class party in the coalition was the Socialist. The oldest and best organized of all the San Sebastian groups, the Socialists also enjoyed the advantage of strict party discipline, a relatively clearly defined program, and a stable source of political support in their trade union, the UGT. Alienated from the Radicals because of their reputation for opportunism, the Socialists—despite an initial reluctance to permit significant regional autonomy—were drawn to Republican Action and the Radical Socialists by anticlericalism and by the willingness of these two groups to experiment with major social reform.

It would be unwise to exaggerate the differences in outlook of the various parties, however. Although opposing factions gradually arose within the San Sebastian coalition, allegiances remained fluid during the first few months of the Republic, and the parties were separated as much by their political styles as by their policies. The problem of leadership in the Provisional Government was solved without difficulty. The two principal cabinet posts went to the most conservative elements in the coalition in a continued attempt to reassure the nation as to the moderation of the Republic. The Progressive leader, Alcalá Zamora, became prime minister, and his chief lieutenant, Maura, assumed the Ministry of the Interior. Lerroux, the best known of the bourgeois leaders, was shunted off to the honorific post of Minister of Foreign Affairs, which satisfied his vanity without arousing the distrust with which the Socialists and Catalans in

regarded by the other San Sebastian factions, see Miguel Maura, *Así cayó Alfonso XIII* (Mexico, 1962). In 1933 the Radical Socialist leader, Ángel Galarza, publicly declared that the only veto imposed in the Revolutionary Committee had been against having a Radical head the Treasury. The ruin of the Radical's reputation began during the *semana trágica* of 1909, on which Joan Connelly Ullman's excellent *Spain's Tragic Week* (Cambridge, Mass., 1968) should be consulted.

particular would even then have regarded his intervention in domestic affairs. Azaña, a relatively unknown figure who was to become the great man of the future, was made Minister of War. Because of their importance to the coalition if it was to continue to enjoy the support of the urban working classes, the Socialists were given three posts. Fernando de los Ríos, Francisco Largo Caballero, and Indalecio Prieto were charged, respectively, with the Ministries of Justice, Labor, and Finance.

The initial harmony within the coalition facilitated agreement on the agrarian question. Although the peasantry had been tranquil since 1921 and had played an insignificant role in the overthrow of the monarchy,[3] it was axiomatic for all parties that some sort of agrarian reform must be instituted. The impetus toward reform which had developed since 1900 was too strong to be disregarded.[4] Moreover, the Provisional Government, having upset the established political order, was faced with the threat that more radical elements, especially the Anarchosyndicalists, might seize the initiative and carry Spain into a social revolution. Finally, the pivotal Socialist party, without which the coalition could scarcely survive, was committed to significant agrarian legislation.[5] As a result the Provisional Government bound itself to agrarian reform in its very first declaration of principles. Its pledge was couched in vague terms which reflected the government's confusion at finding itself so suddenly in power as well as its desire to calm the fears of the propertied classes. Nevertheless, the promise of redemption for the peasantry was unequivocal:

> Private property is guaranteed by law and is consequently not expropriable except for public utility with due indemnity. Nevertheless,

3. Although even the cacique-controlled rural vote was less predominantly monarchist in the elections of 12 April than was once thought, the Republic had already been proclaimed long before the peasant ballots could be counted. Nor were there any important peasant strikes, riots, or demonstrations in April 1931, despite attempts of writers like Bruno Minlos (*Campesinos de España: En lucha por la tierra y la libertad* [Buenos Aires, 1937], pp. 27–28) to create a mythology to the contrary. On the rural vote during the elections see Juan J. Linz, "The Party System of Spain: Past and Future," *Party Systems and Voter Alignments,* ed. Seymour M. Lipset and Stein Rokkan (New York, 1967), pp. 231–36.

4. Although pre-1931 efforts to institute land redistribution helped create the impetus toward reform that the Republic inherited, they had so little influence on the specific policies adopted by the Republic that I have not concerned myself with them in the text. A brief discription is given instead in app. E.

5. The Socialists always claimed that it was they who caused the San Sebastian coalition to include agrarian reform in its program (e.g., *El Obrero de la Tierra,* 17 September 1932). Moreover, the Socialists published a fairly specific list of objectives within a few days after the proclamation of the Republic (*El Socialista,* 23 April 1931).

the Government, conscious of the conditions in which the immense mass of peasants lives, the neglect of the rural economy and the incongruence of rural rights and present legislation, adopts as a norm of policy the recognition that agrarian legislation should correspond to the social function of the land.[6]

The government did not make any specific decisions as to how to fulfill this commitment until the cabinet meeting of 21 April, when a compromise among the various parties was reached. The Socialists agreed to postpone measures affecting the heart of the agrarian problem, the redistribution of land, until the Constituent Cortes had been elected. Lands were not to be seized by decree because "the agrarian reform . . . must be made taking into account an infinite number of factors, with great serenity and assurance, with the help of the technical services that exist in Spain, and with the intervention of the Cortes." On the other hand the government agreed that partial measures to freeze the existing situation and prevent landowners from escaping the consequences of future agrarian legislation need not await parliamentary approval. Further, decrees were to be used to solve lesser rural social problems.[7]

The Provisional Government's Decrees

On the basis of this agreement to permit immediate partial reforms, a series of edicts was promulgated whose importance can scarcely be exaggerated. The initiative was taken by the Socialist cabinet ministers, especially Largo Caballero, the Minister of Labor. Alone among the San Sebastian parties, the Socialists had developed a specific agrarian program. They now proceeded to carry out part of this program by decree.

Of the six major groups of edicts that were enacted between 28 April and the opening of the Cortes on 14 July, two were primarily concerned with tenant farmers and the rest with field laborers. As one of its very first measures, the Provisional Government forbade the expulsion of small tenants, except for noncultivation or failure to pay rent. This was done to forestall a wholesale cancellation of leases by owners who rightly feared that the proposed agrarian reform would attack leased property with special severity. Tenants who voluntarily abandoned their leases were given the right to demand payment for any necessary improvements they had made on the farm.[8] Tenants and sharecroppers were further benefited

6. Translation of *The Times* (London), 16 April 1931.

7. *El Debate*, 22 April 1931. The press statement was issued by Fernando de los Ríos, the Socialist leader who often served as government spokesman on agrarian matters during the early months.

8. Ministry of Justice decree of 29 April 1931. The texts of most of the decrees

when the government permitted them to petition the local courts for reduction of their rents if these exceeded the assessed taxable income of the
farm or if the crop had been poor.[9]

The second group of measures on behalf of tenants was directed
against subleasing. When renting large properties, owners were to be
obliged to give preference to formally constituted workers' societies that
had registered with the government rather than to individual tenants. The
change was to take effect gradually as existing leases expired and would
not affect small plots personally cultivated by the tenants who leased
them.[10] Although the edict had the effect of benefiting Socialist rural
locals, it must not be dismissed as merely a piece of class legislation. The
idea of collective leasing as a remedy to the problem of subleasing had
been popular in Catholic circles since the trienio bolchevista. Indeed, the
principal Catholic newspaper welcomed the edict and urged its readers to
take advantage of its provisions.[11]

To benefit field hands, a decree of 1 July established an eight-hour
day for most agricultural tasks.[12] This constituted a de facto raise in
wages, since owners were now forced to grant overtime pay whenever
they required a longer workday, as they almost inevitably had to do during harvest. The Provisional Government also created agricultural "mixed
juries," whose chief function was to supervise the labor legislation of the
Republic and provide an institutional means for collective bargaining.
All serious labor disputes had to be submitted to the arbitration of these
boards, but their decisions were not binding: employers could refuse to
accept their findings, and unions were free to strike if they gave eight
days' notice once the dispute had been heard.[13] Nevertheless, because of
the supervisory and punitive faculties of the juries (they could levy fines
against infractions of general labor legislation or of local agreements that
had been accepted by both sides), their power was considerable.

---

mentioned in this section are conveniently collected in the *Manual de la reforma
agraria* (Madrid, 1932) prepared by the publishing house of El Consultor de los
Ayuntamientos y de los Juzgados Municipales.

9. Ministry of Justice decree of 11 July 1931.

10. Ministry of Labor decree of 19 May 1931; regulation of 8 July 1931.

11. *El Debate,* 23 April and 21 May 1931.

12. Ministry of Labor decree of 1 July 1931. An edict of 9 May 1931 had already extended the industrial accident law of the monarchy to agricultural workers.

13. Ministry of Labor decree of 7 May 1931. The obligatory arbitration of labor
disputes that threatened to erupt into strikes was not part of the original edict but
was added by a decree of 29 May. The juries were "mixed" in the sense that equal
numbers of owners' and workers' representatives were elected to them (thus leaving
the balance of power in the hands of their presidents and vice-presidents, who were
usually appointed by the government).

None of the measures described above was in itself particularly controversial. As mentioned, the collective lease decree was accepted by the Catholics and was in any case to begin to operate only as existing leases expired and as the state created credit facilities for the workers' societies. The edicts on behalf of small tenants put into effect principles that had long been accepted by social reformers of many different schools. The mixed juries were an application to agriculture of the institutional means for collective bargaining that Primo de Rivera had established for manufacturing industries. The eight-hour day and overtime pay were also already customary in industry and had the additional advantage of being sanctioned by such international bodies as the International Labor Organization. Only as time passed and the consequences of these measures became apparent—the thousands of petitions for rent reduction with which tenants flooded the courts,[14] the increased cost of agricultural production as wages soared, the bias of juries whose presidents and vice-presidents were usually appointed by the Socialist-controlled Ministry of Labor[15]— did they begin to be subject to widespread attacks.

The two remaining edicts were objects of greater controversy. The first of these, the *términos municipales* decree of 28 April, in effect established agricultural labor frontiers on the borders of each of the nine thousand municipalities in Spain. Farmers were obliged to hire workers who lived within the municipality; only when the supply of these was exhausted could outsiders be employed.[16] The decree was justified as necessary to combat unemployment and in fact partly fulfilled this purpose in the plains of Andalusia and Estremadura as the influx of migrant harvest labor from Portugal and Galicia was stopped. Yet it quickly became apparent that the decree created as many difficulties as it solved. The Galicians were, after all, Spaniards who were deprived of a traditional source of income. Workers in the small satellite villages that surrounded the larger townships were also cut off from their normal places of employment. Peasants in mountain villages who depended on seasonal work in the plains were similarly handicapped. Moreover, local workers tended to pervert the decree by stretching out tasks so as to ensure themselves longer periods of employment and by resisting the importation of skilled workers from other villages even when persons with the same skills were not

14. On the Ministry of Justice's efforts to clear the courts, see its decrees of 31 October, 13 November, 10 and 29 December 1931, and 26 March 1932.

15. According to Francisco Largo Caballero, *Discursos a los trabajadores* (Madrid, 1934), p. 37, 374 of the 473 jury presidents and vice-presidents had been appointed by the government as of 1933. Workers and owners had been able to agree on candidates in only 99 cases.

16. Ministry of Labor decree of 28 April 1931.

available locally. In almost every imaginable way, then, rural economic life was threatened with disruption by the attempt to make the labor supply conform to economically artificial municipal boundaries.

The *laboreo forzoso* decree of 7 May was even more controversial when it was first enacted. To prevent owners from sabotaging its agrarian program by withdrawing their lands from cultivation, the Provisional Government threatened that if they did not continue to farm according to the normal "uses and customs" of each region, their properties would be turned over to local workers' societies.[17] Because normal "uses and customs" could be so variously defined, the owners feared that the decree would be used to force them to open pasture lands to cultivation or, worse still, that it would become a means for the de facto seizure of all their lands. Nor were these fears unjustified at first: the decree initially entrusted its execution to municipal boards that were under great pressure from local labor organizations to extend its provisions as much as possible so as to provide employment for the workers.

Neither of these two decrees was applied in its original severity. The Provisional Government quickly made it clear that it intended the laboreo forzoso edict as a precautionary measure, not as the opening wedge for a general seizure of properties. The decree was to apply only to lands that had already been plowed, and its administration was placed in the hands of provincial boards of technicians less subject to local pressures.[18] As for the términos municipales edict, an endless series of executive orders and decrees strove to make it economically more rational by exempting certain occupational groups from its provisions and by creating intermunicipal units that would permit workers in the small satellite village access to their usual places of employment.[19]

Yet neither of the two measures was repealed. The laboreo forzoso decree as a precautionary measure appears to have been accepted by all parties in the San Sebastian coalition. The términos municipales edict, on the other hand, was a special concession to the Socialists. By making employers dependent on a more limited labor supply, it indirectly helped to raise rural wages. More important, however, was the fact that under

17. Ministry of National Economy decree of 7 May 1931.

18. Ministry of National Economy order of 12 May 1931 and decree of 10 July 1931. As an example of the continuous readjustments necessary to maintain the efficacy of the decree without placing excessive pressure on the owners, the *Manual de la reforma agraria* reprints eight other measures on laboreo forzoso between 12 August 1931 and 19 August 1932.

19. The *Manual de la reforma agraria* reprints nine measures, most of them concerned with more than one occupational group, which tried to adjust the términos municipales edict to economic realities. Several dozen intermunicipal units were also created in 1931.

the "right to work" principles of the monarchy, few agricultural unions were secure because their strike power could always be broken by mass importations of unorganized migrant laborers. The labor frontiers established by the decree of 28 April removed this weapon from the hands of the owners and provided the Socialists with the indispensable basis on which they were to build their vast network of rural locals during the first year of the Republic.[20]

In their totality the agrarian decrees of the Provisional Government constituted a revolution without precedent in Spanish rural life. For the first time the balance of legal rights swung away from the landowners to the rural proletariat. The range of the decrees and the rapidity with which they were promulgated are breathtaking in retrospect. New conditions had been created in the countryside long before an agrarian reform bill reached the Cortes for discussion. And since the Cortes, after it convened, translated into law all of the decrees except those governing leases, the benefits of this agricultural revolution seemed assured of permanence.[21]

A price had to be paid for these improvements, however. In the case of the términos municipales edicts the costs were direct: the decree created an exceedingly cumbersome framework for economic life and never succeeded in resolving the problem of the hundreds of thousands of peasants in mountain villages who had been cut off from seasonal employment in the plains.[22] As for other measures, nearly all had the effect of raising the expectations of the peasantry beyond the capacity of the state or of the economy to satisfy them. Thus the tenants whose suits for rent reductions could not be heard by the overcrowded courts began to withold payments without legal sanction. Most local unions refused to accept the limited definition given to the laboreo forzoso decree and instead invoked it to justify the invasion of unplowed pastures. The establishment of the mixed juries and of the eight-hour day meant only that wages would be higher *when work could be found*, not that the field hands had been assured of steady employment. This last problem in par-

20. The membership of the FNTT, the Socialist peasant federation, rose from 36,639 in June 1930 to 392,953 in June 1932. For further details, see below, p. 292.

21. Most of the decrees were ratified as laws on 9 September 1931. The edicts affecting tenants were supposed to be incorporated into a general lease law, but this law was not enacted until 1935—and then under much more conservative auspices.

22. That workers in satellite villages cut off from employment in near-by large townships also suffered great hardships is indicated by the fact that two years later the Ministry of Labor was still engaged in the creation of economically more realistic intermunicipal units. According to IRA, *Ley de bases y disposiciones complementarias que afectan a las juntas provinciales* (Madrid, 1933), pp. 315–23, twenty-nine such units had to be created in the first six months of 1933.

ticular should be stressed. Although almost all of the decrees and much
of the future agrarian legislation of the Republic were justified as measures against unemployment, no solution was ever found to the unemployment inherent in Spanish rural society and aggravated by the effects of
the world depression. The traditional *alojamiento* system was in some
municipalities replaced by a special local tax whose proceeds were to be
used to feed the unemployed.[23] Special subsidies were also given to the
villages for distribution among the jobless.[24] A massive three-year public
works project was announced for Andalusia and Estremadura.[25] But the
resources of the state were so limited in comparison to the magnitude of
the problem—particularly as both Republicans and Socialists were still
bound by doctrines of fiscal orthodoxy that prevented them from acting
energetically in some spheres—that there could be no direct and continuous subsidies to the unemployed.[26]

There were also costs of another nature. The opposition to the decrees
among the landowners themselves was to have been expected and need
not concern us here. More important was the fact that the Catholic press,
which at first had been friendly toward the Republic and had even favored some of the lesser agrarian edicts, also joined in the protest. The
honeymoon period, during which most major political factions greeted the
Republic warmly, ended definitively when the urban riots and church
burnings of 10–12 May revealed anew the deep cleavages in Spanish society which the nearly universal disrespect for Alfonso had tended to obscure. But its termination had already been forecast by the opposition to
the agrarian decrees. Two days before the riots occurred both *El Debate*,
the Catholic organ, and *La Época,* a conservative journal, attacked the
laboreo forzoso decree as a "Draconian measure without parallel in Europe." [27]

23. Ministry of Labor decree of 18 July 1931.

24. Ministry of Finance decrees of 4 and 6 May and 18 June 1931.

25. Under the project 337 million pesetas was to be spent between 1931 and
1934, mostly (85.8%) for road repairs and construction. The project was never fully
implemented, however, and of the money actually disbursed, irrigation works received
a far greater share than had originally been planned. An immediate 10-million-
peseta grant was also distributed (*El Sol,* 29, 30 July 1931).

26. The fiscal orthodoxy of the Provisional Government—so contradictory to its
daring social legislation—is revealed in the preamble to the decree creating the
Caja Nacional Contra el Paro Forzoso, the only institution directly charged wi h
alleviating unemployment: "It is society in general and each profession in particular
which should create institutions to facilitate employment and meanwhile give unemployment subsidies. To the state corresponds the function of stimulating the
establishment of such institutions and of augmenting the means at their disposal"
(Ministry of Labor decree of 25 May 1931).

27. *El Debate,* 8 May 1931, and *La Época,* 9 May 1931.

Initial Conflict over the Agrarian Reform

If the agrarian decrees had aroused opposition among the conservative groups who had acquiesced to the establishment of the Republic, they had been enacted without serious conflict within the Provisional Government. The euphoric mood of the San Sebastian parties at finding themselves in power, their preoccupation with the myriad problems of creating a new regime, their unawareness of the full consequences of the edicts, as well as the willingness of the Socialists to accept modifications in the two most controversial measures, help explain this remarkable fact. The coalition would not, however, be able to maintain its unity in the face of the strains created by the results of the Cortes elections of 28 June or those that arose once discussion began on the actual redistribution of land.

The elections for the Constituent Cortes had two principal effects. On the one hand, because the elections were held while the Republic was in its first flush of glory and its opponents were so disunited as to be unable to agree even on whether they should participate in the balloting, the Republicans gained a far larger popular vote than they would have received had times been normal. The size of the Republican majority in the Cortes was exaggerated still further by the operation of the new electoral law, which rewarded winning coalitions with approximately 75 percent of the seats in each province or urban electoral district, no matter how small their plurality had been.[28] These facts, together with the continued refusal of the Anarchosyndicalists to present candidates, resulted in a parliament that was unrepresentative of the nation both on the Right and on the extreme Left. Except for the twenty-four-man Agrarian minority, which based itself on the small peasant proprietors of Old Castile, and the thirteen-man Basque Autonomist party, there were no conservative factions of importance in the Cortes.[29] As for the Anarchosyndicalists, their views were advocated only by a handful of bourgeois extremists who had broken off from the Radical Socialists.

Although the unrepresentative nature of the Cortes was ultimately to have grave consequences, the impact of the elections on the distribution of power within the San Sebastian coalition was of more immediate import. Having helped secure the acquiescence of enlightened conservatism to the establishment of the Republic, Alcalá Zamora and Maura were dis-

28. The electoral law is best explained by Linz, "The Party System of Spain," *Party Systems and Voter Alignments*, pp. 238–39.

29. The then very small Catalan Lliga, and a handful of independent conservatives increased the total rightist strength to about 10 percent of the 470 Cortes deputies.

illusioned in their hope that this segment of opinion would thereupon organize itself into parties and exert a continuous influence on Spanish political life. The tensions that had arisen since April, the inability of conservatives to agree on a leader or cause, the discouragement engendered by the new electoral law, together with the basically contradictory and exaggerated premises from which Alcalá Zamora and Maura operated, explain this failure. The Progressive party itself remained small, and no new groups with which it might ally arose to its right. In consequence power within the coalition shifted to the left.[30] That this was not reflected by an immediate redistribution of ministerial posts was due to the fact that the two groups that had benefited most from the elections—the Socialists and the Radicals—were antagonistic to each other. Until such time as one or the other could ally itself to the small Left Republican factions that collectively held the balance of power, Alcalá Zamora and Maura retained their positions and the distribution of office within the Provisional Government (which now reconstituted itself as the first regularly appointed government of the Republic) remained unaltered.

The agrarian question was to play an important part in the resolution of this latent conflict within the coalition. On the surface all factions were united in emphasizing the urgency of a sweeping reform, particularly since the Andalusian peasantry was finally showing signs of a return to its revolutionary past.[31] The basically rhetorical nature of many of the commitments—and the confusions and contradictions that characterized the rest—began to be revealed after 20 July, when the Technical Commission established in May to draft agrarian legislation for the consideration of the Cortes submitted its proposal.

The Technical Commission—headed by the jurist Felipe Sánchez Román and deepily influenced by Pascual Carrión and Ricardo Flórez de Lemus, an agronomist and an economist, respectively, who had been closely associated with the pre-Republican movement for reform—took the rhetoric of the political leaders to heart. The logic of the proposal it submitted was extremely simple. The rapid settlement of landless peasants

30. The distribution of Cortes seats within the San Sebastian coalition was approximately as follows:

Socialists	117	Republican Action	26
Radicals	93	Progressives	18
Radical Socialists	59	ORGA	16
Esquerra	32		

31. For the increased agitation of the Andalusian peasantry, see below, chap. 11. As to the rhetoric of the political leaders, even so relatively conservative a person as Maura was calling for agrarian reform "within a matter of months, or if possible, weeks." (*El Sol*, 16 June 1931).

could be achieved only if the state abjured all unnecessary expenditures and all possible legal complications while concentrating its energies on Southern Spain, where the maldistribution of property had its worst social consequences. The way in which these seemingly unexceptional principles were to be translated into action surprised many of the political factions, however.

There was to be no expropriation of property as such, at least not in the immediate future. To expropriate, the approval of the Cortes was necessary, and peasant settlement would consequently be delayed. More important, if the state expropriated it would have to pay compensation, thus diverting financial resources that might more productively be used to supply the settlers with the animals, tools, and credit they would need to begin cultivation. Instead of expropriation there was to be a "temporary occupation" of those portions of the large estates in Southern Spain which surpassed certain size limits. Since these temporary occupations were to be of unspecified duration, they in effect resurrected the obligatory leases that had formed the heart of the agrarian proposals of the ministers of Charles III in the late eighteenth century. The land was to remain the property of its owners, but only in the flexible medieval sense of that word, not in the rigidly exclusive sense adopted by nineteenth-century liberalism. The proprietary interest of the owners was to be recognized in that they would receive modest rents from the new settlers. But the settlers were to be given the same permanent use of the land which the medieval peasant had enjoyed.[32]

Settlements were to take place either individually or collectively. If the farm occupied was already leased to small tenants, they were to remain as its permanent settlers. Otherwise the land was to be delivered to "Peasant Communities" whose members were to decide by majority vote whether to till it collectively, or individually on a cooperative basis. The state was thus to be relieved of the responsibility for deciding this politically controversial issue. The Communities themselves were also intended to be nonpolitical. All three principal authors of the Commission's proposal were bourgeois experts who favored the Communities not for ideo-

32. For the medieval distinction between the *dominio eminente*, which would continue to be enjoyed by the owners, and the *dominio útil*, which would pass to the settlers, see p. 58, n. 40. The agrarian program of Charles III is briefly described in app. E. I may be overstressing the similarities between temporary occupations and these ancient practices, since the Commission did not debar the possibility of future expropriation in favor of the state. By minimizing the importance of expropriation so long as the settlers were given effective control of the land, however, the Commission was clearly "reviving principles which have slept the sleep of centuries," as Alcalá Zamora was later to say in a somewhat different context (*El Sol*, 26 August 1931).

logical reasons, but solely as a necessary technical solution to the problem of the inability of inexperienced individual settlers to manage their lands unaided.

The Technical Commission set as its goal the settlement of from 60,-000 to 75,000 peasant families annually, expecting that at this pace the reform could be completed within twelve to fifteen years. Even without paying compensation (since there would be no expropriation), the state would have to expend some 200 to 250 million pesetas annually, or about 7 percent of the national budget at the time, to finance so rapid a settlement.[33] The funds necessary were to be secured in part by the imposition of a special graduated surtax on large properties, thus forcing the latifundios to help pay for their own liquidation. At the same time, since the surtax applied to northern and central Spain as well as to the South, it would permit an indirect extension of the reform even to those regions in which the state would not undertake peasant settlements. By making large property expensive to maintain everywhere, the surtax would cause large owners voluntarily to divest themselves of some of their holdings.

One other feature must be mentioned. The Technical Commission's proposal was to affect only especially large owners and to strike at each of these with equal force. The sole criteria by which the lands to be temporarily occupied in Southern Spain were to be determined were the size, wealth, and arability of their owners' total holdings throughout the nation. No differentiation was to be made between nobles and nonnobles or between absentees and "direct cultivators." If a person held the equivalent of 300 hectares of grain lands throughout Spain, or if he possessed smaller properties that nevertheless produced more than 10,000 pesetas assessed taxable income, the excess portions of his properties were to be seized so long as they were capable of sustaining permanent cultivation. Even simpler criteria were established for the application of the graduated surtax. All owners whose assessed taxable income exceeded 10,000 pesetas would pay this special tax, even if their holdings were nonarable pasture or forest exempted from the temporary occupations.[34]

To complete the program, the chairman of the Technical Commission recommended that it be put into effect immediately by decree and only later be submitted for Cortes approval. Sánchez Román rightly feared that Cortes debate would delay the reform and weaken the principles which underlay it.

33. The Commission estimated that it would cost from three to four thousand pesetas to help establish each new settler (private notes of Pascual Carrión). Most other estimates, both of the Right and Left, came to similar conclusions.

34. The text of the Technical Commission's draft can be found in Carrión, pp. 421–32, and in the daily press of 21 and 22 July 1931. In interpreting the bill I have relied heavily on Carrión's private notes.

The Republic, which had often posed as a revolutionary regime, now had at its disposal a revolutionary measure by which it might have proceeded rapidly to a redistribution of property. The Commission's program was technically excellent: it provided simple, direct, and efficient instruments of reform and had the added advantage of affecting only a few thousand of the very largest landowners in Spain. Moreover, since the proposal was presented as an emergency measure against rural unemployment, it carried its own justification. But the Commission did not represent any political party: its views were only those of a handful of individuals who had misunderstood the mood of the government and had had, moreover, the temerity to resurrect the specter of reform by decree. As a result the proposal was completely defenseless against the storm of protest that arose.

The landowners themselves were, not surprisingly, terrified. A new agricultural pressure group, the Agrupación Nacional de Propietarios de Fincas Rústicas, was rapidly created to fight the measure.[35] The Agrarian parliamentary minority introduced a tactic that it was to use repeatedly in the future as it called for the immediate convocation in Madrid of a "Great Assembly" of landowners to intimidate the government into rejecting the proposal.[36] The conservative and Catholic press published excited editorials that objected to almost every feature of the draft. The decision to occupy portions of all large farms, not only of those that were "misused," was especially controverted.[37]

The protest within the San Sebastian coalition was nearly as great. The Radical party bitterly rejected the measure, attributing its "primitiveness" and "absurdness" to the "frivolity" and "bad faith" with which it had been drafted.[38] The Progressive leaders, Alcalá Zamora and Maura, also found the measure much too drastic.[39] The most influential liberal journal, El Sol, criticized the proposal for setting impossibly high goals.[40] The Socialist party also joined in the attack, though for quite different reasons, which will be examined shortly. Faced with so united an opposition, the few Left Republican leaders and journals who at first had mildly sup-

35. For the Agrupación's objections to the Commission's draft, see its hurriedly printed pamphlet, *Informe sobre el proyecto de ley de reforma agraria* (Madrid, 1931).

36. *El Debate* and *El Sol*, 22 July 1931.

37. See the editorials in *El Debate*, 21, 23, 24 July and 6 August 1931.

38. Statement of Diego Hidalgo, the Radical party spokesman on agrarian affairs, in *El Sol*, 21 August 1931.

39. Alcalá Zamora immediately convened the cabinet and spent almost two hours grilling the Technical Commission leaders on their proposal (*El Sol*, 24 July 1931).

40. Editorials of 26 July and 11 August 1931.

ported the measure quickly abandoned it.[41] Within a week of its publication, the Technical Commission's draft was utterly routed. The tactical errors committed by Sánchez Román, Flórez de Lemus, and Carrión undoubtedly contributed to the hostility with which their proposal was greeted.[42] But the fundamental cause for the rejection was that their program was too radical for most of the San Sebastian parties.

In the crisis that had arisen, Alcalá Zamora took command. Under his guidance the cabinet rejected direct intimidation and prohibited the "Great Assembly" of proprietors. But at the same time it granted the burden of the proposed assembly's demands by promising that the proposal would not be enacted by decree.[43] During the weeks that followed, three cabinet meetings were held to determine the fate of the rest of the measure. It was finally agreed to abandon the Technical Commission's draft completely and make a fresh start by appointing a ministerial committee, headed by Alcalá Zamora himself, to draw up a new bill.[44]

We do not know for certain what arguments Alcalá Zamora used to convince his colleagues. There is no evidence that anyone feared an immediate military uprising if the Technical Commission's draft were approved. The government may have doubted its ability to control the

41. Azaña was the only major republican leader I could find who supported the proposal (in a speech of 17 July 1931 reprinted in Manual Azaña, *Una Política: 1930–1932* Madrid, 1932, pp. 38–39. Since he spoke before the draft was publicly released, however, it is possible that he did not know its full provisions). Among Left Republican journals, *El Crisol*, 11 August 1931, alone gave support. On the other hand, the Radical Socialist parliamentary delegation expressed reservations from the start (El Sol, 22 July 1931). Incidentally, my practice of capitalizing the term "Left Republican" is not, strictly speaking, correct since no party of this name was founded until 1936. To follow any other practice, however, would involve us in endless pedantries that would only serve to complicate the text.

42. Having deeply offended the Socialists by shunting aside their suggestions for reform, the three leading figures of the Technical Commission apparently constituted themselves into an ad hoc committee that pushed ahead with its proposal despite the opposition of most of the other Commission members. These cavalier tactics did not detract from the merits of the program presented, but they did prove politically costly. For criticisms of the way in which the Commission was run, see *El Socialista*, 6 August 1931; *El Sol*, 11 August 1931; and FNTT, *Memoria que presenta el Comité Nacional al Congreso ordinario que ha de celebrarse en septiembre de 1932* (Madrid, 1932), pp. 251, 261–63. One Socialist leader later suggested that some of the disagreements might have been worked out had the program not been prematurely leaked to the press (UGT, *Boletín*, June 1932, p. 122).

43. *El Debate*, 23 July 1931. For other assurances of Alcalá Zamora to the landowners, see *El Debate*, 7, 9, 11 August 1931. The Catholic journal actively encouraged the prime minister in his new role, converting him once more into the moderating hero many conservatives had expected him to be when the Republic was first established.

44. *El Debate* and *El Sol*, 24 July; 6, 11 August 1931.

peasants, however, for the proposal had been released in the midst of the Anarchosyndicalist general strike in Seville, when many persons desperately feared that the rural masses would rise in support of the urban workers.[45] The strongest likelihood is that the prime minister centered his case around the danger that a radical reform would set off the long-threatened landowners' revolt. If large owners were attacked indiscriminately, and if they were not assured of compensation at least for those labors they had completed at the time their farms were seized, how could they be expected to sow the winter crops that would have to be planted within the next three months? Since the state itself lacked the resources to take over all large properties immediately, economic disaster would follow unless the owners were given greater security and guarantees that any new investments they might make in the land would not be lost.[46]

Although his objections were extremely well founded, Alcalá Zamora's views could not have triumphed so easily as they did had he not received the active support of the Socialists. The PSOE-UGT had rejected the Technical Commission's proposal as not sufficiently radical and had called instead for a higher surtax, the inclusion of more land, and the settlement of a greater number of peasants (150,000 during the first year and a minimum of 100,000 annually thereafter).[47] Yet they followed this strong stand by cooperation with the most conservative segment of the San Sebastian coalition to sponsor a much more limited measure.

The reason for this contradictory stance of the Socialists would seem to lie in their fear that the Radicals were winning the struggle for the allegiance of the Left Republican factions.[48] If they were right, then

45. For the Seville troubles of July 1931 and the sense of public panic that accompanied them, see below, pp. 296, 298–99.

46. For the cabinet's fears that the owners would not sow, see *El Sol* 11, 12, 30 August; 2 September; 4 October 1931. Alcalá Zamora himself stressed the need to give the owners guarantees against arbitrary seizures in his Cortes speech of 25 August and in his interview with *El Sol*, 26 August 1931.

47. *El Socialista*, 22, 23 July 1931.

48. Thus *El Socialista*, 23 July 1931, after speaking of the Technical Commission's provision that the cabinet might in the future extend the reform outside Southern Spain, commented: "Wait and see how the genuinely bourgeois and reactionary governments that the cunning Lerroux-Azaña partnership is about to bring us will use these facilities for expanding social justice. It did not take long for the bellicose Minister of War [Azaña] to be won over to the spiritual rancidness of his new chief. Recently he gave a speech of muffled reactionary tones on the religious question, for him nonexistent, and . . . on the Catalanist myth, for him a living issue now that the very workers of Catalonia have rejected it." This was said of a man who within three months emerged as Lerroux's chief enemy, the Socialists' closest ally, and Spain's leading anticlerical. The reference to the "Catalanist myth"

the occupations authorized by the Technical Commission's draft might indeed turn out to be "temporary" as a new, implicitly anti-Socialist government ousted whatever peasants had been settled. Only by actually expropriating the land could this danger be avoided.[49] The Socialists' continued insecurity in the new regime led them to discount the probability—so feared by the landowners themselves—that the very "vagueness" of the Commission's proposal would result in a permanent occupation of large properties, because the peasants, once settled on the land, would prove extremely difficult to dislodge. Instead the PSOE-UGT accepted a much more moderate program in the vain hope that its less ambiguous legal foundations would prove unalterable. The potentially most revolutionary proposal produced by the Republic prior to 1936 was discarded mostly because the bourgeois Republicans would not accept the enormous political risks it entailed, but its demise was facilitated by the blindness of the Socialists to its revolutionary possibilities.

Assured of Socialist support,[50] Alcalá Zamora personally presented his new draft to the Cortes on 25 August. He was so confident of quick approval that he simultaneously created local and provincial juntas to collect data and administer the reform as soon as it went into effect. Alcalá Zamora's proposal retained the graduated surtax and reaffirmed the goal of settling 60,000 to 75,000 peasants annually. In every other way, however, the Technical Commission's program was significantly modified.

The Technical Commission had wanted to attack all large properties equally on the basis of their size and wealth. Alcalá Zamora restricted the reform to three types of land: those that lay in irrigation zones but had not been irrigated, those that were continuously leased, and noble properties of "feudal" origin. Owners who "directly cultivated" their lands according to "good use and custom" were specifically excluded from the reform. The full effect of this exemption can be understood only if it is remembered that in Spanish legal parlance "direct" cultivation usually does not mean personal cultivation of the kind that a small peasant proprietor gives to his lands. Any owner who takes some part in farm management or invests some capital is normally considered a direct cultivator, even though his contribution may be small. Consequently Alcalá Zamora ex-

---

revealed the continued antipathy of the Socialists toward regional autonomy, which in fact *was* supported by most non-Socialist Catalan workers.

49. For Socialist insistence on expropriation and their protests against the "vagueness" of temporary occupations, see the dissenting opinion they presented to the Technical Commission's draft in FNTT, *Memoria,* pp. 260–62.

50. Both Largo Caballero and Fernando de los Ríos cosponsored Alcalá Zamora's bill. Although the former may have acted only by virtue of his office as Minister of Labor, de los Ríos took an active part in the drafting of the measure and was profusely thanked by the prime minister in his Cortes speech.

cluded not only those owners who ran their own farms through hired labor but also those who depended on estate managers and those who provided their sharecroppers with some of the tools, animals, or seeds they required.

There was one potential exception to this exemption. In the speech that accompanied his proposal, Alcalá Zamora seemed to be inviting the Cortes to expand the expropriation provisions to include direct cultivators who by themselves or with their immediate families held so much (20%) of a given township that they might be said to dominate personally its economic life.[51] Since this attack on economic *caciquismo* would scarcely affect the larger Southern municipalities, however, and since the Cortes itself would have to put it into operation, the fact remained that Alcalá Zamora's impassioned rhetoric against certain scapegoats—the nobility and the absentees who leased—disguised his willingness to exempt most large properties from the reform.

Since expropriation had been decided upon, the fatal question of compensation arose. Here, too, Alcalá Zamora reversed the main thrust of the Technical Commission's attack but at the same time offered one class of sacrificial victims—the nobility—on the altar of Republican radicalism. A fair market price for land in 1931 might be considered equivalent to approximately thirty times its taxable income.[52] Nobles were to receive only ten to twenty times this sum, depending on their total income. By contrast, nonnoble victims of the reform would be paid full market value. They would receive thirty-three times the taxable income of their estates, whatever their total income might be. There was also some discrimination in the way in which the compensation would actually be paid. All owners expropriated would be paid mostly in cash, since payment by means of bonds was to begin only when the indemnification exceeded the very considerable sum of 500,000 pesetas. But whereas these bonds would be nonnegotiable for only five to ten years in the case of bourgeois owners, the nobility could not dispose of them for ten to twenty years.[53]

If Alcalá Zamora's proposal was far more moderate than that of the Technical Commission, it by no means completely destroyed the possibil-

51. It is difficult to decide what Alcalá Zamora's intentions were here. His bill mentioned only those economic caciques who fell into one of the other categories of expropriation, but the violent attacks in his speech against the "dominators" of village life seemed to include direct cultivators as well.

52. This estimate is based on the assumption that a fair market price is equivalent to ten times the real net income of a farm and that in 1931 the assessed taxable income of land was no more than one-third of its real net income.

53. The text of Alcalá Zamora's draft appears in *D.S.* 26, 25 August 1931, app. 9. His important speech presenting the measure is given in ibid., pp. 572–77, and in the daily press of 26 August 1931.

ity for significant reform. As will be remembered from Chapter 3, the nobility and the absentees who leased held between them considerable quantities of land. A lesser amount was also to be made available by owners in irrigation zones who did not irrigate. The Cortes might open still more territory to settlement by giving a strict interpretation to the "good use and custom" clause and by acting upon Alcalá Zamora's apparent willingness to allow expropriation of direct cultivators who could be considered economic caciques. Moreover, if the prime minister had reduced the amount of land available for the reform, he had not moderated the indirect attack on large property which the Technical Commission had hoped to stage through its graduated surtax. Since this tax continued to apply to nonnoble direct cultivators, large estates of all kinds would gradually have been eroded over the course of time.

Alcalá Zamora's program also had two positive advantages. By focusing its attack against the nobility, the absentees, and the caciques, his bill appealed to the lowest common denominator of radicalism among the San Sebastian parties. Even the most timorous among the Republican factions could rally to the cause as it was now defined. Equally important, Alcalá Zamora's proposal provided a basis on which the acquiescence to agrarian reform of the Catholics and conservatives might have been secured.

In contrast to the reception it accorded the Technical Commission's report, the moderate-conservative press greeted the new draft with such warmth that a return to the honeymoon period of the first month of the Republic seemed in the offing. *El Debate*, the Catholic organ, recovered its enthusiasm for change as it told its readers: "Government precautions and a strengthening of the Guardia Civil are not enough to defend public order. Reforms are necessary [and these] cannot be achieved in any way other than that which the government proposes: by seizing lands, legally expropriating them, turning them over to the workers, and giving [the settlers] the means by which to cultivate them." The government must even be allowed "exceptional powers" in carrying out this "necessary and urgent" task. *El Debate* concluded: "We who more than once counseled Primo de Rivera to use his extraordinary powers to undertake this reform cannot now place obstacles in the path of the Republican government." [54]

To be sure, the Alcalá Zamora draft was in some ways still too advanced for the Catholics and conservatives. They considered both the surtax and the compensation provisions for feudal lands discriminatory. They felt that no distinction should be made between feudal and nonfeudal lands and that a tax on all incomes, rather than just on agricultural in-

54. *El Debate*, 27 August 1931.

comes, should be established to finance the reform.[55] Equally important, they thought the goal of settling 60,000 to 75,000 peasants annually should be abandoned, since it was manifestly impossible to achieve if compensation were to be paid. *El Debate* estimated that under the compensation provisions at least one thousand pesetas would be paid for each hectare of expropriated land. If each settler was to receive 10 hectares, 750,000 hectares would have to be expropriated and 750 million pesetas paid to former owners every year. Because the state would also have to help the settlers get established, the total annual expenditure on the reform would exceed one billion pesetas. Since the annual national budget was only 4 billion pesetas, the state could not settle the envisaged number of peasants and still pay compensation.[56] Either the rate of settlement or the rate of compensation would have to decrease. For *El Debate* the solution to this dilemma was to reduce the rate of settlement. Had there not been a sudden shift in the temporary balance of forces within the San Sebastian coalition which had given birth to the Alcalá Zamora proposal, the Constituent Cortes might possibly have agreed.

The parliamentary revolt against the prime minister had two principal origins. The Socialists' collaboration with Alcalá Zamora was so contradictory to their most fundamental aspirations that it could not long be maintained. The Socialist parliamentary delegation seems to have been more aware of this fact than either Fernando de los Ríos, who cooperated in drafting the new agrarian bill, or the editors of *El Socialista*, who initially accepted the proposal without protest.[57] Evidence of pressure from the ranks began to appear as individual deputies called for more drastic action and as the PSOE Cortes delegation met with de los Ríos on three separate occasions within two weeks to discuss the new measure.[58] The extent of the contradiction became still more apparent as parliamentary debate opened on Article 42 of the draft constitution. At precisely the same time as the Socialist cabinet ministers were accepting Alcalá Zamora's defense of direct cultivators, the Socialist-led Constitutional Commission was emphasizing not the inviolability of property but its social function. Article 42 read: "The state, which presently recognizes private property in direct relation to the useful function which its owner fulfills through it, will proceed in a gradual way toward its socialization." No

55. Ibid., 29 August 1931.
56. Ibid., 12, 15 September 1931. Martínez de Velasco, head of the Agrarian minority, raised the same objections in stronger form in an interview with *El Sol*, 5 September 1931.
57. Editorials of 26 and 27 August 1931.
58. *El Sol*, 3, 5, 12 September 1931. At one of the meetings Prieto and Largo Caballero, who had not cooperated so actively as de los Ríos on the proposal but who presumably had voted for it in the cabinet, were also present.

qualifications or limitations were stated. Indeed, although the Article gave the usual assurances that "the penalty of confiscation of goods will not be imposed," it went on to say that "where social necessity requires, the Cortes can establish expropriation without indemnification." [59]

The other indispensable element in the political transformation that now began to occur was the rapprochement between the Socialists and the various Left Republican parties. That this had taken so long to establish was due primarily to the Socialist fear that the Left Republicans would betray them in favor of Lerroux and to the PSOE's reluctance to admit regional autonomy. Now they began to realize that Azaña by no means shared the "spiritual rancidness" of the Radical chief, and, after considerable inner struggle, they accepted the aspirations of the Catalans. The specific bases for the reconciliation were laid during the month of September. On 14 September Azaña joined the Socialists in demanding that the Constituent Cortes continue in session after the Constitution had been approved so that the future government might have a "frankly leftist" orientation.[60] The refusal of the Left Republicans to join the Progressive and Radical parties' attack on Article 42 and on the passage in the constitutional draft which defined the new regime as a "Republic of workers" was also important.[61] Another major step was taken during the week of 23 to 28 September when the Socialists finally reconciled themselves to Catalan autonomy.[62] The increasing cooperation between the bourgeois and working-class Left became still more evident during the first days of October, when they joined together to demand the abolition of the priv-

59. The text of the Article appears in *El Sol*, 14 August 1931; parliamentary debate began on 27 August, two days after the Alcalá Zamora proposal was presented. The Socialist chairman of the Constitutional Commission was Luís Jiménez de Asúa, who later expressed his amazement at the ease with which the Commission accepted without modification Marxist formulations (Carr, p. 605).

60. For the first flurries of the struggle over whether the Constituent Cortes should be dissolved and new elections held after the Constitution had been approved (as the Republican Right, which had done badly in the June elections, desired), see *El Sol*, 8, 9, 12, 15 September 1931. The Socialists, who could scarcely hope to improve their parliamentary position, adamantly refused to accept dissolution and warmly welcomed Azaña's support on this issue.

61. For these conflicts, see the daily press from 28 August to 8 October 1931. In the article on property the demand for the "gradual socialization" of property was finally dropped in favor of the much more innocuous formula that property was "subordinated to the interests of the national economy." The ideological connotations of the definition of the new regime as a "Republic of Workers" were softened by adding the phrase "of all classes."

62. *El Sol*, 24–29 September 1931. Ironically, it was Alcalá Zamora who resolved the Cortes conflict over whether the principle of Catalan autonomy should be stated in the Constitution, whereas the Socialists resisted almost to the bitter end.

ileges of the Church and when Alcalá Zamora's agrarian bill was reported out of the parliamentary committee to which it had been submitted.

The Cortes Committee on Agriculture drastically altered the Alcalá Zamora draft and recommended a program almost as sweeping as that of the Technical Commission. The exemption of directly cultivated lands was abolished, although the moderates retained enough power in the Commission to prevent such farms from being listed in the order of preference which was established for expropriation.[63] No longer were all lands cultivated according to "good use and custom" to be exempt; an owner would have to prove that his property was a "model farm" in order to escape expropriation. The compensation provisions were also severely revised. Most owners would receive not thirty-three but from ten to seventeen times the taxable income of the lands seized. In addition, compensation was not to be granted mostly in cash and partly in regular state bonds as under the previous proposal. Rather, the entire indemnification was to be paid in a new issue of nonnegotiable securities, whose earnings, moreover, were to be subject to the special surtax on agrarian property inherited from the Technical Commission and Alcalá Zamora drafts.

The nobility was singled out for even harsher treatment. Alcalá Zamora had suggested discriminatory treatment only of their "feudal" lands—by which he seemed to mean the lands over which they had held solely jurisdictional rights (señorío jurisdiccional) prior to 1811 but had nevertheless usurped as private property after the Cortes of Cadiz abolished private jurisdictions. His justification was that these lands did not constitute legitimate property.[64] The Cortes Commission draft expanded Alcalá Zamora's attack to include practically all inherited noble properties which dated back to the time when the Property Registers were founded in the 1840s, thus affecting lands acquired during the early phases of the desamortización as well as señorío jurisdiccional properties. Moreover, many of these lands were now to be expropriated without compensation, except insofar as their owner could prove he had made permanent improvements on them. For the first time in modern Spanish history the penalty of confiscation of property was recommended in an agrarian reform measure.[65]

63. The ambiguity in the draft can be seen by comparing its Articles 7, 9, and 24. On balance, it is clear that directly cultivated lands were to be seized, and the draft was opposed by the conservative press on these grounds.

64. For the differences between jurisdictional and property rights, see above, pp. 59–60.

65. The text of the draft appears in *D.S.* 51, 7 October 1931, app. 2, and in the daily press of 8 October. The señorío jurisdiccional lands of the nobility were to be confiscated if an owner held more than three hundred hectares throughout Spain; the

The Agricultural Committee's revisions amounted to a total rejection of the Alcalá Zamora proposal. The new draft had been forced through by the Left Republican and Socialist representatives over the strong opposition of the Committee chairman and some of its most prominent members.[66] As in the Constitutional Committee and in the Cortes itself, the changes wrought by the June elections in the balance of power within the San Sebastian coalition finally took effect as the Left Republican parties began to cooperate among themselves and established ties with the Socialists.

Alcalá Zamora suddenly found himself isolated on all fronts. His first threat to resign, on 6 October, was precipitated by the continued debates on the constitutional article that concerned property rights, though his knowledge of the direct rebuff about to be administered to his agrarian bill may also have played a part.[67] One week later, on 14 October, after the revisions of his agrarian bill were formally announced and after the Cortes voted for the disestablishment of the Church, together with the expulsion of the Jesuits and the nationalization of their property, Alcalá Zamora made his resignation final. The withdrawal of the Progressive leader removed from the scene the figure most responsible for gaining the acquiescence of the established classes to the Republic and marked the first open split in the San Sebastian coalition.

If the religious issue was both the immediate and the most important cause for Alcalá Zamora's resignation, the property question—which most writers have failed to stress—was also fundamental. Even had the disestablishment of the Church not been approved, it is difficult to see how the prime minister could have stayed in office after the agrarian program to which he had committed himself so completely had been rejected. The religious issue provided him with a popular cause by which to extricate himself from a generally intolerable situation, but the seeds of conflict had already been sown by the struggle over agrarian reform.

Property Registry lands, if their owner possessed more than one thousand hectares in any given province.

66. The Left Republicans and Socialists held twelve of the twenty-one seats in the Committee. The chairman was Juan Díaz del Moral, author of the famous treatise on rural anarchism.

67. The Committee's drastic revisions of the Alcalá Zamora draft were public knowledge as early as 3 October, when *El Debate* reported their main features.

7: The Azaña Government in Search of an Agrarian Reform Law

The Split with the Radical Party

The split in the San Sebastián coalition did not immediately alter the nature of the Republic. A few of those Republicans who had, as Miguel Maura expressed it, only "put on a revolution to prevent a revolution"[1] left the cabinet, but their departure did not give complete freedom of action to those who conceived of the Republic as a revolutionary force in its own right. The four Left Republican parties and the Socialists were not so strong a creative force as they had been an obstructive one during the last weeks of Alcalá Zamora's government. They had not yet worked out policies in common; moreover, the Left Republicans did not wish to cut entirely their ties with the Radicals. The Radicals were the second-largest party in the Cortes, by virtue of their ninety-three seats. Without their support a Left Republican-Socialist coalition would be left with a relatively small majority, since it would command the allegiance of only some 250 of the 470 deputies.[2] The new cabinet, headed by the Republican Action leader Manuel Azaña, thus attempted to appease the Radicals, even though their views on social matters were not much more advanced than those of the Progressives.

These fundamental political realities affected the fate of the proposal of the Committee on Agriculture. The Radical position was most conservative precisely on the agrarian question. The Committee draft also had been greeted by a storm of protest in the Catholic and conservative press.[3] The conflict therefore was not abated by the change in government. It only shifted its basis as the Alcalá Zamora draft was forgotten and the dis-

---

1. *New York Times,* 14 June 1932. Maura followed Alcalá Zamora in abandoning his ministerial post.

2. The Socialists held 117 seats in the Cortes; the four left Republican parties, 133.

3. See especially *El Debate,* 9 October 1931.

senting bills submitted by two Committee members—Diego Hidalgo, the principal Radical spokesman on agrarian affairs, and Juan Díaz del Moral, member of the prestigious Group at the Service of the Republic—provided new alternatives around which moderates and conservatives might rally.

The two new measures followed the Alcalá Zamora draft in trying to direct the reform against selected scapegoats so as to divert it from direct cultivators. Needless to say, the nobility remained subject to discrimatory treatment. Díaz del Moral recommended that all their properties that dated from 1811 be seized, not merely their señorío jurisdiccional lands. He also gave a new justification for the despoilment of the nobility. Anticipating Azaña by a year, he claimed that the aristocracy was politically dangerous to the Republic and demanded that its economic power be destroyed out of an "elemental instinct of self-preservation." [4] For Hidalgo, discrimination took another form. Cleverly achieving the effects of confiscation without abandoning the principle of indemnification, he recommended that señorío properties be compensated at their declared values in 1830, ninety-nine years earlier!

Absentee owners who continuously leased their lands remained the other principal victims of the two projects. Here, too, Díaz del Moral and Hidalgo expanded on the Alcalá Zamora draft by recommending that the state seize lands let to sharecroppers (not solely those leased to tenants), even if the owner had provided some of the capital necessary for the operation of the farm.[5] A still more substantial alteration—one that affected noble properties as well—was that whereas the Alcalá Zamora and Committee on Agriculture drafts expropriated owners only insofar as their total holdings throughout Spain exceeded the equivalent of three hundred hectares of grain lands, the two new measures recommended seizure of the properties mentioned in their entirety.

To increase their emotional impact, both bills added two categories of scapegoats that had not been included in previous measures. The rural properties of the fallen monarch—which, as Díaz del Moral admitted, were small and unimportant—were to be appropriated for the reform. The same fate was to befall lands purchased for the purpose of "speculation," whatever that vague term might mean in the stagnant economy of rural Spain.

In their financial provisions both of the new measures coincided in

4. Juan Díaz del Moral and José Ortega y Gasset, *La reforma agraria y el estatuto catalan* (Madrid, 1932), pp. 51–55.

5. The Hidalgo bill in particular contained a much more restricted definition of what constituted direct cultivation (and thus a broader definition of absenteeism) than was customary in Spanish legal terminology.

reviving Alcalá Zamora's principle of paying nonnoble owners the full market value of the lands seized, although the procedures they outlined for determining the worth of a farm were much more cumbersome. Neither Díaz del Moral nor Hidalgo was willing to accept the surtax on large agricultural properties, however. The former did not mention the tax in his proposal; the latter once again resorted to a clever formulation which, while appearing to retain the surtax, in fact emasculated it almost completely.[6]

The Díaz del Moral and Hidalgo drafts tried to restrain the effects of the agrarian reform in one other way. In all earlier measures the structure of the administrating agency of the reform was left undefined, thus giving the government in power the freedom to constitute it as it might wish. The new drafts both carefully specified that the execution of policy be entrusted to large councils dominated by bureaucrats and technicians so as to ensure that radical initiatives would be avoided.[7]

Because of their moderation, the two dissenting bills were warmly supported both in Catholic circles and among landowners. The recently established Unión Económica, which united industrial and agrarian interests into what was to become the most powerful pressure group in Spain, even went to the point of reprinting the two measures in a pamphlet intended for public distribution.[8] As had been the case with Alcalá Zamora earlier, both Díaz del Moral and Hidalgo provided a basis on which the approval of the moderates and the acquiescence of the conservatives could have been secured for the agrarian reform. Nor would their recommendations have made significant reform impossible. If they emasculated the surtax and created an unwieldy administrative agency, they also opened more land to settlement than would have been available under the Alcalá Zamora proposal by authorizing the seizure of noble and absentee properties in their entirety and by tolerating a somewhat broader—though still decidedly restricted—application of the

6. Hidalgo resorted to the patently hypocritical device of basing the surtax on the "nude" value of the land, discounting "all improvements due to the labor of man or to the use of capital." Both bills would also have softened the financial consequences for the expropriated owner by paying him in cash or regular state bonds, not in the special nonnegotiable issue recommended by the Committee on Agriculture.

7. The Hidalgo bill was the more bureaucratic, with twenty-two members on its central administrative board, as opposed to seven in the Díaz del Moral proposal. Both measures also established huge three-hundred-man auxiliary boards consisting of provincial representatives who were to be consulted only on matters concerning their provinces.

8. Unión Económica, *Ante la reforma agraria* (Madrid, 1931). For the Catholic reaction, see *El Debate*, 3 November 1931.

reform to direct cultivators.[9] Díaz del Moral's bill had the added advantage that it relied upon obligatory leases similar to those advocated by the Technical Commission rather than on expropriation as such. Thus the state would have been saved the enormous financial burden of compensation.[10]

The Socialists could not accept either measure. The cumbersome procedures in the Hidalgo draft seemed intended to prove the Radicals right in their assertions that the agrarian reform could not be completed quickly but must be the work of several generations. The exclusion of most direct cultivators from the reform, although ensuring that Spain would not undergo the economic collapse which Díaz del Moral feared if the land passed from experienced entrepreneurs who on the whole tilled their farms reasonably well, meant that the majority of the day laborers would not receive land.[11]

Azaña tried to sidestep the conflict that loomed within his new government by allowing the Agricultural Committee draft to remain tabled and concentrating his attention on securing passage of the remaining articles of the Constitution. The Socialists would not allow themselves to be diverted, however. Before the Cortes had convened, Fernando de los Ríos had announced that "the agrarian reform must be well under way before autumn." [12] Autumn had come and gone, but nothing had been accomplished. On 31 October, after a two-week truce, the Socialists forced the cabinet to agree to return to the original plan for simultaneous Cortes discussion of the agrarian reform rather than waiting, as Azaña had hoped, until the Constitution had been approved. In return the Socialists agreed to resubmit the October draft bill to the Committee on Agriculture in an attempt to work out a compromise with

9. Besides expropriating direct cultivators who did not irrigate properties that lay in irrigation basins, both measures specifically included economic caciques and added lands that lay in the *ruedos* of the villages. This last concept is somewhat complicated and will be explained shortly.

10. For Díaz del Moral's description of the advantages of eighteenth-century device of obligatory permanent leases, see his *Reforma agraria*, pp. 68–69. The property valuations mentioned earlier were for the purpose of determining the basis on which the rent to be paid by the settler should be calculated. The texts of the Díaz del Moral and Hidalgo bills appear in *D.S.* 51, 7 October 1931, apps. 3 and 5, respectively.

11. Díaz del Moral (*Reforma agraria*, pp. 32, 34, 38) openly admitted that most workers could not be settled under his proposal. For him, the "indisputable rights" of landless laborers should be satisfied in agriculture as in industry—by legislation regulating salaries and working conditions, not by turning over to the workers the means of production.

12. *El Debate,* 21 June 1931.

the Radicals. The revisionist campaign, which had never wholly subsided, now increased in tempo as the conservative opposition attempted
to influence the Committee proceedings. The Catholic press, previously
content to attack the first Committee draft as merely Socialist in character, now likened it to the legislation of Soviet Russia. The Agrarian
party, with strong Catholic support, called a protest meeting of 22,000
rural proprietors in Palencia.[13]

Azaña's hopes of compromise between the Socialist and Radical
viewpoints proved vain. Far from modifying Socialist demands, the Left
Republican Committee members apparently supported them more actively than before. As a result the new bill reported to the Cortes on
26 November was more radical than its predecessor. All the features that
had aroused opposition remained intact—the graduated surtax, the goal
of placing 60,000 to 75,000 settlers annually, the confiscation of most
noble properties, and so on. The expropriation of directly cultivated land
was now unequivocably authorized. In addition, the anticlerical spirit
that had arisen since the debates on disestablishment made itself felt as
the few remaining Church lands were subjected to seizure.[14] The most
significant change, however, was in the compensation provisions. Under
the first Committee draft nonnoble owners were to receive from ten to
seventeen times the annual taxable income of their farms. The revised
version established almost confiscatory rates for the larger properties.
Land was to be capitalized at only twice its annual taxable income for
that portion of the income which exceeded 200,000 pesetas, at four times
annual income for the portion between 100,000 and 200,000 pesetas, and
so forth. Only the very smallest owners would receive anything approaching the market value of their lands.[15]

The Socialists appeared to have been vindicated in their refusal to
accept the Technical Commission's proposal. By unequivocably including direct cultivators, the new bill opened up as much land to settlement
while avoiding what the Socialists had regarded as the hazardous device of temporary occupations. Yet the Agricultural Committee's draft

13. Ibid., 1, 3, 9 November 1931.

14. Judging from the savage attacks on Church properties in *El Socialista*'s edi-
torial of 29 November 1931, the Socialists seem to have been as responsible as the
Left Republicans for the addition of this provision, which needlessly (since the
Church had very few lands to contribute to the reform) created new enemies.

15. The text of the new Agricultural Committee draft appears in *D.S.* 81, 26
November 1931, app. 8. The new bill partly compensated for its extremely severe
rates of capitalization on the larger properties by recommending more generous indemnification for the smallest farms and by paying all owners in semi-negotiable bonds
rather than in a completely nonnegotiable issue.

suffered the same basic defect as its predecessor of four months earlier: it was not politically viable.

This fact quickly became apparent. *El Sol* and *El Socialista* might predict that the new draft would receive immediate parliamentary approval.[16] But as *El Debate*—more perceptive to political realities than its two principal competitors during this entire period—recognized, the Left Republican–Socialist majority was greater on the Agricultural Committee than in the Cortes at large.[17] The opposition of the huge Radical party hardened as its leader, Alejandro Lerroux, cried *"Reforma agraria, sí! Reforma agraria socialista, no!"* [18] The Group at the Service of the Republic, which had done so much to turn intellectual opinion against the monarchy, followed Díaz del Moral in criticizing the new measure. As the similarities between the Díaz del Moral and Hidalgo proposals testify (both were once again submitted to the Cortes), this elite group clearly was closer to the despised Radicals than to the Left Republican purists on the agrarian question. The Progressives, the Agrarians, the Basque Nationalists, the Catalan Lliga, and the fairly numerous independent deputies of both moderate and conservative orientation, also resisted the new draft with varying degrees of intensity.

Given the existence of so formidable an opposition, *El Debate* calculated that even if the Committee bill were presented for Cortes discussion, it would not be approved. The Left Republican–Socialist majority was not large enough to overcome the widespread resistance, especially since some Left Republican deputies were lukewarm in their support and could be expected to draw away once prolonged debate had begun. A compromise would have to be effected in which the

16. *El Socialista*, 29, November 1931, thought the bill might be approved by the Cortes "during the coming week." *El Sol*, 2 December 1931, thought the bill would "not require many days to convert itself into law." It might be added that upon having a day to think over its initially favorable reaction to the bill, the liberal journal decided that Díaz del Moral was right in his fears of economic catastrophe if direct cultivators were attacked and began to support his program (*El Sol*, 3 December 1931).

17. Cortes committees usually consisted of twenty-one members. Parties were allotted seats in accordance with their strength in the Cortes. Since it was impossible to reflect party strength exactly, or to include representatives from the fairly large number of independent deputies (normally moderate or conservative in their viewpoints), the position of the Left was usually stronger in committee than in the Cortes. Hence the repeated phenomenon of committees that returned bills more extreme than the Cortes could accept. The position of the chairman was not decisive, as proven by the fact that Díaz del Moral consistently opposed the bills his Committee on Agriculture recommended.

18. *El Debate*, 5 December 1931.

principles of the Díaz del Moral and Hidalgo bills would be merged with those of the Committee draft. The resulting law, said *El Debate*, would be "radical but practicable." [19]

Azaña came to the same conclusion as *El Debate* and this time succeeded in convincing the Socialists of the political realities involved. The government did not attempt to place the Committee proposal on the Cortes agenda. It remained tabled until the Constitution was approved, the new president of the Republic elected, and the Constituent Cortes temporarily recessed. The flurry of bill drafting, which had produced six major proposals in four months, temporarily ceased. The Republic passed into its second calendar year with the forces in the San Sebastian coalition further from agreement on the agrarian reform than when they had first assumed office.

In fact, although concessions to Republican unity could still be made, as in the election by an overwhelming majority of Alcalá Zamora as the first president of the Republic, the San Sebastian coalition had by now disintegrated almost completely. On 14 December, three weeks after they had been rebuffed in the Committee on Agriculture, the Radicals took advantage of Azaña's need to reconstitute his cabinet as the first constitutional government of the Republic to bring their clash with the Socialists into the open. Lerroux demanded that Azaña reduce Socialist representation in the new cabinet. The move boomeranged when Azaña, forced to choose between the two parties, decided in favor of the Socialists.[20]

The temperamental differences that separated the idealistic Left Republican leader from the opportunistic Radical chief do not suffice to explain Azaña's choice. The Socialists were Azaña's sole avenue of approach to the working classes and his only assurance that these classes would remain loyal to the Republic rather than succumb to the Anarcho-syndicalist cries for total opposition. The Socialists also promised to be more pliable allies, since there was no group other than the Left Republicans to whom they could turn. Finally, only the Socialists would give Azaña the support required by his plans for the sweeping renovation of all aspects of Spanish life. If he allowed himself to depend on the Radicals, even his democratic reforms would inevitably be diluted.

19. Ibid.

20. Salvador de Madariaga, *Spain: A Modern History* (New York, 1958), pp. 387–89, 416. Madariaga attributes the split largely to the personal antipathy of Azaña for Lerroux and stresses the enormous political consequences of the alienation of the Radicals. "Even as a big river can be traced back to a slender brook, so the Spanish Civil War may be said to begin on that day when Azaña made up his mind that he could not go hand-in-hand with the Radical Party."

Because of the disorganization of the Right during the June elections and the failure of Alcalá Zamora and Maura to convert the Progressives into a mass party, the Radicals were the only moderate political force of national scope. As a result, until the latter half of 1933, when the Catholic CEDA arose to offer them an alternative, many conservatives flocked to the Radical party and further reduced whatever truly progressive tendencies remained to it from its earlier history.[21] Given Azaña's conception of the Republic, he could not have tied himself to such an unambitious and equivocal force.

Azaña's Agrarian Reform Bill in the Cortes

The new Azaña government, which was to rule Spain for nearly two years, gained in homogeneity by the departure of the Radicals but did not thereby augment its ability to translate its decisions into legislative enactments. An opportunity to clarify the complex political situation that had arisen since June was allowed to pass when Azaña once again rejected demands for new elections and encouraged the Constituent Cortes to reconstitute itself as the first regular parliamentary body of the Republic. The danger of an enlarged conservative opposition was thus avoided, but a price was paid: relations between the Azaña government and the Cortes remained confused and unstable throughout the next two years. The difficulties were of a special kind. Until mid-1933 there was no real danger that the government could be forced out of office. The Left Republican–Socialist coalition controlled a small majority of the Cortes seats, and the opposition parties were in any case unable to unite among themselves. Some sense of a common bond among all Republican factions survived, despite the Radical and Progressive defections from the government. Azaña quickly established himself as the great man of the Republic and had no serious rivals for this role, even though Lerroux intermittently attempted to challenge him. However, since no corresponding consensus existed on specific programs of action, the curious spectacle arose in which a government whose continued existence was accepted had to engage in agonizing struggles to secure parliamentary approval for its proposals. Azaña's legislative program was constantly in danger of being undermined by the defection of a handful

21. *La Luz*, 23, 29 February 1932, contains excellent editorials warning Lerroux against the danger of attracting followers not by the virtues of his program but merely because he provided the most convenient focus for an anti-Azaña campaign. The fact that the Radicals were the only other national party besides the Socialists, along with their doctrinal differences, helps explain the intensity of the conflict between them. See Madariaga, p. 385, and *El Obrero de la Tierra*, 20 February 1932.

of his own deputies or by the determined opposition of the parties outside his coalition.

Although the full extent of the resulting paralysis was not immediately apparent, it was quite clear that the government would have to retrench on the agrarian reform program embodied in the two Agricultural Committee bills. On 21 December, in a speech in Barcelona, Azaña gave notice of his cabinet's new orientation by referring to the agrarian reform as a matter of such complexity that it could only be resolved slowly and would be the work of more than one generation. On the same day Marcelino Domingo, the Radical Socialist leader who had just taken over the Ministry of Agriculture, announced that the last Agricultural Committee bill would be withdrawn and a completely new bill drafted for presentation to the Cortes when it reconvened in January.[22]

The new year did not bring with it the revised draft promised. It was not until late March that the government finally submitted its new proposal to committee. The delay in inaugurating the reform, already long, was extended another three months. Why did this new delay occur? In the latter part of January Marcelino Domingo explained that a pause was necessary so that the passions stirred during the previous year might have a chance to cool.[23] Probably more important was the fact that the sense of urgency which had been shared by all political leaders during the previous year had diminished. The fear of a general peasant rising subsided toward the end of 1931 as the Anarchosyndicalists proved unable to organize the landless workers into an effective revolutionary force.[24] Even the gruesome events at Castilblanco, to be described later, came to be regarded as an isolated outbreak and did not resurrect the specter of widespread peasant revolt.[25] The time of year also probably contributed to the government's inaction. The most favorable season for undertaking settlements, the period after the summer harvest and before the fall sowing, had passed and many months remained before it would appear again.

The most important single reason for the delay, however, was the need of the Left Republicans to work out with the Socialists a compromise measure that would have a better chance of speedy Cortes approval than did the draft of the Committee on Agriculture. The point in dispute between the Socialists and Left Republicans was not, as so many writers

22. *El Debate*, 22 December 1931.

23. *New York Times*, 24 January 1932.

24. See below, pp. 303–04, 314.

25. The Castilblanco rising brought many demands for the reorganization of the Guardia Civil but only a few for immediate agrarian reform.

have asserted,[26] whether the reform should take a collectivistic or an individualistic form. Although the Socialists obviously preferred collective cultivation, they had never insisted that this was the only way in which the expropriated lands should be used. Indeed, all the Socialist proposals contained generous provisions for individual settlement.[27] The Socialists asked only that the development of a collective sector be tolerated within a still largely individualistic agricultural economy. And although they hoped that this collective sector would eventually become large, they did not maintain that it should be created entirely as a result of the land reform bill.[28]

The Left Republicans, in turn, had always conceded the need for some collectivization. Many experts on agriculture counseled collective cultivation of the large unirrigated estates in Spain, particularly after the extremely individualistic solution adopted in the Eastern European "Green Revolutions" proved so disastrous economically. The Technical Commission's bill, for example, had provided the settlers the freedom to choose between individual and collective cultivation of the land.[29] A collectivistic-individualistic dispute existed, but it formed only a small part of a larger conflict. It has been exaggerated in retrospect because of its ideological implications and because of the propagandist uses to which it was put by the conservative opposition. In 1931 and 1932 it was not the major source of conflict between the Left Republicans and the Socialists—nor even between the moderate-conservative opposition and the Azaña coalition.

The real issue that separated the Left Republicans and Socialists was the same that had prevented agreement during 1931. The funda-

26. For example, Brenan, p. 243.

27. See, for example, the PSOE's first statement of policy under the Republic (*El Socialista*, 23 April 1931) and Articles 11 and 12 of the dissenting bill presented to the Technical Commission (FNTT, *Memoria*, p. 250). Moreover, during the entire period in which Domingo was drafting the new proposal, the Socialist press did not campaign for a strengthening of the collectivization clauses but for the addition of such features as agricultural credit, the redemption of *foros*, and the regularization of leases.

28. For this and for further discussion of the Socialist position, see below, chap. 12.

29. Pascual Carrión, in interviews with me, stressed the Eastern European experience as one of the fundamental reasons for the Technical Commission's decision to permit collective cultivation. Moreover, the eloquent writings of Joaquín Costa on "colectivismo agrario" had long since convinced much of Spanish liberal opinion that a strong indigenous communalistic tradition existed in Spain. As will be seen in the next chapter, the question as to whether or not to give settlers full property rights to the lands they received was also not a serious source of contention between Left Republicans and Socialists.

mental question was how profound the reform should be and how it could be made consistent with the resources of the state. There is no source from which the internal debate within the Azaña government can be reconstructed. Few of the memoirs left by the important figures in the cabinet touch upon this struggle.[30] Nor did the Socialist press ever break the silence. From the nature of the bill submitted to committee on 24 March, however, it is evident that the Left Republicans succeeded in convincing the Socialists to allow major concessions in order to formulate a program more palatable to the opposition.[31]

The new bill was a much softened version of the Agricultural Committee drafts. The violent attack on noble property was abated. Confiscation was proposed only for those properties that were considered illegitimate—that is, for the señorío jurisdiccional lands usurped during the nineteenth century. All legitimately acquired property, whether noble or nonnoble, was to be compensated. The rates of capitalization were much more generous than those of the second draft of the Committee on Agriculture and ranged from five to twenty times the assessed taxable income. Moreover, although payment was to be mostly in seminegotiable bonds, a small fraction of the indemnification was to be in cash. The financial pressures on all owners were further alleviated as the progressive agricultural surtax was discarded. The ambitious goal of settling 60,000 to 75,000 peasants annually was also dropped. The strain of the reform on the financial resources of the state was further reduced as a relatively low budget was suggested for the reform.

The retreat was by no means complete. A program of decisive reform was envisaged. The new bill called for the expropriation of direct cultivators, although it set higher limits for the property such owners could retain. Accepting the initiative contained in the Díaz del Moral and Hidalgo drafts, Domingo's proposal took what was to prove the

30. Marcelino Domingo's *La experiencia del poder* (Madrid, 1934) is particularly disappointing in this respect. A few hints of what was happening in the cabinet are given in Domingo's interview with *La Luz*, 30 January 1932.

31. According to a passing reference in the recently published diary of Azaña, it was not Largo Caballero, the future leader of the maximalist current in Spanish socialism, who put up the greatest resistance. After claiming, in his usual arrogant manner, credit for eliminating the "harshest and most alarming" features of the Agricultural Committee draft in a cabinet session held on 1 February 1932, Azaña went on to say: "As to Prieto, who [once asserted that he] 'never believed in the agrarian reform,' he says that it is now beginning to become viable. Largo [Caballero] also gives in easily. The one who resists the most is [Fernando de los] Ríos, who has a type of intellectual fanaticism and argues on the basis of entelechies. At times, he seems a spoiled child" (Manuel Azaña, *Obras completas,* ed. Juan Marichal [4 vols. Mexico, 1968], *4,* 323).

fatal step of recommending the seizure of *all* systematically leased lands, whatever their size. It also made concessions to the Socialists by giving preference in settlement to workers rather than to tenants or small owners and by allowing the settlers to obtain only the usufruct and not the property title to the land. Finally, owners were still to be compensated at only a fraction of the value of their lands.[32]

The relative moderation of the bill must have surprised those who resisted earlier measures. The first reaction of the Catholic press was one of mild approval, and the conservatives briefly refrained from criticism.[33] Yet because the proposal continued to attack direct cultivators and to pay low compensation, it was not acceptable to either segment of opinion, particularly after it was rushed through the Cortes committee without significant alteration. Catholic speakers began to assail it as "less erroneous than previous measures, but still contradictory, incomplete, and mistaken in its fundamental principles." [34] The various associations of landowners launched a new revisionist campaign, both on their own initiative and through the Unión Económica.[35] Finally, on 10 May, when parliamentary debate began, Díaz del Moral and Hidalgo once more placed their dissenting bills of October on the Cortes agenda.

It would be impossible to discuss in detail the Cortes debates that followed. The discussion continued for four solid months, from 10 May to 9 September 1932. Agrarian reform was debated at least briefly in forty-six of the seventy-one sessions that were held during this period. The *Diario de las Sesiones* devoted almost three-tenths of its total space to reprinting the speeches presented. Except for the Constitution itself, no other issue—not even Catalan autonomy or the Church issue—was

32. The text of the Domingo bill appears in *D.S.* 142, 24 March 1932, app. 2. Since most of the bargaining between the Left Republicans and Socialists, who controlled the Cortes Committee on Agriculture, had been done beforehand, the bill was reported to the floor very quickly and without significant change (*D.S.* 149, 5 April 1932, app. 3).

33. *El Debate,* 27 March 1932. The moderately conservative *Times* (London), 9 April 1932, thought that the Azaña government's compromise had guaranteed the salvation of the Republic.

34. Antonio Álvarez Robles, *La reforma agraria española* (Palencia, 1932), p. 39. Álvarez Roble's speech of 2 May 1932 is perhaps the most eloquent statement in print of Catholic views on the agrarian question.

35. The Unión Económica called two general meetings during this period to protest the new bill. For the first, see Unión Económica, *Memoria de la asamblea económica-agraria celebrada en Madrid los días 26 y 27 de abril de 1932* (Madrid, 1932). For the second, see *La Época,* 23 May 1932. After its brief initial silence, *La Época* played an extremely active role in the revisionist campaign, devoting ten front-page editorials and reprinting three major speeches against the reform between 19 March and 19 April.

so exhaustively discussed. Judging from the Index to the *Diario*, it seems likely that well over one thousand separate speeches, requests for information, interpolations, rectifications, and other such parliamentary maneuvers occurred during the debates.[36]

The most important single reason for the extraordinary length and complexity of the debates was the Agrarian minority's campaign of obstruction. This small group of twenty-four deputies, assisted by a few conservative independents, displayed such vigor and perseverance that it almost succeeded in rendering the Left Republican–Socialist majority inutile. The tactics employed in the campaign were quite simple. Given the highly varied agricultural conditions that existed in Spain, innumerable inequities and technical faults could be found in a general document such as the Domingo bill. Each of these failings was dwelt upon at length. In addition, in order to get the maximum benefit from their protest, the Agrarians refused to present only a single amendment to each article which would embody the position of the minority as a whole. Rather, each deputy consumed some of the Cortes's time by presenting an amendment of his own. For example, Agrarian deputies presented twenty amendments to the relatively uncontroversial first article, a ratio of almost one amendment for each party member.[37] And, as an indication of the determination of some of the deputies, Cándido Casanueva, a representative from Salamanca who appears to have been the leader of the floor battle, spoke against the reform in twenty-four separate sessions.

Yet the Agrarian campaign could not have prospered had not other factors also been operative. The huge Radical party never showed the unity or determination of the Agrarians, but it did struggle to modify the bill so as to adjust it more closely to the Hidalgo measure.[38] During

36. The Index of the *Diario* requires twenty-two folio-size pages to classify the debates on the Constitution, fourteen pages for the agrarian reform, eleven pages for the Catalan Statute, and seven pages for the Law of Confessions and Religious Congregations, the principal piece of anti-clerical legislation. The debates on the agrarian bill cover 29.0 percent (938 out of 3,238) of the pages in the *Diario* for the period from 10 May to 9 September 1932. My estimate of "well over one thousand" separate interventions is based on a sampling of the Index. By comparing this figure to the number of pages required to reprint the debates, it will be noted that after the grand orations of the preliminary discussion were over, interventions tended to be short, in keeping with the Agrarian minority's tactics of confusing the Cortes by raising a multiplicity of technical objections to the bill.

37. *El Obrero de la Tierra*, 25 June 1932.

38. Thus the principal Radical spokesmen, Diego Hidalgo and José Maria Álvarez Mendizábal, intervened, respectively, in eleven and fifteen of the forty-six debates in which the agrarian question was discussed. These and other statistics in this section are compiled from the Index to the *Diario*.

the first two months of the debate in particular, most deputies from northern Spain, even some of those affiliated to the Left Republicans, also intermittently opposed features of a bill which, because it had been designed with Andalusia and Estremadura in mind, did not correspond to political and economic realities in the provinces they represented.[39]

Still more important, perhaps, was that El Debate proved right in its prediction of so many months before that the Left Republican commitment to the reform would wither in the face of a prolonged debate. For the Galician and Catalan regionalists, the bill was essentially irrelevant since it scarcely touched the foro and rabassaire problems. The Esquerra, moreover, was totally preoccupied with the statute of Catalan autonomy, which was alternating with the agrarian reform on the Cortes agenda. As to the nonregional parties, the predominately urban, middle-class orientation of Republican Action and Radical Socialist members quickly became apparent as the deputies of these two groups fled from the Cortes whenever agrarian reform was mentioned.[40] But the Left Republican rank and file was not alone in its inactivity. The party leaders never fully brought the weight of their support to the measure. In marked contrast to the valiant struggle the liberal Catholic minister, Jiménez Fernández, waged three years later in defense of his proposals, Domingo intervened in the debates only twice during the first three months. Azaña did not put in a single appearance during the long and difficult summer. Even the three Socialist cabinet ministers—perhaps because they feared to encroach upon Domingo or thought that their appearance would lend support to the charges that the bill was Socialist-inspired—did not intervene. While the luminaries of the Republic flocked to the debates on the Catalan Statute, the agrarian reform was left in the hands of backbenchers.[41]

As a result, the dreary round of debates dragged on throughout the summer. Night sessions might be called, the length of speeches might be limited, the Socialist party might even ask its deputies to abstain from

39. For the protests of several Galician deputies, for example, see La Época, 9, 10 June 1932. The failure of the bill to correspond to conditions in northern Spain is discussed below, chap. 8.

40. The inability of most deputies to stomach debates on the agrarian question had already manifested itself during the previous year (see del Cano, Ante la reforma agraria, pp. 3–5) and was to lead to truly alarming absenteeism from the Cortes in the following summer, when the lease bill finally came up for discussion (see below, pp. 272–73).

41. Thus Maura, Lerroux, Unamuno, and Ortega y Gasset did not participate in the agrarian debates at all. The Socialist position was defended almost entirely by Lucio Martínez Gil, head of the FNTT.

rebuttals whenever possible so as to speed debate[42]—but little progress was made. Preliminary discussion alone consumed more than five weeks. Approval of the first article required a fortnight. The second article benefited somewhat from the procedural changes and needed only a week for acceptance.

By early August, three months after debate had begun, only the first four of the twenty-four articles had been approved. Discussion on the controversial fifth article, which dealt with the types of land to be expropriated, had bogged down under the weight of the seventy amendments presented to it.[43] Among the twenty articles not yet examined, several were capable of provoking heated opposition. Such basic questions as the exceptions to the reform, compensation for expropriated land, and the uses to which this land should be put had not yet been broached. It seemed that the Agrarians might succeed in talking the bill to death. The supporters of the bill were increasingly fatigued by the unending amendments, the petty disputations, and the difficulty of comprehending the multitude of technical issues raised. Attendance continued to decline as the summer wore on; if only 189 of the 470 Cortes deputies voted on the first article, no more than 177 were present for the vote on the second. The government itself appeared discouraged. The Minister of Agriculture, Domingo, was rumored to be trying to get the Socialists to accept a compromise with the Agrarians.[44]

The legislative paralysis ended abruptly as a result of the unexpected events of 10 August 1932. On that date General Sanjurjo, hero of the Moroccan campaigns and recently head of the Guardia Civil, attempted to launch a military coup. With better planning, his pronunciamiento in Seville might have been supported by garrisons elsewhere and the Second Spanish Republic might have passed away as quickly as had the First. As it was, the revolt was a complete fiasco and collapsed within a day. Sanjurjo tried to flee but was arrested. His attempt to destroy the Republic succeeded only in temporarily reviving its lost unity and vigor. The threat of a return to the monarchy temporarily discredited the political Right and caused all those who had participated in the establishment of the Republic to close ranks briefly in a mild form of sacred union. With the resuscitation of the spirit of San Sebastian, the Agrarian minority's power to obstruct debate—which had always depended upon the acquiescence of the Radicals and the irresolution of

---

42. *La Época*, 26 May and 1, 15, 25 June 1932.

43. See Joaquín Arrarás, *Historia de la Segunda República Española* (2 vols. Madrid, 1956), *1*, 361–66, for amendments presented to this and other portions of the bill.

44. Ibid., p. 414.

other Republican groups—disappeared. Thus the reform bill was saved in large measure by an accidental occurrence. Without Sanjurjo's revolt it is doubtful that it could have passed the Cortes without major modifications.

Sanjurjo's revolt also made possible a fundamental radicalization of the reform. Azaña started the process with a fiery speech on 16 August, in which he demanded that the rebels be punished by confiscation of their rural properties for use in the agrarian reform. On 18 August a Radical Socialist deputy, Juan Botella, took a more significant step. Using as justification rumors that the Sevillian nobility had aided Sanjurjo, Botella tried to revive the extreme antiaristocratic proposals of the previous year by asking the expropriation without compensation of all noble properties, not of the señoríos alone.[45] Although doubts remained as to the legality of retroactive punishment, the Cortes could scarcely deny Azaña's request. A special law of 24 August was passed, outside the framework of the agrarian bill. Its importance was mostly symbolic. Since none of the rebels were landowners of consequence, their total holdings in Spain did not exceed forty thousand hectares.[46] The mood of the Cortes had not, however, become sufficiently radical to allow Botella's amendment to prosper. It received little support, even from the Socialists,[47] and died on the floor within a few days.

The matter would have ended there had not several members of Azaña's Republican Action party suddenly reintroduced the same amendment on 7 September, the penultimate day of debates on the agrarian bill.[48] When it, too, began to encounter opposition, its real author, Azaña, abruptly entered the Chamber and for the first time used his enormous personal influence—an influence he had been unwilling to risk while the bill had been slowly dying during the summer months—to decide the outcome of a debate on agrarian reform. The eloquence

45. *D.S.* 220, 18 August 1932, pp. 8052–54, gives the text of Botella's speech attacking the nobility. *D.S.* 221, 19 August 1932, app. 3, contains the text of his amendment.

46. *BIRA* (January 1933), pp. 53–56, lists the holdings of the persons implicated in the revolt.

47. Although the Socialists sometimes advocated confiscation of noble lands, they did not tend to single out the nobility for such harsh treatment as did many of the bourgeois Republicans, whose model for revolution remained France of 1789–94. Thus the FNTT's agrarian draft of June 1931 did not discriminate against the nobility; nor did the Socialists play an important role in the post-Sanjurjo drive to confiscate all aristocratic holdings. (See the speech of the FNTT head, Martínez Gil, in *Boletín de la UGT de España* [March 1933], p. 94.)

48. *D.S.* 231, 7 September 1932, app. 20. Luís Bello headed the group of Republican Action deputies who sponsored the amendment.

of his speech was overwhelming. The Republic is revolutionary, he said, and must adopt standards of revolutionary justice. Sanjurjo's revolt had shown that if the Republic did not destroy its enemies, they would destroy it. Even if the nobility had not actively participated in this revolt, the economic base on which its power rested must be crushed so that it would be unable to aid any future rising. Moreover, the confiscated noble lands would provide the means for a rapid and inexpensive reform, which in turn would guarantee peasant support of the Republic.[49]

Azaña's rhetoric did not entirely convince the Cortes, despite its generally cooperative mood since 10 August. There was no legal proof that the nobility had helped Sanjurjo. Although lists compiled later of persons suspected of having "given aid or allegiance to the rebels" reported 31 titleholders out of a total of 194 individuals accused, these lists were prepared by the government itself and did not represent convictions in courts of law.[50] Moreover, to attack all of the approximately two thousand nobles in Spain because of the actions of thirty-one individuals was scarcely equitable. To prevent a prolonged Cortes debate, Azaña quickly worked out a compromise. It was decided that not the nobility as a whole but only the upper nobility, the *grandeza*, would be penalized. The amendment was further softened by applying confiscation only to those *grande* lands already subject to expropriation under the reform bill, not to all grande lands. The upper nobility was therefore allowed to retain its forest and pasture lands and the equivalent of from three hundred to six hundred hectares of grain lands.[51] But the basically arbitrary nature of Azaña's proposal was not altered. Only two of the thirty-one alleged noble rebels belonged to the upper aristocracy; all 262 grandes in Spain were to be penalized for the actions of two of their fellow titleholders.[52]

In this revised form the amendment was approved.[53] Its incorporation into the final law undermined the agrarian reform in the long run. One of the basic concessions of the Domingo bill had been its rejection of the seizure of property without compensation. The bill allowed confiscation of señorío jurisdiccional lands, but only because they were not

49. Azaña's speech is printed in *D.S.* 232, 8 September 1932, pp. 8674–76.

50. DGRA, orders of 10 October and 22 December 1932.

51. For further details on the confiscation of grande properties, see below, pp. 223–24.

52. A list of the grandes potentially affected by the amendment appears in DGRA, order of 15 October 1932.

53. It was passed by a vote of 227 to 25 (*D.S.* 232, 8 September 1932, pp. 8679–81). The fact that the amendment was approved by less than an absolute majority of the deputies raised important doubts as to its constitutionality, since Article 44 of the Constitution permitted confiscation of property only under such circumstances.

considered to be legitimately held. This exception was obviously based to some extent upon a legal euphemism, but the fact that the euphemism was maintained was important. A second fundamental principle was also violated. The Domingo bill had made no class distinctions. In theory, señoríos were to be confiscated not because they belonged to the nobility but because they were illegitimate. Other noble lands were to have been indemnified in the same way as nonnoble properties. The Azaña amendment reversed all this, thereby raising doubts in the minds of some of his most sincere supporters[54] and giving the conservative opposition martyrs through whom it could discredit the reform as a whole. To be sure, these unhappy consequences might have been rendered unimportant had Azaña actually used the vast amounts of grande lands to settle landless workers and root the Republic among the peasantry. Unfortunately, as we will see, Azaña proved to be a Robespierre only in his rhetoric, not in his actions.

The Sanjurjo revolt produced no other specific change of equal importance, but the atmosphere of the Cortes debates was entirely transformed. In less than a month the impossible had been accomplished, and all the remaining articles were passed. On 9 September 1932 the bill as a whole was approved by an overwhelming majority of 318 to 19. The majority was not composed solely of the votes of the parties in the Azaña government. Most deputies in the parties that had participated in the original San Sebastian coalition also approved. Such important leaders as Lerroux, Hidalgo, and Maura abandoned the reservations they had expressed earlier and gave their sanction. The only group which voted en masse against the law were the Agrarians.[55]

Support for the Agrarian Reform Law was not as unanimous as the Cortes vote indicated, however. Many of those who expressed their approval proved only fair weather friends who resumed their opposition to the law as soon as the spirit of Republican unity produced by the Sanjurjo revolt died down. One hundred and thirty deputies, more than one-fourth of the total Cortes representation, did not vote at all but either abstained or were not present. Among them were such distinguished figures as Juan Díaz del Moral and José Ortega y Gasset.[56] Most

54. For example, Felipe Sánchez Román and Ángel Ossorio y Gallardo both expressed serious reservations. The great liberal newspaper, *El Sol*, approved the confiscation of rebel lands (editorial of 18 August 1932) but not of those of the nobility (editorial of 21 August 1932).

55. The roll call on the vote can be found in *D.S.* 233, 9 September 1932, pp. 8716–19.

56. Many other intellectuals actively supported the law, however. For example, Unamuno and Pérez de Ayala voted in its favor.

important of all, the Cortes that approved the law had never been truly representative of the nation. Conservative and Catholic opinion was not adequately represented because of the electoral system and the atmosphere in which the June 1931 elections had been held. The extreme Left was almost wholly unrepresented, since the Anarchosyndicalists had rejected the validity of the Republic from the beginning and had refused to present candidates. As will be seen in more detail, their opposition to the Agrarian Reform Law, which they regarded as a hoax, was particularly bitter. The only non-Agrarian deputy to vote against the law was José Antonio Balbontín, the bourgeois extremist who most consistently reflected Anarchosyndicalist views.

It had taken a year and a half to find a temporary consensus even within an unrepresentative Cortes dominated by parties which, despite their many differences, still retained some ties to each other. A similar consensus was never to be found in the nation as a whole. The reasons for the failure of the law to gain general national support are complex. They have to do in part with the nature of the law, in part with the way it was administered, and in part with the manner in which the peasantry accepted the promise which the law held for them. These topics are the subject of the next four chapters.

8: The Agrarian Reform Law of September 1932

Lands to Be Expropriated

The Agrarian Reform Law of September 1932[1] was a document of extraordinary complexity. Because it incorporated numerous compromises among strongly opposed forces, some of its provisions were vague and others were mutually contradictory. In general the law was milder than most of the "Green Revolution" legislation in Eastern Europe and the agrarian reform laws of Mexico. Nevertheless, because it envisaged so profound a transformation of the existing system of land tenure, the law must be considered revolutionary in its implications.

Article 5 of the law established no fewer than thirteen categories of expropriable land. Only seven were sufficiently important to warrant description.[2] The basic regulation was stated in paragraph 13 of the Article. No individual might own more than a certain amount of land within a single township; this amount varied according to the type of land owned. The maximum property limit in each municipality for vineyards was set at between 100 and 150 hectares; for orchards, from 100 to 200; for olive groves, from 150 to 300; for grain lands (which constituted about three-quarters of the tilled land in Spain), from 300 to 600; and

1. The text of the law appears in *D.S.* 233, 19 September 1932, app. 2, in the *Gaceta* of 21 September 1932, and in IRA, *Ley de Bases y disposiciones complementarias,* pp. 287–306. This last source also conveniently reprints the texts of most of the supplementary orders, decrees, and regulations discussed in this chapter.

2. The other categories of expropriable land were: (a) lands voluntarily sold to the Institute of Agrarian Reform; (b) lands sold on the open market on which the Institute wished to exercise option (both categories were unimportant because the price asked for the lands would be too high for the Institute to pay); (c) leased lands of public corporations (unimportant because very few properties of this sort existed); (d) lands that had passed to the state in default of taxes (unimportant because such lands tended to be poor in quality and small in size); (e) lands acquired for speculative purposes (unimportant because it was never administered). All these categories form part of Article 5 of the law.

for partly cultivated pasture lands, from 400 to 750 hectares. No special limit was established for privately irrigated lands; in lands irrigated through state-financed projects, however, no owner was to be allowed to retain more than from ten to fifty hectares in each municipality.[3] The specific limit within these ranges was to be decided by the provincial juntas of the Institute of Agrarian Reform in accordance with the quality of the land in each region. If an owner held more than one type of land, the juntas were to determine the amount exempt from the reform by applying certain coefficients established by the Institute.

Only if the land had certain special characteristics could amounts below these limits be seized. In two cases lower property limits were in effect established. In some municipalities application of the standard limits might leave an owner sufficient land to enable him still to dominate local political and economic life. Additional amounts could be expropriated from such economic caciques until each retained no more than one-sixth of the total land surface and one-fifth of the assessed land value of the municipality in question. Because these special limits were to be calculated on the basis of the property of each individual, not of family groups (one of the several concessions to the opposition which Domingo had included in his bill), the attack on economic caciquismo was not nearly so strong as in the drafts of the Committee on Agriculture. Nevertheless the provision could serve as an important instrument of reform, particularly in the smaller townships.

The second exception had a wider scope. In Southern Spain, where the rural population does not live scattered throughout the countryside but is concentrated in relatively few villages widely separated from each other, the land near the village assumes a special importance. The distant lands cannot be worked by small peasants unless new homes are built for them near the plot they are to till, a task which, on a national scale, would be prohibitively expensive and technically unfeasible.[4] Only the neighboring—or *ruedo*—lands are easily accessible for small-scale individual cultivation. Thus larger portions of the ruedo than of other lands were to be made available for resettlement. This logic underlay some of

3. The low limits established by this provision were justified on the theory that the owner had benefited enormously by the state-sponsored conversion of his lands to irrigation and should repay society for the "unearned increment" gained. A similar concept was to guide much of the legislation of the Franco period, though Franco has allowed owners to retain far larger quantities of land than would have been possible under the Republic.

4. The Franco government has solved this fundamental problem by the construction of elaborate new villages, but only at the cost of slowing land distribution considerably and limiting it to a few small areas in Spain.

the proposals of Charles III. It was revived during the Republic primarily by the Socialists, who hoped that if sufficient quantities of land were reserved to individual settlers near the villages, opposition to the collective cultivation of the large estates that lay at a distance would diminish. As it was finally formulated in the agrarian law, the ruedo clause subjected to expropriation all lands not cultivated by their owners which lay within two kilometers of the village, so long as the owners retained in the municipality property assessed at one thousand pesetas—the equivalent of approximately twenty hectares of grain lands.[5]

Only four types of land could be expropriated in their entirety: señorío jurisdiccional lands, badly cultivated lands, continuously leased lands, and lands in irrigation zones that had not been converted to irrigated farming. As mentioned above, properties descended from the señoríos were considered to be illegitimately held. The attack on the three other types of property was justified primarily on economic grounds. Owners who undercultivated or failed to irrigate reduced the productive and employment capacity of the nation; those who continuously leased drained off capital from their farms. All three provisions contained safeguards against their arbitrary use. Failure to irrigate applied only when owners who lived within zones serviced by dams and aqueducts did not build the secondary works necessary to bring water to their lands. Undercultivation was to be determined by independent technical analysis, not by executive fiat. Continuous leasing was considered to exist only when a farm had been rented for twelve consecutive years, and even then widows and other persons who could not themselves have worked the land were exempted.

None of these special categories of expropriable land were especially radical. Some dated from as far back as the eighteenth century. Others had formed part of the moderate reform proposals of the 1907–21 era.[6] During 1931 the Alcalá Zamora, Díaz del Moral, and Hidalgo drafts all had attempted to base the reform exclusively on the expropriation of the señorío, leased, and undercultivated lands. If the rentiers, some nobles, and those who neglected their properties were to be dispossessed by the law, they would be ruined on the basis of principles nominally accepted by most of the moderate-conservative opposition. The landowners who did not fall into these categories were not threatened with economic

5. The average taxable income per hectare of all lands was thirty-one pesetas in 1930 (Carrión, p. 54). Since grain lands are less valuable than most other cultivated lands but much more valuable than forest and pasture, I have estimated the average taxable income of a hectare of cereal land to be fifty pesetas.

6. For information on these proposals, see app. E.

extinction or even with being reduced to family-size operators. This becomes readily apparent when the standard property limits established by the law are examined more closely.

As mentioned earlier, the struggle over the agrarian reform had centered around the extent to which direct cultivators would be subject to expropriation. The Domingo bill had made two major concessions to the opposition prior to the opening of the Cortes debates. The maximum property limits established by the Technical Commission draft and maintained by the Committee on Agriculture bills had been converted into the lower limits of the ranges mentioned at the beginning of this chapter. Thus, rather than permitting each owner to keep no more than 300 hectares of grain lands, the law authorized him to retain from 300 to 600 hectares, depending on the decision of the provincial juntas. Still more important, the new limits were calculated not on the basis of an owner's total property throughout the nation, as in all previous official proposals, or even on his total property within each province. Only those portions of an owner's holdings which happened to exceed the maximum property limits within any given municipality could be expropriated.

In addition to these two major concessions—for despite the disclaimers of the Azaña government, it is impossible to describe them by any other name[7]—the moderate-conservative opposition succeeded in softening the expropriation provisions of the Domingo draft in still another way during the Cortes debates. All owners who directly cultivated their lands would be allowed to keep an additional 25 to 33 percent above the standard property limits established.[8] Since "direct cultivation" continued to be so broadly defined that most owners, even some who would elsewhere be considered absentees, qualified for the premium,[9] the true

7. The substitution of ranges of maximum property limits for a single set figure was justifiable in that the reform could be adjusted to the quality of the land in each region. However, because the range of choice was in every case above the limits proposed previously, this introduction of flexibility in the law seriously weakened its attack upon direct cultivators. The altered basis for calculating the maximum limits was even more clearly a concession to the opposition. It would be absurd to take seriously the Azaña government's contention that, since the property tax was paid on the basis of holdings in each municipality, there was no way of knowing how much land each owner possessed throughout the nation. None of the previous official proposals saw this as a problem (the moderate Alcalá Zamora draft, for example, would have forced the owners to report their national holdings, on pain of heavy fines). The Agrarian Reform Law itself made grandeza lands subject to confiscation on the basis of each grande's national, not local, holdings.

8. For the precise manner in which this premium was to be calculated, see DGRA, order of 19 August 1933.

9. This point of sufficient importance to warrant further documentation. "Direct cultivation" customarily did not mean personal cultivation in the sense that a family

property limits created in the law were not from 300 to 600 but from 400 to 750 hectares of grain lands: that is, from 1,000 to 1,850 acres. Consequently, among those whose lands did not fall into the special categories of expropriation mentioned earlier, only the very largest would be affected by the reform. Even among these, many would escape since their properties were scattered over several municipalities, in each of which they could keep the maximum amount allowed. The one group still threatened with economic extinction were the grandes, who, in addition to having been singled out for confiscation, were the only owners who did not benefit from the favorable system of calculating property limits on a municipal basis.

The position of the existing propertied class was further safeguarded by the fact that the law applied only to arable land—that is, to agricultural land in its narrowest sense. Forest and pasture lands not suitable to continuous cultivation were exempted from the reform unless they were of señorío jurisdiccional origin or unless a single owner held in such lands more than one-fifth of the total land surface of a municipality. Because nonarable land could not be seized, even the rural wealth of the grandeza would to some extent be preserved. They would be ruined as agricultural entrepreneurs but might survive as stockbreeders or in forestry. The lower nobility was still less seriously affected, and many nonnoble owners would emerge from the reform with their properties practically intact. Because of the generous treatment of direct cultivators and the exemption of nonarable land, the capitalistic nature of Spanish land tenure was to be only modified, not totally destroyed, by the expropriation provisions of the law. Control of the basic means of agricultural production would continue to rest in the hands of relatively few.

Yet if the expropriation provisions of the law were comparatively moderate and equitable, the existing system of Spanish land tenure was so thoroughly unbalanced that their effects were revolutionary. A very large proportion of the land in Spain came to be included in the Inventory of

---

operator personally tills his lands. When personal cultivation is meant, Spanish legislation, both before and after 1932, usually so specifies. For example, Article 5 of the collective lease decree of 19 May 1931 excludes from its effects tenants who work their lands "personally or together with members of their families." Similarly, the Franco draft bill of 2 January 1962 permits an owner to reclaim protected leased lands only if he "proposes to cultivate them directly and personally." Thus any form of management of nonleased farms and even most types of sharecropping arrangements can be considered "direct cultivation." The point where "direct cultivation" ceases in such contracts varies, but during the Republic both Article 22 of the Agrarian Reform Law and Article 43 of the 1935 lease law agreed that so long as an owner contributed as much as 20 percent of the capital involved in cultivation, he could not be considered a lessor.

Expropriable Property, in which estates affected by the reform were registered. This proportion varied considerably from province to province
as well as within provinces, but it remained high almost everywhere. In
Seville, for example, 65.4 percent of all lands in Utrera and 40.7 percent
of those in Marchena were listed in the Inventory. In Badajoz 69.5 percent of the immense municipality of Badajoz, 53.3 percent of Olivenza,
and 53.4 percent of Albuquerque were subject to the reform. In the
smaller townships it was not unusual for three-quarters of the land to be
included in the Inventory. In a few the proportion rose to more than 90
percent.[10] Since the reform primarily affected arable lands, the proportion of cultivated land threatened was considerably higher in all cases.

In Southern Spain in general it seems safe to say that more than one-
third of the total land surface and about half of the cultivated area fell
into at least one of the categories of expropriable land. This was certainly
the case in the three principal latifundio provinces of Badajoz, Cordova,
and Seville. As can be seen in Table 25, Inventory lands there constituted from 32 to 42 percent of the total land surface, and from 46 to 53
percent of all cultivated lands.

TABLE 25   PROPORTION OF LAND AFFECTED BY AGRARIAN REFORM LAW IN CORDOVA,
SEVILLE, AND BADAJOZ

| | All Lands | Cultivated Lands | Inventory Lands | Inventory Lands as Percent of: | |
				All Lands	Cultivated Lands (estimated)
	(thousands of hectares)				
Cordova	1,248	644	405	32.4	46.6
Seville	1,406	833	590	41.9	52.8
Badajoz	2,165	1,035	790	36.5	46.3

SOURCES: Compiled from the Registro and *AEPA: 1959–60*, p. 369.

NOTE: Registro data were lacking for three counties in Cordova, so the figures
refer to only 92 percent of that province. I have assumed that approximately 25 percent
of the Inventory lands in Seville and Cordova and 40 percent in Badajoz were not
cultivated.

Thus on the basis of principles moderate in themselves, enormous
quantities of land were included in the Inventory. Only a relatively small
proportion of these lands were actually to be expropriated, of course. The
bulk of the Inventory lands pertained to directly cultivated estates from
which only the portions that exceeded the established size limits could be
seized. Nevertheless, all the land listed was heavily penalized indirectly

10. Registro de la Propiedad, volumes for Badajoz and Seville.

in the sense that it lost much of its commercial value and could no longer be freely disposed of by its owner. This important fact is so often overlooked that it deserves some emphasis. Depreciation of land values and restrictions upon property transfers are an unavoidable part of any large-scale agrarian reform. Existing property relations must be frozen to some extent if owners are not to escape expropriation simply by selling part of their lands or by dividing them up among family members. So many owners had already taken precautionary measures of this kind during the eighteen months in which the reform was being debated that the law declared all such property transfers retroactively invalid.[11] After the law went into effect, owners were not actually prohibited from selling their lands, but since this act did not remove the estates in question from the Inventory of Expropriable Property, they were not likely to find any buyers except speculators.[12] Even owners who did not wish to sell would be hurt, since credit institutions would be reluctant to grant loans against such risky collateral as that represented by farms included in the Inventory. There were more direct consequences as well. In the señorío jurisdiccional and grandeza lands, which were to be the first properties expropriated, the government prohibited the cutting of trees, the sale or slaughter of livestock, and even changes in the pattern of cultivation to prevent the owners from realizing the maximum capital gains possible before their farms could be confiscated.[13]

If the injury to the interests of the large owners was great, it was for the most part unavoidable once expropriation, rather than a slow and indirect redistribution of property through a heavily graduated surtax, had been decided upon. The reform could not obtain enough land unless it relied both on paragraph 13 (which affected direct cultivators) and on the special categories mentioned; neither paragraph 13 nor the other categories could be administered unless existing property relations were partly frozen. The same cannot be said for failure of the law to limit it-

11. Article 1. The favorite device used by owners was to grant their land in "undivided partnership" (*pro indiviso*) to their children. Since the law allowed each individual within such partnerships to retain the maximum size limits authorized (another of the ways in which the effects of the law were softened), the owners hoped that a considerable quantity of land might thus be retained without the inconvenience of actually breaking up the estate.

12. Lands might be sold or mortgaged so long as the property deed carried the notation that the farm was included in the Inventory and the sale was not made for the purpose of escaping the reform. In the case of grandeza lands, buyers were specifically warned that such lands would continue to be expropriable without compensation (DGRA, orders of 6 May and 14 July 1933).

13. Ministry of Agriculture decrees of 1 October 1932 and 18 September 1933. The prohibition against the unauthorized cutting of trees was extended to nonnoble Inventory farms by the Ministery of Agriculture decree of 24 January 1933.

self to an attack on the large properties alone, as did the Technical Commission draft. Two of the special categories in the law, its ruedo and its lease provisions, were formulated in such a way that they encompassed the lands of a regrettably large number of small and medium proprietors.

The inclusion of absentees who systematically leased had originated with the Alcalá Zamora bill, whereas ruedo lands had first been made subject to expropriation in the Agricultural Committee draft of October 1931. As initially formulated, neither of these two categories would have affected small and medium owners, since they applied only to those farms whose owners held the equivalent of more than 300 hectares of grain lands throughout the nation. As the strength of the opposition to the seizure of directly cultivated lands became apparent, however, the reform began to be redirected toward a much more widespread expropriation of these two types of land. This reorientation was facilitated by the fact that the moderate opposition seemed willing to accept it: the Díaz del Moral and Hidalgo drafts both expanded the ruedo clauses of the agricultural committee draft and proposed the expropriation of absentee properties without limit or exception. The Socialists also contributed by fighting for a more universal occupation of the ruedo properties.[14] As a result the Domingo bill tried to offset the concessions it had made to the direct cultivators by radicalizing the lease and ruedo provisions of the earlier official proposals. Lands continuously leased for twelve or more years were to be seized in their entirety, whatever their size; farms in the ruedos could be taken so long as their owners did not personally cultivate them and held more than the equivalent of twenty hectares of grain lands elsewhere in the municipality.

The effects of these two clauses varied widely from region to region. The impact of the ruedo legislation on northern and central Spain can best be discussed in a later context. The consequences of the lease clause fortunately were mitigated during the last-minute rush to gain Cortes approval for the law by a compromise that exempted from expropriation small leased properties in those two regions. Lessors there who owned fewer than 400 hectares throughout the nation could not be expropriated.[15] Had a concession of this type not been made, the law might never

14. The Socialists had tried to get the Technical Commission to include ruedo legislation (FNTT, *Memoria,* p. 249). That they were not satisfied with the Agricultural Committee's disposition of the problem is indicated by Juan Morán's attempt to add a rider that would authorize the seizure of all ruedo properties (*D.S.* 51, 7 October 1931, app. 4, and 82, 27 November 1931, app. 6). The Left Republicans apparently resisted these efforts, because the Domingo bill was somewhat less severe in this particular than the final law.

15. The compromise was not reached until 8 September, the hectic penultimate day of the debates. See Francisco Díaz de Arcaya, *La reforma agraria de 15 de*

have been enacted and certainly could not have been administered. The urban middle classes of Madrid, Bilbao, and Barcelona were composed largely of descendants of small holders who retained ownership of family plots in their native villages which they rented to peasants who had not emigrated. Even some urban workers were rentiers in this sense.

In Southern Spain, as mentioned earlier, great benefits accrued to the reform from the ruedo clause because of the pattern of widely scattered village settlements. Whether or not these benefits outweighed the political costs is open to debate, however. Many medium owners who might have remained neutral became active enemies of the reform because their lands in the ruedos were threatened. The lease provision, on the other hand, was unquestionably mistaken in its formulation. The ruedo legislation at least exempted small owners with less than the equivalent of twenty hectares of grain lands. No such limitation relieved the scope of the lease clause. There was no effort to distinguish between different categories of rentiers in the South. The lessor with two hectares as well as the lessor with two thousand was to be expropriated.

Though not nearly so common as in northern or central Spain, small rentiers were nevertheless numerous in the South. As a result of the lease clause, and with some assistance from the ruedo provision, the reform ended by injuring more small and medium owners than it did large proprietors, even in Southern Spain. This rather startling outcome of a law directed against the latifundistas must be stressed. Inadvertently, because of these two clauses, the law actually claimed more small victims than large. For example, among the eleven principal latifundio provinces, the greatest number of owners was affected by the reform not in Seville, Badajoz, Cordova, or Cadiz, where property concentration reached its height. As can be seen from Table 26, Granada, where small leased farms were common because of extensive irrigation, had half again as many owners and almost three times as many farms listed in the Inventory as any other Southern province. The matter can be put in another way. In Southern Spain as a whole, Inventory owners were almost twice as numerous as all large owners listed in the Cadastre. Since many large Cadastral owners were exempted from the reform because they owned only nonarable pasture or forest, however, it seems safe to conclude that the proprietors subjected to expropriation were three times as numerous as the large Cadastral owners of arable land.

All these persons were alienated to no real purpose. As can be seen in Table 27, where I have tried to analyze the effects of the Agrarian

septiembre de 1932 (Madrid, 1933), pp. 30–31. Díaz de Arcaya provides probably the best summary of the changes effected in the Domingo bill during the Cortes debates.

TABLE 26   INVENTORY OF OWNERS AND FARMS IN THE ELEVEN PRINCIPAL LATIFUNDIO PROVINCES

	Inventory Owners		Inventory Farms	
		As Percent of All Cadastral Owners with over		As Percent of All Cadastral Farms over
	Number	250 Hectares	Number	250 Hectares
Granada	4,203	570	47,304	6,089
Caceres	2,713	219	18,503	1,276
Badajoz	2,346	130	12,017	828
Seville	2,013	164	14,716	1,226
Malaga	1,899	423	8,960	2,018
Cadiz	1,766	270	8,109	1,300
Cordova	1,685	160	7,803	760
Toledo	1,358	126	16,487	2,403
Jaen	962	116	6,976	928
Ciudad Real	891	58	11,811	988
Huelva	633	127	2,030	363
Totals and Averages	20,469	185	154,716	1,522

SOURCES: El Obrero de la Tierra, 1 July 1933 and Carrión, Latifundios, Table 2 and the unnumbered table facing p. 70.

NOTE: There are fewer Inventory owners than Cadastral owners in Ciudad Real, because so many of the Cadastral owners there owned forest and pasture lands exempted by the Agrarian Reform Law.

Reform Law in two of the most important latifundio provinces, the lease and ruedo provisions swelled enormously the ranks of those injured by the reform without making sizable quantities of land available for redistribution. In Seville the owners of less than 100 hectares constituted 45 percent of all Inventory owners but held only 3.5 percent of the Inventory lands. In Badajoz the situation was still worse. By not excluding rentiers who leased less than 100 hectares, Inventory land there was increased by 3.2 percent at the cost of more than doubling the number of Inventory owners. To be sure, a greater proportion of the smaller properties than of the large was actually to be seized when expropriation occurred, so that in practice the amount of land for settlement was probably augmented by at least eight or nine percent. Nevertheless it is clear that the loss in territory which would have resulted from the exemption of owners with leased farms of less than 50 or 100 hectares would not seriously have hampered the reform. The same might be said to a lesser degree for those large owners with fewer than 250 hectares, who are also described in Table 27.[16]

16. My figures for the total number of owners in Table 27 differ from those of

TABLE 27 PROPORTION OF SMALL OWNERS AFFECTED BY AGRARIAN REFORM LAW IN BADAJOZ AND SEVILLE

	Badajoz	Seville
All Inventory Owners		
Number of owners	2,202	1,657
Total holdings (hectares)	789,868	589,781
Average holding (hectares)	359	356
Inventory Owners with less than 100 hectares		
Number of owners	1,106	746
Total holdings (hectares)	25,630	20,851
Average holding (hectares)	23	28
As Percent of All Inventory Owners	50.2	45.0
As Percent of Total Inventory Area	3.2	3.5
Inventory Owners with from 100 to 250 hectares		
Number of owners	288	264
Total holdings (hectares)	49,989	44,566
Average holding (hectares)	170	169
As Percent of All Inventory Owners	13.8	15.9
As Percent of Total Inventory Area	6.2	7.6

SOURCE: Registro de la Propiedad, volumes for Badajoz and Seville. See n. 16 for further information.

Another tactical error of perhaps even greater importance was the failure to limit the geographical scope of the law. Once again the wisdom of the Technical Commission draft becomes apparent. Once again the Socialists, in their anxiety to make the reform as universal as possible, seem primarily responsible for the unfortunate departure from the principles outlined in that proposal. The Technical Commission recognized that the state did not have the resources to carry out land redistribution everywhere and sought to limit expropriation to those provinces in Andalusia, Estremadura, and La Mancha in which the agrarian problem was most grave. Owners in other parts of the nation were to be affected only in the sense they they would pay the proposed surtax that would finance the reform in Southern Spain. The Socialists insisted that agrarian reform apply to the entire nation and found unexpected support among conservatives who saw that an "equitable" application of the law might make it unadministrable.[17] The final compromise between the Left Republicans and

El Obrero de la Tierra presented in Table 26 because, in the smaller holdings, I counted the several individuals included in pro indiviso and other forms of joint ownership as a single owner. Thus the proportion of small owners affected by the law was even greater than my figures indicate.

17. As mentioned earlier, the Socialists had objected to the Technical Commission draft because it applied only to the South and had tried to persuade Alcalá

Socialists accepted the worst consequences of the Socialist viewpoint without substantially increasing the field of operation outlined by the Technical Commission.

In most of its provisions the Agrarian law was applicable to the entire nation. Provincial juntas of the Institute of Agrarian Reform were established in northern and central as well as in Southern Spain. A census of potential beneficiaries was also to be carried out there. Northern owners were obliged to register their lands in the Inventory. These lands suffered the same liabilities as those of Southern owners. In short, everything proceeded as though lands everywhere were to be expropriated and peasants settled. But the land could not in fact be seized except in fourteen southern provinces in which the agrarian problem was considered urgent. In the remaining thirty-six provinces the law stated that land redistribution could occur only in "subsequent stages . . . at the request of the government and through a new law voted in the Cortes." [18] There was only one exception: señorío jurisdiccional and grande lands could be confiscated immediately anywhere in Spain. For other types of property, expropriation was threatened even though the state had neither the ability nor the immediate inclination to carry out the threat.

Under the compromise, administrative resources were to be wasted without benefit to the state or to the peasantry. Technicians who could be used more effectively elsewhere were diverted to provinces where their services were not really necessary. The Institute was forced to supervise elections for delegates to provincial juntas that had no real functions to perform. Institute offices were flooded by petitions and declarations from owners whose lands could not be seized.

The proportion of expropriable farms in the Inventory from northern and central Spain provides a gauge of the administrative difficulties created, and of the political opposition that was unnecessarily aroused. Of the 879,371 farms affected by the reform, only 154,716, or 17.6 per-

---

Zamora to extend his proposal to the entire nation. For the Agrarian minority's emphasis on equitability, see Díaz de Arcaya, p. 29, and Gregorio Peces-Barba, *La Ley de Reforma Agraria* (Madrid, 1933), pp. 340–41.

18. Article 2. The provision for future application of the reform outside Southern Spain had made more sense in earlier official proposals, since only cabinet approval would have been necessary. The Domingo draft added the requirement for Cortes approval in another of its vain attempts to disarm opposition to the reform, particularly among the Radicals. Needless to say, since the Cortes had been reluctant to permit the seizure of most lands in Southern Spain, it was extremely doubtful that it could ever be persuaded to permit the extension of the law to northern and central Spain.

cent, lay in the eleven latifundio provinces to which the Technical Commission had wished to limit operations. Another 11.5 percent were located in the three Southern provinces added in subsequent official drafts.[19] More than seven-tenths of the farms lay in provinces where expropriation could not begin until new enabling laws had been approved by the Cortes. Of even greater importance, had the reform been limited to the eleven principal latifundio provinces, only 20,460 owners would have been affected even after the small and medium holders encompassed by the ruedo and lease provisions are taken into account. As the law was written, 79,554 owners were forced to register their property. The enemies of the reform were increased fourfold: more than two-thirds of all Inventory owners came from northern and central Spain.[20] Moreover, the inclusion of these regions greatly increased the number of small and medium owners injured by the law. Despite the exemption of most leased properties there, the proportion of such Inventory owners was probably even greater in the northern and central provinces than in the South.

In retrospect it is clear that the ruedo clause undid the simplification of the reform achieved by limiting the application of the lease provision in the north. Many owners whose lands were exempted from expropriation despite the fact that they were systematically leased found these same lands subject to seizure as ruedo farms. The reason for this is simple. The human geography of northern and central Spain is different from that of Southern Spain. The large, nucleated village is rare; the population is scattered in thousands of tiny hamlets that lie relatively close to each other. For example, in only three of the thirty-six provinces in which expropriation was planned for "subsequent stages" of the reform was the average size of the municipalities more than 130 square kilometers. In ten of the thirty-six, municipalities were so numerous that their average size was less than thirty square kilometers; in another twelve it was less

19. The Technical Commission proposed application of the reform only to the eleven provinces mentioned in Table 25. Under Socialist pressure, the Committee on Agriculture had added the peripheral latifundio provinces of Salamanca and Albacete, where Socialist locals were strong. The Domingo bill added Almeria, apparently more because of the extraordinary poverty of that exceptionally arid region than because of political pressures or the presence of many large estates.

20. *El Obrero de la Tierra*, 1 July 1933. The figures for Inventory owners were as follows: 20,400 had lands in the eleven Technical Commission provinces; 4,047 held property in the three provinces added later, where the reform was also immediately to go into effect; 55,047 were proprietors in the 36 central and northern provinces, where land redistribution could not take effect until an enabling law had been passed by the Cortes.

than fifty.[21] The ruedo clause, which affected an area of approximately 12.6 kilometers in each village,[22] would have relatively little impact on the municipalities of the South, since their average size was so large. In the twenty- and thirty-square-kilometer municipalities of the Cantabric and Mediterranean coasts, however, the ruedos included half the village area.[23] As mentioned earlier, persons with land in the ruedos did not need to be large owners in order to fall under the threat of expropriation. So long as they did not personally cultivate their holdings and retained in the village property with a taxable income of one thousand pesetas, all their ruedo lands might be expropriated. Because of the human geography of their native regions, the maximum property limit for most northern owners in effect became not three to six hundred hectares of grain lands but only some twenty hectares.

The lease and ruedo clauses, together with the extension of the law to northern and central Spain, ended by creating eighty thousand victims of the reform in a nation where perhaps ten or twelve thousand large agricultural proprietors existed. These three provisions also encumbered the Institute with paperwork for almost 900,000 farms, when the same effects could have been achieved by dealing with perhaps 30,000 or 40,000. The Agrarian Reform Law did not do what it was intended to do. It injured small and medium proprietors at least as severely as large; it endangered more property that it could not immediately use for peasant settlements than property that it could use. The Socialists must bear primary responsibility for these ineptitudes. Having accepted categories of expropriation which were moderate in themselves, they insisted on ap-

21. Compiled from INE, *Anuario Estadístico: 1934*, p. 4. Regional differences in the average size of municipalities were as follows:

Average Size of Municipality (square kilometers)	Number of Institute Provinces	Percent of Institute Provinces	Number of Other Provinces	Percent of Other Provinces
Under 30	None	—	10	27.8
30 to 50	1	7.1	12	33.3
50 to 100	5	35.7	10	27.8
100 to 130	None	—	1	2.8
Over 130	8	57.1	3	8.3
Totals	14	100.0	36	100.0

22. Since the radius of the rough circle that ruedo lands described around each village was two kilometers, the total area affected amounted to approximately 12.6 square kilometers ($a = \pi r^2$). The circle was not perfect, because measurement did not begin at the village center but at the end of the built-up area.

23. This fact was pointed out in vain to the Cortes by the Galician deputy, Reino Camaño (*D.S.* 206, 6 September 1932, p. 7333).

plying them too rigidly. The opponents of the law also bear responsibility. Had they foreseen the effects of these provisions and concentrated their attacks upon them, they would have discharged their obligations with honor. As it was, they protested against the other features of the law more strongly than against these. The "injustice" of paragraph 13, not the misapplication of the lease and ruedo principles, was stressed. The retroactive annulment of property transfers made to avoid expropriation was denounced, not the extension of the law to northern and central Spain.[24] By attacking essential features of the law, the opposition lost sight of its unessential features and caused others to do the same. By trying to deflect the reform away from the large direct cultivator, it helped deflect it toward many small and medium owners.

One should not pity too much the small owners affected by the law. In the final analysis they were all rentiers, although of an entirely different order from those giants who monopolized the Spanish earth: no owner who personally cultivated his lands was to be evicted. Nor should one exaggerate the political importance of the alienation of the small owner, though this would be more difficult to do. The small proprietors were more numerous but much less powerful than the large. Even if the law had not encompassed them, many small and medium owners would still have joined in combating it, especially in northern Spain where Catholic and conservative influence was strong. Yet the inescapable fact remains that the misapplication of the law prevented the reform from developing into what it might have become: a crusade against the excessively rich in which all might join.

Compensation to Be Paid

All expropriated owners, except the grandes and the lesser nobles who held señorío jurisdiccional lands, were to be compensated for their losses. However, none would receive equitable compensation. For the most part this was unavoidable. A poor nation like Spain which lacks important nonagricultural sources of income faces three basic economic realities when it plans large-scale agrarian reform. First, it cannot pay full market value for the lands seized. If it could, agrarian reform in the usual sense would become superfluous: the state would need only to purchase estates as they were voluntarily placed on the market by their owners. Second, the state cannot pay in cash even the low compensation

24. For example, the Unión Económica, in its *Asemblea Económica-Agraria de abril de 1932*, attacked the retroactivity provisions and the inclusion of "direct cultivators" but failed to mention either the ruedo clause or the extension of the reform to the northern and central provinces.

it does allow unless it is willing to resort to the printing presses. Had cash been paid in Spain, 600 or 700 million pesetas would have been necessary, even under the inequitable provisions of the law, to compensate the expropriation of one million hectares. Such expenditures were clearly impossible for a state whose annual budget averaged four billion pesetas, especially since the costs of actually settling the peasants would be almost as great as the expenses of compensation. Third, regular state bonds can be used in the place of cash only at the risk of financial chaos. The emission of sizable quantities of regular bonds to individuals who had not voluntarily accepted them and would immediately try to convert them into cash would quickly devalue all bond issues. The use of special but freely negotiable bonds would also be impossible unless the state were willing to accept universal speculation of the kind that accompanied the emission of assignats in revolutionary France.

Yet economic necessity alone does not explain the harshness of the compensation provisions of the law. The Azaña coalition obviously regarded the largest owners as enemies. It wanted not only to destroy their economic power in agriculture, but hoped also to prevent them from acquiring control of other fields of economic activity with the liquid assets they received for their lands. Thus the compensation provisions were more digressive than they need have been because they were intended to serve political as well as economic ends. The smallest owners were to receive relatively fair compensation under the circumstances (about two-thirds of the market value of their lands); the largest owners were to be paid at almost confiscatory rates. This can readily be seen in Table 28. Because the rates of compensation were increasingly unfavorable as the taxable income of farms increased, the owner of a 300,000-peseta farm was to be reinbursed not with ten times the amount paid the owner of a 30,000-peseta farm but with only five times that amount. The proportion of the compensation to be paid in cash was even more digressive. The owner of the 300,000-peseta farm would receive only half as much cash as the proprietor of the 30,000-peseta farm, not ten times as much. As a result the largest owners would find almost all their assets tied up for at least ten years (only one-tenth of the special issue in which the compensation was to be paid could be transferred annually) in bonds which, although they bore an annual interest of five percent,[25] brought them far less than their previous income and prevented them from reinvesting their capital in other fields.

At first glance the compensation provisions of the law, not its cate-

25. The 5 percent interest rate was low only in relation to what an owner usually earned from his land. It was comparable to the rates paid for other bond issues (*Anuario Estadístico: 1934*, pp. 535–56).

TABLE 28   COMPENSATION FOR EXPROPRIATED LAND UNDER 1932 AGRARIAN REFORM LAW

Taxable Income[a] (pesetas)	Rate of Capitalization[a] (each portion, percent)	Percent[a] Paid in Cash	Estimated Market Value[b] (thousands of pesetas)	Compensation Due[b] (thousands of pesetas)	Amount Paid in Cash (thousands of pesetas)
Less than 15,000	5	20	450	300	60
to 30,000	6	15	900	550	82
to 43,000	7	14	1,290	735	104
to 56,000	8	13	1,680	898	117
to 69,000	9	12	2,070	1,043	126
to 82,000	10	11	2,460	1,173	129
to 95,000	11	10	2,850	1,291	129
to 108,000	12	9	3,240	1,399	126
to 121,000	13	8	3,630	1,499	120
to 134,000	14	7	4,020	1,591	111
to 147,000	15	6	4,410	1,673	100
to 160,000	16	5	4,800	1,755	88
to 173,000	17	4	5,190	1,832	73
to 186,000	18	3	5,580	1,905	57
to 199,000	19	2	5,970	1,974	39
200,000 and over (e.g., 300,000)	20	1	9,000	2,539	25

a. Article 8. The rates of capitalization refer to each income level mentioned, but the percentage paid in cash refers to the total compensation due. Thus the first 15,000 pesetas of a 100,000-peseta farm would be capitalized at 5 percent, the next 15,000 at 6 percent, the next 13,000 at 7 percent, and so on; whereas 10 percent of the entire amount due would be paid in cash.

b. Author's estimates, based on the assumption that market value was equivalent to 30 times taxable income (see Appendix B). All calculations refer to the highest taxable income in each category (i.e., 15,000; 30,000; 43,000; 56,000; and so on).

gories of expropriable property, appear to be its truly radical feature. They were severely criticized even by loyal supporters of the Azaña regime.[26] Non-noble direct cultivators were permitted to keep large quantities of land, but for those lands that were expropriated they seemed destined to receive almost confiscatory compensation. In practice, the effects of these provisions were less damaging than they appeared be-

26. El Sol, 21 August 1932, attacked the principle of basing compensation on tax returns on the grounds that the state itself had set the low tax assessments in the Cadastral areas and had not pushed the Cadastre fast enough to prevent owners from declaring still lower valuations in the rest of the nation. This attitude contrasts with the usual liberal notion that "poetic justice" was finally being meted out to the owners. El Sol also criticized the extremely retrogressive scale on which cash payments would be made, as well as the use of a special rather than a regular bond issue to provide the rest of the compensation.

cause they applied only *to each farm as it was expropriated,* not to the total property of an owner throughout the nation, within each province, or even within each municipality.[27] The truly confiscatory rates of compensation and of cash payment primarily affected properties with taxable incomes of more than 60,000 or 70,000 pesetas. Although the total holdings of many owners exceeded these figures, there were very few individual farms of this worth.

TABLE 29   AVERAGE TAXABLE INCOME OF LARGEST CADASTRAL HOLDINGS

Size of Holdings (hectares)	Number of Holdings	Average Taxable Income (pesetas)
500 –1,000	2,775	15,229
1,000–2,500	1,074	25,553
2,500–5,000	164	39,346
Over 5,000	59	64,357

SOURCE: Compiled from DGP, *Memoria 1928,* pp. 121, 132.

Fairly conclusive proof of this fact can be found in Table 29, where the Cadastral data for the portions of Spain which had been surveyed as of 1928 are summarized. Even when the large properties in regions not yet surveyed are added to the 1928 totals, there were probably not more than 1,200 properties in Spain which fell under the compensation provisions governing 30,000-peseta income farms,[28] not more than 250 that were affected by the provisions for 40,000-peseta farms, not more than 100 whose taxable income surpassed 60,000 pesetas, and not more than 10 to 20 that were assessed at over 100,000 pesetas. Moreover, most of the very largest properties probably belonged to the grandeza, so that they would in any case have been expropriated without compensation. In short, the most radical provisions of the law would have next to no victims! Although the Azaña government intended otherwise, large owners would normally be compensated at almost the same rates as the small. Only a handful would be indemnified at less than half the market value

27. The property that owners might retain was calculated on the basis of total holdings in a municipality, but compensation was determined by the value of each separate farm as it was being expropriated (Article 8).

28. This conclusion is substantiated by recent data. In 1958 the Franco government placed farms with more than 170,000 pesetas taxable income into a special (more severe) tax category. A taxable income of 170,000 in 1958 pesetas was equivalent to a taxable income of approximately 32,000 in 1933 pesetas (according to García de Oteyza, "El Producto Neto," p. 13, taxable income increased by a factor of 5.26 between 1935 and 1957). There were 1,076 farms in Franco's special tax category in 1958, approximately the same number as one would expect on the basis of my calculations.

of their lands and receive less than ten percent of that value in cash. In its political objectives the law again failed to achieve its aims. Had the compensation provisions been calculated on the basis of the total property of each owner, they would have had the political effects desired. Since they applied only to each farm as it was expropriated, the more drastic categories of compensation merely added new grounds on which the inequity of the reform could be attacked without substantially benefiting either the state or the peasants.

The fact that the compensation provisions were more radical in appearance than in reality was especially important because in the long run the state would depend almost entirely on the expropriation of properties that required indemnification. The grandeza and señorío lands that could be expropriated without compensation were sufficient only to initiate the reform, not to bring it to its conclusion. The sanguine hopes that the grandeza lands would open up millions of hectares for resettlement proved illusory.[29] Azaña's amendment of 8 September had authorized the confiscation of grandeza lands only when their owners had exercised the honorific privileges of their rank. Of the 262 grandes in Spain, only 176 had exercised these prerogatives; the rest were children, or persons not active in court circles.[30] Of the 176 individuals subject, a handful were exempted "in recognition of the eminent services" they or their families had performed for the nation.[31] A far greater number were not affected because they did not own rural properties or held so little land

29. For evidence that these hopes were retained even after the grandeza properties began to be counted, see BIRA (January 1933), p. 55. In my account I stress the relatively small size of the grandeza lands, not to discount the popular notion that they were immense—ninety-nine grandes did after all hold about 2.5 percent of the cultivated surface of the nation—but to bring this notion into a more realistic perspective.

30. DGRA, orders of 15 October 1932 and 28 May 1933 list, respectively, all grandes and those who had exercised their prerogatives.

31. The Duke of Vergara, descendant of Columbus, was so exempted, as was the Duke of Ciudad Rodrigo (known in England as the Duke of Wellington). Very little land was lost by these exemptions, however, since none of the truly large owners, not even those who could legitimately claim to have performed "eminent services," was excused. Far more important were the grandes who remained unaffected because they had not exercised their prerogatives. The nineteen individuals so excluded in the six provinces I studied in the Registro held 45,601 hectares, or about one-fifth as much as the 238,234 hectares owned by grandes subject to confiscation. It was also absurd to exclude the personal property of wives of the grandes, who were often large landowners in their own right (they held 19,731 hectares in the six provinces studied). If a class was to be attacked, all its members should have been affected equally. The compromises Azaña was forced to accept on the grandeza provisions probably lessened the amount of land available gratis to the state by some 25 or 30 percent.

that they did not fall within the categories of expropriation. As a result the threat of confiscation could be carried out against only 99 grandes whose agricultural holdings amounted to 577,359 hectares.[32] Although this was an impressive sum in terms of the average property held by each grande, it was hardly enough to permit the settlement of more than sixty thousand peasants, a small fraction of the million or more landless workers and tenants which the advocates of the reform felt must be placed if the agrarian problem were to be solved.

Nor would the amount of land available gratis to the state notably be increased by the addition of the señorío jurisdiccional properties of the remaining nobility. If the proportions that existed in the six major latifundio provinces held for Spain as a whole, the lesser nobility and the 153 grandes not subject to confiscation owned no more than 700,000 hectares of expropriable land.[33] Of this total approximately 15 percent had been recently purchased,[34] and most of the rest probably derived from earlier purchases or from the inheritance of lands obtained through royal grants whose legitimacy could not be disputed. It seems unlikely that more than 150,000 or 200,000 hectares of señorío lands still remained in the hands of nobles not already subject to confiscation under the grandeza clauses. As a result the state would be obliged to pay compensation for more than 90 percent of the approximately 9 to 10 million hectares necessary to give the reform the scope its sponsors planned.

The costs of the reform would be increased still further by two spe-

32. *BIRA* (March 1934), p. 169, and IRA, *La reforma agraria*, pp. 47–48. The size of the agricultural holdings of the ninety-nine individuals actually affected was as follows:

Total Holdings (hectares)	Number of *Grandes*
50,000–79,147	2
25,000–50,000	3
10,000–25,000	9
5,000–10,000	13
1,000–5,000	38
Under 1,000	34

33. The holdings of the ninety-nine grandes constituted 45 percent of the total noble holdings in the six provinces I have studied (238,234 hectares out of 529,423 hectares). If the same proportions held true in the rest of the nation, total noble holdings everywhere would amount to 1,283,020 hectares. See above, pp. 72–73, for further details.

34. In the twenty-four municipalities and nine counties in which I studied the means by which property had been acquired, 13.4 percent of total noble holdings had been purchased by the *present* title holders. See above, p. 69.

cial types of remuneration which had to be paid on all properties, even those subject to confiscation. As will be remembered, the Technical Commission draft had been rejected in large part because it provided no solution to the fundamental dilemma as to how the state might ensure that owners threatened with expropriation would continue to farm until such time as their lands were actually turned over to new cultivators. The Agrarian Law sought to overcome this difficulty in two ways. First, so as to prevent the complete drying up of credit, the state was obligated to repay whatever mortgages might exist on an expropriated estate. Since these payments were to be made in one lump cash sum, the immediate costs of the reform were raised enormously. The final costs were also increased, even though the mortgages paid would be deducted from the compensation due the owner. The grande and señorío lands that seemingly were to come to the state gratis in fact required some expenditure of funds if they were mortgaged. Moreover, the mortgages outstanding on farms entitled to compensation in many cases exceeded the artificially low valuations established by the indemnification provisions of the law.

The other type of special remuneration—intended to ensure that farmers would continue to invest their own capital and labor in their farms until they could be expropriated—had more subtle effects. Before settlement could begin, whoever actually cultivated the land—either the owner himself or the tenants who rented it from him—had to be reimbursed in cash for standing crops and for preparatory plowings. The value of these crops or labors was to be paid at their real worth, not according to an arbitrary schedule of compensation established by the Institute. Potentially, the cash expenditures required for this type of compensation could be enormous. In practice, these costs could be largely avoided by planning expropriation for the period between the late summer harvests and the fall plowings, in any case the most logical season for settlements since it meant the least possible disruption of the yearly production cycle. A de facto seasonal schedule for the application of the reform was consequently established by the existence of this second type of special compensation. As will be seen, Azaña's coalition proved so fragile that even the minor time limitations that this schedule imposed had disastrous consequences.

The financial difficulties that confronted the reform would have been far less significant had the graduated surtax of most of the 1931 proposals been retained. In fact, the abandonment of this surtax was one of the Azaña government's very first concessions to the opposition. The surtax Domingo said, was "erroneous and unjust" because it affected only landowners; the state should obtain the revenues necessary for the reform by a general tax that would apply to industrial and commercial incomes as well.[35] Domingo's reasoning contained one central fallacy. The reformers of the late nineteenth and early twentieth centuries had attached the stigma of illegitimacy only to large rural proprietors. There was no similarly unfavorable consensus of opinion on which to base an attack against other types of capitalists.[36] The Azaña cabinet belatedly recognized this fact. Having sponsored a law that would revolutionize Spanish landholding, it hesitated to propose a strong tax measure that would insure a more equitable distribution of wealth in other fields of economic activity. The income tax bill presented to the Cortes on 15 October 1932 was so timid that its rates varied from only one percent on incomes that exceeded 100,000 pesetas to a maximum of 7.7 percent on incomes of more than a million pesetas.[37] The extraordinary inconsistency in the Azaña policies can be fully appreciated only if it is remembered that average per capita income in 1932 was 1,075 pesetas. Persons who did not earn more than 93 times this income therefore escaped the income tax altogether, and its very modest maximum rates affected only those few individuals who earned almost 1,000 times as much as their fellow citizens![38] A law of this sort applied to the United States in 1968 would mean that persons who earned less than $317,316 would

35. Marcelino Domingo, interview with *La Luz*, 30 January 1932. While acting as spokesman for the decision, however, Domingo may have pressured into it by Azaña and the Minister of Finance, Jaime Carner (Azaña, *Obras completas, 4,* 323). It will be remembered that the substitution of a general income tax for the agricultural surtax had been one of the major objectives of the Catholic and conservative opposition in 1931.

36. This inconsistency of attitude was not confined to Spain, of course. Nineteenth- and early-twentieth-century European history is crowded with persons like Herbert Spencer who would not dream of restricting the freedom of industrialists and merchants but who lightheartedly spoke of vast expropriations of rural property.

37. The text of the bill appears in the daily press of 15, 16 October 1932. The "reactionary" Lerroux governments later lowered the income at which taxation would start to 70,000 pesetas and raised the maximum rate to 11 percent on incomes of over two million pesetas (if any such existed). By contrast, England had imposed a tax of 10.2 percent on incomes of over 50,000 pounds as early as 1903 and during World War I raised it to 63.7 percent.

38. If average income per actively employed individual (2,871 pesetas in 1932) rather than per capita income is used, taxation did not begin until a person earned 35 times as much as other economically active individuals and the maximum rate did not apply until he earned 348 times as much (INE, *Primera mitad del siglo XX,* p. 139). To be fair, it must be said that since some of the existing taxes, particularly the *utilidades* levied on businesses and the heavy duties on luxury imports, indirectly affected the wealthy much more heavily than other groups, they did not escape taxation quite so completely as these figures suggest. Also, the idea of an income tax was nowhere so fully accepted in the 1930s as it has since become; less dramatic instances of fiscal timidity can be found in France and pre-Hitlerian Germany.

pay no income tax and that only those earning over $3,400,000 would pay as much as 7.7 percent!

So ludicrous an income tax could in no way help finance the agrarian reform: during the three years in which it was levied it never contributed more than 0.03 percent of total state revenues.[39] Yet even the grievous error of abandoning the agricultural surtax in its favor was not irredeemable. For all its weaknesses, the September law permitted the state to use a large part of its resources on the more productive of the two major expenditures necessary in land reform: providing settlers with the means of beginning cultivation rather than compensating owners for the farms they had lost. A rapid reform could thus be launched on the basis of existing state income. During the first year or two, when the land needed could be secured gratis from the grandeza and señorío farms, the state could probably meet the goals established in the 1931 draft bills and settle 60,000 or 70,000 peasants annually with an expenditure of from 250 to 300 million pesetas.[40] In later years, as the grandeza lands were exhausted, the pace of settlement might decrease because of the greater cost of expropriation. Nevertheless, relatively rapid reform remained financially feasible so long as Azaña was willing to devote to it the equivalent of 6 or 7 percent of the national budget—a not unreasonable sum. This fact seemed to have been implicitly recognized in the law, which allowed the government to allot whatever sums it deemed practicable. Only one check was imposed: so as to prevent an unsympathetic cabinet in the future from destroying the reform by completely neglecting it, the law guaranteed the Institute of Agrarian Reform a minimum annual budget of 50 million pesetas.

Peasant Settlements

The Institute was normally to secure possession of land by adjudicating whatever claims the owner might make, formally expropriating his farm, and paying him the compensation due. The law also permitted

39. Out of total state revenues of 4.6, 4.4, and 4.5 billion pesetas in 1933, 1934, and 1935, respectively, the income tax provided only 10, 11, and 13 million pesetas, about one-thirtieth as much as the tax on tobacco. It is difficult to estimate what revenues the agricultural surtax would have produced had it been maintained, but a sum of 70 to 80 million pesetas does not seem unreasonable if the surtax had been calculated on the basis of total assessed income throughout Spain, rather than in each municipality (receipts from the existing land tax oscillated between 391 and 422 million pesetas from 1931 to 1935).

40. Calculated on the basis of the generally accepted estimates that it would cost from three to four thousand pesetas to provide each settler with the tools, animals, and seeds he would need to start cultivation.

a speedier, less expensive, and less definitive method of procedure. The
Institute might "temporarily occupy" the land "in order to anticipate
settlements while expropriation is being carried out." [41] Temporary occupations were viewed as exceptional measures, not as the fundamental
instruments of reform envisaged in the Technical Commission draft. If
expropriation had not taken place within nine years after occupation,
the land was to be removed from the Inventory and returned permanently to its owner. Temporary occupations gave flexibility to the
reform. They also lowered the immediate costs of settlement. The owner
of the farm received an annual rent of four percent of its value for so
long as it was occupied, but the payment of compensation and of any
mortgage charges was avoided until expropriation actually took place.

Some of the lands expropriated might be used in reforestation, in
irrigation works, or for the creation of experimental farms. Their chief
use, of course, was to be for peasant settlements. In the case of most
small and medium-size leased properties, "settlement" meant nothing
more than a change in status of the tenants who cultivated them. If
a tenant had worked a plot of less than twenty hectares for six or more
years, he was normally to be given use of the same land in emphyteusis.
Larger tenants who had worked their lands for thirty or more years
were also to receive emphyteutic possession, even if these lands were so
extensive as to have a taxable income of 5,000 pesetas.[42] In most other
farms land redistribution was to occur in a physical as well as in a legal
sense. "Settlement" on these farms would mean a much more profound
and difficult change, because new cultivators would assume the active
management of the soil.

In the provisions governing this second type of settlement, the
September law contained an ambiguity that resulted from differences
between the Socialists and the bourgeois Republican parties. As mentioned earlier, the Left Republicans conceded the need for organizing
settlers into groups. Inexperienced workers could not successfully manage the land by themselves but needed a cooperative framework in
which to begin farming. Moreover, the Institute would encounter insuperable administrative difficulties if it attempted to deal with hundreds
of thousands of individual settlers instead of with a few thousand Peasant
Communities that would act as intermediaries between the settlers and
the state. Thus the major question was not whether organized groups
should be settled but only which groups should be placed. The Left

41. Article 9.
42. Approximately one hundred hectares of grain lands would be required to
produce a taxable income of five thousand pesetas—a sign that the law was not directed against even relatively large tenants who did not sublease.

Republicans preferred that the Peasant Communities be created as entirely new groups. The Socialists had an existing trade union organization to defend. If ad hoc Communities secured the use of the soil, their locals would become superfluous and would rapidly disintegrate. The Socialists therefore insisted that existing labor organizations be allowed to constitute themselves as Communities and obtain possession of occupied farms.

The law settled the conflict by permitting both alternatives. It authorized the provincial juntas to inscribe four categories of settlers in their Census of beneficiaries to the reform. Three categories included only individuals: agricultural workers without any land, owners who held less than ten hectares,[43] and tenants or sharecroppers who rented less than ten hectares. The remaining category consisted not of individuals but of "legally constituted agricultural workers' societies which have been in existence for at least two years."[44] Preference in settlement was to be given to the agricultural workers and to the workers' societies;[45] small owners were to be placed next; small tenants or sharecroppers received least preference in lands other than those they already tilled. The question of collective versus individual cultivation was also handled by compromise. Once the Peasant Communities received land, they were to decide by majority vote how to farm it. The Socialist unions would presumably vote for collective cultivation, but otherwise the individual solution would probably prevail.

The same reasons that counseled settlement in Peasant Communities also led to the conclusion that the property right to the land should be retained by the state, not sold to the settlers.[46] The necessity of pur-

---

43. The law actually benefited owners who "paid less than fifty pesetas tax," about the sum a person would pay on ten hectares of grain lands. The results of the Census are reproduced in Table 24.

44. Article 11.

45. During the hectic last week of debates the Socialists succeeded in adding an amendment whereby preference in the settlement of unirrigated lands "will always be given to workers' organizations who have solicited it for the purposes of collective cultivation" (Article 12). Had this clause been applied literally, it would have led to a completely Socialistic agrarian reform, since unirrigated lands constituted perhaps 95 percent of the territory available for settlement. As far as I can discover, the amendment remained a dead letter on the national scale. The Socialist press never campaigned for its enforcement; the opposition press never singled it out for criticism. It may have created conflict on the local level, however. According to Juan José Vergara, former director of the IRA office in Toledo, UGT locals in the Malpica region fought the settlement of unaffiliated workers on the basis of this amendment.

46. The prohibition of individual purchase appeared indirectly in Article 8, Section g, which mentioned only the possibility of the state surrogating itself in the rights previously held by the owner. It should be noted that state retention of the

chasing the property right, it was argued, could only be a burden upon the settlers, since it would force them to divert resources that they could better use to purchase livestock, tools, and other items necessary to cultivate the soil successfully. Even if the state gave them the property title without charge, there would be danger: the purpose of the reform might be undone as the weaker settlers mortgaged or sold their lands to the economically more powerful. In the individualistic Communities, then, the settler received only emphyteutic possession of his lands. Most of the major attributes of property were his: he retained the full fruit of his labors and was not required to turn his produce over to the Community; he could be dispossessed of his lands only in case of "fraud, habitual negligence, transgression against another Community member, repeated failure to fulfill his duties, or some other grave cause"; he might pass his lands on to his heirs.[47] The property rights that he lacked were those of selling, mortgaging, and leasing his lands, all attributes important to an established farmer in a purely capitalistic economy but not essential to the untried, dependent day laborer whose credit needs would presumably be met by state institutions.

State retention of the property title aroused widespread protest, especially in Catholic circles. They felt that the peasant was being rescued from subordination to the large owner only to become a tenant of the state. The concepts of "property and sovereignty are being merged once more," as in the Middle Ages, they objected: "The servitude of the glebe is being revived."[48] Although accurate in pointing out the continued dependence of the worker, these statements failed to mention that the large owner had been a crueler master than the existing Spanish state, which had no totalitarian ambitions and remained subject to rules

property title, seemingly socialistic, also accorded with liberal interests in that it guarded against the possibility that some of the collective Communities might develop into "Soviets" and permitted the state to intervene in the defense of any settler against whom Community opinion might have turned in the individualistic communities.

47. The specific rights of the settlers were not detailed in the Agrarian law but are given in the Ministry of Agriculture decree of 7 September 1933, especially in Articles 8, 12, and 17. The causes for eviction from the Community applied mostly to settlers in the collectivistic Communities, where each member was assigned specific duties, rather than to settlers in the individualistic Communities, whose communal obligations were minimal. Because of the confusion caused by Catholic propaganda on this subject, it should also be noted that if the settler in the individualistic Communities was denied certain property rights, he retained as much or more freedom as settlers placed by the conservative Besada law of 1907 (see app. E).

48. These charges, repeatedly employed in the Catholic and conservative press, were most eloquently stated by Álvarez Robles, p. 58, from whom the quotations were taken.

of law and dictates of electoral opinion, could be. Moreover, if "glebes" were being created, they were glebes in which no demesne existed; where the lord—that is, the Community council—was elected; which the peasant could leave at will and recover the value of whatever improvements he had made on his plot. The proper historical parallel was neither Soviet Russia nor manorial Europe but Mexico, with its *ejido* pattern of settlement.

Yet because Spain was much more bourgeois in its attitudes than Mexico, the refusal to allow settlers to purchase the land conflicted with the prevailing system of values and was used to discredit the law.[49] The stigma might easily have been removed by a concession in the first of the two major types of lands specified in the reform: those already divided into small units in which redistribution was simple and economic success certain because the only change was one in legal status. The small tenants who previously cultivated the land they now "settled" had proven their ability to survive unaided even while paying exorbitant rents; the reform would not have been seriously endangered had they been allowed to buy the land. But in this as in other features of the law, the Azaña coalition—above all, the Socialists—unimaginatively relied on the strict application of principle instead of adopting a flexible approach to the problems that faced it. The Minister of Agriculture, Domingo, attempted to quiet the protest by stating during the Cortes debates that the government did not consider the exclusion of settlers from full ownership irreversible and promised that they might be allowed to purchase their lands at some future date.[50] This possibility was not incorporated into the law, however, where it might have done more to undermine the attacks of the opposition.

Other Provisions

The law was to be administered by the Institute of Agrarian Reform. The nature of this Institute was not defined in the original draft bill. During the Cortes debates the government accepted an amendment introduced by the Radical spokesman, Hidalgo, which established the main features of the new organization. Authority in the Institute was to

49. Many Republicans tried to legitimize the denial of full property rights to settlers by appealing to the Spanish tradition of emphyteutic leases, or *censos*. This tradition lacked the force of the ejido heritage, however, so that the attempt to revive "principles which have slept the sleep of centuries," as Alcalá Zamora once put it, was a failure.

50. Quoted in Arturo Mori, *Crónica de las Cortes Constituyentes de la Segunda República Española* (13 vols. Madrid, 1932), 7, 559–74. Mori provides an acceptable summary of the lengthy debates on the law.

reside not with its Director General but with an Executive Council "composed of agricultural technicians, jurists, representatives of the official agricultural credit organizations, owners, tenants, and agricultural workers." [51] The Hidalgo amendment guaranteed a technical and juridical presence on the Council and provided a structural check to administrative tyranny, because the Council could act only by majority decision. The Azaña government still retained considerable freedom to create the type of Council it wished, however, because the exact proportion of delegates from each group was left undefined, as was the total size of the body. The way in which the government chose to exercise its power of appointment proved to be one of the more important causes for the failure of the reform.

The government also retained great freedom in determining the nature of the juntas, which were the provincial counterparts of the Executive Council. Although these juntas could not undertake expropriation on their own initiative, they were important because they compiled the Census of beneficiaries and determined the precise maximum size limits for directly cultivated property in each municipality. The juntas included equal numbers of representatives elected by the workers' organizations and by the landowners, respectively. The government retained final control, because the tie-breaking vote was held by the junta president, who was appointed by the Institute. A technical orientation was also guaranteed in that the heads of the official provincial agricultural services sat on the boards in an advisory capacity.

Subprovincial juntas, which the Socialists supported and which all previous official bills had proposed, were rejected in the law so as to prevent branches of the Institute from becoming too directly subject to local political pressures. The several hundred local juntas created (on paper, at least) by Alcalá Zamora in August 1931 were disbanded.[52] The field work necessary for the reform was to performed entirely by a corps of technical personnel organized into provincial delegations and responsible to the Institute in Madrid. By these means local initiative was reduced to a minimum and centralized control over the reform retained. Thus there was little danger that the reform would degenerate into a series of uncoordinated seizures of estates by local authorities.

The September law did not limit itself to the redistribution of land in large estates. It also reaffirmed a number of other commitments for

51. Article 3. It will be remembered that Hidalgo had proposed an even larger and more cumbersome council in his dissenting bills to the Agricultural Committee drafts.

52. See chap. 6. Apparently these local juntas had remained completely inactive during the year in which the Agrarian law was being debated.

basic structural reforms which had emerged out of the confusion in which the San Sebastian coalition had first approached the agrarian question. Thus the law outlined principles on which general lease legislation should be based. It also declared redeemable the *foros* of Galicia and the *rabassa morta* contracts of Catalonia and promised detailed specific legislation on these matters. The law pledged the creation of a National Agrarian Bank, necessary to rescue existing small farmers from dependence on local moneylenders and to provide credit for new settlers under the reform; the latter task was particularly important as the settlers would never be able to rely upon private credit sources to any significant extent because they could not mortgage the lands they would receive. Finally, reflecting the impact of Joaquín Costa's writings on *colectivismo agrario* and expressing Republic's vision of itself as the redeemer of all the many wrongs in Spain's past history, the law promised to restore to the villages those common lands of which they had been despoiled during the desamortización of the nineteenth century.[53]

This reaffirmation of old commitments was in a sense a testimony to how little had been accomplished during the year and a half in which the agrarian reform had been debated. If an instrument for the redistribution of large properties now existed in the September law, other problems of nearly equal importance still had to be set aside with vague pledges for their eventual solution. The resistance encountered by the Agrarian law in the Cortes suggested that these pledges would not be easy to honor. Nor was the spirit with which the Azaña government approached the problems still outstanding very promising. The cabinet expended its greatest efforts in defending the severe formulation given by the law to the primarily ideological problem of the recovery of the common lands. By contrast, the commitment to the creation of a National Agrarian Bank was added only at the last moment, even though such a bank was absolutely essential to the successful implementation of the September law in a nation where private credit institutions were notorious for their reluctance to provide capital for agricultural enterprises, and where the most important public institution had in half a century issued rural loans that averaged out to less than one peseta per hectare of cultivated land.[54]

These same criticisms cannot be levied against one other important matter on which the law also touched only briefly. The dedication of the Azaña government to the expansion of irrigation was implied only in the law's final article, which authorized tax relief and exemption from

53. Articles 21, 22, 23.
54. Gonzalo de Reparaz, *Pobreza y atraso de España* (Valencia, 1932), p. 16.

expropriation for builders of new irrigation facilities. In an arid nation like Spain, new irrigation is in itself a type of land reform since it multiplies jobs and stimulates small-scale cultivation. Because the agrarian law did not feature it more prominently, it has been severely criticized—especially by Franco's new technocrats—on the grounds that it failed to understand the importance of this indirect means of reform and placed exclusive reliance on more controversial and less certain political solutions.

This criticism is unjustified. The September law did not legislate on irrigation because such legislation had already been enacted in the Irrigation Law of 13 April 1932. This was the most effective statute of its kind in the history of Spain, because it authorized the state to construct the secondary works necessary to bring water from the main canals to the farms and forced the beneficiaries—who had for so long frustrated all irrigation schemes by refusing to invest in them—to repay the costs or risk expropriation. Other, grander projects for the irrigation of entire new regions of Spain were also being drawn up by Indalecio Prieto, the Socialist Minister of Public Works, and Lorenzo Pardo, the great hydraulic engineer of the Primo de Rivera era.[55] Nor did the Republic limit itself to planning. Although motivated partly by the need to ameliorate unemployment through public works, the normally parsimonious Azaña government allocated large amounts of money to irrigation. Primo de Rivera, who emulated Mussolini in deriving the maximum publicity from his hydraulic projects, had spent an average of 40 million pesetas on irrigation during each of his last three years in power. The Republic spent an annual average of 80 million pesetas during its first two years, and in 1933 allotted 158 million pesetas, almost four times the Primo de Rivera average.[56] No other state expenditure increased by so much.

The criticism of the Azaña coalition on this point is really a criticism of its unwillingness to rely exclusively on long-range, indirect means of social amelioration and its insistence that immediate land redistribution of the type outlined in the September law was also necessary. Azaña and his allies understood the efficacy of irrigation perfectly well but also recognized that—as the Franco regime has since proved—irrigation alone was not enough. Although so greatly at variance with the facts,

55. For a succinct description of the most daring of these plans, see *The Times* (London), 29 August 1933, and A. Ramos Oliveira, *Politics, Economics and Men of Modern Spain: 1808–1946* (London, 1946), pp. 462–64. It might be added that the work of Prieto and Pardo has constituted the basic fund of ideas from which the vast irrigation programs of the Franco government have unfolded.

56. *Anuario Estadístico: 1934*, pp. 344, 478.

the criticism has stuck, because the consequences of the attempt to redistribute land by direct means proved so catastrophic that they overshadowed all else and because the Azaña government was so short-lived that it was unable to fulfill its grandiose irrigation schemes.

A blindness and inflexibility of another sort did characterize the agrarian law, however. The consequences of the excessively literal application of the lease and ruedo principles have already been discussed, as have the unnecessary complications created by the extension of the law to northern and central Spain. The blanket refusal to allow settlers to purchase title to the plots they received must also be criticized, as must the more confiscatory rates of compensation established in the law. Finally, it was a grievous error not to rely more on indirect fiscal means of reform such as the Technical Commission's proposed surtax on large properties or Diego Hidalgo's heavily graduated inheritance tax. Some of these weaknesses were due, of course, to the compromises the Azaña coalition was forced to accept in the Cortes. Others, however, could easily have been avoided with better planning and more imagination.

Yet the September law did fulfill its central purpose: it made available enormous quantities of land at prices the state could afford to pay. If the Azaña government proved willing and able to act energetically, the reform might prove a success and the many errors committed would be rendered unimportant. It was the misfortune of the Republic that Azaña interpreted the revolutionary document to which his government had given birth in the most limited manner possible and failed to take advantage of the extraordinary powers it conferred on him.

9: A Law in Search of a Government

The Intensification of Cultivation Decrees

A great distance has always separated the laws of Spain from the realities they are supposed to regulate. Advanced social legislation was not difficult to find in Spanish statute books even during the monarchical era; what was rare was its energetic application. The important question in the autumn of 1932 was how the Azaña government would choose to interpret the sweeping mandate it received when the Agrarian Reform Law was passed by so overwhelming a majority. In administering the law would it try to undo the compromises it had been forced to accept during the long Cortes debates, or would it stay within the limitations imposed by the law and apply its provisions cautiously? The tenor of Azaña's speech against the grandeza on 8 September and the radical atmosphere created by the Sanjurjo revolt suggested that the more adventurous path would be chosen.

In its first important test after the law was passed, the Azaña government did indeed act resolutely. It faced a complex situation resulting in part from the bumper wheat crop of the summer of 1932, by far the largest in the history of Spain.[1] This crop could not in any case have been absorbed by the existing domestic market. The inevitable surplus was increased by an error of the Minister of Agriculture. Domingo, expecting the harvest to be poor, had authorized the importation of small

1. The wheat crop of 1932 was 5.0 million metric tons as against the previous high of 4.4 million metric tons in 1925. The average for the previous decade (1922 to 1931) was only 3.85 million metric tons. The truly astonishing 1932 crop was not due to new lands being put under cultivation as a result of the laboreo forzoso decrees, as the enemies of Azaña charged. There were 4.2 million hectares sown as opposed to an average of 4.1 million from 1922 to 1931 (INE, *Primera mitad del siglo XX*, p. 32). The true reasons for the increase were the long-range improvements in Spanish agricultural productivity and, above all, the unusually favorable climatic conditions in 1932.

quantities of less expensive foreign grains. The sudden appearance of so great a surplus of wheat, a crop that accounts for one-fifth of the value of all Spanish agricultural production, drove prices down to their lowest level since 1924.[2] It also had far-reaching political consequences since the approximately two million wheat producers injured by the collapse in prices never entirely forgave Domingo, whose wheat importations were made the scapegoat for the disaster.[3] The immediate effect of the crisis, however, was to renew the struggle between the larger landowners and the government over whether the principle of obligatory cultivation first established in the *laboreo forzoso* decree of May 1931 and repeatedly reasserted in other official measures was still binding.

The resistance of the owners was undoubtedly motivated in part by their desire to sabotage the agrarian program of the Azaña government, which had recently culminated in the September law. It would be unjust, however, to deny that very pressing economic considerations also influenced them.[4] Between the fall in wheat prices and the steady rise in wages which had resulted from the *términos municipales* law, the mixed juries, and the eight-hour day established in 1931, all employers found themselves faced with a profit squeeze that was aggravated by the drying up of sources of credit. The movement to withhold land was not centered in the traditional trouble spot of Andalusia, despite repeated threats of local employers' associations to stop sowing. The profit squeeze was less intense in that region, because the rich soils permitted relatively high yields. Moreover, if the Andalusian owner did not sow, he would receive no income, since there was little alternative use for his land. In Estremadura the situation was quite different. The profit squeeze was more deeply felt because yields were lower; lands left unsown would represent less of a loss to their owners, since the livestock

2. Wheat prices fell from an average of 500 pesetas per metric ton in 1928–31 to 440 pesetas in 1932. Montojo Sureda, p. 113.

3. A vicious campaign was instituted against Domingo on the grounds that he profiteered from the importations (his wife was reputed to hold shares in the importing mills). In fact, the importations were authorized because Spanish economic intelligence was so faulty and because the large wheat producers, hoping to drive prices up, deliberately held back information on the stocks they had at hand. Moreover, the importations amounted to only 0.3 million metric tons, or less than six percent of the domestic crop. Greater importations than this had been authorized in ten of the years between 1900 and 1931 (INE, *Primera mitad del siglo XX*, p. 95). On this whole question, of decisive importance for the Republic, see Montojo Sureda, pp. 38–40.

4. Adolfo Vázquez Humasqué, Director General of the IRA, himself gave "hatred of the regime" as the last of the several reasons that motivated the owners to withhold land in 1932 (article in *La Luz*, 10 May 1933).

that constituted an important source of wealth in Estremadura could graze on them.[5]

Apparently spontaneous in its origins, the movement to withhold land began to be organized systematically toward the beginning of October. The issue assumed national importance when the governor of Salamanca prohibited the Salamanca Landowners' Federation from sending out speakers to urge uncommitted owners not to sow.[6] Under the leadership of José María Gil Robles, later head of the Catholic CEDA, the Agrarian minority opened a campaign in the Cortes to win for the owners the right not to cultivate so long as wheat prices remained low.[7] The government, still flushed with confidence after its recent legislative victories and troubled by the spread of organized owner resistance to Badajoz and Caceres,[8] did not allow Gil Robles's speeches to go unchallenged. Domingo sternly warned that "those who say they will not sow will fall under grave sanctions similar to those recently agreed upon by the cabinet against [the Sanjurjo rebels]. He who does not sow will be expropriated."[9]

Yet it is doubtful that the government would have reacted as it did had it not also been confronted by the danger of peasant upheaval. Estremadura, which was dominated by the Socialists, had on the whole remained quieter than Andalusia since the proclamation of the Republic. There were many local outbreaks, some extremely serious, but these tended to be isolated and accidental. Toward the end of September, however, peasant agitation suddenly spread. The workers, who had had little employment since the summer harvest, continued their normal protest. But now they were joined by the *yunteros,* who formed a large proportion of the agricultural population in Estremadura. As mentioned earlier, the yunteros differed from other Spanish tenants or sharecroppers, because in the mixed agricultural-pastoral economy of Estremadura the lands they cultivated constantly changed; consequently, the "floating" leases they held had to be renewed very frequently.[10] When owners

5. On the complex interrelationship between agriculture and stockbreeding in Estremadura, see the description of the *yuntero* system in chap. 4.

6. *La Tierra,* 3 October 1932. The Landowners' Federation of Salamanca was particularly active during 1932 and 1933, because it was led by the three great stalwarts of the Agrarian minority—Casanueva, Lamamié de Clairac, and Gil Robles —who had been elected deputies from the province.

7. The Cortes debates on noncultivation are well summarized in *El Socialista* and *La Luz,* 18–22 October 1932.

8. On owner resistance in Badajoz, see *El Socialista,* 27 October 1932. On Caceres, see the report of the IRA technicians quoted in *El Obrero de la Tierra,* 4 February 1933.

9. Quoted in *El Socialista,* 22 October 1932.

10. For further details see above, Chap. 4.

suddenly began to refuse to grant new leases and chose instead to keep their land in pasture, the yunteros were driven to desperation. If they were denied land, the animals and tools that were their only possessions would be lost and they would be reduced to the status of day laborers. It was the intervention of the yunteros which gave a more threatening character to the disturbances in Estremadura. Workers had long been accustomed to enter farms to demand work or to seize crops. Now the yunteros themselves began to invade the large estates in order to plow up portions of them. A number of violent clashes occurred in which blood was shed. The tension probably reached its height in the county of Llerena (Badajoz), one of the few areas dominated by the Communists, when a revolutionary strike involving eleven villages began on 10 October. But the Socialist areas were also shaken by disturbances.[11] The government justly feared "that the isolated, sporadic action of some peasant groups would become coordinated and lead to a general upheaval." [12]

The response of the Azaña cabinet was intelligently conceived. Military force, which had been used against the peasants earlier in Andalusia, was politically impossible in the Socialist stronghold of Estremadura.[13] Moreover, repression would only encourage the recalcitrant owners. An immediate application of the Agrarian Reform Law was considered, only to be rejected as illegal, because the law did not permit land seizures of any kind until the property in question was included in the Inventory, on which work had not yet begun.[14] Instead the Azaña government decided to overcome both owner resistance and peasant protest by re-

11. My account is drawn primarily from *El Sol* and *El Debate* of September, October, and November 1932. The incidents of disorder were too numerous to list here, but the most violent among them were as follows. On 16 October a Socialist group attacked and almost killed a village official in Puebla del Prior; on 7 November several workers disarmed and beat three Guardias Civiles in Navalvillar de Pela; on 14 November the Guardia Civil wounded two workers in Oliva de Mérida and killed another in Castillo de Llerena; on 17 November another worker–Guardia Civil clash left six peasants injured. Several of these clashes occurred during invasions of farms for which large groups, which sometimes numbered in the hundreds, usually assembled.

12. Adolfo Vázquez Humasqué, as quoted in *BIRA* (March 1933), pp. 284–88.

13. The repression of Anarchosyndicalist outbreaks in Andalusia is discussed in chap. 11. The role of the Socialists during this entire period is mysterious. The Socialist press and the three major Socialist congresses (PSOE, UGT, and FNTT) held in late September and October criticized the owners' provocations but did not actively campaign for the transfer of lands to the yunteros. If the Socialists were responsible for the solution finally given to the problem, their influence was exercised behind closed doors by the three Socialist cabinet ministers.

14. Marcelino Domingo as quoted in *BIRA* (May 1933), p. 611.

viving the concept of temporary occupations outlined in the Technical Commission draft of the previous year.[15]

On 1 November a decree calling for the "intensification of cultivation" was issued as "an urgent measure for the relief of the present unemployment crisis." [16] Technical personnel were immediately to examine all large estates that remained uncultivated to determine what portions of these could be plowed without detriment to the stockbreeding activities of the farm. These portions were to be turned over to landless peasants for the two-year agricultural cycle characteristic of Estremadura. Thus the settlers would be able to sow a catch crop in 1932–33 and follow it with a major cereal crop in 1933–4. Once this latter crop had been harvested—that is, by September 1934 at the latest—the settlers were to pay the owner a rent and vacate the land. Presumably by that time the application of the Agrarian Reform Law would have progressed to the point of making other lands available for permanent settlement. The first decree applied only to Badajoz, which had experienced the most serious labor troubles. Its provisions were quickly extended to Caceres, Cadiz, Ciudad Real, Cordova, Granada, Malaga, Salamanca, and Seville.[17] In mid-December the province of Toledo was added.[18]

Despite the enormous geographical extension it had given them, the government regarded the Intensification of Cultivation decrees primarily as an indirect means of forcing owners to farm and intended to apply them only in those few localities where labor unrest was so acute that there was no way out except to give the peasants land. At first, the decrees seemed to have served their purpose. The campaign to withhold land from cultivation came to a halt. The peasant disturbances in Badajoz gradually diminished, although they were still sufficiently serious in late December to cause Domingo to take the uncharacteristic step of threatening that peasants who invaded farms would lose their right to become settlers under the Agrarian Reform Law.[19]

15. The Intensification of Cultivation decrees were "nothing more than the Technical Commission draft" put into practice (Domingo, *La experiencia del poder,* p. 226). The single major difference was that they limited temporary occupations to two years rather than extending them indefinitely.

16. Ministry of Agriculture decree of 1 November 1932, Article 1.

17. Ministry of Agriculture decrees of 4, 11, and 12 November 1932.

18. Ministry of Agriculture decree of 17 December 1932.

19. Domingo's bill to this effect appears in *D.S.* 286, 28 December 1932, app. 15. The bill never emerged from committee, partly because of the altered political situation produced by the Anarchosyndicalist rising of January, and partly because of Socialist opposition. *El Obrero de la Tierra,* 14 January 1933, mildly chides Domingo for having presented it, on the grounds that many farm invasions were trumped-up affairs in which owners called the police whenever workers exercised

In early January, however, the situation once again worsened. The Anarchosyndicalists launched a major revolt in Barcelona on 8 January, which was accompanied by brief risings in several other important cities. In the countryside, approximately a dozen villages were seized by in-surgents in Andalusia and in the region of Valencia. The quick crushing of the revolt, together with the fact that most of the peasants in Badajoz and Caceres were affiliated with the Socialists rather than the Anarcho-syndicalists, kept the insurrection from spreading to Estremadura. Never-theless, it had the effect of reviving the earlier peasant protest, particu-larly as it coincided with the approach of spring plowings which in-creased the anxiety of those yunteros who remained without land. In the latter half of January, Estremadura witnessed a new wave of farm in-vasions which appears to have been considerably more serious than that of October 1932. The government was more reluctant than ever to adopt repressive policies against the Socialist militants because of the recent Anarchosyndicalist rising, and because it was still shaken by the political uproar that followed the senseless massacre of twenty peasants by the state police at Casas Viejas (Cadiz) on the last day of that rising.[20] In consequence, new concessions were made. Domingo gave de facto recognition to many of the farm invasions by disguising them as legal settlements under the Intensification decrees. The technical standards by which the IRA personnel were to select the lands to be occupied were in many cases abandoned. In the province of Caceres, a political personage, the governor general of Estremadura, was allowed to make settlements on his own initiative.[21]

Because of the January disturbances, the government ended by temporarily occupying some 120,000 hectares instead of the 30,000 or 40,000 it had originally intended to seize.[22] Yet it was not stampeded into

their customary right to enter estates to search for firewood or gather acorns. Until police archives are opened, or an intensive study of the provincial and local press is made, it is indeed difficult to decide which invasions were serious.

20. For further details on Casas Viejas and the Anarchosyndicalist insurrection of January 1933, see chap. 11. La Luz and El Socialista provide the best coverage of the new wave of farm invasions in the national press, but for this period in partic-ular a study of the local press is also needed. The movement apparently began in Caceres, with large-scale farm invasions in Navalmoral de la Mata and Trujillo. The Communists again falsely claimed credit for the protest; Mundo Obrero was filled with hysterical predictions of general peasant revolt until mid-February.

21. For a surprisingly bitter denunciation of the nontechnical orientation of this second stage of the Intensification decrees, see Vázquez Humasqué's article in La Luz, 10 May 1933.

22. Vázquez Humasqué, La Luz, 8 March 1933, said that only 20,000 hectares were occupied during November, originally intended to be the chief period for the application of the decrees. Other evidence is that only 31,560 hectares had been

a wholesale transfer of all types of land. Although authorized to do so, the government did not invoke the decrees at all in Cordova, Granada, and Malaga, as can be seen in Table 30. It also successfully resisted local

TABLE 30 SETTLEMENTS UNDER INTENSIFICATION OF CULTIVATION DECREES

	Municipalities Affected	Farms Affected	Area Occupied (hectares)	Peasants Settled
Badajoz	57	642	53,146	18,699
Caceres	84	661[a]	45,209[a]	13,871[a]
Cadiz	18	72	7,645	2,394
Toledo	15	103	5,106	1,575
Ciudad Real	13	52	4,357	1,852
Seville	18	28	3,843	724
Salamanca	16	34	3,719	893
Jaen	1	1	280	100
Totals	222	1,593	123,305	40,108

SOURCE: *BIRA* (October 1933), pp. 52–60.

a. Of the Caceres totals, 558 farms, 35,684 hectares, and 11,683 persons were settled under the authority of the governor of the province, not by technical personnel of the Institute.

pressures for the seizure of grazing lands whose cultivation was not economically feasible, as in the immense Valley of Alcudía in Ciudad Real.[23] In Toledo the decrees were applied to but fifteen of the forty-seven municipalities that petitioned to be included under their provisions.[24] And of the 1,022 estates, mostly in Badajoz and Caceres, that actually were settled by IRA personnel, only small portions, never the entirety, were turned over to the yunteros.[25]

Thus the decrees did not entirely lose their original character as primarily precautionary measures. Many of the lands opened to temporary occupation had never been plowed previously, but a sizable proportion merely replaced lands that the yunteros would have received had not the owners begun their drive to withdraw their farms from cultiva-

---

turned over to settlers by IRA personnel by the end of January 1933 (*BIRA* [January 1933], p. 423).

23. *BIRA* (April 1933), p. 423.

24. *BIRA* (June 1933), pp. 701–23.

25. According to *BIRA* (October 1933), p. 57, the average size of the 1,022 farms settled by IRA personnel (there are no similar data for the farms in Caceres settled under the authority of the governor general of Estremadura) was 459 hectares, of which an average of 86 hectares, or about one-fifth, was turned over to the yunteros.

tion.[26] In a few localities the stockbreeding industry may have been slightly damaged, but on the whole it was not. Best of all, the government's policy of restrained concessions seemed to have tided the nation over the labor crisis that had occurred, and to have guaranteed that there would be time to apply the regular principles of settlement outlined in the Agrarian law.

The Squandering of the Impetus for the Reform

Unfortunately the Azaña government did not use the breathing spell it had gained to good advantage. The problems it had to face in executing the September law were, of course, far more complex than those connected with the implementation of the Intensification of Cultivation decrees. The scope of the law was far broader; not a few lands in a few provinces but most lands in many provinces were affected. The lands seized were not to be returned after a two-year interval but permanently expropriated. Inexperienced day laborers, not experienced and essential'y self-sufficient yunteros, were to receive custody of most of the lands appropriated. Farms could not be occupied at will but only after the procedures established in the Agrarian Reform Law had been followed. The state could not depend on the payment of rents by the settlers to reimburse the owners but had itself to pay compensation, much of it in cash, both to the owners and to their creditors. A larger body of technical personnel, who could be recruited only slowly, was necessary to administer the Agrarian law. Moreover, representative organizations for owners, workers, and tenants had to be recognized in each province, and elections had to be held to fill the seats on the provincial juntas of agrarian reform. The appeals of owners subject to expropriation had to be heard. Definitive censuses of the beneficiaries of the reform had to be compiled in each village.

The list of tasks to be performed was thus seemingly endless. Had more been done to prepare for the reform during the year in which the Azaña government awaited the end of the Cortes debates, some of these tasks might have been speedily completed. As it was, even with the best administration the prerequisites of the reform could not have been established in the first few months after the law finally received Cortes

26. In Badajoz approximately 60 percent of the land made available was previously unplowed (*BIRA* [March 1933], p. 265). In Caceres, where the owners' drive to withhold land from cultivation was more highly developed, most of the territory settled merely replaced lands from which the yunteros had been evicted (*El Obrero de la Tierra*, 4 February 1933). I was not able to secure information on other provinces.

approval in September. Once these crucial months had passed, there was strong reason to wait still longer—until the following September—before seriously undertaking the implementation of the law. The agricultural year for most grain crops began in October or November; for most of the other annually sown crops it started in February or March. Once the land had been plowed and crops sown, expropriation became both less desirable and prohibitively expensive. The farm operators who had begun a crop year should be allowed to complete it. If they were not, compensation would have to be paid for the crop as well as for the land. The impact of this kind of compensation could not be softened by payments in state bonds. Thus if the lack of greater preparation from October 1931 to September 1932 for the administration of the reform is excused, Azaña and Domingo cannot justly be criticized for not transforming the property structure overnight. Unless they were willing to act extralegally, which they were not, the law and the season of the year in which it was approved imposed too many limitations. Rather, their competence must be evaluated by what they accomplished given the limitations within which they had to work.

Domingo seems to have been primarily responsible for the first fundamental mistake. As a concession to the Cortes opposition, the September law provided that the Institute of Agrarian Reform be "governed by a Council, composed of agricultural technicians, jurists, and representatives of the official Agricultural Credit organization, of the owners, of the tenants, and of the agricultural workers." [27] The law did not define the composition of the Council in any greater detail, however. Nor did it specifically determine the relative powers of the Executive Council and of the Director General of the Institute, though it was clear that the law intended the Council to "govern." Thus, although the law oriented the Institute toward committee rather than individual rule, it by no means completely tied the hands of the government. Domingo might easily have avoided most of the difficulties inherent in committee rule—particularly the necessity for extended debates and for compromise decisions—without violating the provisions of the law.

Instead, in his decree of 23 September 1932, Domingo organized the Institute in such a way as to exaggerate all of the tendencies established in the law. All important decisions were to be made by the Executive Council. The Director General was to have little power. He would usually preside over the Council in place of the Minister of Agriculture, its nominal head. As chairman he could "initiate and order" the matters the Council was to discuss. He was also to act as liaison between the

27. Agrarian Reform Law, Article 3.

Council and the rest of the government. But his chief role was that of "head of personnel" of the Institute, who would "dictate the orders and instructions necessary for the fulfillment of the decisions of the Executive Council." [28]

The Director General's lack of power might not have rendered the Institute ineffective had Domingo created a compact Council capable of quick decisions. Instead he created a gigantic body of twenty-one members. Though his decision to include two "agricultural technicians" was understandable, he exceeded his obligations when he selected three "jurists" from the major professional corps in Spain. To the representative of the "official Agricultural Credit organization" he added a representative of the Mortgage Bank, a bank that no longer devoted many of its funds to agricultural loans. Though the law did not require it, representatives of four governmental organizations—the Ministry of the Treasury; its subsidiary, the Dirección General de Propiedades; the Ministry of Public Works; and the National Economic Council—were also seated. A veterinarian was also needlessly appointed, as was, still more inexplicably, an architect. Apparently Domingo thought that because the Institute might occasionally require technical advice on matters in which these persons were competent, they should be given voting rights on all questions that arose. Only the representation of those who were directly affected by the law—the owners, the workers, and the tenants—was limited. Each of these groups could elect through their several organizations two delegates to the Executive Council. [29]

Since the Minister of Agriculture and the Director General of the Institute also had voting rights, a body of twenty-one members was established when the provisions of the law might have been satisfied by a body half that size. Domingo's intention apparently was to anticipate objections to decisions of the Council by tying to it every governmental agency and extragovernmental group that had an interest in agrarian affairs. Since the government would itself name most of the delegates, he did not seem to fear that intense conflicts might arise between the several points of view represented.

Domingo's conception of the structure of the Institute did not go unchallenged. The organizational decree had been issued in the name of the entire cabinet, but the three Socialist ministers either had not been consulted or did not realize its implications. [30] Immediately upon release of

28. Ministry of Agriculture decree of 23 September 1932, Articles 11, 12, and 13.

29. Ministry of Agriculture decree of 23 September 1932, Article 8.

30. The silence of the three Socialist ministers during this period is strange, especially since the FNTT had suspected that the organizational structure of the

the decree, the Socialist National Federation of Agricultural Workers (FNTT) lodged a violent protest. The FNTT did not object to the division of power between the Director General and the Executive Council. Its attack was directed entirely at the "bureaucratic" composition of the Council. As they saw it, the two worker representatives in this body would be completely overshadowed by the eleven representatives of the governmental agencies, the banks, and the professional juridical corps, not to mention the veterinarian and the architect. If the Council is not reconstituted, the FNTT charged, "the implementation of the agrarian reform in Spain will fail." Those directly affected by the reform should be given greater representation and the technical and bureaucratic personnel should have only advisory, not voting, powers. Otherwise "the legitimate hopes placed by the working classes in the Agrarian Reform Law will be defrauded." The "bourgeois elements" will unite against the Socialists, and "the Law will be administered badly, with great delay, and with prejudice to the workers." [31]

For six weeks a crisis raged. The FNTT appealed to the UGT and the Socialist party, both of which were holding national congresses, and received their unanimous (though not especially enthusiastic) support.[32] Equally important, though the FNTT had suffered all the vicissitudes of the Cortes debates on the Agrarian law in silence, it now, for the first time, opened a public campaign against a decision of the government. It directed its local units to send protests to the Minister of Agriculture and, for a month, filled the pages of its journal, El Obrero de la Tierra, with the hundreds of responses it received.[33]

The conflict was resolved in the latter part of November by a compromise which, though attacked by El Debate as a sellout to the Socialists,[34] was on the whole a victory for Domingo. Although worker representation was increased from two delegates to six, the technical and bureaucratic personnel lost neither their seats nor their voting rights; consequently they continued to hold the balance of power in the Council. The only real effect of the Socialist protest was to make an already unwieldy body still more so. The tripling of the workers' delegation had to be matched among the owners if the principle of parity were to be maintained. Thus

IRA might be unfavorable to it several weeks before the Domingo decree actually appeared (*El Obrero de la Tierra*, 3, 17 September 1932).

31. *El Obrero de la Tierra*, 1, 15 October 1932.

32. PSOE, *XIII Congreso del Partido Socialista Obrero Español del 6 al 13 de octubre de 1932* (Madrid, 1934), p. 580.

33. *El Obrero de la Tierra*, 22, 29 October 1932; 5, 12, 9 November 1932.

34. "Thus, the agrarian reform is born dead. . . . The agrarian reform is at the service of the Socialists" (*El Debate*, 10 November 1932).

the size of the Council increased from twenty-one to twenty-nine members, most of whom, moreover, had official alternates who had to be informed of the proceedings and who sometimes sat at Council meetings.[35] Since the Socialists had not tried to expand the functions of the Director General, an office they apparently felt they would never fill, the now completely unmanageable Council continued to exercise all real power.

Having seen his agrarian reform proposal almost destroyed by obstructionism in the Cortes, Domingo had created a miniature Cortes of his own, in which, as Azaña contemptuously put it, "questioning periods, interpellations, orders of the day" and all the other apparatus of Spanish parliamentary life would become necessary.[36] Indeed, the Council proved less an executive than a legislative and judicial body. Its membership was so large and so many points of view were represented that its first year was spent in reproducing on a smaller scale the debates that had occupied the Cortes during most of 1932. The struggle was no longer over what provisions should be included in the law but over how the law should be interpreted. Should the ruedo provisions apply to the lands surrounding each hamlet or only to those near incorporated villages? How should the privileges whose exercise would subject the grandes to confiscation be defined? Should partially cultivable pasture lands be included in the reform or should they be excluded under Article 6 of the law? Procedural matters also occupied an inordinate amount of the Council's time. Several sessions were devoted to acting upon the appeals of individual grandes who requested exemption from confiscation. Several others were taken up with disputes that arose over the elections of representatives to the provincial juntas.[37] Though many of the questions debated were of great importance—an indication of how much had been left unsettled in the last-minute rush to approve the September law—the discussions were more

35. The revised decree appeared as Ministry of Agriculture decree of 4 November 1932.

36. Manuel Azaña, *Memorias íntimas de Azaña*, ed. Joaquín Arrarás (Madrid, 1939), p. 92 (entry for 28 September 1932). Part of Azaña's diary was stolen by Nationalist sympathizers during the Civil War. The passages chosen for publication by the Franco government were obviously intended to discredit both the man and the Republic. While unauthentic in the sense that they were taken out of context the passages themselves not only seem to be genuine but are also representative of certain aspects of the prime minister's personality. Azaña was inclined to be contemptuous, as is repeatedly proven in the complete text of those portions of his diary that were not stolen. These latter have recently been published in a masterful edition by Juan Marichal as vol. 4 of Manuel Azaña, *Obras Completas* (Mexico, 1968).

37. My account is drawn mostly from *La Luz* and *El Obrero de la Tierra* of December 1932 to June 1933. Both journals presented better summaries of the Council meetings than did *BIRA*, a generally dull and uninformative publication.

bitter and prolonged than they should have been. The representatives of the landowners were not alone in protracting the debates. As Vázquez Humasqué, the first Director General of the IRA, later said, "Our greatest struggle [on the Council] was not with the landowners but with their agents . . . the juridicial representatives of the *notarios*, the registrars of property, et cetera." [38] The narrow, excessively precise concerns of the governmental technicians who sat on the Council must also have contributed to the slowness of its actions.

Once it had set in, the paralysis of the Council was not easily cured. The Socialists tried to speed deliberations by demanding that subcommittees be created to deal with specific questions and that sessions of the entire Council be held more frequently. Neither proposal was accepted by a majority of Council members.[39] The Directors General could neither impose their authority over the Council nor act in its stead. Vázquez Humasqué, the first occupant of the office, was dismissed in early February, apparently because of a conflict over the implementation of the second stage of the Intensification of Cultivation decrees.[40] Domingo either had difficulty finding a successor willing to accept so thankless a task or could not decide what sort of person he wished to fill the job. Consequently, for the next two months Ramón Feced, an associate of Domingo in the Radical Socialist party, served as acting chairman of the Council in addition to his regular job as Undersecretary of Industry. In April this arrangement broke down as, with much fanfare, Domingo named himself Director General. Yet, burdened as he was with the many other duties he later so often lamented, Domingo could not spare the time to run the Institute. After four months of this unhappy experiment, under a heavy barrage of criticism, the Minister of Agriculture stripped himself of his self-imposed responsibilities.[41] Thus not until early July 1933, when Dionisio Terrer was named to it, did the office of Director General resume even the limited functions it had performed under Vázquez Humasqué.

The mistakes, the hesitations, the confusions that marked the organization and administration of the Institute, also characterized the presentation of the supplementary agrarian legislation mentioned in the closing

38. Quoted in *BIRA* (July 1936), p. 26.

39. *El Obrero de la Tierra,* 4 February and 24 October 1933. The organizational decree required the Council to hold two weekly meetings. It rarely exceeded its statutory obligations.

40. I have not been able to discover the reasons for Vázquez Humasqué's dismissal, but aside from his opposition to the government's legalization of some of the spontaneous seizures of land during the second stage of the Intensification decrees, he seems to have pressed for faster action on the supplementary agrarian program.

41. See below, pp. 251–52, for details on Domingo's rise and fall as Director General of the IRA.

paragraphs of the September law. Enactment of a general lease law, the redemption of foros and rabassa morta contracts, the creation of a National Agrarian Bank, and the recovery of the common lands had repeatedly been promised since the earliest days of the Republic. Even prior to the opening of the debates on the Agrarian law, in April 1932, Domingo had told newsmen that he had already prepared draft bills on leases and agricultural credit which would "soon be submitted for cabinet study" and, presumably, for Cortes approval.[42] After the debates on the September law were over, the Minister of Agriculture once again stressed that quick action could be expected and even went to the point of promising to present a bill for the recovery of the common lands to the cabinet within a week.[43]

In fact, the last three months of 1932 went by without any sign of the supplementary agrarian program. In early January the government took the fatal step of opening Cortes discussion on the bill implementing the anticlerical clauses of the Constitution. This diversion of parliamentary attention from social problems may perhaps be excused on the grounds that, after the passage of the Catalan Statute and the Agrarian Reform Law, the religious question remained the only major issue on which there had been no important piece of specific legislation. Yet the government gave no indication that it was preparing for a resumption of the debates on its social program once the anticlerical bill had been approved and legislative symmetry restored. Domingo again failed to submit the agrarian bills he had promised; more important, in the latter part of February, Azaña neglected to include the supplementary agrarian laws as part of the legislative program the Constituent Cortes would have to fulfill before he would consider its mandate ended and the time for new elections at hand.

Whether unconscious or deliberate, Azaña's significant omission served to rally those concerned with an extension of the agrarian reform. The Socialist press issued much more urgent demands for the appearance of the supplementary program.[44] The government's negligence also began to be attacked in some of the bourgeois Republican journals.[45] Yet even so, considerable time still had to pass before the first steps were taken toward converting the long-standing commitments into legislative realities. Domingo finally broke his silence on 6 April, when he submitted a draft bill

42. Quoted in *Revista de los Servicios Sociales-Agrarios* (May 1932), pp. 164–65.

43. *La Luz,* 19, 26 October 1932.

44. *El Socialista,* 26 February 1933; *El Obrero de la Tierra,* 11, 18, 25 February 1933.

45. *La Luz,* 27 February and 1 April 1933.

on leases to the agricultural committee of the Cortes. After another two
months had passed, in late June, Domingo made public his proposal on
the National Agrarian Bank.[46] The recovery of the common lands had to
wait still longer; it was not until late July that the Minister of Agriculture's
bill on this question appeared.[47] As for the foros and rabassa morta contracts, the Azaña government was to fall from power without having given
legislative form to its pledges that these would be made redeemable.

The Character of Left Republican Leadership

The vacillation and disorder with which the agrarian program was
conducted during the first half of 1933 seemed to reflect the personality of
Domingo. Azaña surpassed even his usual levels of disdainfulness when
he wrote in his diary:

> The most unattainable thing in the world is precision and detail in
> anything from Domingo. Even the Spanish he speaks is made up of
> vague, general and inappropriate expressions. It is not that Domingo
> is stupid, but his mind is oratorical and journalistic, without keenness
> or profundity. . . . His lack of acquaintance with rural affairs is
> total.[48]

Azaña's characterization was not entirely just. Domingo had discharged
with honor his previous post as Minister of Education in the Provisional
Government. Even in agrarian matters he could act effectively when con-

46. Domingo had released a preliminary proposal on the Agrarian Bank in
early May to test the reaction of the private banks whose collaboration he wanted.
The definitive version of the proposal was not made public until late June (*El Sol,*
7 May and 24 June 1933).

47. The recovery of the common lands, which in 1932 seemed to have been
scheduled as the first order of business after the approval of the Agrarian Reform
Law (see chap. 8), had been delayed because of major differences in the cabinet
as to how it should be carried out. I have not been able to discover any of the
details, but some information is given in Aureli Joaniquet, *La reforma agraria a
Catalunya* (Barcelona, 1933).

48. Azaña, *Memorias íntimas,* p. 90 (entries for 6 June and 6 July 1933). To
judge from the complete text of portions of his diary recently edited by Juan Marichal,
Azaña started with a relatively favorable impression of Domingo but had come to
despise him as early as 13 July 1932. In his diary entry for that date (*Obras completas,* 4, 437), Azaña reacted to Domingo's suggestion that the Catalans be persuaded to withdraw their Statute of Autonomy (which was encountering serious
opposition in the Cortes) with: "That's what Domingo is like: whenever confronted
by any difficulty, he runs. Don't lead, don't govern; stay in power by being facile,
that is to say, by being useless, by being a failure. Yet Domingo hopes to carry out
the agrarian reform, a thousand times more difficult than the Statute!"

fronted with a limited problem forced upon him by events, as he proved by the Intensification of Cultivation decrees. Moreover, Domingo was not free to devote all his energies to the agrarian question. Until it was reorganized in June 1933, the ministry he led was in effect a hydra-headed Ministry of National Economy, concerned with all the problems of industry, mining, and commerce—as well as of agriculture—in a depression economy.[49]

Yet it was true that Domingo knew little about the social crisis in the Spanish countryside. Prior to his entry into political life he had alternated as a journalist, playwright, and novelist. After 1917, when his part in the Renovationist movement of that year made him something of a public hero, he also turned to writing political commentaries, especially on problems of education, which became his forte. He was extremely prolific. By 1937 he had published twenty-six books: ten plays, three novels, and thirteen other works on education and political affairs.[50] But he was so removed from the rural social crisis that in the two political testaments he published during the year before the establishment of the Republic, he scarcely mentioned the need for agrarian reform.[51]

Perhaps it was because of his awareness of his limitations that Domingo claimed to have accepted the Ministry of Agriculture—"the most difficult ministry, the ministry with the most disagreeable tasks to perform, the most unpopular ministry"—with reluctance.[52] The forebodings he felt on that occasion[53] proved justified. The office—which seems to have come to him because the Radical Socialists had proved best able to work with the Socialists as the agricultural committee of the Cortes was hammering out its drafts in 1931—brought him little but misery. The wheat importations of 1932 began the destruction of his reputation. The fiasco of the agrarian reform lost him most of his remaining credit, even within his own party.[54] Yet though Domingo could not dominate the problems he had to face, he continued to heap new responsibilities upon himself, as when he assumed the director generalship of the IRA. Nor would he al-

---

49. Domingo, *Experiencia del poder*, pp. 176–80, provides a heartfelt catalog of the manifold responsibilities of the Ministry.

50. For the titles, see his *España ante el mundo* (Mexico, 1937).

51. Marcelino Domingo, *A donde va España?* (Madrid, 1930), and Alicio Garcitoral [pseudonym], *La ruta de Marcelino Domingo* (Madrid, 1930).

52. Domingo's speech of 7 June 1933, in Partido Republicano Radical Socialista, *Texto taquigráfico del Cuarto Nacional Ordinario* (Madrid, 1934), p.469.

53. Azaña's diary (*Obras Completas*, 4, 273) makes clear that Domingo indeed would have preferred to remain Minister of Education. See also Domingo's 16 June 1933 Cortes speech ("I was not the man, when the Republic was founded, designated for this mission I now hold") and his *Experiencia del poder*, p. 175.

54. See below, pp. 262–68, 277–79.

low himself to be transferred to a ministry whose problems were less complex and more in keeping with his previous skills and interests. An opportunity for escape from the morass into which he had fallen presented itself during the cabinet crisis of June 1933, but Domingo refused to take it. In the artfully invective words of Azaña:

> Marcelino is anxious to retain the Ministry of Agriculture. It is a question of *amour propre*. He hopes to undo the past. People blame him for the failure of the application of the agrarian reform, and he either has great confidence in his skills or is absolutely blind, because instead of seizing the first chance to skip out, he insists on continuing in his post.[55]

For all these reasons Domingo was not able to provide the decisive lead that might have revived the agrarian reform. This "good-hearted but weak"[56] man issued statement after statement in which he promised that the application of the Agrarian Reform Law would soon begin. But he so clearly lacked command of the situation that his words came to be treated with ridicule by all. Perhaps it was his bombastic pronouncements and dilettantism that ultimately most discredited him. Upon "resolutely assuming" the director generalship of the IRA, he was later to say, "I abandoned my office in the ministry to seclude myself" with the problems of agrarian reform.[57] To the press he bravely proclaimed that he was bringing a new impetus to the Institute and immediately set off on a whirlwind tour of the trouble spots of Andalusia.[58] Yet three months later his energies had so flagged and he had accomplished so little that the same journals that had enthusiastically accepted his promises of April were sarcastically advising him to stop his "motor jaunts, his Sunday speeches, his visits to trade fairs abroad, his writing of comedies and dramas," and devote himself to the solution of the social agrarian problem.[59]

However, Domingo was not alone to blame for the "open and complete disintegration evident in all things related to the agrarian reform"[60] in the spring and summer of 1933. Azaña must also be held partly responsible. For a short time after his dramatic intervention in the Cortes debates on 8 September 1932, he spoke of the Agrarian Reform Law as "the best work" of the Republic, because it would create a new social class on which

55. Azaña, *Memorias íntimas,* p. 92 (entry for 6 June 1933).
56. Ibid., p. 90 (entry for 6 June 1933).
57. Domingo, *Experiencia del poder,* p. 227.
58. *La Luz,* 1, 3 April 1933.
59. *La Luz,* 4 July 1933.
60. *Economía Española* (May 1933), p. 133.

the democratic regime could firmly base itself.[61] One also suspects that the strong hand of Azaña was behind the Intensification of Cultivation decrees of November 1932. But his renewed interest did not last long. Though privately highly critical of the form Domingo gave to the Executive Council of the Institute,[62] Azaña does not seem ever to have used his influence in an attempt to reshape the Council into a more effective body. And, as mentioned previously, his policy statements during the winter of 1932–33 gave exceedingly low priority to the supplementary agrarian program.

Azaña's limited conception of his duties is probably best revealed in the budgets that his government allotted to the Institute. The Agrarian Reform Law had set 50 million pesetas as the minimum annual allocation for the Institute, a figure slightly larger than 1 percent of the total national budget, or less than half of what was spent on the Guardia Civil. Azaña felt that his obligations were fulfilled when this minimal sum was granted. For the last three months of 1932 the IRA received 8 million pesetas. In the 1933 budget, the first full budget to include the Institute, only the mandatory 50 million pesetas was provided.[63] Vázquez Humasqué asked that the administrative expenses of the Institute be included under the Ministry of Agriculture budget so that the entire IRA allotment could be used to finance settlements. His request was rejected.[64] The niggardliness of these first allocations may have been partly due to the assumption that since the Institute was not fully operative, it could not yet absorb a larger sum. Yet there was more behind it. When asked about his future plans for the agrarian reform by two French Socialist leaders in early 1933, Azaña replied that "the rhythm of the Law's application will depend upon the state of finances." [65] Thus the "state of finances," not the need to settle peasants, was to receive priority. Having helped unbalance the life of the nation by his threat to seize land, Azaña now refused to unbalance his budget. He once again ended the year with a perfect record of fiscal responsibility.[66] The Robespierre of the 8 September 1932 speech had proven himself a Necker.

61. Manuel Azaña, *En el poder y en la oposición* (1932–34) (2 vols. Madrid, 1934), *1*, 22.

62. Azaña, *Memorias íntimas*, p. 92 (entry for 28 September 1932).

63. *BIRA* (April 1933), pp. 443–57.

64. Report of Vázquez Humasqué to the IRA Executive Council as cited in *El Obrero de la Tierra*, 24 December 1932.

65. Jules Moch and G. P. Moch, *L'Espagne Républicaine* (Paris, 1933), p. 49.

66. The fiscal orthodoxy of the Azaña government was remarkable for a new, supposedly radical, regime. Azaña closed both of his years in power with a budget surplus, achieved partly as a result of the successful flotation of bond issues. In Azaña's defense it must be remembered that almost one-fourth of the national budget

The roots of Azaña's passiveness were not entirely dissimilar from those of Domingo's ineffectualness. Despite the great differences of intellect and personality in the two men, they shared a common heritage. It was not that they and their fellow Republicans were unconcerned with agrarian affairs—the influence of Joaquín Costa and of his "colectivismo agrario" was too strong for this to be possible. But theirs was a sentimental attachment to a distant and imperfectly understood objective. The Republican parties during the monarchy were almost entirely urban-based and Europe-oriented. They had been nurtured on anticlericalism, antimilitarism, and antimonarchism. Among the Catalans, regional autonomy was another issue that aroused passionate devotion. Toward agrarian reform the attitude of the Republicans was almost as ambiguous as that of their nineteenth-century predecessors who neglected to enlist the peasantry in their fight against absolutism. A change had taken place since the turn of the century, of course. Years could no longer go by without a Republican deputy rising in the Cortes to demand agrarian reform, as had still been true in the pre-World War I era. Costa, the Green Revolutions of Eastern Europe, and the alliance with the Socialists had changed all that. Yet, as suggested earlier, the deepest emotions of these heirs to the French Revolution were awakened by the antiaristocratic implications of the agrarian reform rather than by the reform itself.[67]

Azaña perfectly typified these attitudes. Prior to 1931 his myriad writings—for he, too, was a novelist, playwright, and social critic, though of a far higher caliber than Domingo—centered around the anticlerical theme, with some attention after World War I to the excessive power of the military.[68] After 1931 his concerns do not seem to have changed. His work as Minister of War in the Provisional Government created his reputation; his October 1931 speech against the Church launched him into the premiership. On agrarian matters he eloquently pleaded for reform in a number of speeches during the first enthusiastic months of the Republic but thereafter remained silent. Except in two instances, one searches in

---

was already tied up in servicing the enormous national debt of 20.8 billions (INE, *Anuario Estadístico: 1943*, p. 461). As in other impoverished nations, the burden of the past was so great that the needs of the present and future could not easily be met except by persons willing to employ drastic methods.

67. There were exceptions to the ambiguous Republican attitude, of course. For example, Álvaro de Albornoz, co-leader with Domingo of the Radical Socialist party, included an eloquent plea for agrarian reform in his introduction to Gabriel Morón, *El Partido Socialista ante la realidad política de España* (Madrid, 1929). Yet even Albornoz failed to do much to defend reform after the Republic was established.

68. For a discerning analysis of Azaña's early writings, see Juan Marichal's introductions to the first two volumes of Azaña's *Obras Completas* (Mexico, 1966).

vain in the three volumes of his collected speeches for more than a passing
reference to what was, after all, probably the most urgent question of the
day.[69]

This lack of deep involvement with the agrarian reform must stand
as a basic reason for the poor implementation of the September law.
There had always been an unresolved internal contradiction in the agrarian program of the Republic. Though milder than some of the bills which
preceded it, the Agrarian law was nevertheless revolutionary in its implications. It seriously threatened the strongest economic class in Spain, cut
off sources of credit, placed much of the land in an anomalous position in
which it was controlled fully neither by its owners nor by the state, and
awakened the hopes of the impoverished peasantry. To have been consistent with so revolutionary a measure, revolutionary means should have
been used to put it into effect. But the Azaña government lacked the emotional commitment necessary to accept the risks involved in such measures. At bottom the position of most Left Republicans was not very different from that of such distinguished moderates as Díaz del Moral. They
feared that if the reform were implemented too rapidly it might lead to
massive owner resistance or degenerate into a chaotic series of peasant assaults on the large estates. Either of these eventualities would produce
enormous dislocations in the agricultural economy and condemn Spain to
what *El Debate* had once described as "one or two years of Russian hunger." [70] Domingo seems to have been especially haunted by these fears. In
his speeches he repeatedly referred to the post-World War I experience
of Eastern Europe, particularly to Communist Russia, which "is still paying for the economic upheaval caused by the cry . . . 'the land for those
who work it.' " [71] In June 1933 he summed up his defense of his activities
as Minister of Agriculture by saying that whatever else he might be accused of, "I am certain that I have prevented an economic crisis." [72]

Yet to go from the rejection of a "simplistic, delusory, and disruptive
cry like that issued by Lenin" [73] to the almost complete paralysis of policy
which characterized Spanish agrarian affairs in 1933, an extraordinary
naïveté and optimism were also required. As was so often to prove the
case in other matters, the Left Republicans (and, as will be seen, the Socialists) were crippled in agrarian affairs by the conviction that since they

69. This point is stressed by Ramos Olivera, p. 337. One gets the same impression of a basic lack of interest, particularly after he had become prime minister,
when leafing through Azaña's diary (*Obras completas, 4*).

70. *El Debate*, 3 November 1931.

71. Domingo, *Experiencia del poder*, p. 218.

72. *Cuarto Congreso*, p. 469.

73. Domingo, *Experiencia del poder*, p. 221.

were the true repository of the highest aspirations of Spain, they would continue to rule until they had put their policies into practice. The ideal would somehow convert itself into the real. The landowners' campaign to convince the nation that the pitiably small achievements of the reform were not worth its cost would not succeed.[74] The peasants, led to expect rapid land redistribution, would remain patient while only some ten to fifteen thousand of their numbers were settled each year.[75] The Azaña government's naïvely optimistic assumption that it held a semipermanent mandate to power underlay the excessively technical orientation it gave to the agrarian reform. Its implicit self-righteousness enabled it to excuse what others might consider its incompetence.

The simultaneous lack of conviction and overconfidence of the Left Republicans sharpened the contradictions inherent in the reform. Not only did Azaña refuse to use revolutionary means to implement a revolutionary measure; he did not even employ his full legal powers. During the first half of 1933 the government could have carried out settlements at least equal to those accomplished under the Intensification of Cultivation decrees without overstepping the bounds of legality, burdening the state with intolerable debts, or setting off a wave of uncontrollable peasant invasions of the large estates. As it was, only a handful of the estates that belonged to the Sanjurjo rebels and the *grandeza* were seized. This is not to say that the nine months that had passed since the approval of the September law were entirely wasted. The legalistic apparatus for future reform was created. The Inventory of Expropriable Property had been completed, though tardily. The Census of beneficiaries to the reform was well under way. Juntas had been established in all fifty Spanish provinces. Technical personnel had been recruited—a difficult task[76]—and dispatched to the fourteen provinces where the reform was immediately applicable in its entirety. Some of the ambiguities in the Agrarian law had

74. The sensitivity of the Left Republicans to the landowners' campaign was simply astounding. All of Vázquez Humasqué's articles in *La Luz* of February through April 1933 touch upon it, and Domingo gives it great emphasis in his *Experiencia del poder*, pp. 225–26, 230–31.

75. Vázquez Humasqué proposed the settlement of 13,000 to 15,000 landless laborers and the conversion of 5,000 small tenants into proprietors (presumably under the still-unenacted general lease legislation) as an ideal annual goal in his *La Luz* article of 2 January 1933. In his articles of 17 and 27 February, however, he accepted a figure of 10,000 annually as a more realistic objective.

76. Though the problems of technical recruitment in Spain were not as great as those encountered by underdeveloped nations outside Europe, there was always a scarcity of trained personnel. For example, the head of the IRA technical corps in the extremely important province of Toledo was a recent university graduate with but a year of practical experience.

been ironed out in the quasi-legislative sessions of the Executive Council. In short, all was ready for the serious implementation of the agrarian reform. How strongly the Azaña government would have acted must remain a matter of conjecture, because it was just then, in the late summer of 1933, that its time ran out. Azaña's assumption that he would continue to enjoy popular support for an unlimited period proved false. He was never given the opportunity to make up for the time lost in the last three months of 1932 and in the first six months of 1933. As Esteban Martínez Hervas, president of the Socialist Peasant Federation, had once put it, the agrarian law had for too long remained "a law in search of a government" [77] willing to apply it

77. Quoted in *El Obrero de la Tierra*, 1 May 1933.

10: The Fall of Azaña

Casas Viejas and the By-Elections of April 1933

The strength of the Azaña government had been slowly waning since January 1933. The floundering of the agrarian reform was not the only cause. A number of other factors, most of them related, to be sure, to the rural social crisis, were equally responsible. Perhaps the most important single cause for the eventual collapse of the regime was an accidental occurrence that took place in an obscure village of southern Andalusia. The Anarchosyndicalists had been waging a desperate war against the Republic almost from its inception. On 8 January 1933 the FAI gave the signal for a national rising. Police stations and army barracks were assaulted throughout Spain; for two days street battles raged in Barcelona. Yet like all previous Anarchosyndicalist efforts, the poorly prepared January revolt was hopeless from the start. The urban masses did not rise to overthrow the state. Almost everywhere the movement depended upon a few militants who were easily defeated. By 11 January the revolutionary movement seemed to have ended. But on that day the peasants of Casas Viejas suddenly took up arms.

The revolt at Casas Viejas was a "tardy spark from an already spent conflagration." [1] When news of the Anarchosyndicalist rising elsewhere finally reached this tiny hamlet in Cadiz, the local militants raised their red and black banner, declared the advent of anarchy, and proceeded to assault the barracks in which the few guardias assigned to the village had taken refuge. The siege was unsuccessful, because reinforcements soon arrived to relieve the local police detachment. Most of the rebels and much of the neutral population fled to the mountains, but a small group barricaded itself in the home of one of the leaders of the revolt, Seisdedos, and began shooting at the police. An Assault Guard, sent to negotiate with the rebels, was taken hostage. In the

1. Ramos Oliveira, p. 298.

siege that followed, the rebels wounded two more Assault Guards. The counterfire of the troops was less effective. Machine guns were brought up, but proved useless against the stone building. Grenades and bombs were thrown, but failed to explode.[2] Since complete darkness had by now fallen, the local commander decided to call off the attack until dawn.

At about two in the morning, however, a ninety-man detachment of Assault Guards suddenly arrived from Madrid by way of Jerez de la Frontera, where it had spent most of the day putting down another outbreak. Nervous and exhausted, its captain, Manuel Rojas, countermanded the local commander, ordered the Seisdedos house set on fire, and stationed his men with their rifles trained at its only exit. A woman and a child who had been in the house were allowed to escape unharmed. As its other occupants emerged, they were not taken captive but were shot. Seisdedos and his daughter, Libertaria, remained behind and were immolated.

The tragedy did not end there. Enraged at the sight of the charred body of the Assault Guard taken hostage earlier, Rojas ordered his troops to drag any men they could find to Seisdedos's hovel to view the horrible consequences of the village rising. Twelve peasants were assembled. One of them apparently gave Rojas an insolent look. His nerves frayed, Rojas opened fire. His subordinates followed suit. The bullets did not cease until all twelve villagers lay dead.[3]

A furor of protest swept the nation. The Republic had come into being as a humanitarian regime that would deliver Spain from the excessive police brutality of the monarchy. Its fundamental claim to moral superiority was thus violated by the massacre at Casas Viejas, especially as it had been perpetrated by the Assault Guards, a force created by the Republic for the specific purpose of avoiding the savagery of the Guardia Civil. It was not the Anarchosyndicalists alone who protested. Sincere Republicans were also deeply disturbed.[4] In the parliament the hotheads

2. As the *La Tierra* article on Casas Viejas put it, "Bombs in Spain, those thrown by the forces of public order just as much as those thrown by the revolutionaries, seem to have been rendered useless in advance." Quoted in José Peirats, *La CNT en la revolución española* (3 vols. Toulouse, 1951–53), 1, 56.

3. My account of Casas Viejas is drawn from Arrarás, 2, 80–86; *El Sol* and *El Debate*, 13–16 January 1936; Peirats, 1, 56–58; Henry Buckley, *Life and Death of the Spanish Republic* (London, 1940), pp. 95–96. Ironically, one year earlier an Anarchist congress had cited Casas Viejas as an especially difficult village to organize, because the peasants there had been "anesthetized by [bourgeois] politics." Federación de Trabajadores Agrícolas de la Comarca de Cadiz, *Memoria del Primer Congreso Comarcal* (Jerez de la Frontera, 1932), p. 9.

4. For example, see *Cuarto Congreso*, pp. 250–57, 340–43, and 419–20.

among the Left Republicans—no Socialists ever joined them—used Casas
Viejas to criticize the moderate policies of Azaña. Had the peasants been
given the land promised, they said, there would have been no revolt.[5]
The Radicals also strongly joined in the assault, especially since they
saw an opportunity to curry the Anarchosyndicalist vote. But perhaps
the most bitter attacks came from those who had previously demanded
that peasant revolts be "put down in blood." [6] The conservative groups
all suddenly found that their deepest humanitarian sentiments had been
offended. As one of them put it, the slaughter at Casas Viejas was "the
consequence of the policies of a regime which should call itself not republican, but barbaric." [7]

The hopes among the opposition parties that the incident could be
used to bring down the government were not fulfilled. Though they sent
an unofficial Cortes deputation to Casas Viejas and forced the cabinet
to agree to an official parliamentary investigation, they could not prove
that Captain Rojas's excesses were due to orders from the Ministry of
the Interior, much less from Azaña. A vote of confidence on 16 March
1933, two months after the furor had started, supported the government.
The issue was closed in the Cortes.

But things were never again the same. The most important specific
consequence of Casas Viejas was that it gave the Radicals the excuse to
go into open opposition once more. Lerroux's denunciatory speech of 3
February 1933 formally ended the *union sacrée* atmosphere created by
Sanjurjo's revolt five months before.[8] The intangible consequences of
Casas Viejas were probably even more important. Azaña, who was
forced to defend his government before the Cortes on eight separate occasions during the two months of the Casas Viejas controversy,[9] never recovered his former authority. In fact, though the entries in his diary
suggest that he hardly knew of Casas Viejas while it was happening, the
rumor persisted that he was the person most responsible because, when

5. The speech of Eduardo Ortega y Gasset, leader of the left wing of the
Radical Socialist party, as cited in Arrarás, 2, 87, 89.

6. *El Debate*, 23 September 1931.

7. The speech of General Joaquín Fanjul, an Agrarian deputy, as quoted in
Arrarás, 2, 91.

8. For the attitude of the Radicals, see Partido Republicano Radical, *Libro de
Oro* (Madrid, 1935), especially pp. 244–46, in which Lerroux made an appeal for
Anarchosyndicalist support by accusing Azaña of a lack of "tact and cordiality" in
handling labor disputes. Like Fanjul, Lerroux was a leopard who changed his spots
when it was to his advantage.

9. Frank Sedwick, *The Tragedy of Manuel Azaña* (Columbus, Ohio, 1963),
p. 122. Azaña appeared so frequently partly because Casares Quiroga, then Minister
of Interior, was ill and unable to defend himself.

asked what to do, he had shouted *"Tiros a la barriga, a la barriga."* [10]
So strong did the slogan "the Government of Casas Viejas" become that
ten months later even poor Domingo, who had nothing to do with the
orders given the troops, was driven from an electoral meeting with cries
of "Murderer!" and "Casas Viejas!"

Just as the Casas Viejas controversy was passing its peak, another
blow struck the Azaña regime. On 23 April 1933 special elections were
held in 2,653 villages to select 19,103 municipal councilors. The special
balloting was necessary because the councilors chosen during the elections of 12 April 1931 (the elections which brought the Republic into
being) had been unseated by the Provisional Government, either because their seats had not been contested or because of charges of irregu-
larities in the voting. For two years the villages in question had been
ruled by committees appointed by the Provisional Government. Since
the old *cacique* system had thus presumably been destroyed, most observers expected a victory for Azaña's forces. The government itself in
a statement of 11 April expressed its belief that "the elections will show
how much public opinion has changed in the rural districts of Spain." [11]

In fact, the elections showed only that the peasants no longer voted
for a monarchy, not that they accepted Azaña's version of the Republic.
Though the parties represented in the Azaña coalition collectively won
more seats than any single opposition group, they received only about
one-third of the total vote. Dramatic reversals of political fortunes
occurred. The Agrarian minority, which had won about 5 percent of the
Cortes seats in the elections of June 1931, won more than 20 percent of
the councilor posts. By contrast, the Socialist party, the largest group in
the Constituent Cortes, won fewer seats on municipal councils than
their long-time rivals, the Radicals, and less than half as many as the
resurgent Agrarians.[12]

In retrospect the government's defeat seems less surprising than does
Azaña's confidence that the elections would buttress his position. Most
of the villages that voted were hamlets located in Old Castile or Navarre,
precisely the areas in which clerical influence was strongest and the

10. "Shoot them in the guts, in the guts." For a standard denunciation of
Azaña on this count, see Melchor Fernández Almagro, *Historia de la República
Española* (Madrid, 1940), pp. 63–64.

11. Quoted in Arrarás, 2, 116. The Socialists seem to have been less sure of
victory than Azaña. Throughout March and April, *El Obrero de la Tierra* conducted
an intensive campaign to get out the vote.

12. As in all other Spanish elections, the precise distribution of seats by parties
is difficult to determine, partly because party affiliations were so weak. My figures
are drawn from *Anuario Estadístico: 1934,* p. 651, and Arrarás, 2, 117. Arrarás
presents perhaps the best conservative interpretation of the elections.

tradition of peasant rebellion least developed. Most of the intended reforms of Azaña were irrelevant to the small peasant proprietors who dominated the rural social structure of these two regions. Whatever benefits might have accrued to them from the Republic were overshadowed by the losses they had suffered from the fall in wheat prices in 1932 and the rise in labor costs produced by the agrarian decrees of the Provisional Government. Had the elections been held in regions where day laborers or tenant farmers made up the bulk of the population, the results might have been quite different. As it was, of the 2,653 *ayuntamientos* contested, fewer than 100 were located in Western Andalusia and Estremadura.[13]

For these reasons Azaña was justified in rejecting demands for his resignation or for changes in his government. The municipalities that had voted were "rotten boroughs," he said. They did not represent so much as 10 percent of the total national population. It would be ridiculous to interpret the decision of so "inert," so "docile," a segment of the population as a repudiation of the mandate of the government. Instead, he claimed, the government should be congratulated for having to some extent penetrated these last strongholds of "monarchism and caciquism."[14] Yet the fact remained that however unrepresentative they may have been, the only elections held in Spain since the ebbing of the enthusiasm of the first few months of the Republic had gone against Azaña.

Strains within the Azaña Coalition

Casas Viejas and the defeat in the April elections helped speed the decomposition of some of the parties in the Azaña coalition. As mentioned, except for the Socialists, these were all new groups that had been formed more or less accidentally after the coup of 1923 had destroyed the political system of the Restoration Monarchy. They lacked the firm organizational base and long political heritage that might have enabled them to weather the stresses present in Spain in 1933. The party most seriously affected was the Radical Socialist, the largest group in the Azaña coalition after the Socialists. Unlike the Galician ORGA and the Catalan Esquerra, the two regional parties in the coalition, the Radical Socialists did not have a central purpose so dominant as to bind them together under almost any circumstances. Unlike Azaña's Republican Action party, they lacked an unquestioned leader who could impose unity by the force of his personality. The Radical Socialists accepted the general objectives of the Republic, but because they were so loosely knit, they did not agree

13. *Anuario Estadístico: 1934*, p. 651.
14. Quoted in Arrarás, 2, 118.

on specific means. A small left wing of the party, headed by Eduardo Ortega y Gasset, regarded the Azaña program as too moderate and called for the wholesale confiscation of all noble lands and the dissolution of the Guardia Civil. The rest of the party was divided along different lines. So long as the Azaña coalition was successful, the party followed the two leaders—Marcelino Domingo and Álvaro de Albornoz—who held cabinet posts. Once Azaña's fortunes began to decline, a group of right-wing dissidents, headed by Félix Gordón Ordás, began to gain power.[15]

The disaffection within the Radical Socialist party—which first found serious expression in Gordón Ordás's seven-hour speech of 5 June to the Fourth Radical Socialist Congress[16]—is worthy of extended discussion, because it centered to a large extent around opposition to the agrarian reform. Even though the Azaña government had done little to implement the September law, profound changes had been occurring in Spanish rural society as a result of the early decrees of the Provisional Government. As explained in Chapter 6, the términos municipales act and the creation of agricultural mixed juries caused an enormous increase in wages, both directly and indirectly in that they greatly strengthened the Socialist rural unions. If laborers had thereby benefited whenever they could find jobs, most other rural social classes—not the large owners alone—had been injured. Small and medium owners and tenants also depended to some extent upon hired labor and therefore found their production costs increasing at precisely the time when the prices they received for their produce were declining.[17] This fundamental contradiction between rising wages in a depression economy of falling prices did not fully manifest itself in 1931 or 1932, because the Socialist unions were not yet firmly established, the mixed juries were not yet wholly functioning, and prices had not yet dropped significantly. By 1933, however, wages had approximately doubled over their 1931 levels,[18] while prices had declined sig-

15. Gordón Ordás had by no means been unimportant prior to 1933. In the 1932 elections for the party's Executive Committee, he received as many votes as Domingo and more than Albornoz. Because he did not hold a ministerial post, however, his influence was less than that of his rivals until Azaña's prestige began to fall.

16. The speech, which requires over one hundred pages to reprint, appears in *Cuarto Congreso.*

17. As noted in chap. 4, 24.0 percent of all entrepreneurs with less than five hectares of land used some hired labor in 1962. For entrepreneurs with from five to twenty hectares, the figure rose to 31.4 percent, and for those with from twenty to one hundred hectares, it soared to 53.0 percent. In the 1930s even more nonfamily labor must have been required by small and medium operators, since Spanish agriculture was much less mechanized.

18. A full-scale investigation of the changes in rural wages would be extremely

nificantly because of the surplus wheat crop of 1932 and the closing of
agricultural export markets.[19]

The tensions in the Spanish countryside were further aggravated by
the fact that the términos municipales act and the rise in wages produced
mixed benefits even among the landless workers. As mentioned previously, the municipal labor frontiers clearly injured workers from mountain villages who sought employment in the plains, even though the
Azaña government tried to ease their lot on several occasions by temporarily lifting the application of the términos municipales law during the
harvest season.[20] More important in contributing to the conflicts of the
summer of 1933, however, was the attempt of most employers—large,
medium, and small—to escape the profit squeeze in which they found
themselves by hiring less nonfamily labor than before. The flexible labor
requirements of agriculture were eminently suited to this purpose. In
contrast to industry, many agricultural tasks can be dispensed with
if an entrepreneur thinks that the extra yields they would produce would
not repay the added labor costs.[21] Such retrenchment, though economically rational from the point of view of the entrepreneur, intensified the
already grave problem of unemployment and constituted a declaration of

difficult, but considerable evidence exists to support my estimate that earnings approximately doubled between 1931 and 1933. At the proclamation of the Republic,
hourly wages averaged about 4 pesetas for male nonharvest labor and about 5.50 to
6 pesetas for harvest labor. In 1933 the mixed juries established harvest wages of
11 pesetas in Salamanca, 10.75 pesetas in Toledo, 10 pesetas in Albacete, 9 pesetas
in Ciudad Real, 8.75 in Huelva, and 8.50 in Cordova. To this must be added the
overtime pay (usually 25 percent) that had to be given to those who worked more
than eight hours, the travel time that the employer had to pay (workers usually were
given 12 to 15 minutes' pay for each kilometer they had to walk to work beyond the
first two), the meals the owner frequently had to provide at his own cost (especially
if he wished to avoid the travel pay involved in permitting workers to return to
town for lunch), and other such innovations introduced by the Republic. The best
source on this difficult question is Ministerio de Trabajo, *Anuario español de política
social, 1934–35*, ed. Mariano González-Rothvoss (Madrid, 1935), which reprints several dozen mixed jury contracts of 1932 and 1933.

19. According to Higinio Paris Eguilaz, *El movimiento de precios en España*
(Madrid, 1943), p. 39, products of annually sown plants collectively experienced the
following price evolution (1926–30 = 100): 1931, 102; 1932, 103; 1933, 92; 1934,
99; 1935, 96. Prices for products of perennial plants fell even more severely since
fruit exports to England were cut drastically by the Ottawa agreements of 1932, and
France, the largest buyer of wines, prohibited further imports in 1933.

20. This was accomplished by decrees that declared an entire province a single
intermunicipal unit for the duration of the harvest. Some twelve to fifteen such decrees
were issued during the Azaña era.

21. The implications of this distinction between dispensable and indispensable
tasks are imaginatively explored by Juan Martínez Alier in *La estabilidad de latifundismo*, his field study on the latifundio economy of Cordova.

war to the rural labor unions. The Socialists in particular fought back strenuously. Socialist village authorities invoked the laboreo forzoso legislation with greater frequency.[22] The Socialist-controlled Ministry of Labor openly exerted pressure on the mixed juries to reach decisions still more favorable to the workers.[23] The FNTT inaugurated a major campaign for the *turno riguroso,* the obligatory hiring of workers from the local unemployment offices *in the order in which they had registered.* This innovation would end discrimination against union members and grant everyone an equal opportunity for the jobs available, but only by destroying completely the owners' freedom to select their own personnel.[24]

The economic difficulties of the small and medium producers, together with the increased aggressiveness of the rural labor unions, began to engender in many Left Republicans an active hostility toward the agrarian reform as it had thus far been conceived. The legislation of the Republic had neglected the small owner and tenant in favor of the worker, they said, but even the worker had not truly benefited, since the higher wages he received were secured at the cost of more frequent unemployment. A major change of direction was necessary. The dissidents insisted that the disastrous términos municipales act be repealed outright. The impartiality of the mixed juries must be assured by replacing the Ministry of Labor appointees who headed them with technicians selected through competitive civil service examinations. Municipal and provincial authorities in Andalusia and Estremadura must be prevented from exercising their power solely on behalf of the workers. All laborers must be "effectively guaranteed the right to work, whatever their ideology or union affiliation." While the past was being undone, a new balance must be created in benefit of the small producers. The National Agrarian

22. For a particularly glaring abuse of the laboreo forzoso decree by local Socialist authorities, see *La Luz,* 23 July 1933. During the municipal elections of April 1933 the Socialists had urged the peasants to vote so they could gain control over the local committees that administered this measure under the supervision of regional boards.

23. The flagrant interference of Largo Caballero in decisions of the agricultural mixed juries of Salamanca and of the garment workers' jury in Madrid were the keystones of the increasingly intense anti-Socialist compaign waged by *El Sol* and *La Luz* during June and July 1933. Since both papers (but especially *El Sol*) were passing through financial crises which they tried to solve by attracting right-wing investors, however, their interpretations should be used with caution.

24. Largo Caballero's attempt to impose the turno riguroso in the summer of 1933 was a major cause of the severe confrontation between the FNTT and the Landowners' Federation of Salamanca. See especially *El Sol,* 11 July 1933. On the Socialist campaign for the turno riguroso in general, see *El Obrero de la Tierra* for June and July 1933.

Bank must be established immediately to provide them with credit. The frequently postponed lease bill must finally be presented for Cortes discussion. Small owners and tenants must be given equal rights with the workers in all existing legislation, particularly in undertaking collective leases.[25]

Gordón Ordás had not yet worked out in detail this long litany of projected modifications of the agrarian reform when he made his speech of 5 June to the Fourth Radical Socialist Congress. But the main direction of his thought was clear. So, too, were its profound political implications. The Republic, he charged, had mistakenly accepted the false Marxist dichotomy between exploiters and exploited and stood in danger of losing the support of the middle groups who in fact constituted the bulk of society. The only effect of the Republic's social legislation thus far had been to give the Socialists excessive power, which, according to Gordón Ordás, they tended more and more to misuse.[26] Unless the bourgeois Republicans checked the Socialists, social and economic instability would increase and the Republic would be permanently endangered. Specifically, the Left Republican coalition should try to retain the allegiance of the Socialists only upon its own terms. If in the process this allegiance were lost, as the dissident Radical Socialists fully expected, the loss could be offset by a renewal of the former collaboration with the Radical party. Thus the crux of Gordón Ordás's argument was that a basic error had been committed in December 1931, when Azaña chose to work with the Socialists rather than the Radicals. This mistake must now be corrected. The San Sebastian coalition must be reconstituted, and if any party had to be excluded it should be the Socialists.

Gordón Ordás's call of 5 June for a more moderate Republic undoubtedly encouraged Alcalá Zamora in his decision to dismiss the Azaña government three days later. However, the president already had sufficient reasons of his own for attempting to create a new political balance. Aside from Casas Viejas and the unfavorable results of the April municipal elections, the position of the government had been undermined by its bill on religious congregations. Presented to the Cortes in January, perhaps in the hope that its anticlericalism would enhance

25. The demands mentioned summarize points 1, 3, and 6 to 13 of the twenty-three-point program presented by the Radical Socialist dissidents to Azaña on 7 July 1933 as the price for their continued collaboration (the text appears in El Sol, 9 July 1933). The program's fourteenth point called for the quick recovery of the common lands as a concession to Republican radicalism, of which Gordón Ordás claimed to be the true representative.

26. In proving his point of the growing irresponsibility of the Socialists, Gordón made effective use of pronouncements in the Socialist press, some of which are quoted in chap. 12, where I discuss the change of mood among the Socialists.

Republican unity, the bill had encountered unexpectedly strong resistance on the floor. The Agrarian minority and the Basque Nationalists made full use of the techniques of harassment they had refined in the struggle over the Agrarian Reform Law during the previous year. The Radical party, engaged in a campaign of obstruction against Azaña and increasingly driven away from its strongly anticlerical past by the logic of its political situation, also contributed to the parliamentary stalemate. Even when the government majority finally succeeded in pushing the bill through in mid-May, its victory was compromised. Catholic organizations of every type announced that they would never accept the measure, particularly its provision for the closing of all Catholic schools except seminaries.[27] Alcalá Zamora—who, after all, had left the Provisional Government in large part over the religious issue—showed his disapproval first by refusing to sign the enactment and then, on 8 June, by taking advantage of Azaña's attempt to introduce minor ministerial changes to withdraw his confidence from the cabinet.

This first major exercise of presidential power proved abortive. Despite the repeated ovations Gordón Ordás's speech had received, neither the Radical Socialist party as a whole nor any of the other Left Republican factions in the Azaña coalition were yet ready to abandon the Socialists and come to terms with the Radicals. Within four days the Azaña cabinet was reconstituted. But as the summer wore on, the tide of battle turned. Many of the objections of the dissident Radical Socialists were valid ones. Economic instability continued, social disorder constantly increased, and the Socialists, frightened by the weakening of their position, began to issue irresponsible statements that lent further substance to Gordón Ordás's charges.

In consequence of this and of the continued paralysis of Domingo, many other former allies of the government joined in the chorus of criticism against it. Felipe Sánchez Román, the distinguished jurist who had headed the Technical Commission in 1931, struck two major blows against Azaña's agrarian policies in late June when he demanded the abolition of the términos municipales act and the curtailment of the Inventory of Expropriable Property.[28] The growing disenchantment of

27. An especially good short analysis of the background to Azaña's bill on religious congregations is given by Brenan, pp. 235–38.

28. Sánchez Román's speeches are reprinted in *La Luz*, 16, 21 June 1933. It should be stressed that he attacked the Azaña government much more from the Left than did Gordón Ordás, emphasizing, for example, a more vigorous settlement of landless workers rather than the favoring of tenant farmers. Nevertheless his criticisms often coincided with those of the Radical Socialist dissidents, particularly in regard to the términos municipales law. Sánchez Román's opposition to the inventory

La Luz during the spring of 1933 culminated in almost daily attacks on the way in which the agrarian reform was being carried out. In early July, after a major change in its editorial staff, *El Sol*, the most prestigious of all Republican journals, also entered the anti-Socialist camp.[29] These events inevitably affected the increasingly bitter struggle within the Radical Socialist party between Gordón Ordás and Domingo, the chief advocate of continued collaboration with the Socialists. The dissident leader scored a major victory in early August when the Executive Committee of the party accepted most of his proposals.[30] Although the Radical Socialists were not yet sufficiently united to provoke a cabinet split, Azaña could no longer count on the unquestioning allegiance of the largest bourgeois party in his coalition. Lerroux, the Radical leader, had finally succeeded in convincing an important segment of the Left Republicans at least to consider his version of what the Republic should be.

Azaña Fails to Regain the Initiative

It was under these pressures that the Azaña government finally began to show signs of awakening from its long torpor. Most of the measures taken in June and July 1933 have been mentioned previously. The Ministry of Agriculture, Industry, and Commerce was split into two parts so that Domingo could devote himself exclusively to rural affairs. The IRA was once again given a full-time head when Domingo resigned as Director General in favor of Dionisio Terrer. The general lease bill finally emerged from the Cortes committee in which it had languished since April. The government at long last made public its proposals for a National Agrarian Bank and for the recovery of the common lands.

All of these actions might have proven effective had they been taken in the fall of 1932 or in the spring of 1933. In the atmosphere of disintegration which reigned during the summer of 1933, however, they were futile. The consequences of the government's earlier lack of preparation

---

of Expropriable Property stemmed from its senseless inclusion of so many small and medium owners (see chaps. 8 and 13).

29. The change in editorial staff occurred on 6 July and was immediately reflected in *El Sol*'s policies. One month after hailing Azaña as "the man who represents all the virtues of the Republic," the liberal journal had joined Gordón Ordás in criticizing him for overdependence on the Socialists (issues of 14 June and 15 July 1933). On the complicated (and somewhat distasteful) maneuvering that preceded the policy shift see Arrarás, *Segunda República Española, 2,* 181–2, and Azaña, *Obras completas, 4,* 457–58.

30. A good short summary of the complicated struggle within the Radical Socialist party is presented in Arrarás, *2, 197.*

—and of its decision in January to turn the attention of the Cortes from social problems to the religious issue—can best be seen in the fate of the general lease bill, the only part of the supplementary agrarian program which actually came up for parliamentary discussion.

The importance of the lease bill can scarcely be exaggerated. As mentioned earlier, the Agrarian Reform Law was not immediately applicable to northern and central Spain; nor did it provide for the expropriation of leased properties of under four hundred hectares there. Thus it did not benefit the hundreds of thousands of tenants who, outside Southern Spain and certain portions of the Levante, were the chief oppressed class in rural society. As enunciated by Domingo, the lease law was to be for northern and central Spain what the September law was to the South. It would help the tenant by establishing minimum six-year leases that were automatically renewable unless the owner himself wished to undertake personally the cultivation of the farm.[31] Rents charged for the leases were to be moderate; in no case could they exceed the assessed taxable income, which in turn fluctuated between one-third and one-fourth the real income of the land. Even these rents could be revised by appeal to the special arbitration boards for leased rural property, which were to be established in each locality. Moreover, if the weather were so unfavorable as to result in a catastrophic crop loss, the rent was automatically to be reduced or entirely forgiven. Subleasing was prohibited. If a tenant died, his sons could continue on the farm in his stead. If for any reason the lease came to an end, the owner was to be obliged to repay the tenant for any necessary improvements made on the farm. No longer could the owner appropriate these without charge.

Besides seeking to curb the greed of the owners and to force them to share some of the risks of cultivation, the Domingo lease program also tried to ensure that each tenant would have a chance to convert himself into a proprietor. All tenant farmers were to be given the right to make the first offer when the farms they worked were sold. To prevent deceit they could also upset any arrangement made later between the owner and another purchaser by offering to match the sale price. Still more important, any tenant who had worked the same land for more than twenty years (and, as the enemies of the proposal were quick to point out, most tenants could eventually hope to fulfill this requirement because of the automatically renewable six-year leases) could force the owner to sell him the farm at twenty times its assessed taxable income. This provision, which gave the tenant "access to the property right," was at the heart of the proposal. In effect, it was a major land reform

31. Tenants could, of course, continue to be evicted for nonpayment of rent, property destruction, and other such offenses.

law in itself. Though the state would intervene only in the sense that the local courts would supervise the process of transfer, the tenant himself would eventually be allowed to "expropriate" the owner at a very advantageous price. Thus the exclusion in the September law of most leased properties in central and northern Spain would not prevent a radical redistribution of property there.

Despite its potentially far-reaching effects and the fact that the Cortes committee radicalized its provisions somewhat, the lease bill probably enjoyed the best chance of success of any aspect of the agrarian program of the government, since it was more in keeping with the philosophical presuppositions both of the Left Republicans themselves and of the opposition. Gordón Ordás had not only made neglect of the tenant farmer a cardinal feature of his attack against Domingo but had also created an Alianza de Labradores de España to unite tenants, sharecroppers, and small peasant proprietors under Radical Socialist auspices.[32] The Radical party of Lerroux had also loudly championed the tenant farmer. The Catholic solution to the agrarian problem had always been that tenants, not inexperienced workers, should become proprietors by being allowed to purchase the land they worked after a certain period of time. This, too, had been the crux of the agrarian reform proposals of such moderates as Díaz del Moral in 1931 and 1932.

Given this lack of ideological opposition, it seems almost certain that the lease bill would have passed the Cortes without difficulty had it preceded, not followed, the Agrarian Reform Law. It is also probable that it would have succeeded had it—not the anticlerical bill—been presented to the parliament in January 1933. By late July, however, when floor discussion finally began, the lease bill was condemned to relive the agonies to which the much more controversial September law had been subjected prior to the Sanjurjo revolt. Once again the Agrarian minority led the opposition. During the six weeks of debates prior to the fall of the Azaña government, this small group of conservative deputies centered its attack upon two key provisions of the Domingo bill. First, though accepting the principle of regulated rents which had for so long formed a central precept of Catholic social thought, the Agrarians protested that it was unjust to the owner to prohibit rents from ever

---

32. For the exaggerated hopes Gordón Ordás held for this organization, which he claimed to be 150,000 strong, see his interview with *El Sol*, 16 July 1933. I was unable to discover much about the Alianza except that it published a newspaper (of which few copies apparently survive) called *La Voz del Campo*. In any case, with the breakup of the Radical Socialists in September, the Alianza seems also to have lost whatever importance it had once enjoyed, although a shadow organization continued to function at least as late as November 1935.

exceeding the taxable income of a farm. Second, though ratifying the principle of "access to the property right"—another fundamental concept of Spanish Catholic social philosophy—they insisted that the tenant pay the owner the full market value of his lands, not the much lower figure of twenty times the taxable income proposed by the government.

If the Agrarian position permitted significant improvements over the existing situation in which the tenants had no rights at all, it also seriously weakened the force of the Domingo bill. The Agrarians insisted that in areas in which the Cadastre had not been completed—that is, in some two-thirds of northern and central Spain—rents be determined in each case by the courts. In effect, the small tenants, inexperienced in litigation and lacking the resources necessary to wait out court decisions, were invited to match legal wits with the proprietors. The proposed Agrarian modifications of the access principle were perhaps even more damaging. If tenants were forced to pay the full market value of the land they worked, only a very few could ever hope to convert them-selves into proprietors.[33] Yet once again this tiny minority, which held less than six percent of the Cortes seats, succeeded in imposing its will upon the parliament. After an eleven-day struggle, from 8 August to 19 August, its version of how rents should be regulated was accepted.[34] After a nine-day floor battle, from 25 August to 3 September, its modifica-tions of the access clause also emerged triumphant.[35]

As during the debates on the September law, the success of the Agrarians was based upon the apathy or acquiescence of much larger parliamentary groups. The Radical party as a whole once more revealed

33. Under these conditions the chief advantage of the access provision would be that the tenants could pay for the land over a long period of time rather than immediately. The Agrarians, in the strange mixture of hypocrisy and idealism which characterized their attitude toward the lease bill, recognized this and asked for payment in twenty annual installments rather than the ten for which Domingo had provided. They also strengthened the Domingo proposal slightly by allowing tenants to exercise their access right after having occupied the land for fifteen, not twenty, years.

34. The final compromise was that rents could not exceed the assessed taxable income where the Cadastre had been completed (mostly in the South) but would be fixed by the courts where it had not. Thus owners would not be penalized for the slowness with which the Spanish state had been surveying the land.

35. The debates on the lease bill are well summarized in *La Luz, El Sol,* and *España Económica y Financiera.* The intensity of the debate is suggested by the fact that the lease bill was discussed in 23 of the 25 Cortes sessions held between 27 July and 7 September 1933, and 439 of the *Diario de las Sesiones's* 939 pages during this period were devoted to this subject. The perseverance and energy of the Agrarian deputies during this struggle are amazing. They introduced literally hundreds of amendments, and one of their deputies, Cándido Casaneuva, spoke on the bill in 17 different sessions.

its moral bankruptcy by taking an ambiguous position in the discussion.[36] The dissident Radical Socialists, who had so loudly championed the tenant farmer during the preceding two months, remained strangely silent.[37] Most important of all, the Agrarian onslaught failed to arouse from their passivity the Left Republican deputies who had never joined in criticism of Azaña.

The truth was that even the most devoted of Azaña's followers were tired. The parliament had sat for too long. In the twenty-five months since it had first convened as the Constituent Assembly on 14 July 1931, the Cortes had enjoyed only two short recesses, which together totaled seven weeks. Out of the 556 weekdays that remained, the Cortes had held sessions on 396. Because so many critical issues had been discussed, many of these were double sessions that extended far into the night. A constitution had been approved; an important region had been given autonomy; the property structure had been questioned; the religious basis of the nation had been revised; new taxes and electoral laws had been discussed; ways to relieve the economic crisis and the social disorder were constantly debated. The deputies had for too long been called upon to answer too many insoluble problems. And now, for the third year in succession, a recess had been denied, and the Cortes was obliged to endure the hottest Madrid summer in decades. Only the Socialist deputies were so well disciplined as to attend the sessions under these conditions, and even they had to be constantly reminded of their duty.[38] Among the Left Republicans, rarely were so many as half the deputies present.[39]

Ironically, now that their forces were in full dissolution, the Left Republican leaders finally tried to provide the strong leadership that for so long had been lacking. Even Azaña's legendary self-confidence was shaken by the high rate of absenteeism among his followers. As mentioned, Azaña had intervened in the Cortes debates on the Agrarian Reform Law only once. Neither before nor after this intervention had he ever addressed the Cortes on agrarian matters. Now, after a month

36. Except for José María Álvarez Mendizábal, none of the Radical deputies seem to have taken an active part in the debates. According to Casanueva, the Radicals at one point were willing to abandon the principle of regulated rents entirely (La Luz, 19 August 1933).

37. Gordón Ordás, for example, did not speak on the lease bill at all.

38. For such reminders, see El Obrero de la Tierra, 22 July and 12 August 1933.

39. El Socialista, 25 August 1933, analyzed the Left Republican participation in roll call votes of the preceding two days and found that whereas an average of 44.4 percent of the Socialist deputies had voted, only 18.6 percent of the Radical Socialists, 9.7 percent of the Esquerra, and 3.1 percent of the ORGA deputies had cast ballots. Only Azaña's small Republican Action party matched the Socialist record, as 46.1 percent of its deputies cast votes.

of the agonizingly slow progress on the lease bill, Azaña appeared before the parliament to denounce the "tyranny of the minority" exercised by the Agrarian minority and to decry the "lack of spirit" among the Republican deputies. Unlike his speech against the nobility a year earlier, Azaña's plea of 25 August 1933 brought no apparent response. Debate continued to drag on so slowly that on 30 August Azaña once more sought the rostrum, this time to utter a more threatening discourse.[40] But once again he succeeded in proving only that the magical power that once surrounded his person had disappeared.

It was in this atmosphere, too, that Domingo finally began to take measures for a serious application of the September law. The Inventory of Expropriable Property had been completed, the provincial juntas established, the technical personnel of the Institute recruited. There could be no further excuse for delay, especially since a new agricultural year was drawing near. Dionisio Terrer, the new Director General of the IRA, spent most of August touring Andalusia. At the end of that month the Institute sent special delegates to nine of the latifundio provinces to request the provincial governors to assist them in preparations for settlements.[41] The provincial juntas in the latifundio regions at long last announced the specific maximum size limits applicable to expropriable farms in each locality.[42] On 2 September 1933 Domingo took the drastic step of reorganizing the Institute so as to end its long paralysis. What should have been done before was finally decreed. A five-man Permanent Commission, which included a single representative from each major group in the Executive Council (the owners, tenants, workers, jurists, and technical-bureaucratic personnel), was empowered to act in place of the entire Council. Since both Domingo and Terrer retained their votes, they could easily dominate this now compact body.[43] The absurdity of debates among twenty-nine individuals was ended; the views of only seven men would have to be considered when settlements were made.

Domingo did still more. The decree of 2 September gave the Director General the power to settle certain matters on his own authority,

---

40. Azaña's two speeches are reprinted in *En el poder y en la oposición, 1,* 159–66, 167–76. Domingo appeared in defense of the lease bill only once, possibly because he had been so discredited that his words no longer carried weight in the Cortes.

41. Ministery of Agriculture order of 31 August 1933.

42. These limits, which in general tended to apply the minimum limit within the range of permissible limits established in the Agrarian Reform Law, are reprinted in *BIRA* (October 1933), pp. 2–50.

43. Ministry of Agriculture decree of 2 September 1933.

without reference even to the Permanent Commission.[44] It also took the administration of the laboreo forzoso decree out of the hands of the technical departments of the Ministry of Agriculture, which had failed to enforce it, and placed it under the IRA, where it might again be used as the revolutionary instrument it had originally seemed to be. On 7 September a further step was taken. Domingo issued a decree that determined the structure and functions of the Peasant Communities to whom expropriated land was to be delivered.[45] At this time, too, rumors began to circulate that the government had secured massive financial backing for the reform from foreign bankers.[46] Thus almost exactly a year after the Agrarian Reform Law had been enacted, everything seemed ready for its application.

But Azaña and Domingo had waited too long. The day after Domingo's reorganization of the Institute, special elections were held to choose fifteen members of the Tribunal of Constitutional Guarantees, the supreme court that was to determine the legality of legislative enactments. Although the people did not vote, the balloting could legitimately be regarded as an expression of popular sentiment, since approximately 35,000 councilors from the ayuntamientos throughout Spain formed the special electoral colleges. The results were essentially the same as those of the municipal elections in April, even though "rotten boroughs" no

44. The most important of these new powers was that the Director General could authorize temporary occupations (though not expropriations, which still had to be referred to the Council) of farms in the Inventory. He could also permit expenditures of less than 100,000 pesetas on his own authority.

45. Ministry of Agriculture decree of 7 September 1933. The principal provisions of this decree were discussed in chap. 8.

46. This strange episode is most fully reported in *El Sol*, 6–8 September 1933. The rumors, which usually spoke of a foreign loan of 400 million pesetas, had enough substance to be accepted by so conservative a journal as *España Económica y Financiera*, 9 September 1933, p. 848. Yet neither Domingo nor any of the other Republican leaders later mentioned the loan when recounting their plans for implementing the reform in the fall of 1933 had they stayed in power. It also seems improbable that so large a loan could have been forthcoming on acceptable terms unless the government was willing to pledge part of Spain's enormous gold reserves, an unlikely possibility given the Azaña coalition's fiscal orthodoxy. This last point is interesting. Despite the backwardness of its economy, Spain in the 1930s had the fourth largest gold reserves in the world in absolute terms (only the USA, France and Britain surpassed it; Germany's reserves sank from half to one twenty-fifth those of Spain between 1932 and 1936). In comparison to gross national product, Spanish reserves were probably greater than those of any other nation except France (League of Nations, *Statistical Yearbook, 1936–37* [Geneva, 1937], p. 238). Yet none of this vast wealth was tapped to support domestic reforms; it lay stagnant in government vaults until the Civil War, when it was shipped to Russia for safekeeping only to be permanently lost.

longer cast the only ballots. Only one-third of the successful candidates were sponsored by parties in the Azaña coalition. The Radicals alone won almost as many seats as did the combined coalition forces. Most important of all, an open enemy of the regime, the financier Juan March, was elected to one of the seats from the prison cell into which the Republic had placed him for misappropriation of state funds during the Primo de Rivera era.

The new electoral reversal might not in itself have been enough to bring Azaña down. But it was only the latest proof that Azaña could no longer successfully govern the nation. The lease bill was being obstructed by a tiny parliamentary minority.[47] The bill for the recovery of the common lands was still tied up in committee. The proposal for the creation of an agrarian bank had never even been presented to the Cortes, because throughout the summer it had been openly attacked by the great Spanish banks, both private and semiofficial, on whose collaboration the success of the proposal depended.[48] Ever since March the various landowners' associations throughout Spain had been holding mass rallies to protest the agrarian program and social disorders in the countryside. Just before the Tribunal elections, as Domingo was proclaiming his renewed determination to apply the agrarian reform, these associations announced that they would cap their antigovernment campaign by holding a gigantic rally in Madrid on 18 September at which 100,000 landowners from all parts of Spain were to gather to demonstrate their opposition.[49]

It was true that Azaña could still muster a majority in the Cortes. In fact, when Lerroux asked for his resignation after the Tribunal elections, Azaña countered by demanding a vote of confidence, which he won by 146 votes to 3. But his success was only proof that the memory of their past unity prevented the members of his coalition from openly

47. Casaneuva, the Agrarian spokesman on rural affairs, had stated that his group had no serious quarrels with the lease bill after the Agrarian position on rents and access had been accepted (*La Luz*, 1, 2 September 1933). It seems likely, however, that political expediency would have driven them to attack both the collective lease provisions (which in themselves were not particularly controversial: the Unión Económica, for example, scarcely mentioned them in its long critique of the lease bill in *Economía Española* [May 1933], pp. 81–118) and the extension to sharecroppers of all the benefits granted to tenants (Domingo himself had opposed this provision, but it was added to the bill in Cortes committee).

48. On the Agrarian Bank, see Ramos Oliveira, pp. 342–43, 469–70; *El Socialista*, 30 August 1933; *Economía Española* (June 1933), p. 69, and (July–August 1933), pp. 7–8.

49. This rally, organized by the Confederación Española Patronal Agrícola, one of the members of Unión Económica, was intended to be the largest conservative demonstration ever held in Spain.

attacking each other. In the words of the Socialist historian Ramos Oliveira, the members of the Azaña coalition

> still regarded each other with affection, but [also felt] the melancholy disillusionment of partners to a childless marriage. They dragged out their existence in power, hoping that the death of the government would bring them release, a much more pious solution for all concerned than a scandalous divorce.[50]

Azaña won his vote of confidence, but fewer than one-third of the Cortes deputies—and only three-fifths of those formally aligned to his government—bothered to cast ballots. Alcalá Zamora was perfectly justified in regarding this as no vote of confidence at all and in asking, on 8 September, for the resignation of the government. The President may not have acted entirely from the highest motives. Some claim that he resented Azaña's fame and wanted to expand his own powers by appointing a more pliable prime minister;[51] others contend that Alcalá Zamora was determined not to allow the closure of the Church schools, scheduled to take effect in October.[52] Whatever the truth of these accusations, sufficient cause existed on constitutional grounds alone for Azaña's dismissal.

The Breakup of the Left Republican–Socialist Alliance

Any hope Azaña may have had that his second dismissal would prove as short-lived as his first was destroyed on 10 September by the results of the second stage of the Tribunal elections. Among the six judges chosen by the Bar Association and the law school faculties, one was José Calvo Sotelo, the closest associate of Primo de Rivera; two others also had monarchist inclinations. The alternatives now open to the Left Republicans were either to participate in a new government under Lerroux in the hope of reaching a modus vivendi or to make any new government impossible so as to force Alcalá Zamora to dissolve the Cortes and call new elections. Since only the Socialists adamantly refused to participate in a Lerroux government, Azaña decided the issue on 11 September by permitting his followers to join the Radical leader temporarily while each party decided its policy for the future. Cortes sessions were also suspended for a month so that Lerroux would not have to face a vote of confidence prematurely.

50. Ramos Oliveira, p. 484.
51. Ibid., pp. 480–81; Madariaga, pp. 419–20.
52. Madariaga, p. 420; Gabriel Jackson, *The Spanish Republic and the Civil War: 1931–1939* (Princeton, 1965), p. 107.

During that month the process of decomposition of the Azaña coalition reached its culmination. At an Extraordinary Congress of the Radical Socialist party, the split between Gordón Ordás and Domingo became final.[53] The dissident leader received the support of a majority; Domingo walked out of the Congress and founded an Independent Radical Socialist party. Since a Left Radical Socialist party had been founded earlier by Eduardo Ortega y Gasset, the largest Left Republican group was now split into three segments. Even more important, the Socialists took the Republican decision to join Lerroux, however temporarily, as confirmation of their fears that the liberal bourgeois parties were scheming to exclude them permanently from office. As Prieto was later to put it, "On September 11, 1933, the Republican parties cancelled all their agreements with the Socialist party. From that day forward we consider ourselves totally, absolutely, and completely free and independent of any obligations we once may have held." [54]

The Socialists and the remaining Left Republican members of the Azaña coalition were able to unite only to bring down the Lerroux government when the Cortes reconvened on 2 October. They would not have been strong enough even for this had not the Agrarians and other conservative deputies also wished for Lerroux's fall. But although the Agrarians acted from the hope that Cortes eléctions would follow, the Azaña forces still resisted this solution. Only after five days of cabinet crisis did the remaining Left Republicans accept the inevitability of a Cortes dissolution.[55] The events of 11 September repeated themselves as all Republican parties agreed to join a caretaker government headed by Lerroux's lieutenant, Martínez Barrio, which would supervise the elections. The Socialists, who were beginning their tragic descent into irrationality, refused to participate and once more cried vainly that they had been betrayed.

The breakup of the Radical Socialist party and, above all, the alienation of the Socialists guaranteed that the elections would go against what had once been the Azaña coalition. Even had these events not occurred, the Azaña forces would have encountered almost insuperable

53. The proceedings of the congress are reprinted in Partido Republicano Radical Socialista, *Texto taquigráfico del Tercer Congreso Nacional Extraordinario* (Madrid, 1934).

54. Cited in Arrarás, 2, 209–10. Azaña still generously held out a friendly hand to the Socialists. In reply to Prieto he said: "Our collaboration is ended. You are about to take a new road; we continue along our former path. But between you and us there will always remain the invisible bridge of the emotions we shared in the past and of our mutual service to the Spanish fatherland" (Azaña, *En el poder y en la oposición, 1,* 215).

55. Arrarás, 2, 210–11.

difficulties. The nation at large was even more tired of the continuous innovations than the Cortes deputies had been. Part of the liberal middle-class vote had been alienated by the "barbarity" of the government at Casas Viejas. An even larger proportion was frightened by the increasing social disorder. The Catalans had less reason to vote as unanimously as in 1931, because regional autonomy had been achieved. The peasant proprietors of Old Castile still suffered from the effects of the collapse of wheat prices. Believers from every social class—particularly women, who were to be allowed to exercise the ballot for the first time[56]—were driven away from Azaña by his anticlerical legislation. Finally, the Anarchosyndicalist CNT, which had permitted its followers to vote in 1931 so as to rid Spain of the hated monarchy, now prohibited their vote in order to destroy the equally hated Republic. Perhaps as many as three-quarters of a million workers who had supported Republican candidates two years earlier in Andalusia, Aragon, the Levante, and Catalonia now abstained.

The opposition to Azaña was also no longer the timid, disorganized force it had been in June 1931. The monarchists, who had then been in so total a state of disarray that they could not even decide whether to vote, had recovered their sense of purpose. More important, the Catholics had been driven by the anticlerical legislation to organize themselves for the first time into effective political parties. These united into the Confederación Española de Derechas Autónomas, the CEDA, headed by the former Agrarian deputy José María Gil Robles. Well financed and intelligently led, the CEDA soon converted itself into a powerful force that used all the modern devices—giant rallies, marches, youth organizations—to influence public opinion. The Falange party of José Antonio Primo de Rivera, son of the former dictator, was also founded, but it proved weak and unimportant when the votes were cast.

Only if the Left Republicans and Socialists had been able to unite with the Radicals to reconstitute the San Sebastian coalition that had won the 1931 elections might they have been able to overcome such obstacles. As it was, Azaña's followers made the fatal error of not uniting even among themselves. As will be remembered, the electoral system devised by the Provisional Government rewarded triumphant parties or coalitions, however slim their margin of victory, with approximately 75 percent of the seats in each electoral district. Now the Socialists refused, except in a few districts, to present a united list of candidates with the Left Republicans. The feeling that they had been betrayed was the main reason for their decision. They seem also to have believed that the frag-

56. The women's vote was especially important since out of a total electorate of some 13.2 million, women outnumbered men by approximately 550,000.

mented liberal bourgeois parties could not materially aid their candidates.[57] Because of Socialist blindness, what would in any case have been a defeat became a rout. The parties that had once formed the Azaña coalition received 39 percent of the votes but only 20 percent of the Cortes seats.[58] The Left Republicans suffered most deeply. Domingo's Radical Socialists (and those of Gordón Ordás) were virtually wiped out. Azaña's Republican Action party retained but five seats. The Galician Autonomy party kept six. The Catalan Esquerra, with nineteen deputies, was reduced to half its former size. The Socialists also paid a price. Formerly the largest party in the Cortes, they fell to third place, behind both the CEDA and the Radicals. Instead of 116 deputies, they now had only 59.

Victory went to the Right. The CEDA alone returned 110 deputies, more than the combined total of the Left. The Agrarians increased their strength to thirty-six deputies. Basque Nationalists, Traditionalists, Renovationists, and other conservative deputies accounted for another sixty seats. But though they had more often formed electoral alliances, the Right was in fact no more united than the Left. The CEDA and the Agrarians could usually work together except insofar as Christian socialist elements within the CEDA advocated more progressive social legislation than the Agrarians could tolerate. Both parties were separated to some extent from the Basques, whose main concern remained regional autonomy. The greatest differences existed with the two openly monarchist parties, the Traditionalists and Renovationists. Though both the CEDA and the Agrarians included many monarchist sympathizers, neither party was ready openly to disavow the Republic.

The disunity within the Right, and the fact that all the Right deputies together held but 206 of the 470 seats, threw the balance of power in the Cortes to Lerroux's Radical party. With approximately one hundred seats, it was by far the largest Center group.[59] For the next two years

57. Largo Caballero appears to have thought that the Socialists could retain about one hundred Cortes seats, though he predicted that the "intermediate parties" (i.e. the Left Republicans) would be annihilated at the polls (*Discursos a los Trabajadores*, pp. 98–99, 105).

58. Brenan, p. 314, states that the Left Republican parties obtained 640,000 votes and the Socialists 1,733,000 in the electoral districts where they ran separately. In the few electoral districts where they combined forces, they won some 750,000 votes. Thus they garnered a total of 3.1 of the 8.0 million votes cast, even though they gained but 94 of the 470 Cortes seats.

59. There were also a number of smaller Center groups. The most important of these were the Lliga (the rival to the Esquerra among the Catalan regional autonomy parties), with twenty-five seats; the followers of Miguel Maura, with eighteen seats; and Alcalá Zamora's old Progressive party, with three seats.

the fate of Lerroux and of Gil Robles were inextricably intertwined. Lerroux, who might have united with the Left Republicans had they been willing to accept his leadership prior to the elections, was now inevitably bound to the CEDA, because the forces of the Left were so reduced that he could not have formed a majority coalition with them even had he wished to do so. On the other hand Lerroux held great power over Gil Robles, because the CEDA would be forced to risk its recently acquired power in new elections if it was not willing to work with the Radicals.

An Evaluation of Azaña's Achievement

The collapse of the Azaña government did not mean the immediate end of agrarian reform. Ramón Feced, the former associate of Domingo who had acted as Minister of Agriculture during the short-lived Lerroux government of September 1933, and Cirilo del Río, a friend of Alcalá Zamora who headed the Ministry of Agriculture after October, kept the IRA functioning despite the political crises. Dionisio Terrer was replaced as Director General by Juan José Benayes (previously head of one of the IRA departments), but most of the other Institute personnel stayed at their posts. The Permanent Commission Domingo had established just before his fall continued to expropriate property. In fact, though Domingo might have followed a faster pace of settlement had he remained in office,[60] the Institute under Feced and del Río probably distributed more land than under Domingo.[61] Even in this, poor Domingo proved ill-fated. The machinery of reform he had finally succeeded in putting together was used to the credit of others.

Nevertheless the fall of Azaña did raise the possibility of future reversals. The structure Azaña had built was an extremely fragile one. Even if the settlements under Feced and del Río are taken into account, the Agrarian Reform Law had not been translated into deeds that would be difficult to undo. By the end of 1933 the Institute had settled only 4,399 peasants on 24,203 hectares. As can be seen in Table 31, there was no single province in which so much land had been transferred as to alter significantly the existing rural social structure. Another 20,133 hectares had been seized from the Sanjurjo rebels under the law of 24 August 1932, but even fewer settlers seem to have been placed on these

60. Even this is not certain, however, as will be explained shortly.

61. It is extremely difficult to determine when the expropriation of land was agreed on, but the summaries of the meetings of the Executive Council reprinted in the *BIRA* seem to point to the conclusion that Feced and del Río settled more land prior to the end of the year than had Domingo.

TABLE 31   SETTLEMENTS UNDER AGRARIAN REFORM LAW AS OF 31 DECEMBER 1933

	Settlers	Hectares
Jaen	2,500	905
Toledo	680	10,960
Cadiz	640	3,941
Cordova	211	3,048
Ciudad Real	150	2,166
Seville	140	2,503
Badajoz	78	680
	4,399	24,203

SOURCE: *BIRA* (December 1933), pp. 202–03.

NOTE: All the land seized was formally expropriated except for that in Cadiz and for 2,309 of the 10,960 hectares in Toledo, which were settled under the temporary occupation clause. I do not know the reason for the improbable settler-area ratio in Jaen.

lands, perhaps because they consisted mostly of pasture or forest.[62] Thus neither the Socialist goal of installing 100,000 to 150,000 peasants annually, nor the Technical Commission's goal of 60,000 to 75,000, nor even Vázquez Humasqué's modest objective of 10,000 to 15,000 annual settlements had been fulfilled. Two and one-half years after the proclamation of the Republic, only 45,000 hectares had changed hands to the benefit of some 6,000 or 7,000 peasants.

Thus, the only real accomplishment of the Azaña regime in land redistribution was the Intensification of Cultivation decrees. But although these settled some forty thousand peasants and significantly transformed agricultural life in Badajoz and Caceres, they were only temporary measures. The yunteros were given use of the land only until the harvest of 1934 was gathered. Unless new properties were found for them, they would be left landless within a few months of Azaña's fall.

Since so little had been done to redistribute land, the greatest accomplishments of the Republic undoubtedly remained the Provisional Government decrees of April and May 1931, for which Azaña could claim little credit. The wages of most field hands had risen considerably since 1931. The position of tenants also improved as their rents and contracts were more strictly regulated. Yet these achievements, too, rested on precarious foundations. High wages depended upon the términos municipales law and the mixed juries, the two most unpopular innovations of the Republic. As for tenants, the transitory enactments governing

62. *BIRA* (December 1933), p. 20. No figures for the numbers of peasants settled on these lands were reported. The 20,133 hectares seized represented almost exactly half of the 40,000 hectares held by the Sanjurjo rebels.

leases had not yet been embodied in a permanent lease law and therefore might easily be reversed when the new Cortes took up the question of general lease legislation. In every sense, then, Azaña's agrarian reform remained an expression of intent rather than of fact.

The major limiting factor on what the Radicals and the CEDA could do if they were able to settle differences among themselves was not anything Azaña had accomplished but the strength of the rural labor organizations. During the two and one-half years of the Republic the peasantry had once more begun to stir. Thus far it has been possible to speak of parliamentary developments with only occasional reference to the existing social situation. However, in 1934, 1935, and, above all, in 1936, political developments were determined largely by the ebb and flow of peasant protest. For these reasons we must retrace our steps in part and analyze the development of the latent civil war in the Spanish countryside after the proclamation of the Republic.

Before turning to this subject, however, it would be worthwhile to dismiss explicitly the rather powerful myth that the Azaña government would have launched a massive agrarian reform in the fall of 1933 had it remained in office. Both Azaña and Domingo had certainly been shaken out of their apathy by the criticisms to which they had been subjected during the summer. Yet they no longer commanded the resources necessary to translate their wishes into action. Domingo was completely discredited, and his sweeping pronouncements were treated with contempt even by those who had most reason to fear them.[63] The Left Republicans were thoroughly disunited and could not have endured the extremely long parliamentary struggles that would have been necessary to pass first the remainder of the lease bill, then the proposal for the recovery of the common lands, then the draft for the Agrarian Bank, and finally the promised foro and rabassaire legislation. Because no adequate financial basis had been established for the redistribution of land under the September law, Domingo would have had to rely on inexpensive temporary settlements of the Intensification of Cultivation type. But these and all other important actions dependent on decrees would have been impossible, because the President, Alcalá Zamora, would not have given the weak government he saw before him the counter-

63. For examples of the contempt in which Domingo was held by representatives of almost all sectors of the political spectrum, see *El Sol*, 18 July 1933; *La Luz*, 29 July 1933; *Economía Española* (July–August 1933), p. 15; and *España Económica y Financiera*, 9 September 1933. Even those tied to him, like the Socialists (who were grateful for his support of their continued collaboration in the cabinet against the Radical Socialist dissidents) and Azaña, did not believe that Domingo would prove capable of energetic and effective action. As evidence, see the entry for 27 August 1933 in Azaña's *Memorias íntimas* and *El Socialista*, 30, 31 August 1933.

signature required by the Constitution. Even had Domingo proved able to secure decree powers, however, the peasantry—now much more highly politicized than during the wave of farm invasions of January 1933 which led to the second stage of the Intensification of Cultivation decrees —would almost certainly have pressed for more drastic action which, if granted, would at a minimum have produced immediate defections from the governmental coalition.

Azaña and Domingo, in short, were irrevocably caught in the web they had spun for themselves by their lack of preparation in 1931 and 1932 and by their apathetic application of the reform in early 1933. Only by the exercise of dictatorial powers—which they did not desire and whose consequences they would not have been able to face—could they have settled more than the ten or fifteen thousand peasants they had set as their goal in the spring of 1933, before the process of political deterioration had advanced significantly. The promise of the agrarian reform was therefore not destroyed either by Alcalá Zamora or by the Center-Right governments that followed Azaña. Its demise was due rather to its inherent difficulties and to the ineffective and contradictory attitudes that had for so long characterized its chief sponsors.

11: Anarchosyndicalism and Spontaneous Peasant Protest

Economic and Organizational Background

In January 1933 Vázquez Humasqué explained to the peasantry that the slow, cautious application of the Agrarian Reform Law was necessary because "otherwise it would not be a law, but a revolutionary act which could lead to the disorganization of the agricultural economy, beyond which lies chaos." [1] In fact, though agricultural production remained surprisingly high,[2] rural society had already begun to disintegrate by the time he spoke. While the parliamentary struggle over the September law and the complementary agrarian program had been going on in Madrid, an even more intense struggle had been unfolding in the Spanish countryside: the struggle of the peasantry to gain immediate possession of the land.

To some extent this struggle stemmed neither from the Azaña government's agrarian legislation nor from the policies of the workers' organizations but from the economic conditions of the time. The Republic had the misfortune to coincide with the world economic depression, which, although it never affected Spain as deeply as the more industrialized na-

---

1. *BIRA* (January 1933), p. 7. The passage comes from a radio address in which Vázquez Humasqué pleaded with the peasants to stop the invasions of farms which led to the second stage of the Intensification of Cultivation decrees.

2. In comparison with the average for 1929 and 1930, over-all agricultural production from 1931 to 1935 was as follows (1929 and 1930 = 100):

1931 = 96.8	1934 = 114.6
1932 = 114.7	1935 = 102.4
1933 = 97.8	

Compiled from Higinio Paris Eguilaz, *Política económica de España: 1939–49* (Madrid, 1949), p. 19. These figures suggest that if the aforementioned profit and credit squeezes caused partly by the Azaña government's agrarian policies created difficulties for farmers, they did not become so severe as to make continued production impossible.

tions, sufficed to upset its always precarious economic balance. The exodus from the countryside caused by the industrial boom of World War I and of the Primo de Rivera era was reversed: the rural population swelled as workers dismissed from factories and mines fell back upon agricultural pursuits.[3] Agricultural export crops were left unsold as the industrial nations, their principal buyers, adopted autarkical policies.[4] The crops that enjoyed only a domestic market also suffered, though in this case it was the surplus wheat crops of 1932 and 1934 which were primarily responsible for the fall of prices. In individual regions special disasters occurred which added to the general economic crisis. The extraordinary preoccupation of the Provisional Government with Andalusia resulted not only from that area's tradition of peasant revolt but also from the fact that a severe drought in the fall of 1930 had restricted the acreage planted in grains for the next year and a terrible frost then killed most of the olive crop, the other great staple of the region.[5] In La Mancha a crisis of longer duration was developing as phyloxera, which for the most part had by-passed the vineyards of Ciudad Real in the 1890s, suddenly began to spread after 1927.[6]

If these occurrences seriously injured the small producers, both owners and tenants, agricultural workers were still more severely affected. Unemployment among them was already great when the Republic was proclaimed. A Ministry of Labor survey during the last days of the monarchy estimated that the loss of the 1930–31 olive crop left about one-third of the workers in Jaen and Granada without jobs at what should have been a peak season of employment.[7] The extent of unemployment in Spain as a whole during this period and during the early months of the Republic is

3. Reverse migration of this sort is not unusual in times of crisis in recently industrialized societies, where urban workers have not yet lost their agricultural skills and interests. In Republican Spain it was probably intensified by the términos municipales law and other legislation, which gave workers a better chance of finding jobs in the countryside than in the cities. Although no figures are available, some information on this phenomenon appears in Jesús R. Coloma, "La Intensificación de Cultivos," *BIRA* (April 1933), pp. 425–31, and IRA, Provincial Delegation for Seville, "Memoria," Folder 41/0—1, IRA Archives.

4. As mentioned earlier, fruit and, above all, wine production fell drastically from their 1929 and 1930 averages, partly because of the import restrictions adopted by France and England. This fact may help explain the virulence of social conflicts in Jerez, La Mancha, and Valencia, as well as the conversion of the La Rioja area of Aragon to anarchism.

5. Ministerio de Trabajo, *Crisis agraria andaluza*, pp. 9–14. The 1930–31 olive crop was the worst since 1912.

6. Carlos Morales Antequera, *La agricultura en la provincia de Ciudad Real* (Madrid, 1942), pp. 5–6.

7. Ministerio de Trabajo, *Crisis agraria andaluza*, pp. 110–14.

unknown, since national surveys were not made. In June 1932, however, the Ministry of Labor estimated national unemployment to be 446,263 workers of all types. Of these, 258,570 were agricultural workers, even though the cereal harvest was then at its height.[8] In 1933 more systematic records began to be kept, so that the pattern of unemployment can be traced from that year onward. Of a total non-self-employed population of perhaps 4.0 million, which included approximately 1.9 million agricultural workers, the average unemployment officially recorded from July 1933 to July 1936 was as given in Table 32.[9]

TABLE 32   AVERAGE UNEMPLOYMENT FROM JULY 1933 TO JULY 1936

	Total Unemployment	Agricultural Unemployment	
		Number Unemployed	Percent of Total Unemployment
1933 (July–Dec.)	593,627	382,965	64.5
1934	667,263	409,617	61.4
1935	696,989	434,054	62.4
1936 (Jan.–July)	796,341	522,079	65.6

SOURCE: Sindicato Vertical del Olivo, *El paro estacional campesino* (Madrid, 1946), p. 3. See n. 9 for some of the problems involved in interpreting these data.

A striking feature of Spanish unemployment was that although it did not reach the proportions recorded in Germany, England, or even France, it proved more constant. The partial recoveries experienced elsewhere did not occur in Spain. Although most of the increase seems to have occurred before mid-1932,[10] unemployment mounted constantly from 1930 to the end of 1933. In 1934 and 1935 the situation stabilized, but in 1936 the

8. Cited in Moch, p. 269.

9. Like all other Spanish statistics, the unemployment figures presented in Table 32 must be used with caution. Not all the workers listed were totally unemployed. Partly unemployed workers—defined as those working fewer than six days a week —were also included. Since no more exact breakdown was ever provided, it is difficult to estimate how desperate the condition of the partly unemployed really was. One would assume, however, that most of the partly unemployed must have been without jobs at least half the week, otherwise they would not have registered with the Ministry of Labor's placement offices. It is also difficult to decide to what extent the apparent rise in unemployment from 1933 to 1936 merely reflected better reporting from more towns and villages. The Ministry of Labor, on the basis of adjusted figures that took into account the increase in the number of units reporting, claimed that unemployment actually decreased from an average of 687,930 in 1934 to 674,161 in 1935 (Ministerio de Trabajo, *Boletín* [February 1936], p. 239). This slight drop would not alter the conclusions presented in the text, however, if it did indeed occur.

10. Unemployment in June 1932, the only month in the earlier period for which figures exist, was already almost as high as it was to be in June 1934 (446,263 for the former; 483,984 for the latter).

number of those without work began to rise once more. What level it would have attained had not war, that great user of men, intervened is uncertain. From 1931 to early 1934 unemployment may have been aggravated by the términos municipales decree and the owners' desire to free themselves from the aggressiveness of the rural trade unions. In 1936 political turmoil was undoubtedly an important cause of the employment crisis. Yet even in 1935, a year of peace during which the Republic seemed to have achieved a balance favorable to the propertied classes, there were no real signs of recovery.

The gloomy spectacle of unemployment formed a constant backdrop to the history of the Republic. It was a catastrophe with which none of the governments of the period knew how to deal. The Provisional Government and the Azaña regime, so daring in other legislation, proved timid in this respect. Their answer to the crisis was the traditional one of public work projects and municipal relief, albeit they supported them much more generously than had been customary. No institutional means for handling the problem on the national level were created except for the weak Caja Nacional Contra el Paro of 1931, which provided small subsidies to the unemployment funds established by various professional organizations.[11] In 1935 the successors of Azaña created the somewhat more ambitious Junta Nacional Contra el Paro as the administrative agency for a coordinated program of public works. At no time, however, was regular unemployment insurance provided. The direct expenditures of the national government for the relief of unemployment remained infinitesimal. From 1931 to 1933 they must be expressed in tenths of one percent of the national budget. By 1934 the sums allotted had almost reached one-half of one percent of the budget. In 1935 they rose to approximately three-quarters of one percent. Only in the first quarter of 1936 did direct allocations increase significantly; even then they accounted for only two percent of all state expenditures.[12]

To what extent was this widespread and continuous unemployment responsible for the intense rural agitation that characterized the Republic? There seems no reason to deny the common sense conclusion that the relation between the two was very strong. Table 33 lists the eleven provinces in which total agricultural unemployment averaged more than ten thousand workers a month between July and December 1933. It was in these same provinces, nine of which lay in the latifundio zones, that labor unions achieved their highest membership and rural unrest was most severe. The correlation is not a perfect one, to be sure. There is a point at which

11. See above, p. 171, for further details on this fund.
12. INE, *Anuario Estadístico: 1950*, pp. 482–83. Incidentally, the Center-Right governments of 1935, not the Popular Front, were responsible for the 1936 increase.

TABLE 33 PROVINCES WITH MOST ACUTE AGRICULTURAL UNEMPLOYMENT IN JULY–
DECEMBER 1933

	Wholly Unemployed	Partly Unemployed	Total Unemployed
	(thousands of agricultural workers)		
Jaen	29.0	16.8	45.8
Badajoz	21.4	12.8	34.2
Cordova	15.6	8.9	24.5
Seville	13.6	10.6	24.2
Granada	11.0	10.0	21.0
Valencia	8.0	12.9	20.9
Malaga	11.8	9.0	20.8
Toledo	11.4	8.5	19.9
Murcia	7.5	7.8	15.3
Caceres	9.0	6.1	15.1
Cadiz	7.7	2.9	10.6
Total: 11 Provinces	146.0	106.3	252.3
Total: Rest of Nation	59.5	71.1	130.7
11 Provinces as Percent of Nation	71.0	59.9	65.9

SOURCE: Ministerio de Trabajo, *Estadística del paro involuntario en el segundo semestre de 1933* (Madrid, 1934), pp. 8, 36, 92, 120, 148. See n. 9 for an explanation of the difference between wholly and partly unemployed.

deprivation deadens the soul; this was the case in Jaen, where unemployment was highest but where peasant resistance never became so ferocious as in Seville, Cordova, or Badajoz. In Cadiz the strength of the Anarchist tradition gave to rural upheavals a vehemence that the level of unemployment alone cannot explain. In Murcia the relative weakness of this tradition caused the peasants to accept their lot more passively.

But unemployment alone was not responsible for the tension in the Spanish countryside. It has been an historical truism since Toqueville that the masses usually rise when some measure of hope is added to their desperation. The Spanish peasant was no exception. At the turn of the century the myth of the general strike and the initial success of a number of industrial walkouts in Barcelona precipitated the wave of rural agitation of 1903–04. After World War I the Bolshevik Revolution and rumors that the king was about to redistribute property were partly responsible for the much greater convulsions of 1918–20. In 1931 the proclamation of the Republic and the repeated promises of land stimulated the excitable temperament of the peasantry once more. The Republic was scarcely one month old when groups began to invade farms to demand immediate application of the agrarian reform.[13]

13. The first farm invasion reported in the national press occurred in Yuncos (Toledo) (*El Debate*, 21 May 1931).

Even when it became apparent that the land would not be redistributed immediately, these exaggerated hopes did not die out. Political parties and labor organizations continued to promise great changes. Equally important, the traditional weapons used to control peasant agitation were no longer as efficacious as in the past. Because of the términos municipales law, landowners were less able to reduce the workers to submission by importing migrant labor. The former intimacy among the village squires, the ayuntamiento, and the Guardias Civiles, who together had dominated rural life for so long, was also upset by the Republic. More radical municipal governments were elected or appointed after 1931; less conservative provincial governors were named; the freedom of action of the local police was curtailed. The rural oligarchy of old was by no means left completely powerless. The Republic failed to take the elementary step of transferring the Guardias Civiles and the powerful secretaries of the ayuntamientos to other villages where they would be separated from their former associates.[14] Nevertheless many of the local restraints of the past were removed, and the working classes enjoyed greater power than ever before. So long as this state of affairs continued and the national government abstained from launching general repressions, the moods of despondency which had so often wrecked workers' movements in the past did not recur.

The simultaneous hope and desperation of the rural masses, together with the weakening of the old local restraints, brought about the most extraordinary increase in the size of labor organizations in the history of Spain. The Spanish proletariat continued to be polarized into the two great groupings of the monarchical period, the Anarchosyndicalist CNT and the Socialist UGT. The relative strength of the two organizations, however, was no longer what it had been during the *trienio bolchevista*, when the CNT could still claim more than three times the membership of the UGT. During the intervening years the UGT had consolidated its position and was ready to cast off its role as junior partner. Largo Caballero's cooperation with Primo de Rivera paid off handsomely as the UGT not only remained intact during the dictatorship but even increased its numbers slightly. The advantage of the UGT was heightened during the early months of the Republic. While the CNT was wasting its strength in futile opposition, Socialist control of the Ministry of Labor (and thus of most mixed juries) secured serious consideration for UGT demands and gave it an effective platform from which to recruit. As can be seen in Table 34, by 1932 the UGT had five times as many followers as during the trienio and had become the largest labor organization in Spanish his-

14. See the speech of Gordón Ordás in *Cuarto Congreso*, pp. 186–87.

TABLE 34   UGT MEMBERSHIP FROM DECEMBER 1922 TO JULY 1932

	Local Sections	Members	Index of Membership
December 1922 (just before the rise of Primo de Rivera)	1,198	208,170	100
December 1929 (just before the fall of Primo de Rivera)	1,511	228,501	110
December 1930 (interim period between dictatorship and Republic)	1,734	277,011	133
December 1931 (after eight months under the Republic)	4,041	958,451	460
July 1932 (after fifteen months under the Republic)	5,107	1,041,539	500

SOURCE: UGT, *Memoria y orden del día del XVII Congreso que se celebrará en Madrid los días 14 y siguientes de octubre de 1932* (Madrid, 1932), p. 61.

tory. Though reliable statistics are not available for the remaining years of the Republic, it seems probable that the numerical superiority of the UGT over the CNT was not reversed, at least not until the Civil War introduced new conditions.[15]

A still more dramatic change occurred in the relative strength of the two organizations among the rural masses. The Anarchists had awakened the peasantry during the late nineteenth century, whereas the Socialists had largely ignored the existence of the agrarian problem. A reversal of positions began during the trienio bolchevista: the UGT abandoned its Marxist preconceptions and tried to attract peasant support, and the CNT came increasingly under the control of the industrial unions of Barcelona. One of the first acts of the UGT after the fall of Primo de Rivera was to establish a separate peasant federation, the FNTT. The success of this organization, formally constituted in April 1930, exceeded the fondest hopes of its founders. Within two years it had registered a twelvefold increase

15. The numerical superiority of the UGT to the CNT during the Republic is not generally recognized, in part because Miguel Maura, in a November 1934 speech to the Cortes (*D.S.* 123, 16 November 1934, pp. 4843–44), stated that police records for "the first months of 1934" estimated 1,577,547 Anarchosyndicalists in Spain as opposed to 1,444,474 Socialists and 133,266 Communists. Though this estimate has been widely reprinted, it does not seem valid. Maura had been out of the cabinet for more than three years and had no access to police records. As will be seen shortly, his estimate contradicts all other available evidence. It is especially improbable that the CNT surpassed the UGT in "the first months of 1934," since the Anarchosyndicalists were still recovering from the suppression that followed their insurrection of December 1933. Finally, Maura so exaggerates the Communist following as to make his other figures suspect.

in membership. With 392,953 affiliates in 2,541 local unions, the FNTT was in June 1932 half again as large as had been the entire UGT during the monarchy. Because Socialist strength in the countryside rose at a much higher rate than in the cities, the FNTT accounted for more than half of the spectacular increase in UGT membership after 1930. In practice, the FNTT may not have been "the strongest arm of the UGT," [16] but it certainly could have become such. Seven Socialist deputies in the Cortes officially spoke in its name; its weekly newspaper, *El Obrero de la Tierra,* enjoyed a circulation of over eighty thousand;[17] most important of all, the rural federation accounted for approximately 40 percent of the total UGT following.

By June 1932 the FNTT had developed into the first Spanish rural labor organization that could justly claim national power. As can be seen in Table 35, it quickly spread beyond the old Socialist strongholds of Badajoz, Caceres, and the mountainous portions of Cordova to achieve a paramount position in most of La Mancha and Eastern Andalusia. It disputed the dominance of the CNT in such traditional Anarchist centers as Seville and the Levante. It even developed some strength in a few provinces of Old and New Castile.[18] Only in Galicia, in certain of the most traditional Anarchosyndicalist areas (Catalonia, Cadiz, and Aragon), and in those regions in which the rural social structure did not produce class consciousness (northern Old Castile and the Biscay Coast) did the FNTT organizational drive fail.

The development of the more amorphous CNT cannot be described with equal precision. The two major Anarchosyndicalist congresses held during the Republic—those of June 1931 and May 1936—were convened as the CNT was beginning to reorganize itself after periods of repression. Therefore the membership of approximately 550,000 reported by each congress cannot be taken as indicative of CNT strength at its peak.[19] During most of the Republic the CNT was unquestionably stronger than it had been during the trienio bolchevista, when it had commanded the

16. Moch, p. 228.

17. FNTT, *Memoria,* p. 246, claims that the circulation of *El Obrero de la Tierra* rose from 32,000 in January 1932 to 84,100 in June 1932. Both figures seem too high, but I have no evidence to the contrary.

18. For example, as of 30 June 1932 the FNTT claimed 11,009 members in valladolid, 9,092 in Cuenca, and 8,113 in Avila (FNTT, *Memoria,* p. 239).

19. CNT, *Memoria del Congreso Extraordinario celebrado en Madrid los días 11 al 16 de junio de 1931* (Barcelona, 1932), pp. 11–21, reports that 535,565 members were represented at the First Extraordinary Congress. *Solidaridad Obrera,* 6, 7 May 1936, reports that 559,294 members were represented at the Second Extraordinary Congress. The forces that backed Pestaña and split off from the CNT from 1932 to 1936 are included in both reports.

TABLE 35   GROWTH AND GEOGRAPHICAL DISTRIBUTION OF FNTT MEMBERSHIP IN 1930–33

	Local Unions	Members
A. Growth of FNTT Membership, 1930–33		
April 1930	157	27,340
June 1930	275	36,639
April 1932	2,233	308,579
June 1932	2,541	392,953
June 1933 (estimated)	3,319	451,337
B. Geographical Distribution, June 30, 1932		
Estremadura	*335*	*65,389*
Badajoz	110	36,673
Caceres	125	20,708
Salamanca	100	8,008
La Mancha	*316*	*64,072*
Toledo	159	34,477
Ciudad Real	92	18,278
Albacete	65	11,317
Upper Guadalquivir Valley	*197*	*69,063*
Jaen	93	32,663
Cordova	64	21,003
Seville	40	15,397
Eastern Andalusia	*119*	*31,934*
Malaga	87	21,120
Granada	32	10,814
Levante and Southeast	*391*	*56,649*
Valencia	149	24,121
Alicante	105	11,250
Almeria	84	10,920
Murcia	53	10,358
All other provinces and regions	*1,183*	*105,846*

SOURCES: For "A.," see Jules Moch and G. P. Moch, *L'Espagne Républicaine* (Paris, 1933), p. 228. *El Obrero de la Tierra*, 17 September 1932, 16 September 1933. For "B.," *El Obrero de la Tierra*, 17 September 1932, or FNTT, *Memoria que presenta el Comité nacional al Congreso ordinario que ha de celebrarse en septiembre de 1932* (Madrid, 1932), pp. 238–40. The Salamanca figures are surprisingly low, since the provincial federation there was very active. The FNTT was weakest in Catalonia (1,027 members) and Galicia (5,838 members).

loyalties of almost 700,000 workers.[20] But we do not know by how much it surpassed its trienio following. According to one report, CNT membership in January 1932 was 862,000.[21] Another source states that the number of followers had risen to approximately one million by the end of 1932.[22]

20. At the 1919 Congress 699,369 affiliated and 56,723 unaffiliated members were represented (CNT, *Congreso de 1919*, pp. 11–34).
21. Moch, p. 312.
22. Manuel Ramírez Jiménez, "Los grupos de presión en la Segunda República

There is only one estimate, highly suspect, which claims that the CNT had surpassed its 1919 following by as much as 50 percent.[23] Thus the more destructive role played by the Confederation during the Republic was due more to its change in policy after the trienio than to its increase in numbers.

Even less can be said about the numerical strength of the rural sections of the CNT, since the records of its two congresses, which provide the only relatively reliable membership figures available, rarely distinguished occupational groupings. The CNT unquestionably retained control of the lower Guadalquivir valley and exerted considerable influence in the Levante, that other traditional center of rural anarchism. But prior to 1936 it did not expand significantly beyond its former geographical limits. There was one major exception: rural anarchism in Aragon and La Rioja increased considerably from what it had been during the trienio. The primary reason for this was the total conversion to anarchosyndicalism of the city of Saragossa during the *pistolero* era of 1920–23. By the time of the Republic, Saragossa had become, after Barcelona, the greatest center of urban anarchism in Spain; from it, Anarchist influence spread to the surrounding countryside.[24]

Yet though neither the CNT as a whole nor its rural branches matched the spectacular increase in membership of the Socialist organizations, they played an extremely important role in the history of the Republic. Because the CNT adopted a policy of implacable hostility toward the new regime, the social upheavals, both rural and urban, were much more severe than they would otherwise have been. Social tranquillity could not have been expected, given the economic and psychological condition of the working classes. Without anarchosyndicalism, however, the worst outbreaks of chaos would have been avoided. The CNT in effect tried to convert what would have been a continuation of the perennial private war of the peasantry against their masters into a revolutionary struggle for the overthrow of the Republic. Though it did not succeed in its ultimate objective, it contributed to the fall of Azaña and did much to discredit the

---

Espanola" (Ph.D. dissertation, University of Granada, 1964), p. 198. Ramírez gives the International Labor Organization as the source of his estimate.

23. See note 15 for the reasons for which I consider Miguel Maura's estimate suspect. For 1934 the figure of 800,000 members given by the *Anuario español de política social, 1934–35,* p. 115, seems much more reasonable.

24. The influence of Saragossa seems paramount in the conversion of Aragon. Though there was severe local unemployment in La Rioja because of the drastic decline in wine exports, Aragon as a whole does not seem to have been badly off in this respect, since the extensive irrigation works under construction offered many jobs (Ministerio de Trabajo, *Boletín* [April 1935], p. 456). None of the provinces with acute agricultural unemployment listed in Table 31 are in Aragon.

very idea of a Republic. For this reason our study of rural social disorder must begin with an analysis of the relations between the CNT and the peasantry.

The Failure of Revolutionary Anarchosyndicalism

That the CNT should oppose the Republic was not surprising. To the Anarchosyndicalists, the Republic was a capitalistic regime that by its very nature would continue to oppress mankind. Its promises of improvement were all false, and were made with the intention of diverting the workers from the path of revolution.[25] This was especially true of the agrarian reform. The only type of reform that the CNT could accept was the immediate confiscation without compensation of all large properties and the total abolition of all taxes, rents, and mortgages on small properties. There could be no delay, no compromise, no partial measures of any kind. The state should in effect turn over the land to the poor and then dissolve itself. Anything else would be ineffective and should be rejected.[26] What, then, should the attitude of the CNT be toward a Republic that refused to follow this course? The June 1931 Congress, called to hammer out CNT policy toward the new regime, resolved that the Confederation should remain "in open war against the State." [27] The "essential mission" of the rural unions was not to obtain land for their members by cooperation with the agrarian reform but to work for "the revolutionary preparation of the rural masses, their constructive preparation for the Anarchosyndicalist social experience," which would come in "that decisive battle when the *campesinos* and the industrial proletariat rise together to crush capitalism." [28]

Although all factions agreed on this theoretical stance toward the Republic, a major dispute arose as to when the "decisive battle against capitalism" should begin and how "open" the war against the state should be in the meantime. The older leaders, who had been prominent in the relatively moderate CNT of the trienio, recognized that though the Republic might be the enemy of the workers, it was in many ways an improvement

25. See the keynote address of Rudolph Rocker, the IWW delegate to the June 1931 Congress, in CNT, *Congreso Extraordinario de 1931*, pp. 24–25. "The greatest danger confronting the CNT in Spain today is the democratic danger," precisely because the workers might accept its false promises and be led away from their hatred of capitalism and the state.

26. Ibid., pp. 107–08.

27. A resolution of the congress cited in Peirats, *La CNT*, 1, 43. "Open war," of course, did not necessarily mean active war—at all odds, not until the extremist faction won control of the CNT.

28. CNT, *Congreso Extraordinario de 1931*, p. 107.

over the monarchy. The new regime, they said, was after all "the product of a revolutionary event" and thus should arouse some sympathy, however slight, among the Anarchists. Moreover, its establishment was "an event in which, directly or indirectly, we participated." [29] The Republic, then, could be tolerated for a short time. Its overthrow should occur only through a rising of the masses as a whole after they had been generally converted and carefully prepared, not through immediate action by an audacious minority. As one moderate manifesto put it, "We wish a Revolution born out of the deepest feelings of the people . . . not the Revolution offered us . . . by some individuals who . . . inevitably would convert themselves into dictators the day after their triumph." [30] Should a policy of insurrection be adopted, it would fail because "everything is left to chance, everything depends on the unforeseen." Those who advocate this policy "believe in the miracles of the holy revolution as though the revolution were some panacea, and not a tragic and cruel event which forms man only through the suffering of his body and the sorrow of his mind." [31]

The old CNT leaders—Pestaña, Peiró, López—were opposed by a younger generation, bred in the gun battles of Barcelona in 1920–23, which rejected any modus vivendi, however temporary, with the Republic. These new men—Durruti, the Ascaso brothers, and García Oliver—had organized a purely Anarchist secret society, the Federación Anarquista Ibérica, whose purpose was to mold the CNT into an instrument for immediate revolutionary action.[32] For six months a struggle raged between the FAI and the followers of Pestaña and Peiró. Partly because of the state of disorganization in which the CNT emerged from its repression under Primo de Rivera, partly because of the youth and audacity of the FAI, the struggle gradually went against the moderates. Although the FAI played little part in the church burnings of May 1931 in Madrid, it seems to have been instrumental in spreading them to other parts of Spain, particularly Malaga. In July 1931 FAI elements led an armed

---

29. Cited in Peirats, 1, 42. The "indirect participation" referred to was the support given by the moderate CNT leaders to a republican manifesto in 1930 (ibid., 1, 24–25) as well as other similar forms of collaboration (Brenan, pp. 199–200).

30. The manifesto of the *trentistas* (the thirty moderate CNT leaders who broke away or were expelled from the Confederation in January 1932) as cited in Peirats, 1, 44–48.

31. Ibid.

32. Brenan, pp. 249–52. In the late 1920s, many anti-reformist but not necessarily revolutionary leaders, such as Manuel Buenacasa, also gravitated to the FAI. After 1931, however, they dropped away and the organization fell exclusively into the hands of extremists.

assault on the Central Telephone Building in Madrid. During the same month they helped give to the four-day general strike in the city of Seville its revolutionary overtones. In August the FAI seems to have provoked the serious street clashes between Anarchosyndicalist and Socialist workers in Bilbao.[33] In September it led a violent general strike in Barcelona which left sixteen dead.[34]

The Provisional Government contributed indirectly to the success of the FAI by sometimes meeting the Anarchosyndicalist challenge with excessive brutality. In so doing the government in a sense was overcompensating for its failure in its first great test. The church burnings of May could have been stopped by the slightest show of force. Spontaneous in origin, they had spread only when the idealistic qualms of certain Left Republican leaders, especially Azaña, against "shedding the blood of Republicans" appeared to grant the incendiaries immunity.[35] This error was never repeated. For example, when the government encountered resistance during the Seville general strike of July, it used artillery to destroy CNT headquarters and refused to investigate an incident in which the police seem deliberately to have killed four workers who were "trying to escape." [36] As a result of the church burnings and the Seville strike, a new mobilized police force, the Assault Guards, was created to deal with the Anarchosyndicalist menace. After the Barcelona general strike, a harsh "Law for the Defense of the Republic" was enacted which gave the government strong emergency powers for use against strikes it considered illegal. All these measures vindicated those within the CNT who cried hatred toward the Republic.

The clash between the FAI and the moderate CNT leaders reached its peak after the September general strike in Barcelona. Pestaña publicly protested that "sporadic acts of violence can only lead to dictatorship" and was in turn publicly denounced by Durruti.[37] The FAI won a major victory in October when the moderates lost control of the chief Anarchosyndicalist journal, Solidaridad Obrera.[38] Though Pestaña and Peiró were not formally expelled from the CNT until three months later, the new course the Confederation would follow was charted. For the next two years the CNT-FAI launched against the Republic the most ferocious and unceasing opposition ever directed by any proletarian group against any

33. Times (London), 14 August 1931.

34. Ramos Oliveira, p. 298.

35. For the truly remarkable story of the Provisional Government's response to the church burnings, see Maura (then Minister of the Interior), pp. 241–75.

36. Enrique Vila, Un año de república en Sevilla (Seville, 1932), pp. 128–30.

37. The Times (London), 2, 4 September 1931.

38. Brenan, p. 253.

Spanish regime. The CNT-FAI now occupied, "in its fashion, an historical position comparable to that of the Bolsheviks in Russia in 1917." [39] It retained the mass following that its organization along Syndicalist lines had given it, but reverted to the earlier Anarchist tradition of insurrection. On three separate occasions during the next two years, Anarchosyndicalist revolutions of national pretensions were proclaimed.

The first (and least important) insurrection occurred in January 1932 when miners, textile workers, and peasants in the upper Llobregat Valley of Catalonia proclaimed the establishment of *comunismo libertario*.[40] The second was launched in January 1933 in Barcelona but was accompanied by gun battles in the cities of Madrid, Valencia, Cadiz, and Seville.[41] The third insurrection broke out in December 1933, soon after the elections that unseated the Azaña coalition. This time Aragon was the focus, though there were repercussions in Madrid, Valencia, La Corunna, Cadiz, and Seville.[42]

For our purposes the most interesting aspect of these insurrections was that they were seldom effectively seconded by rural locals. This fact has been obscured by the notoriety achieved by Casas Viejas, one of the few Andalusian villages to support the January 1933 rising. For example, although peasants in the Llobregat valley itself joined miners and industrial workers during the first major revolt, there was almost no peasant response elsewhere. Apparently the only exceptions were two villages in Teruel where municipal archives, a church, and Republican flags were burned as militants proclaimed the revolution.[43] The rural areas of Andalusia seem to have remained entirely quiet. Peasant inactivity during the Llobregat rising may be explained on the grounds that the revolt itself was partly fortuitous, not the result of extensive previous planning. But in the more consciously prepared Barcelona rising of 8 January 1933 there was also no general peasant response. Four Levante villages were briefly seized by insurgents; in one the rebels fought so well that four Guardias Civiles were killed.[44] In Andalusia there were short-lived risings in six

39. Joaquín Maurín as quoted in Carlos Rama, *La crisis española del siglo XX* (Mexico, 1960), p. 154.

40. Arrarás, 2, 255–64; Brenan, p. 254.

41. *El Sol* and *El Debate*, 9–16 January 1933.

42. Ibid., 9–13 December 1933. Between the January and December insurrections there had been a formidable eighteen-week strike in the construction industry in Barcelona, which was supported by strikes in Saragossa, La Corunna, Oviedo, and Seville (Brenan, p. 254).

43. These were the villages of Castel de Cabra and Alcoríza. José Gutiérrez Ravé, *España en 1932: Anuario* (Madrid, 1933), p. 36.

44. On the basis of the Levante insurrections, Peirats, *1*, 54–55, has devised a five-stage anatomy of Anarchist village risings in general. At an agreed hour the rebels suddenly enter the homes of those with weapons, disarm them, and take over the

rural villages besides Casas Viejas.[45] The December 1933 insurrection
was the only national CNT effort to receive important peasant backing,
but in this case, too, the response was geographically limited. Fifteen villages of La Rioja and Aragon, where the insurrection had its center, experienced serious social upheavals. Elsewhere there were important outbreaks only in four villages of Estremadura (where Socialists and Communists may have joined with the Anarchosyndicalists) and in one of the
larger rural towns of Cordova.[46]

What was true of the national CNT insurrectionary efforts was also
true within Andalusia itself. Little effective cooperation existed between
the Anarchosyndicalist unions of the major Andalusian cities and their
rural counterparts. This was evident in the first and perhaps most severe
of the Andalusian urban upheavals: the four-day Seville general strike of
July 1931 in which some thirty workers were killed and some two hundred
wounded. The fear that the peasants, as yet untested, would join the urban strikers was especially great since Dr. Pedro Vallina, a saintly dema-
gogue in the old Anarchist tradition, had repeatedly uttered threats to the

---

ayuntamiento. The rest of the village, "intimidated, remains neutral." The Guardia
Civil outpost is surrounded and negotiations start for its surrender, with the captured
mayor often acting as intermediary. If the police refuse to leave the village, a siege
begins. Meanwhile, property records are burned, telephone and telegraph wires are
cut, and comunismo libertario, together with the abolition of private property and
money, is proclaimed. When reinforcements arrive the rebels "more or less resist
according to how long it takes them to realize that the revolution is not general in
all Spain and that they are isolated in their magnificent effort." Then they flee in
disorder, pursued by the troops. Mass arrests, beatings, and tortures follow. Generally,
while in control of the village, the rebels do not commit personal violence against
any but the guardias, if these resist. El Debate, the Catholic journal, agrees on this
point. In the December 1933 La Rioja risings, no private individuals, not even the
local priests, were in any way molested (El Debate, 14 December 1933). Personal
vengeance is minimal, because in the New Jerusalem all, including former enemies,
are to see the light and become brothers. But, as was proven in the Civil War, should
anyone refuse the benefits of the new order, then "a bullet in the head for this compañero—without hate, of course, without hate . . . After all, compañero, death is
nothing" (Brenan, p. 194).

45. The Levante village revolts occurred in Ribarroja, Betera, Pedraba, and
Bugarra. In Andalusia there were serious struggles in Casas Viejas, Arcos de la Frontera, Medina Sidonia, Alcalá de los Gazules, Sanlúcar de Barrameda (all in Cadiz),
Utrera, and La Rinconada (both in Seville). El Sol and El Debate, 9–16 January
1933; Peirats, 1, 55).

46. The La Rioja and Aragon village insurrections were too numerous to list
here. In Caceres serious outbreaks occurred in Navalmoral de la Mata, Oliva de
Plasencia, and Malpartida; in Badajoz, Villanueva de la Serena; in Cordova, Bujalance
(El Sol and El Debate, 9–13 December 1933). The Bujalance troubles flared up
anew when a truck transporting some of the eighty arrested militants was ambushed
and the prisoners set free (El Debate, 16, 17 December 1933).

effect that the Andalusian countryside would "burn" if the government "byzantinized" and did not turn over the land to the workers immediately.[47] Yet when the opportunity arose the peasantry did not revolt. Vallina managed to gather a few dozen peasant supporters in villages near Seville but was arrested on the second day of the outbreak while trying to lead them into the city. With Vallina gone the peasant threat evaporated. Two small villages declared sympathetic general strikes; militants, many of whom were probably not peasants, assaulted jails and other public buildings in Dos Hermanas, Carmona, and Utrera. Elsewhere the peasants remained quiet.[48]

There was also a failure to coordinate action among the CNT rural locals. Peasant strikes were never effectively linked together in the several provinces of Andalusia or the various regions of Spain. United action within a single province was sometimes attempted but could not be maintained. The provincial strike that came closest to success—and the rural strike that received the greatest support from the national CNT as well as from the Andalusian urban unions—was the walkout called by the Seville Federation for 19 May 1932. The strike was nominally directed against the mixed juries established by the Provisional Government at the urging of the Socialists. The Anarchosyndicalists violently opposed these arbitration boards and their urban counterparts on the grounds that they were "a constant threat to the direct action tactics of the CNT, and, as a result, a violation of our revolutionary principles." Like the other "corporative measures" by which the Socialists were trying to institutionalize the labor struggle, the boards increased the power of the state.[49] Moreover, the boards (partly because the Anarchosyndicalists themselves refused to elect delegates) had fallen under the control of the Socialists—those "castrators of the will and spirit of the workers." [50] The Seville Federation,

47. *El Sol*, 9 June 1931. The government's fears were increased by the fact that it suspected separatist elements, headed by Commandante Ramón Franco (brother of General Francisco Franco and one of the military heroes of the overthrow of the monarchy), of plotting a general revolt based upon a peasant rising. These fears had caused the government to keep Andalusia under martial law from the time of the church burnings in May to late August, except for a brief interlude during the Cortes elections of late June. On Franco's threatened left-wing revolt, see Vila, pp. 93–97, 142–45; *El Sol* and *El Debate*, 25–30 June, 4–5 August 1931. Blas Infante's Andalusian regionalists, who strongly supported Vallina, were also suspected of complicity.

48. My account of the Seville general strike is drawn from *El Sol* and *El Debate* of 20–26 July 1931. One of the reasons why peasant support was minimal was that some of the Socialist locals, especially the very large Ecija local, met to pass resolutions against participation.

49. *Solidaridad Obrera*, 14 May 1932.

50. Ibid., 16 June 1932.

then, was fighting an important battle of principle for the entire CNT; if its strike forced the government to dissolve the boards in Seville, they might also be successfully challenged elsewhere.[51] The preparations for the strike were extensive, and care was taken to announce the walkout well in advance so as to satisfy the legal requirements and deny the authorities any excuse for immediate repressive action.

The cautious preparations proved vain. Just before the strike was to begin, the police in Morón and Montellano announced the discovery of huge caches of arms, allegedly for use in an insurrection for which the strike, if successful, would be the signal. Whether these were in fact the intentions of the CNT or whether the Republic was not above using certain of the repressive tactics of the monarchy is uncertain. The Azaña government had already intimated that it would not tolerate the strike, because the grain harvest was "sacred" [52]—a tactic that was to backfire against the Socialist two years later. In any case, the Law for the Defense of the Republic was invoked as soon as the arms were discovered, CNT centers throughout the province were closed, and union leaders were arrested. Strikes nevertheless broke out in sixteen villages; in several they were accompanied by bloody clashes. Some of the villages unable to participate gave vent to their frustration by burning machines and crops. For a time it seemed that the disturbances would spread throughout Andalusia. The Cordova Federation at one point announced its support of the Seville strike but drew back when its leader reached an agreement with the provincial governor which satisfied local CNT objectives. Urban workers in Seville, Málaga, and Cadiz declared general strikes in support of the peasants, but since these did not begin until twelve days after the start of the rural disturbances the tide of peasant defeat could not be stemmed. The national CNT organization enthusiastically backed the Seville strike in its pronouncements but ordered no other supporting action.[53]

The Seville strike, which seemed to have completely ended by 2 June, flared up anew on the sixteenth. This time it died out much more quickly because of police surveillance and the exhaustion of the workers. The only effect of the two strikes was to throw the Andalusian CNT into disarray. The head of the Cordova Federation, who had backed down after initially supporting the strike, was ousted. Charges of treason filled the air as a conflict developed between the regular CNT leadership and

51. Ibid., 14, 17 May 1932.

52. Ibid., 17 May 1932.

53. My account is drawn from *Solidaridad Obrera* and *El Sol,* 18 May–4 June 1932.

Dr. Vallina—that "popular idol bred by the ignorance of the peasantry" [54] —who, in the end, was expelled from the Confederation.[55]

Andalusian rural anarchism seems never to have recovered from these blows. United harvest strikes were declared in other provinces during the summer of 1932, but these were easily crushed, occasionally by application of the principle that the strikes were illegal because the harvest was "sacred." [56] The Seville Federation declared a new provincial strike during the harvest of 1933, but it was only a pale shadow of its predecessor.[57] Thereafter the only important instance of what may have been coordinated action was clandestine in form. In the fall of 1933 a series of farm burnings, which originated in the Jerez de la Frontera-Medina Sidonia region of Cadiz, spread rapidly to other parts of Spain. From August to November, several hundred farms and forests, though apparently relatively few farm buildings, were set on fire.[58]

Why did rural anarchosyndicalism fail so completely? In part, the neglect of Andalusia by the national CNT-FAI was at fault. This neglect in turn reflected the fundamental change in the relative importance of Catalonia and Andalusia. The predominance of Andalusia in the Anarchist federations of the 1870s and 1880s had disappeared after the turn of the century and was but a distant memory. The two ancient centers of Spanish anarchism were no longer in any sense equal. Urban anarchosyndicalism had far outdistanced rural; Catalonia far overshadowed Andalusia.[59] This was especially true because Catalonia was now flanked by a

54. *Solidaridad Obrera,* 16 June 1932.

55. *El Socialista,* 1 November 1932.

56. *La Tierra,* 23 September 1932. For a list of other repressive measures of the Azaña government during the summer of 1932, see the declaration of the CNT Regional Confederation for Andalusia and Estremadura in *Solidaridad Obrera,* 14 October 1932.

57. The second Seville provincial strike is described in *El Sol* and *El Debate,* 31 May–5 June 1933.

58. For example, from 29 August to 7 September 1933 *El Debate* lists twenty-seven different villages in which such fires occurred. *La Luz,* 29 August 1933, devotes a full page to listing several dozen other conflagrations. In Casas Viejas alone, twenty farms were burned (*El Obrero de la Tierra,* 19 August 1933). *The New York Times,* 2 September 1933, suggests that some of the fires may have been set by owners who feared their lands would be expropriated, but this is doubtful since the landowning classes had by then come to regard Domingo with contempt.

59. According to the reports of the various Anarchist or Anarchosyndicalist congresses, the proportion of Andalusian membership—both urban and rural—varied as follows: 1873, 61.2 percent; 1882, 59.3 percent; 1919, 13.3 percent; 1931, 20.1 percent; 1936, 27.9 percent. Since the proportion reported in 1919 was probably unrepresentatively low, however (the congress was held after the trienio passed its peak in Andalusia), and since the 1936 proportion was too high (it included

new Anarchosyndicalist stronghold in Saragossa. The ties between these two regions were so much more intimate than those maintained by either with any other part of Spain that one may safely speak of a new geographical bloc within the CNT. The FAI leaders—Durruti, the Ascasos, and García Oliver—were all from Barcelona and Saragossa. The major insurrections of the CNT-FAI originated and found most of their response within these two regions. And it was this bloc, with some assistance from the neighboring Levante, that was to carry on the Civil War for the Anarchosyndicalists after Andalusia had fallen to the Nationalists.

The northern, urban orientation of the CNT-FAI may also help explain the failure to create a national peasant federation like that formed by the Socialist or like the Anarchosyndicalist FNAE of the 1913–18 period. The establishment of such a federation was contemplated for a time. At its June 1931 congress the CNT authorized a committee on peasant relations to revive the old FNAE newspaper, La Voz del Campesino and to call, "as soon as possible," a national peasants' congress, which was to found a separate rural federation.[60] In January 1932 a spokesman for the committee stated that the proposed congress would soon convene.[61] In May 1932 Solidaridad Obrera mentioned anew the need for peasant union.[62] But there was so little real interest that the congress never met and the federation was never founded. The national peasant journal, which might have provided an alternative means of communication, was no more successful. Though La Voz del Campesino began publication in Jerez de la Frontera in 1932, it was abandoned during the same year.[63] Thereafter the idea of a separate rural federation was revived only by moderate groups, which may have maintained ties with the sindicatos de oposición organized by the ousted CNT leader, Pestaña.[64]

The lack of greater unity within Andalusia itself had other causes. In all the port cities of the region—Cadiz, Málaga, and Seville—the An-

Estremadura as well as Andalusia) it seems safe to assume that Andalusia contributed about 20 percent of CNT membership throughout the twentieth century.

60. CNT, Congreso Extraordinario de 1931, p. 108.

61. Federación de Trabajadores Agrícolas de la Comarca de Cádiz, Memoria del Congreso celebrado en enero de 1932, p. 9.

62. Solidaridad Obrera, 17 May 1932.

63. Campo Libre, 2 November 1935.

64. Tierra Libre, a peasant journal of national pretensions, began publication in Sueca (Valencia) in 1934 but perished the same year. In mid-1935 Campo Libre, the third national peasant journal, was founded in Madrid. Though this newspaper survived into the Civil War, it had to overcome determined boycotts on the part of FAI extremists during its early months (Campo Libre, 21 December 1935). Apparently the idea of a national peasant federation had been dropped by the time Campo Libre appeared, because it spoke only of the need for regional unity.

archosyndicalists were engaged in a bitter struggle with the Communists for control of the workers. Though the CNT retained its dominance, none of the cities could give the countryside the strong lead that Saragossa provided to the peasants of Aragon. The effort to establish regional links among the rural locals themselves also failed, perhaps because it seems to have been sponsored by moderate groups not controlled by the FAI. Three committees were set up to create a regional peasant federation, but none survived for more than a few months.[65] Finally, the Anarchosyndicalist-Communist rivalry on occasion directly divided the existing peasant leaders.

But neither these factors nor the strong feelings of village particularism fully explain the failure of the peasants to rise en masse, as Vallina had threatened they would. The most important reason was that the Provisional Government, once it had shed its illusions that the Republic could be preserved without bloodshed, adopted extremely harsh measures against the Anarchosyndicalists. The traditional local restraints of the cacique system had weakened, but in areas dominated by the CNT the government replaced them with new restraints of its own. The leftist journal *La Tierra* complained that the blades of bayonets outnumbered the blades of grass in the Andalusian countryside during the 1932 harvest.[66] And in fact—given the enormous increase in police forces which occurred during the first year of the Republic—there is every reason to believe that police surveillance in Andalusia was far greater than it had been under the monarchy.[67] At first—from the time of the church burnings until after the July 1931 Seville general strike—the Provisional Government seems to have reacted to the Anarchosyn-

65. The first two committees, based in Jerez and Utrera, were extremely short-lived. The third committee, established in Morón in December 1935, managed to hang on until the Civil War, though it was still pitifully pleading for support when that cataclysmic event occurred (*Campo Libre,* 21 December 1935 and 13 June 1936).

66. *La Tierra,* 23 September 1932.

67. There are no figures on the geographical distribution of police forces, but the rise in total police strength is indicative. From 1912 to 1919 the Guardia Civil, then the only national police force in Spain, numbered approximately 20,000. Its strength was increased during the *trienio* to 26,500, at which level it remained through the Primo de Rivera era. With the advent of the Republic, the Corps was expanded to 27,817. Moreover, an entirely new force, the Assault Guards, which numbered 11,698 by 1932, was created. Thus, within a year of the proclamation of the Republic, total police forces were half again as numerous as under the dictatorship, or twice as numerous as they had been in 1918. Equally important, the striking power both of the Assault and of the Civil Guards was increased in that both Corps were motorized under the Republic. (*Pequeño Anuario Estadístico de España, 1936,* p. 85.)

dicalist menace in a state of panic. After its fear that the whole of Andalusia would erupt had passed, it continued to apply repression in a highly deliberate manner. The main reason why the Anarchosyndicalists could not organize the peasantry into a more effective revolutionary force was that their declaration of "open war" against the Republic provoked the Republic to declare war against them in turn. Although it may be naïve to believe that without the Republic's policy of unremitting suppression the Anarchosyndicalists would have achieved "a pacific and constructive collaboration with the new State," there can be no question that "half the Spanish proletariat" was indeed placed "outside the law." [68]

Yet there was a limit to what the state could do. It could crush the great FAI insurrections in Catalonia and Aragon so rapidly that there was no time for the Andalusian peasantry to respond. It could check the spread of united labor agitation within Andalusia itself, as it proved during the July 1931 and the May 1932 Seville strikes. But it could not maintain so constant and universal a presence as to prevent local outbursts. It was in this last sense that the removal of some of the old local restraints had importance. There were literally hundreds of isolated village disturbances in Andalusia during the first two years of the Republic. It would be pointless to try to catalogue all these incidents, which ranged from brief invasions of farms to local insurrections. Nor could such a catalogue be complete without a systematic study of the local and provincial press, a herculean task that was beyond my capacities.[69] Some idea of the situation that existed during most of the period from 1931 to 1934 can be conveyed, however, by recounting some

68. Rama, p. 157.

69. Because I relied exclusively on the national press, my description of peasant upheavals is very inadequate and can serve only to outline the major problems and trends. I chose *El Debate* rather than *El Sol* (the other great newspaper of the period) as my principal source because I feared that the latter, a strong supporter of the Azaña coalition until mid-1933, might conceal Socialist excesses. This choice was probably mistaken, as I have since concluded that *El Sol* provided somewhat more complete coverage without sacrificing objectivity. I did, however, examine major incidents in both papers and used *El Sol* alone during the many periods when *El Debate* was suspended (the Provisional Government and Azaña muzzled the opposition press with shocking frequency). I also consistently employed the FNTT weekly, *El Obrero de la Tierra*, as a counterbalance to *El Debate* and turned to the Anarchosyndicalist press on the few occasions when its publication was permitted during major clashes between the CNT-FAI and the state. Perhaps mistakenly, I did not use either the highly biased monarchist journal, *ABC*, or the leftist daily, *La Tierra*, whose sensationalistic reporting vitiated its great merit as the national newspaper that devoted the most space to rural upheavals.

of the outbreaks reported in the national press during the first great period of trouble, the fall of 1931.

In August 1931 severe strikes took place in Bujalance and Baena after the governor of Cordova banned a provincial walkout planned by the CNT. At the same time peasants in Moraleda de Zafayara (Granada) tried to seize land, and prolonged strikes broke out in Écija and Estepa, two of the larger agricultural towns of Seville.[70] In early September day laborers in Doña Mencía (Cordova) assaulted a Guardia Civil outpost after the police tried to stop a demonstration.[71] During the same month a series of strikes that were to last until the late spring of 1932 began in the Jerez and Arcos de la Frontera region of Cadiz,[72] and in Corral de Almaguer (Toledo) a rural conflict left four or five peasants dead.[73] October began with a gun battle between strikers and the Guardia Civil in Pozoblanco (Cordova) which produced several wounded.[74] A week later a similar clash in Gilena (Seville) left two dead and five wounded.[75] Meanwhile a series of strikes in the Sierra Morena regions of Cordova and Ciudad Real assumed revolutionary proportions and—in the Villa-nueva de Córdoba area at least—had to be quelled by infantry and military aircraft.[76]

These local outbreaks could not, individually or collectively, overthrow the Republic. In this sense the CNT—so long as it remained "only a loose union of local and regional organizations, each of which formulated its own policies and acted at decisive moments without a common plan" [77]—was powerless to achieve its ultimate objective. Yet its unrelenting opposition did succeed in weakening the Republic. The atmosphere of insecurity created by CNT local risings helped turn countless voters against Azaña in the 1933 elections. Equally important, they caused Azaña to adopt policies of stern repression which sometimes backfired—most notably at Casas Viejas, which probably damaged Azaña's position more effectively than all of the other rural upheavals

70. *El Debate* and *El Sol*, 12–16 August 1931.

71. *El Debate*, 8 September 1931.

72. *El Obrero de la Tierra*, 23 April and 7 May 1932, claims that, beginning in September 1931, the CNT launched four important strike waves in this region.

73. *El Sol*, 23 September 1932.

74. Ibid., 2 October 1932.

75. Ibid., 10 October 1932. One of the two persons killed and two of the five injured were Guardias Civiles.

76. *El Debate* and *El Sol*, 8–13 October 1931.

77. Asociación Internacional de Trabajo, *Informe para el Congreso Extraordinario del 6 de diciembre de 1937* (typeset copy, apparently not intended for public distribution, located in the Labadie Collection of the University of Michigan, Ann Arbor).

put together. In short, the Anarchosyndicalists, unable to carry out their type of revolution, prevented the Republicans from fully realizing their own revolutionary dreams. In the end the excesses that inevitably resulted from the "dictatorial" policies that the CNT forced upon Azaña cost him even the support of many liberals who believed that "democratic" methods could be applied at all times against all opponents.

But the Anarchosyndicalists, too, paid a price. By rejecting all the means (including the redistribution of land) by which the Republic was trying to benefit the workers, and by bringing down upon itself the wrath of the state, the CNT failed to attract many of those workers who might otherwise have joined its ranks. It was for this reason that the CNT did not experience the same spectacular rise in membership as the Socialist organizations. This, too, was why it did not expand significantly beyond its traditional geographical limits. In these respects the more flexible and less doctrinaire CNT of the trienio bolchevista had been relatively more successful. Under FAI leadership the CNT became a destructive force that in the end seemed also to be destroying itself. Throughout the latter half of 1933 its power was on the wane. After the national insurrection in December the cumulative effect of the repressions it invited finally reduced it to a belligerent force of secondary importance. Though the CNT was still able to launch an impressive strike in the construction industry in Saragossa during the spring of 1934, the Socialists generally dominated the labor scene. Only when the political bankruptcy of the conservative governments that succeeded Azaña led to the Popular Front victory in the elections of February 1936 did the CNT again begin to revive. This time it achieved its true objective, though no longer entirely through its own efforts. The Republic collapsed, and the Anarchosyndicalists could at long last test their dream of a stateless society.

Latent and Spontaneous Civil War in the Countryside

It would be unjust to attribute to the Anarchosyndicalists, or to the Communists,[78] exclusive responsibility for the continuous social upheaval

78. Until the formation of the Popular Front government in 1936, the Communists were as hostile to the Republic as the Anarchosyndicalists. The party was still so weak and unimportant, however, that its rural activities can still be relegated to a footnote. Probably the most important Communist-inspired outbreak occurred in Antequera (Malaga) in March 1932, when the Holy Week festivities were turned into an occasion for convent burnings and semi-insurrectionary riots (El Debate, 30–31 March 1932). Communists also seem to have played a role in the aforementioned Corral de Almaguer and Villanueva de Córdoba agitations of September and October 1931, as well as in the January 1933 wave of farm invasions in the

in the Spanish countryside. The CNT-FAI policy of total opposition did not create but only intensified the spontaneous war waged by the peasantry against its old enemies, the landowners and the Guardia Civil. In this war the intensity of feeling often rendered organizational affiliations unimportant. Chaos frequently descended upon villages where organized labor units did not exist. It also visited villages affiliated with the Socialist UGT and FNTT, though, as will be abundantly proven in the next chapter, both organizations advocated nonrevolutionary policies during the Azaña era. Nor was violence initiated by the workers alone. The propertied classes did not passively accept the new order but frequently took their defense into their own hands. Local units of the Guardia Civil did not always exercise restraint in suppressing illegal manifestations but sometimes reverted to their tradition of what might be called "preventive brutality" toward the peasantry. Thus the story of rural unrest during the Azaña years cannot be summarized entirely under organizational headings. It must also be told in terms of individual cases in which conscious planning for revolt of the Anarchosyndicalist or Communist type did not exist.

The FNTT's support of the Republic and rejection of insurrectionary tactics did not mean that the Socialists condemned themselves to inactivity. The FNTT was deeply engaged in a power struggle with the old rural oligarchy. In this struggle the weapon of the strike was energetically used. During the 26 months from April 1930 to June 1932 FNTT groups participated in no fewer than 925 strikes.[79] Though most of these were minor local efforts, some had a wider scope. This was especially true in the few instances in which the provincial federations of the FNTT invoked their great power.[80] In 1931 the Salamanca Federation threatened, but apparently did not call, a provincial walkout, and the Badajoz Federation staged a two-day general strike to protest alleged excesses of the Guardia Civil.[81] In 1932 the Jaen Federation ordered

---

borderlands of Caceres and Toledo. Finally, Communists tried to steal some of the Anarchosyndicalists' thunder by calling a strike of their own to coincide with the CNT's Seville provincial strike of May–June 1932. There is no way of measuring the number of peasants who followed the Communists. Though their greatest gains seem to have been made in Malaga, at the expense of the Anarchosyndicalists, the Socialists were also occasionally concerned with the danger of Communist penetration (see, for example, *El Obrero de la Tierra,* 22 April 1933).

79. FNTT, *Memoria,* p. 140. The causes, locations, durations, and results of the strikes are listed on pp. 112–39.

80. In addition to provincial strikes, neighboring villages sometimes also combined forces. The most important instance of such collaboration seems to have occurred in Jaen, when four villages managed to maintain a walkout for twenty days (*El Debate,* 7, 10, 20, 21, 26 September 1933).

81. Ibid., 29 September and 29–31 December 1931.

a one-day demonstration to demand the immediate application of the laboreo forzoso decree, and the Toledo Federation proclaimed a provincial strike against the terms—not the principle—of the harvest contract decided upon in the local mixed juries.[82] In 1933, because of the increase in unemployment and the deterioration of relations between the Socialists and Azaña, provincial strikes became more frequent. In May the Toledo Federation again struck for higher wages and for stricter application of the términos municipales law.[83] In June the Seville Federation struck against the use of agricultural machinery in the harvest, so as to increase the number of jobs available.[84] In July the Salamanca Federation brought its long-standing dispute with the provincial Landowners' Association to a head by going on strike in response to a threatened lockout.[85]

All these strikes had political implications, of course, but only once did a Socialist provincial federation openly use its power for political ends. This occurred in the Badajoz strike of December 1931, which sought the ouster of the provincial governor and of the provincial commander of the Guardia Civil. As will be seen, the Badajoz demonstration was also the only provincial strike accompanied by major physical violence. All the other provincial efforts passed without serious bloodshed, since the Socialists did not try to convert them into revolutionary upheavals and the police—restrained because of Socialist participation in the government—did not suppress them as such.[86]

On the local level the responsibility of the FNTT for the rural chaos of the Azaña period was more direct. Although neither the national nor the provincial FNTT organizations ever openly approved such methods, the local units often encouraged workers to invade farms, either to plow land or to demand work. Aside from the two great waves of invasions which swept Socialist-dominated Estremadura in October 1932 and

82. Ibid., 26–28 March and 25 May 1932.

83. Ibid., 19 May 1933.

84. Ibid., 7–10 June 1933.

85. Ibid., 9–15 July 1933. For the background to the strike, see *Economía Española* (June 1933), pp. 117–47, and *La Luz, El Socialista,* and *El Sol* for June and July 1933.

86. The March 1932 Jaen strike produced a few clashes that left some wounded but no dead. The most serious occurrence of the May 1932 Toledo strike seems to have been that the provincial governor, who was touring the villages to calm the strikers, was mobbed in his car at Escalonilla and had to flee. In the June 1933 Seville strike, two harvesting machines were burned at Morón; by contrast, twelve had been destroyed during the Anarchosyndicalist strike in the same town a week earlier (*El Debate,* 29 May and 7–10 June 1933). The other provincial FNTT strikes all passed without serious violence, except for the December 1931 Badajoz strike.

January 1933, there were many dozen—perhaps even several hundred—local incidents. In fact, it would seem that the number of farm invasions to plow land—though not to demand work or to steal crops—was greater in Socialist than in Anarchosyndicalist districts. This was partly because many yunteros were affiliated with the Socialists, whereas the Anarchosyndicalists recruited mostly day laborers who lacked the instruments necessary for cultivation. The existing use of the land was also important: in Estremadura there was much untilled land that could be plowed, whereas in Andalusia most arable land was already cultivated. Finally, FNTT militants could count on relatively more lenient treatment from the police. Though numerous, the farm invasions had serious social conseqences only during the period of the Intensification of Cultivation decrees. Normally they were tentative probes to test the intentions of the authorities. When they were resisted, the peasants quietly evacuated the land. Bloodshed occurred, but only rarely.

The rapid growth of the FNTT locals also led to a struggle between them and the civil authorities, especially in villages where conservatives retained control of the ayuntamiento. In most cases the struggle was waged by means of demonstrations and strikes intended to drive the authorities from office. Sometimes it was resolved by violence. In 1932, for example, the mayors of El Gordo (Caceres) and Pedro Muñoz (Ciudad Real) were beaten by FNTT members for failing to support worker demands.[87] Toward the end of the same year a municipal councilor was killed, and the mayor and the local judge were wounded by Socialist militants in Benitalga (Almeria) when the two local factions squared off for battle on the feast day of the patron saint of the village.[88] In 1933 Socialists killed the mayor of Belalcázar (Cordova);[89] later in the year the mayor of a village in Valencia was shot and wounded, also because of his consistent opposition to Socialist demands.[90] In the two latter cases the assaults seem to have been premeditated, though perhaps only by a few excited individuals who acted independently of the local FNTT leadership.[91]

87. *El Debate*, 25 July 1932; *El Obrero de la Tierra*, 28 January 1933.

88. *El Obrero de la Tierra*, 25 February 1933. Feast days were often occasions for such battles, since they provided both leisure and, because of the religious processions, provocation.

89. *El Debate*, 26 March 1933.

90. Ibid., 18 May 1933 (the village was Herrera del Río Pisuerga).

91. Sometimes the situation was reversed. In Salvaleón (Badajoz) the Socialist mayor cooperated closely with the FNTT. On May Day, 1932, a group of workers gathered in front of the mayor's house to serenade him with the "Internationale." The Guardia Civil arrived and ordered them to disperse. When the workers refused, the police fired into the crowd, killing three and wounding one. They thereupon

Even on the local level, however, the FNTT units did not play the same sinister role as the CNT peasant unions, though they were far more numerous and subject to less constant police surveillance. This conclusion seems unavoidable even when the opposition Catholic press, which may have tended to exaggerate Socialist excesses (since the Socialists, not the Anarchosyndicalists, were the principal political opponents of the Catholics), is used as the chief source of information. No instance is recorded during the Azaña era in which FNTT locals tried to seize villages and proclaim the revolution. No great caches of arms were ever uncovered in FNTT centers. The cutting of electric and telephone wires, the destruction of agricultural machinery, the burning of farms, and the other forms of sabotage so characteristic of the Anarchosyndicalists rarely accompanied FNTT activities. Violence occurred in the Socialist strongholds, but principally because the FNTT had absorbed so many new members that it could not completely control its followers.[92] Their misery was too great, their hatred too intense, and their expectations too unlimited for them always to accept the spirit of restraint that guided the Socialist leadership prior to 1933. Consequently, Socialist as well as Anarchosyndicalist areas were capable of producing the most horrible excesses. This was proven in Castilblanco, whose story, as the first great cause célèbre of the peasant war (it occurred a year before Casas Viejas), deserves to be told.

A tiny unincorporated hamlet in the arid hill country of southern Badajoz, Castilblanco lay in a region dominated by the Socialists. Though no FNTT unit had yet been formally established, Socialist influence was sufficiently strong for the hamlet to join in the December 1931 political demonstration ordered by the Badajoz Federation against the civil governor and the Guardia Civil. The strike produced a number of serious incidents. In Feria a clash with the peasants left two guardias wounded, a peasant dead, and several other peasants injured. In Puebla de Alcocer there was brief gunplay, though no casualties. But it was in Castilblanco that truly terrible events occurred. Their precise course is disputed. According to one version, the guardias peacefully approached a large group of demonstrators, who suddenly fell upon them with

---

arrested the mayor for "provocation." The Socialists attributed the Salvaleón incident to a long-standing struggle for power between the progressive mayor and the local police commander, who was affiliated with the caciques who had formerly controlled the town (*El Obrero de la Tierra*, 3, 14 May 1932).

92. It must always be remembered that the Socialist peasant following increased more than twelvefold in two years and that the overall UGT membership increased almost fivefold. Under these circumstances it is remarkable that the national Socialist organizations retained as much control of their followers as they did.

knives. This would explain the ease with which the rifle-bearing police were disarmed. According to another version, the police tried to break up the demonstration by firing first into the air and then into the crowd, killing one peasant and wounding another. This would help explain the blood lust that seized the mob, for it was not satisfied with killing the guards but began with shovels and machetes to hack apart the corpses, severing the heads and gouging out the eyes. And around the monstrous remains the women of the village are said to have formed a circle and danced.[93]

The revenge of the Guardia Civil was almost more terrible than the act itself. Its commander, General Sanjurjo, announced that the corps would "not tolerate cowardly attacks upon itself in the future." As though to prove his words were not vain, as well as because of the horror that the fate of their comrades must have generated among them, the police for a time abandoned all restraint in dealing with labor disturbances, meeting each of them with gunfire. Three days after Castilblanco two peasants were killed and three wounded by Guardia Civil bullets in Zalamea de la Serena (Badajoz). Two days after Zalamea a striker was killed and another wounded in Calzada de Calatrava (Ciudad Real), and two strikers died and eleven were wounded in Epila (Saragossa). On the same day the revenge of the corps made itself felt as far away as Valencia, where two peasants were killed and ten wounded in Jeresa. At the same time in Puertollano (Ciudad Real) another striker was shot down. On 5 January 1932, six days after Castilblanco, the revenge of the Guardia Civil—long honored by the propertied classes as "La Benemérita" (The Worthy One)—reached its height. The local detachment at Arnedo (Logroño) killed seven and wounded thirty when it fired repeatedly into a crowd of industrial workers peacefully demonstrating in front of the town hall. Four of the dead were women, a fifth was a child.[94] Symbolically, all this occurred as the Constituent Cortes was assembling for the first time as the regular legislative body of Spain. The agenda for the first two days is a capsule history of the Second Republic. The opening session was devoted not to celebrations of the successful establishment of constitutional rule but to the events at Castilblanco. The second session was taken up by debates on Arnedo.[95]

93. My account is drawn principally from *El Sol* and *El Debate,* 2–5 January 1932. *El Obrero de la Tierra* never issued a complete report on Castilblanco; indeed, it scarcely mentioned it except to deny that an FNTT local existed there (one was established soon thereafter, however, as we learn from FNTT, *Memoria,* p. 186).

94. *El Debate* and *El Sol,* 2–6 January 1932.

95. *D.S.* 93, 5 January 1932, pp. 2989–3005; *D.S.* 94, 6 January 1932, pp. 3015–18.

Between the two extremes these names represented, the Republic and the Cortes were to be destroyed.

The week between Castilblanco and Arnedo was the most terrible in the history of the clash between the "Benemérita" and the peasantry, but it was by no means unique. In October 1932 the same fatal duality of mutual excesses seemed about to be reborn. On 6 October a mob of peasants in the Anarchosyndicalist village of Arroyomolinos de Leon (Huelva) attacked and wounded several guardias. On the seventh the local detachment in Socialist-dominated Fuensalida (Toledo) fired into a peasant demonstration, killing two—a father and his infant child—and wounding several.[96] Even before Castilblanco the same fatal duality had manifested itself in Montemolín (Badajoz), a village in which no organized labor unit existed. Peasants trying to storm the ayuntamiento were fired upon by two guardias, one of whom they managed to disarm and lynch, while the other made his escape behind a steady stream of fire.[97] The instances of such bloodshed, too numerous to be described fully here, were not limited by party, by time, or by place, except insofar as they occurred primarily in the latifundio provinces. They were the inevitable product of the workers' demands for complete independence and of the authorities' refusal or inability to grant it.

To the violence resulting from the enmity between police and peasants must be added that stemming from the ancient hatred between peasants and landowners. The latter did not passively accept the new state of affairs. Although they did not yet organize the vigilante societies that were to appear in 1936, the owners often took the law into their own hands. Since they, not the workers, held most of the privately owned firearms in the countryside, the damage they were able to inflict was considerable. Most of the casualties occurred as owners tried to force off their farms peasants who had invaded them to plow or to demand work. Others took place as villages split into opposing factions and battled in the streets.[98] In a few instances the owners' resistance assumed more sinister forms. Perhaps the most terrible of these was the slaughter at Castellar de Santiago (Ciudad Real) in December 1932. This, too, deserves to be related.

96. *El Debate*, 7, 8 October 1932.
97. Ibid., 14 June 1931.
98. In my reading of the daily press I counted ten incidents in which owners killed or seriously wounded a large number of peasants without intercession of the police. There were also six incidents in which the peasants killed or seriously wounded owners while invading farms. All but two of these sixteen incidents occurred in the latifundio provinces.

The FNTT members in Castellar had repeatedly protested that they were being denied work during the olive harvest because of their political affiliations. They demanded that women be refused employment until all men had been hired, so as to prevent wives of unorganized laborers from taking jobs away from them. When the mayor tried to leave town without granting their demands, some of the workers stoned the bus on which he was departing and injured him. A friend of the mayor got out his rifle, shot at a worker, but was knifed by another worker before he could do further damage. Rage seized the local landowners. They formed a lynch party, proceeded to the house where the worker guilty of the knifing had taken refuge, broke open the door, and dragged him outside. The "Benemérita" tried to intervene but were forced to stand back while the worker was murdered. The owners then returned to the house and killed another worker who had hidden there. Their thirst for blood still not satisfied, and the police no longer trying to stop it, the lynch party headed for the home of the local FNTT leader. When it did not find him there, it began a house-to-house search until the victim was uncovered and assassinated.[99] The barbarism of the established classes at Castellar matched that of the peasants at Castilblanco, that of the Guardia Civil at Arnedo, and that of the Assault Guards at Casas Viejas. In each case the unrelieved tension that gripped the Spanish countryside exploded into an outburst of primitive savagery.

Azaña never found a solution to the rural tension. Rather than decreasing as time went on, social disorders increased. This can be proven through the strike statistics of the Ministry of Labor, despite the fact that they recorded only a small fraction of the legitimate strikes that occurred and completely ignored all other forms of social protest.[100] In the last six months of 1930 only 27 agricultural strikes were recorded. In 1931, when the Republic was established, the total rose to 85. In 1932 they numbered 198. In 1933 the total was 448, of which 245 occurred before Azaña was unseated in September.[101] The violence of rural upheavals also increased insofar as can be judged by a reading of the

99. My account is drawn from *El Obrero de la Tierra*, 17, 24, 31 December 1932. The Socialist account would seem accurate, since it was not denied in the Catholic press.

100. On these and other inadequacies of Spanish strike statistics, see notes 25, 41 and 44 in chap. 5.

101. Ministerio de Trabajo, *Boletines* for each month. The number of strikers and of workdays lost in agricultural strikes also increased from 1932 to 1933 (there are no figures for 1931). In 1932 strikers numbered 90,802 and 809,431 days were lost. In 1933 the number of strikers rose to 240,609 and the number of days lost to 2,056,863. As mentioned, strike statistics are especially inadequate in these respects, so that my figures should be taken only as representative of trends.

daily press. Excluding the general bloodshed that accompanied the three CNT-FAI national insurrections, the number of rural clashes in which deaths were reported rose from ten in 1931, to fifteen in 1932, to twenty-six in 1933.[102] Needless to say, clashes in which persons were only wounded or in which only property damage occurred were far more numerous.

Theoretically, Azaña might have restored peace by crushing all labor organizations, both national and local. But peace of this sort would have been bought at too high a price. In the political sphere total repression would have required Azaña to abandon his entire legislative program, since it could not survive Cortes opposition without Socialist support. In the social sphere suppression would have meant a return to the stagnation and injustice of the monarchy, since, as of old, the workers would be the only class to pay the price for the reestablishment of order. Neither of these consequences was acceptable to Azaña, either psychologically or politically. Whatever his failings, he did sincerely believe in reconciling the workers with Spanish society, thereby ending the deep class cleavage that threatened to destroy it. Thus Azaña might relentlessly persecute the CNT, but he never sought utterly to proscribe it. With the passage of time he hoped that even this extremist organization might soften its stand and accept his socially progressive Republic.

Could Azaña have restored peace by speedier application of the agrarian reform? One can only speculate. From May to August 1931, when the Provisional Government was seized by a paroxysm of fear that the peasants would rise en masse, events seemed to be heading in the direction of an attempt to buy social tranquillity by rapid land redistribution. Once the general revolt failed to materialize, however, the feeling of urgency passed and a false confidence that the Republic could ride out its troubles characterized official action thereafter. The endless Cortes debates, the cautious application of the September law, and the delay in presenting the supplementary rural legislation all proceeded without reference to the growing civil war in the countryside. Only in the Intensification of Cultivation decrees did Azaña give in to peasant protest, and in this case he acted almost as much in opposition to the owners' refusal to cultivate as in response to the social chaos.

102. My figures are undoubtedly too low. The responsible national press reported rural upheavals only sporadically, and I have made no systematic analysis of such sensationalistic national journals as *La Tierra* or of the provincial press. That even an opposition paper such as *El Debate* was restrained in its reporting is interesting. It constantly spoke of the "anarchy in the countryside" but made no attempt to blow up each incident in such a way as to provoke a sense of terror in its readers. On the whole the Spanish press in the 1930s maintained surprisingly high standards of reporting for such troubled times.

What would have happened had more land been distributed more rapidly? There are a few important signs that the effects would have been beneficial. Had the actions of the government disproved the Anarchosyndicalist claim that the Agrarian Reform Law was a hoax, it is possible that it might have weaned away many CNT followers. Though most Anarchosyndicalist locals followed the policy of the national Confederation and refused to have anything to do with any official measures, some were not impervious to the promise of land. On the only occasion on which the government acted vigorously, a few CNT locals broke their earlier resolutions and asked that the Intensification of Cultivation decrees be applied to their villages.[103] The fact that peasants who had received land thereafter did not participate in social upheavals also gave cause for hope. Judging from the attention they received in the opposition press, the only beneficiaries of the Intensification decrees or of the September law who remained a source of trouble were those of Espera (Cadiz). But the disturbances in Espera were very modest in comparison to some of the incidents we have been describing. The settlers there split into two factions and could not agree as to how to work the land they had received. A few workers in each faction were assaulted, and production was seriously disrupted, but there was no general violence. Espera proved only that in this one instance collective cultivation could not succeed, not that the peasantry did not appreciate the gift of land.[104]

It would be naïve, however, to think that more rapid land transfers could have restored complete social tranquillity. Badajoz, the province in which more peasants received land than any other, did not thereby become an island of peace, because the majority of the peasants were inevitably by-passed even by the relatively energetically applied Intensification of Cultivation decrees. In truth, Azaña was faced with a problem that defied perfect solution. Unless he were willing to abandon all thought of legal action and abdicate the power of the state by permitting unopposed peasant seizures (a course of action which, aside from being psychologically and politically impossible for him, might have led to a military rising or full-scale civil war), most peasants would inevitably remain without work or land for the immediate future. So

103. Adolfo Vázquez Humasqué in *BIRA* (March 1933), pp. 258–60. On the other hand, the IRA office in Seville stated in a 1934 report ("Memoria sobre el estado social en Seville," folder 41/0/1, IRA archives) that no CNT locals had as yet solicited land. This contrasted not only with the Socialist, but also with the Communist locals, which showed the "greatest eagerness" to receive land.

104. On Espera, see *BIRA* (October 1934), pp. 942–43, and *El Obrero de la Tierra*, 19 August 1933.

long as these conditions continued upheavals would occur. Rural chaos was the price Spain was paying for its poverty and its past neglect of the peasantry; upheavals could not be stopped unless the old local restraints, which in turn meant social stagnation, were reimposed.

The importance of the failure to distribute land more quickly lies elsewhere. The Anarchosyndicalists had proved unable to overthrow the Republic. So long as the Socialists remained committed to the democratic regime, peasant unrest in most of the nation remained uncoordinated and ineffective. But because Azaña offered them no concrete achievement by which their faith might be sustained, some Socialist leaders and many of the rank and file members became disillusioned and were able to change the course of the party. Once the restraint exercised by the Socialists was removed, what might have been the birth pangs of a new rural order proved instead part of the death throes of the Republic.

12: The Radicalization of the Socialists

Socialist Moderation Prior to 1933

The change of attitude in the Socialist party was of such momentous importance to the history of the Republic that it seems worthwhile to stress once again the extent to which the movement had been reformist in the past. Spanish socialism preached the utopian goal of the classless society but placed this goal in the distant future and rejected violence as a means of reaching it. As one observer put, it the Socialists spoke in "cold and dry voices"[1] that stressed organization and education, not the miraculous transformation that the Anarchists proclaimed. Even in the great wave of hope that washed over the Left in 1917–20, the followers of Pablo Iglesias did not succumb to the temptations that swayed important elements in sister parties elsewhere in Europe. Though they made a few tentative approaches to the CNT and sought for a time to join the Third International, the Socialists remained chiefly "in contact with the republicans, and [were] more concerned with sociopolitical evolution than with the rapid establishment of the dictatorship of the proletariat."[2] The one decisive action of the UGT during the trienio bolchevista, the general strike of August 1917, occurred not in opposition to the bourgeoisie but with the acquiescence of Republican and Catalan groups. When the Army crushed this strike with considerable bloodshed, a seemingly lasting "aversion to so-called 'catastrophic' movements was introduced into Spanish Socialism."[3]

This nonrevolutionary orientation survived the death of Iglesias and served as the basis on which the new UGT chief, Largo Caballero,

1. Díaz del Moral, p. 224.
2. The Marquis of Torrenueva as quoted in IRS, *Córdoba*, p. 137.
3. Julio Álvarez del Vayo, *The Last Optimist* (New York, 1950), p. 210. Maura also believed that "The experience of 1917 had taught [the Socialists] a lesson they could never forget" (p. 73). Unfortunately, these statements proved true only for Julián Besteiro, not for Largo Caballero, the other leader of the 1917 strike.

worked out his modus vivendi with Primo de Rivera. The Socialists rejected Communist and Anarchosyndicalist overtures for common action against the dictatorship. Instead UGT leaders quickly accepted positions on governmental committees, and, in 1925, Largo Caballero himself agreed to sit on Primo de Rivera's Council of State. Although the co-operation between the Marxists and this "fascist" lessened as the years passed, the Berenguer government, which in 1930 replaced the collapsed dictatorship, calculated that the "frankly governmental" behavior of the Socialists "during the past six years" could be expected to continue. "Despite the enormous unemployment crisis, the social legislation [of the Primo de Rivera era] has caused Socialist workers to resist insurrectionary appeals, and their leaders to refuse to cooperate with movements of agitation and revolt." In cataloguing its resources, the Berenguer government considered the Socialist party, which "at the present moment not only does not constitute a danger to public order, but is a guarantee of it," as the only political group on which it could rely except for Primo de Rivera's Unión Patriótica.[4]

This estimate proved too sanguine. The Socialists broke their ties to the moribund monarchial regime and realigned themselves with the Republicans and Catalans. Yet even in this shifting of alliances they proceeded cautiously. Their representatives at the meeting of August 1930 which established the San Sebastian Pact were sent only as observers. Before agreeing to support the antimonarchial revolutionary effort, the Socialists demanded assurances that Army opposition to a republic would be neutralized.[5] The general strike they called in support of the Jaca rising in December 1930 was a tentative effort to which they did not commit their full strength.[6] In short, during the transition from the monarchy to the Republic, bourgeois forces acted more confidently and aggressively than did the Marxist prophets of revolution. The admittedly indispensable contribution of the Socialists to the birth of the Republic was made not in the streets—all insurrectionary acts of the transitional period originated outside their ranks—but in the ballot boxes, where urban workers helped give Republican groups their sweeping majorities in the municipal elections of 12 April 1931.

4. Report of General Bazán, as quoted in Dámaso Berenguer, *De la Dictadura a la República: Crisis del Reinado de Alfonso XIII* (Madrid, 1935), pp. 52–53.
5. Maura, pp. 70–73; Julio Álvarez del Vayo, "Spain under the Republic," *The American Socialist Quarterly* (Summer 1932), pp. 34–35.
6. The Socialists attributed the feebleness of the strike to the fact that the garrison at Jaca revolted prematurely and gave the police warning. Enrique Santiago, *La UGT ante la revolución* (Madrid, 1932), pp. 80–82.

After the proclamation of the Republic Socialist policy became more moderate than ever. To be sure, there was a split in party ranks over whether Socialists should sit in the new government, but it lacked the revolutionary overtones of the early disputes among the Anarchosyndicalists. A group headed by Julián Besteiro, professor of logic at the University of Madrid, took the orthodox position that no party leader should accept a cabinet post, because Socialist objectives were ultimately too incompatible with those of the Republicans. Socialists might sit in the Cortes (in fact, Besteiro became its first speaker), but to share in the execution of policy would serve only to dilute the ideological purity of the movement.[7] Largo Caballero, on the other hand, insisted that collaboration be complete. The Socialists had made significant organizational gains by their association with Primo de Rivera; they could expect much greater advances by working with the Republic. Since Largo was now warmly seconded by Indalecio Prieto,[8] his viewpoint easily carried the day. The embarrassment and distrust that had characterized the Socialists' cooperation with the dictatorship disappeared. The hesitancy of the Berenguer period was also swept away. Once the Republic was established, collaboration became open and enthusiastic. The predominant mood in the party as a whole and of Largo Caballero in particular was one of almost childlike optimism. Of all the varied groups that held high exaggerated hopes for a Republic which, after all, had been won without much sacrifice or struggle, the Socialists were second to none in their expectations.[9]

This is not to say that all was perfect harmony. Whether because of the explicitly moral basis of their philosophy, or because their policy in regard to Primo de Rivera could so easily be considered opportunistic,[10] the Socialists' stance was often one of extreme self-righteousness. They enthusiastically cooperated with the Republicans but nevertheless felt morally superior to this "mosaic of parties, of little cliques, of *caudillismos*," some of which (the Radicals) were "low, mean and self-seeking." [11] Though they themselves had done nothing to resist Primo de

7. Gabriel Mario de Coca, *Anti-Caballero* (Madrid, 1936), p. 42.

8. Prieto had opposed cooperation with Primo de Rivera but became the most constant supporter of collaboration with the Republic.

9. So late as 13 February 1932, *El Socialista* was saying: "In truth, there is no political or class organization more optimistic than our own."

10. For example, Enrique Santiago's *UGT ante la revolución* is essentially an attempt to refute the charges of opportunism. All Socialist publications during 1931 were filled with documents that tried to prove that the Socialists had, in fact, valiantly stood up to the dictatorship.

11. Santiago, pp. 109–10.

Rivera's coup, they decried the fact that "the liberal spirit of the Spanish bourgeoisie had fallen so low" as to accept military rule.[12] Finally, though the initiative for the creation of the Republic lay elsewhere, they tended to arrogate to themselves the title of its only true defenders.[13]

Mixed in with this sense of superiority were equally dangerous fears of persecution by a bourgeois society that might prove still hostile. The obsession with press criticisms, which was to become almost paranoiac in 1933–34, already existed in nascent form in 1931. At precisely the moment when Azaña gave concrete proof of his reliance on the Socialists by choosing to build his coalition with them rather than with the Radicals, a member of the UGT Executive Committee was saying, "They fight us furiously from all sides . . . The Spanish bourgeoisie . . . squanders its money in buying up writers so that from certain periodicals they can attack us with rage, with calumny, with defamations." [14]

But since these disturbing traits did not yet affect policy, the Berenguer government's estimation proved correct once that government itself had fallen. After April 1931 local and provincial leaders sometimes embarked on disruptive courses of action, but the national leaders and organizations did indeed exercise their influence to "guarantee public order." The Republic was unfortunate to have inherited so irreconcilable a working-class organization as the CNT but was fortunate to have as a countervailing force so responsible a group as the early UGT. In this sense the Socialist pose as the chief defenders of the Republic was justified. Without this bulwark among the proletariat, the Republic could neither have come into being nor have survived for more than a few months in the form that Azaña gave to it. The existence of a progressive republic was predicated on the moderating influence exercised by the PSOE-UGT on the working classes.[15]

The agrarian policies of the Socialists clearly illustrate the truth of these assertions. For the first two years of the Republic, the reasonableness and restraint of the FNTT were little short of remarkable. For example, when the May 1932 strike of the CNT in Seville threatened to spread,

12. Manuel Cordero, *Los socialistas y la revolución* (Madrid, 1932), pp. 47–50.

13. This claim became especially frequent after 1933 but was also common during the first months of the Republic.

14. Santiago, pp. 8–9. See also the violent attack of *El Socialista*, 23 July 1931, on Azaña himself (cited in note 48 of chap. 6).

15. Even so conservative a journal as the London *Times* recognized this fact (see its editorial of 2 September 1931). At first *El Debate* also was not blind to the importance of the Socialists as a force for social order, although it slowly altered its position and with tragic short-sightedness began to taunt "the working-class movement of the Right" with the possibility that it might lose its following to the CNT.

El Obrero de la Tierra, the FNTT organ and its chief means of communication with its followers, rushed to aid the Azaña government in localizing the disturbances.

> There are moments in which it becomes necessary to join in a struggle, not for wage increases or shorter working days, but to defend ideals. Then one sacrifices whatever is necessary. Are we in one of those moments now? We say no! Now that the Republic, a democratic regime which permits us amply to develop within the law, has been restored, all we workers have the duty to consolidate it. This can be achieved by increasing the national wealth, by complying with our obligations in our work, and by avoiding strikes whenever possible.[16]

The Anarchosyndicalist tendency toward violent, insurrectionary acts was especially abhorrent to the Socialists because it involved "playing with the lives of the workers without practical purpose." [17] When the CNT Seville Federation launched a new provincial strike in June 1932 the FNTT again accused its leaders of "deceiving" the *campesino.*

> They spoke to him of immediate revolution . . . put a weapon into his hands and threw him into the fight. The outcome could not have been anything but disastrous, because it was not an ideal which motivated [the campesino] but hatred. And when rancor rules, redemption cannot follow, because there is no foundation in ideals for it.[18]

To try to achieve the classless society by insurrectionary means is like "filling the ocean with sandbags, thinking that roads from continent to continent can thus be built." [19] The only effect of an insurrectionary policy, warned *El Obrero de la Tierra,* will be to turn the nation against the working classes.

Socialists believed that the position of the workers could be bettered only by pacific means and that even these could not assure immediate improvements. The proletariat must retain faith not in the immediate but in the ultimate efficacy of the legislation of the Republic. The FNTT repeatedly warned its members not to expect too much too soon from the

16. *El Obrero de la Tierra* (henceforth, *OT*), 21 May 1932. In saying that a democratic regime had been "restored," the editorial was referring to the First Republic of 1873–74, which the Socialists eulogized during this period.

17. *OT,* 18 June 1932

18. Ibid. This theme was often echoed by local unions and provincial congresses of the FNTT. See, for example, the resolutions passed at the Regional Congress of Andalusia and Estremadura in *OT,* 13 February 1932.

19. *OT,* 18 June 1932.

Agrarian Reform Law: "An agrarian reform cannot be completed in a year or two";[20] "It is impossible to achieve in a single stage an improvement of this magnitude and whoever maintains the contrary shows that he is an enemy of the workers";[21] "The reform that is planned will require years before it can be carried out in full. At first, it will benefit some by giving them land and others because the decrease in the labor supply will make it easier for them to find work. Later these benefits will spread to one group after another until the reform has been completed."[22]

Even when the agrarian reform had been completed it would not be, "nor can it be, the complete solution for the rural social problem. The emancipation of the workers from the system of wages . . . requires time, the education of the workers, and perseverence."[23] Nor would the new rural social structure that was finally created be wholly socialistic. "In these moments in which we live, it cannot be socialistic . . . To impose collective cultivation [everywhere] by a law would be a grave error, because in many places our campesinos do not have sufficient preparation to put into practice the magnificent ideal of collectivization."[24] Why then should the Socialists support the Republican agrarian reform bill? Because "This is the most advanced proposal drafted in Spain up to the present. Even though it does not satisfy us completely, it is a good point of departure for later advances."[25]

It was this spirit that sustained the Socialists during the long Cortes debates on agrarian reform. They frequently objected to the obstructionist tactics of the Agrarian faction and occasionally called for the inauguration of the reform by decree.[26] But neither the UGT nor the FNTT used their immense power outside the Cortes to speed action. No demonstrations, no mass rallies, no strikes aimed at intimidating the parliament, were called; these remained exclusively the tactics of the

---

20. Speech of Lucio Martínez Gil (secretary general of the FNTT) as quoted in *OT,* 26 March 1932. See also the editorial of *El Socialista,* 2 February 1933.

21. *OT,* 5 February 1932. The FNTT Regional Congress of New Castile even went to the point of formally resolving that "We firmly believe that the agrarian problem cannot be solved in a short time" (*OT,* 17 April 1932).

22. *OT,* 5 February 1932.

23. Ibid.

24. *OT,* 23 January 1932.

25. *OT,* 26 March 1932. Ten months later *El Socialista,* 20 January 1933, was still saying: the Agrarian Reform Law "should not be deprecated because it is not Socialist. Except for Russia and Mexico, there has never been a more radical, more effective or more promising agrarian reform."

26. *OT,* 5 March, 25 June, 23 July, and 6 August 1932.

Right. The FNTT's moderation and optimism also allowed it to acquiesce to the successive modifications of the agrarian reform by which many of its initial demands were discarded. The law did not settle 75,000 peasants a year, or apply immediately to the whole of Spain, or grant as low compensation to the owners as the Socialists had originally requested.[27] But even though these concessions sometimes seemed to render the Agrarian Reform Law "an aspirin to cure an appendicitis," as Largo Caballero is reputed to have said,[28] the Socialists nevertheless welcomed it.

As previously noted, a brief conflict between Socialists and Left Republicans broke out in late September 1932 when Domingo gave the workers practically no representation on the IRA Executive Council. Once this crisis passed, the FNTT returned to its normal attitude of hopeful expectation. *El Obrero de la Tierra* continued to urge the Azaña government to present its supplementary agrarian program to the Cortes without further delay, but none of its editorials was couched in very strong terms. Indeed, the Socialists were still capable of great enthusiasm as late as January 1933. The village of Espera (Cadiz), where the first collective farm was formally established, was hailed as "the Covadonga of the *reconquista agraria*" and likened to "the port of Palos" from which Columbus sailed to discover new worlds.[29] Moreover, two months later, although few collectives had been established elsewhere, individual settlements lagged, and the supplementary agrarian legislation had not been presented to the Cortes, the Socialists were still willing to accept Domingo's promise that more rapid settlements would begin in the autumn. *El Socialista* tried to pacify those FNTT members who were becoming impatient by explaining that an excessively rapid reform would be "counterproductive." The peasants, it said, "despite their hunger," are capable of waiting; there is no danger of "Communist penetration" among them because they "are awake." [30]

27. FNTT, *Memoria*, pp. 248–49, 261. Azaña paid public tribute to the Socialists' willingness to accept the many modifications in their agrarian reform bill (*The Times* [London], 19 July 1932).

28. Quoted in Brenan, p. 263. For a more typical Socialist response, see Julián Besteiro's statement in *OT*, 24 September 1932.

29. *OT*, 28 January 1933.

30. *El Socialista*, 29 March 1933. Strong support also continued to come in from FNTT locals. For example, the Ejea de los Caballeros organization, in a letter to *OT*, 15 April 1933, urged peasants to cut off all ties with the Anarchosyndicalists, because their tactics consist of "direct action which results in a few wounded, a few dead, and another few thrown in jail. Sum total: misery and ruin for many humble families without any practical gain. We, the Socialist caciques, achieve our ends through legal means and without ruining humble homes."

The Socialists Lose Their Sense of Perspective

Yet beneath the surface Socialist confidence was gradually being eroded by the slowness of the implementation of the Agrarian Reform Law. A major shift in attitude began to occur after the municipal elections of 23 April 1933 shattered the Socialists' illusion that they held a permanent mandate to power and reminded them of their political mortality.[31] Within the FNTT the change was signaled by a May Day editorial written by Esteban Martínez Hervas, its president, who attributed the lack of peasant support in the April elections to the timidity with which the agrarian reform had been applied. Martínez Hervas also first voiced the lament that was to be repeated so often by both Socialists and Left Republicans: the Republic had made a tragic mistake in not applying the reform by decree when it first came to power. "We have lost almost two years by not having broken the back of caciquismo with the agrarian reform, by not having put it into effect in August 1931," when the Technical Commission draft was rejected. For the first time, also, a major Socialist leader implied that Domingo was too weak for his post and dismissed the Institute of Agrarian Reform as "useless" and "unwieldy." Ominously, Martínez Hervas went on to warn that the patience of the workers was not limitless and that the preparations for the reform must quickly be completed. Manuel Sánchez, head of the important Cordova Federation, echoed Martínez Hervas's warning. Until now the peasants have restrained themselves, he said. But if "they are deceived once more we will all suffer the consequences. . . . It will be catastrophic should the masses lose confidence in the possibility of bettering themselves through legal means." [32]

Although the FNTT continued to support the Azaña government and rejected all thought of revolutionary action,[33] its pronouncements thereafter assumed an increasingly critical form. The failure to implement the Agrarian Reform Law began to be attacked bitterly, as was Azaña's failure to present the supplementary agrarian legislation to the Cortes.

---

31. The ministerial crisis of 6 June and the increasing hostility of the Radical Socialists intensified this feeling of insecurity. Thus *El Socialista,* 4 July 1933, warned that "We must become alarmed over the possibility that a new ministerial crisis will surprise us, as did the last one, with the agrarian reform not yet implanted."

32. *OT,* 1 May 1933.

33. For example, *OT,* 13 May 1933, attacked the Anarchosyndicalists for initiating "bloody, disorganized, obscure struggles which benefit only the capitalists. . . . In each . . . the number of counterrevolutionaries increases because everyone believes that if the Anarchosyndicalists were to triumph, there would be no peace and order."

A new theme was stressed during the harvest of 1933, when, because the crop was poor, unemployment became widespread and owners discriminated against Socialists in hiring. Beginning with an editorial of 3 June 1933, *El Obrero de la Tierra* launched an intensive campaign against this economic "persecution of the workers." It demanded that the términos municipales law be buttressed by new legislation that would force employers to hire workers in the order in which they had registered with the local unemployment offices: the employer should have no choice in selecting his personnel. If this "turno riguroso" were not established, the FNTT organ continued, the government should provide unemployment benefits to the workers, inaugurate massive public works projects to provide jobs, and apply the laboreo forzoso decrees seriously so that more land would be brought under cultivation. Finally, the Azaña government should begin to seize lands immediately if it hoped "to raise the spirits of the campesinos, who are gradually losing faith in the application of the Agrarian Reform Law." [34]

In the latter part of July the Cortes debate on Domingo's general lease bill added a new reason for disillusionment. The success of the Agrarian minority in obstructing the debates and the absenteeism among the Left Republican deputies brought angry protests. Azaña's appearance on the Cortes podium to rally his Republican followers in support of the bill did not mollify the FNTT. *El Obrero de la Tierra* continued to complain that, even though the bill was less radical than previous drafts, the Socialists alone were willing to fight for it.[35]

The FNTT's crisis of confidence reached its peak during the final days of the Azaña government. On 11 August the Executive Council of the IRA voted on the meaning of a sentence in the Agrarian Reform Law which could be interpreted either as automatically exempting from expropriation all stockbreeding estates that had never been cultivated or as excluding only those in which the land was so bad that it could not be tilled at least once every three years. The issue was of critical importance, particularly for the Socialist stronghold of Estremadura, where there were large tracts of marginal land. When the vote went against them the Socialists seem to have abandoned all faith in the IRA. The decision was called the most "counterrevolutionary" act of the Institute; instead of attempting to include every inch of land under the Agrarian Reform Law, the Institute was permitting considerable quantities to escape. For the first time *El Obrero de la Tierra* used the phrase that was to become the standard Socialist slogan as it referred to "this wretched Institute

34. *OT*, 3, 10 June; 1, 8, 15, 22 July; 26 August 1933.
35. *OT*, 22 July; 12, 19 August; 16 September 1933.

which, rather than the Institute of Agrarian Reform, should call itself
the Institute of Anti-Agrarian Reform." [36]

On 9 September, the day after Alcalá Zamora dismissed the Azaña
government, a still sharper break occurred. At a meeting of its National
Committee, called before Azaña's dismissal and held at a time when it
was by no means certain that Lerroux would succeed in forming a new
government, the FNTT agreed "to view with displeasure the negligence
with which the Ministry of Agriculture (still headed by Domingo) has
applied the Agrarian Reform Law." The National Committee went on
to state that "the delay has prejudiced to an extraordinary degree the
interests of the working classes and has permitted the large landowners
. . . to develop such overweening self-confidence that they are constantly
challenging the rural masses." Consequently the FNTT for the first time
formally declared that if necessary, it would "organize a campaign of
agitation throughout the nation to force the implementation of the
law." [37] The disenchantment of the FNTT was now complete. Had the
Azaña government been restored to power, it could have regained the
confidence of the Socialist peasant federation only by drastic revisions
of its personnel and program.

The temporary (and necessary) decision of the Left Republicans to
serve in the "governments of Republican concentration" of Lerroux and
Martínez Barrio further alienated the FNTT. Nor did it show regret
when the suicidal policy of refusing to form electoral coalitions with the
Left Republicans produced the truly disastrous electoral defeat of November. The loss of the elections was basically the fault of "the so-called Left
Republicans, who because of their apathy . . . and political immorality"
had not seized the historic opportunity presented them in 1931 to win
the masses but had instead "handed democracy over to the enemy." Was
reconciliation possible? "During 1933 we have witnessed the end of an
experiment which has taught us how to regulate our future relations with
the Republican parties. . . . All Republicans, some through positive
treason and others by neglect, have proven themselves more on the side
of the bourgeoisie than with us." [38]

But the transformation of the Socialists did not stop with the cutting
of their ties to the Republicans. By February 1934 the FNTT, which had
meanwhile fallen under more extreme leadership, was issuing semirevolutionary pronouncements. *El Obrero de la Tierra* was converted from an
organ of information to a platform for agitation. The first declaration of
the new FNTT National Committee carried the heading "We declare

36. *OT*, 19, 26 August; 28 October 1933. See also *El Socialista*, 12, 27 August.
37. *OT*, 16 September 1933.
38. *OT*, 16, 30 December 1933.

ourselves for the revolution!"[39] Succeeding issues of the FNTT journal appeared under such banner headlines as: "The first measure of the triumphant revolution must be the socialization of the land!" and "Without revolution there will never be agrarian reform!"[40] The column that summarized the activities of the IRA assumed the title "The Institute of Anti-Agrarian Reform." The doctrine of collectivization received new emphasis. For the first time the achievements of the Soviet *kolkhozes* were regularly praised.[41]

Even more extreme utterances originated outside the FNTT. On 20 April 1934, in a speech to the Socialist Youth Organization, Largo Caballero discarded all caution:

> Things of such a nature are going to happen in Spain that the working class must issue some statement to justify its future actions. . . . At a given moment, the proletariat unquestionably will rise and strike violently at its enemies. Let them not say that we are uncivilized beasts because our actions then will correspond to their actions now. And in that moment, let not those whose hearts have been hardened be surprised if we have cast aside useless sentimentality. Once the working class is in power, they cannot expect an armistice from those whose children are now dying because they are denied employment.[42]

Why had so major a change occurred in the attitude of the Socialists? The question is more difficult to answer than may at first appear, because of both its intrinsic complexity and the lack of monographic studies on the functioning of the UGT and PSOE. One fact, however, is certain. The common notion, that the Socialists were driven into revolution because the reactionary policies of the new Lerroux governments reduced the workers to such misery that they had no choice but to strike back, is inadequate. The radicalization of the Socialist movement began before Lerroux came to power; the policies of his governments were by no means as black as they have been painted; and the available evidence suggests that the initiative for the new Socialist stance came as much from the party leaders themselves as from the rank and file.

As will be seen in greater detail in the next chapter, Lerroux did not immediately stop the application of the agrarian reform. In fact, though he eventually intended to modify the September law, his governments continued to administer it in such a manner that they actually settled

39. *OT*, 3 February 1934.
40. *OT*, 10 February and 3 March 1934.
41. *OT*, issues of 3 February 1933 onward.
42. Largo Caballero, *Discursos a los trabajadores*, p. 132.

more peasants than had Azaña. Nor were the far more numerous settlements under the Intensification of Cultivation decrees undone. All the
colonists placed were to be allowed to remain on the land until the fall
of 1934, the normal period of settlement authorized in the decrees. For
most of the colonists it seemed that even this deadline might not apply.
They were implicitly promised that they would retain their lands indefinitely.[43]

Lerroux's reaction was directed instead against three other measures.
The character of the mixed juries, previously so favorable to the workers,
began to alter as Lerroux replaced many of the personnel appointed by
Largo Caballero. There was also some desultory discussion of making
the newly conservative character of the boards permanent by revising
the law so that only county judges or other bureaucratic personnel could
serve as their presidents.[44] The universally unpopular términos municipales law, which while protecting the Socialist locals against migrant
labor also injured many unaffiliated workers, was sabotaged almost
immediately. Even before the November elections Lerroux decreed that
twelve Southern provinces would be considered single labor units: owners
might hire workers from any municipality in each province, though they
still could not legally employ extraprovincial labor.[45] After the elections
the Center and Right began to plan for the outright repeal of the law
everywhere in Spain.[46] Finally, the turno riguroso agreements that had
been forced upon a few of the mixed juries by Ministry of Labor pressure
during the summer of 1933 were canceled. Only if the juries had unanimously agreed to this innovation would employers be obliged to hire
workers in the order in which they had registered with the local employment offices rather than being allowed to choose freely among all those
inscribed.[47]

More important than these specific measures taken by the new government was what might be called a "reaction by inaction." Most labor
laws were not repealed, but they were weakened by not being enforced

43. This complicated question is discussed in the next chapter.

44. Although this idea was discussed from the beginning, a law revising the
structure of the arbitration boards was not presented to the Cortes until 11 June
1935 (D.S. 201, app. 5) and not passed until 16 July 1935 (D.S. 223, app. 1).

45. Ministry of Agriculture decrees of 20 September to 4 October 1933. Fines
owed by employers who had violated the law were also rescinded.

46. A bill to revoke the términos municipales law was presented to the Cortes
on 11 January 1934 (D.S. 20, app. 8).

47. Ministry of Labor decree of 26 September 1933. For the controversy over
Largo Caballero's attempt to foist the turno riguroso on the mixed juries during the
summer of 1933, see above, p. 265.

as energetically as under Azaña. As a result the old rural oligarchy was able to recover many of its former positions of local power and from these sought to reduce the peasantry to submissiveness once more. The rendering of old accounts seriously hurt the working classes.[48] Although there is no evidence of widespread eviction of tenant farmers in 1934, owners were probably able to break many contracts. Discrimination against Socialist militants in hiring was undoubtedly very common, especially in the areas where the turno riguroso had previously been operative. Most important of all was the fall in wages. Because of the Azaña government's efforts, Spain had probably been the only nation in the world in which wages had actually risen during the Depression. With state protection withdrawn, wages fell to more "natural" levels.

On the whole the condition of the working classes unquestionably worsened, but does not seem to have deteriorated so badly as to justify desperate revolutionary retaliation. There was no wholesale repeal of past laws, no sudden increase in the number of unemployed,[49] no deliberate persecution of the workers by the national government. The most catastrophic event was the drop in wages in the countryside (in the cities, where wages had not risen as rapidly under Azaña, they did not fall as drastically under Lerroux). Even so, wages remained much higher than they had been during the monarchy.[50] And though the institutional means of protecting workers' interests were weakened, the Socialists were by no means reduced to their pre-Republican impotence. The mixed juries continued to function with full worker representation. Socialist mayors and councilmen still controlled hundreds of villages and towns. Above all, strong Socialist unions had been established in most of Spain, and the basic working-class weapon of the strike could still be employed to defend the peasants against the worst excesses of the owners. Indeed, strikes were called with great frequency in both industry and agriculture during the early months of 1934—without, incidentally, provoking such

48. That the established classes took advantage of the greater neutrality of the state to settle accounts that had accumulated during the previous two years is undeniable. See, for example, Gil Robles's attack on the "suicidal egoism" of the owners in El Debate, 6 March 1936.

49. See the unemployment statistics above, p. 286.

50. It is exceedingly difficult to determine what wages were actually being paid during this period. The wage agreements reached in the mixed juries remained high, but these were frequently evaded. On balance, given the fact that the Socialist unions were still strong and the national government still occasionally attempted to enforce the mixed jury decisions (see, for example, Ministry of Labor order of 24 February 1934), it would seem unlikely that wages fell much below their 1932 levels until after the Socialist defeat in the FNTT harvest strike and the October revolution—that is to say, in the unionized areas at least, they probably remained one-third to one-half again as high as they had been prior to 1931.

severe repression as Azaña had directed against the Anarchosyndicalists.[51]

Was the change in the Socialist attitude justified by Lerroux's abandonment of democratic practices? There is no evidence to support the
frequent Socialist charge that the November 1933 elections had been
dishonest. It was precisely to ensure that the elections would not be
"made," as they had so often been under the monarchy, that Left Republicans had accepted posts in Martínez Barrio's caretaker government.
Nor did Lerroux try to strengthen his advantage once the elections were
over by retroactively declaring some of their results null (as the Provisional Government had done in the municipal elections of 1931 and as
the Popular Front was to do in the elections of 1936). If the new Cortes
were not representative—and they were not—it was largely because the
Socialists, in refusing to form electoral alliances, had blindly disregarded
the consequences of an absurd electoral law they themselves helped
devise.[52] Aside from alleged electoral dishonesty, there was really nothing with which even the Socialists could charge Lerroux. The new
premier did not, for example, ignore the Cortes and govern by decree.
Indeed, it would have been impossible for him to do, since Alcalá Zamora, who had proven that he would not tolerate excessive use of the decree power, was still president.

Two other dangers are frequently cited to justify the new Socialist
stance. Lerroux might ally himself with the Right, or be forced to bow
to its united power, and so begin to follow an openly reactionary course.
Worse still, Gil Robles might himself form a government, since the CEDA
was the largest single party in the Cortes. Should this occur, the Republic might be overthrown and the Socialist organizations destroyed. The
Socialists had many reasons to suspect that these were the intentions of
the Catholic leader. Because of his desire to attract monarchist support,
Gil Robles did not unequivocally state his acceptance of the Republic
but spoke of the "accidental" nature of governmental forms. His electoral
campaign had been conducted largely on the basis of anti-Marxist slogans.
In several of his pronouncements he seemed to accept violence as a
legitimate means of action, though one wonders to what extent he was
merely echoing the phraseology that Largo Caballero had begun to use.
Some of the CEDA techniques—the organization of youth groups, the
holding of mass rallies, the glorification of the party leader—resembled
those of fascism. The change in the international political climate gave
all these factors special meaning. Although Hitler's rise to power had

51. From January to the end of May 1934, there were 98 agricultural and 441
industrial strikes (Ministerio de Trabajo, *Boletines* for each month).

52. As mentioned previously, the Left received almost 40 percent of the
popular vote but only 20 percent of the Cortes seats.

little immediate impact on Spanish thought, it began to haunt the Socialists after they lost their emotional moorings in the Republic. Even more relevant was the destruction of the Austrian Socialists in February 1934 by the Catholic leader Dollfuss. Would Gil Robles someday prove to be the Spanish Dollfuss?

Strangely enough, perhaps the best critique of the true import of these two dangers was given by one of the Socialists most responsible for the change in party outlook. In a remarkable but little-known article in *Foreign Affairs* of April 1934, Luís de Araquistáin, who had been Spanish ambassador to Berlin during Hitler's rise to power, dismissed one after another of the apparent dangers that faced the Socialists and the Republic. The monarchy was so discredited that it could not be restored: "In the twentieth century, when monarchies fall, they fall forever." "Fascism of the German or Italian type" was also impossible in a nation where "there are no demobilized men . . . no hundreds of thousands of young university men with no future, no millions of unemployed. There is no Mussolini, nor even [*sic*] a Hitler; there are no imperialistic ambitions or sentiments of revenge. . . . Out of what could Spanish fascism be concocted? I cannot imagine the recipe." A military coup was possible but did not seem likely to Araquistáin. The submission of Spain to Primo de Rivera had been "more apparent than real. . . . The very stones would rise against a [new] military dictatorship." Moreover, "There are few regiments whose officers can count unconditionally on the noncommissioned officers and men." [53] The case of Dollfuss was not mentioned, but the means by which an Austrian-type coup could be staged in Spain were all discounted.[54]

Did the danger then lie in the fact that the Right would gain permanent control of the Cortes? Not at all. Araquistáin forecast that the heterogeneous CEDA would split: part would merge with the Agrarians to form a single conservative but nonmonarchical party; the remainder would join the existing monarchical groups, themselves "numerically unimportant." The Right would be further weakened once the Basques achieved regional autonomy, because they would then concentrate on

53. Luís de Araquistáin, "The Struggle in Spain," *Foreign Affairs* (April 1934), p. 470. The view that officers could no longer control their men, and that if a military rebellion occurred it would favor the Socialists, was frequently expressed by Largo Caballero as well as by Prieto. See Largo Caballero, p. 97, and Mario de Coca, pp. 120, 142–43.

54. It is not clear whether Araquistáin wrote the article before Dollfuss's destruction of the Austrian Socialists, but this event in itself should not have altered the Socialist viewpoint so completely, since it had been foreseen as early as the summer of 1933.

local affairs and ignore the national scene.[55] Nor did Araquistáin see any possibility that Lerroux's Radicals could form a permanent coalition government with the Agrarians and the CEDA. Inevitably, the Right and Center would split. Thus "Everything points to the fact that the life of the present Cortes will be brief . . . a few months, perhaps." In the new elections that would become necessary, it was "possible that the Republic will recover its political equilibrium and that parliament will again function efficiently." [56]

If all this were true, and if it were also true that there was no immediate danger that the Anarchosyndicalists would steal the Socialist following,[57] why then should Araquistáin end his article on an ominous note? "One thing, however, is clear. The first and relatively peaceful stage of the Spanish political revolution terminated with the elections of November. They ushered in a new stage which will not be so peaceful and will probably be less political and more social." Moreover, "Another electoral mix-up like the last will finish the Republic as a parliamentary regime. For many it is, in fact, already finished; they look only for extra-parliamentary methods.[58]

If the first part of Araquistáin's analysis was correct, how could the second part be accurate unless the Socialists themselves chose to make it so? If the Socialists had borne so many an "electoral mix-up" in the past, why could they not bear yet another? Why was the Republic "already finished" as a parliamentary regime if the Socialists themselves had not abandoned their democratic heritage? This is the context within which the change in Socialist policy must be discussed. There is no question that they had legitimate cause to oppose the new regime so long as that opposition was limited to parliamentary action and non-revolutionary strikes. But to refuse to accept a new period in the wilderness, and to strive for the complete victory of a new "social Republic" that would replace the "bourgeois Republic" established in 1931,[59] was to adopt the policy of the Anarchosyndicalists.

The governments of late 1933 and early 1934 were not blindly reactionary. The Radicals were only opportunistic, the CEDA only conservative. Conditions were not so threatening that the Socialists had

55. Araquistáin, "Struggle in Spain," p. 461.
56. Ibid., p. 471.
57. Ibid., pp. 467–69. The willingness of the Socialists to enter into alliances with the Anarchosyndicalists on both the local and national level also suggests that they did not fear that their following would be stolen.
58. Ibid., p. 471.
59. For references to a "second revolution" that would overthrow the "bourgeois" Republic and establish a new "social" Republic, see *OT*, 10 February 1934, and Largo Caballero's speeches as quoted in Mario de Coca, pp. 119–21.

inevitably to strike out on a revolutionary path. Many Socialist leaders recognized this. Besteiro, who had fought against such close collaboration with Azaña, now fought against such complete opposition to Lerroux. The Socialists, he said, should be "neither so progovernmental" as they had been "nor so antigovernmental" as they were becoming.[60] They had been wrong to expect miracles from the Republic in the first place. The new events should teach them to discard dangerous illusions of immediate victory and return to the central Marxist truth that Socialism could not be established until further historical evolution had occurred. The "bourgeois Republic" should not be rejected, because the "social Republic" could be established only at the cost of so much bloodshed that its very purpose would be defeated.[61] Some of the other older leaders, like Andrés Saborit and Trifón Gómez, also opposed the change in outlook. And though Prieto, to his everlasting regret, fell in with the activists, he certainly would not have initiated the new militancy.

Ironically, the Socialists were led away from parliamentary democracy in 1934 by precisely the man who had most energetically advocated collaboration with the Republic in 1931. The shift in Socialist policy was in large part a reflection of the change in Largo Caballero's personal outlook. Why Largo Caballero altered course is unclear: his biography remains to be written. Salvador de Madariaga and other writers stress the influence of his two new advisers, Luís de Araquistáin and Julio Álvarez del Vayo.[62] Gabriel Mario de Coca, in a brilliant defense of Besteiro's policies, attributes the change to Largo's lack of grounding in Socialist doctrine. According to this writer, because Largo lacked historical vision he could not place the vicissitudes of political fortune in their proper perspective but was subject alternately to great hope and great despair.[63] When writing for a foreign audience Araquistáin had enough critical ability to recognize how limited were the dangers confronting the Socialists; Largo Caballero may sincerely have believed that a catastrophe was approaching unless the Socialists took preventive action.

To these factors must be added others. The Azaña period of rule had been a bitter disappointment to Largo Caballero in that it revealed

60. Mario de Coca, p. 82. Largo Caballero attacked Besteiro's efforts to moderate the Socialist position by implying that he was treasonous: "How can one explain that when there were Socialists in the government [Besteiro opposed collaboration], whereas as soon as the Socialists left the government comrades appeared who suddenly want to embrace the Republic?" (ibid., p. 131).

61. Ibid., p. 132.

62. Madariaga, p. 450.

63. Mario de Coca, passim.

the timidity and lethargy with which even the most advanced elements of the bourgeoisie approached questions of paramount concern to the workers. It had also caused him deep personal disappointment. Though other Socialist leaders, particularly Prieto and Besteiro, had easily been integrated into the new order—and received praise on occasion from even the conservative opposition—Largo Caballero had remained an isolated figure, never really accepted by most of his Left Republican allies, satirized in the press for his propensity to extravagant statements,[64] criticized for his intimate connection with such unpopular measures as the términos municipales and laboreo forzoso decrees. The coolness with which he had been treated sharply contrasted to the cult of personality that began to develop around his figure after the Left Republican-Socialist alliance had collapsed. Largo Caballero could not long resist the crowds that shouted "All power to the Socialists" in response to his electoral speeches of late 1933 or reject the flattering words with which men like Araquistáin encouraged him in his new role:

> Rarely has the fate of a people been so tied to a man as that of Spain is now tied to Largo Caballero. . . . Their destinies [have been] merged in an intense historic drama. The awareness of this drama makes us think of Largo Caballero and of Spain with an inner tremor: a tremor such as we would have felt in the presence of Lenin in October 1917; the tremor inspired by great men in whose hands lie the momentous decisions of history.[65]

Since Prieto supported the militants, and since the Socialist rank and file did indeed suffer great hardships, Largo gained control of the Socialist movement without difficulty. After a short, bitter struggle in January 1934 Besteiro and his followers were ousted from the Executive Committees of the Socialist labor unions. In the FNTT, where Largo's forces won their first victory, Martínez Gil and Martínez Hervas were replaced by a young militant, Ricardo Zabalza.[66] It was from this time onward that *El Obrero de la Tierra* openly declared itself "for the revolution."

64. The most famous of these was his threat that the Socialists would "launch a civil war" if the Constituent Cortes were dissolved so that new elections could be held after the Constitution had been approved (*El Socialista*, 24 November 1931).

65. Araquistáin's introduction to Largo Caballero, *Discursos a los trabajadores*, pp. xii–xiii. At precisely the same moment (March 1934) as he was writing these words, Araquistáin was attacking the Anarchosyndicalists in "Struggle in Spain" for "maintaining by the magic of violence what cannot possibly be preserved by reason or by the experience of history" (p. 469).

66. *OT*, 20 January and 3 February 1934; Mario de Coca, p. 131.

Defeat and Disaster

Yet though they now often spoke like Anarchosyndicalists, the Socialists still retained a somewhat more accurate conception of the realities of power than did their erstwhile opponents. They declared their belief in the inevitability of proletarian victory but knew that a working-class rising might in fact be crushed.[67] Consequently the Socialist cry for a second revolution was not unconditional. Socialists continued to sit in the Cortes and on such governmental bodies as the mixed juries and the Institute of Agrarian Reform. By their threatening statements they hoped to prevent the Lerroux government from using its parliamentary majority to revise the Azaña legislation. The new rhetoric was also intended "spiritually" to prepare the workers for the revolution. The "material" preparation for a revolt was to be achieved as the Socialists secretly armed themselves. But the call for insurrection was not to be sounded until the Socialist leaders felt that a rightist coup against the Republic was imminent. Specifically, the Socialists declared that they would not tolerate the formation of a government by Gil Robles or permit any of his followers to be seated in any future Center cabinets. Since Lerroux and Alcalá Zamora, for reasons of their own, also had no desire to give power to the CEDA, the seriousness of Socialist intentions was not tested for several months. In the meantime the cold war that had risen continued to be waged by means of threatening speeches and frequent, though uncoordinated, strikes.

Only in one instance prior to October 1934 did the Socialists act more strongly. As the harvest of 1934 approached, the new FNTT leaders were seized by a mood of excitement. The harvest gave peasants power over the landowners since demand for labor was then strongest and crops would rot if not gathered. It was also the period of greatest danger to the workers, who counted on their harvest earnings to carry them through the rest of the year. Because of the renewed strength of the rural oligarchs in 1934, there was every reason to expect that wages would be low and that Socialist militants would not be hired. The situation was rendered especially critical by the fact that the revocation of the términos municipales law was soon to be discussed in the Cortes: unless the Socialists invoked their extraparliamentary power, the law was sure to be repealed since most deputies, not those of the Center

67. Throughout the spring of 1934 the Socialists vacillated between inflammatory cries for revolution and precautionary statements warning their followers not to act without adequate "material" preparation. See *OT*, 17, 24 February 1934, and Largo Caballero, pp. 141–42, 156.

and Right alone, opposed it.[68] Thus, through the same mixture of defensive and aggressive motives that characterized the Socialist movement as a whole, the FNTT decided to unleash for the first time its hundreds of thousands of followers.

The sequence of events began on 25 April when the Toledo Federation, at that time probably the largest and most militant branch of the FNTT, announced that it would strike for the adoption of the turno riguroso. On 28 April the FNTT took up the cry and demanded, in addition to the turno riguroso, the prohibition of the use of harvest machinery and the establishment of special local committees to supervise the fulfillment of harvest contracts throughout the nation. Three days later the FNTT went far beyond the immediate harvest contracts. In its May Day proclamation it proposed the formation of a Frente Campesino to unite all agricultural workers, including the Anarchosyndicalists, behind a demand that all expropriable land in the IRA inventory be turned over to collectives within the next six months. The Frente Campesino was also to force the Cortes to pass legislation regarding leases, common lands, and agricultural credit. At its meeting of 11–12 May— convened the day after the parliament began to debate the términos municipales law—the FNTT National Committee merged the specific harvest demands and the general demands for immediate fulfillment of the agrarian reform into a single ten-point program. If this program were not accepted, it threatened, a national harvest strike would be called on 5 June.[69] After some hesitation the UGT and the Socialist party gave their approval to the FNTT initiative.[70] From 12 May onward *El Socialista* vigorously applauded the peasant strike as a struggle for the rights of all workers.

The government, confronted with a clear challenge to its authority, followed a flexible policy. On the one hand the debates on the revocation of the términos municipales law were pressed to a conclusion on 24 May. The Minister of the Interior, Rafael Salazar Alonso, who regarded the strike as revolutionary in intent, was also given a free hand. In the last

68. For example, Martínez Barrio's Radical Democratic group, which consistently voted with the Left in 1934 and 1935, supported repeal of the law (*D.S.* 87, 24 May 1934, p. 3114). *El Sol*, the liberal journal, was delighted by its revocation (issue of 24 May 1934).

69. *OT*, 1, 5, 12 May 1934.

70. Some members of the UGT Executive Committee considered a national strike too risky and counseled instead a series of regional strikes, to be declared as harvest time approached in each of the agricultural regions of Spain. Zabalza successfully held out for a single mass effort but after its failure bitterly reproached the UGT industrial federations for not lending more active support. See Zabalza's retrospective account in *OT*, 18 April 1936.

week of May, reviving the tactic employed by Azaña against the Anarchosyndicalists, Salazar Alonso prohibited the strike on the grounds that the harvest was "sacred." *El Obrero de la Tierra* was temporarily suspended, local strike meetings were prohibited, and many local leaders were arrested.[71] On the other hand many cabinet members, especially Cirilo del Río, the Minister of Agriculture, José Estadella, the Minister of Labor, and Ricardo Samper, the prime minister who had temporarily replaced Lerroux, were anxious to avoid a showdown. On 24 May the government ordered field inspectors of the Ministry of Labor to prevent discrimination in hiring and urged the rural arbitration boards to agree quickly on harvest contracts favorable to the workers.[72] On 2 June the government made further concessions by strengthening the legislation that obliged owners to hire workers only through the local employment offices (though not necessarily in the "rigorous order" the Socialists required) and by authorizing its field inspectors to assign additional workers to each owner in areas where unemployment was severe. Meanwhile the harvest contracts issued by the local arbitration boards established minimum wages that were as high as those that had prevailed during the Azaña era.[73]

For a brief moment it seemed as though the FNTT would back down because of these concessions and because public opinion was so obviously unfavorable to a strike that threatened the loss of an entire year's harvest.[74] But the peasant federation had gone so far that retreat would seem surrender to the hated Salazar Alonso, who had exacerbated

71. *El Socialista*, 29, 30, 31 May 1934. There was good cause (particularly if the tradition of press censorship established by the Azaña government is taken into account) for the suspension of *El Obrero de la Tierra*. Its last two issues (12, 19 May 1934) were filled with semirevolutionary proclamations. According to Enrique Esperabé de Arteaga, *Los partidos políticos en España* (Madrid, 1951), pp. 254–55, the FNTT tracts that circulated in the villages were even more violent in tone.

72. Ministerio de Trabajo, *Boletín* (July 1934), pp. 45–46.

73. For example, the arbitration board of Seville agreed to wages of twelve pesetas, slightly higher than those of the previous year (*El Sol*, 26 May 1934).

74. Ibid., 1, 2 June 1934. Since the wide variations in Spanish climatic conditions create a spread of as much as two months in the time in which the crop is collected in various regions, there was no danger that the entire crop would in fact be lost. Nevertheless, because this possibility was stressed both in the FNTT's threats and in Rightist propaganda, it seems to have been generally believed. Moreover, the strike could unquestionably have led to the loss of an important part of the Southern crop, which in itself would have been a catastrophe of major proportions. Ironically, the 1934 harvest turned out to be the largest in Spanish history (see chap. 13, n. 25), with the result that Spain was confronted not with scarcity, but with the almost equally troublesome problem of how to keep wheat prices high when there was so great a surplus.

the situation by his inflammatory speeches against the Socialists. More-over, although the Frente Campesino had not materialized, the FNTT's recently concluded agreement with the Andalusian branch of the CNT would have to be disavowed. On 3 June the FNTT renewed its demands for the turno riguroso, the prohibition of the use of agricultural machinery throughout Spain, and the establishment of local supervisory committees. It also required that these and all other harvest concessions be applied during the entire agricultural year.[75]

By its action the FNTT ended any hope for a negotiated settlement. Since the local committees were to be elected, control of labor relations would pass to groups that would usually favor one class, the workers. To apply harvest wages during other periods of the agricultural year would render Spanish agriculture uneconomical. To surround the owners with all the restrictions the Socialists demanded would in truth destroy economic freedom. Moreover, given the militancy of Zabalza, it seems probable that had the government accepted his new demands, the FNTT would then have revived its earlier program for the immediate, revolu-tionary application of the agrarian reform. The FNTT's refusal to com-promise left the government few alternatives. Had Salazar Alonso been more moderate, he might have abstained from suppressing the strike long enough to see whether it would die out on its own. But had the strike continued, no government could have refrained from intervention. More than partial loss of the harvest, on which the livelihood of Spain depended, was involved. The question to be decided was whether the Socialist labor organizations could compel the state to do their will. Isolated and alone (not a single Left Republican leader or journal sup-ported the strike), the Socialists took their first stumbling step along the road Largo Caballero had pointed out to them.

At the outset it seemed as though the strike might have some chance of success. According to the official statistics, strikes were declared in no fewer than 1,563 municipalities. The movement was centered in the latifundio provinces, in part because it was mostly there that the harvest had actually begun. About half of the villages in Ciudad Real, Cordova, and Malaga issued strike proclamations; in Badajoz, Huelva, and Jaen one-fourth of the pueblos called work halts. Yet because of the pre-cautionary measures taken by the government, the success of its con-ciliatory tactics in weaning away the moderates, and the confusion that had been sown among the workers by the continuous fluctuations in FNTT policy, the threat was never so serious as it appeared. Most of the strike proclamations were symbolic gestures of defiance or attempts to vindicate FNTT honor; they led to actual work stoppages in only

75. *El Sol* and *El Socialista*, 2, 3, 4 June 1934.

435 of the 1,563 municipalities in which they had been issued.[76] Since prompt governmental repression and strict press censorship guaranteed that the strike would not spread further, the course of battle began to turn against the Socialists almost immediately. On 10 June the FNTT issued its first admission of defeat by permitting small farmers to resume their harvesting activities (since the work stoppage was to be total, strikers had tried to prevent harvesting on small as well as on large farms). On the same day the Caceres Federation broke the united front and ordered its members to return to work. One by one the other provincial federations followed suit until by 20 June the strike had completely ended.[77]

Violence could not be avoided in so widespread a movement: an analysis of the official press releases indicates that some thirteen persons were killed and perhaps two hundred injured. But many lesser strikes had resulted in as much bloodshed. The fact that casualties were relatively few was due in part to the restraint of the Socialists. Though they were pursuing semirevolutionary goals, the Socialists were not yet ready to use revolutionary means. No municipalities were seized; no major caches of arms were uncovered. Indeed, the Socialists sacrificed their largest labor federation without even ordering their industrial unions to declare sympathetic strikes. But the Samper government also exercised restraint. Alcalá Zamora refused Salazar Alonso's request that martial law be imposed.[78] Most of the casualties occurred in clashes between strikers and nonstrikers rather than in conflicts in which the Guardia Civil participated. Arrests were exceedingly numerous: some seven thousand farm workers were imprisoned.[79] But incarceration was used more as a preventive than as a punitive device. Most of the prisoners were released within a few days, the rest within a month.[80] Even the Socialists criticized the government less for repressing the workers than for unseating municipal governments

76. Ministerio de Trabajo, *Boletín* (July 1934), p. 47.

77. My account is taken from *El Sol* and *El Socialista*, 6–20 June 1934. Both newspapers published essentially the same news because of the government censorship.

78. Esperabé de Arteaga, p. 256.

79. The Socialist Cortes deputies asked for and received a list of those imprisoned (*D.S.* 105, 25 June 1934, p. 3968), but this list was apparently never published. My figure of seven thousand prisoners—which is the highest that I encountered—comes from *El Debate*, 18 July 1934.

80. Based on the fact that the Madrid Socialists arranged a welcome for three hundred prisoners from Estremadura who were returning from prison on 7 July, less than a month after the strike ended. Since these prisoners appear to have been strike leaders, ordinary workmen were presumably released almost immediately. The lack of appeals for amnesty in the Socialist press would also seem to support my conclusions.

that had aided the strikers and for violating the principle of parliamentary immunity by arresting four Cortes deputies suspected of leading strikers. Yet even in this respect the government did not act vengefully. The arrests of the Cortes deputies seem to have resulted from the excessive zeal of local police officials; only one deputy was detained for more than a night. And though complete figures are difficult to find, it appears that no more than thirty or forty of Spain's nine thousand municipal governments were unseated.[81]

The strike nevertheless had catastrophic consequences for the FNTT. Although the peasant federation continued to function, most of its local units were not reorganized. Not until 1936 did the morale of its followers recover from their complete defeat in an effort on which so much had been staked. Instead of reasserting Socialist power, the strike squandered all of the organizational gains made since 1931 and gave the rural oligarchy complete control of the Spanish countryside. The workers were reduced to reliance on whatever protection the national government might offer them. Since most Anarchosyndicalist locals had already been rendered impotent, the peasantry of Spain became an inconsequential revolutionary force. The extent of the collapse is suggested by the strike statistics of the Ministry of Labor. During the first five months of 1934 ninety-eight agricultural strikes occurred in Spain. During the six months after the June strike only twenty strikes were recorded. In 1935 peasant power declined still further. During the whole of that year work stopped briefly on only fifteen occasions.[82] Needless to say, all other manifestations of peasant independence, especially the farm invasions that had once been so frequent, also ended.

The disastrous outcome of the FNTT strike did not deflect the Socialist leaders from the dangerous path they had been following since the collapse of the Azaña coalition. Events unfolded with tragic fatality. In early September Gil Robles announced that he would no longer acquiesce in the exclusion of his followers from office. The Socialists immediately replied with strikes and threats of revolution, and so normally cautious a man as Prieto cast himself in the unwonted role of arms runner in Asturias. Monarchists and other reactionaries countered with inflammatory statements designed to increase the turmoil.[83] It was against this background of tension that Alcalá Zamora decided that Gil Robles's

81. *El Debate*, 26 July and 1 August 1935. For a very different account of the June strike (less critical of the FNTT and more critical of the Samper government), see Jackson, pp. 134–38.

82. Ministerio de Trabajo, *Boletines* of each month.

83. Jackson, pp. 140–46, gives a good account of the extreme friction that arose during the late summer of 1934.

demand could no longer legitimately be denied. On 4 October he asked Lerroux to form a government that would include three CEDA ministers. Though Gil Robles himself was not seated and the Radicals retained control of the critical Ministries of War and of the Interior, a wave of panic seized the Left. Azaña and other Left Republican leaders did not call for revolutionary resistance but sent vehement protests to the president, declaring that he should have dissolved the Cortes rather than give in to the Catholics. The Socialists, trapped by their past rhetoric, proclaimed a revolutionary general strike.

Despite Largo Caballero's frequent cries for the "spiritual" and "material" preparation of the workers, the masses had in fact not been very well prepared. In most of the nation the general strike either failed completely or remained a relatively mild affair. In Madrid tranquillity was restored after the police repulsed a few Socialist militants who tried to take over the Ministry of the Interior. In Barcelona the Socialists had little to do with the tragic series of events by which Luís Companys, head of the autonomous Catalan government, was driven to declare the independence of Catalonia within a new Federal Republic.[84] But the failure in the rest of the nation was overshadowed by the extraordinary response of the miners of Asturias. The rising there was the greatest in Spanish history. Indeed, nothing like it had been seen in Western Europe since the time of the Paris Commune. Only after the rebels had been assaulted by overwhelming military force for a fortnight were they completely vanquished.[85] Yet in truth even the Asturian rebels never had a chance, since the rising was not general throughout Spain. The aid that the peasantry might have offered had been uselessly squandered during the June strike. Only a handful of villages rose to support the Asturian revolt.

As a result of the October Revolution the Socialists were finally given real cause for the grievances they had felt for so long. Moorish troops of the Foreign Legion perpetrated unspeakable atrocities in

84. The Catalan government had been in conflict with Madrid throughout the summer of 1934, because the Tribunal of Constitutional Guarantees had struck down the Ley de Cultivos by which the Generalitat, in the absence of legislation from the Cortes, tried to grant the rabassaires the right to purchase the lands they worked. For reasons of space, and because of the lack of a close connection between this problem and that of the latifundios in Southern Spain, I have chosen not to discuss the rabassaire controversy in detail. Good summaries appear in Joaquín Maurín, "El problema agrario en Cataluña," *Leviatan* (August 1934), pp. 42–50; Emilio Giralt, "El problema rabassaire," *Revista de Trabajo* (1964), pp. 68–71; and Balcells, *El problema agrarí a Catalunya*. See also my chap. 4 for an overview.

85. For two excellent accounts of the Asturias rising and its consequences, see Brenan, pp. 284–92, and Jackson, pp. 148–68.

Asturias. Approximately fifteen to twenty thousand workers were imprisoned; this time they were not released immediately after the danger of revolution had passed. Azaña was imprisoned for three months as his enemies shamelessly tried to implicate him in the Catalan revolt. Companys was jailed, the government of Catalonia was disbanded, and the Statute of Autonomy was suspended. Hundreds of municipal governments were unseated throughout Spain. Largo Caballero was imprisoned for almost a year, though in the end he had to be acquitted for want of legal evidence of his complicity in the revolt. Prieto fled to Paris, where he remained in exile. Martial law was lifted after two months, but a "state of alarm" remained in effect for more than a year. All of these actions finalized the split between the Left Republicans and the Center on the one hand and between Largo Caballero and the "bourgeois Republic" on the other. That the CEDA proved not to be fascist, that the military did not use the October Revolution as an excuse for a coup, that the Socialist party and its trade unions were not proscribed and the Cortes continued to meet, were no longer of importance to many Spanish political leaders. The hatred with which they regarded each other had become profound. Most of the Left no longer accepted the legitimacy of the Republic as defined by their opponents. The "true" Republicans cut off all ties with the "false."

Yet the October revolution did have two potentially positive effects. By revealing the folly of insurrection, it restored Prieto to his senses. From this time forward Prieto tried to break the spell Largo Caballero had cast over the Socialist party so as to lead it back to its former close collaboration with Azaña's Left Republicans. The revolution also cleared the air within Spain by permitting the CEDA to assume the cabinet responsibilities to which it was entitled and by removing the threat of insurrection by the working classes. The hands of the Center and Right were no longer bound. If they could reach an understanding with each other they could reshape the Republic in accordance with the principles they had so often professed. If they succeeded in revising the Azaña legislation wisely, even the negative consequences of the Asturias rebellion might eventually be overcome as the Republic found a new consensus on which to base itself. The revision of the agrarian legislation would be especially important, since it would affect so many millions of voters. Nor was it impossible to conceive that the Center and Right might lead an intelligent "revolution from above." Ironically, one of the three CEDA ministers whose inclusion in the Lerroux government had provoked the Socialist revolt was Manuel Jiménez Fernández, a moderate who quickly proved himself the most able and energetic Minister of Agriculture in the history of the Republic.

13: The Failure of the Center-Right

The Balance That Was Destroyed by the October Revolution

If local landowners had immediately taken advantage of the change in political climate produced by the elections of November 1933 to drive down rural wages, the Center governments prior to the October Revolution had done little—aside from the repeal of the términos municipales law—either to revise the agrarian legislation of Azaña or to enact new legislation on problems Azaña had not touched. There were two exceptions, one of which had, strictly speaking, nothing to do with the agrarian reform. In order to placate his monarchist followers, Gil Robles forced the Cortes to grant amnesty to the Sanjurjo rebels in April 1934. The lands confiscated from the rebels were thereupon returned to their former owners unless they fell under one of the categories of expropriation established in the Agrarian Reform Law, in which case they were retained by the IRA.[1] This measure, irresponsible in that it constituted a symbolic renunciation of the Left, had little effect on peasant settlements since the total property of the rebels was very small. The second exception concerned the settlers under the Intensification of Cultivation decrees. As mentioned earlier, two types of settlement had occurred under these edicts: the first carried out by IRA personnel and carefully observing all of the legal requirements established in the decrees, the second sponsored as an emergency measure without due regard for legal forms by the governor general of Estremadura. The legality of the latter settlements was being contested in the courts by owners who wished to recover their land. In February 1934 the Cortes resolved the question by a law that had mixed consequences. On the one hand the legal suits were voided and all yunteros settled by the governor general were al-

1. Law of 24 April 1934 and Ministry of Agriculture decree of 4 May 1934. The owners also had to reimburse the Institute for any improvements and for mortgages paid on the lands that were actually returned.

lowed to remain in the land. On the other the September 1934 deadline for the evacuation of the land originally established by Azaña in the decrees was made irrevocable for this group of settlers.[2]

Otherwise the legislative basis for the agrarian reform remained unchanged. Gil Robles and several other CEDA deputies jointly introduced a bill for the revision of the September law shortly after the new Cortes began to hold sessions.[3] Martínez de Velasco, head of the Agrarian party, also drafted a proposal in January 1934, although he did not present it to the Cortes until November.[4] In addition to these private bills, three official measures were submitted by Cirilo del Río, the Minister of Agriculture in every cabinet from October 1933 to October 1934. His first proposal, presented in February 1934, centered on the general lease legislation that had provoked such heated discussion in the Cortes during Azaña's final month in power.[5] His two other projects, submitted on his last day in office, were probably intended as his legacy to the new Center-Right government then being formed. One revived in essentially unaltered form Domingo's bill for the recovery of the common lands.[6] The other called for a moderate revision of the Agrarian Reform Law.[7] Except for del Río's lease bill, none of these measures was reported out of the Cortes Committee on Agriculture.

There were two basic reasons for this legislative inactivity. First, the Center and the Right were not united among themselves. If a large group of right-wing CEDA deputies worked in tandem with the monarchists and some Agrarians so as to void all previous legislation, there was also an important moderate branch of the CEDA that collaborated with the Radicals and other smaller parties to modify, not destroy, the Azaña legacy. Cirilo del Río, a Progressive, was an outstanding example of the latter group. The preambles to his bills were studded with tributes to Domingo. His lease bill differed from Domingo's mainly in that its collective lease provisions were somewhat weaker; the controversial attempt to tie rents to the assessed taxable income was retained, as was the tenant's "access to the property right."

A second fundamental reason was that the Left—a considerably larger minority in the new Cortes than the Right had been in the old— was not powerless to act in its own defense. Until October 1934 both Socialists and Left Republicans actively participated in the Cortes and

2. The text of the law is in *D.S.* 38, 20 February 1934, app. 2.
3. *D.S.* 41, 23 February 1934, pp. 1178–84.
4. Martínez de Velasco's bill was dated 24 January 1934, but it was presented to the Cortes in *D.S.* 126, 22 November 1934, pp. 4945–54.
5. *D.S.* 41, 23 February 1934, app. 4.
6. *D.S.* 113, 1 October 1934, app. 22.
7. Ibid., app. 21.

sat on its Committee on Agriculture. They could thus attempt to obstruct discussion on matters unfavorable to them or, at the least, to
swing their weight behind the moderate Center and Right deputies who
resisted the proposals of the reactionaries.

That this balance of forces effectively prevented a wholesale repudiation of the Azaña heritage is unquestionable. Had the Left been powerless, and the Center and Right united behind reactionary policies, it
would be difficult to explain the Agricultural Committee's refusal to
report Gil Robles's agrarian reform bill or Martínez de Velasco's failure
to submit his own project to committee for so long.[8] The heterogeneous
composition of the Committee also helps explain why it altered del Río's
lease bill so little. A few provisions favorable to the owners were added,
but the central features of the Minister of Agriculture's moderate draft
were left intact.

What was true in committee was also true on the Cortes floor.
During the debates on the revision of the Intensification of Cultivation
decrees, the extreme Right sought to oust immediately the yunteros
placed by the governor general of Estremadura, without waiting for the
end of the agricultural year, and to establish the illegitimacy of the
much larger number of settlements that had been made by IRA personnel.[9] Neither effort prospered. In fact, by refusing to reaffirm the
deadline that nominally affected the IRA settlements, the Radicals implicitly supported the leftist position that the overwhelming majority
of yunteros should be permitted indefinite possession of the lands they
had received. The same pattern asserted itself a few months later, in
June 1934, when several right-wing CEDA deputies tried to take advantage of the hostile reaction aroused by the FNTT harvest strike to
cut off appropriations to the IRA. After a fierce three-day battle in which
the Left and Center joined hands to oppose them, the conservative extremists were defeated.[10] Only in the case of the universally detested
términos municipales law, where the Socialists could not even count on
the suport of their Left Republican allies, was an innovation of the
Azaña era completely discarded.

8. The Gil Robles and Martínez de Velasco bills were not reported out of
committee until 28 March 1935 (*D.S.* 179, app. 8), long after the October Revolution had pushed the Cortes to the right.

9. For these efforts, sponsored by right-wing CEDA deputies (Azpeitia, Casanueva, Rodríguez Jurado) and by the Agrarian party chief, Martínez de Velasco,
see *D.S.* 25, 19 January 1934, app. 8; *D.S.* 28, 25 January 1934, app. 10; *D.S.*
30, 30 January 1934, app. 4. The strong opposition of the Radical party spokesman,
Álvarez Mendizábal, is evident in his debate with Azpeitia, *D.S.* 31, 31 January
1934, pp. 800–09.

10. *D.S.* 101–03, 19–21 June 1934, pp. 3785–3909.

Nor was the application of Azaña's legislation drastically altered. Juan José Benayes, the Director General of the IRA after September 1933, had risen to his post from a lesser position to which Domingo had appointed him. The IRA was reorganized by del Río, but essentially along lines that Domingo had first suggested.[11] Nor did the Radicals reduce the IRA budget: they continued to allot fifty million pesetas annually, the same amount that Azaña had granted. None of the lands seized under the September law were returned to their former owners. In fact, the rate of expropriation was faster than before. In the sixteen months between September 1932 and December 1933 the Institute settled 4,399 peasants on 24,203 hectares. During the first nine months of 1934 del Río placed 6,269 settlers on 81,558 hectares.[12] Nor was the settlement of peasants in collectives abandoned, though the IRA technicians sometimes may have used their influence to get settlers to vote for individual cultivation within cooperatives. Six of the nine farms settled as of 1935 in Seville were farmed collectively.[13] In Toledo four of the ten farms seized were collectively exploited.[14] The application of the reform was not abandoned for the same reasons that its legal basis was not revised in the Cortes. Del Río and Lerroux were not reactionaries, the Center and Right did not agree on a common program of action, and the presence of Socialists on the Executive Council of the IRA gave the Left the power to obstruct unfavorable decisions.

Yet although the agrarian reform was not undone, it was not carried forward very far. The whole question of its future remained in a state of suspension for more than a year. The reform as defined by the Azaña coalition generated little enthusiasm within either the Center or the Right. It remained the law of the land mainly because no consensus existed within these highly heterogeneous blocs as to what changes

11. Ministry of Agriculture decree of 4 December 1933. Del Río abolished the Permanent Commission established by Domingo just before Azaña's fall and weakened the authority of the Director General somewhat. On the other hand the Executive Committee was reduced from twenty-nine to seventeen members, and the Director General retained greater powers than he had enjoyed during most of Domingo's tenure in office.

12. *BIRA* (March 1934), pp. 174–75, and (September 1934), pp. 694–95. Most (71,149 hectares) of the land occupied was formally expropriated; only 10,409 hectares were seized under the "temporary occupation" provisions of the 1932 law.

13. IRA, Servicio Provincial de Sevilla, "Informe-resumen sobre el desarrollo de las fincas explotadas por sociedades y Comunidades de Campesinos durante el año agrícola 1934–35," [folder 41/0–1 IRA Archives].

14. IRA, Servicio Provincial de Toledo, "Memoria sobre el estado económico-social-agrícola de las Comunidades en esta provincia" (report dated October 1935), folder 45/0–1, IRA Archives.

should be made. Cirilo del Río might have been more successful in establishing his moderate program as the permanent basis for reform had his own Progressive party wielded more power or had the Radicals commanded a parliamentary majority and been more passionately committed to the cause of national regeneration. As it was, the Minister of Agriculture remained the faithful caretaker of a policy that everyone to some degree disputed but that no one was able to replace.

All this changed after the October Revolution. The threat of working-class opposition outside the Cortes was ended. The Socialists who were not in prison or in exile abandoned their seats on the Executive Council of the IRA and on the Cortes committees as a sign that they no longer recognized the legitimacy of the Center-Right government. The Radicals, who severed all ties with the Left Republicans by their admission of the CEDA into the cabinet and by their unprincipled harassment of Azaña after the Catalan revolt, were driven into the arms of the Right. Finally, as a catalyst in the new situation, Manuel Jiménez Fernández, the CEDA Minister of Agriculture, arrived on the scene.

The Ordeal of Jiménez Fernández

Plump, rasping in voice, unprepossessing in appearance, Jiménez burned with an inner fire. Professor of canon law at the University of Seville, he was later to spend much of his life studying Bartolomé de Las Casas, the great sixteenth-century Dominican friar who stirred the conscience of Spain to the plight of the American Indians under the conquistadores. Something of Las Casas's thirst for social justice and combative spirit seemed already to have entered Jiménez Fernández's soul. He also shared Las Casas's blustering self-confidence and naïve faith in the essential goodness of human nature. Jiménez was certain that he could infect the Cortes with his enthusiasm for helping the poor and even believed that with a few basic changes in the Azaña legislation the reform could be made acceptable to the landowners themselves. Reassured by the presence of a responsible government that did not regard them as enemies, Jiménez said, the landowners would "respond marvelously" to his appeals and "voluntarily cede" lands to those who needed them.

Yet if the new Minister of Agriculture distinguished himself from most of his fellows by the vigor with which he pursued his goals, he nevertheless remained a typical product of liberal Spanish Catholicism in many of his attitudes. He passionately proclaimed the need to modify the existing property structure so that the land would serve its "social function" but could not entirely discard his respect for the "legitimate rights" of property. In practice, this meant an acceptance of what was in any case a political necessity for any CEDA minister—the principle that adequate compensation must be paid for lands seized. Jiménez Fernández also shared the traditional Catholic prejudice in favor of the small tenant over the landless worker. He saw as the object of agrarian reform the creation of small, independent homesteads, to be held by the settler as property with a minimum of reliance upon the state. This objective could be achieved most speedily and securely by settling small tenants, who had tools and animals of their own as well as active experience in the independent management of the land. In these beliefs, too, political necessity operated, since Spanish Catholicism for decades had tended to write off the landless workers as hopeless converts to socialism and anarchosyndicalism. Yet Jiménez's preference for the tenant was almost obsessive in its intensity.[15]

These prejudices must be kept in mind in evaluating Jiménez Fernández's often misunderstood decree of 2 January 1935. The decree had three essential parts. It ordered that during 1935 the IRA not expropriate outright any property but rather make settlements exclusively under the "temporary occupation" provisions of the September law or on farms voluntarily rented to the IRA by their owners. Second, preference in settlement was to be given to tenants and sharecroppers who possessed their own instruments of cultivation. Finally, the decree established a goal of ten thousand settlers for the year.[16]

These measures clearly redefined but did not "kill" the agrarian reform, as some writers have since asserted. There is no reason to doubt Jiménez's explanation that he was merely being realistic in establishing a goal of ten thousand settlers for 1935; after all, not many more colonists had been placed during the previous two and one-half years, and the Azaña government itself had announced a similar figure as its objective for 1933 before it was pushed by rural upheavals to more extravagant pledges.[17] Nor did the exclusive reliance on temporary occupations indicate an intention to return the lands to their owners at some future time. Rather, this legal device was invoked to permit the IRA to postpone payment of compensation until a new law had established more equitable

15. These impressions of Jiménez Fernández's personality are based on his Cortes speeches, a long interview with *El Debate*, 1 January 1935, and two personal interviews with him in 1961 and 1962.

16. Ministry of Agriculture decree of 2 January 1935.

17. See above, chap. 10. It might be added that if the rate of land redistribution under Jiménez during the last three months of 1934 (1,505 settlers on 13,045 hectares—*BIRA* [December 1934], pp. 2–5) was lower than that established by del Río, it was remarkable that any land transfers at all occurred in the turbulent atmosphere that followed the October Revolution.

rates of indemnification.[18] In short, the January decree was intended to start the IRA functioning along lines that it was expected would be embodied in the new agrarian legislation, not to destroy it altogether.

Jiménez Fernández sponsored one other transitional measure during his first three months in office. As mentioned previously, the Intensification of Cultivation settlements were scheduled to end in the fall of 1934. Although the Center parties, during the debates on the settlements sponsored by the governor general of Estremadura, had implicitly promised that the tenure of the yunteros placed by the IRA would be extended, Cirilo del Río had done nothing to redeem this pledge, presumably because of the extreme political tension that had preceded the CEDA's entry into the cabinet in October. Jiménez Fernández therefore arrived in office just as both types of Intensification leases lapsed and yunteros began to be expelled from their holdings. Realizing the urgency of the problem, he immediately drew up a bill that would force owners to extend all existing leases—including those that had originated with the governor general —for another agricultural year and presented it on 5 November, at the very first session held by the Cortes after the October Revolution. The bill cleared committee with surprising speed, and the floor debates were also brief. At the last moment the monarchists marred Jiménez's performance by calling for a quorum vote, a tactic which blocked definitive approval of the bill until late December.[19] It was by now too late in the year for the yunteros to plant winter wheat, but they could still sow spring crops. By their rear-guard action the monarchists had placed the yunteros in a much more difficult position than Jiménez had intended, but at least he had succeeded in his main objective of staving off for another year the threat of total defeat and expulsion that had faced these small tenants and sharecroppers.

So long as he dealt only with transitional measures, Jiménez Fernández did not encounter insurmountable opposition from the newly resurgent right wing of the Cortes. The attempt of the monarchist deputies to prevent the extension of the yunteros' leases ultimately failed. The continued seizure of Inventory lands under the temporary occupation device was accepted without significant protest. Jiménez's calvary began only after he turned from transitional to permanent legislation. The first major test arose in connection with del Río's general lease proposal, which had

18. As explained in chap. 8, only an annual rent, not over-all compensation, was paid on temporarily occupied lands.

19. The bill was presented in *D.S.* 115, 5 November 1934, app. 13, and was reported out of committee in *D.S.* 119, 12 November 1934, app. 1. Debates continued from 21 to 30 November. The obstruction of the monarchists prevented definitive approval of the bill until *D.S.* 143, 21 December 1934, app. 28.

been favorably reported out of committee before the October Revolution and which was presented for floor discussion in the early part of December 1934.

Jiménez not only accepted his predecessor's draft but, just before debate began, submitted a new bill that would strengthen the controversial "access to the property right" provisions of the general proposal. Del Río had asked that owners be forced to sell land to tenants who had farmed it for fifteen consecutive years. The Commission of Agriculture had revised the time requirement to twenty years. Jiménez's new project aimed to reduce the period of waiting to only twelve years on most lands.[20]

The extent to which Jiménez, in thinking that he could actually improve on the del Río bill, had miscalculated his power became apparent very quickly. Almost immediately a coalition of extreme-right-wing deputies began to form in opposition to the permanent structural reforms envisaged in the bill. The most vituperative opponent of the measure was undoubtedly José Antonio Lamamié de Clairac (a leader of the Traditionalist party who had been one of the chief spokesmen of the old Agrarian minority under the Constituent Cortes). Other monarchists, and a few members of the newly restructured Agrarian party, were also active.[21] But the heart of the opposition was provided by the right wing of Jiménez's own party, led by Mateo Azpeitia, Cándido Casanueva, and Adolfo Rodríguez Jurado, the CEDA's principal representatives on the Agricultural Committee. All three men, who like Lamamié had from 1931 to 1933 been members of the old Agrarian minority, had fought the lease bill in committee[22] but had been unable to revise it because of the combined Left Republican–Socialist opposition and the independent attitude maintained at the time by the Radicals. Under the conditions created by the October Revolution, however, they could no longer be stopped.

The floor battle was grueling. For thirty almost consecutive sessions[23]

20. The text of Jiménez's "access to the property right" bill appears in *D.S.* 132, 4 December 1934, app. 6.

21. The Agrarian minority in the Constituent Cortes had grouped together most of the conservative deputies who did not belong to regionalist parties. After the 1933 elections, since both monarchist and Catholic members had withdrawn to form their own parties, the Agrarians became a conservative but pro-Republican group, without specific ideological ties, which lay somewhat closer to the center of the political spectrum than in 1931–33. A monographic study of both manifestations of the party would be useful. One wonders, for example, the extent to which the past collaboration of Lamamié de Clairac and Casanueva, who had been the chief spokesman on rural questions of the old Agrarian minority, facilitated their unofficial joint action against Jiménez.

22. They had presented a dissenting opinion to the committee findings (*D.S.* 101, 19 June 1934, pp. 3778–80).

23. The Cortes debates extended from *D.S.* 133, 5 December 1934, to *D.S.*

Lamamié de Clairac and the right-wing CEDA deputies ripped away one after another of the progressive features of del Río's bill. The minimum duration of leases had been set at six years; it was now reduced to four years in most lands. Rents had been tied to the assessed taxable income of the land; they could now be set at whatever level the owner desired— the tenant's only recourse would be to institute litigation for rent reduction. The tenant's right of first option should the farm be sold was rendered ineffective, because the penalties against deceit on the part of the owner were removed. The access to the property right, even in the moderate form in which it had appeared in the committee draft, was rejected outright. The arbitration boards for leased property, which del Río and Jiménez had expected would supervise lease conditions, were disbanded; all appeals from the tenants were to be judged by the traditionally conservative local courts.

Nevertheless, even after the alterations made by the extreme Right, the bill granted tenants certain privileges they had not enjoyed in the past. During disastrous crop years the tenant could demand a reduction in rent. He could also force the owner to pay part of the legal costs of the new contracts, to make some repairs on the farm, and to contribute toward the cost of insurance against crop failure. If the tenant left the farm he could demand payment for any necessary improvements he had made. Moreover, he was assured of at least a four-year lease, which he could usually renew thereafter, and could exercise the somewhat theoretical right of first option mentioned earlier.

The parliamentary skill of Lamamié de Clairac and his CEDA allies, which they had so effectively employed in the Cortes battles of 1932 and 1933 while members of the old Agrarian minority, was again demonstrated as they succeeded in turning precisely these improvements to their own advantage. Before an owner could be asked to accept all these new conditions, they argued, he should be given the right to recover the land if he decided he would rather farm it himself; this right was especially necessary because owners had been prevented from evicting tenants since 1931, when the Provisional Government froze existing leases. The Cortes accepted these rationalizations and, in consequence, attached to the bill a new set of "transitory provisions" which, for the time being at least, permitted it to be used to persecute rather than aid the tenants. Owners were given the power to end existing leases as soon as they expired. If they had already expired and the tenant remained on the land by virtue of the Azaña decrees, the owner could recover the land at the end of the 1935 harvest. Verbal contracts (which were exceedingly common) could also

171, 14 March 1935. The text of the bill as finally approved appears in *D.S.* 172, 15 March 1935, app. I.

be ended as soon as the crop had been gathered. Any court sentences of eviction which had been suspended by Azaña could be put into effect immediately. It is true that in all these cases the owners could recover the land only if they planned "directly to cultivate" it themselves. However, since "direct cultivation" was so broadly defined in Spanish legal usage, any owner who wished to rid himself of a tenant could do so easily. This was particularly so since Lamamié and his associates had also managed to pervert some articles of the law by which Jiménez had been trying to establish a more socially beneficial type of sharecropping arrangement in such a way as to further undermine the security of tenure of all lessees.[24]

Jiménez did not remain silent during the assault on the lease bill as he might have on the excuse that he was preoccupied with trying to solve the crisis in wheat prices (the 1934 crop was even larger than that of 1932, and an enormous surplus had been left unsold).[25] Instead he passionately fought back against the right wing of his own party. On twenty-one separate occasions the Minister of Agriculture appealed to the conscience of the Cortes and warned Catholics that they were violating the most precious principles of their faith.[26] As he was defeated on specific issues, Jiménez reintroduced them to the Cortes under new guise. Even after the parliamentary debates had ended, he did not rest but continued to call for adoption of the access to the property right principle and for a more restrictive definition of "direct cultivation" so as to prevent the mass evictions that the transitory provisions seemed to threaten.[27]

Nor did the ordeal to which Jiménez had been subjected on the lease bill discourage him from pressing ahead with important new legislation. Once again the yunteros of Estremadura, whose one-year renewal of leases was due to expire in a few months, were his immediate concern. But the implications of his "increase of small farming areas" bill, which was presented to the Cortes in February 1935, were far greater in scope. Whenever there were small cultivators who lacked land on which to employ

24. Law of 15 March 1935, transitory clauses 1–3.
25. The wheat crop was 5.0 million metric tons in 1932 and 5.1 million metric tons in 1934. Thus the two best crops in the history of Spain up to that time occurred under the Republic, an indication of how little the social disturbances that occurred affected conditions of production, in the short run at least.
26. To which Lamamié de Clairac replied: "If you persist in trying to steal our lands by quoting encyclicals, we shall end by becoming schismatics" (quoted in Mendizábal, p. 231).
27. Jiménez sought to accomplish this by allowing owners to claim "direct cultivation" only if they lived in the village where the land was located, in the case of small farms, or if they lived close to the village, in the case of farms of over sixty hectares (El Debate, 23 March 1935). He fell from office before he was able to secure cabinet approval for his proposal.

their animals and tools, the IRA was to be empowered to turn over to them up to 25 percent of any estates over three hundred hectares in size, so long as this did not prejudice the existing agricultural or livestock activities of the estate. The bill as written applied only to Badajoz, where the yuntero problem was gravest; it also limited the temporary occupations to a period of two years.[28] Yet as its opponents pointed out and Jiménez defiantly admitted,[29] the principles established in one province would soon be extended to others and the settlements, though intended as temporary, would tend to become permanent. In essence Jiménez was seeking to make the Intensification of Cultivation decrees—and thus the spirit of the 1931 Technical Commission proposal—a regular instrument of state policy.

Needless to say, Jiménez was no more successful in securing approval of his small farming areas bill than he had been in preventing the drastic alterations of the general lease law. In truth, his position was hopeless. Since only a few Left Republicans and Socialists still attended Cortes sessions, he was forced to rely on the support of the handful of deputies from the Center and Right who did not suffer from the growing moral bankruptcy of their parties. Cirilo del Río fought for progressive legislation. So did Álvarez Mendizábal, who seemed to be emerging as the voice of conscience of the Radicals. But the major party leaders sat back and allowed events to take their course. This was especially true of Gil Robles, whose personal moderation had been indicated by his choice for Minister of Agriculture of Jiménez rather than Casanueva, Azpeitia, or Rodríguez Jurado—all of whom had previously been more intimately connected with agrarian affairs. The CEDA chief dared not risk splitting his party by taking sides in the conflict that had arisen. As a result Jiménez found himself increasingly isolated. By the end he had become the victim of bitter personal attacks. The use of the term "the white bolshevik" to describe him became current.[30] "You may pretend to be a defender of the Right," cried one CEDA deputy, "but we all know that you are really in the employ of the Left." [31] Even Jiménez's integrity was ques-

28. The text of the bill appears in *D.S.* 146, 23 January 1935, app. 15. It was rejected by the Cortes Committee on Agriculture but revived as a private motion by the Radical party spokesman Álvarez Mendizábal. The measure was tabled after two brief debates in February and March and was dropped entirely after Jiménez lost his cabinet post.

29. *D.S.* 166, 27 February 1935, p. 6677.

30. Jiménez did not flinch before such attacks. For example, when accused of being a Socialist, he replied: "If Socialism means a system which attempts to reform society . . . when things are bad, then I am a Socialist" (*D.S.* 172, 15 March 1935, p. 6965).

31. *D.S.* 166, 27 February 1935, p. 6678.

tioned. The only reason that he was so progressive in agrarian affairs, his enemies asserted, was that his own wealth would not be affected since it rested entirely on urban properties.[32]

The amazing thing is that Jiménez was able to hang on for so long. His strong sense of party loyalty prevented him from walking out of the CEDA: like Prieto and Besteiro among the Socialists, he reluctantly accepted decisions of which he did not approve and tried to reverse them from within his party. The CEDA also could not benefit from a complete break with Jiménez, and he continued to enjoy a close personal relationship with Gil Robles. Consequently, he remained at his post until the end of March 1935, when a cabinet crisis offered everyone concerned the opportunity to end the friction that had arisen while saving appearances. Jiménez was not renamed to the Ministry of Agriculture. In fact, though he was soon given the honorific position of vice-president of the Cortes, he was never again allowed to hold a cabinet post.

Would the CEDA have been able to gain the support of the peasantry had Jiménez succeeded in stirring its conscience? His general lease proposals were, in their own way, certainly as advanced as those of Domingo. There can also be no question as to his passionate devotion to the yunteros. The outcome of his plans for the revision of the Agrarian Reform Law, had he been given time to carry them out, is somewhat harder to surmise. From various statements he made (he never submitted a formal proposal to the Cortes), it seems that the main features of his program would have been the following. Confiscation of grande lands would stop: after so much Catholic propaganda against such confiscation no other course was politically possible. Compensation for non-grandes would increase and would be paid mostly in cash and in a regular bond issue rather than in the special, non-negotiable issue provided by the 1932 law. The hundreds of thousands of small farms threatened by the ruedo and lease provisions of the 1932 law would no longer be expropriable. The law would not be applied uniformly and automatically even against large properties. Rather, a "case" approach would be adopted whereby the law would be invoked chiefly against large estates located in townships in which acute social problems existed.

On the other hand Jiménez saw that equal compensation could not be paid for all lands. Indemnification would continue to be inversely proportionate to the total wealth of each owner. The "origins" of the property would also be taken into account (i.e., proven señorios and, possibly, lands obtained through mortgage foreclosures would be reimbursed at lower rates than other properties).[33] Moreover, a new graduated tax would be

32. D.S. 172, 15 March 1935, p. 6965.
33. Jiménez mentioned the above features as part of his plan for the agrarian

applied to all land to help finance the reform and to encourage "the natural tendency among owners voluntarily to dispose of their holdings as the progressive tax makes ownership too great a burden." [34] Jiménez would also have improved the 1932 law in one other way. Its maximum property limits would apply to a person's holdings throughout Spain, not to those in each municipality, thus opening vast areas to expropriation.

There were dangers in Jiménez's approach to the reform, of course. Despite the revenues from his progressive tax, the state would have been hard pressed to find the money necessary to pay the more equitable compensations allowed. Moreover, Jiménez saw the Agrarian Reform Law principally as another means of helping the tenant farmers and tended to accord the secondary importance to settlement of day laborers. For this latter reason in particular, Jiménez's plans—which in many ways resembled the moderate bills sponsored by Diego Hidalgo and Juan Díaz del Moral under the Provisional Government—could have succeeded only partly in providing the mass support on which the Republic could be built anew. The allegiance of tenant farmers and sharecroppers might have been gained, but the redistribution of land would have proceeded too slowly to win over the field hands. As regards political groupings, Jiménez might have conciliated some of the Left Republicans but could not have appeased the newly militant Socialists. Yet even granting that he could have enjoyed only limited success, there can be no doubt that the defeat of Jiménez Fernández was one of the central tragedies of the Republic. The transformation of the CEDA into a socially conscious Christian Democratic party, which was Jiménez's central purpose, was never accomplished. The polarization of Spanish society, which might have been checked by a show of generosity on the part of the triumphant Right, continued apace.

The Triumph of the Reactionaries

Once Jiménez was defeated, all hope of serious social reform passed away. The Ministry of Agriculture soon fell into the hands of the Agrarian party. In the Cortes the balance of power was indisputably held by the monarchists, Agrarians, and the conservative wing of the CEDA, all of whom tended to reject the possibility of social improvements through legislative action. The only reason for the present sufferings of the peasants,

---

reform in his interview with El Debate, 1 January 1935. For his desire to penalize mortgage foreclosures, see D.S. 82, 16 May 1934, pp. 2850–52.

34. The progressive surtax was not mentioned in the El Debate interview. However, he later stressed this in the Cortes (D.S. 166, 27 February 1935, pp. 6677–78) as well as in my interviews with him.

their spokesman Lamamié de Clairac once said, was that the natural conditions that had preserved a social balance in the past had been upset. If the confidence and freedom of action of the owners were restored, workers would once again find employment and tenant farmers would soon recover the land they had held before.[35] The progressive Catholics, like the nonrevolutionary Socialists, did not follow what would have been the most honorable course. They were too distrustful of the Left to break with the CEDA and contented themselves with the hope that the improvements they would introduce into the program of the extreme Right would compensate for the features they did not like. The Radicals and independents, with a few exceptions, drifted along with the tide since they lacked any real foresight or courage.

Yet no immediate change was made in the status of the agrarian reform. In fact, it seemed that the Cortes would recess for the summer without having discussed a revision of the 1932 law. But suddenly, on 3 July 1935, the new Minister of Agriculture, Nicasio Velayos y Velayos, submitted a new draft bill. Since the Committee on Agriculture was by now completely controlled by conservatives, it cleared the bill within two days —unprecedented speed for Spanish legislative committees.[36] On the Cortes floor, however, the situation was somewhat more fluid. The Left Republicans strongly protested the new measure and found perhaps unexpected support from del Río and such Radical spokesmen as Álvarez Mendizábal and Samper, all of whom were willing to accept some modification of the 1932 law but not the measure that had been placed before them. José Antonio Primo de Rivera—son of the late dictator, leader and sole deputy of the Falange—added to the difficulties of the government with a dramatic speech in which he denounced the bill as yet another manifestation of the moral bankruptcy of the traditional parties of the Right and went on to expound his own somewhat romantic vision of what agrarian reform should be. Most important of all, Jiménez Fernández demanded the addition to the bill of a progressive surtax and of a substitute for the access to the property right provision that had been defeated during the debates on the lease bill.[37]

The second day of debates was almost as unfavorable for the government as the first. Del Río, Primo de Rivera, and the Left Republican Claudio Sánchez Albornoz once again put their oratorical skills to good

35. *D.S.* 172, 15 March 1935, pp. 6972–73.

36. The text of the Velayos bill is in *D.S.* 216, 3 July 1935, app. 1; of the committee report, in *D.S.* 218, 5 July 1935, app. 28. Velayos was a leading number of the Agrarian party.

37. The texts of these several speeches can be found in *D.S.* 228, 23 July 1935, pp. 9357–82.

use.[38] Although these three men represented only a small fraction of the Cortes deputies, it seemed for a moment fully possible—given the luke-warmness of the Radicals and the sense of deception among the CEDA moderates—that they might succeed in blocking debate until the Cortes were forced to adjourn.[39] Faced with this prospect, the government hastily worked out a compromise. The liberal Catholics were the key to the situa-tion. Jiménez Fernández was granted his substitute for the access prin-ciple: owners had not been obliged by the lease law to sell land to tenants after a certain number of years, but tenants who had fulfilled the time re-quirements were now permitted to petition the IRA for preferential grants of whatever lands it had available. A "homestead" (*patrimonio familiar*) clause, sponsored by Antonio Álvarez Robles with the support of Jiménez, was added to give tenants and small owners still greater preference in set-tlements.[40] Concessions were also made to the Radicals. Álvarez Mendizá-bal's "social utility" amendment,[41] to be explained shortly, was accepted. Señoríos jurisdiccionales would continue to be confiscated if the Institute could prove in court that they had indeed been illegally appropriated—a nod to the Radicals' antiaristocratic past. But the conservative majority in the Cortes refused to accept any really substantial modifications of their program. For example, Álvarez Mendizábal's demand that rates of com-pensation vary according to the total wealth of owners was rejected, and Jiménez Fernández was persuaded to drop his proposal for a graduated surtax after he had won preferential treatment for the tenant farmers.

Once these negotiations with the moderate opposition had been com-pleted, the bill was assured of easy passage. The Left Republican depu-ties, aware of the hopelessness of their situation, issued a declaration in which they vowed to undo the law as soon as they returned to power and

38. *D.S.* 229, 24 July 1935, pp. 9395–9419. José Antonio's discourses during these two sessions have special historical importance in that they have served as the voice of conscience—unfortunately usually ignored—on agrarian affairs of the Franco regime since the Civil War.

39. Attendance at Cortes sessions had been extremely low for the previous several weeks, and there was no possibility that the Radical leaders in particular could discipline their deputies to forego their summer recess if debates on the bill stalled. Unlike the Constituent Cortes, which for all its defects was capable of almost superhuman efforts, the 1933–35 parliament was an old-style, cynical body that had to have its vacations.

40. Because so much land would have been required to satisfy these two provisions (the IRA, for example, was authorized to devote up to 50 percent of its funds annually to the fulfillment of the "access" principle), the law would have ended by excluding day laborers from the reform almost completely. Thus, one of the law's principal defects resulted more from liberal Catholic preoccupation with small tenants and owners than from the policies of the extreme Right.

41. *D.S.* 219, 9 July 1935, app. 18.

then walked out of the Cortes en masse—the first time they had taken such action.[42] With the Left Republicans gone, the liberal Radical spokesmen quickly abandoned their few remaining objections.[43] The parliament had debated the Agrarian Reform Law of 1932 for five months; debate on the 1935 law lasted five days. As though to confess its shame at the indecent haste with which it was approving so vital a measure, the Cortes passed the bill by voice vote. But even had a roll call vote been taken, the outcome would have been the same. After the surrender of the Radicals and the walkout of the Left Republicans, only a few scattered individuals—del Río, Primo de Rivera, and one or two others—remained who would have voted against the measure.

How did the "Law for the Reform of the Agrarian Reform," [44] as it was officially dubbed, revise the Azaña legislation? At first glance the categories of expropriable property seem not to have been altered drastically. Direct cultivators remained subject to expropriation; the maximum size limits of old were retained, as were the penalties against señoríos, undercultivated lands, and unirrigated lands in irrigation zones. Only the ruedo provisions and those calling for the expropriation of small leased property were dropped, but these were precisely the worst features of the 1932 law and had been denounced by many moderates. The real change made in the 1935 law was more subtle. The categories of expropriation were for the most part rendered meaningless by the repeal of the Inventory of Expropriable Property—that is, of the legal restrictions that prevented direct cultivators from altering the status of their farms in order to bring them below the size limits at which they could be seized. In the future only owners who did not want to escape expropriation need suffer it. All others could avoid the reform merely by ceding part of their land to their children or by selling it to their neighbors. The legal restrictions on property transfers had indeed caused hardships, but to remove them entirely—instead of only on small farms, as had originally been planned [45] —was to end all hope of serious reform.

42. D.S. 230, 25 July 1935, pp. 9440–47. Incidentally, the dignified speeches by which Gil Robles tried to salve the Left Republicans' pride and to convince them to remain in attendance offer further evidence of his essentially nonfanatical and nonvindictive temperament.

43. The pathetically rapid collapse of Álvarez Mendizábal is documented in ibid., pp. 9456–59. Samper put up a somewhat stronger resistance.

44. The official texts are in D.S. 231, 26 July 1935, app. 26, and D.S. 232, 24 September 1935, app. 4.

45. The complete abolition of the Inventory was accomplished during the debates. The Minister of Agriculture, Velayos, like all of his predecessors, had asked only that the hundreds of thousands of ruedo and small leased farms, which were penalized to no real purpose (see above, pp. 212–19), be dropped from it.

A still more central change was made in the compensation principles of the 1932 law. The principle of confiscation of property was repudiated except in the case of señoríos that could be proven to have been illegitimately acquired. Contrary to what is so often asserted, the grande lands seized since 1932 were not returned to their former owners, although the Institute now had to pay compensation for them. The really important change in the compensation provisions, however, concerned owners who had never been threatened with confiscation—the bourgeoisie who controlled more than nine-tenths of the land in Spain. The indemnification they received was no longer to be determined automatically on the basis of retrogressive multiples of the assessed taxable income of their farms. The terms of sale were to be fought out in each case between representatives of the owner and of the Institute. If no agreement could be reached, the traditionally conservative county courts were to decide the final sale price. If the owner was still not satisfied, he could carry his case to the supreme court. Obviously proprietors could hold out for nothing less than the full market value of their lands. And since compensation was to be paid in regular state bonds, the value of which would be determined by their market price on the day of sale, owners expropriated by the state would often be better off than those who tried to sell their lands to private buyers. The bonds could be converted immediately into cash, whereas most private buyers were unable to put together enough money to pay off at once the full price of the farm. In this sense it made little difference that the Inventory of Expropriable Property had been repealed. The conditions of compensation had been made so attractive that, as del Río put it, "Proprietors will line up to beg that their farms be included in the agrarian reform." [46]

The compensation provisions so increased the cost of expropriation that they could have been reconciled with the stated objective of a profound agrarian reform only if the budget of the Institute had been multiplied five or six times. Instead the 1935 law took the figure of 50 million pesetas, previously the minimum budget of the Institute, and converted it into the maximum budget permissible. The explanation that budgetary restrictions were necessary because otherwise the bonds issued as compensation would flood the bond market and drive down the value of all securities is patently false. A securities market of the size of Spain's—in which some 20 billion pesetas' worth of state bonds were outstanding—was easily capable of absorbing 150 to 200 million pesetas of new issues annually. Alternately, reliance on the bond market could have been lessened by accepting the graduated surtax on agricultural property which

46. *D.S.* 228, 23 July 1935, p. 9358.

had been proposed by so many moderates since 1931. The budgetary limitation is perhaps the best single evidence of the hypocrisy of the conservatives who controlled the Cortes. Despite their rhetorical concern for the plight of the peasant, they really desired no reform at all, whether it be collectivistic or individualistic, Socialist or Catholic.

These three critical changes killed the agrarian reform for all practical purposes. For two or three years—even after paying off the grandes whose farms had been seized in the past—the state might have purchased enough land to put up a pretense of reform. The Institute had done so little in the past that, alone among Spanish government agencies, it had accumulated a large surplus that could be used to this end.[47] But once this surplus had been exhausted, land redistribution would practically stop. José Antonio was exaggerating only slightly when he estimated that reform on these terms would take 160 years to complete.[48] As Cirilo del Río said, the 1935 law was in fact "not a plan to reform the agrarian reform, but a plan of agrarian counterreformation." [49] Even the tenant farmers and small proprietors, of whom the law spoke so lovingly, would not really have been helped, since no more than three or four thousand of them could have been settled annually.[50]

Yet the 1935 law contained one provision that had revolutionary implications. In order to justify the abolition of the Inventory and to mollify such moderates as Álvarez Mendizábal and Jiménez Fernández, the government accepted their "case" approach to the reform. It would be unjust, the argument ran, to expropriate automatically all properties of a given type merely because they happened to fulfill certain characteristics. But

47. As of the end of 1935 the IRA had received budget allocations totaling 158.3 million pesetas. Because almost all the land seized was grande property that was not compensated, and because the IRA was so sluggish, its budgetary surplus amounted to 95.8 million pesetas—in other words, a state agency had performed the miraculous feat of spending only 40 percent of the monies it received.

48. José Antonio calculated that the 8 to 10 million hectares necessary to complete the reform would cost about 8 billion pesetas, which at 50 million pesetas annually works out to 160 years.

49. D.S. 228, 23 July 1935, pp. 9357–58.

50. It is worth mentioning, however, that the 1935 law handled the question of converting the settlers into proprietors more intelligently than had the 1932 law, which primarily for ideological reasons had insisted on state ownership. The settlers were to be given a choice (after a period of time which varied from two to six years) of either buying the land from the state under very generous terms of payment or accepting it under a *censo* (emphyteutic lease) arrangement in which they would enjoy most of the advantages of ownership without any of its costs. Sufficient safeguards were included to prevent the reaccumulation of property, the diversion of resources from productive needs to the payment of mortgages, and most of the other dangers foreseen by the bourgeois technicians who in 1931–32 had supported the Socialists in denying settlers the property right.

should the seizure of a property really be necessary to solve an urgent social problem, the Right would prove that it could act with greater vigor than the Left. Thus, in addition to its right to occupy the properties included in the categories of expropriation, the state was given the power to seize for purposes of "social utility" any farm in Spain, whatever its size or condition. Within the framework of the 1935 law, the radical principle of social utility meant little, since the Institute was starved for funds and an owner could delay seizure by litigation over the terms of compensation. Once separated from that framework, however, the social utility clause in itself could provide the legal basis for the most revolutionary actions, as was to be proved in 1936.

The 1935 law was important mainly as proof of the moral bankruptcy of the Center-Right coalition. Its application during the coalition's remaining six months in power did nothing to redeem its authors. Most of the rest of 1935 was spent in reorganizing the IRA so as to end any vestiges of independence it might have retained and to exclude permanently all Socialist representation from it.[51] Even the budget surplus accumulated by the Institute was not tapped to provide a semblance of energetic reform; rather, every administrative decision seemed to be aimed at reducing still further the scope of the 1935 law.[52] By the end of the year moderate Catholic journals like El Debate (which originally supported the law) were crying out against the lethargy that had settled over "this regrettably all too famous Institute." As in the past, the nation was being forced "to wait, perhaps hopelessly," for action.[53]

Yet the 1935 law did not have any immediate negative consequences for the peasantry. No lands taken under the 1932 law were returned; none of the settlers on them was expelled. Indeed, in its own slow manner, the Institute continued to occupy farms voluntarily offered by their owners.[54]

---

51. DGRA Orders of 17 October, 7, 30 November and 7 December 1935. The chicanery employed to exclude the Socialists makes these orders unpleasant reading.

52. This remained true after the Ministry of Agriculture passed out of the hands of the Agrarian party on 29 October 1935. The generally more centrist Chapaprieta and Portela governments that succeeded to power acted like conservatives on agrarian affairs. Even Álvarez Mendizábal did not follow the progressive inclinations he had shown in the Cortes debates during his tenure in the Ministry of Agriculture, just before the Popular Front elections. His decree of 8 February 1936, for example, set up very complicated procedures for land redistribution, which would have delayed considerably the application of the 1935 law. On this decree, see El Sol, 12, 15 February, and 1 March 1936.

53. El Debate, 1 January 1936.

54. No statistics were ever published on the amount of land occupied by the IRA after December 1934. Judging from the meetings of the IRA Executive Council as summarized in BIRA, a number of farms voluntarily offered by their owners were

The reasons for the deterioration in the condition of the Spanish peasantry during 1935 lie elsewhere. Perhaps the greatest harm on a national scale was done by the "transitory provisions" of the general lease law. No statistics exist, but, to judge from the frequent cries of dismay uttered in the Catholic as well as in the liberal press,[55] several thousand owners must have taken advantage of their right "directly to cultivate" their land in order to evict their tenants. Moreover, many other owners undoubtedly used the threat of eviction to force tenants to accept higher rents. In Estremadura the consequences of the expiration of Jiménez Fernández's yunteros law must have been catastrophic. Since none of the governments after March 1935 had any interest in extending the protective legislation, most of the yunteros were evicted from the land, and those who were allowed to remain were forced to pay higher rents. The condition of the day laborers also probably worsened, although this was mostly the result of the useless self-destruction of the Socialist labor unions during the previous year. Few of the rural locals of the FNTT functioned; strikes were almost unknown; the arbitration boards fell increasingly into conservative hands; the national government did nothing to check the power of the rural oligarchy. Consequently wages continued to decline and, though there was no increase in general unemployment until the very end of the year, Socialist militants who had not been jailed after the October Revolution must have been subjected to unmerciful discrimination in hiring.

The Center-Right parties were called upon to pay the price for their generally reactionary program after the October Revolution somewhat sooner than anyone had expected. In the fall of 1935 financial scandals broke out which discredited Lerroux so completely that he was forced to resign as prime minister. Alcalá Zamora turned to a distinguished moderate, Joaquín Chapaprieta, but the new prime minister's program of fiscal austerity (which included plans for somewhat heavier taxation) soon brought him into conflict with the CEDA and other conservative parties, without whose support no cabinet could function. It seemed as though the President might now be forced to ask Gil Robles to form a government. But personal antipathy and a lingering suspicion that the Catholic leader might try to restore the monarchy or establish a corporative state caused Alcalá Zamora to reject this alternative. Instead he decided to dissolve parliament and called upon an ex-Radical, Manuel Portela, to form a government that would guide Spain through the elections. Alcalá Zamora

---

purchased. No compulsory seizures of lands took place after 1 July 1935, however. Even the "temporary occupations" utilized by Jiménez stopped.

55. For Catholic protest that the general lease law was being misused, see *El Debate*, 4, 17 July 1935, and 1 January 1936.

gambled that Portela would be able to found a new Center party to re-place the discredited Radicals as the basis for a moderate Republic.

The President could not have been more mistaken in his expectations. A new Center party could not be created overnight. The organizational problems were too great, and there was no figure of national stature to lead it. Some of those who had previously voted for the Radicals turned to the Left in disgust at the hypocrisy and inaction of the 1933–35 period, and others, frightened by the rhetoric of Largo Caballero's Socialists, sup-ported conservative candidates. Lerroux's Radicals had died; Portela's party was stillborn. The Center disappeared almost completely as a po-litical force in the elections of February 1936.

The struggle was fought almost entirely between the Right, organized for electoral purposes into a "National Front," and the Left, organized into a "Popular Front." And though the Right increased its popular support considerably,[56] the victory went to the Left. For this victory of its op-ponents the Right had only itself to blame. The sterility of its program had wiped away, at least temporarily, all of the disputes that had divided the Left in the 1933 election. The tenant farmers and day laborers voted against it en masse. Catalonia turned to the Left once more to avenge itself on those who had suspended its regional autonomy. The Anarcho-syndicalists temporarily put aside their hatred of Azaña and allowed their hundreds of thousands of followers to cast ballots. Above all, despite Largo Caballero's initial opposition,[57] the Socialists agreed to enter into electoral alliances with the Left Republicans once more. The tragic mis-take of 1933 was not repeated: a slate of Popular Front candidates ap-peared in every electoral district of Spain. With its lost unity restored, the Left proved unbeatable. Its popular support exceeded that of the Right by only some 500,000 votes, but because its electoral alliances were firmer than those of the Right, the electoral law that had prevailed since 1931 converted its relatively small popular majority into a very large majority in the Cortes. The Popular Front seated 258 deputies, as against 152 for the Right and 62 for the Center. Azaña returned to power: the Left re-covered its freedom of action once more.

56. As usual, the electoral statistics are very poor. Madariaga, p. 445, gives 4.2 million votes to the Left and 3.8 million to the Right. Brenan, p. 298, gives 4.7 million to the Left and 4.0 million to the Right. In either case the new supporters the Right picked up from the ruins of the Radical party raised its total vote far above the 3.4 million votes it scored in the 1933 elections.

57. Indalecio Prieto et al., *Documentos socialistas* (Madrid, 1935), pp. 20, 56–57, 145–47.

14: The Destruction of the "Bourgeois" Republic

Largo Caballero and the Beginnings of Peasant Revolution

The Popular Front government elected on 16 February 1936 bore little resemblance to the Azaña government of 1931–33. The dissimilarity was not caused primarily by the alliance with the Communist party. This latter group was still too small to be decisive and, in any case, had moderated to some degree its earlier policy of implacable hostility toward the Republic. The major difference—a difference that also clearly separated the new Spanish regime from the Popular Front government elected in France three months later—lay rather in the attitude of the revived Socialist movement. No longer was it the moderate reformist movement of old. Disillusioned by the failures of the first Republican era, maddened by its near destruction during the second, the dominant wing of Spanish socialism, headed by Largo Caballero, continued against Azaña the same perilous tactics of direct action it had employed against Lerroux and the "fascists" in 1934. For Largo Caballero, the electoral alliances to which he had agreed were only temporary: he sought permanent collaboration not with the progressive elements of the bourgeoisie, his associates of 1931–33, but with the Anarchosyndicalists and the Communists, the working-class groups he had formerly despised. Only upon occasion did the maximalist leader actually call for the overthrow of the bourgeois government,[1] but he constantly encouraged the workers to take over all of the functions of the state. This can be easily documented through the pronouncements of *El Obrero de la Tierra*—the FNTT organ, which remained under the direction of Ricardo Zabalza and his followers—and *Claridad*—the journal Largo founded when he was unable to win control of the editorial board of *El Socialista*.

In 1931–33 the Socialists had accepted the fact that technicians

1. For example, in the speeches quoted in *Claridad,* 19 March 1936, and *La Libertad,* 16 June 1936.

play an indispensable role in any nonrevolutionary agrarian reform. Only if the new settlers received technical counsel could they survive the difficult first years of cultivation; only if technicians chose the lands to be settled could the agricultural economy be saved from total disruption. Now the FNTT disregarded all technical considerations, claiming (with much reason) that, "It was because of these considerations that the land problem was not solved during the first two years of the Republic." [2] "If agrarian reform is to be carried out, the findings of the technicians must be replaced by the simple wisdom of the campesinos. No one knows better than they which lands should be worked, how they should be cultivated, or when the moment to till them has come." [3] Should the IRA reject the FNTT's demands and continue to employ technical help, the peasant federation threatened violence. In a message to Vázquez Humasqué, once again Director General of the Institute, it cried:

> Señor Vázquez Humasqué! Listen to what our comrades say! Their opinion can be condensed into this one rancor-filled cry! "The technicians SHOULD BE HANGED!" You can save the disloyal engineers, inspectors and department chiefs—saboteurs and incompetents all— from the gallows in only one way! BY THROWING THEM OUT! [4]

Nor was the FNTT willing to await parliamentary action and a new legal basis for the reform. The existing laws, "well interpreted," [5] provided a sufficient basis for the redistribution of land. "The truth is that there is no bad law when the people take the initiative and give it its proper interpretation." [6] Consequently:

> The working classes should not adopt a passive attitude, leaving to the government the task of converting its promises into deeds. They must press their initiative. . . . It is not enough to be vigilant. . . . It is not enough to urge the government forward. . . . All legislation requires as a precondition some overpowering reality which makes [its application] inescapable. . . . We must begin to think of giving the government of the Popular Front the foundation it needs in order to solve the great problems of the Spanish countryside. We must present it with the solution already made, so that it need only give its legal sanction through the appropriate decrees. . . . We must settle the agrarian problem by ourselves in such a way

2. *OT,* 7 March 1936.
3. Ibid.
4. *OT,* 14 March 1936.
5. *OT,* 1 March 1936. See also *Claridad's* invocation to the peasants to "self-interpret" laws in its 9 April 1936 edition.
6. *OT,* 11 April 1936.

that the Popular Front government need only give legal form to realities which the peasant organizations have already created.[7]

The peasants should themselves enter estates and seize them: "Señor Azaña talks of 'civilized methods.' These may be all right for those who eat three hot meals a day, but our campesinos do not figure in these ranks." [8] What were the peasants to do if the Guardia Civil resisted farm seizures? The FNTT's ultimate hope was to subvert the police forces or to replace them with a people's militia. *El Obrero de la Tierra* made impassioned pleas to the guardias to remember that they themselves were "sons of poor peasants . . . [and should] feel pity and affection toward the campesinos, knowing as they do the misery they suffer." [9] It also appealed "to all our Socialist, Communist and Syndicalist comrades" to form militias in order to protect themselves and the agrarian reform "from the fascists—and when we speak of fascists we refer to those of the CEDA as well as to those of the Falange." [10] In the immediate situation the FNTT did not wish for bloody encounters with the guardias but was not willing to abandon the policies that might lead to such confrontations. "These are our instructions to the farm workers [who have seized land]. AVOID CLASHES WITH THE FORCES OF PUBLIC ORDER. BUT NOT ONE STEP BACKWARD! HERE I AM AND HERE I STAY!" [11]

These words did not fall upon deaf ears. The tranquillity that had prevailed in the countryside since the failure of the FNTT harvest strike in the summer of 1934 was deceptive. Under the surface the Spanish peasantry had been driven by what Gil Robles once called the "suicidal egotism" of the owners into the most profound radicalization of its history. The process had begun with the decline in wages in 1934 but had accelerated rapidly in 1935, particularly after the defeat of Jiménez Fernández and other moderates cleared the way for a total removal of state protection from the peasantry. The abandonment of the yunteros; the expulsion of tenants; the rent increases that had been made possible by the "transitory provisions" of the Lease law; the fall of wages not only

7. *OT*, 29 February 1936.
8. *OT*, 28 March 1936.
9. *OT*, 21 March 1936.
10. *OT*, 28 March 1936. The FNTT claimed that village militias were necessary, because landowners had been forming "so-called hunters' societies" that terrorized the villages with the consent of the Guardia Civil. It seems to have toyed with the idea of having the militias federate regionally. See *OT*, 29 February, 11, 18 April 1936; *Claridad*, 15 April 1936; and the article by Ilya Erenburg in *Leviatan* (July 1936), pp. 13–16.
11. *OT*, 28 March 1936.

to their 1931 or 1932 levels but probably to below those that had prevailed under the monarchy—all were recent grievances that called for vengeance. So, too, was the slogan of *"Comed República!"* ("Go eat the Republic") with which many owners had taunted peasants who had begged for jobs in 1935, pleading that their families were hungry.

In addition, the very gods seemed to conspire against social harmony in the Spanish countryside. A nation whose greatest natural liability had always been too little rain now suddenly began to suffer from too much. The damage was not caused by savage storms or by hail. Rather, from December 1935 to the beginning of March 1936—precisely the period in which the political changeover was occurring—the southern two-thirds of Spain was subjected to steady, unceasing downpours. During these three and one-half months little work could be done in the fields, and when the rains finally stopped the soils were flooded and the grain crop was in large part lost.

The 1936 rains were by far the heaviest of the century, exceeding the previous record of 1916 by some 40 percent. Only Aragon, the northern Mediterranean, and the Cantabric Coast regions were not seriously affected. Enormous crop losses resulted. A Ministry of Agriculture survey dated 1 June estimated that the 1936 wheat harvest would be approximately 50 percent as large as that of 1935 (a normal year) in Estremadura, 53 percent as large in New Castile, 71 percent as large in Old Castile, 79 percent as large in Western Andalusia, and 85 percent as large in Eastern Andalusia. For the nation as a whole the crop was expected to be 74.4 percent of the 1935 harvest, or 73.4 percent of the average crop from 1931 to 1935.[12]

Every existing rural social conflict was aggravated by this climatological aberration. Throughout the late spring and early summer of 1936 labor-employing entrepreneurs were more than normally reluctant to accept worker demands for higher wages, since they themselves were faced with financial losses. Smaller tenants and owners desperately sought to ward off economic disaster by agitating for drastic rent reductions or new lands on which to farm. But the consequences were felt most immediately by the laborers. For three months they had been left with little work and, because of the crop losses, the future did not hold promise of more constant employment. The dimensions of their problem can be seen in official unemployment statistics. In 1935 agricultural unemployment had averaged 434,656. In the first six months of 1936—in part, at least, because of the rains—it rose by 20 percent to 522,079. By contrast, nonagricultural

12. On the rainfall, see *El Sol*, 4 March and 19 July 1936; on the expected crop losses, see Montojo Sureda, *Trigos y harinas*, pp. 45, 113.

unemployment during the same period increased by only 5 percent—from 262,335 to 274,262.[13]

This deterioration in the position of the peasantry combined with the great sense of hope engendered by the electoral victory of the Popular Front to produce an even more spectacular rise in union affiliation than that which had followed the proclamation of the Republic in 1931. We lack the statistics that would enable us to chart the chronological course or exact size of this increase, but it appears probable that the labor organizations had recovered their 1933 membership by mid-April and had far surpassed it by mid-July. The increase took place in most of Spain and seems to have resulted from the adhesion of small owners and tenants as well as from that of the day laborers. The Socialists were by no means the only group that benefited. In Guadalajara, for example, the Anarchosyndicalists were able for the first time to establish an important rural following. The province of Cuenca, previously nonpoliticized, quickly found itself divided into Anarchosyndicalist and Socialist camps.[14] The small Communist peasant union also made significant strides.[15]

Yet if social tension had become general, it continued to be most intense in the latifundio regions and was most effectively organized by the Socialists. Both these facts became evident during the first major confrontation between the peasantry and the new regime, the great wave of farm seizures of March 1936. The chain of events began on 3 March in Cenicientos, a small mountainous hamlet in Madrid, when its inhabitants marched out to occupy a pasture that they claimed had formerly constituted part of the village common lands. The neighboring village of Nombela quickly followed their example.[16] Within the next

13. Sindicato Vertical del Olivo, *El paro estacional campesino*, p. 3.

14. For CNT gains in Guadalajara, see *Campo Libre* during the spring of 1936. The Cuenca situation is best described in an unpublished report in the IRA Archives. The exceedingly poor crop expectations in New Castile (see above, n. 12) may help explain the sudden radicalization of both provinces. On the other hand labor recruitment was as successful in the northern, forestal belt of Cuenca as in its southern, cereal-growing region.

15. The Communists in 1936 began to seek peasant support much more actively than before. For example, on 8 June, they began publication of a new weekly, *La Voz del Campo*, which was devoted exclusively to rural affairs. This must have represented as substantial investment, as the quality of the photographs and paper used, as well as the sophistication of the writing, was far superior to that of *El Obrero de la Tierra* and most other working class newspapers, including those that the Communists themselves had published prior to 1936.

16. *OT*, 14 March 1936. It should be noted that the Azaña government maintained a severe censorship on all organs of information throughout 1936, thus making it impossible to reconstruct events, whether farm seizures, strikes, or demonstrations, with exactitude.

few days land was also seized in several villages of Salamanca and Toledo.[17] On 17 March numerous farm invasions took place in the irrigated *huerta* of Murcia. On the eighteenth the province of Madrid once more became the center of activity as the villagers of El Tiemblo reclaimed "former common lands." [18]

Thus far the farm invasions seemed to have resulted primarily from spontaneous local action and occurred either outside the latifundio belt or in peripheral latifundio provinces. The Azaña government desperately sought to prevent the invasions from spreading, particularly to Estremadura, whose yunteros had been converted by their severe fluctuations in fortune into the most highly politicized peasant group in Spain. On 3 March, even before news of Cenicientos had reached him, Mariano Ruiz Funes, the new Left Republican Minister of Agriculture, issued a decree inviting the yunteros who had been evicted in 1935 to petition for a return of their lands.[19] On the fifth he ordered the IRA to expedite the petitions within thirty days.[20] On the twelfth, during a whirlwind tour of Badajoz and Caceres, he changed the time limit and promised that "40,000 yunteros will be settled within a week." [21] On the fourteenth he dropped the exemption of pasture lands that had restricted the application of the earlier edicts.[22] On 20 March, justifying himself under the social utility clause of the 1935 Agrarian Reform Law, he eliminated all other exemptions and authorized the IRA to occupy immediately any farm anywhere in Spain if it seemed socially necessary.[23]

These efforts all proved vain. Even before the Cenicientos invasion, the FNTT had begun to organize for 15 March a nationwide demonstration to demand the immediate redistribution of land. After a personal confrontation between Zabalza and Azaña, it backed down to the extent of calling off the demonstration.[24] But on 20 March, when Ruiz Funes's

17. Burnett Bolloten's superb study, *The Grand Camouflage* (London, 1961), p. 21, is probably mistaken, however, in accepting a Communist newspaper estimate that land seizures occurred in ninety villages in Salamanca. A movement of this scope would have resulted in government action and would have been mentioned in other journals, despite the censorship.

18. *El Debate*, 18 March 1936; *OT*, 4 April 1936.

19. Ministry of Agriculture decree of 3 March 1936. The various decrees and orders mentioned in the text are reproduced in the *BIRAs* of 1936.

20. IRA Order of 5 March 1936.

21. *El Debate*, 11, 12 March 1936.

22. Ministry of Agriculture decree of 14 March 1936.

23. Ministry of Agriculture decree of 20 March 1936. The critical difference between the "social utility" clause in this decree and in the 1935 law, aside from the radical temperament of the government that would apply it, was that in the decree prior compensation was not to be paid expropriated owners.

24. *OT*, 1–15 March 1936; *El Sol* and *El Debate*, 9–13 March 1936.

self-imposed deadline had passed with only three thousand yunteros settled, the FNTT authorized its Badajoz Federation to launch a massive assault on farms throughout the province. At 5:00 on the morning of 25 March some sixty thousand peasants—more than half of the adult male rural population of Badajoz—marched upon some three thousand previously selected farms, cried "*Viva la República!*" marked out the limits of the areas they were to cultivate, and began to plow.[25] The precision and perfect order with which this gigantic mass of people acted were impressive. *Claridad* joyfully exclaimed:

> When historians of the future look for the event which marked the great turning point in the history of Spain, some of them will certainly point to our Estremadura, where the first mass occupation of lands occurred. . . . Even if they succeed in ousting the Estremenian peasant from all of the lands he has occupied and is now working, historical conditions can never again be the same.[26]

As the FNTT expected, Azaña could do nothing against so overwhelming a popular movement. Troops were rushed into the province and, at one point, were apparently even authorized to fire upon the peasants if it proved necessary in order to evict them. In several villages the peasants were frightened by this show of force, as well as by the numerous arrests that accompanied it, and evacuated the land. But so little real headway was made that on 28 March the government agreed to release the prisoners and to legalize the seizures. On 30 March the troops were withdrawn, whereupon many of the peasants who had been frightened off the land a few days earlier once more invaded the farms to reclaim their plots.[27] The tactics of the FNTT could not have been more successful. By a single decisive act the peasants had occupied far more land than had been granted to them in the previous five years.

The Badajoz invasions did not, however, set off a new chain reaction of farm occupations. To judge from the heavily censored press, a few isolated farm seizures occurred in April, but there were no further massive assaults upon the land. This was in great part due to the end of

25. The most complete report of the Badajoz invasions appears in *OT*, 4 April 1936. This issue, published in defiance of the censorship, apparently was seized before it could be distributed in Spain. I have seen a copy in the U.S. Department of Agriculture library in Washington, D.C. Other sources sometimes mention eighty thousand invaders, but this figure seems too large.

26. *Claridad*, 7 April 1936.

27. Since Spanish papers were silenced, the best source for the aftermath of the Badajoz invasions is *La Nación* (Buenos Aires), 27–31 March 1936. This journal estimates that twenty thousand peasants reinvaded farms after the troop withdrawal, but, again, the estimate may be too high.

the spring plowing season, which removed the temptation to stake out claims on uncultivated land. After a month of relative tranquillity, however, a new source of conflict arose in connection with the signing of the grain harvest contracts. Here, too, the Azaña government had tried to ward off trouble by concessions to the peasants. Although the términos municipales law as such was not revived, its substance was granted in that the turno riguroso, demanded by the Socialists since 1933, was made obligatory.[28] The municipal judges and other state functionaries who had been appointed presidents of the mixed juries during the conservative biennium were dismissed in favor of persons more favorably disposed toward the workers.[29] Exceedingly heavy fines were levied against owners who violated the labor contracts.[30]

Once more the conciliatory gestures of the state proved vain as Spain entered into the most severe strike wave in its history. In the two and one-half months between 1 May and the outbreak of the Civil War on 18 July, the Ministry of Labor recorded 192 agricultural strikes, as many as during the whole of 1932 and almost half as many as during that entire year of trouble, 1933.[31] The scale of the strikes was considerably greater than it had been previously. Although there were relatively few provincial walkouts, the FNTT and the CNT both launched frequent country- or district-wide efforts. The isolation of the countryside from the city also began to be overcome as urban and rural strikers lent each other support. Finally, in several instances Socialist, Anarchosyndicalist, and Communist unions were able to act in unison, something which would have been impossible three years earlier.[32] The new dimensions these changes gave to the labor struggle were best revealed in Malaga during the first two weeks of June. A province-wide peasant strike, called mostly under CNT auspices on 2 June, quickly snowballed as the FNTT and Communist locals supported it and the industrial, construction, and dock workers of the provincial capital and of Antequera went out on

28. Ministry of Labor decree of 27 March 1936.

29. Personnel changes probably occurred from the February elections onward. The universal unseating of the 1935 jury presidents however, was not authorized until a Ministry of Labor decree of 30 May 1936.

30. For example, owners in Seville were fined from 500 to 2,000 pesetas, the equivalent of from 42 to 168 times the average daily wage paid to field hands.

31. Ministerio de Trabajo, *Boletines* for each month. Industrial strikes apparently increased even more rapidly than agricultural. From 1 May to 17 July 1936 there were 719 industrial strikes, more than in the whole of any previous year.

32. The best, though still very incomplete, sources on the strikes are the "Social Conflicts" columns of such newspapers as *El Sol, El Debate,* and *ABC.* On the cooperation between UGT and Communist locals, see also Bruno Minlos, *Campesinos de España,* p. 3.

sympathy strikes. At some points in the conflict as many as 100,000 peasants and urban workers seem to have been involved—by far the largest turnout for any rural-inspired strike in Spanish history, except for the June 1934 national walkout of the FNTT.[33]

The frequency and intensity of rural strikes were such that even the Anarchosyndicalist journal, *Solidaridad Obrera,* was driven to remind its readers that strikes were "double-edged weapons which sometimes turn against those who use them." [34] For the first time under the Republic, the old conservative lament that strikes were seriously damaging agricultural output seems to have been borne out by the facts. In several regions the struggle over work contracts was so prolonged that parts of the wheat and barley harvests were lost.[35] Strike demands also posed a longer-range threat to production. The mixed juries for the most part set wages at from eleven to thirteen pesetas for harvest labor.[36] This meant more than a doubling of 1935 wages and an increase of some 20 percent over the pay scales of 1933, a year in which the profit squeeze on producers was so great that it contributed to the disintegration and electoral defeat of the Azaña coalition.[37] The increase in labor costs, moreover, was not confined to the payment of higher wages. Strikers also successfully demanded the introduction of structural reforms that would solve the problem of unemployment. However just they may have been, the unemployment funds and the agreements to hire permanently a certain number of workers which farm managers were forced to accept added considerably to their expenses.[38]

33. *El Sol* and *El Debate,* 2–16 June 1936.

34. Quoted in *El Sol,* 24, 25 June 1936. Another indication of the extent of the strikes was provided by Bagaría in *El Sol,* 28 June 1936. This famous cartoonist, playing upon the constitutional definition ("a Republic of workers of all classes"), asked whether it would not "have been better to call the new regime a Republic of workers on strike."

35. For the testimony of a liberal source, which had modified its semi-conservative stance of late 1933 and 1934 and had since 1935 once again become usually sympathetic to the workers' demands on this question, see *El Sol,* 23, 27 June and 3, 9 July 1936.

36. Compiled mostly from press reports, since the *Boletin* of the Ministry of Labor did not reprint the agreements reached in the mixed juries during this period. Some wage demands went as high as seventeen pesetas, but these were exceptional.

37. See above, pp. 263–65.

38. For example, in Cadiz the CNT forced the owners to hire a worker permanently for every twenty hectares farmed. The plan was operative in the entire province (*El Debate,* 19 June 1936). In Almendralejo (Badajoz) owners agreed to sponsor a permanent unemployment fund after a sixteen-day FNTT harvest strike (*Claridad,* 11, and 17 June 1936; *El Debate,* 12 June 1936). A similar arrangement had been worked out earlier in another Badajoz town, Fuente de Cantos (*El Sol,* 20 March 1936).

Production costs were further increased by a number of other factors not directly related to strike demands. The obligation to hire labor according to the turno riguroso meant that totally inexperienced and unwilling workers had to be accepted from the local employment offices. This was a major calamity, since the registers of these offices were crammed with the unemployed of every imaginable field of economic activity, who had signed up as harvest laborers since they could be sure of getting a job in agriculture if they could only wait until their turn came up.[39] The quality of work seems also to have been affected by slowdown agreements among the workers. By June both the liberal press and government officials had accepted as just the owners' demands that wage concessions be made conditional on the fulfillment of minimal standards of output.[40] Finally, labor costs were significantly raised by the increasing misuse of the *alojamiento* principle, either on the part of workers themselves who invaded farms in gangs and forced owners to grant them employment, or by harassed local officials who sought to still labor unrest by assigning farm managers far more workers than they needed.[41] Taken together with wage raises and the structural reforms intended to reduce unemployment, these changes in the normal patterns of labor relations meant that the real rise in labor costs over 1933 was not some 20 percent, as the difference in pay scales would suggest, but more on the order of 50 or 60 percent. The contrast wth 1935 was of course still greater. It would seem safe to estimate that labor costs almost tripled during the first few months of Popular Front rule.

The full extent of the social tension that gripped the Spanish countryside in the spring and early summer of 1936 cannot be understood, however, if we confine our discussion to organized land seizures and strikes. Just as the electoral victory of the Center-Right in 1933 had permitted the established classes to revenge themselves upon the workers in hundreds of small ways, most of them in defiance of the law, so, too, the

39. The fact that so many industrial and service workers sought rural jobs is, of course, another explanation for the disproportionately high 1936 increase in officially recorded agricultural unemployment mentioned earlier. The articles of Pedro Pedromo in *El Sol*, 15–19 July 1936, greatly stress the negative consequences of the turno on the economy of Badajoz

40. See particularly *El Sol*, 26, 30 June 1936.

41. On the alojamiento principle, which obliged owners to employ extra workers during labor crises, see above, pp. 102–03. The principle had also been misused during the trienio bolchevista as gangs of laborers intimidated farm managers to force them to grant work (Díaz del Moral, p. 216), but at that time its misuse was confined to the province of Cordova, lasted only "some weeks," and did not enjoy the support of municipal officials. Consequently, the comparisons sometimes made between the two periods are misleading.

victory of the Popular Front gave the workers license to impose their will with impunity. The major difference was that whereas the continued existence of rural labor unions and the ambivalence of the Center governments prior to the October Revolution had provided a period of transition before complete owner dominance could be established, the change in climate of rural life in 1936 was almost immediate. All the excesses that had begun to appear toward the end of the first Azaña era found expression on a larger scale. Intimidation of all those who did not belong to the labor unions seems to have become the order of the day. Perhaps the most constant source of trouble was the gangs of workers who entered farms to force their managers to grant work.[42] The stealing of animals and crops, and the cutting of trees for firewood or for lumber also became common, although there was no repetition of the farm burnings of the autumn of 1933. The anticlericalism of the first Azaña era reappeared in far more acute form. Priests were harassed unmercifully; churchgoers were made to feel that it was unsafe to attend Mass.[43] Nor did the Popular Front's decision to unseat all conservatively oriented municipal governments end the labor unions' struggle for local political dominance, since the unions considered most of the progressive Republican ayuntamientos that were appointed as too reactionary to be accepted.[44] Because of these pressures, the life of the established classes in many ways became as insecure as had been that of the Socialist and Anarchosyndicalist militants in late 1934 and 1935. They enjoyed only one advantage: sufficient financial reserves to enable them to abandon their homes and farms and seek refuge in the cities. This option they apparently exercised by the thousands.[45]

42. The Agrarian deputy, José María Cid, made these self-alojamientos the chief theme of his important Cortes speech on "The Anarchical Situation in the Countryside" (D.S. 54, 1 July 1936, pp. 1743–53).

43. This, at least, was the testimony of dozens of former village residents with whom I talked in Madrid in 1961–62. There is no more reason to doubt its validity than there is to question the equally undocumented leftist assertion that owners generally adopted the brutal and mindless slogan of "Go eat the Republic!" when dealing with hungry workers in 1935. The tragedy of Spain after the October Revolution was that neither side showed generosity in triumph.

44. The dissolution of perhaps half the ayuntamientos in Spain, both those elected in 1933 and those appointed during the conservative biennium, was one of the first acts of the Popular Front. On the continued potential for conflict, see El Sol, 26 February 1936.

45. Personal testimony and Cid's Cortes speech (D.S. 54, 1 July 1936, p. 1745).

Azaña and Prieto Struggle to Reestablish Control

The Popular Front government, composed—because of the abstention of the Socialists and Communists—entirely of bourgeois Republicans who did not share the revolutionary temperament of the working classes, had little choice but to give way before this strong tide of protest. The use of the coercive powers of the state to check the proletariat might have been effective had it been applied against the small scale disturbances that occurred before the Badajoz farm invasions of 25 March and the great strike wave that swept the nation from late April onwards. Once the proletariat had been allowed to reorganize itself and develop a sense of self-confidence, however, massive repression of the type that would by then have become necessary was politically impossible. Azaña and his followers had come to power largely on the basis of the working-class vote and depended for their Cortes majority on the Largo Caballero Socialists. A policy of repression would also carry the risk of delivering power once more to the Right, which had proven that it opposed not only the agrarian, but all reform. Moreover, Azaña had reason to hope that if he rapidly fulfilled some of the workers' demands, the mass agitation might end and a calm be restored within which the democratic Republic of 1931–33 might be fully revived. In his gamble he counted heavily on the support of Indalecio Prieto, who had broken with Largo Caballero and sought to bring the Socialists back into the Republican fold. Prieto did not enjoy nearly so much influence over the masses, or even upon the local committees of the PSOE, as did the maximalist leader. Nevertheless, he controlled a majority on the Executive Committee of the Socialist party, commanded the allegiance of perhaps half the Socialist parliamentary deputies, and controlled the official party organ, *El Socialista*. If Azaña opted for repression Prieto would lose all chance of using these positions of strength to steal away some of Largo Caballero's present following, particularly in the UGT. If concessions were allowed it was possible that the indispensable basis of the first Azaña government, the restraint exercised by the Socialists over the workers, might be restored.

From the very first, then, Azaña's new government worked frantically to satisfy working-class grievances. The desperate measures taken to prevent the spread of farm invasions to Estremadura have already been noted, as have the imposition of the turno riguroso and the changes made in the mixed juries. The Institute of Agrarian Reform was also drastically reorganized. All the powers of the Executive Council were transferred to the Director General, who was henceforth able to act in a "dictatorial" fashion.[46] A new legislative basis for reform began to be laid on 19 April, three weeks after the Cortes convened, when Ruiz Funes submitted not one but five agrarian bills for parliamentary approval. The most important of these reduced (by from 16.6 percent to 62.5 percent, depending on the type of land) the maximum property limits that had been allowed under the 1932 Agrarian Reform Law, restored compensation to more or less what it had been during the first Azaña era, and permitted the state full freedom to seize any farm for reasons of social utility. The scope of land redistribution was also vastly enlarged by a bill that allowed municipalities to recover their lost common lands under much easier conditions than those outlined in Domingo's unsuccessful proposal of 1933.[47] At the beginning of May two further measures were added to the Cortes agenda. One voided the 1935 general lease law in favor of legislation similar to that which Domingo had sponsored in 1933.[48] The second embodied the principle of land reform through taxation which had been rejected by the Azaña government in 1931 and subjected landowners to graduated surtaxes of over 100 percent when their assessed incomes exceeded approximately twenty thousand pesetas.[49]

In contrast to the first Azaña era, these measures were energetically pushed forward once they had been introduced. Ruiz Funes spent much of his time in the Cortes defending his proposals from attacks from the Left and the Right. On the whole he was successful. His bill to restore land to all tenant farmers who had been evicted during the conservative biennium was passed on 2 June.[50] A radicalized version of the 1932 Agrarian Reform Law, which was to serve as a temporary basis for

46. Ministry of Agriculture decree of 3 March 1936. *El Debate,* 6 March 1936, first characterized the Director General's new powers as "dictatorial," but Vázquez Humasqué also employed the term (*BIRA* [June 1936], p. 43).

47. The texts of these and the other three bills, to be mentioned later, appear in *D.S.* 19, 17 April 1936, apps. 5–9.

48. *D.S.* 22, 29 April 1936, app. 1.

49. *D.S.* 26, 7 May 1936, app. 18. The proposed surtax rose from 25 percent on assessed incomes of approximately 6,500 pesetas, to 50 percent on 10,000, to 100 percent on 20,000, to 125 percent on 70,000, and to 150 percent on those over 200,000. Though the bill was radical in comparison to past proposals and in its attempt to place an added burden on the now exceedingly hard-pressed owners, the very slow graduation of rates on incomes of more than 20,000 pesetas lessened its effectiveness. Since the tax that was actually paid was approximately one-seventh of the assessed income, and since this income in turn oscillated between one-half and one-fourth real income, most owners would end up paying no more than a total of 10 to 12 percent of their gross income, or approximately 20 to 25 percent of their net earnings (see app. B).

50. *D.S.* 38, 2 June 1936, app. 9

action until the new permanent measure described above could be passed, received parliamentary approval on 11 June.[51] The potentially revolutionary bill for the recovery of the common lands formed the topic for debate during the last eight Cortes sessions prior to the outbreak of the Civil War.[52] The important plan for a graduated agricultural surtax was presented for discussion during the last sitting of the parliament.[53]

Nor were the activities of the Institute of Agrarian Reform suspended while the government awaited the outcome of the parliamentary debates. As can be seen in Table 36, the pace of land redistribution established

TABLE 36   SETTLEMENTS UNDER POPULAR FRONT: CHRONOLOGICAL ANALYSIS

	Peasants Settled	Area Occupied (hectares)
March	72,428	249,616
April	21,789	150,490
May	5,940	41,921
June	3,855	55,282
July	6,909	74,746
Totals	110,921	572,055

SOURCE: *BIRA* (March–July 1936).

NOTE: Of the July totals, 40,166 hectares were expropriated before July 17 and 34,580 after. Since the IRA seems to have planned the latter occupations prior to the outbreak of the Civil War, I have included them in this table. The slight discrepancy between the total settlements given here and in Table 37 reflects discrepancies in the *BIRA* data. See nn. 54–56 for further information.

in March and April was not maintained, but this reflected the end of unauthorized peasant farm invasions which were subsequently legalized, not a return of the IRA to its former sluggishness. The monthly average of almost five thousand peasants settled and fifty thousand hectares occupied during May and June was considerable, given the fact that the planting season had passed. In July, as the harvest was ending and the planting season approached once more, the IRA again began to step up the rate of land transfer, this time apparently on its own initiative, without the immediate pressure of de facto peasant farm seizures.

Taking the period as a whole, far more land was redistributed from March to July than in the entire previous history of the Republic. As is shown in Table 37, settlements had been made in almost all of the latifundio provinces and were beginning in other parts of Spain as well.

51. *D.S.* 43, 11 June 1936, app. 7.
52. *D.S.* 52–60, 26 June–10 July 1936.
53. *D.S.* 60, 10 July 1936, app. 8.

TABLE 37   SETTLEMENTS UNDER POPULAR FRONT: PROVINCIAL ANALYSIS

	Peasants Settled	Area Occupied (hectares)
Estremadura	*83,767*	*297,165*
Badajoz	49,809	125,331
Caceres	31,388	113,446
Salamanca	2,570	58,388
La Mancha	*18,166*	*174,945*
Toledo	10,153	145,954
Ciudad Real	6,219	26,224
Albacete	1,794	2,767
Andalusia	*11,733*	*94,309*
Cordoba	5,300	34,935
Seville	2,070	19,702
Huelva	1,849	7,701
Cadiz	1,626	24,358
Jaen	693	8,271
Granada	195	1,342
Other Provinces	*677*	*6,771*
Saragossa	546	5,455
Madrid	81	808
Avila	50	508
National Totals	114,343	573,190

SOURCE: *BIRA* (March–July 1936).

In two provinces, Badajoz and Caceres, approximately one-third of the adult male rural populations received some land.[54] Moreover, the official IRA figures used in compiling the table probably significantly understate the amount of land which was actually redistributed. For example, the daily press mentioned in July a number of land settlements, particularly in Albacete, Jaen, Madrid, and Zamora, that were not included in the IRA reports. Also, in a speech at Valencia, Ruiz Funes stated that as of 19 June, 192,183 peasants had been settled on 755,888 hectares. If the Minister of Agriculture's figures were correct (and there is no reason to doubt them), the true extent of settlements by the outbreak of the Civil War must have been almost twice that reported in Table 37.[54]

The great question that must forever perplex students of modern Spain is whether Azaña's gamble would have succeeded if the military insurrection of 18 July had been postponed. Would the energetic agrarian reform he instituted have calmed the peasantry without unduly injuring

54. For Ruiz Funes's speech see *El Sol*, 23 June 1936. In compiling Tables 36 and 37 I have relied on the IRA statistics despite their obvious inadequacy because they alone permit us to establish some idea of the rhythm and provincial distribution of the settlements.

other classes? A variety of evidence can be cited to support the argument that it would have. First, the government seemed gradually to be re-establishing its control over the redistribution of land. The massive farm invasions of March did not recur; nor was there any peasant group in Spain which possessed the tools, animals, experience, and organization that had enabled the yunteros of Estremadura to triumph so easily. The IRA was able to maintain a technically manageable rate of settle-ment from May onward. The practice of seizing farms in their entirety, which had characterized the peasant occupations of March, was replaced by the expropriation of small portions of each farm, the loss of which would not necessarily prevent the existing farm operators from con-tinuing to cultivate.[55] The plots of land granted to the settlers were also economically more viable. As can be seen in Table 36, the farm occupa-tions of March and April had left an average of only about four hectares for each settler. From May on, this average rose to almost ten hectares.[56]

There were also indications that the Largo Caballero Socialists might prove less revolutionary in their deeds than in their rhetoric and that, even if they were to continue on a revolutionary path, they would not be able either to carry the entire Socialist movement with them or to achieve the firm alliance with the Anarchosyndicalists which was necessary for working-class victory. For example, no real evidence has ever been presented that any of the working-class groups had worked out a specific plan of revolt, and the Socialists frequently allowed to pass events—such as the Guardia Civil massacre of the peasants of Yeste (Albacete)[57]—which might have been used to increase revolutionary

55. This encouraging change in policy should not be overstressed, however, since the *BIRA* data are especially inexact, and frequently contradictory, on this point.

56. *BIRA* (March–July 1936). In July only the number of settlers was re-ported, but I assumed that the trend of May and June continued and that each received ten hectares. Ruiz Funes's Valencia speech also suggests that the plots granted to settlers increased in size, although he gives much smaller average-size figures than those reported in *BIRA*. Thus he states that 91,919 yunteros (all of whom had pre-sumably been settled in March or April) received 239,198 hectares, for an average of 2.6 hectares, whereas 100,264 "heads of families" (most of them presumably settled after April) received 523,690 hectares for an average of 5.2 hectares. It is difficult to see how settlers could have survived on such small plots without sup-plementary wage labor or sharecropping, both of which sources of income would be more difficult to obtain given the fear that must have gripped the owners and the reduction in the amounts of land they had at their disposal. In short, as will soon be seen in greater detail, the settlements made were only the first stage of a wider battle, not a full solution of the problems of the settlers who received land.

57. The massacre at Socialist-dominated Yeste might easily have been turned into a second Casas Viejas had the Caballeristas so willed. The clash began when a twenty-five man Guardia Civil detachment tried to prevent a large group of peas-

fervor to the breaking point. The massive strike of early June in the province of Malaga ended with a series of bloody street clashes between UGT and CNT militants in the provincial capital.[58] A few weeks later, in the critically important construction and maintenance workers' strike of Madrid, the UGT abandoned its CNT allies and voted to accept arbitration, apparently in the fear that continuation of the month-long strike had become too risky.[59] At about the same time, in early July, the liberal journal *El Sol*, which had been extremely pessimistic about the ability of the moderate Socialists to contain the maximalists, suddenly saw in the results of two intraparty elections reason to hope that the tide had been turned.[60]

As to the strenuous efforts of the Left Republican cabinet to safeguard the interests of other social classes while carrying forth its concessions to the workers, there can be no doubt. Its acceptance of the principle of tying rural wage increases to the fulfillment of minimal work standards was an important step toward undoing the economically catastrophic consequences of the turno riguroso and the slowdown agreements of the workers. The rationalization of land redistribution was a still more significant measure of economic reconstruction. And if the government's agrarian reform program was far more radical than anything that had preceded it, it was also more intelligently conceived and would have hurt fewer owners. For example, maximum property limits were lowered so as to encompass some of the large farms that had previously remained outside the scope of the reform, but the ruedo clause, which had needlessly threatened thousands of small and medium proprietors, was dropped. Compensation terms for large owners were very harsh, but small owners who were expropriated would be paid almost the full market

---

ants from cutting down trees on privately owned land that had once been municipal commons. A peasant apparently stabbed one of the guardias, whose colleagues thereupon went on a rampage, killing seventeen peasants and wounding fifteen others. Casualties among the guardias were one killed and fourteen wounded. (*El Sol*, 6 June 1936; *OT*, 6, 13 June 1936). It should be noted that Yeste was exceptional. Usually the police followed orders not to fire and the peasants temporarily retreated (only to filter back later) whenever confronted by a show of force. In consequence there seems to have been less bloodshed in the countryside in 1936 than one would expect, given the turmoil of the times. Nevertheless, Yeste alone cost more lives than the FNTT's 1934 national harvest strike.

58. *El Sol*, 11–13 June 1936.

59. Jackson, pp. 220–21, lays special emphasis on this point, and *Claridad* did indeed strongly urge UGT members to return to work. It should be noted, however, that the government-sponsored settlement was so unusually favorable to the workers that Largo Caballero can scarcely be thought to have sacrificed their interests for the sake of Republican unity.

60. *El Sol*, 2, 8 July 1936.

value of their lands.[61] The government also reduced some of the sources of ideological opposition among the middle classes by rejecting the principle of confiscation, except for the Sanjurjo rebels; by allowing settlers to purchase the land they received if they so wished rather than insisting that it remain the property of the state; and by actively pursuing an access to the property right law.[62]

An equally imposing list of reasons, however, suggest that Azaña would have failed. If Largo Caballero was indeed moderating his position, he was doing so in an extremely inconsistent way. His rhetoric remained violent, and his closest collaborators vaunted themselves that "We Spanish Socialists are now more advanced, more communistic, than the Communist party." [63] He accepted the government's extremely favorable settlement of the Madrid construction strike but rejected its attempt to tie rural wage increases to the fulfillment of minimal work standards, as well as the goal of 100,000 peasant settlers annually which the Left Republicans advanced as a basis for compromise.[64] The intraparty electoral victories of the Prietistas were dismissed by the Caballeristas as the result of fraudulent counting of votes by the Socialist party's National Committee.[65] Even had the Caballeristas proved wrong and suffered another defeat in the party congress scheduled for October, this probably would not have meant that the Socialist movement as a whole would have returned to its former policy of collaboration with the Left Republicans. Caballero's strength was far greater in the UGT than in the PSOE, and the split between him and Prieto had become so deep that he would probably have preferred a party schism to surrender. In short,

61. The compensation provisions of Ruiz Funes's proposed agrarian reform law are too complicated to be discussed here, but they centered upon the assignment of relatively equitable land valuations that were thereupon reduced by from 25 percent to 40 percent on medium and large, but not on small, properties.

62. This is not, of course, to say that these features of Ruiz Funes's agrarian bills would have survived the opposition of the Caballeristas and the Communists in the Cortes. For example, the cabinet apparently did not want to restore the controversial provision calling for confiscation of grande property (such confiscation was not mentioned in any of the measures submitted, to the surprised delight of the Catholic and conservative press), but began to change course under pressure by mid-June.

63. Luís Araquistáin, in an interview with The New York Times, 26 June 1936.

64. On the question of minimal work standards, see El Sol, 26, 27, 30 June 1936. The goal of 100,000 settlers annually was most specifically enunciated by Vázquez Humasqué in a speech of May 23 (reprinted in BIRA [July 1936] pp. 42–44). Similar statements of governmental intentions by Ruiz Funes are reported in El Sol, 14 May and 9 June 1936. By contrast, the Caballerista National Committee of the FNTT called for the resettlement of all lands by October and the expenditure of one billion pesetas (some 22 percent of the national budget) on agrarian reform and unemployment relief (OT, 18 April 1936).

65. See Claridad, 2–8 July 1936.

the evidence concerning Caballero's intentions and his ability to secure a stronger institutional base from which to implement them is at best mixed. It is quite clear that he had no specific plan of revolution but equally clear that he was not prepared to abandon the maximalism that had wreaked havoc on the Republic.

The economic situation, in the countryside at least, was even less promising. The enormous rise in labor costs and continuous social unrest had begun to make the traditional system of agriculture impossible. For the first time, large numbers of farm managers seem to have been driven to the point of actually preparing to abandon cultivation.[66] Those who did continue to farm could probably have done so only by refusing to hire all but the most indispensable outside labor. Both responses would inevitably have led to a further decrease in production and increase in unemployment, which in turn would have produced new pressure for still more massive land seizures and still more aggressive application of alojamientos. This process had already begun to unfold during late June and July when the Caballerista and Communist press launched their campaign for the immediate seizure of lands belonging to the relatively few owners who were prepared to lose an entire year's harvest rather than pay the cost of collecting it.[67] By the fall the conflict would have become far graver, since many owners who were willing to harvest crops that were already standing would have refused to make the new investment of again plowing and sowing their lands. Under these circumstances it is difficult to imagine how a new and far greater wave of farm invasions could have been prevented, even though there were no peasants who were so well organized as the yunteros of Estremadura had been.

The rapid collapse of the traditional system of agriculture did not mean that a viable new system would replace it. Massive land transfers were in themselves incapable of restoring social or economic stability. This was proven by the experience of Badajoz, in which at least one-

66. For landowner threats to abandon cultivation, see *El Sol*, 26, 30 June; 4, 5, 15 July 1936. It is of course impossible to determine the extent to which these threats were seriously meant. Both their tone, which, in contrast to 1931–33 was more pleading than it was arrogant, and the fact that the government itself regarded labor costs as exorbitant (see *El Sol*, 10, 14, 30 June 1936) suggest that continued cultivation had indeed become uneconomical.

67. The Caballerista-Communist campaign centered around the old theme that the owners were abandoning cultivation in order to sabotage the Republic. This seems unlikely, since the owners were very badly organized (most of the pressure groups created in 1931–33 seem to have disintegrated during the conservative biennium, when they were no longer essential to defend owner interests) and because of the enormous economic loss that abandonment of a standing harvest implied (all previous campaigns of resistance by the owners had been mounted during the fall or spring plowing seasons, not during harvest).

third of the rural population had received land in March and April [68] but which seems to have been in complete chaos on the eve of the Civil War. Thousands of peasants wandered around the province in a futile search for jobs; farm managers of any importance continued to be subjected to repeated alojamientos, and small owners lived in constant fear that they, too, would become victims of the workers' aggression as the definition of the words "bourgeois" and "fascist" expanded to include property of every size. [69]

The catastrophic conditions in Badajoz resulted to an extent from the winter rains and the harvest strikes, both of which had been especially severe in that province. The late date at which the settlers had taken over their lands was also important. More fundamental, however, was the fact that without state credit even the relatively self-sufficient yunteros were unable to farm the lands they had seized. Credit, which was as much a key to successful reform as land itself, was precisely what the Left Republican government could not have provided if it acquiesced to settlements on the scale the Caballeristas were demanding and which the steadily deteriorating economic situation seemed to require. The resources of the Spanish state were barely compatible with the announced goals of paying compensation to the expropriated owners and settling 100,000 peasants annually. [70] Were more settlers than this to receive land, the moderating provisions of the agrarian legislation before the Cortes, together with the attempts of the IRA to provide technical guidance and

68. The active rural male population of Badajoz numbered approximately 150,-000. Since this figure included owners, well over one-third of the rural proletariat received land even if the minimal estimate of 50,000 settlers reported in *BIRA* (see Table 37) is used. If Ruiz Funes's much higher estimate is accurate, then probably more than half of all Badajoz workers and tenants received some land.

69. Based on the eyewitness reports of Pedro Pedromo in *El Sol*, 15–19 July 1936. It should be stressed that *El Sol*, as objective a source as we have for these troubled times, was deeply preoccupied by the fate of the small owners and tenants, whom it considered to have been more severely injured by the social and economic crisis than were the large holders themselves (see particularly the issues of 13 and 19 June and 3 July 1936).

70. Assuming that each settler would receive only five hectares, that the compensation rates envisaged in the new agrarian law would work out to 500 pesetas a hectare (the equivalent of some 42 days of harvest wages and about half of what most non-working class sources estimated that the land was really worth), and that each settler could successfully start cultivation with credits of 1,500 pesetas (instead of the 3,000 pesetas considered necessary by all observers in 1931–33), the cost of successfully settling 100,000 peasants would have come to some 400 million pesetas annually, an absolute maximum for the impoverished Spanish state. In practice, of course, compensation would have had to have been abandoned, and credits to the settlers could not have exceeded by much the 338 peseta average that Ruiz Funes announced had been paid to the 1936 settlers as of 19 June.

financial help to the colonists, would have become totally meaningless. The Left Republicans would have been forced to preside over a revolutionary confiscation of lands, which, because it was incapable by itself of solving the social and economic problems of rural Spain, could only have resulted in further turmoil whose consequences they would not have been able to control.

Two other factors must also be taken into account in judging the chances for success of Azaña's policy of conciliation. First, because of the excessive spring rains the 1936 wheat harvest was by far the worst in the history of the Republic. In June the Ministry of Agriculture forecast a crop of only 3.2 million metric tons, or 73.4 percent of the average crop from 1931 to 1935.[71] This might be a blessing to the large landowners and merchants who had built up stocks in 1934 and 1935 that they could now sell at high prices, but it was a catastrophe for the small owners and tenants who could not hope to recoup the loss that so great a drop in their production represented through the higher prices that would be paid for the small quantities they did harvest. Thus a new source of social dissension, which because of the importance of wheat would have ramifications in every aspect of the economy, was added to the long list we have already mentioned. Second, although Caballero's maximalism had temporarily diverted attention from the Anarchosyndicalists, this group was rapidly increasing its strength and had in no way softened its ideological opposition to the Republic. Given its repeated recourse to revolution in 1931–33, when circumstances were much less favorable, it is difficult to believe that the CNT-FAI could long have abstained from a new insurrectionary effort.[72]

71. Montojo Sureda, *Trigos y harinas,* pp. 43, 113. The economic implications of so great a drop in production become clearer if it is remembered that in the 1930s wheat accounted for 22.1 percent of the value of all Spanish agricultural production (INE, *Primera mitad del siglo XX,* pp. 30, 35). If the estimates were accurate (the eruption of war prevented final statistics from being gathered), the 1936 crop was the worst since 1914.

72. A monographic work on the ambiguous role of the Anarchosyndicalists in the spring of 1936 is desperately needed since the superb work of José Peirats, *La CNT en la revolución española,* does not answer the questions I have raised here. Had an Anarchosyndicalist insurrection occurred, it undoubtedly would have been seconded by some of the Socialist locals, but not necessarily by Largo Caballero, always braver in rhetoric than in action. In this case, it probably would have been defeated easily and may have served as the catalyst for the formation of a semi-dictatorial government of Republican concentration which (as will be explained shortly) seems to me to have been the only alternative by which the Left Republicans and Prietistas could have ended the growing chaos. Thus, a small possibility did exist that the Left would have put its house in order had the military insurrection

We are unavoidably led to the conclusion that Azaña could have ended the increasing social disorders in the countryside—together with the much bloodier disorders in the cities—only by imposing the Republican dictatorship for which Miguel Maura and others had begun to call.[73] But one wonders whether this was any more possible for him politically and psychologically than it had been in February and March, when the working-class groups were far weaker than they had subsequently become. If Largo Caballero had somewhat moderated his cries for the overthrow of the Republic, it was in large part because the Popular Front government, in its desire to placate the workers, had acted as his instrument. Had it changed course and sought to reimpose its authority, the alienation of Caballero and of the Communists would again probably have become total.[74] This does not necessarily mean that the Caballeristas would have rebelled and have had to be put down by military force. The peasantry in particular had on several occasions in the past, including one so recent as June 1934, been checked by a relatively minor show of strength. However, a confrontation with Caballero would have led at least to a constant cold war of the type that had been waged against the Anarchosyndicalists since 1931. With the working classes united against him, Azaña would inevitably have been forced to rely on a government of Republican concentration in which the CEDA and other political forces still further to the Right would have played an increasingly important part. While such an alliance might eventually have laid a firm basis for the Republic, it implied a permanent abandonment of

---

been delayed. Nevertheless, given the conditions of the times and the attitude of Azaña and Casares Quiroga, it is scarcely to be wondered that the Right was unwilling to trust its fate to such an eventuality.

73. The urban violence, which, in contrast to the rural, claimed many dead, is described in a number of general histories, particularly in Arrarás, *Segunda República,* and José Plá, *Historia de la Segunda República Española* (4 vols. Barcelona, 1940). Nevertheless, monographic work is also necessary here, particularly on the relationship of the *pistolero* atrocities (which have usually been treated in isolation) to the massive strikes that occurred.

74. The Communist reaction, of course, is especially difficult to estimate because of the party's international connections. Although its propaganda was generally less hostile to the Left Republican cabinet than that of the Caballeristas (probably because of its greater interest in maintaining the fiction of perfect unity within the Popular Front), its specific legislative demands were even more aggressive than those of the other working-class groups and could not have been abandoned without a complete reversal of policy. Nevertheless, even more than the Caballeristas, the Communists may well have backed down after a show of force by Azaña, particularly if this was carried out in such a way (against Anarchosyndicalist militants, for example) as to allow them to save face.

many Left Republican dreams and could not have saved Spain from a long period of trouble. The workers' gains in power had been so great since February 1936 that any attempt to redress the balance would have been impossible without retrenchment at least as harsh as that which had been imposed in 1934–45.

All of these speculations are, of course, vain. Whether or not the radicalization of the workers would eventually have led to the establishment of a "social" Republic, it served to radicalize and unite the previously divided Right. The struggle between the moderate and extreme Left for dominance within the Popular Front was decided by the military insurrection of 18 July. The Left Republican government, lacking other means of defense, was very quickly rendered dependent on the working-class organizations that supplied its troops. Possession of the land was now decided by its geographical location. Where the military rebellion was defeated, the local Socialist and Anarchist organizations seized the land and the state legalized their action.[75] Where it was successful, the settlers placed by the Republic were for the most part ousted from their holdings.[76] In both zones the changes were effected by violence. In both, the phrase "applying the agrarian reform" become a grisly

75. It is impossible to determine exactly how much land was seized by working-class organizations in Republican Spain because of the shifting lines of battle and because the seizures only gradually found their way into governmental statistics as they were retroactively legalized by the IRA. The scope of the latter problem is apparent in the two main sets of figures we have—that IRA "settlements" encompassed 3.9 million hectares as of May 1937 (IRA, *Reforma agraria en España*, p. 67) and had risen to 5.7 million hectares as of May 1938 (cited in Pierre Vilar, *Historia de España*, p. 152). Since the period between the two dates mentioned was characterized by a drastic reduction of the territory in Republican hands and by a major Communist-sponsored decollectivization drive in Aragon, it seems likely that the extra 1.8 million hectares "settled" reflected not new collectivizations, but the late registration of collectivizations that had occurred immediately after the military insurrection. In trying to reconcile the evidence available, I have come to the conclusion that approximately one-third of all lands and (since collectivization occurred mainly on arable land) between half and two-thirds of all cultivated land in Republican Spain were seized. By a cruel irony, the victims were predominately small and medium holders, since most of the latifundio districts had fallen to the Nationalists almost immediately after the outbreak of hostilities and consequently were not included in the IRA reports.

76. The official Nationalist position distinguished between settlements made under the Popular Front, which were immediately undone on the grounds that they were illegitimate, and the lesser settlements made earlier, the legitimacy of which was accepted until 1941, when the entire legacy of the IRA was liquidated. In some areas, however, particularly those under the control of General Quiepo de Llano, the yunteros who had received temporary grants of land in the spring of 1936 were also allowed to remain on their holdings until the end of the war.

THE DESTRUCTION OF THE "BOURGEOIS" REPUBLIC

euphemism for the murder of class enemies, each of whom, if fortunate, received his plot of land in which to be buried. Agrarian reform as a matter of law rather than of force was finished in Spain. The brave experiment of the Republic had failed catastrophically.

15: Could the Disaster Have Been Avoided?

The Inadequacies of the Liberal Democratic Solution

Perhaps the most disagreeable duty of the historian is the necessity to assign responsibility for complex historical occurrences. Summary judgment inevitably involves the abstraction of the object to be judged from many of the contexts in which it existed, and therefore places the historian in even greater danger than usual of falling victim to Charles Kingsley's dictum that "history is a pack of lies perpetrated by the living upon the dead." When dealing with politically controversial questions like the origins of the Spanish Civil War, the historian also runs a second risk. His capsule judgments, which, however hard he might try, cannot do full justice to the labyrinthine events he has been treating, will be perverted still further and used by one faction or another for its own purposes. For these reasons, I follow the custom of appending a conclusion to my book with great reluctance. The only claim I make for the observations that follow is that they seem to me less untruthful than others that might be (and have been) made.

It should be obvious from what has preceded that I consider the agrarian reform of the Republic to have been one of those unfortunately all-too-frequent events in human history from which no one emerges with much credit. The Right unquestionably bears heavy responsibility, both moral and political, for the disaster that occurred. Morality would have no meaning if, after contrasting the insensitivity of most of the Right to the sufferings of the Spanish peasantry with the willingness of most of the Left to attempt social amelioration, we did not applaud those who rejected the status quo and were moved by noble dreams.[1]

1. Except for Jiménez Fernández and a handful of others, who on the Right shared Azaña's estimable hope that "in our country a profound transformation of society would be accomplished while sparing us the horrors of social revolution" (speech of 14 February 1933, quoted in Ramos Oliveira, p. 472). And how is one to excuse, for example, these deputies who gratuitously subjected the yunteros to a

In connection with its political responsibility, the Right misused from October 1934 to February 1936 the considerable power it had obtained after the self-destruction of the Left in the Asturias and Catalan revolts —misused it to break up labor unions, drive down rural wages, evict tenants and yunteros, and defeat Jiménez Fernández's compromise measures. By each of these acts of "suicidal egoism," as Gil Robles later described them, the Right intensified the polarization of society that had begun in 1933 and contributed to the creation of the conditions that would eventually erupt into civil war.

Nevertheless, it would be false to attribute exclusive or even primary political responsibility for the failure of the agrarian reform to the Right, if only because it lacked the political power to translate its wishes into reality except during the sixteenth-month period between the October Revolution and the Popular Front elections, when it rose to the position of *primus inter pares* in the Center-Right coalition. For example, the long delay in enacting an agrarian reform law in 1931–32 was not caused by the Agrarian minority, the chief rightist force in the Constituent Cortes. Until May 1932, no serious parliamentary discussion occurred on agrarian matters; the repeatedly discarded legislative drafts that appeared during the first year after the overthrow of the monarchy reflected a struggle within the triumphant Republican coalition itself as to what sort of reform should be undertaken. From May to September 1932 the Agrarians' efforts to obstruct debate could easily have been defeated had the other 94 percent of the Cortes deputies shown any real enthusiasm for the Domingo draft. Once the September law had been enacted, the Right can be considered to have contributed to its faulty administration only to the extent that the major Spanish banks refused to join in the creation of a National Agrarian Bank to provide credit to the settlers. But this refusal did not occur until the summer of 1933, long after all real impetus for reform had been lost.

After the Right itself obtained a share of power in the elections of November 1933, it by no means waged an uncompromising struggle for the immediate or total reversal of the Azaña legislation. On the agrarian question the Right was divided into several distinct groups, none of which was able to establish its supremacy until after Jiménez Fernández tried to alter the status quo that had existed since the fall of Azaña. The agrarian bills drafted in early 1934 by Gil Robles and Martínez de Velasco were relatively moderate measures that significantly revised only the compensation provisions of the 1932 law. The lease bills sponsored

month of added suffering by insisting upon a quorum vote in November and December, 1934, even though it was apparent that Jiménez's extension of the yuntero leases would be approved by the full Cortes?

by del Río and Jiménez Fernández were almost as advanced as those of Domingo. And if outside the parliament the landowners succeeded in driving down rural wages, they were not yet able to reimpose the miserable salaries paid under the monarchy or evict the tenant farmers whose leases had been frozen by Azaña.

As to the responsibility of the traditional Right[2] for the outbreak of the Civil War, it consists mainly in the fact that the generally reactionary policies it followed in 1935 helped create the polarization of society which permitted violence to erupt after the Popular Front elections. As mentioned earlier, the lack of generosity of the Right to those over whom it enjoyed a temporary ascendancy and its blindness to its own long-term self-interest helped produce a catastrophe from which the Right would suffer almost as much as other segments of society. During 1936 itself, however, the Right can scarcely have been expected to accept passively the new trend of events, since the point at issue was no longer which of several different versions of limited, state-controlled reform would be adopted, but whether a revolutionary peasant onslaught upon all lands could be prevented. The moral culpability of the Right in supporting the revolt of the generals is also lessened by the fact that the Left had earlier, and probably under less provocation,[3] resorted to an insurrection whose eventual consequences were as unforeseeable as those of the military rising.

The causes for the failure of the reform are, therefore, to be found chiefly among the Center and Left parties that brought the Republic into being. The role of the Center, particularly of the Radical party, was

2. The Carlists, the Falangists, Calvo Sotelo's monarchofascists, and several military leaders had, of course, deliberately sought to provoke a confrontation for years. These persons and groups, however, were antagonistic to the parties of the traditional Right (the CEDA, the Agrarians, and the Lliga) and enjoyed very little influence in Spanish politics in general prior to the wave of hysteria that swept the country in the spring of 1936.

3. In 1934, prior to the Socialist rebellion, there was no change in the fundamental institutions of government and no wholesale annulment of the legislation of the Constituent Cortes. In 1936, by contrast, the legislative innovations of the previous two years were immediately undone. At the same time the basic political institutions of the Republic were threatened as thousands of municipalities were replaced by "executive committees," the President of the Republic was ousted by legal trickery, the leading politician of the opposition, Calvo Sotelo, was assassinated by a group which included off-duty state police, and legislation was introduced by the Communists to ban most parties outside the Popular Front on the grounds that they were "fascist." As to the comparative personal plight of the millions of followers of the Right and Left, who is to say that the psychological terrors experienced by the former in the spring of 1936 were less legitimate a cause for rebellion than had been the economic hardships through which the latter had passed prior to October 1934?

almost exclusively negative. During the Azaña biennium it sought to limit the scope of the legislation proposed by the Socialists and Left Republicans. During the conservative biennium it tried—particularly before it lost some of its maneuverability as a consequence of the October Revolution—to prevent a complete reaction in agrarian affairs. Unfortunately it was more successful in the first period than in the second. The long delay in securing Cortes approval for an agrarian reform law, and the absurd compromises that were eventually incorporated into it, were caused far more by the need to obtain Radical acquiescence to the Domingo bill, both while it was being drafted and during the floor debates, than by the parliamentary obstruction of the Agrarian minority. In 1934, on the other hand, the Radical attempt to strike a balance between conservative demands and continued adherence to the Azaña legacy neither stopped the landowners from instituting a severe (though not unlimited) reaction in the countryside nor dissuaded the Socialists from launching their revolution. By 1935 the opportunism that had always been the major flaw of the Radicals triumphed as they abandoned all real efforts to serve as a moderating force and allowed themselves to be swept along by the rightist tide that predominated after Jiménez Fernández was defeated.[4]

The responsibility of the Left is more complicated, since, until the military insurrection of 1936, it was by far the most continuously active force in Republican Spain. The confused and contradictory nature of Left Republican and Socialist objectives is apparent from beginning to end. Neither the Left Republicans nor the Socialists supported the Technical Commission draft of July 1931, perhaps the most promising agrarian proposal advanced under the Republic. Both groups accepted the worst possible compromises during the period when the Domingo bill was being drafted: the agricultural surtax and the measurement of maximum

---

4. The moral insensitivity of the Radicals was beautifully captured by Azaña in commenting on the reception accorded by the Center-Right parliament of 1934 to a speech by Prieto.

> I was present at the session of the Cortes on Wednesday last. What a spectacle! We saw there a pathetic scene: we saw a man [Prieto], pierced in his sensibilities as a Socialist, as a Republican, and as a Spaniard by the gravest, most painful, most acute anxieties; we saw him shattered by the inner struggle of conscience; we saw him implore the whole Parliament for a just solution, a way out; we saw him call upon the Government to fulfill its obligations, and before this moving, awful spectacle do you know what most of them did? They laughed! [Speech of 11 February 1934, quoted in Ramos Oliveira, p. 500.]

Unfortunately, Azaña's words can be used equally well to describe how the Popular Front Cortes dismissed pleas for moderation from such responsible leaders Jiménez Fernández and Gil Robles in 1936.

property limits on a national rather than a municipal basis were discarded, whereas the ruedo provision and the prohibition of the sale of land to even the most self-sufficient settlers were maintained. During the Cortes debates the Left Republicans did little to break the deadlock that arose as a result of their own half-heartedness, the covert opposition of the Radicals, and the obstruction of the Agrarians. After the September law was approved, Domingo gave a highly bureaucratic orientation to the reform, Azaña further weakened it by stringent budgetary limitations, and the Left Republicans in general displayed little interest in fulfilling their promise of supplementary agrarian legislation. Having accepted these errors without public protest until the summer of 1933, the Socialists suddenly panicked and adopted an intransigent position in which they refused first to accept any modification of such controversial measures as the términos municipales law (a concession that might have cut the ground from under the Left Republican dissidents) and then rejected electoral alliances with the progressive bourgeois parties.

If the shock of the November 1933 electoral defeat helped the Left Republicans overcome their lethargy in agrarian affairs, it facilitated the birth within the Socialist movement of a revolutionary current whose effects were to be disastrous. The Socialist rhetorical exaggeration of the dangers posed by the early Lerroux governments laid the basis for the October revolution and, in turn, for the strongly conservative reaction of 1935. After the Popular Front elections of 1936 the continued revolutionary orientation of the Caballeristas undermined the power of the government and so terrified large sectors of the population that the military insurrection of July enjoyed widespread popular support. As to the Left Republicans in 1936, they had learned enough from their previous errors to try to match their rhetoric with deeds while abstaining from unnecessary provocations of moderate and conservative opinion. Yet, having failed to oppose the extralegal actions of the working classes immediately after the February elections, which a limited show of force might still have been effective, they were unable to halt the disorder and the deterioration of state authority which were the truly important questions of the day.

In the final analysis, then, the failure of the agrarian reform was due primarily to the inconsistency and ultimate incompatibility of the two great forces that made up the Azaña coalition. Had the Left Republicans and Socialists been able to stick to a united program of action, the reform would not have gotten off to so bad a start, could not have been revised so easily during the conservative biennium, and would not have escaped so completely from the control of the government in 1936. Accidental occurrences and the personal deficiencies of some of the major leaders contributed to the errors that were committed. The incompetence of Domingo, the indifference to rural affairs of Azaña, the foolhardiness and lack of perspective of Largo Caballero, the coincidence of the Republic with the world depression, all helped destroy the agrarian reform. But more fundamental reasons, which had to do with the very essence of the Republican experiment and which were by no means unique to Spain, were also operative.

As I mentioned in the Introduction to this study, the Spanish reform, like all democratic efforts at land redistribution, was based upon two fundamental assumptions: that the enlightened bourgeoisie would commit themselves firmly to the reform and that the peasantry would accept the promise of state action and patiently await its fulfillment. Neither of these two assumptions proved valid. Agrarian reform is both peripheral to and presents a great dilemma for the liberal philosophy that has traditionally inspired the bourgeois Left in capitalist societies. The bourgeois Left is based primarily on the urban middle classes and the intellectuals, whose principal concerns historically have been not agrarian reform but the removal of obstacles to political and cultural freedom. Thus in Spain the overthrow of the monarchy, the disestablishment of the Church, the creation of a lay system of public education, and the granting of regional autonomy motivated Azaña and his followers far more than did any purely social improvements. The Left Republicans were led to espouse agrarian reform partly to gain the support of the Socialists for their political and cultural reforms, partly because they considered it necessary for the maintenance of social order, and partly because the humanitarian instincts of their liberal philosophy dictated the freeing of the peasantry. None of these reasons were sufficient to sustain them once the tremendous cost of the reform, as well as its inevitable violation of the respect for property rights and for individual economic opportunity which have constituted the core of the liberal philosophy, became apparent. As a result they began to hedge upon their commitment almost as soon as the Agrarian Reform Law was enacted.

The peasantry also proved unable to fulfill its part of the tacit agreement on which the Azaña coalition was based. By a tremendous effort and with the help of the great improvements that had occurred in rural wages and lease conditions, if not in the redistribution of land itself, the Socialists managed to keep peasant protest under control in 1931 and 1932. By the summer of 1933, however, even the wage improvements had come to seem irrelevant, and the peasantry was rapidly evolving, first with Socialist acquiescence and later under Socialist leadership, in a revolutionary direction. The open confrontation that occurred might have been delayed had not Alcalá Zamora dismissed the Azaña government in September 1933, but it is difficult to see how it could have been avoided entirely even had Azaña stayed in office.

The split between the enlightened bourgeoisie and the working classes, as well as the strain that the reform placed upon the Spanish economy, gave to the conservative opposition the opportunity to reassert its power. Once again the democratic nature of the Republican regime contributed to the failure of the agrarian reform. Had the Republic come into being through a violent revolution in which the propertied classes had been crushed rather than by a withdrawal of confidence from the monarchy in which they to some extent participated, or had these classes subsequently been terrorized into submission by an energetic and united coalition of the Left, they could not have checked the process of reform in 1934 or reversed it in 1935.[5] Nor could they, when parliamentary means had failed them and the apparent submission of the bourgeois Left to the revolutionary working classes threatened them with extinction in 1936, have given effective support to the military insurrection.

The disastrous outcome of the Republican experiment does not, of course, imply that all democratic efforts at agrarian reform are destined to fail. Small quantities of land have been redistributed by democratic means in both India and Italy since the end of World War II. The agrarian reform schemes recently adopted in South America may also prove successful.[6] Indeed, democratic land reform might not have failed even in Spain in 1931–36 had the Republic remained truer to its bourgeois origins and adopted the limited program sponsored by the Radicals, Progressives, and the Group at the Service of the Republic in 1931. Under these circumstances—in which a purely bourgeois coalition, rather than the by no means inevitable Left Republican–Socialist coalition that actually was

5. Pedro González-Blanco, *La tierra de España y la reforma agraria* (Valencia, 1931), p. 27, expressed this central truth well while speculating as to the kind of agrarian reform law the Provisional Government would produce. "True revolutions," he observed, "usually undertake radical expropriations; that is to say they do not pay compensation and sometimes go to the point of expropriating the heads of those who protest. The Republic, which came into being through a compromise, must indemnify [the proprietors whose lands it seizes]."

6. Judging from past experience, however, it seems more likely that the South American reforms will remain façades behind which only minute quantities of land will actually be redistributed. As for India, the modest (in relation to the enormous size of the country) postindependence reform has been facilitated by the passivity of the peasantry and by the fact that the reform has consisted mostly of the transfer of property titles to already existing small units of cultivation, rather than the economically more difficult task of breaking up large estates. In Italy, the small-scale reform of the 1950s was successful largely because it coincided with an extraordinary industrial boom which allowed the agrarian problem to be transcended by drawing the peasants away from the land.

established, would have set the tone of the Republic—the contradictions that later arose might have been avoided. The Left Republicans would not have been subject to so many fluctuations in policy; the Socialists would have developed neither the power nor the expectations that later made possible their October insurrection; the propertied classes would not have had as much reason to support the military adventure so unanimously.

Yet if it is obvious that very limited reforms can be carried out by democratic means, especially when facilitated by propitious circumstances such as those that existed in Italy and India, the experience of Spain in the 1930s suggests that the Western model of peaceful, constitutional change is not feasible for large-scale land redistribution. During the Republic, reliance on equitable procedures and technical controls proved ineffective. The magnitude of the threat that the Agrarian law posed to the propertied classes did not permit them to tolerate its fulfillment. The magnitude of the promise offered the peasantry was equally intolerable. They could not be prevented from trying to gain immediately what they were told they would eventually acquire under the law. As for the urban middle classes, their lack of a direct interest in the reform and its inevitable violation of many of the most fundamental principles of their value system combined to turn them against it whenever difficulties threatened.

The failure of the agrarian reform in Spain was in part caused by accidental factors, especially the world depression and the extraordinary international ideological division of the 1930s. The fundamental cause for its failure lay in the difficulty of reconciling the greatness of the objective with the limited means used to accomplish it. A profound revision of the structure of landed property, in all but the industrialized nations whose life is not based upon such property, is the revolutionary act par excellence. As such, society will not stand still while the reform is being carried out by the gradual methods of compromise which lie at the heart of democratic action.

The Inadequacy of the Revolutionary Solution

As Laurence Shoup, one of my graduate students, just pointed out to me, the preceding section, by emphasizing the inadequacies of the liberal democratic approach to agrarian reform, seems to imply that I consider revolution to have been the only possible solution to the land problem in Spain. This is not my intention, and such a conclusion would obviously conflict with the tenor of my remarks on the consequences of the radicalization of the Socialists after 1933. Unfortunately, there are no simple solutions to many historical problems. If the liberal democratic approach is inadequate in many situations, so too is the Left Marxist or Anarchosyndicalist emphasis on unremitting revolutionary action.

One of the difficulties with the Left Marxist approach is that revolution is neither fully predictable nor controllable. During the Republic, for example, it is clear that the political situation was most fluid immediately after the overthrow of the monarchy. If the Provisional Government had chosen to act in a social revolutionary manner or if the peasantry had forced it to so act by small scale upheavals that played on Republican fears of a general peasant uprising, sufficiently large quantities of land might have been transferred in 1931 to give a decisively different orientation to the reform. These possibilities existed only as abstractions, however; in the concrete circumstances of Spain in 1931 they had no reality.

The Provisional Government could not choose to act in a Jacobin manner because it was not composed of Jacobins nor confronted with the kinds of desperate dangers that might have allowed Jacobinism to articulate itself among those in whom it existed in embryo. The Republic, to repeat myself, did not result from bloody struggle but from a rather mysterious shift in opinion that created an antimonarchical consensus. Pacific, not violent, methods had proven efficacious. Change had occurred within the framework of the law, not outside it. The established classes were not uniformly considered to be enemies; rather, the support of important sectors of them was thought to be essential.[8] For the Provisional Government to abandon the tactics which up to that point had been so successful and threaten the consensus on which it rested would have required that its members possess so strong a theoretical commitment to social revolution that they could place the apparent lesson of their immediate past in its proper perspective. Such a commitment did not exist among them, and there is little point in belaboring persons for not having adopted policies that were psychologically alien to them. Moreover, it is useless to bewail the fact that these persons and not others came to power. Had the leaders of the Provisional Government been other than they were, the consensus on which the overthrow of the monarchy was built would probably not have existed. In short, the very circumstances that gave birth to the Republic guaranteed that it would not voluntarily turn to immediate state-sponsored social revolution.

The peasantry might indeed have forced the Provisional Government to abandon its natural predisposition to legal, pacific tactics had it applied pressure upon it. Most of the Republican leaders in the spring and summer of 1931 were so fearful of widespread peasant revolt that they

8. See chap. 7, particularly pp. 162–64, in support of these assertions.

would probably have sought to stem it by more drastic reforms had it begun to manifest itself. But it did not. Peasant rebellion became a significant force after 1933, not in 1931 when it might have been politically more efficacious. Important though it was, the central cause for this fatal delay was not the moderating influence of the Socialist movement upon the peasantry. Could a group that in April 1931 controlled perhaps 60,000 out of a total rural proletariat of over two million have exerted such influence unless it coincided with peasant aspirations at that time? Far more fundamental was the fact that the early twentieth-century tide of peasant revolt had been broken by the collapse of the trienio bolchevista and the long period of economic prosperity under Primo de Rivera; it could not immediately be restored even by so decisive an event as the overthrow of the monarchy. The experience of the Anarchosyndicalists and Communists, who desperately tried to set the tide in motion once more, is instructive. Dr. Vallina, despite his enormous personal popularity, could gather together only a handful of peasants in support of the Seville general strike of July 1931; CNT and Communist recruiters in general were so distant from the prevailing peasant mood that both organizations remained primarily urban based even so late as 1936. By contrast, the nonrevolutionary Socialists experienced a five-fold increase in peasant membership during the first year and, at their peak in 1933, may have united as many as 500,000 rural followers.

Social revolution could not be unleashed in 1931, when it would have been politically most opportune, because it had no basis in objective reality either within the Provisional Government or among the peasants. By 1934, the second of these prerequisites had begun to be established and social revolution became possible. Its consequences, however, only served to point to another of the major difficulties that characterize the revolutionary approach to politics—its inability to calculate the strength of the reaction that it will engender.

Because of what occurred in Germany and Austria, the lesson of the 1930s is often taken to be that working-class reformism facilitates the seizure of power by the extreme Right. Had the German and Austrian Socialists been more militant, it is said, neither Hitler nor Dollfuss would have come to office. Although this interpretation may be valid in these cases (the possibility that greater militancy might only have resulted in a still more rapid Nazi triumph leaves room for doubt), the opposite was true in Republican Spain. As has been abundantly indicated in the text and need not be repeated here, so long as the working-class Left remained reformist, the Right remained relatively weak and restricted itself to parliamentary action. By charting a revolutionary course after 1934, the Spanish Socialists succeeded only in removing all obstacles to the ascendancy of the most reactionary elements within the traditional Right during 1935, and in shifting power to hitherto isolated radical-rightist military and political groups in 1936. Insurrectionary tactics did not save the Republic, but only helped destroy it by polarizing society. Had the Socialists at least made an effective bid for power the consequences of their actions might be more easily forgiven. But, like the Anarchosyndicalists on many previous occasions, they became so caught up in their illusion that, in 1934, they could not see that disunion within their own ranks and the lack of support from other segments of the Left made successful revolution impossible, and, in 1936, they vastly underestimated the hidden strength and resources of the rightist groups to which their maximalism had helped bring so much popularity.

The point I am trying to make should be clear by now. In many parts of the underdeveloped world today, where peasant protest is buttressed by the urge for national liberation and faces as its chief domestic enemy a ruling class that is so corrupt and unyielding that it has isolated itself from every vital segment of society, social revolution may indeed be a viable solution. In countries like Spain in the 1930s, where these conditions were not fully developed, it was not.

If I am correct in thinking that both major types of solution to political problems in recent history were inadequate in Spain, was there any way in which the catastrophe that overtook the country might have been prevented? I have already suggested one alternative: the Republic might have avoided facing up to the problems it inherited had Lerroux's goal of a purely bourgeois alliance between Radicals and Left Republicans triumphed in the fall of 1931 rather than Azaña's Left Republican–Socialist coalition. Had this occurred the Republic would have been merely another of the many dull, ignoble regimes that stifle human aspirations rather than striving to fulfill them. While costs of this kind are not to be minimized, who can deny that they are rendered insignificant in comparison to the costs of civil war and a generation of dictatorship that Spain was eventually called upon to bear? Under Lerroux, peace would have been bought at the price of mediocrity and opportunism, but might not even such a peace have been preferable to what actually took place?

Yet since human beings would be little more than automatons were they permanently to stifle their aspirations out of fear of the suffering that striving to fulfill them might eventually bring, the negative alternative that Lerroux represented is not satisfying. The question, rather, is whether there was any way in which the Azaña government, having chose to address itself to the most profound problems of Spain, could have successfully solved them? Given the persons who made up that government and the attitudes that influenced them at critical moments, the answer is probably no. Had they been different, however, the agrarian reform may have prospered and a progressive Republican regime might perhaps have established itself as the enduring form of government in Spain.

Since Azaña's ultimate objectives could scarcely have been bettered,[9] the differences that may have proven beneficial have less to do with aspirations than with personal temperaments and tactical conceptions. The whole history of the Republic might have been different, for example, had the Left Republicans matched in sheer perseverance the rightists of the old Agrarian minority who fought first against overwhelming odds to weaken Domingo's proposals and then, in 1935, succeeded in turning Jiménez Fernández's lease bill to their advantage. Had the Left Republicans in 1931 and 1932 been sufficiently technically competent and concerned to gather the fundamental data necessary for the proper formulation and application of the reform, they might have avoided some of the errors written into the September law and the administrative paralysis that discredited the IRA in 1933. Had they not been so consumed by their outdated ideology, they would not have wasted so much of their energy on scoring largely symbolic victories over the Church and might instead have engaged in "reform-mongering" to gain Catholic acquiescense to the social changes that were the truly important issues of the day. Had their conception of legality not been so narrow, they might have instituted not one but a series of Intensification of Cultivation decrees to deliver significant portions of land to the peasantry while the Agrarian Reform Law was being debated and the IRA established.

This list can be extended almost indefinitely, but to do so would be to recapitulate much of the book and violate what I said earlier about the uselessness of lamenting that the Republican leaders were not other than they were. My central point can be easily made. The Republic would probably have failed even under the best leadership because the circumstances under which it functioned were so unpropitious and the problems it faced so complex. Insofar as there was any chance of success, however, it could have been fulfilled only if the Left Republicans and early Socialists had mixed with their liberal humanitarianism greater technical competence and a more intelligently focused radicalism. It is not enough for

9. Azaña showed far greater sensitivity both to regional and (in abstract form, at least) social aspirations than is characteristic of most statesmen, whether Spanish or of other nations. Even in connection with the religious problem, his obsessive anticlericalism did not have as its goal the destruction of the Catholic faith but rather a revision of the relationship between Church and society such as that which had occurred in France.

those who want to institute change to have noble aspirations. They must at the same time see social realities as they actually are rather than through ideological prisms, and must have the courage to establish tactical orders of priority so as to avoid chasing after the unimportant or becoming entangled in a web of legalism when dealing with that which is significant. Liberal humanitarianism is not enough, nor is radicalism. What is needed is a more effective blend of the two than existed during the Spanish Republic.

Appendix A:

Sources of Information on Modern Spanish Land Tenure

The Catastro de la Riqueza Rústica, inaugurated in 1906, is the oldest and only continuous source of information on Spanish land tenure in the twentieth century. Its purpose is to provide accurate data on which to base a uniform and equitable land tax.[1] The need for a Cadastral Survey arose because the *amillaramiento* system of taxation used earlier permitted widespread tax evasion. Under this system a tax quota was assigned to each township, which thereupon calculated the amount owned by each proprietor on the basis of his property declarations. Since it was in the interest of the township to reduce its collective tax burden, taxable land was often concealed, and the quality of the land reported was frequently misrepresented. Needless to say, the large owners probably benefited most from this falsification, because they were politically so much more powerful than the small owners. The state could not effectively counter the falsified municipal claims, since it lacked adequate information of its own and depended on the municipalities to administer the tax. So considerable did the concealment of land become that, according to one author, more than one-third of the land in the South escaped taxation altogether.[2] Since the land reported was taxed at below its true value, the total loss of revenue to the state was even greater. Thus on the 21 million hectares surveyed by the Cadastre as of July 1928, the new tax valuations were more than double those reported on the same land under the amillaramiento system.[3]

Despite the extraordinary increases in state revenues it permitted, progress

1. Gabriel García-Badell, *El catastro de la riqueza rústica en España* (Madrid, 1944), pp. 46–53. This volume presents probably the best technical description of the development of the Cadastre. A shorter, and more politically conscious, analysis is given by Francisco Molina de Palma, "Contribución territorial rústica," *Información Comercial Española* (August 1964), pp. 115–23.

2. Julio Senador Gómez, *Castilla en escombros* (Valladolid, 1915), p. 18. According to this author, concealment reached its height in Granada, where almost 60 percent of the land went unreported and untaxed.

3. DGP, *Memoria 1928*, pp. 161–63, contains valuable information on the area surveyed, tax assessed, and budget allotted to the Cadastral Service for each year from 1906 to 1928.

of the Cadastre was exceedingly slow until 1919. Impressive strides were briefly made after World War I, when budget allocations for the Cadastre were tripled. The pace slowed down once more in 1925, however. Possibly because of loyalty to the landowning class from which he had sprung, Primo de Rivera did not apply to the Cadastre his usual policy of expanding and expediting state services. Expenditures on the Cadastre were cut by more than one-third, and the role of the Geographical Institute, which was interested in a technically perfect but time-consuming topographical survey, was increased at the expense of the Cadastral Service of the Treasury, which advocated a rapid if less scientifically accurate survey.[4] After the establishment of the Second Republic, new procedural disputes prevented significant advances. The Civil War further retarded progress. As a result the Cadastre began to approach completion only after 1953, when aerial photography, which permitted rapid surveying at relatively low cost, was generally introduced.[5] By the end of 1959, 42.8 million hectares had been surveyed: except for a few scattered counties in the north, the whole of Spain was covered. A process that would have required less than twenty-five years, had the 1919–24 pace of surveying been maintained, ended by necessitating more than a half century of sporadic and ill-organized effort.

This history of the Cadastral Survey, together with the still more chaotic history of the publication of the Cadastral findings,[6] explains some of the

4. Primo de Rivera cut the budget for the Cadastre from 8.7 million pesetas in 1923 to approximately 5 million pesetas after 1926 (DGP, *Memoria 1928*, p. 163). For the struggle between advocates of a topographical survey and sponsors of more rapid techniques, see Enrique Alcaraz Martínez, *El catastro español* (Barcelona, 1933), and García-Badell, *Catastro*, pp. 54–89.

5. Some 10.8 million hectares were surveyed between 1953 and 1959, thanks to aerial photography.

6. The three principal publications of Cadastral findings are the 1928 *Memoria* of the DGP, Pascual Carrión's *Los latifundios en España*, and the article by García-Badell in *REAS*, January–March, 1960. Cadastral data were published in other sources at other times, but these reports were either concerned with single provinces or, in the case of one *Memoria* (DGP, *Memoria sobre los trabajos realizados durante los años 1944–48* [Madrid, 1949]), did not add important information. The accuracy of the 1928 *Memoria* and of García-Badell's article has never been disputed. Carrión, on the other hand, has been severely criticized by political conservatives on the grounds that he falsified the Cadastral information to which he had access while a member of the Technical Commission of 1931–32. I did not find these criticisms to be justified. Carrión was a strong partisan of agrarian reform, but his prejudices affected only his text, not the validity of the statistics he presented. A careful comparison of Carrión's figures with those of the 1928 *Memoria* failed to reveal any discrepancy. The only possible source of inaccuracy I could discover was that in parts of Badajoz and Huelva, Carrión relied not on Cadastral data but on hastily gathered reports for technicians preparing for the agrarian reform. Because I consider Carrión's information generally valid, I have used it extensively. It is far more detailed than García-Badell's article. It also has two advantages over the 1928 *Memoria*: it covers 2.8 million more hectares and gives information on the township, instead of only on the provincial level.

many problems that confront the researcher into modern Spanish land tenure. First, because only unreliable amillaramiento data exist prior to 1906, it is difficult to learn how the modern Spanish property structure evolved from its nineteenth-century antecedents. Second, because the Cadastre was completed so slowly, there is no statistical information on land tenure in Spain as a whole prior to 1959. Either the regional information available in earlier years must be considered in isolation, or, if a national setting is desired, the 1959 data must perforce be used despite their noncontemporaneous nature. Third, because Cadastral findings were published in widely varying degrees of completeness, the information available at different times and for different regions is extremely uneven. Data are especially scarce for the post-Civil War period, when, possibly because the Franco government feared to revive the agrarian question, only the number of owners or holdings in each Cadastral category has been reported. Statistics on the total income or total area controlled by each type of owner or holding have been suppressed. Thus the relatively complete findings for the 1928–30 period in Southern Spain are only partly comparable to the skeletal findings published for that region in 1959. Also, since Northern Spain was surveyed entirely after the Civil War, its property structure cannot be known in the same detail as that of Southern Spain, for which an extensive body of information exists for at least one moment in time.

Several other problems, not directly related to the historical development of the Cadastre and common to all published Cadastral reports, also confront the researcher. Since most of the difficulties, together with their practical implications, are discussed as they arise in the main body of this work, they need only be summarized here. The following problems are especially significant.

1. The tendency of the Cadastre to overstate the number of owners and thus understate the average area and income controlled by each, because it includes gardeners and counts "true" owners once in each of the several municipalities in which they may own property: as a result there were some 6.0 million Cadastral "owners" in 1959, but the total agricultural population of Spain numbered only 4.6 million persons.

2. The failure of the Cadastre to distinguish in its reports between municipal and individual ownership, with the consequence that the collective importance of large owners and large estates is overstated—especially in Northern and Central Spain, where considerable municipal lands still exist.

3. The failure of Cadastral reports to distinguish between irrigated and unirrigated lands within cultivated lands, or to distinguish cultivated lands as a whole from pasture and forest lands: as a result heated controversy exists over what type of land the large owners and large estates control.

4. The failure of Cadastral reports, even prior to the Civil War, to indicate the total amount of land encompassed by each category of its area classifications for owners: thus it is impossible to determine with exactitude the average area controlled by each owner. This defect would be less significant if owner income figures—which prior to Franco were presented in

full—could be related to the owner area list: that is, if we could establish at least the average income of owners in the various area categories. Because income figures were never presented in terms of area figures, however, precision is impossible in this respect as well. Fortunately these defects exist only in relation to owners; prior to the Civil War, area as well as income information for holdings was fully disclosed, and the two concepts were presented as functions of a single basic list of holdings, thus permitting statistical correlations between them.

5. The failure of the Cadastral reports to use finer gradations in their categories of classification frustrates depth and richness of analysis. For example, in the 1928–30 period the highest income classification was 5,000 pesetas. Thus the moderately wealthy owners—those with tax assessments of 6,000 or 7,000 pesetas—cannot be distinguished from the enormously wealthy owners—those with assessments of 25,000, 50,000, or 100,000 pesetas. The absence of finer gradations is also troublesome when one tries to give statistical definitions for such loose terms as "small," "medium," and "large" owners or holdings. For example, since no Cadastral report has ever used any area classification between 10 and 50 hectares, the researcher must separate "small" from "medium" holdings at the 10-hectare level, even though 20 or 25 hectares would probably be more appropriate to Spanish agricultural conditions. Similarly, 150 or 175 hectares would probably be the most acceptable statistical demarcation between "medium" and "large" holdings, but because the Cadastre includes no classification between 100 and 250 hectares, the researcher is left with equally disputable alternatives in forming his definitions.

These failings, present even in the best of the Cadastral statistics, will explain the necessity for the rather elaborate methods required in Chapter 1 to answer some of the questions on Spanish land tenure. Two other defects not discussed in the text merit brief explanation here.

1. As mentioned, the property of owners is never considered as a whole but only as it exists within each municipality. Theoretically, holdings are still further subdivided: they are considered not only within municipal limits but also within the limits of the sectors into which each municipality is divided in order to create manageable zones of investigation for the surveyors. Thus if an estate crosses a municipal border it is recorded as two holdings; if it also crosses a sector border within either municipality, the Cadastre records it as three holdings. In practice, the resulting overstatement of the number of holdings is not nearly so great as is the case with owners, despite the fact that sector divisions do not affect the latter. Small and medium holdings are rarely transversed either by municipal or by sector boundaries, since these boundaries tend to conform to some permanent physical feature (such as a creek or a road) that would also normally serve as the boundary of a small or medium holding. The possibility of serious distortion arises only among large estates, since such estates may include within themselves the topographical features utilized to demarcate sectors and municipalities.[7] Thus whereas

7. See DGP, *Memoria 1928*, p. 42.

small and medium holdings in the Cadastre statistics usually reflect true units of exploitation, large estates probably occupy greater areas and produce greater incomes than those statistics suggest.

2. My use (in Chapters 1 and 2) of the taxable income as a rough indicator of the nature of the land, although justified on the whole, has some dangers attached to it. The Cadastral "income" does not register yearly fluctuations in true income. Rather, it operates as do most other property taxes: it assigns a semipermanent value to the land and then deduces the approximate income that can be derived from it. Although a few variables are taken into account, the formulas used in both calculations are essentially standard. Thus the skill with which a given farmer cultivates his land and markets his produce does not seriously affect the final assessment. Since annual declarations of income do not exist, the question of false reporting is also not significant. The chief danger in using the taxable income as a gauge of the quality of the land is that although the Cadastre does not register minor variations, it does reflect the over-all use of the land. The same land would be taxed differently if left in pasture than if plowed. A farm is assessed differently after it has been irrigated than before. Thus because the Cadastre is not concerned with the ultimate natural potentialities of the land,[8] we cannot be sure from the taxable income whether a given estate remains untilled because it is of poor quality or only because its owner neglects it. All cultivated land is obviously arable, but we do not know what portions of uncultivated lands may also be arable. Nor can we tell from the Cadastre whether an unirrigated field devoted to grains could have water brought to it. There is no way of overcoming these difficulties. The taxable income is the most sensitive statistical guide we have, but it must be supplemented by other methods of approach, some of which I have used in Chapters 2 and 3.

Despite these several limitations, the Cadastre remains indispensable for the study of Spanish land tenure. When millions of owners and tens of millions of holdings are involved, a basic statistical framework is absolutely necessary if discussion of property structure is to consist of more than a trading of impressions. For all its failings, the Cadastre was the only general statistical account of Spanish landholding prior to 1953. Even though new sources appeared after that date, the Cadastre continues to provide the most complete and accurate statistical record.

II

The Cadastre has been supplemented since 1953 by two separate studies of Spanish land tenure. These are the 1953 and 1956 Encuestas Agropecuárias of the Junta Nacional de Hermandades (the rural branch of the National Syndical Organization) and the 1962 Agrarian Census of the National Statistical Institute.

8. To tax the land on its potential productivity rather than its actual use would in itself be an important step toward agrarian reform and was repeatedly proposed as such. The Franco government has recently begun to attack the land problem by such taxation.

The Encuestas Agropecuárias may be dismissed quickly. At first sight they appear to enjoy two great advantages over the Cadastre: they were completed within a few weeks and thus reflect Spanish land tenure at a single moment in time; their published findings made the crucial distinction between land tenure in irrigated and unirrigated lands, although they did not go on to separate unirrigated land into cultivated, pasture, and forest components. Unfortunately these merits are overshadowed partly by the narrow scope of the Encuestas—they were concerned only with the size of holdings and did not attempt to determine the total property of owners—and, more important, by the unreliability of their findings. The Encuestas were conducted through questionnaires sent from the central syndical office to the local Farm Brotherhoods. A study of the completed questionnaires reveals that the local unions often failed to follow instructions and submitted carelessly drafted, impressionistic reports.[9] The task of accurately determining the property structure in their locality was probably beyond the capacity of the local Brotherhoods, especially since they were also expected to provide a variety of information on other matters, such as the agricultural population and livestock and forest resources.[10] Nor did the handful of individuals who made up the statistical section of the Hermandades office in Madrid command the resources necessary to check the local returns for accuracy. The Encuesta findings thus possess slight value, except possibly in establishing a rough approximation of the property structure in irrigated lands. Their frequent use in scholarly works of the late 1950s and early 1960s testifies to the paucity of more substantial information during the post-Civil War period.

The 1962 Agrarian Census is a much more serious effort to fill in the many intelligence gaps that exist in Spanish agrarian affairs. Its method of gathering data is more sophisticated than that of the Encuestas, combining sampling techniques with the use of questionnaires directly administered by employees of the National Statistical Institute. The scope of the project is broader even than that of the Cadastre, since the Census tries to relate its data on land tenure to such variables as crops grown, irrigation, use of fertilizers, the status of the farm operator (owner, tenant, or sharecropper), the number of workers each farm operator employs, and so on. It also improves on the Cadastre by taking as its basic unit not holdings as such but the total area (which in Spain usually consists of several separate holdings)

9. The completed questionnaires are located in the offices of the Statistical Service of the Junta Nacional de Hermandades headquarters in the National Syndical Organization Building in Madrid.

10. The population data obtained in the Encuestas are also unreliable on a local level. A sampling of the results for sixteen villages in Seville showed that clearly impossible results were reported for at least one occupational grouping in eleven of the villages. I used the population data of the Encuestas in chap. 3, mainly because the local errors seem to cancel each other out on the provincial level and because they are the only studies to provide an occupational analysis of the agricultural population prior to the mechanization of agricultural tasks and to the great rural exodus of the late 1950s and early 1960s.

cultivated by each farm operator. The Census thus has already greatly enriched discussion on land tenure. Nevertheless, it can only supplement, not replace, the Cadastre, if only because its purposes are different. It is interested in land tenure in the operational rather than in the property sense: it is concerned with farm operators, not farm owners per se. Consequently it places outside its purview one of the groups that is central to our study—the large farm owners who do not work their lands but lease them to tenants and sharecroppers.

III

All the sources discussed thus far share the common characteristic of being impersonal statistical accounts. None answer the question central to any study of the political and social implications of land tenure—the identity of the large owners.[11] For this information we must turn to another source: the Inventory of Expropriable Property compiled by the Institute of Agrarian Reform in 1933. The farms and owners included in the Inventory are summarized in 254 volumes, which are housed in the Instituto de Colonizatión (Institute of Land Settlement) in Madrid and entitled Registro de la Propiedad Expropiable del Instituto de Reforma Agraria. The information in the Registro stems from declarations that owners whose lands were potentially subject to expropriation under the Agrarian Reform Law of 1932 were obliged to submit to the Registrars of Property in each county in which they held land. The specific items listed in the Registro, together with their value for the researcher, are as follows:

1. The name (together with the noble title if such existed), age, place of birth, and marital status of each owner: this information is the most important single contribution of the Registro. It provides the researcher with a basis from which he can (a) transcend municipal boundaries and arrive at some estimate of the total property held by a given owner in broader regions; (b) determine the background of each owner at least to the extent of deciding whether he pertained to the nobility; (c) determine whether the owner was directly involved in political, industrial, or financial affairs by checking the names of local and national governmental officials or of directors of industrial firms; (d) determine whether the owner was related to other large owners or to political, financial, or industrial figures; (e) determine whether the owner was native to the region in which he held property or whether, because born in another region, he was probably an absentee.[12]

2. The name, location, and boundaries of each farm possessed by each

11. There is one exception. Since 1957 such information has been provided by the Cadastral Service on the very largest owners, those whose assessed taxable income exceeded 170,000 pesetas in any province.

12. In their official declarations to the Registrars of Property, owners were also obliged to state their place of residence as well as their place of birth. Unfortunately this information (along with the present occupations of the owners) was not recorded in the Registro and has been lost.

owner in each municipality: this information is unimportant to the general researcher except insofar as the names of the largest farms enable him to use the detailed data sometimes compiled by the Institute of Agrarian Reform on the farms which it expropriated.[13]

3. The principal crops grown on each farm: the potential importance of this category is reduced by the fact that the Registro summarized this information in the briefest and vaguest manner possible.

4. The size of each farm, which indicates whether an owner kept his property in large units, probably run by farm managers, or whether the property consisted of a multiplicity of small plots, probably let to tenants and sharecroppers.

5. The category of expropriable property established in the Agrarian Reform Law into which each farm fell: this information, though often omitted or inexact, is important because it tells us whether the property had been leased over a long period of time, whether the land remained unirrigated despite a legal obligation of an owner to introduce irrigation, and so on.

6. The manner in which each farm was acquired: this is important in establishing trends in the movement of property. For example, was the nobility expanding its holdings through new purchases, or did it rely on the lands it had inherited?

7. The mortgages and other charges on each farm, which in turn constitute a measure of the economic stability of the owners: unfortunately this information is recorded in such a disorganized and illegible manner that it is very difficult to use.

The deficiencies of the Registro may be summarized as follows:

1. Either because some Registrars of Property did not submit copies of the information they had condensed from the owners' declarations or because such copies were lost, the Registro is not complete. In the six southern provinces that I studied, for example, records were not available for three counties in Cordova and two in Toledo.[14] These omissions are not of great significance, however, since it seems that at least 90 percent of the counties in Spain did report.

2. The Registro does not report all lands but only those potentially sub-

13. A large section in the Institute of Agrarian Reform Archives consists of reports on individual farms that either had been or were about to be expropriated. I did not use many of these reports or much of the very extensive documentation that exists on former common lands. Needless to say, they would be of considerable importance for any technical study of Spanish agriculture during the 1930s.

14. The Registro may also be incomplete in the sense that some of the supplementary lists submitted by the Registrars of Property were lost because they were not bound together with the main list (small parts of the Registro are still unbound; most of the remaining volumes seem to have been bound in their present form only after the Civil War). For most counties only the single main list appears. This defect is probably not serious, however, since most of the existing supplementary lists include only landowners whose possessions were so small that they were overlooked the first time around.

ject to expropriation. In one sense, this is an advantage to the researcher, because if the millions of small peasant proprietors in Spain were also recorded,
it would become more difficult than it already is to pick out the important
landowners from the mass of documentation. In another sense, a major problem arises. In general the Agrarian Reform Law affected only cultivated
land. Forest lands, enclosed pasture lands that had never been cultivated,
and *esparto* lands not capable of sustaining permanent cultivation were specifically excluded from its provisions. However, there were two exceptions to
this exclusion which cause some lands of this type to be included in the
Registro. The *señorío jurisdiccional* lands of the nobility and all properties,
whether noble or not, which covered more than one-fifth of the surface
of any municipality were expropriable. Moreover, the noncultivated portions of
primarily crop-bearing farms were also recorded, along with their cultivated
portions. Thus on the one hand we cannot determine the total extent of an
owner's property, since most of his uncultivated properties were excluded;
on the other hand, since some uncultivated land was included, perhaps only
about two-thirds of the property listed in the Inventory as a whole was arable
land, and in some provinces, as was mentioned in Chapter 3, the proportion
was considerably lower.

3. Because the Registro consists of reports prepared by hundreds of
Registrars of Property, the quality of the information varies considerably. In
some counties notations were either omitted or made in the most perfunctory
manner possible. In others, premetrical systems of measurements were occasionally used. One is sometimes even confronted by the problem of the
illegibility of the handwritten inscriptions submitted.[15]

4. Above all, the Registro is extraordinarily difficult to use. Each farm
of each owner in each municipality is recorded, but the material is not further
summarized in any way. Since owners sometimes control more than a hundred
separate holdings in a given municipality, the researcher must spend most of
his time adding figures. Comparative studies of owners in different municipalities are also rendered difficult by the fact that names are never listed in
alphabetical order. Moreover, though the general nature of the land is described, the Registro does not attempt to arrive at a rough numerical approximation of its over-all value. Ultimately, then, though the Registro has
the great advantage of permitting us to get beyond impersonal statistical
terms, its corresponding weakness is that it is nearly unmanageable because
it is so difficult to reduce to statistical terms.

Unquestionably the virtues of the Registro outweigh its weaknesses. It
is in effect a property register for all important owners in Spain which, instead of being scattered about in county seats throughout the nation, is

15. The problem of legibility is aggravated by the allocation of space in the
inscription sheets of the Registro. Great amounts of space were left for such unimportant (to the researcher) items as farm boundaries, but such crucial information
as the crops grown and the mortgages that encumbered the property had to be
crammed into one or two square inches.

located at a single site in Madrid.[16] The wealth of information it contains cannot be fully exhausted except through the efforts of a team of scholars using the most modern machinery and techniques. In this study I have only skimmed the surface for six Southern provinces. Most of the Registro remains completely unexplored.

A brief word may be added about the Archives of the Institute of Agrarian Reform in general. Except for the Registro, there is little of value for the student of the political and social aspects of the land question. Most of the remaining material is extremely technical and is concerned with individual farms or "Peasant Communities." Only a few general reports from the Provincial Delegations of the Institute survive, and these come mainly from Seville. I was not able to discover what happened to the rest of the material. A fire once destroyed a small part of the Archives. Other material was probably destroyed by water seepage (the Archives are housed in the subbasement of the Instituto de Colonización). By far the greatest loss probably occurred during the Civil War when the Institute moved its headquarters first to Valencia and then to Barcelona, taking with it each time the most important material. Why the Registro was left behind, I do not know. Its bulk alone might have discouraged any attempt to move it. Also, it had lost much of its importance, because, during the Civil War, lands were seized spontaneously by the peasants on the grounds that they belonged to "Fascist" owners, not taken after due process by the Institute because they were included in the Inventory. Neither of these reasons is really satisfactory, since most of the material that was moved was probably less important than the Registro. Perhaps the answer is that what I saw in Madrid was a copy of a more orderly and better preserved Registro that traveled along with the Institute each time it shifted location.

16. The Registro has other advantages over the regular property registers kept in each county. Because there is no legal obligation to record property transfers, a considerable amount of land does not appear in the latter. For example, the preamble to the Mortgage Law of 30 December 1944 estimated that the property registers recorded no more than 40 percent of all Spanish land.

Appendix B:

Methods of Estimating Data in Statistical Tables

Tables 1, 2, and 3 of text and Tables A, B, C, and D of Appendix C. My estimates of the areas occupied by different kinds of holdings in Spain in 1959 were calculated by multiplying the number of holdings reported in García-Badell by reduced versions of the average sizes that prevailed for those holdings in Central and Southern Spain in 1930.[1] The degree of reduction depended primarily on what proportion of all holdings of a given category was formed by Northern holdings, which always seem to be smaller than those in the rest of Spain. The reduction was greatest in the smallest-holding categories. For plots of under one hectare it was impossible to arrive at a reasonable estimate except by slashing the 1930 average in half. This seems justified, because in Central and Southern Spain parcels of from 0.5 to 1 hectare constitute a much higher proportion of the "under one hectare" holdings than in Northern Spain, where more than 90 percent of such holdings are in fact less than 0.5 hectare in size.[2] The other small-holding, and the medium-holding, categories were all reduced by approximately 10 percent. The large holdings, located mostly in the Center and the South, were reduced only to the extent of rounding off their average sizes in 1930. There are probably many errors in these estimates, of course, since so many variables are involved; the estimated totals as a whole, however, differ from the true area surveyed by less than one percent.[3] García-Badell reaches (by methods he does not describe) conclusions somewhat different from my own. He estimates that small holdings occupy less of the total area (38.9 percent to my 46.5 percent) and medium and large holdings more (29.3 percent to

1. To have used the 1930 averages themselves would have led to impossible results. Apparently the lands surveyed after 1930 had smaller average areas (and, as will be seen, lower income-area ratios) than the lands surveyed before 1930.

2. In Northern Spain only 2.3 million holdings, or 9.1 percent of the 25.5 million holdings of under 1 hectare, were between 0.5 and 1 hectare in size. In the rest of the nation they were proportionately twice as important, forming 19.9 percent (4.6 out of 23.2 million) of the "under one hectare" holdings (García-Badell, table 2).

3. The true area surveyed in 1959 was 42.76 million hectares, whereas my estimates give results of 42.91 million.

my 24.9 percent and 31.8 percent to my 28.6 percent, respectively).[4] These estimates seem mistaken to me, particularly in regard to small holdings, where it is scarcely possible to assign lower average sizes than I did.

Similar methods were employed to arrive at the income estimates for holdings in Spain as a whole in 1959. I determined the income-area ratios that prevailed for each category of holding in Central and Southern Spain in 1927 (the 1930 figures were not sufficiently detailed on this point) and applied slightly reduced versions of these ratios to the area estimates that I had previously calculated. The necessity for reduction in the income-area ratios probably results from the greater proportions of poor land in Northern Spain, where surveying had not yet begun in 1927. Since there was no way of determining what proportions of such lands were included in each category of holding, my reductions of the ratios were relatively uniform. This seems to have produced reasonable over-all results, although in some of the individual categories and regions my estimates are undoubtedly mistaken. García-Badell gives no estimates for income.

The estimated area and income of holdings in Northern Spain were achieved by applying the average size figures and the income-area ratios adopted for Spain as a whole to all Northern holdings of over ten hectares. The resulting area and income were subtracted from the total real area and income, and the remainder was assigned to holdings of under ten hectares. Again, the over-all results seem satisfactory, but there may be significant errors in individual categories or regions.[5]

The accompanying table summarizes the data on which the estimates for both area and income were based. Size is indicated in hectares.

Holding category	Average size: 1930	Average size adopted: 1959	Income-area ratio: 1927	Income-area ratio adopted: 1959
Under 0.5	...⎫ 0.38	0.12⎫ 0.19	...⎫ 175.6	164⎫ 155
0.5–1	...⎭	0.60⎭	...⎭	146⎭
1–5	2.0	1.8	126.2	110
5–10	6.7	6.0	131.7	110
10–50	20.3	18.0	98.5	90
50–100	65.8	60.0	91.5	80
100–250	144	140	84.3	75
250–500	321	320	76.3	70
500–1,000	670	650	73.2	65
1,000–5,000	1,745	1,700	50.4	42
Over 5,000	6,206	6,200	27.3	20

SOURCES: Carrión, *Latifundios*, Table 1, and DGP, *Memoria 1928*, pp. 125, 133.

4. García-Badell, table 7.

5. For Northern Spain as a whole this method of subtraction produced a small-holding area of 7.2 million hectares, as opposed to the 7.0 million hectares that results from applying the national averages to small as well as to medium and large holdings. In some of the subregions, however, the discrepancy is greater.

Table 6 of the text and Tables E and F of Appendix C. Since no area totals were published for owners even in the pre-Civil War period, I was forced to base my estimates on the area occupied by holdings, not owners, in 1930. This time the average size of the holdings in each category was increased so as to take into account the fact that owners frequently possess more than one holding (in 1959 there were 6.0 million owners but 54.0 million holdings—a ratio of 9 to 1). Since multiple ownership was especially prevalent in the "under 0.5 hectare" category (2.1 million owners and 41.8 million holdings—a ratio of 20 to 1), an increase of three-quarters was allowed for owners of this type. An increase of at least one-sixth seemed warranted in the "0.5 to 1 hectare" category, where holdings outnumbered owners by 6 to 1 (1.1 to 6.9 million). Only a 5 percent increase was allowed in the "over 5,000 hectare" category, mainly in order to make every possible concession to the possibility that large owners control less territory than the Cadastre data suggest. Elsewhere I increased the 1930 holding figures by approximately one-eighth. Once more, the over-all margin of error seems to be small: my estimates produce an area of 42.79 million hectares, almost exactly the same as the 42.76 million hectares actually surveyed. García-Badell's estimates again differ from mine, though less than on individual holdings. He gives a slightly lower estimate for small (19.0 percent to my 19.7 percent) and medium (27.5 percent to my 27.9 percent) owners, and a slightly higher one for large owners (53.5 percent to my 52.4 percent).[6]

The regional estimates were calculated by applying the average sizes adopted for Spain as a whole to all owners with over ten hectares in each region, subtracting the resulting area from the real area surveyed, and assigning the remainder to holdings of under ten hectares. This is a somewhat crude device, since there are probably noticeable differences in the average area held by owners of different types in Northern, Central, and Southern Spain. Because there is no way of determining these regional differences, however, I had to use the national averages.

Table 7 of text and Tables G and H of Appendix C. The "estimates" here are not estimates at all but income figures that prevailed in 1955 in the province of Malaga according to DGP, *El Catastro de rústica: Su iniciación y desarrollo* (Madrid, 1955), p. 123. This publication was prepared as a training pamphlet for students of agronomy and is the only publication since the Civil War to state the amount of income actually assessed. I have used the Malaga figures rather than attempting to estimate average income on the basis of the 1930 data, because the Malaga figures produce reasonable results and because the enormous change in the value of the peseta since 1930 would make such estimates dangerous (the only change I made in the

I preferred the method of subtraction, because there are so many millions of small holdings that the slightest variation between their real average sizes and the average sizes I applied would have produced major differences in the total area or total income figures.

6. García-Badell, table 7.

printed Malaga income statistics was in the "under 50 peseta" category, which, as so often happens with Spanish statistics, was obviously inaccurate). When applied to the national data for 1959, the Malaga figures understate the taxable income by about five percent, perhaps partly because of the inflationary trends in Spain between 1955 and 1959. Since this understatement affects only absolute quantities, not proportional relationships (which are the important factor under consideration), I have made no attempt to correct it. The average income of Northern owners was once again calculated by applying the national averages to the large and medium categories and assigning the remaining income to the gardener and small-owner category.

Table 27. I have estimated that the true market value of the expropriable land was approximately thirty times its taxable income by assuming that real net income was three times the taxable income and that a fair market price is equivalent to about ten times the real net income of a farm. Both assumptions may be disputed, but it is the relation of taxable income to real income that is the most troublesome. The chief difficulty is that there were two methods of determining land tax incomes in Spain in 1932—the Cadastre and the amillaramiento system. In the Cadastre zone, which included most of the latifundio provinces, the assessed income in 1932 was usually "less than half" real income and "in many cases" only one-third of that income (Carrión, p. 72). In the amillaramiento zone taxable income was a still smaller proportion of real income because of the tendency of owners to underdeclare their earnings. Although in earlier years amillaramiento owners reported only about half of what they would have been assessed under the Cadastre (see Appendix A), administrative efficiency had increased to the point that by the 1930s they probably declared about three-quarters as much.[7] Thus my over-all estimate—that taxable income averaged one-third of the real income—probably exaggerated the harshness of the compensation provisions for Southern Spain, where the Cadastre was almost completed, and understates it for the rest of the nation. I have not used the relation of net national agricultural income to taxable income to establish a more precise average, because Spanish statistics do not distinguish the portions of that income received by each of the various classes of the rural population. My estimates cannot be far wrong, however. In 1935 net national agricultural income was 9,350 million pesetas and total taxable income 1,309 million

7. For example, in 1959 the Cadastre assigned approximately equal taxable incomes to Madrid, the Balearic Islands, Leon, Lerida, Burgos, and Huesca (ibid., table 4). In 1918, when only Madrid had been surveyed, the other five provinces declared only about half as much taxable income as the Cadastre assigned to Madrid; in 1928, on the other hand, they declared about three-quarters as much as Madrid, even though they were still under the amillaramiento system (DGP, *Memoria 1928*, pp. 30–31). The same pattern can be traced by comparing relative taxation in 1918, 1928, and 1959 in Cadiz, Lugo, and Tarragona, as well as in Ciudad Real and Barcelona.

pesetas[8]—a ratio of 7.14 to 1. But since at least half of the net national agricultural income must have gone to workers, tenants, sharecroppers, and the other nonowners who form most of the rural population, the real ratio of the net income of owners to their taxable income would be roughly 3 to 1.

8. Luís García de Oteyza, "El Producto neto," p. 13.

Appendix C:

Additional Statistical Data on Spanish Land Tenure

TABLE A NUMBER, ESTIMATED AREA, AND ESTIMATED INCOME OF HOLDINGS IN SPAIN AS A WHOLE IN 1959

Holding Category (hectares)	Number of Holdings	Percent of All Holdings	Estimated Average Size (hectares)	Estimated Percent of Total Area	Estimated Percent of Total Taxable Income
Under 10	53,547,993	99.1	0.4	46.5	60.2
10–100	439,404	0.8	24.5	24.9	21.5
Over 100	49,323	0.1	249.0	28.6	19.6
Under 10					
under 0.5	41,815,975	77.4	0.11	10.7	17.5
0.5–1	6,899,123	12.8	0.60	9.6	14.0
1–5	4,243,122	7.9	1.8	17.8	19.6
5–10	596,035	1.0	6.0	8.3	9.1
10–100					
10–50	373,553	0.7	18.0	15.7	14.1
50–100	65,851	0.1	60.0	9.2	7.4
Over 100					
100–250	35,229	0.1	140.0	11.5	8.6
250–500	9,845	—a	320.0	7.3	5.1
500–1,000	3,171	—	650.0	4.8	3.1
1,000–5,000	1,011	—	1,700.0	4.0	1.7
over 5,000	67	—	6,200.0	1.0	0.2

SOURCE: The number of holdings is taken from García-Badell, "Distribución de la propiedad," Table 2. The printed figures contained errors that García-Badell kindly corrected for me.

NOTE: For the method of estimating size and income see Appendix B. The true area surveyed in 1959 was 42.76 million hectares, whereas the estimates produce results of 42.91 million.

a. Unless otherwise stated, a dash (—) indicates less than 0.05 percent in this and all succeeding tables.

TABLE B   DISTRIBUTION OF MEDIUM HOLDINGS IN 1930 AND 1959 (ABSOLUTE QUAN-TITIES)

	Total Number of Holdings (thousands)	Total Area (thousands of hectares)	Total Taxable Income (thousands of pesetas)
Spain (1959)	439	10,675	1,584
North (1959)	104	2,581	399
Center (1930)	58	1,544	37
South (1930)	111	3,067	97
Northern Spain			
Galicia	11.6	293	55.7
Leon and Burgos	13.8	439	38.3
Biscay Coast	10.6	259	57.4
Aragon-Ebro	39.6	950	123.0
Catalonia	28.0	640	125.0
Central Spain			
Old Castile	10.2	269	9.0
New Castile	11.2	325	6.9
Levante	16.2	428	10.4
Southeast	20.5	522	11.0
Southern Spain			
Western Andalusia	39.7	1,085	43.3
Estremadura	24.2	741	26.7
La Mancha	33.2	876	13.5
Eastern Andalusia	14.3	365	13.6

NOTE: Sources and categories estimated are the same as in Table 1, to which this table corresponds. In this and subsequent tables of Appendix C, the income figures for Central and Southern Spain are so low because of the change in the value of the peseta. The regional totals do not add up to the national because of the different dates to which they refer. On those dates the area surveyed in Northern Spain was 11.6 million hectares, in Central Spain 6.9 million, and in Southern Spain 15.5 million.

TABLE C   DISTRIBUTION OF SMALL HOLDINGS IN 1930 AND 1959 (ABSOLUTE QUANTITIES)

	Total Number of Holdings (thousands)	Total Area (thousands of hectares)	Total Taxable Income (thousands of pesetas)
Spain (1959)	53,548	11,954	4,434
North (1959)	26,982	7,217	1,576
Center (1930)	6,240	3,691	168
South (1930)	3,776	4,323	194
Northern Spain			
Galicia	14,457	1,951	473
Leon and Burgos	5,859	1,439	181
Biscay Coast	2,467	868	256
Aragon-Ebro	3,348	1,933	360
Catalonia	851	1,026	306
Central Spain			
Old Castile	2,695	1,266	50.9
New Castile	1,734	1,003	34.4
Levante	1,341	912	55.1
Southeast	470	510	27.1
Southern Spain			
Western Andalusia	839	1,198	68.3
Estremadura	1,032	947	42.7
La Mancha	1,374	1,676	48.7
Eastern Andalusia	531	502	33.9

NOTE: Sources and categories estimated are the same as in Table 2, to which this table corresponds.

TABLE D   DISTRIBUTION OF LARGE HOLDINGS IN 1930 AND 1959 (ABSOLUTE QUANTITIES)

	Total Number of Holdings (thousands)	Total Area (thousands of hectares)	Total Taxable Income (thousands of pesetas)
A. Large holdings defined as those over 100 hectares			
Spain (1959)	49.3	12,277	1,377
North (1959)	8.0	1,764	234
Center (1930)	6.3	1,687	24
South (1930)	22.4	8,120	180
B. Large holdings defined as those over 250 hectares			
Spain (1959)	14.1	7,345	744
North (1959)	2.0	926	110
Center (1930)	2.1	1,080	14
South (1930)	10.4	6,388	131
C. Regional analysis of holdings of over 250 hectares			
Northern Spain			
Galicia	0.3	113	18.0
Leon and Burgos	0.5	234	16.0
Biscay Coast	0.2	75	11.3
Aragon-Ebro	0.8	398	37.3
Catalonia	0.2	106	27.2
Central Spain			
Old Castile	0.4	276	4.0
New Castile	0.4	232	4.7
Levante	0.6	259	2.3
Southeast	0.6	313	3.2
Southern Spain			
Western Andalusia	4.0	2,455	62.9
Estremadura	2.5	1,239	34.7
La Mancha	2.6	1,870	18.4
Eastern Andalusia	1.2	824	14.7

NOTE: Sources and categories estimated are the same as in Table 3, to which this table corresponds.

TABLE E DISTRIBUTION OF OWNERS AND ESTIMATED AREA IN SPAIN AS A WHOLE
IN 1959

Size Category (hectares)	Number of Owners	Percent of All Owners	Percent of "True" Owners	Average Size (hectares)	Estimated Percent of Total Area	Percent of "True" Owner Area
Gardeners	3,128,953	52.3	—	0.4	2.7	—
Small Owners	2,357,667	39.4	82.4	3.1	17.0	17.5
Medium Owners	451,734	7.5	15.8	26.4	27.9	28.7
Large Owners	50,413	0.8	1.8	444.9	52.4	53.9
Gardeners						
0.0–0.5	2,054,592	34.3	—	0.2	1.0	—
0.5–1	1,074,361	17.9	—	0.7	1.8	—
Small Owners						
1–5	1,805,012	30.1	63.1	2.0	8.4	8.7
5–10	552,655	9.2	19.3	7.0	8.6	8.8
Medium Owners						
10–50	401,922	6.7	14.1	21.0	19.7	20.3
50–100	49,812	0.8	1.7	70.0	8.1	8.4
Large Owners						
100–250	27,672	0.5	1.0	155.0	10.0	10 3
250–500	12,320	0.2	0.4	340.0	9.8	10.1
500–1,000	6,491	0.1	0.2	700.0	10.6	10.9
1,000–5,000	3,586	0.1	0.1	2,000.0	16.8	17.2
Over 5,000	344	—	—	6,500.0	5.2	5.4

SOURCE: The number of owners is taken from García-Badell, "Distribución de la propiedad," Table 3.

NOTE: The method of estimating area is explained in Appendix B. The estimates total 42.79 million hectares, as opposed to the 42.76 million hectares actually surveyed.

TABLE F   Regional Distribution of Owners by Area in 1959 (absolute quantities)

| | Gardeners and Small Owners | | Medium Owners | | Large Owners | |
	A (thousands of owners)	B (thousands of hectares)	A (thousands of owners)	B (thousands of hectares)	A (thousands of owners)	B (thousands of hectares)
Spain	5,487	8,434	452	11,929	50	22,428
North	2,196	3,786	134	3,348	9	4,426
Center	1,828	2,444	160	4,290	14	5,943
South	1,228	1,752	146	4,096	27	11,625
Northern Spain						
Galicia	957	1,277	35	795	1	417
Leon and Burgos	385	809	21	495	2	991
Biscay Coast	252	442	16	388	1	455
Aragon-Ebro	360	821	37	968	3	1,794
Catalonia	243	437	26	703	3	770
Central Spain						
Old Castile	673	977	70	1,921	5	2,027
New Castile	332	247	45	1,161	4	2,162
Levante	635	820	23	587	2	826
Southeast	189	400	22	621	3	928
Southern Spain						
Western Andalusia	318	324	43	1,265	9	4,053
Estremadura	368	543	40	1,119	8	3,558
La Mancha	353	555	45	1,215	7	2,939
Eastern Andalusia	192	330	18	497	3	1,075

NOTE: Sources and categories estimated are the same as in Table 6, to which this table corresponds. "A" columns indicate the number of owners in a given category; "B" columns, the estimated area they held. The regional totals fall short of the national because the latter includes the Balearic and Canary Islands.

TABLE G DISTRIBUTION OF OWNERS AND ESTIMATED TAXABLE INCOME IN SPAIN AS A WHOLE IN 1959

Assessed Income Category (pesetas)	Number of Owners	Percent of All Owners	Percent of "True" Owners	Estimated Average Income (pesetas)	Estimated Percent of Total Income	Estimated Percent of "True" Owner Income
Gardeners	3,428,124	57.2	—	98	4.8	—
Small Owners	2,348,882	39.2	91.7	1,231	41.3	43.3
Medium Owners	187,710	3.1	7.3	10,452	28.0	29.4
Large Owners	24,889	0.4	1.0	73,070	26.0	27.3
Gardeners						
0–100	2,074,246	34.6	—	41	1.2	—
100–200	801,292	13.4	—	144	1.6	—
200–300	552,586	9.2	—	246	1.9	—
Small Owners						
300–500	643,613	10.8	25.1	402	3.7	3.9
500–1,000	760,999	12.7	29.7	801	8.7	9.1
1,000–2,000	560,395	9.4	21.9	1,432	11.5	12.0
2,000–5,000	383,187	6.4	15.0	3,179	17.4	18.3
Medium Owners						
5,000–10,000	120,289	2.0	4.7	6,814	11.7	12.3
10,000–20,000	50,851	0.8	2.0	14,977	10.9	11.4
20,000–30,000	16,602	0.3	0.6	22,935	5.4	5.7
Large Owners						
30,000–40,000	8,145	0.1	0.3	34,552	4.0	4.2
over 40,000	16,744	0.3	0.7	91,807	21.9	23.0

SOURCE: The number of owners is taken from García-Badell, "Distribución de la propiedad," Table 5.

NOTE: For the method of estimating average income, see Appendix B. My estimates produce a taxable income of 7,008 million pesetas as against a true taxable income of 7,366 million pesetas. The assessed taxable income in 1959 should be multiplied by four to approximate real income.

TABLE H   DISTRIBUTION OF OWNERS BY ASSESSED TAXABLE INCOME IN 1930 AND
1959 (ABSOLUTE QUANTITIES)

| | Gardeners and Small Owners | | Medium Owners | | Large Owners | |
| | A | B | A | B | A | B |
	(thousands of owners)	(thousands of pesetas)	(thousands of owners)	(thousands of pesetas)	(thousands of owners)	(thousands of pesetas)
Spain (1959)	5,777	3,228	188	1,962	25	1,819
North (1959)	2,297	1,304	58	574	4	288
Center (1930)	866	109	24	64	3	55
South (1930)	833	119	49	113	14	239
Northern Spain						
Galicia	983	455	10	86	—	27
Leon and Burgos	402	181	5	44	—	25
Biscay Coast	278	173	10	92	1	31
Aragon-Ebro	383	296	16	158	1	105
Catalonia	252	198	18	195	2	101
Central Spain						
Old Castile	254	26	6	19	1	21
New Castile	160	19	7	13	1	16
Levante	326	40	9	19	1	11
Southeast	125	24	2	12	—	8
Southern Spain						
Western Andalusia	261	42	18	44	6	110
Estremadura	159	24	12	27	4	70
La Mancha	265	33	11	22	2	30
Eastern Andalusia	148	20	8	20	2	29

NOTE: Sources and categories estimated are the same as in Table 7, to which this
table corresponds. "A" columns indicate the number of owners in each category;
"B" columns, the assessed taxable income of lands held by such owners. The low figures
for Central and Southern Spain are, of course, due to the incompleteness of the Cadastre
in 1930 and to the change in the value of the peseta.

Appendix D:

Methodology Used to Establish Family Relationships and Absenteeism among Large Owners

Family relationships (Table 18). The methods used in drawing up Table 18 are quite simple. Spaniards normally employ not one but two surnames. The basic assumption in the "extended family groups" category was that if a surname was very unusual, those individuals who held it either as their paternal or maternal surname were probably related to each other. In many cases other evidence existed in the Inventory to corroborate this assumption; in some, the surname stood as the only link. Once a surname was chosen, all individuals who shared it were gathered together, the small and medium owners among them were eliminated to avoid irrelevancies that would obscure the true extent of property concentration,[1] and the holdings of the remaining large owners—those with more than 250 hectares throughout the province —were totaled to determine the collective holdings of each extended family group. To enrich the analysis, each extended family was broken down into the number of individuals and sibling groups it included. The number of noble titleholders is also given.

A wide variety of family relationships are included in the extended families, because many different types of individuals may share a single surname. At times the relationship is as close as father and son; in most instances, however, the landowners studied were uncles and nephews, or cousins. In the latter cases, of course, the danger exists that the relationship may have become so distant as to be no longer meaningful. There is also a possibility that a few unrelated individuals may accidentally share a single surname, however unusual that surname might be. Neither of these problems arises with the isolated sibling groups, both those included within the extended families and those "isolated" groups that constitute the table's second category. These are undisputably closely woven units of brothers and sisters, since both surnames of the individuals in question were the same, and additional evidence of family relationship, such as identical inheritance dates and

1. Relatively few members of the large landholding families were without large properties of their own. Only forty-seven individuals related to one of the extended family or sibling groups owned less than 250 hectares throughout the province. Their combined holdings were only 7,095 hectares.

identical birthplaces, was always present. Though described as "isolated," many of these sibling groups were in fact probably related to each other or to some of the sibling groups within the extended families, since they held either the same maternal or the same paternal surname. Because the single surname shared in these cases was not an unusual one, however, I did not consider it adequate evidence of family ties. The same was true for several of the largest individual proprietors, who are included as the third category of Table 18 in order to round off my description of property concentration in Badajoz. Although these persons were without any positive family connections to other large owners, some of their surnames coincided with the more common surnames found in the family or sibling groups. In short, although the interlocking of ownership may be overstated somewhat for the extended family groups, it is understated in the other two categories and in the table as a whole.

Bourgeois absenteeism (*Table 20*). Two major problems confront the researcher. First, he must decide what to do with owners born in the capital of the province in which they held lands (the sole source of information on bourgeois absenteeism, the Inventory of Expropriable Property, lists only the birthplaces of owners, not their places of residence). It may be argued that such persons should not be suspected of absenteeism, because birth may not indicate residence but only that women of means customarily traveled from the rural districts to the nearest city to deliver. Moreover, even if residence could be proven, it need not reflect neglect of the land by the owner, since the provincial capital may be as convenient to his property as any of the villages in which he might live. Although neither argument is entirely convincing, both contain sufficient merit to warrant the exclusion from the findings presented in Table 20 of persons born in the local provincial capitals. It should be remembered, however, that absenteeism of the local provincial capital variety is considerable. For example, in five fertile counties of Seville 16.8 percent of the land belonged to persons born in the provincial capital. Since neither of the two arguments mentioned is particularly compelling in these five counties, it would seem safe to assume that at least half of these owners were true absentees.[2]

A problem of interpretation also arises in connection with bourgeois

2. The arguments are not compelling because (1) the county seats (Carmona, Écija, Marchena, Morón, and Osuna) were all very large towns (their populations in 1930 ranged from 17,500 in Marchena to 30,000 in Écija) with medical facilities of their own, and (2) at least three-quarters of their territories (I excluded from my analysis the townships of Carmona that lie closest to Seville) is more than 50 kilometers from the provincial capital, a considerable distance given the state of road transportation in Spain in the early part of the twentieth century. The quasi-absentee status of owners born in the provincial capitals is also suggested by the fact that, in the sample area used for Table 20, they continuously leased 27.7 percent of their land, whereas only 14.9 percent of the land that belonged to other bourgeois owners not included in the "extraprovincial urban absentee" category was so leased.

owners born outside the province in which their lands were located. Since non-nobles are much more likely than nobles to strike out in search of economic opportunity, one cannot be sure whether an owner whose birthplace was distant from his property still lived there and managed his lands at long distance or whether he had established a new permanent residence close to his lands.[3] I tried to overcome this difficulty by a compromise that undoubtedly understates the frequency of absenteeism. All individuals born in cities of the Madrid and San Sebastian type, or in one of the more glamorous Southern provincial capitals, were listed as absentees on the assumption that economic opportunities are so many and life is so sweet in such cities that residents will rarely move to rural districts. On the other hand persons born in distant rural or semirural communities—including in the latter category such lesser Southern capitals as Ciudad Real and Huelva and such northern capitals as Burgos, Palencia, and Soria—were excluded from the table, because even though many of them undoubtedly remained in their places of origin, most probably bought lands only after they had emigrated to the Andalusian countryside.

3. That there is no such problem with the nobility is indicated by the almost perfect correspondence between my findings on the grandeza and those of Professor Linz on the lesser nobility (see nn. 36, 37 of chap. 3) despite the different methods of measurement employed.

Appendix E:

Pre-Republican Agrarian Reform Proposals

One of the major ironies of Spanish history is that agrarian reform was seriously advocated in the highest political circles long before the age of organized social protest, but once the peasantry actually began to revolt the state found itself without any policy except repression. The first great impetus toward reform came from four ministers of Charles III (1759–88)—Aranda, Campomanes, Floridablanca and Olavide—who believed that by means of a general agrarian law the state could fulfill the threefold objective of stimulating agricultural production, benefiting the impoverished masses, and increasing its own revenues. The chief victims of the reform were to be the Church, the municipalities, and, indirectly, the nobility. The principle upon which the reform was to be based was the delivery of the land to poor peasants not in ownership, but under emphyteutic leases that would be supervised by the state. The peasant would thus acquire permanent use of the land without having to purchase it. The low rents he was to pay would go to the titular owners of the land, who would thus continue to receive some income from their properties. The state would benefit from the increased production and tax revenues that would result from the opening of empty lands to cultivation.[1]

Although the general agrarian law was never enacted, the economic logic behind it could not be denied permanently. More land had to be opened to cultivation as the population expanded, and this could not be done until the soil had been wrenched from the "dead hands" that held it under the ancien régime. This necessity was so compelling that within seventy years of Charles III's death the sweeping land transfers advocated by his ministers had in fact taken place. But if the Church, the municipalities, and, to a lesser extent, the nobility lost their possessions, the beneficiaries of the change were not the poor peasants whom Aranda and Olavide in particular had favored. Partly because of the inexorable financial needs of the state as it staggered

1. On the proposed reforms and the socioeconomic conditions to which they were responding, see Herr, *Eighteenth Century Revolution*, pp. 86–119; Domínguez Ortiz, *Sociedad española*, pp. 255–343; and the brilliant article by Marcelin Defourneaux, "Le problème de la terre en Andalousie au XVIIIe siècle et les projets de réforme agraire," *Revue Historique*, 217 (1957), 42–57.

after 1793 through endless wars and revolutions, and partly because of the introduction of liberal economic thought with its emphasis on the free play of market forces, the immense holdings of the ancient corporations were auctioned to the highest bidders, not granted without charge to those who most needed them. The social objectives of Charles III's ministers were forgotten and only their economic objectives were fulfilled. Instead of an agrarian reform, there was only a *desamortización*.[2]

It is difficult to see how this outcome could have been avoided. Aside from its financial exigence and its acceptance of liberal economic doctrine, the state did not have any immediately compelling reason to attempt the paternalistic settlement that Aranda and Olavide had contemplated: because the peasantry remained quiescent during the first half of the nineteenth century while the property structure of Spain was being transformed, only the economic logic of Charles III's ministers was irrefutable, not their social reasoning. Despite its inevitability, however, one cannot help regret the shift of policy. Huge quantities of land that were politically easily accessible and that might have been used to calm peasant unrest once it began were transferred to wealthy individuals from whom they could not easily be retaken.

The squandering of Church and common lands aroused scattered opposition throughout the nineteenth century, particularly during the First Republic.[3] It was not until the turn of the twentieth century, however, that a new consensus in favor of agrarian reform began to be discernible. There are several reasons for the gradual change in attitude: the European-wide waning of classical liberal economic thought during the last two decades of the nineteenth century had obvious repercussions within Spain; the writings of Joaquín Costa in the late 1890s and early 1900s discredited the desamortización and created a powerful myth of agrarian collectivism; above all, the organizational gains of the Anarchists and Socialists among the peasantry and the rural strike wave of 1903–04 revived fears of general peasant unrest or rebellion. The process of evolution was facilitated by the deaths of Cánovas del Castillo and Sagasta in 1897 and 1903, which opened the Restoration party system to new leaders who were more attuned to popular demands. Although the Liberal party was to prove itself more active in the search for a wider social program, the Conservative party did not lag far behind.

2. The effects of the desamortización are briefly discussed above, chap. 2. On the role of Jovellanos's thought in paving the way for the desamortización, compare Viñas y Mey, *Reforma agraria . . . en el siglo XIX*, pp. 19–22, and Herr, pp. 376–87.

3. Parliamentary opposition to the desamortización prior to 1868 is best discussed by Viñas y Mey. Ministerio de Trabajo, D.G. de Acción Social, *Los reyes y la colonización interior de España desde el siglo XVI al XIX* (Madrid, 1929) describes some of the exceedingly minor resettlement efforts that were exceptions to the general giveaway of lands during this period. Unfortunately, although some information can be found in works like Joaquín Costa, *La tierra y la cuestión social* (Madrid, 1912), no comparable studies have been done for the revolutionary period of 1868–75, or for the Restoration monarchy that followed.

The first important political manifestation of the new attitude was probably José Canalejas's cry, while serving as Minister of Agriculture in the Liberal ministry of 1901, for "the disappearance of the latifundios and the construction of an intermediate class between the great proprietor and the modest cultivator." In 1902, the first major investigation into wages and living conditions of landless workers in Andalusia and Estremadura was undertaken. In 1903, the Institute of Social Reforms was founded to study social problems and recommend ameliorative legislation.[4] During the same year, the king sponsored a widely publicized competition for solutions to "The Agrarian Problem in Southern Spain." [5] In 1905, the Count of Romanones, while serving as Minister of Development in a new Liberal cabinet, made an equally well-publicized tour of the South to focus attention on its problems. During that same year, the new concern of both major parties with agrarian affairs began to be reflected in an outpouring of legislation that continued almost to the end of the decade. Yet if a change of attitude had occurred, it was not so pronounced as to permit radical social experimentation. With one exception, the post-1905 legislation was entirely devoted to agricultural credit, cooperation, and education—all of which were thought to be indirect economic solutions to the social problem—and shied away from direct action.[6] Even that exception—the 1907 law sponsored by Augusto González Besada, Minister of Development in the Conservative cabinet of Antonio Maura—was as much an indication of the distance that remained to be traveled before major land reform would be politically possible as it was of the distance that had already been traversed.

The Besada law created a Junta for the Colonization and Repopulation of the Countryside to settle poor peasants who lacked land. Unfortunately, the name given the Junta was more grandiose than the functions it was allowed to perform. It was not authorized to expropriate private property: Besada specifically rejected the idea that his law in any way forecast an attack upon the large owners, who, he said, "perform an essential function by serving as a model" to smaller cultivators. Nor was it permitted to purchase private lands voluntarily placed on the market by their owners, or common

4. In some ways the most important innovation of this period, the IRS succeeded a weaker Commission of Social Reforms, which had also been founded in response to social unrest after the Mano Negra disturbances of 1883 (see chap. 5). Its guiding spirit was Segismundo Moret, the Liberal politician who stands with Canalejas as the statesman most concerned with social reform in the early 1900s.

5. Although the 1903 competition was the only governmental venture into the field, it was not so unique as is sometimes believed. The Royal Academy of Moral and Political Sciences, for example devoted its essay contests of 1873, 1885, and 1909–11 to similar themes. Moreover, as a glance at the Academy's *Antologia de discursos de ingreso* (2 vols. Madrid, 1963) will confirm, a surprising number of the inaugural speeches of the notables who were admitted were concerned with the agrarian problem. As in the seventeenth and eighteenth centuries there was no lack of proposed remedies in Spain, but only of the ability and will to act upon them.

6. On the rural legislation of the 1905–09 period, see chap. 4.

lands that the municipalities might want to sell.[7] Rather, the Junta was rendered completely dependent upon those common lands that were so worthless to the municipalities that they would be willing to cede them gratis to the State. In consequence, the century's first official attempt to settle peasants turned out to be less a measure of social reform than a land reclamation project of the most primitive and unrewarding sort. The lands opened to settlers in Denía (Alicante), for example, consisted of the summit and slopes of a mountain. In Sanlúcar de Barrameda (Cadiz), sand dunes were eventually rendered arable by the ingenious but cruel method of digging deep pockets into which water from the surrounding slopes would seep.[8] Since the budget of the Junta was not suited to the financing of such herculean tasks on a large scale (it averaged less than one-tenth of one percent of the national budget), it is hardly surprising that the Junta settled an annual average of only 91 peasants and 624 hectares during the eighteen years in which it functioned.[9] Nevertheless, the Besada law was important because by involving the State in the process of resettlement it created precedents upon which others could expand.

The first serious proposal for land reform legislation had to await the coming to power in February 1910 of José Canalejas, the Liberal maverick who for a decade had been trying to convert his party from its traditional laissez faire orientation. The agrarian bill Canalejas presented to the Cortes in June 1911 had three principal parts. The central absurdity of the Besada law was to be eliminated by authorizing the Junta to start settlements on all of the remaining common lands, not solely on those waste portions for which the municipalities had no other use. The Junta was also to be given funds with which to purchase private estates as they were placed on the market. Finally, it could forcibly expropriate private lands that lay in "areas irrigated by hydraulic works financed in whole or in part by the state" if it decided

7. On both counts, Besada and the Maura government lagged behind enlightened opinion. Three years earlier, for example, Segismundo Moret had called for the opening of all the approximately 10 million hectares of remaining common lands to settlement (*D.S.* 190, 7 July 1904, pp. 5682–85), and in the royal competition of 1903, at least 21 of the 66 entries advocated the purchase of private estates as they appeared on the market (Gallardo Lobato, *Problema agrario en Andalucía*, p. 22).

8. As a commentary on the miserable social conditions that existed in Spain, many of the barren lands donated were already being worked by squatters, who were reorganized by the Junta as settlers. In addition to the Junta's own *Boletín*, an excellent summary of its operations appears in Enrique Alcaraz, "The Problems of Home Colonization," International Institute of Agriculture, *Monthly Bulletin of the Bureau of Economic and Social Intelligence,* 26 (1912), 174–94. Also useful is Jupin, *Question agraire en Andalousie*, pp. 145–54.

9. Cristóbal de Castro, *Al servicio de los campesinos: Hombres sin tierra; Tierra sin hombres* (Madrid, 1931), p. 193. A total of 1,679 peasants were settled on 11,243 hectares between 1908 and 1926.

that this was in the "general interest." [10] Although the Junta's field of activity remained sharply restricted, a small breach had finally been made in the century-old tradition of the absolute sanctity of private property.

It is difficult to decide whether Canalejas's bill would have passed the Cortes had he lived. On the one hand, Canalejas acquired greater personal preeminence during his term in office than any other prime minister throughout the entire decade of the 1910s; his bill also enjoyed some political legitimacy in that its most radical provision was associated with the problem of irrigation, the one aspect of agrarian reform that most Spaniards accepted as necessary. On the other hand, the prime minister was undoubtedly in advance of his party. Until the wave of peasant upheaval that followed World War I, land reform was an active concern of only a few far-sighted leaders of the Liberal and Conservative parties and did not generate much enthusiasm among the rank and file. Even for the leaders, the reform had relatively low priority because, so long as the peasantry remained quiescent, other issues were more pressing. These factors, together with the high degree of ministerial instability that characterized the period (eight cabinets governed from 1910 to 1917), resulted in the recurrent spectacle of fairly advanced proposals being presented to the Cortes only to languish in committee or, if favorably reported, to fail to find a place on the Cortes agenda.[11]

The Canalejas bill itself was never brought to a test because, although it was reported out of committee with only slight alterations in May 1912, almost a year after it had been submitted, floor debates had not begun when Canalejas was assassinated in November. His successor, Romanones, was unable to advance the measure during his short term in office.[12] Eduardo Dato,

10. The Canalejas bill appears in *D.S.* 51, 5 June 1911, app. 2, and the committee report on it in *D.S.* 113, 11 May 1912, p. 3094. Cristóbal de Castro conveniently reprints as appendices the texts of this and most of the other official bills mentioned hereafter. For the committee texts, however, the *Diario de las Sesiones* of the Cortes is the only source.

11. The following timetable for cabinet-approved proposals summarizes the pattern:

Bill sponsored by	Date submitted to Cortes	Date reported by committee	Date sponsoring government falls
Canalejas	5 June 1911	11 May 1912	12 Nov. 1912
Dato	13 Nov. 1914	(Never)	9 Dec. 1915
Alba	30 Sept. 1916	(Never)	19 April 1917
Ossorio y Gallardo	11 July 1919	(Never)	20 July 1919
Lizárraga	13 May 1921	14 Dec. 1921	20 Dec. 1921
Maura	2 March 1922	21 March 1922	6 Dec. 1922

In the last two cases, the date in the final column refers to the date at which the Cortes was disbanded and new elections held, rather than to the fall of the sponsoring government.

12. Romanones resubmitted it to the parliament (*D.S.* 196, 6 December 1912, app. 5) but it was buried in committee until his fall on 27 October 1913.

the Conservative leader who most closely paralleled the position that Canalejas had held among the Liberals, reintroduced the bill to the new Cortes chosen in the elections of 1914.[13] But so little impetus remained that this time the bill failed even to emerge from committee.

The main line of development—that of legislation which would permit the direct expropriation and resettlement of modest amounts of land—begun by Canalejas was interrupted after the elections of 1916 by Santiago Alba, Minister of Finance in a new Romanones government. Alba's proposals are of great interest both because of their radical nature and because they represent an alternative approach to the agrarian problem which, unfortunately, was almost totally neglected by the Second Republic in the decisive years from 1931 to 1933. Alba sought to achieve by a fundamental tax reform the three objectives that had once been pursued by the ministers of Charles III: to increase State revenues, expand agricultural production, and at the same time bring about social improvements. In his attempt, he was influenced both by the thought of Henry George, who had acquired a small but active group of followers in Spain, and by the pre–World War I tax program of the English minister, David Lloyd-George.

The central provision of Alba's bill of 30 September 1916 imposed a graduated surtax, which ranged from 15 to 30 percent, on all "unearned increments" in the value of the land. This tax affected both urban and rural properties; among the latter, it sought indirectly to achieve the purpose of the Canalejas proposal by forcing owners either to pay for or dispose of properties they held in irrigation zones, since those properties received an enormous unearned increment in value when water was brought to them. A second graduated surtax was to be placed on all properties (urban as well as rural) that had an assessed taxable income of more than 30,000 pesetas; although the rates of this surtax were low (they ranged from 2 to 6 percent), it was important because it tried to establish the principle that large properties could be discriminated against merely because of their size and wealth. The third surtax was not graduated and affected only rural properties: all estates that contained arable land but were untilled would be obliged to pay 25 percent more than the normal rates. Finally, so as also to force all other owners to make better use of their farms and thus provide greater employment opportunities, Alba called for an alteration in the basis on which the regular land tax was computed so that assessments would no longer be based on the existing use of the land but on its maximum potential productivity.[14]

13. *D.S.* 85, 14 November 1914, app. 2.
14. Some of the ideas of Alba have been applied in highly diluted form by the Franco government. Thus, although he has placed no surtax on irrigated land, Franco justifies the expropriation of small parts of it because of the unearned increment, or *plusvalía,* which the rest receives when water is brought to it. Uncultivated arable lands also pay no surtax but are theoretically subject to other penalties under the "improvable farms" program instituted in 1953. Finally, Franco's 1957 tax reform subjected large farms to more severe taxation, partly through greater emphasis on their potential productive capacity rather than their actual use. The

In addition to these indirect measures, Alba advocated more direct state action. If the owners who did not till their lands failed to make reasonable progress toward cultivation within two years despite the surtax they had to pay, the state could force them to sell at low prices to individuals or peasant associations that would cultivate; if no buyers appeared, then the state could itself expropriate the land and distribute it to small settlers. Major reforms in lease conditions were also proposed. Once the revisions had been made in the assessments for the regular land tax, owners would be prohibited from demanding rents that exceeded the new assessments. If the tenants made improvements in the lands they leased, the owners were obliged to reimburse them. When such improvements increased the value of the farm by more than 50 percent, then the tenant could oblige the owner to sell it to him at the low price of twenty times its assessed taxable income. Nor did Alba neglect the institutional apparatus necessary to buttress his reforms. As a capstone to his tax bill, he simultaneously introduced another measure which called for the creation of an Agrarian Bank that would finance expropriation by the state, the purchase of land by tenants, and the improvements that owners might want to make in order to bring their untilled properties up to the levels of cultivation at which they would be exempt from the penalties mentioned.[15]

Alba's proposals were so far in advance of their times that there was never any chance that the Cortes would approve them. Even if it had, the tradition-bound Spanish bureaucracy lacked the energy, imagination, and sophistication necessary to administer so subtle and complex a program. The bills lay buried in committee during the six months of office that remained to the Romanones government. Alba resubmitted them to the new Cortes elected in 1918 when he returned to the Ministry of the Treasury with the short-lived García Prieto government of that year, but this time he lacked even cabinet support and had to present them as private measures.[16]

Although Alba failed, the climate of opinion was becoming much more favorable to agrarian reform during the two years that separated his ministries. The revolutions in Russia, the massive land redistributions that began to take place in Eastern Europe, and the appearance in Spain in 1917 of peasant protest on an unprecedented scale converted many politicians, however reluctantly, into agrarian reformers. Yet if the apathy that had blocked earlier measures had diminished, the governmental instability that characterized the 1912–17 period concurrently increased to such an extent that effective action still proved impossible. Twelve cabinets headed by eight different men governed between 1918 and 1923, as compared to seven cabinets headed by three different men between 1912 and 1917. Moreover the War and its

Republic, by contrast, ignored Alba almost completely, especially after the early proposals to establish a surtax on all large properties had been defeated (see chap. 6).

15. Both Alba's lease provisions and his proposed Agrarian Bank are, of course, strongly reminiscent of certain aspects of the Azaña program (see chaps. 8, 9, and 10). The texts of Alba's bills appear in D.S. 55, 30 September 1916, apps. 6 and 7.

16. D.S. 100, 26 November 1918, p. 3300 and app. 1.

aftermath intensified other problems—particularly the urban labor problem, the colonial struggle in Spanish Morocco, and the constitutional conflict between the Cortes on the one side and the king and army on the other—to such a degree that despite the greater concern with agrarian reform, no higher priority could be given to it than before.

Once again then, we can only evaluate intentions, not deeds. Two major currents are apparent during the five years between the end of World War I and the establishment of the Primo de Rivera dictatorship in September 1923. The first to appear was the major upsurge in social Catholicism, principally as a reaction to the sudden organizational gains made by the Anarchosyndicalists and Socialists among the peasantry from 1917 onwards. Few Spanish Catholics went to the point of imitating the radical style and tactics of mass organization that characterized the contemporary Popolari movement of Don Sturzo in Italy. Nevertheless, the Southern countryside was suddenly overrun with Catholic organizers and the propertied classes were bombarded with pleas that they help the poor by voluntarily turning over some of their lands to them. In the Cortes, first through individual deputies like Felix Villalobos and then through an informal proto-Christian Democratic group headed by Ángel Ossorio y Gallardo, Catholic-inspired proposals for agrarian reform were placed on the agenda.

Catholic attention centered primarily upon the small tenant farmers, whose numbers had increased but whose social and economic position had deteriorated during the closing years of the World War. The Villalobos and Ossorio y Gallardo bills of 1918 to 1921 sought to prohibit subleasing, protect tenants against excessive rents, and force owners to grant long leases.[17] In the countryside, the local Catholic syndicates tried to obtain collective leases on extensive tracts of land so as to be able to replace the large tenants (arrendadores) who increasingly acted as middlemen between the owners and smaller tenants. Neither initiative was successful. In the parliament, for reasons that I have not been able to discover, the Catholic lease bills attracted much sympathy but considerably less specific support than other more comprehensive measures and so died in committee. As to the local syndicates, after a couple of years of apparent progress they ran up against the fundamental contradiction that always limited the scope of Catholic action in Southern Spain and reduced its chances for permanent success. Reassured by the waning of the rural social crisis after 1920, the large owners who had rallied behind Catholic efforts to bridge class cleavages so long as they felt themselves to be in danger now stopped their financial contributions to the syndicates and became more reluctant to fulfill their "Christian duty" by voluntarily making concessions to the peasants.[18]

17. The Villalobos bill appears in D.S. 60, 19 June 1918, pp. 1829–33. The first Ossorio y Gallardo proposal can be found in the Diario de las Sesiones for 11 July 1919, the second in D.S. 21, 25 February 1921, app. 6.
18. On the Catholic syndicates in action, see Díaz del Moral, passim, but especially pp. 389–410.

The other main line of development that had originated in the crisis of 1917–20 culminated in a bill inspired by the Conservative leader Eduardo Dato and presented to the Cortes, after his assassination, by the Count of Lizárraga, head of the newly created Ministry of Labor in the Allende Salazar government. This bill, dated 31 May 1921, was far more ambitious than any of its predecessors except for the quixotic tax measures of Alba; both its provisions and the reception it received in parliament revealed the transformation that had occurred in the political climate since Canalejas had first attacked the absolute sanctity of private property ten years earlier. The right of the state to settle all remaining common lands and to expropriate private properties in irrigation areas when their owners did not construct the necessary secondary works had by now become a commonplace which aroused no opposition. The bill's assertion of the right to expropriate "privately owned lands that are abandoned, uncultivated, or insufficiently exploited" was also no longer particularly controversial. The radical quality of the bill, rather, lay in its establishment of the principle that the state could expropriate property on the basis of its size alone in case of social necessity. According to Article 10, whenever an owner's property, whether in the form of a single farm or of several scattered plots, exceeded 500 hectares within any municipality, the surplus portions became liable to expropriation. This did not mean that a maximum size limit had been established, since expropriation would not occur automatically, as under the 1932 Agrarian Reform Law of the Republic, but only if the land could be "cultivated with higher yields or with greater benefit for the proletarian classes." [19] Nevertheless, a potential limitation on the size of properties had been created.

The parliamentary reaction to the Dato- Lizárraga bill was surprising, particularly since the Liberal and Conservative parties that had governed Spain since 1875 continued to dominate the Cortes. All previous measures since 1910 had either been buried in committee or, in the case of the Canalejas bill, had emerged in attenuated form. By contrast, the committee that studied the 1921 proposal strengthened it considerably. According to its revised version, expropriation might sometimes begin on properties that exceeded 300, not 500, hectares; even smaller properties might be seized if they lay in the *ruedos,* which were so generously defined that they would have included the entire area of most Spanish villages. The provisions for compensation were also made more radical. Lizárraga had departed from previous measures by proposing that expropriated owners be paid in State bonds, rather than in cash. The committee now added the proviso that this compensation never exceed twenty times the assessed or declared taxable income of the farm, a sum that would in most cases be only about half its market value since tax valuations in the early 1920s were significantly lower than during the Republic. Finally, although the committee did not deny Lizárraga's "case" approach toward agrarian reform, it took a step toward the automatic seizure of farms that exceeded the new size limits by requiring that they be registered

19. The text of the bill appears in *D.S.* 59, 31 May 1921, app. 1.

in an Inventory of Expropriable Property to be maintained by the State.[20]

The Dato-Lizárraga bill was reported out of committee on 14 December 1921, six days before the Cortes was disbanded and new elections scheduled. Earlier this coincidence of events would have meant the death of the proposal. As a further indication of the change of attitude that had occurred, however, Antonio Maura, though formerly little concerned with agrarian reform, reactivated the measure in the second session held by the new legislature. The bill had to pass through committee once more, but was reported out again in the near-record time of three weeks.[21] Sad to record, however, the story ends here. As the Moroccan war, the street-fighting in Barcelona, and the constitutional conflict between king, army, and parliament all built up toward their climax, the agrarian problem once again began to lose its priority. Neither the Cortes of 1922 nor its even shorter-lived successor elected in 1923 found the time to debate the Dato-Lizárraga proposal. The constitutional monarchy's last effort at agrarian reform was destroyed in the death throes of Spanish democracy.

Primo de Rivera did not strongly favor rural social legislation. For him the solution to the agrarian problem lay principally in the expansion of industry to draw off workers from the farms and in the construction of irrigation works to provide fuller employment for those who remained behind. Consequently, his coup opened a hiatus in the line of development that had been unfolding since 1900. The reforms he inaugurated during his first three years of rule were important, but they should be regarded primarily as expressions of his government's desire to eliminate obvious anachronisms and rationalize existing institutions. Thus in 1923 he legalized the position of small peasants who had squatted on State lands. In 1925 he strengthened the system of municipal agricultural credit administered through the *positos* by the creation of a new national rural credit organization. In 1926 he modified the land tax somewhat and sought to bring to an end the centuries-old conflict over the *foros* in Galicia by declaring that those who worked the land could purchase titular ownership. During the same year he abolished the Junta which had been administering the absurd program of settlement via land reclamation of the 1907 Besada law. In its stead he created the Agency for Agrarian Social Action, which operated on the more fruitful principle of helping groups of tenants who could put up 20 percent of the purchase price to buy the large estates they worked, if their owners agreed to sell them. Finally, although he proceeded with it in a dilatory manner that contrasted

20. *D.S.* 106, 14 December 1921, app. 2. The committee did not, however, correct the greatest single weakness of the bill—its proposal of an annual budget of only 8 million pesetas for the administering agency. This limitation alone made the bill far less drastic than the 1932 Agrarian Reform Law, despite the resemblance between several of their provisions and the more generous definition of ruedos (5 as opposed to 2 kilometers) in the 1921 measure.

21. The Maura bill appears in *D.S.* 2, 2 March 1922, p. 14; the committee version in *D.S.* 9, 21 March 1922, app. 5. Maura meanwhile (8 March 1922) had been replaced as premier by Sánchez Guerra.

sharply with his usual impetuousness, Primo also committed himself to the elaboration of a general lease law, the one item of the pre-1923 proposals for which he felt even a minimal sympathy. In September 1925 he ordered the Ministry of Labor to begin circularizing various organizations for their views on what type of lease reform should be essayed.[22]

So long as Primo basked under the general approval that economic prosperity, his victory in the Moroccan war, and his ending of the political instability of the 1918–23 period had brought him, these limited innovations were sufficient. The political atmosphere began to change in 1927, however. Pressure for more profound rural action came not from the peasantry, which sank into almost total passivity after the social conflicts of 1917–20, and only secondarily from the Socialists, who concentrated most of their energies on the implementation of the major structural reforms Primo had introduced in industrial labor relations. Rather, the leading role was taken by the Catholics, the only other political faction of the pre-1923 era that had been permitted to continue functioning under the dictatorship. In 1927 both the liberal Catholic press and the representatives of the National Catholic Agrarian Federation who sat in Primo's newly created National Assembly inaugurated a campaign to force him to speed presentation of the general lease law that had been pending since 1925, and—though less emphasis was placed on this point—to revive the pre-1923 principle that uncultivated arable lands should be expropriated.[23]

Primo remained adamant against the concept of expropriation even in this highly restricted form. The relative success of his Agency for Agrarian Social Action (which in its first three years helped 4,202 tenants buy 21,501 hectares, as compared to the Besada Junta's record of 1,679 peasants settled on 11,243 hectares during eighteen years)[24] obviated for him the need for compulsion. Disregarding the fact that the Agency could not long maintain

22. The best summary of Primo's agrarian legislation is probably Constancio Bernaldo de Quirós, *Los derechos sociales de los campesinos* (Madrid, 1928).

23. See especially Asamblea Nacional, *D.S.* 24, 24 May 1928, pp. 917–25, and *El Debate*, 1 January 1928. Catholics hoped, of course, to use their favored position and Primo's suppression of the Anarchosyndicalists to recruit a larger peasant following. They probably would have failed even had Primo survived, because of their antiquated tactics and self-defeating attempts to emphasize class harmony where none was possible. How, for example, could most self-respecting tenants and small owners in the 1920s swear the oath that was expected of them in Catholic peasant rallies: "We recognize the right of everyone to live *in accordance with the condition in which the Lord has placed him. We consider the rich man as an older brother* in Jesus Christ and as such we respect and love him" (*D.S.* 3, 23 November 1927, p. 37; my italics).

24. Castro, *Al servicio de los campesinos*, pp. 193, 197. The relative cost of the Agency's operations was also much lower because it had only to pay for the land, not buy animals, tools, seeds and technical assistance for the settlers: whereas the Junta paid an average of 7,824 pesetas for every peasant settled, the Agency paid 2,481, and the settler himself contributed another 498 (ibid.).

its initial pace of action and was not suited to conditions in Southern Spain, where tenants lacked both the unity and the capital necessary to take advantage of its services,[25] Primo's ministers asked: why should the State expropriate when owners were offering to sell it more land than it could afford eo buy?[26] The principal thrust of the Catholic campaign, however, was more successful. After repeated pressure, Primo finally submitted a plan for a general lease law to the National Assembly in May 1929. Less radical than the proposals of the 1918–21 period, the measure nevertheless prohibited unregulated subleasing, ensured somewhat longer leases, and permitted rent reductions in case of disastrous crop failure. Caught in a crossfire between those who wanted to strengthen it and those who opposed any type of serious reform, the bill was never brought to a vote in the National Assembly but, in one of Primo's final actions before his fall, had to be issued as a Royal Decree on 21 November 1929.[27]

After nearly thirty years of discussion a single bill concerned with the least controversial aspect of agrarian reform had finally become law, and then only through use of the exceptional powers of the dictatorship. So slight a success could not wipe away the sorry record of the past or give to the Republic that was to be proclaimed a year and a half later a firm basis on which to build. Partly because of the apathy that long characterized the Restoration party system, partly because of the disintegration of government under the challenges of the 1910s and early 1920s, and partly because Primo de Rivera destroyed the reform consensus that was developing in the parliaments of 1921–23 without substituting energetic rural social action of his own, the Republic was forced to start from scratch. In consequence, its already difficult task was rendered nearly impossible.

25. Thus, only 4,873 of the 21,501 hectares settled as of 1929 were in Southern Spain (Castro, p. 197). The cost of the reform would also have increased as the Agency ran out of owners anxious to sell and had to induce others (the overwhelming majority) by paying higher prices.

26. Asamblea Nacional, *D.S.* 24, 24 May 1928, p. 923.

27. The Primo bill and the committee revisions appear in Asamblea Nacional, *D.S.* 43, 1 July 1929, apps. 1 and 4; the brief but bitter debates are reported in the daily press of 6 and 7 July 1929.

Glossary of Spanish Words

alojamiento. The palliative invoked by local authorities during severe unemployment crises whereby landowners were obliged to give jobs to a certain number of workers for a stated period of time. I have coined the term "self-*alojamiento*" to describe situations in which gangs of workers themselves sought to force owners to give them money or employment.

arrendador. In Andalusia, refers to the rich tenants who rented large estates and then often subleased portions of them to poor tenants or sharecroppers.

ayuntamiento. The government or a municipality or the town hall in which that government is housed.

behetría. A form of government in medieval Castile which gave greater than usual rights to the inhabitants of a locality as against their lord.

cacique. An American Indian term meaning "chieftain," employed in Spain to denote the local political "bosses" prominent under the Restoration monarchy.

campesino. Equivalent to the English word "peasant" in that it denotes all poor farmers, whether they be small owners, tenants, or workers.

campiña. In the province of Cordova, the name for the fertile countryside that surrounds the capital city.

censo. Used in the text as equivalent to empyteutic lease—i.e., a long term, usually inheritable lease on which the rent could not be raised.

comunales. Those portions of the common lands that (unlike the *propios*) were not rented to individuals but stayed open for use of all inhabitants.

comunismo libertario. The slogan ("free communism") by which the Anarcho-syndicalists expressed their goal of a communal society which would not be marred, as was that of the Marxian communists, by the continued or heightened use of state power.

desamortización. The vast nineteenth century disentailment of Church, municipal, and noble lands which established bourgeois owners and capitalist economic relationships as the dominant forces in large portions of rural Spain.

foro. An especially permanent and unalterable empyteutic lease common in Galicia which became the object of centuries of litigation and conflict among titular owners, *foreros* (first tenants), and *subforados* (subtenants).

grande. An especially elevated aristocratic rank held by approximately 10 percent of the Spanish nobility in the 1930s. The English word "grandee" is a corruption of this. The *grandes* collectively are known as the *grandeza*.

439

guardia. Used to refer to individual members of the Guardia Civil, the elite national police force which has played so important a role in Spanish history since the 1840s.

laboreo forzoso. The "obligatory cultivation" decree by which the Provisional Government sought to prevent landowners from discontinuing farming but which working class groups often invoked to justify their invasions of unplowed lands.

latifundio. A large landed estate (though rarely of the size of the Roman latifundia) whose owner was frequently referred to as a *latifundista.*

minifundio. The opposite of the *latifundio*—i.e., the fragmented small property which was especially common in Northern Spain.

pistoleros. Literally "gunmen," used particularly in reference to the street gangs of both the CNT and industrialists which terrorized Barcelona between 1920 and 1923.

pósitos. Local granaries which developed some credit functions during the late Middle Ages and which several governments after 1900 unsuccessfully tried to convert into modern credit institutions.

presura. The medieval Castilian custom of legalizing the settlement of empty lands which lay in uninhabited areas that were disputed with the Moslems.

pronunciamiento. Originally the "declaration" by which a military leader justified his call for rebellion, the term has also come to mean a military revolt as such.

propios. The non-*comunal* portions of the common lands which were rented by municipal governments to private individuals so as to raise revenues.

rabassaire. The fairly prosperous peasants of Catalonia who sharecropped lands on what had once been semi-emphyteutic *rabassa morta* (dead vine) leases and who sought to obtain full ownership of the land on advantageous terms during the twentieth century.

semana trágica. The "tragic week" of Barcelona during which some 100 persons were killed and many religious establishments burned in 1909.

señorío. A lord's domain or seignory. *Señorío jurisdiccional* territories were those over which a lord had enjoyed only jurisdictional rights but which he nevertheless appropriated as private property during the early nineteenth century.

términos municipales. The "township" or "municipal boundaries" act by which the Provisional Government sought to stem the flow of migrant labor into rural townships so as to strengthen local labor unions and raise local wages. This was achieved only at the cost of considerable economic dislocation and much hardship to those who relied on migrant labor as a normal part of their income.

trienio bolchevista. The "Bolshevik triennium" of 1917–20 during which Spain passed through its first truly profound labor crisis.

turno riguroso. The Socialist demand that owners be forced to hire workers from local employment offices in the "rigorous order" in which they had registered, so as to prevent discrimination against working class militants.

Selected Bibliography

In drawing up this bibliography, I made no effort to include everything that I used: only those materials which seemed to me of more than passing interest are mentioned. The bibliography is not divided according to types of material employed, except insofar as primary sources are separated from secondary, and published materials from unpublished. Rather, I employed a topical division in which all materials—whether books, articles, or public documents—are included in the division in which they have greatest relevance. In a few cases, I listed a book both as a primary and as a secondary source because it contained important information of both types. A word should be said concerning my handling of publishers. Many Spanish publications, especially those of governmental agencies, have only printers, not publishers in the traditional sense. In such cases, I have considered the author as the publisher.

I should also add that, although I exhausted the sources available as of 1965, when I completed the major portion of my research, I have not attempted to keep up with everything that has been published since. In practice, this meant that I consulted most—though not all—of the new works published between 1965 and 1967, but consciously refrained from making more than incidental use of books that appeared after the latter year. This decision, although unavoidable if my research was not to become endless, was particularly regrettable in connection with three recent publications: the last two volumes of Manuel Azaña's *Obras Completas,* edited by Juan Marichal (México: Ediciones Oasis, 1968); José María Gil Robles, *No fué posible la paz* (Barcelona: Ediciones Ariel, 1968); and, finally, a work that I had the good fortune to consult in rough draft though not in its final form, Juan Martínez Alier, *La estabilidad del latifundismo* (Paris: Ruedo Iberico, 1968).

441

Published Primary Sources

GENERAL STATISTICAL SOURCES

Until the Civil War, the *Anuarios Estadísticos de España* and the *Censos de la población de España* were published by the Direción General del Instituto Geográfico, Catastral y de Estadística. After the Civil War, this agency was reorganized as the Instituto Nacional de Estadística, under whose auspices statistical yearbooks and census findings were thereafter published. Besides these two major sources, there is an historical statistical abstract (Instituto Nacional de Estadística, *Principales actividades de la vida española en la primera mitad del siglo XX* [Madrid, Author, 1952]), which is of great value to the researcher.

SOURCES RELEVANT TO TECHNICAL ASPECTS
OF SPANISH AGRICULTURE AND LAND TENURE

Camilleri Lapeyre, Arturo. "La distribución, por provincias, del producto neto de la agricultura española en la campaña 1958–59." *Revista de Estudios Agro-Sociales,* July–September 1961, pp. 47–60.

Carrión, Pascual. *Los latifundios en España.* Madrid: Gráficas Reunida, 1932.

Consejo Económico Sindical Nacional: Ponéncia Núm. 2. *Situación actual de la agricultura.* Madrid: Author, 1957.

García-Badell, Gabriel. "La distributión de la propiedad agrícola de España en las diferentes categorias de fincas." *Revista de Estudios Agro-Sociales,* January–March 1960, pp. 7–32.

García de Oteyza, Luís. "Los regimenes de explotación del suelo nacional." *Revista de Estudios Agro-Sociales,* October–December 1952, pp. 49–62.

Instituto de Cultura Hispánica. *Estudios hispánicos de desarrollo económico: La agricultura y el crecimiento económico.* Madrid: Author, 1956.

Instituto de Estudios de Administración Local. *Estudios y estadísticas sobre la vida local de España.* 18 vols. Madrid: Author, 1940–50.

Instituto Nacional de Estadística. *Diccionario corográfico, conforme al nomenclátor de ciudades, villas, lugares, aldeas y otras entidades de población del Censo general de 1940.* 4 vols. Madrid: Author, n.d.

———. *Estadística de propietarios de fincas rústicas de España.* Madrid: Author, 1951.

———. *Primer Censo Agrario de España, Año 1962. Resumenes nacionales.* Madrid: Author, 1966.

———. *Primer Censo Agrario de España, Año 1962. Resultados provisionales: Anexo.* Madrid: Author, 1966. The innumerable other publications concerned with the 1962 Agricultural Census published by the INE should also be consulted, particularly the volumes that summarize provincial results.

Instituto de Reforma Agraria. *Boletín,* January 1933–July 1936.

Ministerio de Agricultura. *Anuario Estadístico de la producción agrícola.* Vols. for 1925–35, 1957–60. Madrid: Author, 1926–36, 1958–61.

———, Dirección General de Montes. *Estadística forestal de España.* Vols. for 1954, 1959. Madrid: Author, 1955, 1960.

———, Servico Nacional del Trigo. *La estructura de las explotaciones trigueras segun datos estadísticos de la cosecha de 1957.* Madrid: Author, 1959.

———, Servicio Nacional del Trigo. *La produccíon triguera nacional y rendimientos por hectárea del secano, por provincias, durante el quinquenio de intensificación de la producción: 1954–58.* Madrid: Author, 1959.

Ministerio de Hacienda, Dirección General de Propiedades y Contribución Territorial. *El catastro de rústica: Su iniciación y desarrollo.* Madrid: Author, 1955.

———. *Memoria de la Dirección General de Propiedades y Contribución Territorial durante el año de 1928.* Madrid: Author, 1931.

Ministerio de Justícia. *Grandezas y titulos del reino: Guía oficial.* Madrid: Author, 1959.

Torres Martínez, Manuel. *El problema triguero y otras cuestiones fundamentales de la agricultura española.* Madrid: Consejo Superior de Investigaciones científicas, 1944.

SOURCES RELEVANT TO SOCIAL ASPECTS OF THE AGRARIAN QUESTION

Banco de Bilbao. *La renta nacional de España y su distribución provincial.* Bilbao: Author, 1957.

Delegación Nacional de Sindicatos, Servicio Sindical de Estadística. *El paro obrero en Jaen.* Suplemento a los números 27 y 28 de la *Revista Sindical de Estadística,* III y IV trimestres de 1952.

Díaz del Moral, Juan. *Historia de las agitaciones campesinas andaluzas— Córdoba.* Madrid: Revista de Derecho Privado, 1929. Reprints many valuable documents.

Instituto de Reforma Agraria. *Datos recogidos.* Madrid: Author, 1934.

———. *La reforma agraria en España: Sus motivos, su eséncia, su acción.* Madrid: Author, 1937.

Instituto de Reformas Sociales. *La emigración obrera en España después de la Guerra,* ed. Constancio Bernaldo de Quirós. Madrid: Author, 1920.

———. *Estadística de las huelgas.* Vols. for 1907–20. Madrid: Author, 1908–21.

———. *Información sobre la emigración española a los paises de Europa durante la Guerra.* Madrid: Author, 1919.

———. *Información sobre el problema agrario en la provincia de Córdoba.* Madrid: Author, 1919.

———. *Memoria acerca de la información agraria en ambas Castillas.* Madrid: Author, 1904.

————. *Subarriendos y arrendamientos colectivos de fincas rusticas*. Madrid: Author, 1921.

Ministerio de Agricultura. *Censo electoral de Sindicatos Agrícolas y Comunidades de Labradores*. Madrid: Author, 1934.

————, Sindicato Vertical del Olivo. *El paro estacional campesino*. Madrid: Author, 1946.

Ministerio de Trabajo y Previsión. *Boletín*, Vols. for 1931–36.

————. *Estadística del paro involuntario en el segundo semestre de 1933*. Madrid: Author, 1934.

————. Servicio de Parcelación y Colonización Interior. *La crisis agraria andaluza de 1930–31: Estudios y documentos*. Madrid: Author, 1931.

MEMOIRS; COLLECTIONS OF SPEECHES AND DOCUMENTS; MINUTES
OF POLITICAL PARTIES AND PRESSURE GROUPS; ET CETERA

Agrupación Nacional de Propietarios de Fincas Rústicas. *Informe sobre el proyecto de ley de reforma agraria*. Madrid: Vicente Rico, 1931.

Álvarez Robles, Antonio. *La reforma agraria española*. Palencia: Imp. de la Federación Católica Agraria, 1932.

Ateneo Científico, Literario y Artístico de Madrid. *Algunos aspectos de la reforma agraria*. Madrid: Author, 1934.

Azaña, Manuel. *En el poder y en la oposición (1932–34)*. Madrid: Espasa-Calpe, 1934.

————. *Memorias íntimas de Azaña*, ed. Joaquín Arrarás. Madrid: Ediciones Espanoles, 1939.

————. *Obras completas*, ed. Juan Marichal. 4 vols. México: Edicones Oasis, 1966–68.

Berenguer, Dámaso. *De la Dictadura a la República: Crisis del Reinado de Alfonso XIII*. Madrid: Editorial Plus-Ultra, 1935.

Cierva, Ricardo de la. *Los documentos de la primavera trágica*. Madrid: Ministerio de Información y Turismo, 1967.

Confederación Nacional de Trabajo. *Memoria del Congreso celebrado en el Teatro de la Comedia de Madrid, los días 10 al 18 de diciembre de 1919*. Barcelona: Tip. Cosmos, 1932.

————. *Memoria del Congreso Extraordinario celebrado en Madrid, los días 11 al 16 de junio de 1931*. Barcelona: Tip. Cosmos, 1932.

Congreso de la Federación de Trabajadores de la Región Española celebrado en Sevilla los días 24, 25, y 26 de septiembre de 1882. Barcelona: Tip. Espanola, 1882.

Costa Martínez, Joaquín. *Oligarquía y caciquismo como la forma actual de gobierno en España*. Huesca: Ed. V. Campo, 1927.

Díaz del Moral, Juan, and Ortega y Gasset, José. *La reforma agraria y el estatuto Catalan*. Madrid: Revista de Occidente, 1932.

Díaz-Plaja, Fernando. *La historia de España en sus documentos. El siglo XX, 1923–36*. Madrid: Instituto de Estudios Politicos, 1965.

Domingo, Marcelino. *La experiencia del poder*. Madrid: 1934.

Federación de Trabajadores Agrícolas de la Comarca de Cádiz. *Memoria del Primer Congreso Comarcal celebrado los días 17 y 18 de enero de 1932.* Jerez de la Frontera: Tip. M. Martin, 1932.

Federación Nacional de Trabajadores de la Tierra. *Memoria que presenta el Comité Nacional al Congreso Ordinario que ha de celebrarse en Madrid durante los días 17 y siguientes del mes de septiembre de 1932.* Madrid: Gráfica Socialista, 1932.

Largo Caballero, Francisco. *Discursos a los trabajadores.* Madrid: Gráfica Socialista, 1934.

Maura, Miguel. *Así cayó Alfonso XIII.* Barcelona: Ediciones Ariel, 1966.

Partido Republicano Radical. *Libro de oro.* Madrid: Suc. de Rivadeneyra, 1935.

Partido Republicano Radical Socialista. *Texto taquigráfico del Cuarto Congreso Nacional Ordinario, celebrado en Madrid durante los días 3, 4, 5, 6, 7 y 8 de junio de 1933.* Madrid: Author, 1934.

———. *Texto taquigráfico del Tercer Congreso Nacional Extraordinario, celebrado en Madrid durante los días 23, 24 y 25 de septiembre de 1933.* Madrid: Author, 1934.

Partido Socialista Obrero Español. *XIII Congreso del Partido Socialista Español del 6 al 13 de octubre de 1932.* Madrid: Gráfica Socialista, 1934.

———. *Convocatoria y orden del día para el XII Congreso Ordinario del partido.* Madrid: Gráfica Socialista, 1927.

Peirats, José. *La CNT en la revolución española.* 3 vols. Toulouse: Ediciones CNT, 1951.

Prieto, Indalecio, et al. *Documentos socialistas.* Madrid: Gráfica Sánchez Lara, 1935.

Semanas Sociales de España. *Problemas agrarios de España: Semana Social de Zaragosa (30 de septiembre al 7 de octubre de 1934).* Madrid: Author, 1936.

Unión Económica. *Memoria de la Asamblea Económica-Agraria celebrada en Madrid los días 26 y 27 de abril de 1932.* Madrid: Gráfica Administrativa, 1932.

———. *Ante la reforma agraria.* Madrid: Gráfica Administrativa, 1931.

Unión General de Trabajadores. *Memoria y orden del día del XVII Congreso, que se celebrará en Madrid los días 14 y siguientes de octubre de 1932.* Madrid: Gráfica Socialista, 1932.

Vera, Jaime. *Informe presentado a la Comisión de Reformas Sociales por la Agrupación Socialista Madrileña en el año 1883.* Paris, Ediciones Tribuna Socialista, 1962.

PARLIAMENTARY DEBATES AND COLLECTIONS OF LAWS, DECREES, AND OTHER LEGAL ENACTMENTS

Diario de las sesiones de las Cortes Españolas. Vols. for 1901–23 and 1931–36.

Diario de las sesiones de la Asamblea Nacional. September 1927 to November 1929.

Díaz de Arcaya, F. *La reforma agraria de 15 de septiembre de 1932.* Madrid: Editorial Reus, 1933.

Instituto de Reforma Agraria. *Boletín,* January 1933–July 1936. Each issue reproduced recent agrarian legislation.

————.*Ley de Bases y disposiciones complementarias que afectan a las Juntas Provinciales.* Madrid: Author, 1933.

Manual de la reforma agraria, edited by the staff of *El Consultor de los Ayuntamientos y de los Juzgados Municipales.* Madrid: Imp. de *El Consultor,* 1932.

Martínez-Alcubilla, Marcelo. *Boletín jurídico-administrativo. Anuarios de legislación y jurisprudencia: 1931–35.* Madrid, 1932–36.

Ministerio de Agricultura. *Anuario de la legislación agrícola:* Vols. for 1932–36. Madrid: Author, 1933–36.

Ministerio de Trabajo. *Anuario español de política social, 1934–35,* ed. Mariano González-Rothvoss. Madrid: Author, 1935.

Mori, Arturo. *Crónica de las Cortes Constituyentes de la República Española.* 13 vols. Madrid: Aguilar, 1932.

Contemporary Newspapers and Periodicals

ABC (the leading monarchist daily).

Boletín de la Unión General de Trabajadores (monthly bulletin of the UGT).

Campo Libre (moderate Anarchosyndicalist journal published weekly after mid-1935).

Claridad (organ of the Largo Caballero faction in the Socialist Party after mid-1935).

El Debate (the leading Catholic daily).

Economía Española (monthly organ of the Unión Económica after January 1933).

La Época (conservative daily with strong ties to the leading financial groups).

España Económica y Financiera (a leading conservative business weekly).

La Luz (outstanding liberal daily published 1933–34).

The New York Times.

El Obrero de la Tierra (weekly organ of the FNTT).

Revista Social y Agraria (monthly organ of the Confederación Católica-Agraria).

El Socialista (official organ of the Socialist Party).

El Sol (the principal liberal journal).

Solidaridad Obrera (the leading organ of the CNT).

La Tierra (sensationalistic daily which expressed an Anarchosyndicalist point of view).

The Times, London.

La Voz del Campo (Communist journal which began publication in 1936).

Unpublished Primary Sources

ON TECHNICAL ASPECTS OF SPANISH AGRICULTURE AND LAND TENURE

The most important unpublished source is the Registro de la Propiedad Expropiable del Instituto de Reforma Agraria, of which 254 volumes are housed in the Archives of the Institute of Agrarian Reform (located in the Instituto de Colonización in Madrid). The tens of thousands of ill-organized documents on various farms, townships, etc., also have considerable value. Less important, but still useful, are the inscription sheets for the Encuestas Agropecuárias conducted in 1953 and 1956 by the Junta Nacional de Hermandades. These are housed in the offices of the Statistical Section of that organization, which is located in the Delegación Nacional de Sindicatos in Madrid.

ON SOCIAL ASPECTS OF THE AGRARIAN QUESTION

Instituto de Reforma Agraria. Servicio Provincial de Sevilla. "Informe-resumen sobre el desarollo de la fincas explotadas por sociedades y comunidades de campesinos durante el año agrícola 1934–35." (Undated document located in folder 41/0–1 in the IRA Archives.)
———. "Memoria." (Undated document located in folder 41/0–1 in the IRA Archives.)
———. "Memoria sobre el estado social de los asentamientos en Sevilla." (Undated document located in folder 41/0–1 in the IRA Archives.)
———, Servicio Provincial de Toledo. "Memoria sobre el estado económico-social-agrícola de las comunidades en esta provincia." (Dated October 1935, and located in folder 45/0–1 in the IRA Archives.)
Private notes which Pascual Carrión permitted me to see.

ON THE APPLICATION OF THE AGRARIAN REFORM

The minutes of the meetings of the Executive Council of the Institute of Agrarian Reform, for which I searched in vain for years, finally turned up in the recently opened archive of materials connected with the Civil War maintained by the Delegación Nacional de Servicios Documentales in Salamanca. Although I discovered these important documents far too late to use them (my book was already in its final stages of publication), they should be the starting point of research for future scholars of the agrarian problem during the Second Republic.

Published Secondary Sources

ON HISTORICAL AND TECHNICAL ASPECTS OF SPANISH AGRICULTURE
AND LAND TENURE

Alcaraz Martínez, Enrique. *El catastro español.* Barcelona: Salvat Editores,
1933.

Anlló Vázques, Juan. *Estructura y problemas del campo español.* Madrid:
Editorial Cuadernos para el Dialogo, 1966.

Barthe y Barthe, Andres. *Las grandes propiedades rústicas en España.*
Madrid: Real Academia de Ciéncias Morales y Políticas, 1912.

Cano, Rafael del. *Ante la reforma agraria.* Madrid: Editorial del Norte, 1931.

Carandell, Juan. *Distribución y estructura de la propiedad rural en la provincia
de Córdoba.* Madrid: Sob. de la Suc. de M. Minuesa de los Ríos, 1934.

Carrión, Pascual. *Los latifundios en España.* Madrid: Gráficas Reunidas, 1932.

Concha, Ignacio de la. *La "presura"; La ocupación de tierras en los primeros
siglos de la reconquista.* Madrid: Instituto Nacional de Estudios Jurídicos,
1946.

Gallardo Lobato, Juan. *El problema agrario en Andalucía.* Jerez de la Frontera:
Imp. del "Diario de Jerez," 1904.

García-Badell, Gabriel. *El catastro de la riqueza rústica en España.* Madrid:
Ministerio de Agricultura, 1944.

García Ormaechea, Rafael. *Supervivencias feudales en España.* Madrid:
Editorial Reus, 1932.

González, Julio. *Repartimiento de Sevilla.* 2 vols. Madrid: Consejo Superior
de Investigaciones Científicas, 1951.

Houston, J. M. *The Western Mediterranean World.* London: Longmans,
1964.

International Institute of Agriculture. *Bulletin of the Bureau of Economic
and Social Intelligence,* and *International Review of Agricultural Economics.* Valuable for the pre-1931 period.

Joaniquet, Aureli. *La reforma agraria a Catalunya.* Barcelona: Liberia Bosch,
1933.

Lacarra, José María, ed. *La reconquista española y la repoblación del país.*
Zaragoza: Consejo Superior de Investigaciones Científicas, 1951.

Marichalar, Luís, Vizconde de Eza. *La reforma agraria en España.* Madrid:
Sob. de la Suc. de M. Minuesa de los Ríos, 1931.

Molina de Palma, Francisco. "Contribución territorial rústica." *Información
Comercial Española,* August 1964, pp. 115–23.

Montojo Sureda, Jorge. *La política española sobre trigos y harinas: Años
1900–45.* Madrid: Afrodisio Agudo, 1945.

Naval Intelligence Division, English Admiralty. *Spain and Portugal.* 4 vols.
London: His Majesty's Stationery Office, 1941.

Quirós Linares, Francisco. "La desamortización, factor condicionante de la
estructura de la propiedad agraria en el Valle de Alcudía y Campo de
Calatrava." *Estudios Geográficos,* August 1964, 367–407.

Revenga Carbonell, Antonio. *Comarcas geográficas de España.* Madrid: Instituto Geográfico y Catastral, 1962.

Sánchez-Albornoz, Claudio. *La reforma agraria ante la historia.* Madrid: Tip. de Archivos, 1932.

Senador Gómez, Julio. *Castilla en escombres.* Valladolid: Lib. de Vda. de Montero, 1915.

Viñas y May, Carmelo. *La reforma agraria en España en el siglo XIX.* Santiago: Tip. de "El Eco Franciscano," 1933.

Zorilla, Ángel. *Introducción a la economía agrícola española en relación con la europea.* Madrid: Instituto de Estudios Agro-Sociales, 1960.

On Social Aspects of the Agrarian Question

Bernaldo de Quirós, Constancio. *Bandolerismo y delincuencia subversiva en la baja Andalucía.* Madrid: Anales de la Junta para Ampliación de Estudios e Investigaciones Científicas, 1913.

———. *Los derechos sociales de los campesinos.* Madrid: 1928.

———. *El espartaquismo andaluz.* Madrid: Biblioteca de la Revista General de Legislación y Jurisprudencia, 1919.

Bolloten, Burnett. *The Grand Camouflage.* London: Hollis & Carter, 1961.

Castro, Cristóbal de. *Al servicio de los campesinos: Hombres sin tierra; Tierra sin hombres.* Madrid: Javier Morato, 1931.

Costa Martínez, Joaquín. *La tierra y la questión social.* Madrid: E. de Fortanet, 1912.

Costedoat-Lamarque, Jean. *La question agraire en Andalousie.* Paris: E. de Boccard, 1921 [?].

Díaz del Moral, Juan. *Historia de las agitaciones campesinas andaluzas— Córdoba.* Madrid: Revista de Derecho Privado, 1929.

García Fernández, Jesús. "El moviemiento migratorio de trabajadores en España." *Estudios Geográficos,* May 1964, pp. 139–74.

Hobsbawm, E. J. *Primitive Rebels: Studies in Anarchic Forms of Social Movements in the 19th and 20th Centuries.* Manchester: University of Manchester Press, 1959.

Jupin, René. *La question agraire en Andalousie.* Paris: Libraire du Recueil Sirey, 1932.

MacDonald, J. S. "Agricultural Organization, Migration and Labour Militancy in Rural Italy." *The Economic History Review,* August 1963, pp. 61–75.

Minlos, Bruno. *Campesinos de España: En lucha por la tierra y la libertad.* Buenos Aires: Ediciones "La Nueva España," 1937.

Moret y Pendergast, Segismundo. *El problema social-agrario en España.* Madrid: Hijos de M. G. Hernández, 1904.

Pitt-Rivers, Julian. *The People of the Sierra.* London: Weidenfeld and Nicholson, 1954.

Polo Benito, J. *El problema social del campo en Extremadura.* Salamanca: Tip. de Calatrava, 1919.

Termes Ardévol, José. *El movimiento obrero en España: La Primera Internacional (1864–1881)*. Barcelona: Ediciones Ariel, 1965.

GENERAL TREATISES AND IMPORTANT MISCELLANEOUS WORKS

Álvarez del Vayo, Julio. *The Last Optimist*. New York: The Viking Press, 1950.

Araquistaín, Luís de. "The Struggle in Spain." *Foreign Affairs Quarterly*, April 1934, pp. 461–71.

Arrarás, Joaquín. *Historia de la Segunda República Española*. 4 vols. Madrid: Editorial Nacional, 1956–63.

Brenan, Gerald. *The Spanish Labyrinth*. Cambridge: Cambridge University Press, 1960.

Brugera, F. G. *Histoire contemporaine d'Espagne: 1789–1950*. Paris: Editions Orphys, 1953.

Buckley, Henry. *Life and Death of the Spanish Republic*. London: Hamish Hamilton, 1940.

Buenacasa, Manuel. *El movimiento obrero español: 1886–1926*. Barcelona: Imp. Costa, 1928.

Carr, Raymond. *Spain: 1808–1939*. Oxford: Clarendon Press, 1966.

Cierva, Ricardo de la. *Historia de la Guerra Civil española. Perspectivas y antecedentes*. Madrid: Lib. San Martín, 1969.

Cordero, Manuel. *Los socialistas y la revolución*. Madrid: Imp. Torrente, 1932.

Domínguez Ortiz, Antonio. *La sociedad española en el siglo XVIII*. Madrid: Instituto Balmes de Sociología, 1955.

Fernández Almagro, Melchor. *Historia de la República*. Madrid: Biblioteca Nueva, 1940.

Fuentes Quintana, E., and Fuentes Velarde, J. *Política económica*. Madrid: Doncel, 1959.

Gutiérrez Ravé, José. *España en 1931: Anuario*. Madrid: Imp. Saez Hermanos, 1932.

Herr, Richard. *The Eighteenth Century Revolution in Spain*. Princeton: Princeton University Press, 1958.

Hennessy, C. A. M. *The Federal Republic in Spain: Pi y Margall and the Federal Republican Movement: 1868–74*. Oxford: Clarendon Press, 1962.

Jackson, Gabriel. *The Spanish Republic and the Civil War: 1931–39*. Princeton: Princeton University Press, 1965.

Linz, Juan J. "The Party System of Spain: Past and Future." In *Party Systems and Voter Alignments: Cross-National Perspectives*, ed. Seymour M. Lipset and Stein Rokkan. New York: The Free Press, 1967.

Linz, Juan J., and Miguel, Amando de. "Within-Nation Differences and Comparisons: The Eight Spains." In *Comparing Nations*, ed. Richard L. Merritt and Stein Rokkan. New Haven: Yale University Press, 1966.

Lamberet, Renée. *L'Espagne* (1750–1936). *Mouvements ouvriers et socialistes* (*Chronologie et bibliographie*). Paris: Les Editions Ouvriers, 1953.

Madariaga, Salvador de. *Spain: A Modern History.* New York: Praeger, 1958.

Mario de Coca, Gabriel. *Anti-Caballero.* Madrid: Editorial Engles, 1936.

Marvaud, Angel. *La Question sociale en Espagne.* Paris: Felix Alcan, 1910.

Maurín, Joaquín. *Revolución y contrarrevolución en España.* Paris: Ruedo Iberico, 1965.

Mendizábal, Alfred. *The Martyrdom of Spain: Origins of a Civil War.* London: Geoffrey Blis, The Centenary Press, 1938.

Moch, Jules, and Moch, G. P. *L'Espagne républicaine.* Paris: Les Editions Rieder, 1933.

Morato, Juan José. *El Partido Socialista Obrero Español.* Madrid: Biblioteca Nueva, 1918 [?].

Morón, Gabriel. *El Partido Socialista ante la realidad política de Espana.* Madrid: Editorial Cenit, 1929.

Paris Eguilaz, Higinio. *El movimiento de precios en España.* Madrid, 1943.

Payne, Stanley G. *Politics and the Military in Modern Spain.* Stanford: Stanford University Press, 1967.

Plá, José. *Historia de la Segunda República Española.* 4 vols. Barcelona: Editorial Destino, 1940.

Prados, Jesús. *Los próximos veinte años.* Madrid: Editorial Sopee, 1958.

Rama, Carlos. *La crisis española del siglo XX.* México: Fondo de Cultura Económica, 1960.

Ramírez Jiménez, Manuel. *Los grupos de presión en la Segunda República Española.* Madrid: Editorial Tecnos, 1969.

Ramos Oliveira, A. *Politics, Economics and Men of Modern Spain: 1808–1946.* London: Victor Gollanz, 1946.

Santiago, Enrique. *La UGT ante la revolución,* Madrid: Saez Hermanos, 1932.

Tamames, Ramón. *Estructura económica de España.* Madrid: Sociedad de Estudios y Publicaciónes, 1960.

Valdeavellano, Luís G. de. *Historia de España: De los origenes a la baja Edad Media.* Madrid: Revista del Occidente, 1952.

Vicens Vives, Jaime. *Historia social y económica de España y América.* 5 vols. Barcelona: Editorial Teide, 1959.

Vila, Enrique. *Un año de república en Sevilla.* Sevilla: La Editorial Sevillana, 1932.

Vilar, Pierre. *Historia de España.* Paris: Librairie des Editions Espagnoles, 1960.

Index

Information referring specifically to any of the fifty Spanish provinces is indexed under the name of the province. However, entries for regional divisions (e.g. Southern Spain) should also be consulted for information on the provinces that make up the region (see page xix for a listing of provinces and regions).

GLASSBORO STATE COLLEGE